an individual with a unique pattern of   :ss.
Educators and other professionals must   ind
building on the strengths of deaf peopl

D0116308

It is doubtful that any area of compa   less
light than the education of children who are deaf or   the
American School for the Deaf was established in Hartford, Connecticut, in 1817, the
field has been rife with controversies that have consumed the attention and energies
of its most gifted educators. Consequently, these individuals have been forced to
approach problems from the framework of simplistic either-or, black-white polarities.

I have contended that since its inception education of the deaf has been consumed by three basic questions (Moores, 1990a; 1991; 1993a; 1995a).

1. How shall we teach deaf children?
2. Where should we teach deaf children?
3. What should we teach deaf children?

These simple questions mask complex issues and are heavily influenced by what
one perceives as the goal of education of the deaf. The first question, of course,
addresses the famous (or infamous) "methods" controversy. This is commonly perceived in oral versus manual terms: Should we speak or sign with deaf children? If
we choose to use signs, the issue quickly becomes more complicated: Should we
use American Sign Language (ASL) or one of the manual codes on English in coordination with speech? The second question deals with academic placement in settings ranging from residential schools for the deaf to complete integration in classes
with hearing children. The third question involves how much of a deaf child's
school day should be allocated to special areas such as speech, auditory training,
English grammar, Deaf culture, and ASL, and how much to academic areas that
consume the bulk of the school day for hearing children. What are the trade-offs
between the special and general curricula?

An overriding concern is the difficulties deaf children encounter in mastering the
language of the larger society in which they live and the effects of the resulting
communication limitations on many other aspects of their development. A second,
related concern is the insensitivity of hearing individuals to the impact of early
deafness and the debilitating consequences of this insensitivity for deaf children.

Children with hearing can be considered linguistically proficient in every sense
of the word. They have a knowledge of the basic rules of their language. They can
produce a potentially infinite number of novel yet appropriate utterances and, because of their unconscious mastery of the grammatical structure of their language,
can combine and recombine its elements indefinitely. They can produce and understand sentences to which they have never been exposed. They use language in
different ways in a variety of situations to fulfill a number of pragmatic functions.
These children enter the formal educational system around age six armed with an
invaluable instrument for learning—language and communication ability—acquired
without conscious effort on their part or that of their parents.

Excerpt from Chapter 1   Overview: Education of the Deaf

Educating the Deaf

Educating the Deaf

Psychology, Principles, and Practices

FIFTH EDITION

Donald F. Moores
Gallaudet University

HOUGHTON MIFFLIN COMPANY   BOSTON   NEW YORK

To Margery Miller Moores

Senior Sponsoring Editor: Loretta Wolozin
Development Editor: Lisa Mafrici
Senior Project Editor: Carol Newman
Senior Production/Design Coordinator: Jill Haber
Senior Manufacturing Coordinator: Marie Barnes
Marketing Associate: Caroline Guy

Cover Design: Diana Coe/ko Design
Cover Image: Untitled. © 1979 Ibrahim Benoh. Courtesy of NextMonet.com

Credits
Chapter 8, pages 190, 193: Selections from Donoghue, R., 1968, "The Deaf Personality: A Study in Contrasts." *Journal of Rehabilitation of the Deaf,* 2, no. 1; 35–51.
Chapter 9, page 214: American Manual Alphabet. (Used by permission. Copyright © 1976, Kathryn A. Licht.)
Chapter 9, page 226: Selection by Larry Stewart as appeared in *NED Broadcaster,* Vol. 44, No. 1. *Eyes, Hands, Voices: Communication Issues Among Deaf People* (*A Deaf American* monograph). Vol. 40, Nos. 1-2-3-4, 1990.
Chapter 11, page 273: Adapted from D. Calvert & R. Silverman, *Speech and Deafness* (Washington, D.C.: A.G. Bell Association, 1975), pp. 148–156. Reprinted with permission of the publisher, the Alexander Graham Bell Association for the Deaf.
Chapter 12, pages 297–298: From "A Descriptive Study of Developing Literacy of Young Hearing-Impaired Children" by C. Ewolt, *Volta Review,* 87, pp. 109–126. Reprinted with permission of the Alexander Graham Bell Association for the Deaf.

Printed in the U.S.A.

Library of Congress Catalog Card Number: 00-103364

ISBN: 0-618-04289-X

3 4 5 6 7 8 9-FFG-09 08 07 06 05

Contents

10 Early Intervention, Infant, and Preschool Programs   228

11 The Acquisition of English: Teaching and Training Techniques   250

Preface

Perspective

I began work on the first edition of *Educating the Deaf: Psychology, Principles, and Practices* in 1974 out of a sense of frustration over the lack of a definitive resource on educational, social, and psychological aspects of deafness. As a professor at the University of Minnesota responsible for undergraduate and graduate training programs in education of the deaf and as the person responsible for teaching the introductory overview courses, this lack was of particular concern to me. There were several texts dealing individually with psychology and deafness, speech and deafness, literacy and deafness, and audiology and deafness, but they were too narrowly focused on one specialty or another and were not appropriate for students preparing for a career that would require a possession of knowledge and skills involving several seemingly disparate disciplines. This situation was no different from what I experienced when I went through my training to become a teacher of deaf children.

My approach to a course in education of the deaf was similar to that of colleagues in other universities, namely to organize readings from various fields around relevant topics and try to integrate them into some kind of seamless package. My efforts were not very successful. Readings from different fields often assumed a background or professional orientation that did not match those of my students, at least on the surface. There was no continuity and frequently the readings reflected a "deficiency" or pathological view of deafness, representing what some people have referred to as a medical model of deafness. Deafness was seen as a disease to be cured, deaf people were regarded as imperfect hearing people, and their sign language was seem as an unsystematic series of concrete gestures. Deaf people were viewed as a problem to be solved rather than people coping with the everyday world in normal ways. In short, much of the literature did not reflect the reality of the lives of deaf individuals I knew. My goal was to develop a textbook that would meet the needs of deaf and hearing professionals dealing with educational, social, and psychological implications of deafness and to make the textbook as complete, objective, and comprehensive as possible.

I first looked at the course outline I had developed over the years. Essentially, it covered a range of topics similar to that included in the present text—history, causes of deafness, demographic information, academic achievement, curriculum, literacy, cognition, vocational success, and American Sign Language. Given the range of topics my initial thought was to develop an edited textbook with professionals from different backgrounds contributing chapters in their areas of expertise. I discussed this with Dr. Samuel Kirk, my role model from the time I was a Ph.D. candidate at the University of Illinois and he was Director of the Institute for Research on Exceptional Children. I had worked as a research associate at the Institute for Dr. Kirk on the standardization of the Illinois Test of Psycholinguistic Abilities as well as on several deafness-related projects. Dr. Kirk disagreed with my plan for an edited book and suggested that I write one myself. He argued that an edited book would have the same problems as a loose collection of papers and would not reflect a cohesive, integrated perspective. When I told him I did not have sufficient background in many of areas, he responded that I was a young man and that it was time I acquired that background. Although he was too polite to mention it, I knew that the first edition of his classic textbook, *Educating Exceptional Children,* had appeared in 1962 and it definitely was *not* an edited text! After several false starts, I developed drafts of two chapters and sent them to Dr. Kirk. He took it upon himself to mail copies of the drafts to his publisher, Houghton Mifflin, recommending publication. From that point there was no turning back. It took four years to write the first edition, beginning in 1974 to its publication in 1978, as I worked on acquiring the knowledge I needed to get the book into print and to justify Dr. Kirk's faith in me.

My primary sources of knowledge have come from almost a lifetime of interaction with deaf individuals of all ages and circumstances, beginning as a teenaged farm worker at a residential school for the deaf. Since then I have benefited from experiences as a dormitory supervisor, graduate student, honorary member of a deaf fraternity, classroom teacher, summer camp director, Boy Scout leader, football coach, professor, advisor, researcher, colleague, and friend. I have learned much from extensive reading and discussion as well as from teaching college-level courses related to deafness. For forty years, I have been fortunate to be involved in research on deafness, dealing with topics ranging from preschool intervention to vocational adjustment. The organization of content, the review of literature, and the presentation of information in most chapters of the text have been facilitated either by my direct involvement in related research or by my interaction with research colleagues.

I also have had the honor and pleasure of serving as Editor of the American Annals of the Deaf since 1990. The Annals has the dual distinction of being the oldest educational journal in America as well as the oldest English language journal on deafness in the world. The manuscripts we review provide me with up-to-date information on developments and trends related to deafness around the world..

Audience

I wrote *Educating the Deaf* to serve the needs of a broad range of readers, both lay and professional. The text can be a primary source of information on deafness for many individuals, including parents of deaf children, teachers of the deaf, interpreters, specialists in early child development, school and clinical psychologists, social workers, school and rehabilitation counselors, speech and hearing professionals, and special education program administrators at local, state, regional, and national levels. For those individuals *Educating the Deaf* provides a foundation for more intensive specialized study.

Revisions in the Fifth Edition

Examination of the organization and content of the five editions reveals almost revolutionary changes given the ongoing reality of deafness over the short period of little more than one generation. As the first edition was being prepared, Public Law 94–142, (PL 94-142), the *Education for All Handicapped Children Act,* was passed. The act mandated a free *appropriate* public education for all handicapped children in the least restrictive environment, with due process provisions specified. Over time PL 94-142 evolved into the *Individuals with Disabilities Education Act (IDEA),* which broadened the scope of services to include the family and extended the age range to the time of identification of a disability in a child. The very change in title from handicapped to disability provides insight into how public perceptions have improved in a brief time span. The impact of these acts on education of deaf children and the incentive to enroll more and more deaf children in public school programs cannot be overemphasized. The passage of the *Americans with Disabilities Act* (1990) and its reauthorization in 1997, which has been hailed as a bill of rights for disabled individuals, could not have been anticipated at that time of the first edition nor could the *Education of the Deaf Act,* through which Congress has addressed issues specific to deafness and education.

This fifth edition was developed to incorporate new trends and developments in several areas. First among them is the fact that education of the deaf is becoming more and more integrated with general education. At present, more than eighty percent of deaf children are taught in local public schools, most of whom attend at least some classes with hearing children. This influence is felt even in residential schools for the deaf, where traditional curricula are being revised to follow models of local public schools. Of almost equal importance are developments in medicine and biology. The Human Genome Project and the increasing sophistication of cochlear implants offer both exciting possibilities and complex moral issues. In yet another area, significant demographic changes in the deaf student population have occurred in the past several years in terms of racial/ethnic identity and geographic distribution.

The use of ASL (American Sign Language) in the classroom and advocacy of ASL-only instruction was inconceivable by the dominant educators of the deaf only a generation ago. Now, the possibilities of the educational uses of ASL, either alone or complementary with Signed English systems, are receiving the attention they deserve. A related development has been the ascendency of deaf educators of the deaf, at least in residential school settings. This has been particularly gratifying to me. When I was a graduate student at Gallaudet, deaf students could not enroll in graduate programs. The *Deaf President Now* movement arising in the spring of 1988 represented a watershed in which the students, faculty, and staff of Gallaudet successfully insisted on the selection of a deaf president, leading to the appointment of I. King Jordan as the first deaf president of Gallaudet. Since that time, the role of deaf professionals and the public awareness of the capabilities of deaf administrators has been unequivocally altered.

In the face of obvious change in the field, I have tried to deal with the regrettable fact that more progress has not been made. In spite of undeniable improvements, deaf individuals continue to encounter communicational, educational, and social obstacles. To bring order out of this paradox—apparent change and improvement in the face of enduring long-term barriers to progress—I have continued to rely on the work of Fernand Braudel, a distinguished French historian. Braudel has argued that there are three approaches to the study of history; one can focus on (1) events and short-term changes, (2) cycles, and (3) the long-term reality of life, in which change occurs gradually and in incremental steps. Although I am not a trained historian, I believe his tripartite division is helpful in relating events, cycles, and long-term reality to the condition of deaf individuals.

Educating the Deaf, Fifth Edition, continues to include a significant amount of historical material. This is due to my respect for the work done by those who preceded us and to my belief that understanding their efforts will help us build on their successes while avoiding some of their mistakes. The emergence of historians devoted to the study of deaf individuals, their organizations, and their lives have added immeasurably to our knowledge.

As with previous revisions, the most difficult task in the Fifth Edition was to add as much up-to-date information as possible while retaining the most salient aspects of previous work and maintaining consistency. The most painful decisions related to what material to exclude from the book. I only wish that twice as much space were available.

New Resource

One important resource that has been added is the "World Wide Web Resources" appendix, which is located at the end of the text. This appendix contains various websites that provide information on issues facing the deaf and hard-of-hearing community. Online newspapers written by and for deaf people, strategies for parents with hard of hearing children, inspiring stories written by late-deafened adults, and membership guidelines of the country's preeminent deaf associations are only a few topics that can be researched using the websites in this appendix.

New Coverage

Highlights of new or expanded topics in this edition include:

- Ethnic, racial, and social diversity within the deaf community, including federal classifications and disparities in treatment
- The Human Genome Project and genetic engineering
- Treatment of the deaf during World War II and the Holocaust
- Debates on cochlear implants
- Information on proper and improper testing methods, and concomitant issues such as potential misclassification of students
- The correlation between learning ASL and developng literacy

If, in addition to factual knowledge, *Educating the Deaf* manages to convey a feeling of respect for deaf people and the ways in which they function in the world, then I will be satisfied that the effort I devoted to writing this book was worthwhile.

Acknowledgments

My greatest debt is to Margery Miller Moores, whose love, patience, insightfulness and understanding is matched only by her expertise and knowledge of all aspects of our field. This book is dedicated to her with love and respect—a great combination.

The second greatest influence in my educational life has been Samuel A. Kirk, the father of special education. He has been my role model and I will never forget his wisdom and integrity.

In addition, throughout my career I have benefitted from the support and friendship of people with whom I have taught, conducted research, developed books, and shared ideas. They include, but are not limited to, Mac Vernon, Bob Davila, E. B. Boatner, Barbara Griffing, Boyce Williams, Steve Quigley, Jack Gannon, Yerker Andersson, Clara Hamel, Dave Denton, Terry O'Rourke, Frank Bowe, Margaret Walworth, Bernard Bragg, Barbara Luetk Stahlman, Ernie Hairston, Ed Corbett, Art Schildroth, Bob Hoffmeister, Mike Karchmer, Tom Allen, Donna Mertens. Kay Meadow-Orlans, Tom Kluwin, Pat Spencer, Rob MacTurk, Len Kelly, Sue Mather, Gwen Horton, Bob Mobley, Carol LaSasso, Dave Martin, Rich Lytle, and Bill McCrone.

Four people at Houghton Mifflin also deserve special thanks. I first started working with Loretta Wolozin, education editor, in 1975 in the development of the First Edition when I was struggling with the complexities of writing a text for the first time. I am indebted to her for her support of all five editions. Lisa Mafrici, had the dubious distinction of working through the fourth edition with me and Sarah A. Rodriguez took on responsibility for the fifth edition. I want to thank them for their suggestions, promptness, and attention to detail. They were invaluable in helping me through the difficult parts. Also, thanks to Carol Newman for shepherding the text through production for the fourth and fifth editions.

Finally, thanks are due to the following colleagues across the country for their manuscript reading, feedback, and suggestions, during the development of the text:

Margaret Finnegan, Flagler College
Marjorie Harrington, Barton College
John Luckner, University of Northern Colorado
Pamela Luft, Kent State University
Henry Teller, University of Southern Mississippi
Olga M. Welch, University of Tennessee at Knoxville

D.F.M.

Educating the Deaf

CHAPTER

Overview: Education of the Deaf

Introduction

Although education of the deaf is the oldest field of special education in the United States, dating back to the beginning of the nineteenth century, deafness is a condition that remains a mystery to most members of the general hearing community. Traditionally it has been considered a deficit or a disease to be prevented or cured. To many members of the deaf community and to a growing number of hearing people, deafness can be considered within a social context. The first perspective has been referred to as a medical or pathological model of deafness. One criticism of this model, at least in its most extreme form, is that it can lead to the mistaken belief that any deaf person is incomplete, per se, and that wholeness only can be obtained by curing deafness. The second perspective, commonly known as a so-cial/cultural model, holds that deafness constitutes a difference, not a deficiency, that it is part of the human condition, and that it places no limits on social, emotional, intellectual, and academic development. One way to conceptualize this model is to understand that there are not two worlds—a deaf world and a hearing world—but one world in which deaf and hearing people exist and interact on a daily basis. It will be clear in this text that my orientation is with a social/cultural model of deafness but that I am aware of the obstacles facing deaf individuals in a society unaware of the implications of early childhood deafness, which occurs in less than one child in a thousand and usually involves a deaf child with hearing parents with little or no prior exposure to deafness.

One theme that will run throughout this text is the pervasive influence of general education on education of the deaf, an influence that has been growing for more than fifty years. This has been manifested in a variety of ways. In the past most deaf

1

children were educated in residential schools or commuted daily to day schools for the deaf in large cities. The curriculum was specifically designed to emphasize speech, speechreading, and English grammar, with little attention, relative to general education, devoted to content areas such as math, literacy, science, and social studies. Today most deaf children attend the same schools, and sometimes the same classes, as hearing children. To some extent, the curriculum is similar. This is also true for deaf children attending separate day schools and residential schools. As we will learn, however, implementing a general education may be difficult for the large numbers of deaf children who may enter the educational system without having a mastery of the English language and a clear functional communication system.

Federal legislation, technological advances, improved educational services, and growing public awareness have brought about the greatest progress since the establishment of the first school for the deaf almost two centuries ago. The influence of the Deaf community has grown spectacularly, and deaf individuals have assumed their rightful roles both within the Deaf community and in society at large. In addition to the National Association of the Deaf and state associations, an incredible variety of organizations reflect the diversity of the Deaf community. These include Catholic, Jewish, and Protestant organizations; African-American, Hispanic-American, and Asian/Pacific-American organizations; and gay and lesbian organizations. There is even an organization of deaf entrepreneurs.

At the same time, awareness of deafness and opportunities for participation in the general culture have expanded dramatically, in part because of a general trend toward acceptance of diversity in society. American Sign Language (ASL) has generated considerable interest and is being studied by large numbers of hearing individuals. It is now offered for credit in many American high schools and colleges. The presence of deaf students throughout our educational system and the work environment has been a factor in the increased visibility of deaf individuals. There have been a deaf Miss America, deaf actors and actresses, deaf professional athletes, deaf business leaders, and deaf professionals in medicine, the law, and dentistry, to mention a few areas.

Various pieces of federal legislation have benefited the deaf. The Americans with Disabilities Act of 1990 guarantees equal access to information and services for all Americans, and this concept underlies legislation that is of particular interest to deaf individuals. For example, each state is required to have a statewide telephone relay system for deaf consumers at no extra cost to them. Other legislation requires that all television sets sold in the United States be equipped to receive closed-caption broadcasts. Also, some deaf adults and many families with deaf children receive financial support from the federal government through the Social Security Insurance (SSI) Disabilities program.

Federal legislation also mandates a free, appropriate public education for every deaf child from the time a hearing loss is identified through age twenty-one, with individual educational plans for the child and family. Deaf children are being identified and served at younger ages, and academic achievement has improved significantly. More educational options are available; for example, the number of deaf students enrolled in postsecondary education is rising steadily.

**Heather Whitestone, Miss
America, 1995.** *Whitestone is
deaf.*

The record, however, is one of mixed success. In spite of progress, the field of deaf education has been riddled with bitter controversy and conflict. Although educational achievement has improved, it is far below what it should be. Barriers to career advancement for deaf professionals persist. The use of American Sign Language (ASL) for very young children in the classroom, cochlear implants, and educational placement of deaf children are the subjects of highly emotional debate. Many deaf children still fail to master the basic fundamentals of English despite rising expectations. As we progress through this text, we will examine this paradox from different perspectives to gain an understanding of the complexities of the issues and the realities that can lead well-meaning and dedicated individuals to diametrically opposed conclusions.

The successes and failures of deaf students and adults have intensified the paradox. Since the first schools for the deaf were established, educators have expressed concern about deaf students' lack of academic achievement and their poor command of the language of the hearing community. In the United States, the results of decades of standardized achievement testing suggest a severe educational gap between deaf and hearing students, especially in areas related to English, such as reading. However, the fact that approximately 65 percent of deaf graduates of Gallaudet University go on to graduate schools, where they compete on equal terms with hearing students, suggests that the deaf/hearing gap in achievement may be more apparent than real.

This text will attempt to reconcile apparent paradoxes. In some cases, this task will be relatively simple. For example, evidence that standardized tests underestimate the reading abilities of deaf students suggests that this situation has never been as grim as most educators think. In other cases, reconciliation will be quite difficult. How do we reconcile the evidence of massive changes and improvements with the enduring reality of deafness in everyday life? How do we reconcile rapid developments in some areas with only gradual improvements in other areas?

In analyzing the education of the deaf, we can identify one influence as the work of Fernand Braudel, a French historian who has had a significant impact on our understanding of history. Through his study of demography, food, clothing, lodging, and technology, Braudel (1981, 1982) has introduced considerations of everyday life into the domain of history. He argues that material life is a prolongation of an ancient society and economy that change very slowly and hence imperceptibly.

Braudel provides three perspectives from which past and present realities of education of the deaf can be viewed. The first perspective is concerned primarily with *events,* such as the establishment of schools, the passage of important legislation, and the development of influential texts and curricula. This approach places great emphasis on dates.

The second perspective deals with *cycles.* Every society experiences economic, political, and educational cycles of varying lengths. In U.S. education, a cycle runs approximately twenty-five years. In American Education, at present, there is a strong commitment to academic achievement possibly as a result of previoiusly lax standards in the public schools. Across the United States, local and state education agencies introduced changes such as longer school days, competency testing for teachers, testing of students for promotion and graduation, minimum grade-point averages for participation in extracurricular activities, more content courses for high school graduation, restructuring of teacher training programs, and charter schools. The equity-versus-excellence debate has intensified. Simply put, how do we guarantee equal access to all while maintaining the highest possible standards?

The third of Braudel's perspectives is that of the *long term,* the enduring reality. This reality provides a basis against which we can attempt to measure and judge events and cycles.

Through a synthesis of all three perspectives—event, cycle, and long term—we may be able to establish a framework for considering how, where, what, and by whom deaf students should be taught.

Any system of education must be considered within a cultural context. In a pluralistic society such as that of the United States today, educational systems have a variety of purposes, both implicit and explicit, and there is often disagreement over priorities. Frequently, goals conflict with each other, such as the simultaneous goals of excellence and equal opportunity. The idea that children must learn the traditional three Rs (Reading, Riting, and Rithmetic) to be able to function in society has general support. Beyond that are strong differences of opinion about issues such as the roles of religion and moral training, sex education, driver education, and interscholastic sports.

Educational systems are products of particular cultures and are used as vehicles of cultural infusion. Within a relatively homogeneous society, the educational goals of cultural transmission and indoctrination may not be controversial. In our pluralistic society, however, these issues have been the battleground for racial, ethnic, and religious conflict for more than a century. Thus the establishment of "separate but equal" schools for black children was based on political, not educational, considerations. In the past, some groups that disagreed with public school policies chose not to participate in public school education and developed their own school systems, both to preserve their identities and to provide their children with values other than those espoused by public schools. During the same period in which German immigrants and their descendants developed separate schools that used the German language, Irish-Catholic immigrants and their descendants instituted Catholic school systems to protect their children from what they perceived as the undesirable influence of public education dominated by Protestant Anglo-Saxon values (Schrag, 1967). In the eighteenth and nineteenth centuries, separate Catholic schools were established at the college level, including Georgetown, Fordham, Xavier, Notre Dame, and Boston College.

For a variety of reasons, the present tendency is to work for change through the public schools rather than develop parallel school systems. The growth of charter schools, of course, is a result of this tendency. By law, all children are entitled to a free, appropriate public education regardless of race, sex, ethnic status, religion, country of origin, or disabling condition. The conflict, of course, revolves around how and by whom the term *appropriate* is defined. The issues of school busing, placement of children with disabilities, use of languages such as Chinese and Spanish in the classroom, and teaching of unpleasant aspects of American history, among others, raise different and often emotional opinions. The manner in which such conflicts are resolved will have a profound impact on American society for generations to come.

Given the influence of general education, issues that are beyond the control of educators of the deaf will significantly influence the ways deaf children are educated. Throughout history, deafness has been perceived as a pathology and, by extension, deaf individuals have been seen as pathological. The goal has been to either "cure" the deafness or reduce its impact. Without minimizing the constraints deafness imposes on an individual, it is also possible—and, in my opinion, preferable—to view deafness as a social or cultural condition. Rather than thinking of a deaf person primarily as someone with a defect, we should perceive that person as an individual with a unique pattern of characteristics, one of which is deafness. Educators and other professionals must direct their energies toward identifying and building on the strengths of deaf people.

It is doubtful that any area of comparable size has generated more heat and less light than the education of children who are deaf or hard of hearing. Since the American School for the Deaf was established in Hartford, Connecticut, in 1817, the field has been rife with controversies that have consumed the attention and energies of its most gifted educators. Consequently, these individuals have been forced to approach problems from the framework of simplistic either-or, black-white polarities.

I have contended that since its inception education of the deaf has been consumed by three basic questions (Moores, 1990a; 1991; 1993a; 1995a).

1. How shall we teach deaf children?
2. Where should we teach deaf children?
3. What should we teach deaf children?

These simple questions mask complex issues and are heavily influenced by what one perceives as the goal of education of the deaf. The first question, of course, addresses the famous (or infamous) "methods" controversy. This is commonly perceived in oral versus manual terms: Should we speak or sign with deaf children? If we choose to use signs, the issue quickly becomes more complicated: Should we use American Sign Language (ASL) or one of the manual codes on English in coordination with speech? The second question deals with academic placement in settings ranging from residential schools for the deaf to complete integration in classes with hearing children. The third question involves how much of a deaf child's school day should be allocated to special areas such as speech, auditory training, English grammar, Deaf culture, and ASL, and how much to academic areas that consume the bulk of the school day for hearing children. What are the trade-offs between the special and general curricula?

An overriding concern is the difficulties deaf children encounter in mastering the language of the larger society in which they live and the effects of the resulting communication limitations on many other aspects of their development. A second, related concern is the insensitivity of hearing individuals to the impact of early deafness and the debilitating consequences of this insensitivity for deaf children.

Children with hearing can be considered linguistically proficient in every sense of the word. They have a knowledge of the basic rules of their language. They can produce a potentially infinite number of novel yet appropriate utterances and, because of their unconscious mastery of the grammatical structure of their language, can combine and recombine its elements indefinitely. They can produce and understand sentences to which they have never been exposed. They use language in different ways in a variety of situations to fulfill a number of pragmatic functions. These children enter the formal educational system around age six armed with an invaluable instrument for learning—language and communication ability—acquired without conscious effort on their part or that of their parents.

In contrast, profoundly deaf children generally have not acquired a language naturally and automatically (unless they have deaf parents). They need intensive compensatory training. For such children, language is not a facilitating device for the acquisition of knowledge; rather, it is a barrier between them and the full realization of their academic, intellectual, and social potential. Although of normal intelligence, deaf children may find their range of experience constrained by communication limitations. Relative to other children, they lack opportunities to interact fully with and manipulate their environment in meaningful ways. Although deafness itself may have no effect on intellectual potential, it may lead to impoverished communication skills that can limit development severely, unless the children are provided with compensatory tools.

Much of the curriculum in programs for deaf children has been designed to develop the English proficiency that hearing children bring to the educational process. The means by which most deaf children presently learn English is more laborious and inefficient than that used by hearing children. The results in terms of mastery of standard English are below those of hearing children, both qualitatively and quantitatively. In addition, the time devoted during the school day to teaching English inevitably diminishes the time available for teaching other school subjects such as mathematics, social studies, and science. Given the increased emphasis on academic achievement in U.S. education today, educators of the deaf must continually rethink their priorities with respect to the mix between teaching academic content and traditional training that concentrates primarily on communication skills.

The Influence of Public Education

As our public educational systems encounter widespread criticism for their perceived failure, education of the deaf will also experience increased demand for fewer frills, higher achievement standards, and tighter discipline. Certain readily identifiable themes have appeared in several sources within the context of appeals for higher standards and a commitment to excellence (Boyer, 1983; The National Commission on Excellence in Education, 1983).

Even a casual reading of the popular press will forcefully illustrate the interest of the American public in improving public education. Newspapers and magazines are full of discussion about the potential benefits and drawbacks of a national curriculum and national testing standards; of competency testing for beginning and continuing teachers; of phonics versus whole word approaches to reading; and of statewide proficiency tests that students must pass to receive a high school diploma and, by implication, attend college. In many states there is disagreement about whether children of limited English proficiency should take the exams. The same question has come up regarding deaf students who may have mastered subject matter content but who also may have difficulties with standard English. The issue is complicated in the case of the large numbers of deaf students who come from homes where English is not the first language.

Most readers probably are also aware of attempts to compare the academic achievement of American students in math and science to that in other countries as well as across states (National Educational Goals Panel, 1997; National council of Teachers of Mathematics, 1998; Reese, Miller, Mazzeo, and Dossey, 1997). American students appear to do relatively well in science at different grade levels and in mathematics at the fourth grade, but tend to fall below the norm at higher grades. The results have led to a movement to revise teacher training for teachers of mathematics, with emphases on problem solving, interactive technology, and mathematical reasoning. Again, teachers of deaf children must increase their efforts to keep pace.

Educators of the deaf will continue to address sociocultural and communication factors as well as academic achievement, but they must be aware of the dominant emphasis on achievement in basic academic subject matter: math, science, English, and social studies. Because academic achievement of hearing children is receiving greater attention, educators of the deaf must help their students improve in academic achievement merely to maintain their position relative to that of hearing children. To be judged successful academically, deaf students must improve in school achievement at a faster rate than hearing children—a task that will challenge the field to its utmost.

As noted, the implications of developments in education in general for education of the deaf are much greater today than in the past. Historically, most deaf children were educated separately, either in residential schools or in day schools for the deaf. Even when the schools were publicly supported, little or no connection existed between general education and education of the deaf. Today the majority of deaf children are educated in public schools attended by hearing students. With the use of sign interpreters, more deaf students are spending at least part of the school day in classes with hearing students. If this situation is to continue, the emphasis on academic achievement in programs for the deaf must be increased to match that found in general education, and the curriculum in classes for the deaf must be brought into line with the general curriculum.

The extent of the needed changes and their impact on education of the deaf should not be underestimated. For more than two hundred years, the primary emphasis among educators of the deaf has been communication, with academic achievement receiving secondary attention. It is unrealistic to expect a deemphasis on training in communication skills, but a reevaluation of priorities is in order.

Research has established that although the average deaf child is of normal intelligence, most deaf children begin elementary school with deficits in reception and expression of spoken language, in English grammatical skills, and in factual knowledge of the world. Thus, educators and parents must make some difficult trade-offs. Typically, programs for the deaf have concentrated on remediating speech and English grammar. Special curriculum materials and techniques have been developed to help deaf children master the basic sounds of the language, both expressively and receptively. Most programs set aside time for individual or small-group training in speech or in the use of residual hearing. Related lessons may also be incorporated into other parts of the school day, and classes in subjects such as history, social studies, or mathematics may include some degree of training in vocal skills. Most programs, choosing from among available alternatives, employ some kind of language curriculum to teach children the fundamentals of English grammar. The curriculum is far different than that provided for hearing children in English classes; it's designed to teach deaf children English grammar that hearing children have already mastered. History, math, or social studies classes are then frequently used to teach deaf students grammatical constructs (such as subject-verb agreement, past tense, or passive voice) in addition to specific academic content. Even with recent improvements, the deaf child generally devotes far less time to academic subjects than does the hearing child. There is evidence that even in preschool, deaf children spend less time on math or premath instruction than do hearing children. Their math scores at seven years of age reflect this difference (Moores, 1985a). The pattern of reduced enrollment in academic subject matter continues through high school (Moores, Kluwin, and Mertens, 1985; Kluwin, Moores, and Gaustad, 1992; Pagliaro, 1998b).

One of the most consistent findings in educational research is the correlation between achievement and "time on task." Simply put, everything else being equal, the amount of time spent studying or concentrating in class on a particular topic or subject area is positively related to learning and mastery of content. The more time students spend on biology or mathematics, the more they will learn.

The difficulties educators of the deaf face in organizing a school day, week, month, and year should be appreciated. Deaf children cannot realistically be expected to attend school for longer periods of time than hearing children. First, a longer day would be difficult to schedule, especially for children in public schools. More important, a longer day might put too much of a strain on deaf children, who have to maintain visual attention to learn. Deaf children cannot close their eyes or turn away and still follow the progress of a class. Thus school is more tiring for deaf students than for hearing students, who do not need visual contact to understand the teacher or other students.

Although there is evidence that increased concentration on academic subject matter can lead to increased achievement, a reorientation toward academic achievement may be difficult to attain. The training of most teachers presently working with the deaf has emphasized vocal and grammatical skills at the expense of teaching subject matter such as math, science, history, and social studies. Most professionals involved in teacher training have had the same orientation as the author of this text. Thus a reorientation and retraining of teachers and teacher educators is needed. The major thrust must be the development of teachers who possess the same teaching skills as traditional teachers of the deaf, along with more expertise in specific content areas. State and national standards for certification of teachers of the deaf will likely be revised to meet the changing needs.

The situation in the area of mathematics documents the work that needs to be done in bringing teachers of the deaf up to general education standards. Dietz (1995) proposed a national action plan for mathematics education reform for the deaf, with an emphasis on preservice and inservice programs. Pagliaro (1998b) reported that teachers of deaf children from kindergarten through twelfth grade typically did not employ reformlike techniques in their mathematics instruction, but continued to rely on traditional practices such as rote memorization, work sheets, and drill and practice. In a related study on the preparation and professional development of mathematics teachers of the deaf, Pagliaro (1998a) found an insufficient level of mathematics preparation, especially at the high school level. Few held degrees in a mathematics-related field, and only a moderate number sought professional development in the discipline. Clearly, we have a long way to go to provide both equity and excellence to our deaf students.

The equity-versus-excellence conflict in U.S. education dates back to the nineteenth century and is not likely to be resolved soon. The passage of the Americans with Disabilities Act in 1990 and the commitment to provide equality of access to education for all children, especially those from underserved populations—economically disadvantaged groups, individuals with disabilities, and racial and ethnic minorities—will have an enduring impact. Although all of the problems inherent in equality of access have not been resolved, significant progress undeniably has been made. Educators of the deaf must continue to work to maintain the gains in equality of access and, at the same time, redouble their efforts to help deaf children achieve to the highest limits of their academic potential.

Definitions of Terms

To discuss educational programs and services for the deaf, it is necessary to have some reference points for the concept of deafness. At first glance, deafness might seem to be a simple concept that one could diagnose through straightforward audiometric procedures. However, from a developmental and educational perspective, other factors must be considered. In the final analysis, any definition must be functionally oriented and be accepted only within broad limits. It would be no more defensible to classify a child as deaf or hard of hearing solely on the basis of an audiometric examination than it would be to label a child as gifted or mentally retarded purely on the basis of an IQ score. Other factors, such as age of onset of the hearing loss, configuration of the loss, etiology, age of instigation of training, age of fitting and appropriateness of fit of the hearing aid, and family climate, are critical.

A great deal of the confusion among professionals working with children who have hearing losses may be traced to an inability to reach consensus on terminology. In the past, the term *hearing impaired* covered the entire range of auditory impairment, encompassing both the deaf person and the individual with a very mild loss, who may understand speech without difficulty. At present, *hearing impaired* refers to the smaller class better known as the *hard of hearing*. In most areas today, the term *hearing impaired* is not in common use; it is considered a pejorative term and one to be avoided. Although one person's concept of hard of hearing may overlap with another's concept of deafness, *hard of hearing* is usually used to distinguish individuals whose auditory channels are affected but functional from those, the deaf, for whom the sense of hearing is nonfunctional as the primary modality for the development of language. However, no satisfactory definition other than a behavioral one has been developed. The difficulties lie in (1) trying to categorize hearing losses into discrete levels when in reality they exist on a continuum and (2) attempting to generalize from an audiogram alone when so many other factors also may influence the behavior of a child with an acoustical impairment.

One practice that has added to the confusion is the tendency to report an individual's hearing loss on the basis of an unaided audiogram when substantial differences may exist between aided and unaided hearing. With appropriate fitting, training, and education, some children may cross the line separating deaf individuals from those who are hard of hearing. The movement toward early diagnosis of hearing loss and fitting of hearing aids is growing. For example, in some preschool programs for the deaf, each child is now equipped with a hearing aid. It is much more reasonable, therefore, to refer to an individual's hearing loss under his or her normal listening condition. For an increasing proportion of young children in the United States who are hearing impaired, the normal condition includes a hearing aid.

In a report of a committee formed to redefine *deaf* and *hard of hearing* for educational purposes, Frisina (1974) noted that the term *deaf* has been used variously to mean "impairment," "disability," and "handicap." As the committee defines it, deafness is caused by the physical and presently irreversible impairment of the auditory mechanism. The terms *deaf* and *deafness* are restricted to describing the disability caused by the impairment. The disability is expressed in terms of speech reception as measured by speech and other sounds calibrated for frequency and intensity. The *handicap of deafness* is the extent to which a person's overall functioning is limited by the disability of deafness. Although recognizing some negative connotations of the term *deaf,* the committee recommended its retention as a generic term because of legislative and legal precedents. As we will discover, federal legislation since 1975 has reflected a change in focus from the concept of a *handicap* to that of a *disability.*

The committee recommended that the term *deaf* be used only as an adjective, with *deafness* being the preferred term for reference to a state of hearing disability. Again, neither word describes or connotes the degree of disability involved.

The following definitions (Frisina, 1974, p. 3) were adopted by the Conference of Educational Administrators Serving the Deaf (CEASD). They are still used today.

Simple General Definitions

- A *deaf person* is one whose hearing is disabled to an extent that precludes the understanding of speech through the ear alone, with or without the use of a hearing aid.
- A *hard-of-hearing person* is one whose hearing is disabled to an extent that makes difficult, but does not preclude, the understanding of speech through the ear alone, with or without a hearing aid.

Definitions Related to Age at Onset of Deafness

Prelingual deafness refers to the condition of persons whose deafness was present at birth or occurred prior to the development of spoken or signed language. *Postlingual deafness* refers to the condition of persons whose deafness occurred following the spontaneous acquisition of language. Again, use of terminology involves sensitivities. By this definition, all neonates are prelinguistic. A newborn may be either *prelingually hearing* or *prelingually deaf*. A *postlingually deaf* child is a hearing child who became deaf. A *postlingually hearing* child (a rarity at this time) is a deaf child who became hearing. This may become more common if new generations of cochlear implants become more successful.

Many educators now restrict the definition of *deafness* to individuals who have a prelingual hearing loss of 90 dB or beyond, although some educators continue to use a more inclusive range of down to 70 or 75 dB. In general terms, this means that some educators would tend to classify children from 70 to 90 dB as deaf, whereas others would tend to classify these same children as hard of hearing.

Unfortunately, there is no generally accepted definition of the terms *deaf* or *hard of hearing*. Bienenstock and Vernon (1994) found a bewildering lack of consistency in classification across the fifty states that severely complicates the provision of services throughout the country. They reported that Public Law 94–142, the Education of All Handicapped Children Act of 1975, mandates that each state report the disability and educational placement of each child receiving special educational services. According to Bienenstock and Vernon, federal regulations do not use a specific measurable degree of hearing loss to establish eligibility; rather, they provide the following definitions (p. 129):

> *Deaf*—means a hearing impairment that is so severe that the child is impaired in processing linguistic information through hearing, with or without amplification, which adversely affects educational performance.

> *Hard of hearing*—means a hearing impairment, whether permanent or fluctuating, which adversely affects a child's educational performance, but is not included under the definition of "deaf" in this section.

Some states used terms such as *auditorially handicapped,* others *hearing impaired,* and yet others *hearing handicapped*. Some states used two categories—deaf and hearing impaired—while others used two other categories—deaf and hard of hearing. Massachusetts used no category because it does not categorize children who need special services (p. 130). For those states that distinguish the deaf from the hard of hearing, the cutoff may be as low as 65 dB (Georgia) and as high as 92 dB (Nevada). This means that a child who has a 75-dB loss is considered deaf for educational purposes in Georgia and hard of hearing in Nevada. In addition, a child who has a 40-dB loss may be eligible for services in one state and not in another. Finally, some states classify children who have unilateral (one-ear) losses as eligible, and others do not. Bienenstock and Vernon concluded that the inconsistent statistics can lead to invalid research, wasted money, and poor program planning.

Communication Modes and Methods of Instruction

Another area in which we need to establish some working definitions prior to considering substantive issues is classroom communication modes. Throughout this text, we will examine the use of different modes of communication and instruction in different contexts. Despite recent advances and a movement toward utilizing all means of communication, the centuries-old "oral-manual" controversy has generated more confusion than any other question in the field. Thus it is not surprising that professionals on the periphery are not clear about the issues.

Two basic methods of instruction may be identified in the United States: the oral method and total communication. A third approach, the bilingual-bicultural (BI-BI) method, has encouraged a great deal of discussion but has been implemented only on a limited basis to date.

1. In the *oral method,* also called the *oral-aural method,* children receive input through speech reading (lip reading) and the amplification of sound, and they express themselves through speech. As we might expect, there is great variability within the oral method. For example, some programs emphasize the use of residual hearing, others stress the use of vision, and still others balance the two. All programs, however, discourage the use of signs and finger spelling.

2. *Total communication* is a combination of the oral method plus the use of signs and finger spelling. The children receive input through speech reading, amplification, signs, and finger spelling and express themselves through speech, signs, and finger spelling. Signs are differentiated from finger spelling in that signs may represent complete ideas or words rather than individual letters of the English alphabet. Traditionally, signs were used in coordination with speech, necessitating the use of manual codes on English (to be discussed later) and not ASL. Now the trend is toward code switching: alternating between manual codes on English and ASL (Miller and Moores, in press).

3. The *bilingual–bicultural method* uses ASL for all "through-the-air" communication and uses English for reading and writing (Kuntze, 1992, p. 15; Miller and Moores, in press). Speech, auditory training, and manual codes on English are not used in the classroom, but speech and auditory training may be provided on an individual basis.

Confusion exists over the meaning of *total communication* because it is used to refer to a philosophy of education as well as to a mode or method of instruction. A total-communication philosophy endorses the right of every child who is deaf or hard of hearing to communicate by whatever means are found to be beneficial. Communication might occur through speech, signs, gestures, writing, or some other means, depending on the circumstances. In the past, a total-communication class was commonly accepted to mean one that used manual communication (signs and finger spelling) and speech in coordination. This was clearly the case in public school systems with two programs, oral and total communication, in which the total-communication component was simultaneously oral and manual. This situation has changed with the belated but welcome acceptance of ASL within the total-communication framework. As such programs have become more inclusionary by no longer excluding ASL, they have approached the ideal of true total communication.

The oral method was predominant in the United States until about 1970, when total communication (the simultaneous method) began to gain acceptance. Before that time, programs for the deaf followed a completely oral approach, at least throughout the elementary grades. Even in the "manual" schools, simultaneous methods of instruction were not used in the classroom with students below age twelve. It was common practice in such schools to house and teach younger children apart from those of secondary school age. Typically, deaf teachers were not employed with younger children for fear that they would expose the children to sign language. The ascendancy of the oral method can be traced back to the International Congress on Deafness in Milan, Italy, in 1880, which passed a resolution stating that the use of manual communication of any kind would restrict or prevent the growth of speech and language skills in deaf children.

The movement toward the use of total communication came after a series of studies (Meadow, 1967; Stuckless and Birch, 1966; Vernon and Koh, 1970) reported that deaf children who had deaf parents and were exposed to manual communication were superior to deaf children of hearing parents in English skills, academic achievement, writing, reading, and social maturity. The two groups showed no differences in speech. The finding that early manual communication seemed to facilitate overall development with no detrimental effects on acquisition of spoken language came at a time of dissatisfaction with oral-only education in general and with the negative impact of using the oral method in preschools (Moores, 1970a).

Within a short time, a drastic shift occurred. Education of the deaf moved from predominantly oral-only instruction to the simultaneous use of oral and manual means of communication in a majority of programs. Since 1975, classroom instruction in programs for the deaf has focused primarily on total communication (Schildroth and Hotto, 1994). At every level—preschool, elementary, junior high, and senior high—most programs now employ total communication.

The changes in the mode of classroom communication that took place in the 1970s are documented by two surveys of classroom modes of communication, one for 1975–1976 (Jordan, Gustason, and Rosen, 1976) and one for 1977–1978 (Jordan, Gustason, and Rosen, 1979). The first survey, which involved 7,181 classes, showed that total communication was used primarily in 64.3 percent (4,619) of the classes and oral-aural communication in 33.0 percent (2,370). The remaining 192 classes used either the Rochester Method (speech and finger spelling, but no signs) or Cued Speech (a manual system to provide cues for spoken English). Large numbers of programs reported that they had changed from oral-only instruction to total communication. However, because of confusion over the wording of the questionnaire, the extent and date of changes were not clear. Therefore, a follow-up study was conducted (Jordan, Gustason, and Rosen, 1979, p. 350) for the period 1977–1978. Information was gathered on 5,102 classes from 642 programs for the deaf across the United States, a somewhat smaller sample than in the first survey. The study reported that total communication was used in 64.7 percent (3,385) of the classes and oral-aural communication in 34.6 percent (1,807), essentially the same ratio as in 1975–1976. The reported use of the Rochester Method (25 classes) and Cued Speech (12 classes) dropped sharply. Jordan, Gustason, and Rosen (1979) reported that 481 of 642 programs had changed from oral-only modes of communication and 537 programs had changed to total communication. Changes away from Cued Speech, the Rochester Method, and "other" modes of communication were noted. Some programs had both total-communication and oral-aural classes.

Data provided by the Annual Survey of Deaf and Hard of Hearing Children and Youth indicate that by 1975 approximately two-thirds of the children enrolled in programs for the deaf were taught in total-communication classes and approximately one-third in oral-aural classes. Reliance on manual communication appears to increase with age, with 75 percent or more of high school students being taught through total communication. This finding may reflect a greater emphasis on academic content at the secondary level.

The most recent information on the primary mode of teaching (Table 1.1) indicates that 42.7 percent of students are instructed through oral/aural-only modes of instruction and 56.2 percent through some form of manual communication. Of this latter number, 51.2 percent are taught through sign and speech and 5 percent through sign alone, presumably ASL. It may surprise some readers that sign only is the primary mode of instruction with only 5 percent of students. It should be noted that ASL is used in many programs that report the use of sign and speech. It is common for teachers in such programs to switch from sign with speech to sign alone. Moores (1999) has argued that the lines between BI-BI and total-communication programs have blurred to some extent because of the tendency of most total-communication

TABLE 1.1   Primary Method of Teaching with Deaf and Hard of Hearing Students, 1997–1998

Mode	Number	Percentage
Sign and speech	24,083	51.2
Oral/aural only	20,092	42.7
Sign only	2,371	5.0
Cued speech	200	0.4
Other	322	0.7
Total	47,068	100.0

Source: Callaudet Research Institute, *1997–98 Annual Survey of Deaf and Hard of Hearing Children and Youth* (Washington, D.C.: GRI, Callaudet University, 1998), p. 27.

programs now to use both AL and English-based sign systems. This issue will be discussed in detail in a later chapter.

As might be expected, the mode of instruction used is related to a child's school placement and to hearing level. Schildroth and Hotto (1993) analyzed the primary teaching method used with children in four types of placement: residential school, day school, local integrated placement, and local, not integrated placement (see Table 1.2). Rather than use terms such as *total communication, bilingual-bicultural,* and so forth, they used descriptors such as *sign and speech, sign only,* and *auditory/oral only.* In residential schools, 92 percent were taught through sign and speech compared to only 38 percent in local integrated settings, where the majority received auditory/oral instruction. In other settings, 72 percent of children were instructed through sign and speech. The differences in mode of instruction between residential and local integrated students may largely be explained by two factors: age and hearing level. According to Table 1.2, 89 percent of children in residential schools had severe/profound hearing losses, compared to 38 percent in local integrated programs. Also, residential students tended to be older, with 50

TABLE 1.2   Selected Characteristics of Children Who Are Deaf and Hard of Hearing in Four Different Placements, 1992–1993

	Residential School	Day School	Local, Not Integrated	Local Integrated
Degree of Loss				
Less than severe	11%	18%	36%	62%
Severe/profound	89	82	64	38
Primary Instruction Method				
Auditory/oral	4	23	25	60
Sign and speech	92	72	72	38
Sign only	4	5	2	<1
Other	<1	<1	1	1
Age				
Under 14	50	79	81	75
14 and older	50	21	19	25
Ethnic Status				
White	65	47	51	62
Black	20	21	22	15
Hispanic	10	26	19	17
Asian/Pacific	3	3	5	4
Other	3	3	2	2

Source: Adapted from A. Schildroth and S. Hotto, "Annual Survey of Hearing Impaired Children and Youth," *American Annals of the Deaf,* 138 (1993):163–171.

percent fourteen years of age or above compared to 25 percent for children in integrated settings. Also note variation in placement by racial/ethnic status in Table 1.2. In 1993, white students constituted a minority in the combined enrollment in day school and local, not integrated, settings; Hispanic children were underrepresented in residential schools.

Educational Programs and Services

As we have noted, education of the deaf has undergone tremendous changes in recent years. Areas that will receive full treatment in this text include the use of manual communication, the growth of preschool programs, the development of a variety of options at the postsecondary level, cochlear implants, the Human Genome Project, and the provision of more effective services to individuals with multiple disabilities. Impetus for such changes has come from a number of sources: the worldwide rubella epidemic of the middle 1960s, which dramatically increased the number of children born deaf during that period; breakthroughs in the development of powerful wearable hearing aids for children; innovative research on American Sign Language and the systems of manual communication; changing cultural attitudes; and the impact of Public Law 94–142, the Education of All Handicapped Children Act of 1975, and its evolution into Public Law 99–457, the Individuals with Disabilities Education Act (IDEA) of 1990, which was later reauthorized as Public Law 101–476 and amended as public law 105–17 in 1997.

A tripartite perspective encompassing events, cycles, and the long term, however, reveals that some basic questions and issues have come down to us almost unchanged over the past several hundred years. The role of manual communication, for example, still remains a subject of bitter debate in some areas, and the arguments used are essentially the same as those employed by the pro-signing Abbé de l'Epée and the anti-signing Samuel Heinicke in their exchange of correspondence in the eighteenth century (Garnett, 1968; Stedt and Moores, 1990).

Trends in Special Education

Before considering the educational placement of deaf children, we will examine trends in special education that have had both direct and indirect impacts on placement decisions for children who are deaf. Beginning around 1968, a reaction developed against increasingly segregated education for children classified as moderately and mildly handicapped. Concern was particularly high for children classified as educable mentally retarded (EMR) as special educators belatedly became sensitive to the fact that minority children were overrepresented in classes for EMR students. After an article by Dunn (1968) questioned the placement of EMR children in segregated settings, the majority opinion quickly shifted in favor of educating children with and without disabilities in the same classes to the greatest extent possible.

During this period, the term *mainstreaming* came into popular use. For a time, some of its more zealous advocates perceived it as a goal in itself rather than a means to an end.

The cyclical nature of the concept of mental retardation among special educators was illustrated by Kirk (1975), who pointed out that a major reason for the growing popularity of mainstreaming for students who were mentally retarded was that in the past many children had been mislabeled as *retarded* and inappropriately placed in special schools and classes. According to Kirk, in the 1920s and 1930s, the term *mental retardation* was used to refer to individuals whose intelligence quotient (IQ) scores were 70 or below. Over a period of time, the upper limit for children eligible for special classes was gradually raised to 75 or 80—in some places, 85. By 1962, the American Association on Mental Deficiency (AAMD) had defined *retardation* in terms of an IQ one standard deviation below the general population mean IQ of 100. This made an IQ of 85 the upper limit for retardation, thus increasing the potential population for assignment to special classes. As a result, the number of children classified as retarded in special classes in the United States rose from 113,565 in 1952 to 703,800 in 1968—an increase of more than 600 percent in less than twenty years (Kirk, 1975).

The situation had become intolerable for a number of reasons, but especially because placement practices were racially and ethnically discriminatory. There was no educational basis for segregating children based on an IQ score of 85, especially when the children used a language or dialect different from that of the teacher or the psychologist. Mercer (1973) reported that black and Spanish-surnamed children were assigned to classes for students with mental retardation in disproportionate numbers, and Garrison and Hamil (1971) estimated that 25 percent of children in classes for educable mentally retarded students were misplaced.

From 1968 to 1975, the reaction by psychologists and educators of people with mental retardation was dramatic. In 1973, the AAMD changed the psychometric definition of *mental retardation* to require an IQ two standard deviations below the norm rather than one standard deviation. The 1962 AAMD definition included children with a measured IQ of up to 85, whereas the 1973 definition limited the category to those with an IQ of 70 or less. Thus, children with measured IQs from 70 to 85 were no longer psychometrically eligible for designation as having mental retardation.

Educators of students labeled retarded have not been the only professionals to establish overly inclusive criteria for inclusion in a category. As mentioned previously, there is a growing tendency to think of deafness as involving a hearing loss of greater than 85 or 90 dB, in contrast to past standards of 70 or 75 dB. One reason for this trend is the belief that many children with significant residual hearing have been inappropriately labeled as deaf and assigned to special classes or schools. Normal spoken conversation takes place roughly in the 40- to 70-dB range. Many children with severe hearing losses—and some with profound losses—may be able to hear significant amounts of speech with a hearing aid. In the final analysis, a number of factors must be considered, including etiology, type of loss, age of loss, and presence of other handicapping conditions.

Between 1968 and 1975, several court cases dealing with placement and educational services for students with disabilities were decided. (Treatment of these cases appears in Abeson [1972, 1974]; Kuriloff, True, Kirp, and Buss [1974]; and Turnbull [1975].) The two landmark cases were *The Pennsylvania Association for Retarded Citizens* (PARC) v. *The Commonwealth of Pennsylvania* and *Mills* v. *The Board of Education of the District of Columbia,* both of which were decided in 1972. Rulings on these cases declared that practices excluding individuals with disabilities from educational opportunities were illegal. The *PARC* decision established that all individuals with mental retardation had the right to free public education and required the state to identify all such children who were excluded from such education, as well as to evaluate all those already in special classes.

In both the *PARC* and *Mills* cases, it was decided that regular class placement was preferable to placement in special classes, which in turn was preferable to placement in a residential setting. From this it follows that a child with mental retardation—and, by extension, a child who has any disability—should not be placed in a residential school or institution if the education provided is not demonstrably superior to that offered in special classes. If children are removed from the home for educational purposes, the burden of proof, according to the *PARC* and *Mills* decisions, is on the educators.

The court cases dealt with children with more severe disabilities than those who had been classified as EMR for educational purposes, but the trend was clear: movement toward what would be considered a less restrictive environment. This meant "deinstitutionalization" for many children and adults with severe retardation, that is, a return to the communities and the public schools, usually in a special-class setting. For those who previously might have been labeled EMR, the move was from the special class back into a regular classroom.

Public Law 94–142: The Education of All Handicapped Children Act of 1975; Public Law 101– 476: The Individuals with Disabilities Education Act of 1990; Public Law 105–17: The Individuals with Disabilities Education Act Amendments of 1997

In the fall of 1975, as an outcome of the aforementioned trends in special education and the efforts of several advocacy groups for people with disabilities, the United States Congress passed Public Law 94–142, the Education of All Handicapped Children Act. The act mandated a free, appropriate public education (FAPE) for all children with disabilities, and it stipulated procedural safeguards to protect the rights of these children and their parents. The act called for nondiscriminatory testing, assurance of an annual individualized educational plan (IEP), and provision of services in the least restrictive environment (LRE) appropriate to each child's needs (Harvey and Siantz, 1979). The IEP is the key element of PL 94–142. Each year, an IEP must be written for every child who has a disability, describing the child's current performance, outlining educational objectives, and specifying evaluation procedures. Through PL 94–142, parents have the legal right to participate in the formulation of the IEP, and they have the option to accept or reject the IEP or any of its parts. Procedures for resolution have been developed for cases in which differences of opinion arise.

Although PL 94–142 has been viewed in some areas as the "mainstreaming law," the term *mainstreaming* was deliberately excluded from the act, which mandates both an appropriate education and an education in the least restrictive environment. From the beginning of its implementation, the act was interpreted to mean that a range of placement options should be available. Bersoff and Voltman (1979) note that the continuum of alternative services should include instruction in regular classes supplemented by special services, special classes, special schools, home instruction, and instruction in hospitals and institutions. These authors state the following:

> Despite the preference for mainstreaming in PL 94-142, placement of children in regular classrooms may be inappropriate, as recent judicial decisions have held. In *Frederick* v. *Thomas* (1977) the court concluded that Pennsylvania had to identify all learning disabled students. Those students were already receiving an education in regular classrooms but the court found that many such students should be placed in separate classes while others should be provided supplemental support services. Similarly, the court in *Howard S.* v. *Friendswood Independent School District* (1978) found that placement of the plaintiff in regular classes with a resource teacher was an inappropriate program considering the severity of his disability. From these examples, it seems that although placement in regular classes is viewed as desirable under PL 94-142, such a placement will still be open to challenge as being inappropriate for a particular child's educational needs. (pp. 19-20)

The enactment of PL 94–142 and subsequent reauthorizations, including PL 101–476, the Individuals with Disabilities Education Act (IDEA) of 1990, and its 1997 amendment, reflect a continuing evolution in the approach to special education. First, as the name implies, the concern is with disabilities, not handicaps, suggesting a more positive approach to education. IDEA also expands the age range served. PL 94–142 was originally concerned with ages five to eighteen. IDEA authorizes services from time of identification of a hearing loss, or any disability, up to age twenty-one. The scope of services also has expanded from child centered to family centered. The individualized educational plan of PL 94–142 has been replaced by the individual family service plan (IFSP) of IDEA and its amendments.

School Placement Alternatives

Because the growth in options, especially in public school programs, has been a relatively recent phenomenon, a great deal of confusion exists over terminology, a not uncommon situation in our field! Different school districts identify the various options in different ways, making it difficult to interpret reports consistently. The following definitions provide a very simple way to classify the most common types of programs for deaf children:

1. **Residential schools.** Residential school programs provide facilities to house students as well as to educate them. In areas accessible to large populations, substantial numbers of children live at home and commute daily. Children living within commuting distance generally attend on a day basis, and those living farther away stay at school on a residential basis, at least during weekdays. In recent years, approximately 50 percent of students in residential schools for the deaf have attended on a day basis. Most live at home on weekends.

2. **Day schools.** In larger metropolitan areas, programs may be established in separate day schools for the deaf. Children commute to these schools daily, and hearing children are not enrolled.

3. **Day classes.** Day-class programs are classes for the deaf established in a public school building in which the majority of children are hearing. Instruction may be in completely self-contained classes, or children may spend part or most of their time in regular classrooms.

4. **Resource rooms.** Most resource rooms are planned so that children spend most of their day in regular classes, returning to the special class for additional attention, usually in English and in particular academic areas. Whereas day-class programs tend to have several classes in one school, with homogeneous grouping of children, the resource room teacher is generally expected to provide individualized services to students varying in age, hearing loss, and academic achievement.

5. **Itinerant programs.** In itinerant programs, children attend regular classes full time and receive support services from an "itinerant" teacher, who may work with children from several different schools. The support services vary from daily to weekly lessons, depending on a child's individual needs.

With increased individualization of instruction, more complex patterns of placement have been identified. As many as twelve variations of the five basic placements may be in operation in any one state (Moores, 1995b). The labels used are not always consistent with the definitions just given. For example, Texas has a statewide program for the deaf called a *public day-school program,* but the children do not attend separate day schools for the deaf; they are enrolled in day classes, resource rooms, and regular classrooms in public schools that also enroll hearing students.

Many school districts now centralize their programs, especially for high school–age students, to consolidate resources and support services. It is common to have services on a day-class, resource room, and itinerant basis all in one building. Given the requirements of an annual individualized educational plan and the possibility that a child will require different types of placement over a period of years, the concentration of programs in one area reduces the chance of frequent school changes.

In the past, only children with the most residual hearing and the best oral communication skills tended to be placed in resource room and itinerant settings. The use of manual interpreters in regular classrooms has led to an increase in the number of children with profound hearing losses in regular classrooms for at least some academic subjects (Moores, 1990a; Moores, Cerney, and Garcia, 1990).

Patterns in School Placement, 1974–1994

Perhaps the best way to assess the impact of legislation and societal change on the placement of deaf children is to compare enrollment for the fall of 1974 (the year before Pl 94–142 was passed) with the most recent data available, the fall of 1997. The 1975 edition of *American Annals of the Deaf* (Craig and Craig, 1975) has enrollment data for fall 1974, and data for 1997–1998 were obtained from the Annual Survey of Deaf and Hard of Hearing Children and Youth. Table 1.3 summarizes the results. The categories are somewhat different for the 1974 data and the 1997–1998 data, so caution should be exercised in interpreting the data. A major problem in interpretation lies with the fact that instructional setting was not reported for 14,502 children, or almost 30 percent of the total number of students for 1997–1998.

I was informed by a researcher in the Annual Survey that the residential and day-school programs tend to report the instructional setting more than do local schools, so the numbers in local school settings are probably underreported. Also, the numbers of children reported for 1997–1998 in *mainstreamed, self-contained classrooms, and resource rooms* are larger than the total in local schools. This is because some children were listed in more than one category. Finally, the 1997–1998 data do not present separate information for day schools and residential schools, but list both under the category *Special school or center.* Even with all these caveats, the data do show some interesting trends. Most important is a clear movement away from enrollment in special schools and centers, where reported attendance has declined from 28,639 to 10,170, or from 54 percent of the students to approximately 30 percent, probably lower. The instructional setting today is mostly in local public schools, with the single largest category being mainstreaming, which we may equate with receiving itinerant services. Moores (1992a) has noted that the trend away from residential schools started well before PL 94–142. In 1945, at the end of World war II, 76 percent of deaf children attended residential schools, a much higher percentage than in 1974. In 1945 the bulk of the remaining children attended day schools for the deaf. Since 1974 both the number and percentage of children attending residential schools have declined. Most deaf children today do not have the residential school experiences of past generations. Nor do they have the experience of attending day schools in which all children are deaf.

Ethnic Minorities

Although we will explore the subject in detail in later sections, we should note at this point that educational services to deaf individuals from ethnic minority groups typically have been inferior to those provided for most deaf individuals. Until re-

TABLE 1.3 Patterns in School Enrollment, 1973–1974 and 1997–1998

Instructional Setting	1973–1974		1997–1998	
	Number	**Percent**	**Number**	**Percent**
Special school or center	28,639	54.0	10,170	29.9
Residential	(20,564)		—	
Day school	(8,075)		—	
Local public school	22,256	41.9	21,757	63.9
Mainstream	—		(14,748)	
Self-contained class	—		(10,888)	
Resource room	—		(4,748)	
Alternative setting	2,114	4.0	2,135	6.3
Home	—		(638)	
Other	—		(1,467)	
Not Reported	—		14,502	

Sources: W. Craig and H. Craig, Eds, "Directory of Services for the Deaf," *American Annals of the Deaf,* 120(1974). Gallaudet Research Institute, *1997–98 Annual Survey of Deaf and Hard of Hearing Children and Youth* (Washington, D.C.: GRI, Gallaudet University, 1998).

cently, most information has been restricted to the black deaf population, and there is a documented history of discrimination and placement in poorly supported separate schools up until the 1960s.

Historically, estimates of the incidence of deafness among minority populations have been low (Moores and Oden, 1978). Underestimates of the size of a population lead to underestimates of the needs of the population. These needs must be strongly emphasized at present, given evidence that the percentages of minority children in programs for the deaf are higher than the percentages of minority children in the general school-age population. According to Schildroth and Hotto (1995), approximately 40 percent of the deaf school-age population consisted of African-American, Hispanic-American, Asian-American, and Native American children. Of these, African-Americans accounted for approximately 17 percent, Hispanic-Americans for 16 percent, Asian-Americans for 4 percent, and Native Americans and "others" for 3 percent. The numbers of Caucasian and African-American children in programs for the deaf have been declining, with other categories increasing. By 1987, "minority" students accounted for the majority of students in programs for the deaf and hard of hearing in the three most populous states: California, Texas, and New York (Schildroth, 1989).

The Deaf Community

The Deaf community is a unique component of American society. The reader should be aware of its existence and its importance for deaf individuals. The existence of a Deaf community can be traced to the enculturating influence of residential schools for the deaf. The schools served to bring together people with a low-incidence condition (deafness) who otherwise would have been isolated in their home communities. Identifying themselves through the use of a unique language, American Sign Language (ASL), deaf people have developed a community with characteristics consistent with those of an identifiable subculture or ethnic group. As mentioned at the beginning of this chapter, there are local, regional, state, national, and international organizations of the deaf. There are cultural events, athletic competitions, and even a Miss Deaf America pageant. Frequently, deaf people are members of deaf religious congregations, and the rate of deaf intramarriage is quite high. The Deaf community has infused its members with a sense of pride and provided support in difficult times.

Much discussion has centered on the use of capitalization in the terms *Deaf/deaf*. This issue has been addressed most comprehensively by Padden and Humphries (1989) in a book entitled *Deaf in America: Voices from a Culture*. In sociocultural terms, there is a Deaf community with a shared language, American Sign Language, and a shared culture, Deaf culture. Padden and Humphries reject the deficiency/ disease model of deafness and concentrate instead on the social model of a community with identifiable and unique characteristics. Audiological status is only one criterion for membership in the Deaf community. Cultural characteristics and behavior must also be present. Whether or not, or the extent to which, a hearing person can be a member of the Deaf community is a matter of debate and is beyond the scope of a book concerned primarily with education. For our purposes, we will refer to "deaf students," who may or may not become members of the Deaf community. In our experience, a majority of deaf students already belong to or become part of the Deaf community.

Although the Deaf community meets many of the criteria of a linguistic or ethnic minority, the analogy can be carried only to a certain point given the unique nature of deafness and of the deaf population. Reagan (1990), for example, has argued that contemporary concepts of ethnic and linguistic minority group status are too simplistic to describe the complexity of the real-life situation of deaf people. He points out that the situation of a deaf person who is also a member of an ethnic or linguistic minority, such as an African-American or a Hispanic-American, is even more complicated.

Another consideration is the fact that only a very small number of deaf children—approximately 4 percent—have deaf parents, and most deaf children have hearing brothers, sisters, aunts, and uncles. Thus transmission of the culture and of American Sign Language is not familial; it usually takes place through contact with nonrelated deaf peers.

Changes in school placement and in modes of instruction raise questions about the future evolution of ASL and the Deaf community. Most deaf adults in the United States and Canada in the past learned to sign from other deaf students in residential schools. Most schools did not allow signing in class, at least through the elementary grades. Children learned signs from other children, many times surreptitiously. At present, most children attend public day classes. Of those children in residential schools, many reside at home. This means that fewer than 15 percent of all deaf children *reside* in residential schools. With the spread of total communication, most deaf children receive their greatest exposure to signs from hearing teachers in class-rooms, not from deaf peers in dormitories. These children may also use signs at home with hearing parents and relatives. The sign systems hearing teachers use, typically accompanied by speech, are usually manual codes on English and differ from ASL in many respects. There is no doubt that ASL is a viable language and will continue to thrive. However, like all languages, it undergoes constant change, and it will likely undergo extensive modification as the deaf children now in school grow into adulthood.

The changing school placement patterns may alter the character of the Deaf community by changing the self-perceptions of deaf individuals. Because most deaf children attend school at least in the same building as hearing children, the unifying force exerted by the residential school is lacking. As the children now in schools enter adulthood, it will be interesting to observe their impact on the American Deaf community.

The Deaf President Now (DPN) movement, a weeklong, student-led protest in the spring of 1988 that led to the selection of the first deaf president at Gallaudet University, the only higher education institution for the deaf in the world, was a defining moment for the Deaf community. For almost 125 years, Gallaudet had been led by hearing men. For more than 100 years, it had had only three presidents: Edward Minor Gallaudet, Percival Hall, and Leonard Elstad. Each had devoted his entire career to education of the deaf. Following this period, the priority shifted from expertise in education of the deaf to expertise in higher education, and Gallaudet looked to state universities for presidents. From 1969 to 1989, three out of the four individuals selected as president of Gallaudet had been administrators at state universities and had little or no prior exposure to deafness. The selection of the fourth individual in 1988, a hearing woman, sparked the DPN movement.

In 1988, for the first time, the university had a pool of deaf applicants with backgrounds in higher education. Three of the six semifinalists were deaf, and each had substantial experience in higher education and administration in addition to fluent sign communication skills and knowledge of deafness. None of the three hearing semifinalists had experience in education of the deaf or signing skills. From the semifinalists, two deaf candidates and one hearing candidate were chosen as finalists. When the hearing candidate was selected as president, the students protested, boycotted classes, and closed down the university. The person selected obviously had excellent qualifications for higher education but little knowledge of the unique nature of deafness or of the special characteristics of deaf students. Most symbolic to some students was the fact that she would be required to rely on an interpreter to communicate with many of Gallaudet's students until she developed sign proficiency. Because there were deaf candidates with excellent academic skills, the decision by the board of trustees was seen as discriminatory. The students issued several demands, including the selection of a deaf president from among the qualified candidates and a reconstitution of the board of trustees with a majority of deaf members. The demands were supported by the faculty (most of whom were hearing) by a vote of 99 to 5 and by the staff. After a period of confrontation, a deaf academic, I. King Jordan, was named president, and the board of trustees was subsequently reorganized with a deaf majority. The entire DPN movement is described in a book by Gannon (1988), *The Week the World Heard Gallaudet*.

Impact of Diversity

At this point it might be beneficial to address the concepts of race and ethnicity as used by the federal government. At one time or another we have probably all come across the statement that race is an artificial construct but that racism is real. Any attempt to categorize the human race into separate discrete categories is doomed to failure. Humans from different groups have been interbreeding from the beginning of time and will continue to do so. Any classification is inefficient and ambiguous. According to information I received from a colleague who had worked with the Commission on Civil Rights (Moores, 1998), definitions have changed over the past centuries, and states can and do vary from the federal government in their definitions. As I understand it, the federal categories are roughly as follows:

Black not Hispanic

White, not Hispanic

Hispanic

Asian/Pacific Island

Native American

These represent quasi-racial, ethnic, and geographic categories. The term *black* refers to African origin; hence the relationship with the term *African-American*. However, the origins of an African-American need not be completely, or even predominantly, from Africa. Historically, individuals of mixed black and white ancestry have been classified as black and denied civil rights. Typically a person with three white grandparents and only black grandparent has been classified as black. Most African-Americans also have white, Native American, and/or Hispanic ancestry.

The white category, also a social construct, has mistakenly been referred to as European. It also includes individuals from North Africa, the Arabian Peninsula, and Iran. Of course, Syria, Saudi Arabia, and most of Turkey, Israel, and Lebanon are in Asia, but the federal government does not describe them as being of Asian/Pacific origin. Large numbers of white Americans also have black, Hispanic, and/or Native American ancestry.

Hispanic-Americans are classified by ethnicity and not by race in official reporting, thus confusing an already ambiguous situation. Although most Hispanic-Americans identify themselves as white, substantial numbers identify themselves as black or have origins in the indigenous populations of Latin American countries.

The Asian/Pacific grouping is neither racial nor ethnic but geographic, although it does not include all Asians and some categories have changed. At one time Americans from India and Pakistan were classified as white, but now they are included in the Asian/Pacific category.

The Native American category also represents great diversity in terms of origin and tribal definitions of membership, which may include individuals of predominantly white and/or black genetic heritage. In recent years there has been a large increase in the Native American population, mostly because of changes in self-identification from other groups.

Given the ambiguity of classification, and keeping in mind the problems of classification, it is still beneficial to examine trends from the admittedly rough data that have been available. Looking at Table 1.4, we can see some significant shifts in the demographic characteristics of children in programs for deaf children from 1983–1984 to 1997–1998. In essence children classified as white fell from 67 percent to 56 percent of total enrollment, children classified as black declined slightly from 18 percent to 17 percent, Hispanic children went from 11 percent of enrollment in 1983–1984 to 20 percent in 1997–1998, and Asian/Pacific enrollment increased from 2 percent to 4 percent. The actual numbers provide an interesting picture. The numbers of children classified as white declined by 25 percent and those classified as black declined by 14 percent over the period, in spite of the fact that the white and black school-age populations have increased. There are some possible explanations for this situation, but they must remain speculation. Perhaps improvements in medical care and general health in these populations have led to decreases in deafness related to meningitis, mother-child blood incompatibility, complications related to prematurity, and other factors. The answers should become clear over a period of time. On the other hand, the growth of representation from Hispanic and Asian/Pacific populations does represent significant increases in the American school-age population.

TABLE 1.4 Changes in Enrollment by Racial and Ethnic Status, 1983–1984, 1993–1998

	Year					
	1983–1984		*1997–1998*		*Change*	
Racial/Ethnic Category	*Number*	*Percentage*	*Number*	*Percentage*	*Number*	*Percentage*
White	35,069	67	26,372	56	−8,697	−25
Black	9,337	18	7,991	17	−1,346	−14
Hispanic	5,720	11	9,192	20	+3,472	+61
Asian/Pacific	1,130	2	1,946	4	+816	+72
Native American	Not reported		376	1	—	—
Other	1,074	2	756	2	−318	−30
Multiethnic	Not reported		574	1	—	—

Source: A. Schildroth and S. Hotto, "Race and Ethnic Background in the Annual Survey of Deaf and Hard of Hearing Children and Youth," *American Annals of the Deaf* 140 (1995): 96–99.

Summary

It is beneficial to view the past history and present reality of education of the deaf from the three distinct but complementary perspectives of events, cycles, and the long term. Recent years have seen significant improvements in education of the deaf. There is much greater flexibility in modes of instruction and educational placement. Services have improved from preschool through graduate school, and there is evidence of improvement in academic achievement. Although difficulties remain, at least the special needs of deaf children from diverse backgrounds are now receiving attention.

A cyclical perspective reveals that U.S. education has long endured a conflict between the two somewhat antagonistic ideals of equity and excellence in education. Within the context of a rise in overall achievement, school programs must be designed to enable deaf students to increase their academic achievement in order not to lose ground. The goal is to improve achievement while maintaining the advances in equity of access that have been achieved.

Looking beyond cycles, we find that the enduring reality of deafness changes slowly. Relative to hearing people, deaf people may be better off now than they were 25 years ago, but in some ways they are no better off than they were 125 years ago. Then, as now, the greatest problems deaf individuals faced concerned communication with the rest of society.

Concentration on deafness as a pathology or a deficiency can be self-defeating. Deaf children should be allowed to develop their individual strengths and skills. Although deafness can involve restrictions and accommodations, it should also be perceived in a social context. The more deafness is approached as a social condition, the greater will be each child's chances for healthy overall development.

CHAPTER

2

Historical Perspectives: Prehistoric Times to the Twentieth Century

Introduction

Deafness is part of the human condition and exists throughout the world. It is present in all races, in both genders, and from preliterate hunter/gatherer tribes to the most highly industrialized societies. Deafness has occurred in royal families and in the most impoverished social strata.

Deafness was noted in the first literate societies in Egypt and Mesopotamia and occurs in all societies today. Thus, it has probably existed throughout the history of humanity. The fact that genetic deafness itself has a large number of causes and that deafness can be acquired in many ways suggests that it is likely to be found in any large population.

Although deafness has likely always been part of the human condition, its incidence and the conditions under which deaf individuals lived in prehistoric, classical, and medieval times can only be a matter of conjecture. Brief mentions of deafness and deaf individuals in ancient documents provide some fascinating insights, but ancient societies varied so greatly that it is difficult to generalize from the few references available.

Information about deafness and deaf individuals was also extremely limited well into modern times. In the preface to the text *Deaf History Unveiled,* Van Cleve (1993, p. ix) wrote, "As recently as 1970, Deaf history did not exist." The text itself was based on sixteen essays presented at the first International Conference on Deaf History, held in 1991 at Gallaudet University in Washington, D.C., and represents a significant breakthrough. However, all of the essays were limited to Europe and North America, and fourteen of them addressed conditions in the nineteenth and twentieth centuries. The remaining two dealt with Pedro Ponce de León, a six-

29

teenth-century Spanish Benedictine monk recognized as the first teacher of deaf children (Plann, 1993), and the Abbé Charles-Michel de L'Epée, who established the first school for deaf students in Paris in the 1760s (Fischer, 1993).

Nevertheless, the surge of interest in Deaf history promises to add immeasurably to our understanding of conditions in nineteenth- and twentieth-century Europe and North America. Eventually, this interest may extend to the rest of the world and to premodern times.

Acquired deafness may have been more common in the past than at present. In recent times, antibiotics have greatly reduced deafness resulting from meningitis, scarlet fever, and otitis media. It is logical to assume that these and other diseases took their toll on past civilizations to at least the same extent that they did in industrialized societies until the recent past. The absence of prenatal care and nutritional deficiencies also probably had a deleterious effect (Winzer, 1993a).

It is also possible that the incidence of inherited deafness was higher in prehistoric times. Given the limited mobility of the prehistoric world, the concentration of recessive genes was likely high, increasing the probability of inherited deafness in a population. It is doubtful that infanticide, in the areas where it was practiced, had much effect on the incidence of deafness in a population, for even today a diagnosis of deafness frequently is not made until after infancy.

At present, the incidence of genetic deafness, which is usually associated with recessive genes, is higher among homogeneous populations that intermarry than among heterogeneous populations. An example of a modern inbred group with a high incidence of inherited deafness is the native population of Martha's Vineyard, a small island off the coast of Massachusetts, whose inhabitants comprised self-contained communities that had little contact with the mainland and intermarried for several generations. The incidence of deafness on the island was ten times higher than in Massachusetts; in one section, it approached 25 percent (Groce, 1980). The islanders developed their own sign language and easily accommodated deaf members in the life of the community. The incidence of deafness decreased with intermarriage as islanders began to move to the mainland and other populations moved onto the island.

Observations of widely divergent cultural groups indicate the same easy accommodation to deafness. Mallory (1880) noted that young deaf children among the North American Plains Indians used sign language skillfully. In a report on the isolated Tasaday tribe in the Philippine Islands, Nance (1975) noted that only two of the twenty-six tribe members were deaf, yet the entire tribe used a sign language to communicate with those members.

Although individual tribes and cultures may have imposed limitations on deaf individuals and even acted punitively toward them, it is difficult to imagine any culture so dependent on hearing that deaf persons could not participate and contribute. One might argue that the deaf have faced the greatest disadvantage relative to hearing persons in those societies that have been influenced most heavily by the Judeo-Hellenic tradition (that is, in European and American societies) as a result of the greater emphasis placed on the spoken word and its preeminent role in religious as well as intellectual functions. Although all cultures apparently have attached magical and mystical qualities to at least some spoken words, nowhere has this belief been expressed more strongly than in the statement "In the beginning was the Word." Thus there were biblical sanctions against marriages of "deaf-mutes," and during medieval times most deaf persons were not allowed to receive communion because they were unable to vocally confess their sins.

It is not known whether the deaf in other great societies, such as ancient Egypt, Central and South America, Indonesia, China, Japan, Africa, India, and Southeast Asia, labored under similar restrictions. Degerando (1827) suggested that in societies such as ancient Egypt and China, where writing was based on meanings and did not rely on an alphabet, deaf individuals may have been instructed to read. Peet (1851) strongly disagreed with this supposition. Unfortunately, as noted, the only historical information presently available has a basically European framework. However, with Eurocentricism decreasing around the world, pertinent information may be uncovered from unanticipated sources.

The Ancient World

Around 10,000 B.C., hunting and food gathering began to give way to agriculture in the areas that constitute present-day Syria, Iraq, Iran, and Turkey. By the fourth millennium B.C., a peasant agriculture had developed that was capable of supporting villages and small towns. From these beginnings, the valley of Mesopotamia, located between the Tigris and Euphrates rivers, produced the essential foundation of civilization, the literate city-state (Mallowan, 1965).

The ancient world may be thought of as extending from the beginning of recorded history to the fall of the western Roman Empire, around A.D. 500. In terms of territory, the ancient world encompassed the original Mesopotamian kingdoms (Sumeria, Assyria, and Babylon) and Egypt and in time expanded to include areas as widespread as Persia and Rome, but not such equally ancient and sophisticated societies as present-day India, China, and Indonesia.

Formal education as we know it today began in Mesopotamia and Egypt, the first literate societies of the ancient world (Boyd, 1966; Lawrence, 1970). Schooling was necessary to train scribes to function in developing government bureaucracies. The ancient Egyptians and Mesopotamians prized intellectual ability, and highly talented boys (but not girls) had unlimited opportunities for advancement (Laurie, 1907). Excavations of a Sumerian school dating back to 2000 B.C. and the discovery of writing-exercise tablets dating back to 2500 B.C. indicate that these societies valued reading, writing, and mathematics much as present-day societies do (Bowen, 1972).

Although no evidence exists of any attempts to educate the deaf or individuals with other disabilities in the first literate societies, Egyptian society had considerable tolerance of and concern for such persons. Infanticide was forbidden by decree. The Egyptians possessed the roots of concepts basic to most modern civilizations, such as the ideas of conscience, truth, justice, righteousness, one god, and distinctions between right and wrong (Frost, 1947). Ancient Egyptian thought has come down to modern times indirectly through its profound impact on the ancient Jews during their period in Egypt and more directly through the Greek and Roman cultures, which conquered Egypt and absorbed many of its values.

The ancient Egyptians, representing perhaps the most humane society of the ancient world, were the first people to document an interest not only in handicapping conditions but also in individuals with disabilities. In addition to studying causes of and cures for disabilities, they focused on the personal and social well-being of persons with disabilities, especially the sightless. The priests of Karnak trained the blind in music, the arts, and massage. Blind people participated in religious ceremonies and, during some periods, represented a large proportion of the poets and musicians of ancient Egypt.

Although the process of hearing was less understood than the process of seeing, lotions and ointments were used to treat hearing loss. The first known reference to deafness is found in the Egyptian Ebers papyrus (circa 1550 B.C.), which is probably based on even more ancient writing (Feldman, 1970).

The evidence suggests that the attitudes of people in the ancient world toward the deaf were ambivalent at best. In general, the first indications of interest in the deaf were theological and judicial, not medical or educational (Werner, 1932). The major concerns appeared to be defining the legal and religious rights of the deaf. Education for the deaf was not a consideration in societies in which the majority of the population was illiterate. Medically, it was generally believed that curing congenital deafness (that is, deafness present at birth) was impossible.

Classical Greece and Rome

With the ascendancy of Greece and later of Rome, the spoken word continued to be of primary importance, and the situation for the deaf deteriorated. Conditions probably were not as severe, however, as many educators of the deaf have suggested.

Aristotle has been portrayed as a villain because in 355 B.C. he wrote, "Men that are deaf are also speechless; that is, they can make vocal sounds but they cannot speak." Greek philosophers generally believed that thought could be conceived only through the medium of articulate words. Because Aristotle declared the ear as the organ of instruction and believed that hearing made the greatest contribution to intelligence, he has been accused of keeping the deaf in ignorance for two thousand years (Deland, 1931). This idea, coupled with the belief that his statement "Let it be a law that nothing imperfect should be brought up" led to the destruction of deaf children by Spartans, Athenians, and Romans, has made the name of Aristotle anathema among some educators of the deaf.

Aristotle's bad standing is in large part undeserved. His statement, taken out of context, was distorted and misinterpreted. The preceding quote is merely a statement of fact that holds true today: without special training, a child who is born deaf will not learn to speak. In Aristotle's time, speech training did not exist, and thus the conditions of deafness and muteness were considered to be interrelated. In 1851, Peet reported that whereas some biblical passages use the same word, *kophoi*, both for deaf and for dumb (or mute),* Aristotle used separate terms to distinguish between the words *deaf* and *mute* (or *speechless*). Within the context of his writing, the negative connotations attributed to his statement are not justifiable. Moreover, it is doubtful that Aristotle's dictum about imperfection, no matter how abhorrent to present-day readers, actually led to the destruction of many deaf babies. As previously noted, diagnosis of deafness at birth, at which time Greek babies were inspected, is difficult even today because physically normal deaf babies manifest no observable differences from physically normal hearing babies.

The fact that deaf individuals existed and were accepted by Greek society is attested to by the following exchange between Socrates and Hermogenes in Plato's Cratylus (Levinson, 1967):

SOCRATES: And here I will ask you a question: Suppose that we had no voice or tongue, and wanted to indicate objects to one another, should we not, like the deaf and dumb, make signs with the hands, head and the rest of the body?
HERMOGENES: How could it be otherwise, Socrates?
SOCRATES: We should imitate the nature of the thing; the elevation of our hands to heaven would mean lightness and upwardness; heaviness and downwardness would be expressed by letting them drop to the ground. (p. 359)

In passing, we should note that Socrates' "sign" for *heaviness* is similar to the ASL sign for *heavy*. In a later section, we will address the issue of sign language iconicity.

Another ancient writer whose references to deafness have been misinterpreted was St. Augustine, who, during a discussion on "original man," remarked, "For what fault is so great innocence sometimes born blind and sometimes deaf? A defect moreover which is a hindrance to faith itself, according to the Apostle who says, 'So then faith cometh by hearing'" (Fay, 1912, p. 213). Augustine's statement was interpreted as depriving the deaf of immortality (Arnold, 1879; Farrar, 1923), an interpretation Fay (1912) refuted by reference to several other statements by Augustine, among which the most famous is as follows:

If a man and woman of this kind [deaf] were united in marriage and for any reason they were transferred to some solitary place where, however, they might be able to live, if they should have a son, who was not deaf, how would the latter speak with his parents? How can you think he would do otherwise than reply by gestures to the signs which his parents make to him? However a small boy could not do even this; therefore my reasoning remains sound, for what does it matter, as he grows up, whether he speaks or makes gestures, since both these pertain to the soul? (p. 213)

*This is not clear in English translations. For example, Matthew 9:13 reads, "The dumb spoke," and Matthew 9:5 reads, "The deaf hear." Both statements, however, used *kophoi,* a term that had negative implications and also connoted "dull of mind."

The Justinian Code

Around A.D. 300, the Roman Empire was divided into eastern and western segments, with the eastern emperor residing in the Greek city of Byzantium. In A.D. 476, the western Roman Empire fell to German barbarians. The areas of western and central Europe that had been colonized by Rome reverted to barbarian status, and what is known as the Middle Ages in Europe began.

The eastern Roman Empire began its golden age after the fall of Rome. It existed for another thousand years until Byzantium, which had been renamed Constantinople, (and is now Istanbul), fell to the Turks in 1453. This eastern Roman, or Byzantine, Empire preserved many of the traditions of Roman government within the Greek culture and tradition. The Byzantine Empire represented a fusion of Greek classical learning, Orthodox Christianity, and Roman legal tradition (Geanakoplos, 1976). Emperor Justinian, who reigned in the sixth century A.D., directed the development of the Justinian Code, which integrated a thousand years of Roman law and provided the basis for most legal systems in modern Europe (Barker, 1966). The Justinian Code identified five conditions of deafness, as presented by Peet (1851):

> Maintaining the distinction between the deaf and the dumb since the two defects are not always combined, we ordain:
>
> 1. That if one is afflicted with both diseases at once, that is to say, if from natural causes he can neither hear nor speak, he shall neither make a will nor any form of bequest, nor shall he be allowed to grant freedom by manumission nor in any other way. And this decree is to be binding on both males and females.
>
> 2. But where in either male or female, the same condition has been brought about by calamity, not from birth, voice or hearing have both been lost by subsequent disease, then in a case such as one have received an education, we permit him to do his own act all that in the previous case we prohibited.
>
> 3. But if this further misfortune, which so rarely occurs, is to be considered, we should allow a man who was only deaf, supposing the affliction to be from natural causes, to do everything in the nature of making a testamentary bequest, or granting freedom, for where nature has bestowed an articulate voice there is nothing to hinder him from doing as he wishes for we know that certain jurisconsuls have made a careful study of this, and have declared that there is no one who is altogether unable to hear if he is spoken to above the back of the head; which was the opinion of Juventius Celsus.
>
> 4. But those who have lost their hearing by disease can do everything without hindrance.
>
> 5. Supposing, however, the ears are perfect, but though there is a voice the tongue is tied (although on this subject there is considerable differences of opinion among the old authors) yet supposing such a one to be well educated, there is nothing to prevent his doing anything of this nature, whether the misfortune be congenital, or the result of disease, without distinction between males and females. (p. 136)

A reading of the code reveals a number of interesting facts. First, several Roman authors had apparently discussed aspects of deafness and muteness with a wide divergence of opinion and great interest. Although these writings are lost to us, we can deduce that the Romans studied problems of deafness closely enough to realize that complete deafness is a rarity. The method of speaking to individuals "above the back of the head" may refer to the first crude attempts at auditory training. The code also shows sensitivity to differential impacts of adventitious deafness and partial deafness. The Romans gave full rights to individuals who were (1) deaf and mute, but literate; (2) deaf but articulate; (3) mute but hearing; or (4) adventitiously deaf. They denied rights only to those who were deaf and mute from birth and also illiterate. Unfortunately, this apparently included just about all individuals who were born deaf.

The surviving Roman literature mentions only one deaf person by name. This is Quintus Pedius, grandson of the Consul Quintus Pedius, who with Caesar Augustus was coheir to Julius Caesar (Peet, 1851). With the approval of Augustus, Quintus Pedius was instructed in painting; Pliny mentioned him as among the most eminent painters of Rome.

Even with the evidence of the case of Pedius, and possibly a few other individuals of noble background, it never occurred to ancient Greeks and Romans that a person born deaf could be educated. Implicit in section 1 of the code is the belief that a person born deaf would never become literate. The notion that words could be presented directly through writing, manual spelling, and signs without the mediation of speech apparently was inconceivable to the Romans, who, ironically, had developed pantomime to its highest degree.

The lack of education per se would not have been a major handicap in ancient times. In fact, Werner (1932) claimed that the deaf were skilled at crafts and made satisfactory livings in most societies. He reported that deaf farmers, craftspeople, and even soldiers were common in Rome. Noting that Justinian laws contained special conditions for the testaments of deaf soldiers (p. 144), Werner concluded that the army must have abounded with deaf individuals. Given the five categories of deafness in the Justinian Code, the army probably included few, if any, individuals with profound congenital hearing losses, but the number of soldiers with acquired deafness and early mild to severe hearing loss may have been high.

The Middle Ages

With the fall of Rome in A.D. 476, those parts of western Europe that had developed urban centers quickly reverted to an agricultural society, and systems of feudalism arose. Education, culture, and learning were of limited importance. Eventually a number of petty kingdoms were created by the tribes succeeding the Romans. Christian educational institutions, heavily influenced by the unique fusion of pagan culture and the Christian beliefs of Irish scholars, were established along classical models (Geanakoplos, 1976; Graves, 1918). It would take centuries, however, for western Europe to approach the Mediterranean world and the Middle East in terms of education and culture.

If the deaf may be said to have suffered from an attitude of benign neglect during classical periods, their condition following the onslaught on Rome by barbarians was even worse. The early code of nearly every nation in Europe imposed on the deaf civil and religious restrictions that were much more severe than those in the Justinian Code, including deprivation of rights of inheritance, restriction from the celebration of Mass, and denial of the right to marry without the express dispensation of the Pope (Deland, 1931; Peet, 1851). Although the deaf were generally either ignored or discriminated against, references to miraculous cures of deafness and muteness have been found. The most famous cure was effected by John, Bishop of Hagulstad (later known as St. John of Beverly), who worked several miracles among the Anglo-Saxons, including the teaching of speech to a young deaf mute. St. John first had the young man say the Anglo-Saxon *gea* (*yea*) and then taught him to repeat letters, syllables, words, and finally sentences until his speech was normal (Peet, 1851).

No record of an educated congenitally deaf person has been found from the time of Quintus Pedius until the fifteenth century, when Rudolphus Agricola reported the case of a deaf mute who had learned to write (Bender, 1970; Peet, 1851). No details were given concerning name, place, or mode of instruction, and the report was generally dismissed on the grounds that it was impossible to instruct one who lacked the organ of instruction—the ear.

As in Byzantium, no evidence exists of any systematic attempts to educate the deaf in western Europe before the sixteenth century. At a time when illiteracy was the norm, individuals with disabilities received charity, not instruction.

The Spread of Islam

While western Europe was in decline, Byzantium was struggling for dominance with the rapidly expanding power of Islam, the religious faith of the Moslems as set forth in the Koran (Qur'an). Following the death of the prophet Mohammed in 632, Arab tribes broke out of Arabia and spread the message of Islam. Within ten years they had occupied Syria, Palestine, Iraq, Persia, and Egypt and converted the populations. By 718, Moslems had conquered all of North Africa, Spain, and Portugal. Their advance was halted in France in 732 (Lewis, 1966). The conquest of Spain and Portugal by Christians required almost eight hundred years, ending with the fall of Granada in 1492.

During this period, the Byzantine Empire and the Islamic world were far advanced over Europe. Just as the contributions of Byzantium to modern society have been minimized, the accomplishments of Islamic states have been slighted, leading to a western Europe parochialism (Meyer, 1966). The Arabians directly influenced European culture through Moslem Spain and Sicily (Bowen, 1975). The learning not only was Islamic in nature but also reflected the heritage of Greece, Syria, Egypt, and Persia. Spain, which had been heavily colonized by Syrian Arabs (Lewis, 1966), was directly exposed to the traditions of the ancient world while the rest of western Europe was in darkness.

Rhazes (850–920), a leading Arab physician of the period, divided deafness into three categories: impairment, curtailment, and complete loss. He believed that congenital hearing loss could be cured if treatment was initiated within two years. Avicenna, or Ibn Sina (980–1037), perhaps the greatest Arab physician and philosopher, also treated the causes of deafness, using a theory of hearing based on the work of Galen, the ancient Greek physician (Werner, 1932).

Despite all the attainments of the Moslem world, there is no indication of any attempts to educate the deaf. In a study of diseases and disabilities in the Arab world entitled *Disability in Antiquity,* Haj (1970) reported that visual defects were by far the most common type of disability and that the Koran gives special consideration to the blind. Since education was highly oral, it was possible for motivated blind students to succeed even at universities.

Haj reported that deafness was mentioned very infrequently in Arabic literature and reasoned that deaf individuals would face great difficulties in a society that so heavily emphasized the vocal transmission of history, wisdom, and religion. Haj (1970) quoted an ancient source as follows:

> He who lacks hearing is deprived in many respects. He loses ability of communication and debate. He misses the pleasure of sound, of entertainment, and of charming melodies. People are bored in his company and he is a burden to them. He is unable to listen to any of the people's stories and conversation. (p. 159)

The Beginnings of Education of the Deaf

The end of the dark ages for the deaf may be marked by the writings of Girolamo Cardano (1501–1576), a sixteenth-century Italian mathematician and physician, who accepted Agricola's report of a deaf mute who had learned to write. Cardano argued for the importance of teaching the deaf to read and write, believing that many abstract ideas could be explained to them through signs. Apparently, he was the first to realize that written words could represent ideas directly without recourse to speech, presenting his position as follows:

> The deaf-mute can conceive that the word, bread, for example, as it stands written, represents the object which we point out to him. Just as after having seen any object, we preserve its form in the memory and can draw a resemblance of it, so the deaf-mute can preserve in his mind the forms of the written characters, and can associate them directly with ideas; for spoken words represent ideas only by convention, and written words can be made to represent ideas by convention. (Peet, 1851, p. 138)

To some extent, Cardano's ideas were similar to those of the proponents of a "bilingual" approach to education of deaf children in which the majority language, such as English, is acquired through reading and writing (Walworth, Moores, and O'Rourke, 1992). Cardano, of course, did not conceive of the other component: the use of a sign language.

Cardano himself treated the subject only from a theoretical perspective, and he never put his ideas to a practical test. For the beginnings of education of the deaf, as for so many other breakthroughs during the Renaissance and at the start of the modern era, we must look to Spain.

Although exceptions and overlap will always exist, we may discern periods in which major contributions to education of the deaf were made primarily by one nation. Interestingly, national leadership in education of the deaf seems to have been related to political, economic, cultural, and military factors. Thus, the first thrust in education of the deaf was in Spain during the sixteenth century, followed by a flurry of activity, partly influenced by Spanish work, in seventeenth-century Great Britain. This was followed in the eighteenth century by the introduction and spread of the "French method" (described later), which in turn was challenged by the "German method." Proponents of the two methods remained antagonists through-out most of the nineteenth century (with the somewhat more insular British on the periphery) until the "final, complete" victory of the German method in 1880, which coincided with rising German political influence and the smashing German military victory in the Franco-Prussian War.

In the twentieth century, of course, the "final" victory of the German method has been shown to be not so final. Perhaps in the twenty-first century, with the "infor-mation highway" providing universal access to information, educational leadership will not be tied to political or military leadership.

Spain

The honor of being the first teacher of the deaf has been accorded to Pedro Ponce de León (1520–1584), a Benedictine monk who established a school at a monastery in Valladolid where he tutored deaf children of Spanish nobility (Enerstvedt, 1999). Deafness was common among the Spanish aristocracy, including the royal family. Ponce de León was motivated to begin his work by the presence in the monastery of two deaf brothers, Francisco and Pedro de Velasco, members of the wealthy and influential Velasco family (Chaves and Solar, 1974). The presence of recessive genes for deafness in a family that, for financial and political reasons, engaged in consan-guineous marriages had resulted in a large number of deaf children. Francisco and Pedro, for example, were from a family in which five of eight children were deaf (Werner, 1932). The three deaf sisters were sent to convents.

Ponce de León undertook the task of teaching Francisco to read, write, and speak. Francisco, the legitimate heir to the marquisate of Berlanga and the eldest son of the House of Tudor, learned to speak and write and thus gained his inherit-ance (Peet, 1851). Pedro de Velasco's accomplishments were even more spectacu-lar. He studied history, mastered Spanish and Latin, and received a papal dispensa-tion allowing him to be ordained as a priest. Ponce de León also taught two of the Velasco sisters and at least twelve other deaf individuals, most of whom were mem-bers of the Spanish aristocracy (Chaves and Solar, 1974).

"L'Abbé de L'Epée and the deaf mute Joseph." By Ponce Camus. Collection of the Paris National Institute for the Deaf.

Ponce de León's success was widely acclaimed. In a legal document dated August 24, 1578, he himself described his success as follows:

I have had for my pupils, who were deaf and dumb from birth, sons of great lords and of notable people who I have taught to speak, read, write, to pray, to assist a Mass, to know the doctrines of Christianity, and to know how to confess themselves by speech. I have taught them all this. Some attained to a knowledge of Latin; others, taught Latin and Greek, acquired the knowledge of Italian. One who entered the priesthood and undertook a charge and a benefice of the Church, was also able to recite the canonical hours; and several others attained to know and to understand natural philosophy and astrology. Another, heir to an estate and a marquisate, and led afterward to embrace the military profession, learned, in addition to the knowledge above referred to, every kind of exercise and became a noted horseman. Much more, my pupils studied history, and were able to trace the annals of their own country, and also those of other lands. Better still, they proved by the use they made of them that they were possessed of the gifts which Aristotle had denied to them. (Peet, 1851, p. 141)

Ponce de León may be forgiven a somewhat unseemly immodesty if indeed he obtained even some of the results claimed above. If his pupils actually were profoundly deaf from birth, the results are incredible given the circumstances and the fact that he apparently developed his methods without recourse to other sources. Even allowing for a certain justifiable exaggeration concerning two accomplishments previously considered impossible—teaching the deaf to read and to speak—Ponce de León's purported work remains a standard that present-day educators should regard with envy and strive to attain.

Unfortunately, very little is known about the techniques Ponce de León employed. Although he produced a written account of his work, no record of it survives; it was either lost or destroyed. Other writers, including one pupil, suggest that he began with reading and writing and then moved on to speech, and that he used a manual alphabet in instruction. It is unclear whether he used signs.

Covarrubias, a physician to King Philip IV, reported that Ponce de León reversed the usual order of instruction by first teaching the deaf to write, pointing out by finger the things to which the written characters corresponded and then procuring them. Deland (1931) quotes Covarrubias: "And thus we begin by speech with those who hear, so do we as well by writing with those whose ears are closed (p. 57)." This statement preceded by four centuries the position of American linguist Lenneberg (1967a), who argued for the use of graphics in the education of the deaf from the beginning.

Since the Benedictine monks at Ponce de León's monastery worked under a vow of silence except for specified periods of time, they used a traditional system of signs. Most historians agree that this sign system probably formed a basis for the instruction of the Velasco brothers. Plann (1993, p. 8) reported that every newcomer was assigned a paternal older monk who provided instruction in reading, arithmetic, prayers, ceremonies, and the signs used in silent communication. Ponce de León was put in charge of the Velasco brothers. Plann reasons that the brothers, coming from a family with several deaf siblings, had probably developed a system of home signs prior to entering the monastery. She concludes that the communication method employed was likely an amalgamation of signs Ponce de León knew as a monk in a nonspeaking order and the home signs used by the Velascos.

Plann (1993) argues that another monk in a signing monastery might have been the first teacher of the deaf. Fray Vicente de Santo Dominco of the monastery of Estrella taught drawing to Fernando Navarrete ten years before the Velascos began their training. Navarrete, who communicated in signs and was known as El Mudo (The Mute), became a painter at the royal court and was highly literate, being well versed in history and the scriptures.

The most complete account of Ponce de León's methods, which corroborates the preceding description, comes from a passage written in Latin by Don Francisco Velasco:

> While I was a boy and ignorant, *ut lapis* [as a stone] I began to work by copying what my teacher had written; and I wrote all the words of the Castilian tongue in a book prepared to that purpose. Hereupon I began, adjurante Deo, to spell, and to utter some syllables and words with all my might, so that the saliva flowed from my mouth abundantly. Then I began to read history, and in ten years read the history of the whole world. Afterwards I learned Latin. All this was through the great grace of God, without which no mute can exist. (Peet, 1851, p. 149)

After the death of Pedro Ponce de León came a hiatus of more than thirty years in reported efforts to educate the deaf. This may be explained by the loss of Ponce de León's descriptions of his techniques and his failure to train any successors to carry on his work. The next known effort to educate the deaf again involved the Velasco family, this time two generations removed from Ponce de León's students and involving two largely unknown but intriguing personalities, Juan Pablo Bonet and Manuel Ramirez de Carrion. Although they probably worked together for four years, neither referred to the other or to Ponce de León in print, and each claimed to be the originator of a new method of teaching the deaf.

The story has been pieced together as follows. In 1607 Juan Bonet, a soldier of fortune, entered into the service of Juan Fernandez de Velasco, the constable of Castile, whose father (the previous constable) was the brother of the two previously mentioned students of Ponce de León. Upon the death of Juan Velasco in 1613, his widow, Duchess Dona Juana de Cordoba, retained Bonet as secretary to the new constable, Don Bernadino Fernandez de Velasco, then a child of four. The duchess had two other young children, one of whom, three-year-old Luis, had lost his hearing around age two. Bonet took it upon himself to secure help for Luis. In 1615 he came upon Ramirez de Carrion, a tutor and private secretary to the deaf Marquiz de Priego, who agreed to release de Carrion temporarily to work with Luis. Thus, de Carrion worked with Luis from 1615 until 1619, when he returned to the service of the Marquiz de Priego. In 1620, Bonet published the first book ever written on teaching the deaf, *The Reduction of Letters and the Art of Teaching the Mute to Speak.** In the book, Bonet took complete credit for developing the system, making no mention of the work of either Ponce de León or Ramirez de Carrion. Bonet stated, "I began to make a special study of the case, contemplating, examining and turning the matter every way to seek means of supplying the deficiencies of one sense through the remaining senses" (Peet, 1851, p. 150).

Bonet must have known Ponce de León's work, although it is unclear whether he was aware of any of the latter's specific techniques. In an introduction to Bonet's book, Abbot Antonio Perez mentions the pioneering work of Ponce de León (Deland, 1931; Peet, 1851) and criticizes him for failing to teach his skills to anyone else. As for Ramirez de Carrion, Bonet must have either collaborated with him or overseen his work from 1615 to 1620. Because of his refusal to acknowledge the work of others, Bonet has been accused of plagiarism (Carton, 1883) or at least of a lack of generosity (Best, 1943).

**Reducción de las Letras y Arte para Enseñar a Hablar los Mudos.*

Educators of the deaf who have examined Bonet's manuscript express admiration for his insight and understanding of the problems of educating the deaf (Huervas y Panduro, 1795; Tomas, 1920). Deland (1931) stated, "The book shows too intimate a knowledge of the subject not to have been the outcome of actual experience, so unless Bonet worked along with Carrion, he must have preceded him in the education of the talented Luis." Peet (1851) wrote:

> Considering the period at which he wrote, his views are for the most part, remarkably correct, and the course of instruction which he marks out, though little adapted for numerous schools, might, in the hands of an able and zealous private teacher, produce, if perseveringly pursued, and with subjects of good capacity, results not inferior to those ascribed to the labor of Ponce. (p. 152)

Bonet advocated initiating training through the use of a one-handed manual alphabet, which is essentially the same as the alphabet used today in the United States. He attached great importance to early intervention and to the provision of a consistent language environment, positions that only recently have been accepted in the modern world. For example, he insisted that everyone living with a deaf person use the manual alphabet. He also advocated the early teaching of speech on the basis of the manual alphabet and the printed word, arguing that a lack of early speech training is an impediment to later speech development.

Deland (1931) claimed that Bonet's ideas about sense training anticipated twentieth-century methods used in schools for the deaf. To make his point, Deland quoted from a section containing suggestions for teaching similarities and differences among objects in relation to properties such as length, width, color, and weight:

> In this lesson he ought to be well versed; and this can be accomplished, for it is the very threshold of reasoning; and he must learn the words and concepts by which he is to express what he thinks; and with this in view he will have to be asked many questions about different things; some of them are so similar as to demand feeling rather than sight to distinguish them, and these he must weigh in his head, so as to reorganize differences in things that need some consideration. (p. 33)

This incredible passage anticipates aspects of the work of Itard, Sequin, Montessori, Pestolozzi, and Piaget, among others. The implication that thought precedes language is a radical departure from traditional thinking and is the basis of much contemporary work in developmental psycholinguistics concerned with the semantic bases of language. The existing evidence suggests that the work of Bonet, which probably drew heavily on that of Ponce de León, directly and indirectly influenced later work not only with deaf children but also with children with mental retardation and nonhandicapped children.

The third of the early Spanish educators of the deaf, Ramirez de Carrion, was also a person of genius and apparently was highly successful as a teacher of the deaf. His three most eminent pupils—Prince Emmanuel of Savoy, the Marquiz de Priego, and Luis Velasco—were highly literate and successful individuals. Don Luis was the favorite of King Henry IV, who appointed him the first marquis of Frenzo.

Pietro di Castro (also known as Ezechiele de Castro) credited de Carrion with developing a cure for deafness. It was said that de Carrion first put his pupils through a preliminary treatment and then had them shave the tops of their heads and apply nightly a salve consisting of brandy, saltpeter, niter, almond oil, and naphtha. Then he would speak strongly to the crown of the head, and the pupil would "receive" a voice and learn to speak.

Although de Carrion's "cure" has been dismissed as a fabrication, Peet (1851) noted that if the story has any foundation in fact, it suggests that the subjects were only partially deaf. It is interesting to note the similarity between this "treatment" and the statement in section 3 of the Justinian Code—more than 1,100 years earlier—that no one is unable to hear if he or she is spoken to "above the back of the head."

Great Britain

Interest in education of the deaf originally developed in Great Britain in response to a report by Sir Kenelin Digby concerning the remarkable skills of Don Luis de Velasco, whom Digby met while accompanying the Prince of Wales, later Charles I, on a visit of state to Madrid. According to Digby, Velasco was so deaf that if a gun were shot off close to his ear, he would be unable to hear it (Deland, 1931). But his speech was distinct, and he understood what others said so perfectly that he would not lose a word in a whole day's conversation.

Digby greatly influenced the work of English philosopher John Bulwer, who in 1648 published *Philocophus; or, the Deaf and Dumb Man's Friend*. Bulwer made a special study of manual expression and what he considered the natural language of the hand. Deland reported that Bulwer would sign himself Chirosopher, or "lover of the language of the hand." Bulwer's interest in deafness resulted from his friendship with two deaf brothers, Sir William and Sir Edward Gostwicke, with whom he communicated by means of a manual alphabet. Although reports of Don Luis's success led Bulwer to emphasize lip reading as the salvation of the deaf, Bulwer never put his ideas into practice. Thus the honor of being the first educator of the deaf in Great Britain must go to either William Holder (1616–1698) or John Wallis (1618–1703), each of whom actively claimed to have invented the art of teaching the deaf and never referred to the writing of Bulwer or Bonet.

The evidence suggests that Holder was the first to teach a deaf individual in Great Britain, but Wallis was the first to present his results to the outside world. In 1659, Holder started to teach Alexander Popham, the son of Admiral Popham and Lady Wharton. A summary of Holder's method was presented to the Royal Society in 1669. His techniques were similar to those of his Spanish predecessors in that he advocated the use of writing as a beginning step and used a manual alphabet in teaching speech (a two-handed alphabet, not the one described by Bonet). Holder developed specific techniques to teach speech reading skills. These techniques differed from those used by Bonet, for example, who considered speech reading an art that was dependent on the deaf individual's own efforts. Holder relied heavily on context to differentiate not only among sounds that may look alike on the lips (for example, /p/, /b/, and /m/) but also among meanings of the same word in varying contexts. Holder was well aware of the difficulties of speech reading; he stated, "The histories of those who could discern speech by their eye are most of such as having had knowledge of language and a readiness in speaking, falling afterwards into deafness, having lost the use of speech; but still retain the memory of it" (Deland, 1931, p. 52).

Wallis, an Oxford professor and mathematician, began to teach Daniel Whaby, the twenty-five-year-old son of the mayor of Northampton, in 1660. He claimed to have taught Whaby to articulate distinctly within a year. Wallis began with the natural gestures his pupil used and moved on to writing and the manual alphabet before introducing articulation. He differed from Holder and others in that he separated articulation training from the use of the manual alphabet. Unlike Holder, but like Bonet, Wallis placed little emphasis on teaching speech reading.

George Dalgarno (1628–1687), a contemporary of Holder and Wallis, did not actually work with deaf pupils, but he produced a masterful treatise on deafness and education of the deaf in 1680: *Didascopholus; or, the Deaf and Dumb Man's Tutor,* which was reprinted in the *American Annals of the Deaf* in 1857. Dalgarno was headmaster of a private school in Oxford. Although he and Wallis were personal acquaintances, neither mentioned the other in print. Dalgarno's method for the development of language was more natural than the strong grammatical systems employed by Holder and Wallis. He believed language could be developed in much the same way that it evolves in infancy, and he advocated continual use of finger spelling, asserting that a deaf baby could learn in the cradle as readily as any other child if mothers and nurses had "but as nimble a hand as commonly they have a tongue." Dalgarno suggested that the manual alphabet be placed in the back of the hornbook used to teach letters to hearing children in England at that time.

The two-handed manual alphabet Dalgarno recommended was similar to that used by Holder. The letters were located on the fingertips and palms of one hand and were signified by touch from the finger or thumb of the other hand. Alexander Graham Bell used this system two centuries later in Massachusetts with his first pupil, who wore a lettered glove during his lessons (Bruce, 1973).

Dalgarno, echoing the opinion of Cardano in the previous century, emphasized that deaf individuals had potential for learning equal to that of hearing persons and, if properly educated, could obtain the same level of functioning.

The first school for the deaf in Great Britain was established by Henry Baker (1698–1774), who had started by teaching a deaf niece. According to his own reports, he developed a method of instructing his deaf students to read, write, understand, and speak the English language. Like his predecessors, Baker did not acknowledge the existence of other individuals engaged in educating the deaf (if he was aware of them). Baker opened a small, very select private school and never divulged his methods. It has been reported that each pupil was required to post a bond of 100 pounds, which would be forfeited if any of Baker's techniques were mentioned (Deland, 1931).

Neither Baker's school nor his methods survived him. Thomas Braidwood (1715–1806), the first of three generations of leading educators of deaf children, established a school for deaf individuals in Edinburgh in 1767 and is acknowledged to be the most influential early British educator of the deaf. He was joined by his son-in-law and nephew, John Braidwood. The work was later carried on by John's widow as well as by another nephew, Joseph Watson (1765–1829), who established the first nonprivate school for indigent deaf persons in London around 1809.

At one time, Braidwood offered to make his methods public if financial support were forthcoming from the nobility and gentry. Receiving no response to his offer, Braidwood continued to keep his methods a family secret. Eventually, this secretiveness was instrumental in pushing the founder of the first permanent school for the deaf in America to embrace the French method.

Although Thomas Braidwood never published anything concerning his techniques, Francis Green, a Bostonian whose son was enrolled in the Edinburgh school, published a description of his son's education in 1793, which angered the Braidwood family. Subsequently, Watson (1809) published a book based on the Braidwood method. In his program, Braidwood incorporated the two-handed alphabet, gestures and natural signs, and reading and writing. His approach to the development of articulation was elemental, beginning with speech elements and gradually building up to syllables and words.

France

As in Great Britain, efforts in France were motivated by the pioneering work of Spanish educators. However, it is clear that schools and educational systems for the deaf were the product of the French Enlightenment.

In France we again find the familiar controversy over who should be recognized as the individual most responsible for the establishment of educational programs for the deaf. The two best-known claimants for the title were Jacob Rodriguez Pereire* (1715–1790) and the Abbé Charles-Michel de l'Epée (1712–1789), two equally brilliant but otherwise disparate individuals. As with other such controversies, a strong case can be made for either one: Pereire was the first well-known teacher in France; de l'Epée began his work later but was responsible for establishing the world's first public school for the deaf in Paris in 1755.

Technically, neither Pereire nor de l'Epée was the first known teacher of the deaf in France. In a Spanish translation of a book on the life of Pereire, written in French in 1847, Seguin (1932) reported that Pereire's first pupil, M. d'Azy d'Etavigny, had attended school in Amiens along with four or five other deaf children for a period of seven years. The instructor was deaf, and so d'Etavigny learned to express himself

---

*At least nine variations on Pereire's name exist, including Giacobbo Rodrigues Pereire, Jacobo Ridriguez Pereira, Jacob Pereira, and Jacob Rodriguez. When living in Spain and Portugal, Pereire was forced to convert to Catholicism. Rodrigues(z) represented his Christian name and Pereire(a) his Jewish name. Various spellings of all names were influenced by Spanish, Portuguese, and French.

Laurent Clerc. A graduate of the Paris Institution for the Deaf, he became the first teacher at the American School for the Deaf and trained most of the first teachers of the deaf in the United States.

GALLAUDET UNIVERSITY ARCHIVES

by signs. This is but one of many examples of how contributions of deaf pioneers have been overlooked.

Pereire was born in Estremadura, Spain, and migrated first to Portugal and then to France to escape religious persecution. According to Deland (1931), Pereire began teaching his deaf sister before migrating to France. As reported by Mann (1974), however, Pereire started his work after falling in love with a deaf girl. Seguin (1932)—who had obtained some of Pereire's documents from his son, Jacob Rodriguez, and grandchildren—mentions neither of these young women.

Pereire's first known student was a sixteen-year-old boy, d'Azy d'Etavigny. As previously mentioned, d'Etavigny had already been instructed for seven years, from 1736 to 1743. When he entered the College of Beaumont in 1743, he used no speech, and attempts were made to teach him vocal skills using a technique based on the work of the Dutch scholar Johann Amman. This approach failed (Seguin, 1932). Following extensive negotiations, Pereire and the older d'Etavigny entered into a "performance contracting" agreement of the type popular in Great Britain and investigated by several U.S. public schools in the early 1970s. Pereire received one-third of the amount upon initiation of instruction, one-third when young d'Etavigny reached a certain level of competence, and one-third when d'Etavigny had completed his education.

Pereire exhibited d'Etavigny before the French Academy of Sciences in 1749, which reported as follows:

> We find that the progress made by d'Azy d'Etavigny justifies Pereire in hoping that, by his method, congenital deaf-mutes cannot only learn to read, pronounce and understand common words, but also acquire abstract notions, and become capable of reasoning and acting like others. We have no difficulty in believing that the art of lipreading, with its necessary limitations, will be useful to other deaf-mutes of the same class ... as well as the manual alphabet Pereire uses. (Deland, 1931, p. 71)

Following this success, Pereire undertook the education of Saboreux de Fontenay, the godson of the Duc de Chaulnes. De Fontenay became a noted linguist, studying not only European languages but also Hebrew, Syriac, and Arabic (Deland, 1931). Pereire is also credited with teaching other deaf individuals manual communication (Bender, 1970), although he himself was careful to note that de Fontenay suffered from only a partial hearing loss (Degerando, 1827).

Pereire's students were sworn to secrecy concerning his methods, for he intended to keep the methods within his family. Unfortunately, this penchant for secrecy was so strong that at the time of Pereire's death even his own family was unfamiliar with his methods, and despite the efforts of his son, mother, and daughter-in-law, Pereire's work died with him.

Most of what we know about Pereire's techniques came from a letter written by Saboreux de Fontenay, who apparently had little compunction about violating his oath. Pereire employed a one-handed alphabet for the teaching of speech, relied on a "natural" approach to the development of language, developed auditory training procedures for individuals with residual hearing, and used special exercises involving sight and touch in sense training.

Although Pereire did not teach individuals with mental retardation, his work greatly influenced the techniques used later by educators of these students. Itard, a physician at the school for the deaf in Paris at the beginning of the nineteenth century, used many of Pereire's sense-training techniques in his classic work with Victor, the "wild boy" of Aveyron (Lane, 1976). Itard later directed his protégé, Seguin, in the instruction of a child with retardation. Seguin went on to develop the physiological method of teaching individuals with retardation, freely acknowledging his indebtedness to Pereire (Kanner, 1967; Seguin, 1860, 1932). Seguin was convinced that Pereire's secret lay not in his methods of teaching speech but in his physiologically based sense training (Drouot, 1932). Maria Montessori, in turn, studied the work of Itard and Seguin and based much of her method on their endeavors

(Montessori, 1912). The progression in the use of sense training can be traced in a straight line from Bonet in the seventeenth century to Pereire in the eighteenth century to Itard and Seguin in the nineteenth century up to Montessori in the twentieth century, with the principles gradually expanding from work with the deaf that applied to a feral child, to children with mental retardation, and to nondisabled children.

The Abbé de l'Epée apparently was less motivated to keep his methods secret than other early educators of the deaf, such as Baker, the Braidwoods, Pereire, and de l'Epée's German contemporary, Samuel Heinicke. Of course, de l'Epée had the benefit of an independent income, whereas for the above-mentioned individuals, making their methods known to the public could have detracted from the economic well-being of their own families. Because public schools for the deaf did not exist, these teachers were obliged to concentrate on educating children of the rich and powerful. The teaching methods they developed represented the most precious inheritance they could pass on to their progeny.

De l'Epée began his work with the deaf when he undertook the religious instruction of two young deaf sisters. Lacking prior experience with the deaf, he began to develop his own system of instruction. However, his work was soon influenced by three sources. The first source was the sign language used by the deaf in Paris. De l'Epée came to believe that sign language was the natural language of the deaf and was their only real vehicle for thought and communication (McClure, 1969). Although he was not opposed to teaching speech, he regarded it as a mechanical operation and a lower priority than intellectual or spiritual concerns (Garnett, 1968). Fischer (1993) reports a misconception that de l'Epée had invented the sign language used by deaf people in Paris. In fact, a sign language already existed, and de l'Epée modified it for instructional purposes. De l'Epée developed what he called "methodical" signs to supplement the natural sign language. The methodical signs represented both an expanded vocabulary and an attempt to adapt the sign language to French syntax and morphology. The second source of influence was a copy of Bonet's original book on education of the deaf, which a stranger had donated to de l'Epée. De l'Epée reportedly undertook to learn Spanish the same day he received the book (Bender, 1970; Deland, 1931). Finally, de L'Epée was influenced by the work of the Dutch educator Amman, who in 1862 published *Surdos loquins (The Speaking Deaf)*.

Over time, de l'Epée gave decreasing attention to articulation. He was severely criticized for his position on articulation and speech reading (Garnett, 1968), and his seemingly contradictory statements concerning the efficacy and need for teaching speech to the deaf have created a great deal of confusion. De l'Epée's basic position apparently was that he was not opposed to the teaching of speech, but he considered it to be a slow, arduous process. Because he was responsible for the education of large numbers of children, he did not believe he could devote significant amounts of time to articulation. Far more important to de l'Epée was the development of intellectual capabilities.

The strongest personal attacks on de l'Epée came from Pereire and Heinicke. They were especially upset when the Austrian Abbé Stark was trained by de l'Epée and established Austria's first school for the deaf in Vienna in 1789. Heinicke wrote an unsolicited letter to Stark, stating, "The Parisian method of tuition is not simply of no use, but an absolute detriment to the advancement of the pupils" (Garnett, p. 27). The distraught de l'Epée invited both Pereire and Heinicke to visit his school and observe instruction firsthand. Both refused, and thus the battle over methods began. The positions of de l'Epée and Heinicke were set out in private exchanges of letters between them (Garnett, 1968).

De l'Epée was succeeded by the Abbé Roch Ambroise Sicard (1742–1822) in 1790. Sicard continued the work of de l'Epée, relying on the methodical signs, writing, and the manual alphabet. During his tenure, the trend toward greater reliance on natural signs, begun under de l'Epée, continued. This apparently resulted from a tendency for conversation to slow down when signs were used to indicate mood, tense, number, gender, and so on. By the time of Sicard's successor, Roch Ambroise Augusta Belican, a native of Spain, the transition to natural signs and the manual alphabet was complete.

Germany*

Although his methods have not survived, Samuel Heinicke (1729–1784) is generally known as the originator of the German method. A forceful, brilliant, largely self-educated man with an extensive military career, he gravitated toward education of the deaf through his experiences with deaf children as a private tutor and teacher in several German cities. His success brought him wide acclaim and attracted increasing numbers of deaf students. At the invitation of the elector of Saxony, Heinicke established a school in Leipzig in 1778.

Consistent with the spirit of the time, Heinicke was secretive about the specific techniques he employed. In 1782, he wrote to de l'Epée as follows:

> No other method can compare either in point of facility or solicity with that which I have invented and now practice, for mine is built entirely on articulate and vocal language, and upon taste which supplies the place of hearing. . . . My deaf pupils are taught by a slow and easy process to speak both their vernacular tongue and foreign languages with a clear and distinct voice from habit and from understanding. . . . The method which I now pursue as the tuition of the deaf and dumb was never known to anyone besides myself and son. The invention and arrangement of it cost me incredible labor and pains, and I am not inclined to let others have the benefit of it for nothing. By right the publication of it should be purchased of me by some prince, and I defy all the casuistry in the world to argue me out of money that I lawfully and laboriously gain. Such of the deaf and dumb are poor, I instruct gratis, while I made the rich pay in proportion to their wealth, and I often receive more than I demand. (Garnett, 1968, pp. 42-44)

---

*The name *Germany* is used for convenience, for during the period discussed there was no united Germany but a collection of Germanic states and principalities of various sizes.

Heinicke disagreed with the practice of teaching letters before teaching speech, arguing that this went against the natural order of learning. Influenced by the work of Amman—as de l'Epée was, but in a different way and to a lesser extent—Heinicke attached a somewhat mystical quality to the spoken word. He argued that pure thought is possible only through speech, on which everything else depends. Operating from this premise, Heinicke had only to take a small step to conclude that written language is secondary to spoken language and must follow rather than precede it.

Heinicke seemed to be somewhat inconsistent in his support of the primacy of speech, for he developed a theory that the sense of taste can substitute for hearing in the perception of sound. Thus, in his teaching, he related the taste of water to the vowel *a*, wormwood to *e*, vinegar to *I*, and olive oil to *u*.

Unfortunately, Heinicke's son Rudolf died before him, and his other two sons were not interested in the work. His widow and two sons-in-law attempted to carry on, but they met with mixed success, and Heinicke's method did not survive him for long. De l'Epée's work began to exert an influence in Germany, and it was not until the nineteenth century that the German, or oral, method experienced a revival in its native land.

Far more responsible than Heinicke for the ultimate spread of the oral method were John Baptist Graser (1766–1841) and Frederick Maritz Hill (1805–1874). During the period of greatest French influence, Graser opposed the use of the French method and continued his efforts to expand the use of German techniques. He maintained that the two greatest deficiencies in education of the deaf were the use of manual communication and the isolation of deaf children in institutions and residential schools (Gordon, 1885a).

As the political influence of France began to decline in the early nineteenth century, an upsurge of nationalism spread across Europe. In no area was this movement stronger than in the German lands. Thus, Graser's arguments were eagerly put into practice in Germany. Under his influence, all teachers were instructed in the education of deaf children so that they could be integrated into regular classes with hearing children. In 1821 Graser initiated an experimental school along these lines, thus anticipating mainstreaming or "inclusion" (the "latest" American conceptual breakthrough in educating children with disabilities) by 150 years. Under Graser's influence, deaf children were integrated into the public school programs in several German states, but the system was abandoned after a few years because the children encountered difficulties in making academic progress (Bender, 1970; Gordon, 1885a).

Of all German educators of the deaf, the most influential was Frederick Hill, who applied the principles of Pestolozzi to educating deaf individuals. Hill argued that deaf children should learn language in the same way hearing children do—that is, through its everyday use in relation to the daily activities of life—rather than through structured lessons in correct grammatical usage. He strongly believed that speech must be the foundation for all teaching and for all language, involving simple but natural interactions between the child and people in the environment. Although Hill used charts, colored pictures, and special readers, he did not allow the use of the manual alphabet or signs; natural gestures were acceptable only with very young children. Hill was quite active in the training of teachers of the deaf, and his influence spread throughout Germany, the rest of Europe, and eventually the United States. The German, or oral, method appeared to have won the day over the French, or manual, method. The apparent high-water mark for the oral method was the famed Conference of Milan in 1880, which finally proclaimed the superiority of the oral method—a claim that was not to be challenged until after the 1950s, in the Soviet Union and the United States.

Other Nations

Although the major advances in the education of the deaf were achieved in Spain, Great Britain, France, and Germany, work was also progressing in countries such as Norway, Italy, Austria, Russia, Belgium, and Sweden. Numerous individuals in these nations contributed to improving conditions for the deaf. In most cases, educators of the deaf in these countries were influenced, and frequently were trained, by the French and German leaders.

Johann Konrad Amman (1669–1724) deserves special mention, for he influenced the founders of both the French and German methods, de l'Epée and Heinicke, as well as later generations. Amman earned his degree as a medical doctor at age eighteen. Compelled to leave his native Switzerland because of his religious ideas, Amman settled in Holland. He became involved with education of the deaf when he began to teach speech to a deaf child whom he was unable to cure medically. He developed his techniques independently, unaware of similar efforts in other countries. In 1692 he published the previously mentioned *Surdos loquins (The Speaking Deaf)*, and in 1700 he followed with *Dissertation de loquela (A Dissertation on Speech)*.

Amman perceived the nature of speech in a religious sense. He believed that at the time of the fall of Adam and Eve, humanity had lost its "divine speech," which enabled one to effect all things merely by speaking the word (Deland, 1931). According to Amman, even though our spoken language is but a mere shadow of the original language, it is the most important characteristic that humanity possesses; therefore, education of the deaf must have as its primary emphasis the teaching of articulation.

Despite a lack of clarity in his writing, Amman's ideas had a profound impact on several educators of the deaf, especially in Germany. He, as much as Heinicke, may have established the foundation for what was to become known as the German method. Referring to Amman, with whose ideas he strongly disagreed, Peet (1851) stated:

> And many later teachers, especially in Germany, influenced by his views, have strangely held that the power of articulating words was necessary to the full conception and realization of the value of words; and this idea had probably as much influence as anything else, in leading the early German educators to make articulation so prominent a part in their system of instruction. (p. 159)

The Twentieth Century to World War II

At the time of the Conference of Milan in 1880, the situation for deaf Europeans was poor; unfortunately, from that point it deteriorated for the rest of the nineteenth century and through at least the middle of the twentieth century. Essentially, there were no deaf administrators and few, if any, deaf teachers. Education was limited to an elementary level, with a vocational emphasis on unskilled or semiskilled labor. The dominance of oralism was almost complete, and sign languages were repressed, especially in school settings. Schools and government organizations for the deaf were controlled by hearing people. Throughout the period, deaf individuals maintained their organizations and their sign languages, but they were vulnerable minority groups with no control over their own education. Because of a lack of education and training, they were relegated, at best, to dead-end jobs.

The situation in the United States and Canada was also bad, but some factors militated against the worst excesses of the treatment of deaf Europeans. Primary among these was a core of college-educated deaf leaders from Gallaudet College, the only college for the deaf in the world, who provided a sophisticated leadership for the North American deaf community. Although deaf professionals were excluded from leadership positions in general, they remained a factor in residential schools for the deaf and in strong national organizations such as the National Association of the Deaf. However, as we will learn, opportunities essentially were limited to white deaf males.

National Socialism and the Deaf Holocaust

The most horrific period for deaf individuals occurred during the ascendancy of the National Socialists, or Nazis, in Germany and in occupied lands from the mid-1930s to the end of World War II. The extent of the outrages was little known, or little discussed, for generations. To some degree there was a conspiracy of silence. Many deaf survivors, a significant number of whom had been sterilized, felt an undeserved shame for the indignities that had been inflicted on them. Hearing teachers, administrators, religious leaders, deaf leaders, and physicians who participated in the sterilizations and murders were not about to volunteer information.

Gradually, over the years, more and more information has become available, and a breakthrough was made with the publication of a Ph.D. dissertation in 1988 by a hearing German teacher of the deaf, "Klagende Hände." An English translation, "Crying Hands" (Biesold, 1999), is now available. The scope of Biesold's work is enormous. In the 1980s he was able to gather questionnaires from 1,215 deaf Germans who had been sterilized from 1933 to 1945, with the majority of the operations occurring from 1933 to 1935. He accomplished this despite the fact that the records of many schools and ministries allegedly were lost, shredded, transferred, or not available.

With the seizure of power in the 1930s by Hitler and his Nazi party in Germany came a renewed interest in eugenics and in racially based concepts such as "purity of blood" and "racial hygiene." There were two classes of targets. The largest consisted of those Germans who were not of "Nordic" or "Aryan" stock—primarily Jews and Gypsies. The second group consisted of those who were of such stock but who were "biologically deficient" or "hereditarily diseased." This label was applied to a range of conditions, including "hereditary" alcoholism, blindness, deafness, schizophrenia, and manic-depression. Eventually, both classes of targets were judged a threat to national health and purity, leading, in the end, to wholesale murder.

In the 1930s several laws were passed. Chief among these were the Law for the Prevention of Offspring with Hereditary Disease (1933), calling for sterilization and abortion of individuals in nine categories, including hereditary deafness, and the Nuremburg Racial Laws (1935) prohibiting any sexual contact or marriage with Jews or Gypsies. The editor of the *American Annals of the Deaf* (Fusfeld, 1934b) reported that special courts and superior courts on eugenics had been established to carry out the provisions of the law and noted that direct force would be used with those who refused to submit. Later in the year Fusfeld (1934a) reported on the closing of the journal of the Association of German Instructors of the Deaf and Dumb. He referred (p. 357) to an article in another journal by the German educator Hermann Maesse that expressed its attachment to the fundamentals of Nazism, stating that all efforts with the deaf must be justified by what they can contribute to national strength and that all considerations of sentiment, humanitarianism, or individual development must be discarded. Maesse conceded that the deaf could become useful members of society even if they could not bear arms in the military, and he advocated, among other things, the following:

1. Elimination of all nonessentials from the curriculum
2. Contributing to the welfare of the nation as the ultimate aim
3. Curtailment of all effort on behalf of the "backward deaf (i.e., those with mental or physical disabilities)
4. Unfailing allegiance on the part of all teachers of the deaf to the doctrine of National Socialism and to the leader, Adolph Hitler

By 1939–1940 events led to a killing program of disabled Germans that was carried out in secret. It was officially stopped in 1941 when the program became public, but the killings persisted through starvation, medical overdoses, and gassing. According to the notes of a German senator at a confidential meeting of the German Association of Cities, the main reason for secrecy was fear of American intervention. Biesold (p. 162) quotes the notes as follows: "This whole program must be executed with extreme care; there is otherwise the extreme risk that, for example, the United States might use this as a pretext for entering the war." It should be noted that the scientific and medical communities did not oppose the laws and that leading educators of the deaf, many of whom were members of the Nazi party and wore the uniform at work, cooperated in the implementation of the law to the point of reporting names to the police. Perhaps the most chilling case was the distribution of a directive, "A Word to the Hereditarily Diseased Protestant Deaf." Excerpts from a translation (Biesold, p. 39) contain the following statements:

The authorities have ordered that whoever is hereditarily diseased shall have no more children in the future, for our German fatherland needs healthy and sound persons.

...And you, dear friend, you are afflicted with deafness.... How unhappy they [your parents] must have been when they first learned you could not hear!

Now, this is where the authorities want to help you. They want to protect you from transmitting your affliction.

Obey the authorities. Obey even when it is difficult for you. Think of the future of your people and make the sacrifice that is asked of you. Trust in God and don't forget the words of the Bible: We know that all things turn out for the best for those who love God.

Reich Union
of Pastors of the Protestant Deaf

There were even collaborators among the deaf. The Reich Union of the Deaf of Germany (REGEDE) was incorporated into National Socialism, its leaders supported consolidation under Nazi leadership, and all members were enrolled in the Nazi party. Leaders did not hesitate to inform on their "hereditarily diseased" fellows. The Nazi deaf turned on the Jewish deaf, expelling them from deaf associations. Eventually, almost all Jewish deaf Germans were either deported or killed.

There was some resistance. Approximately one-third of deaf individuals marked for sterilization fought it, but they usually lost. Jewish and Catholic doctrine opposed abortion and sterilization, and its leaders opposed the sterilization laws. The Protestant provincial bishop of Wurttemburg, probably at a personal risk, protested the existence of a nearby "euthanasia" center and thus influenced its closing (Biesold, 1999, p. 165). The most notable opposition was provided by a deaf leader, August Veltmenn, head of the Catholic Deaf Association in Munster from 1925 to 1945 (Biesold, 1999, pp. 112–115). He successfully resisted incorporation into REGEDE. Even though his organization had officially been dissolved, it continued to function. He reported that repression came not only from the authorities but also from deaf members of REGEDE, who reported him to the Gestapo several times.

Biesold relates the atrocities of the Nazi era to what he sees as new threats that are now signaled by genetic engineering and the attempts of "humane" genetics to promote sterilization on eugenic grounds. He urges opposition to all such tendencies.

Summary

No evidence exists in recorded history of any systematic attempts to educate deaf individuals before the work of Pedro Ponce de León in Spain in the sixteenth century. The philosophical and practical foundations for education of the deaf were further developed in the seventeenth century through the work of individuals such as Bonet of Spain, Dalgarno of Great Britain, and Amman of Holland, who set the stage for the later establishment of schools for the deaf. The implementation of programs in the eighteenth century by leaders such as de l'Epée of France, Braidwood of Great Britain, and Heinicke of Germany was based on the intellectual legacy of the seventeenth century.

The development and dissemination of effective methods of educating the deaf were hindered by the secrecy employed by many of the leading practitioners. At a time when universal education did not exist and illiteracy was widespread, a teacher of the deaf could survive financially only through the support of well-to-do parents of deaf children. Under such circumstances, it is not surprising that educators were reluctant to share their knowledge.

Every issue presently facing those concerned with optimal development of the deaf was also addressed by their predecessors. A partial list would include areas such as the relation of language to thought, "natural" versus "grammatical" approaches to language development, segregated versus integrated education, the early teaching of reading, the efficacy of speech reading, the development of speech by elemental versus synthetic means, early home education, auditory training, sense training, and information processing via auditory and visual channels. Present educators of the deaf tend to treat each of these topics as having arisen independently of any historical context. It is somewhat humbling to realize that all the issues were treated in one way or another at least two hundred years ago. It is hoped that the preceding brief overview of the work of selected individuals not only will help the reader appreciate their contributions but will also help put into perspective some of the issues that remain unresolved.

CHAPTER

3

Historical Perspectives: The United States from the Eighteenth Century to World War II

Introduction

In considering developments in education of the deaf in the United States, we must keep in mind that the nation today bears little resemblance to that of two hundred years ago. The country grew from a relatively homogeneous, agrarian, isolated nation of 3 million people on the Atlantic seaboard to a pluralistic, post-industrial, continental power 280 million strong.

At the beginning of the nineteenth century, Spain, France, and England together controlled much of what is now part of the continental United States. Sovereignty over large amounts of territory was in dispute, particularly along the boundaries with Canada. At that time, power was concentrated in the hands of Americans of English descent, who constituted approximately half of the population. Black slaves accounted for almost one-quarter of the population, with Germans and Scotch-Irish comprising the only other larger identifiable groups. German settlers tended to cluster in farming communities and maintain the language and customs of their homeland. At the beginning of the nineteenth century, many Germans settled in the Middle Atlantic states, establishing communities such as Germantown, Pennsylvania, and Germantown, Maryland. Scotch-Irish settlers (later called Ulster Irish to differentiate them from Irish-Catholic immigrants) predominated in frontier areas, making up a large proportion of the early pioneers. Under British law slavery was legal in all colonies. Following the American Revolution, although slavery continued in some northern states well into the nineteenth century, most African-American slaves were concentrated in southern states.

Given the realities of life in the United States of the early nineteenth century, illiteracy was not a great obstacle to full participation in society, especially away from the Atlantic Coast. Illiteracy did not limit economic mobility and success. Thus, in 1800, an uneducated deaf person in the United States probably faced no great obstacle due to a lack of education per se and could probably function adequately in society. Deaf children from affluent, educated families, in which education was the norm, typically were sent to Europe for education (Best, 1943).

According to Lee and Stevens (1981), in 1800 approximately 40 percent of the adult population in the North and up to 50 percent in the South was illiterate. By 1840 illiteracy had dropped substantially, especially among adult white males, who were seen as major targets for education. The illiteracy rate for adult white males had dropped to 3 percent in the Northeast and 18 percent in the South. Much of the explanation for the regional disparity lies in the beginning of the Industrial Revolution in New England in the early 1800s, which required higher levels of literacy among workers. Coupled with a New England colonial tradition of education, especially in Massachusetts and Connecticut, the result was the rapid development of a literate population, both male and female. With the advent of the Industrial Revolution, an uneducated deaf person in New England likely faced obstacles to employment and to functioning in society not encountered in other regions. Therefore, community leaders, rather than sending a few deaf children from wealthy families to Europe, worked to establish a school to serve deaf children from a variety of social backgrounds. The result was the first permanent school for the deaf in the United States.

The impact of the Industrial Revolution was only one of many major influences on education of the deaf. The field did not develop in a cultural vacuum; rather, it was shaped by major issues and powerful forces, from "manifest destiny" to slavery, to wars, to depressions, to the continuing influx of immigrants of different nationalities, religious groups, and races. All of these factors influenced how we set our educational priorities and even the way we teach deaf children. This chapter assumes that readers have a working knowledge of U.S. history and thus alludes to major developments only as they relate to education of the deaf.

Early Efforts

Deafness probably existed on the North American continent from the time of settlement of the Native American population. However, the first reference to deaf individuals of which this author is aware was made in 1715 by a visitor to Martha's Vineyard, a small island off the coast of Massachusetts. The visitor noted that one of the local fishers was deaf and also had deaf relatives (Groce, 1980).

Although occasional references to education of the deaf may be found, no evidence exists of any organized attempt to provide for the deaf in the United States before the nineteenth century. Parents who had the financial resources sent their deaf children to Europe to be educated. The Braidwoods' Edinburgh school was apparently the favorite, although Best (1943) reported that a deaf nephew of the future President Monroe was educated in Paris.

Two relatives of Edinburgh students made important contributions to early attempts in education of the deaf. Thomas Bolling, the hearing brother of John and Mary, who enrolled in Edinburgh beginning in 1771 and 1775, respectively, was to be responsible for the establishment of the first school for the deaf in the United States (which, unfortunately, was short-lived).

To Francis Green, the father of Charles Green, who began his education at Edinburgh in 1780, belongs the credit for making the first attempt to establish education for the deaf in the United States. Francis Green was an eclectic and enthusiastic individual. As noted in Chapter 2, Green incurred the displeasure of the Braidwoods by publishing a book on their methods. He was also responsible for having much of the work of de l'Epée translated into English. Following the untimely death of his son in 1793, Green continued his work. In 1803, in the *Palladium,* a Boston-based newspaper, he published an appeal to the clergy of Massachusetts to send him the names of all deaf individuals in the state. In essence, this effort constituted the first census of the deaf in the United States (Deland, 1931). The appeal turned up seventy-five names but no follow-up in terms of establishment of a school.

The first person to work with the deaf in a capacity other than private tutor probably was John Stanford, chaplain to the almshouse of New York City, who in 1810 undertook the education of several deaf children he encountered in his ministry. Stanford apparently tried to teach the children primarily by means of writing, but he experienced little success and eventually gave up working directly with the deaf. However, he maintained an interest in their problems and later was a founder of the New York Institution for Instruction of the Deaf and Dumb (Gallaudet, 1886).

The third attempt to establish an educational program for deaf children in the United States involved the Bolling family of Virginia and the star-crossed John Braidwood, grandson of Thomas Braidwood, who founded the Edinburgh school. Colonel William Bolling, whose three deaf siblings had been educated in Edinburgh, himself had two deaf children, William Albert and Mary. In 1812, the colonel learned that John Braidwood was in the United States and invited him to Virginia to establish a school.

Braidwood had been the headmaster of the Edinburgh school, the most prestigious in Great Britain, for two years. Although a young man with unlimited potential, he was replaced because of intemperance and irresponsibility, and he migrated to the United States under a cloud. Braidwood informed Bolling that he was establishing a school in Baltimore. Bolling sent Braidwood $600 for that purpose, with the understanding that the school would open by July 1, 1812 (Bender, 1970). Apparently the school was never established, and the next thing Bolling heard from Braidwood was that he had been imprisoned in New York for unpaid debts. Bolling paid Braidwood's debts and brought him to Virginia as a tutor for his children. In 1815, Colonel Bolling turned over a family estate to Braidwood and paid him a salary in return for teaching four or five students.

In 1817, Braidwood left Virginia and went to New York, where he tried, apparently unsuccessfully, to establish another school (Gallaudet, 1886). He returned to Virginia in 1818, and the long-suffering Colonel Bolling established a new school in

Manchester, Virginia, this time with the Reverend John Kilpatrick as head and Braidwood as assistant (Best, 1943). Braidwood was affiliated with the school for only about six months, and the school apparently closed within a year or two. Braidwood died "a victim of intemperance" in 1819 (Doyle, 1893) or 1820 (Deland, 1931).

The Establishment of Schools for the Deaf

The honor of establishing the first permanent school for the deaf in the United States belongs to Dr. Mason Fitch Cogswell, Laurent Clerc, a deaf teacher from the Royal National Institute for the Deaf in Paris, and Thomas Hopkins Gallaudet. A graduate of Yale at age eighteen, Gallaudet had completed Andover (Massachusetts) Theological Seminary and was about to enter the Congregational ministry when he became interested in the education of nine-year-old Alice Cogswell, the deaf daughter of a neighbor, Dr. Mason Fitch Cogswell, in 1814. Dr. Cogswell was a surgeon and president of the Connecticut Medical Society. He pioneered techniques of cataract removal and was the first surgeon of record to tie the carotid artery (Boatner, 1959b). Gallaudet undertook to teach Alice some simple words and sentences. His success strengthened Dr. Cogswell's determination to establish a school for the deaf in Connecticut. Following the lead of Francis Green in Massachusetts, Cogswell conducted a census of the number of deaf individuals of educable age in Connecticut. His efforts must have been better advertised, because he came up with eighty names, five more than Green had turned up in the more populous Massachusetts. Using these figures, Cogswell projected a total of more than two thousand deaf persons in the United States, four times Green's estimate of five hundred (Bender, 1970).

In 1815, Cogswell presented his results to a group of community leaders in Hartford. He enlisted their support in establishing a committee to raise funds to send a person to Europe to study education of the deaf. The money was raised in one day. The natural choice was Thomas Hopkins Gallaudet. At first reluctant to give up his ministerial calling, Gallaudet was convinced by the arguments of the group (especially Dr. Cogswell's), and he agreed to undertake the journey. He planned to go first to Great Britain to study the Braidwoods' method and then to Paris to learn the French method of de l'Epée and Sicard. Gallaudet sailed for Europe in the spring of 1815. Upon arrival in Great Britain, he presented himself to the Braidwoods and Joseph Watson and proposed to spend a few months with them, after which he would go to Paris. This would enable him to choose what he considered to be the most effective components from each method (Gallaudet, 1888).

The Braidwood family rejected Gallaudet's proposal, apparently for three reasons. First, the Braidwood method was still considered a family secret not to be divulged on demand. Second, the family was opposed to the French method and saw no advantage in having it connected with their system. Third, John Braidwood was establishing a school in Virginia at that time, and the family was not eager to train a rival in the United States. The fact that the United States and Great Britain had just been at war probably did not help relations.

The Braidwoods told Gallaudet that learning their system would require four or five years and presented a counterproposal. Watson offered to send an assistant to the United States to help establish a school rather than train Gallaudet. Gallaudet rejected this offer on the grounds that he wanted to be trained and did not want to rely on someone wedded to one method. Gallaudet then was offered a three-year residence, in which he would be employed as an assistant. The plan called for him "to be with the pupils from seven o'clock in the morning till eight o'clock in the evening and also with pupils in their hours of recreation" (Deland, 1931). Gallaudet vigorously rejected what he considered an insulting proposal. He made one final attempt, requesting that the Braidwoods release from an oath of secrecy a Mr. Kinniburgh, who had been trained by the Braidwoods and was teaching in Edinburgh. This request was refused, and Gallaudet broke off negotiations with the Braidwoods to go to Paris to study with Sicard, who had met Gallaudet while on a speaking tour in Great Britain.

Gallaudet had developed a great interest in the French method on the basis of the performance of two deaf men who accompanied Sicard on his lectures and responded to audiences' questions on matters ranging from philosophy to the use of signs to convey abstract ideas (DeLadsbut, 1815). Gallaudet was immediately placed in training by Sicard, and he stayed for approximately four months. He prevailed on Sicard to allow a deaf teacher, Laurent Clerc, to return with him, and the two arrived in the United States in August 1816. Although Gallaudet had left for Europe with an eclectic orientation, circumstances dictated that he return with knowledge of only the French system. Although he had rejected Watson's offer of an assistant, he actively sought the services of Clerc. Thus it was that the first teacher at the first school for the deaf in the United States was a deaf individual, whereas in the British system deaf teachers were not employed.

In October 1816, the Connecticut legislature appropriated $5,000 for the school. In the fall and winter of 1816–1817, Gallaudet and Clerc traveled to several cities in the United States to solicit money from private sources. On April 15, 1817, the American Asylum for the Education of the Deaf and Dumb (now the American School for the Deaf) was officially begun. The school opened with seven students and had grown to a total of twenty-one students by the time of the July 1817 annual report. Gallaudet served as principal until he resigned in 1830.

The permanence of the school was ensured in 1819, when the United States Congress gave the school a land grant of a township site of 23,000 acres in Alabama. The school sold the land and established a fund in excess of $300,000. The position of the American Asylum thereby was secured, and its influence was unrivaled by any other school in the first half of the nineteenth century. During that period, the school provided both an education for deaf individuals from other states and leadership in the establishment of new schools throughout the country. In 1819, the Massachusetts legislature decided to support the education of twenty deaf students at the American School for the Deaf. Similar actions were later taken by other New

England states (New Hampshire in 1821, Maine and Vermont in 1825, and Rhode Island in 1845). Even distant states such as Georgia and South Carolina elected to send their children to Hartford until they established schools of their own.

The curriculum of the American School for the Deaf in its early years reflected the ethos of New England at that time: a deeply religious society at the onset of industrialization. In addition to special training in English grammar, the school stressed the five Rs: Reading, Riting, Rithmetic, Religion, and Rules of Conduct (Lee and Stevens, 1981). Students had a superficial exposure to history, philosophy, and literature (Van Cleve and Crouch, 1989). The practical bent of the school is exemplified by the fact that it was one of the first schools in the United States to provide vocational education for its students. A program in individual training was established in 1822, five years after the school opened (Jones, 1918). Students were provided with the skills needed to enter the industrial work force of the time.

Many of the earliest students at the school were adults, and the average age of admittance for the first one hundred students was eighteen years (Valentine, 1994). This resulted in conflict with some of the male students who resisted the paternalistic environment of the school and would slip out at night and return intoxicated. Many of them were dismissed by Gallaudet (Valentine, 1994, p. 63).

The second school for the deaf, the New York Institution for the Instruction of the Deaf and Dumb, opened in 1818. To some extent, it was the product of the unsuccessful efforts of Stanford and Braidwood. At first, the school survived by means of subscriptions, donations, and tuition payments. New York City soon allocated funds for ten day students, and in 1821 New York State made permanent provision for the support of an additional thirty-two students. In essence, this was the first day school for the deaf in the United States, although it soon evolved into a residential school. According to E. M. Gallaudet (1886), the school experienced great difficulties until Harvey Peet was appointed principal in 1831. Peet had been an assistant to Thomas Hopkins Gallaudet in Hartford.

The development of the third school for the deaf in the United States was also heavily influenced by the American School. The beginning of the Pennsylvania Institution for the Deaf and Dumb may be traced to the efforts of David Seixas. Seixas found some deaf children wandering the streets of Philadelphia and began to try to teach the children in his home. In April 1820, the board of directors of the Pennsylvania Institution for the Deaf and Dumb was established, with Seixas as principal. The school was initially supported by "benevolent persons in Philadelphia" (Gallaudet, 1886) but was quickly incorporated by the state of Pennsylvania, and state support for fifty students was approved in 1821. Because of difficulties at the school, Laurent Clerc took a seven-month leave of absence from the American School to replace Seixas as acting principal. During this time, Clerc organized the school, established the curriculum, and trained the teachers. Upon his return to Hartford, Clerc was succeeded by Lewis Weld, another teacher from Hartford. Weld remained in Philadelphia until 1830, when he was appointed to succeed Thomas Hopkins Gallaudet as principal of the Hartford School.

The first three permanent schools for the deaf, in Hartford, New York City, and Philadelphia, were established within three years of one another. The experiences of the schools in New York and Philadelphia were similar in that each was established independently, experienced difficulty, and then turned to the American School in Hartford for a principal to organize the school and establish a curriculum. As a result, the schools had common curricula, teacher-training procedures, and educational philosophies. Relationships were strengthened by movement of teachers and principals from one school to another. These three schools, with the American School as first among equals, would provide the leadership for education of the deaf for generations. Later schools were based on their model, and they provided a great share of the leaders in the field until well after the Civil War (1861–1865).

Because of the network created by the interaction of the three schools and their subsequent contributions to other schools, Laurent Clerc became the most influential figure in education of the deaf in the United States during its first forty years. His impact has extended to the present day (Lane, 1984). Although Thomas Hopkins Gallaudet is justly credited with establishing the first school for the deaf in the United States, a deaf individual—Laurent Clerc—was the first true educator of the deaf. He was responsible for the sign language and sign system used in the classroom. The curriculum he introduced traces back to the work of Bonet in Spain, and elements of it are in use today. Clerc, then, was a bridge between Europe and the United States, and he had the insight to adapt techniques to new situations. On a personal level, he trained many of the first teachers, who later passed on his techniques when they themselves trained new teachers.

Much of the early work in education of students with disabilities had a heavy religious orientation (Kauffman, 1980). Francis Green's appeal to the clergy of Massachusetts for help, the work of Reverend Stanford in New York, and the pioneering efforts of former theological student Thomas Hopkins Gallaudet highlight the influence of religious leaders on the development of programs for the deaf in nineteenth-century United States. This, of course, was an extension of a tradition begun with Pedro Ponce de León in the sixteenth century. One of the major motivations of educators of the deaf was to instruct children in religious matters, and the first schools typically had a strong religious atmosphere. As the century progressed and the population of the United States became more heterogeneous, the issue of separation of church and state—and, by extension, state-supported schools for the deaf—assumed growing importance. Specific religious training was phased out, and a concentration on "moral" training evolved to take its place (Jones, 1918).

The ministries to the deaf were perceived as part of ongoing missions to minister to and convert all classes of individuals who might be considered unfortunate, including those with disabilities, orphans, and the poor. As previously noted, Reverend Stanford had been chaplain of an almshouse in New York City. Thomas Hopkins Gallaudet was the author of several children's books with biblical and moral messages that were translated into several languages. He also worked in prison reform and at the Hartford Retreat, which among other functions served individuals with emotional problems. Finally, he was involved in sending ministers west to combat the infiltration of the Catholic faith and other sects into the rapidly expanding frontiers of the United States (Boatner, 1959b). Gallaudet was descended from French Huguenots (Boatner, 1959b), and a certain antipathy might be expected from the descendant of a group of Calvinist Protestants who had left France generations earlier to escape religious persecution. It is to his credit that he was able to acknowledge his debt to the work of French priests such as de l'Epée and Sicard.

Despite the intellectual leadership of Clerc, the first fifty years of education of the deaf in the United States were controlled by a paternalistic elite: white, Protestant, affluent, hearing, and authoritarian (Moores, 1992a; Winzer, 1981). Valentine (1994) reported that principals at the American Asylum viewed themselves as benevolent, morally correct fathers and deaf people of all ages as children in need of guidance. Winzer (1981) has stated that the first teachers of the deaf were a "tightly-knit male elite, predominantly members of the clergy" (p. 124) and noted that in 1852, thirty-five years after the establishment of the first school, there were only three female teachers in fourteen schools for the deaf (p. 125).

In a paper by Weed (1859) on the missionary element in deaf education, the Reverend W. W. Turner, principal of the American School for the Deaf, stated:

> It is greatly to be desired that teachers of the Deaf and Dumb should keep steadily before them this great object, which was so prominently before the minds of those who introduced the art of teaching mutes into this country—the spiritual elevation of those admitted to their care. The deaf and dumb when they come into our institutions are heathen. (p. 30)

Examples of oppression of deaf people, including professionals, in the nineteenth century abound. At the third meeting of the Convention of American Instructors of the Deaf (CAID) in 1853, it was decided, over the opposition of Laurent Clerc, that the procedure on any question would consist of a voice vote by hearing participants, followed by a show of hands by deaf participants. The question of allowing deaf and female participants to serve on committees was not even raised until the seventh CAID meeting in 1870. The insensitivity of hearing educators is best illustrated by the response of Harvey Peet to the request for voting by a show of hands, as reported in the 1853 (CAID) proceedings:

> Dr. Peet said he would not exactly oppose this motion, but he thought practical application would be found inconvenient. To him it would be altogether the most satisfactory that the question be taken by ayes and noes, the Deaf Mutes themselves voting by uplifting hand. The vote could in no case be simultaneous, because the Deaf Mutes must necessarily have the matter explained.
>
> This, he thought, would be found annoying and calculated to retard business. . . . He proposed that the vote of the Deaf Mutes be taken after the vote by ayes and noes.

Peet's proposal was accepted, and he did not represent a minority view. Lane (1992) identified Peet as superintendent of the New York Institution, first president of CAID, "the dean of American educators of the deaf," and an individual who "had long been the intellectual leader of his profession" (p. 265).

The most dramatic example of the repression under which deaf teachers labored is the reaction of hearing administrators to the request by John Carlin, a deaf artist, poet, and community leader, that schools for the deaf follow a principle of equal pay for equal work and raise the salaries of deaf teachers to the same level as hearing teachers. After pursuing the topic for several years, Carlin submitted his request by letter to the fifth meeting of CAID in 1858. Following are some of the comments published in the meeting proceedings in 1859:

> Mute teachers are not capable of doing that for which we need liberally educated men. (Samuel Porter, American School, Caid, 1859, p. 70)

> He [the deaf teacher] is not in full communion with his fellow-beings and never can be. It is the want of this that incapacitates him for the accomplishment of the higher duties of a teacher. (Reverend W. W. Turner, principal, American School, p. 71)

> It is Mr. Carlin, who is not a teacher and never will be—because he can do a great deal better in his present lucrative and honorable profession. . . . although I have a great deal of respect for him [Carlin], and own that *for a deaf and dumb man, I could never understand how he could get such an education* [italics added]. (Reverend B. M. Fay, principal, Michigan School, p. 73)

> I believe that a man deprived of one important sense is not as valuable as a man who has use of all. I do not subscribe to the doctrine that a deaf and dumb teacher can become as useful as a speaking teacher. (Reverend Collins Stone, superintendent, Ohio School, p. 73)

Harvey Peet decided the issue:

> Beyond a certain point, the deaf mute teacher is not as well qualified to carry on a class as a hearing and speaking man. In the first place, he is not as well educated. There are a great many idioms of the language he does not and can not understand. . . . This is precisely the argument brought forward by all the women's right conventions in the country that I have ever heard of. They say if a female performs certain duties as well as a man, for instance, those of a clerk, she ought to have the same salary that a man gets. I am disposed to doubt and controvert this idea. (CAID, 1859, p. 66)

> The deaf and dumb teachers do not perform as much service as a professor. For instance, they have nothing to do with performing religious worship in chapel. . . . And they are not capable of carrying a class to as high a degree of attainment. It would be very unwise indeed to place a class of four or five years' standing under a deaf mute teacher. (p. 67)

> They are not qualified to carry forward a class of Deaf Mutes, successfully, for over a period of three to four years. (p. 69)

> If I have anything to do with the controlling management of the Institution, I will never allow a deaf mute to go forward with the same class beyond three years. (p. 69)

Lane (1992) presents a different perspective on education of the deaf in the nineteenth century. He claims deaf and hearing professionals had equal status, no medical or pathological model of deafness existed, and academic achievement was much higher. This situation changed, according to Lane (p. 25), when hearing people seized control of education of the deaf. In a review of Lane's text, Moores (1993b) agreed with Lane that deaf people face difficulties even today but maintained that Lane "wants to return to the halcyon days of a past that never was" (p. 5), stating that, on balance, life for deaf Americans was much worse than at present. Fewer than half of deaf Americans ever attended schools at that time, instruction—when available—began late, and whole groups were excluded. Specifically, the first segregated schools for deaf African-American children were not established until after the Civil War.

In a response to the review, Lane (1993, p. 318) argued that education of the deaf was more successful in the past century, quoting from Van Cleve and Crouch (1989, p. 85) an example of what the National Deaf Mute College (now Gallaudet University) expected applicants to the freshman class to know: "arithmetic, algebra to quadratic equations, English grammar, ancient and modern history, geography, physiology, philosophy, and the principles of Latin construction, especially Latin etymology and syntax." Lane compares this situation to the low-achieving pool of deaf high school graduates now available.

In a reply to Lane's response, Moores (1993b) pointed out that in Gallaudet's first two years, only *one* student, Melville Ballard, matriculated under these conditions, and he was admitted as a junior. Van Cleve and Crouch (1989, pp. 84–85) noted that Gallaudet established a preparatory program because most deaf students had only vocational training. Fischer and de Lorenzo (1983) reported that only two schools for the deaf had high schools. Ballard was the only true college student of five students in attendance in 1864–1865 and of twenty-five students in 1865–1866. Fischer and de Lorenzo quoted Edward Minor Gallaudet, the first president of Gallaudet: "As only one of the five young men occupying this building was, strictly speaking, a college student, remarks were often facetiously made, by his mates, as follows: 'The college has gone to the city.' 'The college has gone to bed.' 'The college is taking a bath'" (p. 59).

The Spread of Education of the Deaf

Following the establishment over a three-year period of the schools in Connecticut, New York, and Pennsylvania, only four new schools were added from 1820 to 1844. These were in Kentucky (1823), Ohio (1829), Missouri (1838), and Virginia (1839). The Virginia school was the first in which schools for the deaf and for the blind were placed under a single administration. The Marie E. Consilia Deaf Mute Institution in St. Louis, Missouri, was established by Sisters of St. Joseph from Lyons, France. Around 1910, it merged with the present St. Joseph's School for the Deaf (Gannon, 1981). From 1844 to 1860, just before the Civil War, seventeen new institutions were established.

The growth of the early schools for the deaf occurred in two stages: In the twenty-seven years from 1817 to 1844, only seven schools were established; then, from 1844 to 1860, there was one new school per year. As might be expected, the first three schools were established in metropolitan areas, where a demand for literacy existed. Thus education of the deaf was at first limited to a relatively small part of the United States. With growing industrialization, the system of schools for the deaf in the United States expanded, and by the Civil War it covered the nation.

The Columbia Institution for the Deaf and Dumb in Washington, D.C., founded by Amos Kendall in 1857, deserves special mention. Edward Miner Gallaudet (1837–1917) and Sophie Fowler Gallaudet, the son and the widow of Thomas Hopkins Gallaudet, were appointed superintendent and matron, respectively. In 1864 the school added a collegiate department, which was named the National Deaf Mute College (Gallaudet, 1886). This was later renamed Gallaudet College (and eventually Gallaudet University) in honor of Thomas Hopkins Gallaudet. It remains today the only liberal arts college for the deaf in the world.

Edward Miner Gallaudet (circa 1880).   *First president of Gallaudet College; now Gallaudet University.*

GALLAUDET UNIVERSITY ARCHIVES

The schools founded in the fifty-year period from 1817 to 1867 were primarily residential institutions, though several schools, such as those in New York City and Philadelphia, originated as day schools and apparently had numerous day students (students who lived at home). Although the first three schools were located in the most populous areas of their states (Hartford, New York City, and Philadelphia), subsequent schools tended to be established in areas removed from the major population centers. Schools were founded by state legislatures in Danville, Kentucky; Staunton, Virginia; Jacksonville, Illinois; Cave Spring, Georgia; Fulton, Missouri; Delavan, Wisconsin; Flint, Michigan; and Faribault, Minnesota (rather than in Louisville, Richmond, Chicago, Atlanta, St. Louis, Milwaukee, Detroit, or Minneapolis–St. Paul). In addition to political reasons specific to each state, the placements probably reflected an attitude that the problems of the deaf precluded them from being a part of the larger society. This mindset also influenced the placement of schools and institutions for individuals who were blind or had mental retardation. Frequently, states established schools for the deaf and the blind in the same locality, sometimes with shared campuses and a common administration.

The first long-standing day schools for the deaf were not established until 1869, when the Pittsburgh Day School and the Boston Day School (renamed the Horace Mann School in 1877) opened. The Pittsburgh school later evolved into a predominantly residential facility and is now known as the Western Pennsylvania School for the Deaf. The relatively late development of day schools for the deaf may be explained by the fact that deafness is a low-incidence condition and the early U.S. cities lacked populations large enough to supply the number of deaf children necessary to justify the existence of a day school.

First Attempts at Oral Education and the Common School Movement in the United States

No treatment of education of the deaf in the nineteenth century in the United States would be complete without consideration of the oral-manual controversy that always seemed to be operating just beneath the surface and frequently flared into open hostility. The problem was compounded by disagreement among advocates of manual communication, with some favoring "methodical" signs following English word order, others supporting "natural" sign language with a word order different from that of English, and a somewhat smaller third group relying heavily on the manual alphabet.

Thomas Hopkins Gallaudet's initial plans to combine elements of the manual and oral methods were not realized, and the early schools were basically manual only. They tended to place little or no emphasis on articulation or speech. Two notable exceptions were Braidwood's school in Virginia and an oral school established by the Reverend Robert T. Anderson in Hopkinsville, Kentucky (Jones, 1918). The Hopkinsville school operated from 1844 to 1854, when it closed its doors.

Oral education in the United States had its roots in two quite disparate movements. One movement favored the addition of oral elements to the existing manual methods to produce a combined oral-manual system. The other focused on the establishment of an oral-only system that did not employ manual components.

Although sporadic attempts were made to teach articulation and speech reading from the beginning, most of the effort was limited to the hard of hearing. As early as 1836, Boatner (1937) noted reports of successful instruction in articulation at the American School for the Deaf with students who had lost their hearing in childhood and with adventitiously deaf students. It was believed that attempts to teach oral communication to the congenitally deaf were doomed to failure in the majority of cases. This belief was challenged in 1844 by Horace Mann and Samuel Howe, who returned from a tour of German schools for the deaf convinced of the superiority of the German (oral) method (Deland, 1931; Jones, 1918). They recommended the establishment of an oral school in Massachusetts, a recommendation strongly opposed by the American School. Mann was one of the most influential early American educators. Howe was the principal of the first school for the blind in the United States and coordinated the training of Laura Bridgeman (Lamson, 1878), a deaf-blind individual who was considered the Helen Keller of her time.* Bridgeman was instructed primarily through the manual alphabet, and it is possible that many of the techniques Anne Sullivan used with Helen Keller were based on those previously used with Bridgeman.

The recommendations of Mann and Howe concerning education of the deaf must be considered within a broader cultural context. Mann was in the process of redefining the role of education in the United States and was initiating sweeping changes, especially in New England (Lee and Stevens, 1981). His recommendations for changes in education of the deaf were consistent with his plans for education in general.

Horace Mann acted on the basis of strong moral convictions. He was a leader in the antislavery movement and was a strong advocate for issues ranging from temperance to the establishment of asylums for individuals with disabilities. Deeply shocked by riots in Massachusetts involving poor Irish immigrants, Mann blamed the stresses that the introduction of industrial capitalism and the factory system had brought to New England. The roles of the traditional social institutions of learning— home, work, church, school—were undergoing change. There was a new and growing immigrant population with different religious and family values, and work was no longer home centered. Mann realized that the schools would have to play an increasingly important role if the newcomers were to be "civilized, Christianized, and Americanized" (Lee and Stevens, 1981). He apparently was unaware that most immigrants already thought of themselves as civilized and Christian, if not American.

---

*Interestingly, Howe's position was originally offered to Thomas Hopkins Gallaudet, who declined primarily because he did not want to leave Hartford (Boatner, 1959a).

Mann was impressed by the work of the schools in France in fostering French nationalism, but he was more heavily influenced by the Prussian two-track system of education, which was free, universal, and compulsory. Upper-class children attended a gymnasium and later perhaps a university or a military academy. Children from the masses attended a common school (Volksschule), with some males matriculating at technical schools and some females matriculating at normal schools to be trained as teachers.

As a result of Mann's reorganization of the Massachusetts school system, for the first time American schools functioned as state vehicles, with one object being the socialization of all children into a common cultural world view imbued with a spirit of patriotism. The common schools had a number of different implicit mandates; the main objective was to provide an increasingly diverse school-age population with the skills needed to contribute to a complex, rapidly changing society while simultaneously inculcating the newcomers with the religious and moral values that the dominant society had held when New England was agrarian and homogeneous.

Mann's ideas had a profound impact on American educators, and sweeping changes were initiated. However, the new goals and curricula of the public schools were opposed by two groups that were destined to increase in size and importance throughout the nineteenth century.

From the establishment of the republic until well into the nineteenth century, German-Americans constituted the second largest minority in the United States after blacks. They had made great efforts to preserve their language and culture, sometimes to the dismay of English speakers, and they opposed the monolingual nature of the schools. Language debates in the United States have been going on for more than two hundred years. In 1753, Benjamin Franklin lashed out at the Germans in the colony of Pennsylvania, expressing the fear that their language would soon become dominant (Heath, 1981). Many of the publications of the Continental Congress from 1774 to 1780 were in German as well as in English (Lee and Stevens, 1981). In 1794, a request was made to Congress that some laws of the United States be issued in German as well as in English, a common practice with documents at that time. It was rejected by the House of Representatives by a vote of 42 to 41. The vote eventually gave rise to the legend that German missed becoming the national language of the United States by one vote. In the second half of the nineteenth century, American and British journalists used a highly distorted version of this legend to warn Americans of the extent of German usage and to persuade them that German could receive enough support to become the language of choice in the United States (Heath, 1981). The conflict over the place of German in schools and society in the eighteenth and nineteenth centuries is essentially the same as that over the role of Spanish and other languages today. Heath (1981) stated:

> Throughout the history of the United States, whenever speakers of varieties of English or other languages have been viewed as politically, socially, or economically threatening, their language has become a focus for arguments in favor of both restrictions in their use and imposition of Standard English. . . . Individuals, groups, and the national

government have promoted the idea at different times throughout our history that speaking the same language would ensure uniformity of other behavioral traits, such as morality, patriotism, and logical thinking. (p. 10)

The second minority group to oppose the public schools during this time was the Irish Catholics, who were predominantly poor residents of rapidly growing urban slums. Contrary to popular belief, many of the early Irish-Catholic immigrants spoke Irish rather than English as their first language (Greeley, 1981). However, their opposition to the public schools was religious, not linguistic. They resisted what they interpreted as attempts to impose Protestant religious beliefs on their children. The resistance of the German and Irish immigrants, buttressed by later immigrants, put pressure on the public schools to be open to the use of other languages and to secularize instruction.

A third source of resistance to the efforts of Horace Mann in the 1940s was a group that has received little attention from general education because it includes less than one school-age child in one thousand: the deaf. Mann's and Howe's observations on the oral method caused a sensation in the United States. Dr. Harvey Peet and Reverend George Day (from the New York Institution and the American School, respectively) were sent to Germany to observe the oral method firsthand. They were much less impressed with the results of that method than Howe and Mann were (Deland, 1931; Jones, 1918), declaring that the manual method produced better results and the German method was a feeble one for education and for moral and religious instruction. However, some of the "manual" educators acknowledged the benefits of articulation, at least for some students. Lewis Weld, principal of the American School, had made a trip to Europe before Peet and Day had. On the basis of Weld's report (Weld, 1855), the board of directors of the American School declared:

> The Board of Directors will take efficient measures to introduce into the course of instruction in the school every improvement to be derived from these foreign institutions; and with regard to teaching deaf-mutes to articulate, and to understand what is said to them orally, that they give it a full and prolonged trial, and do in this branch of instruction everything that is practically and permanently useful. (Boatner, 1937, p. 50)

The schools for the deaf at that time were already teaching the five Rs and were in harmony with much of Mann's thinking. The opposition to his ideas centered on the belief that the use of signs was superior for moral and religious instruction. Mann's opposition to signs may have arisen from concern about the use of a system of instruction that had some fundamental differences from spoken English. From our perspective in the twenty-first century, it is interesting to note that in mid-nineteenth-century American education, there was disagreement over the use of home languages other than English in classes, the relationship between religion and the schools, and the use of signs in educating deaf children.

The Establishment of Oral Schools in the United States in the Late Nineteenth Century

The American School for the Deaf was the first school in the United States to hire a full-time speech teacher, Eliza Wadsworth, in 1857. Many believed that the commitment of the American School to oral education was dictated as much by political as by educational considerations and that a major goal was the prevention of the establishment of a competitive school that the state of Massachusetts would favor over the Connecticut-based American School (Report of the Joint Special Committee of the Massachusetts Legislature on the Education of the Deaf and Dumb, 1867).

The person responsible for establishing an oral school for the deaf, despite opposition from the manual faction, was Gardiner Greene Hubbard, a prominent Massachusetts lawyer of distinguished ancestry. His daughter Mabel had lost her hearing through scarlet fever in 1863 at age five (Bruce, 1974). The Hubbard family was opposed to sending Mabel to the American School, preferring to have her tutored orally. Convinced of the success of their efforts, they actively sought the establishment of an oral school. Their effort was supported by the parents of two other young, adventitiously deaf girls: Fanny Cushing, daughter of the governor of Rhode Island, and Jeannie Lippitt, sister of a future United States senator from Rhode Island (Bruce, 1974; Deland, 1931).

However, the effort to establish a school with state support was defeated. Hubbard then founded a private school in Chelmsford, Massachusetts, under the leadership of Harriet Rogers, the tutor of Fanny Cushing and sister of one of the instructors of Laura Bridgeman (Deland, 1931). Hubbard persisted in his efforts at the state level, and in 1867 he succeeded in establishing an oral-only school in Northampton, Massachusetts. Harriet Rogers was appointed the first principal.

A major factor in persuading the Massachusetts legislators was a demonstration given by Jeannie Lippitt, then fifteen, and Roscoe Green, an eighteen-year-old native of Providence who had lost his hearing at age seven (Turner, in Gallaudet, 1868, p. 57). They were able to discuss a variety of topics without recourse to manual communication (Deland, 1931; Gallaudet, 1868).

The fear that with the establishment of the Clarke school the state of Massachusetts would no longer send students to the American School proved to be unfounded. Although in his testimony before the Massachusetts Joint Special Committee (1867, p. 11) Samuel Howe had recommended that no deaf students from Massachusetts be sent to the American School after May 1867, Gardiner Hubbard envisioned the oral school as serving primarily students who had lost their hearing at age three or later as well as those who were hard of hearing. His testimony before the committee included this exchange:

> HUBBARD: If the child were of poor parents, I should not attempt articulation.
> QUESTION: Let him grow up in silence?
> HUBBARD: No, sir; I should send it to Hartford. (p. 10)

In the *First Annual Report of the Clarke Institution for Deaf Mutes,* Hubbard (1868) reiterated his position that the school was established primarily for the deaf and the hard of hearing. Because of the attention given to the oral-manual question, little recognition has been given to two essential policies of the new school that represented major breakthroughs (Hubbard, 1868). First was the setting of the age of admission at five years, when most schools for the deaf required students to be at least ten years of age. Second was the decision to expand the period of instruction from the usual six years to ten years.

Because of the drawn-out controversy surrounding its establishment, many believe that the Clarke school was the first permanent oral-only school for the deaf in the United States. This is incorrect; the first oral-only school was the New York Institution for Impaired Instruction, now the Lexington School for the Deaf. The New York school (not to be confused with the New York Institution, founded in 1818) grew out of a private oral school started in 1864 by Isaac and Hannah Rosenfeld. The Rosenfelds wished to extend the benefits of the training to children whose parents could not pay. Reorganized with substantial philanthropic support, the school opened on March 1, 1867, seven months before the Clarke school (Deland, 1931; Jones, 1918). Bernhard Engelsmann, who had been a teacher in the Vienna Hebrew (oral) School for the Deaf, was appointed the first principal (Deland, 1931). In 1870, the New York legislature ensured the school's stability by providing for the support of students on the same terms accorded those enrolled in the previously established school for the deaf in New York.

Developments in education of the deaf in the mid-nineteenth century occurred during a period of profound changes in the United States. The territory expanded considerably through wars with England and Mexico and through land purchases from Spain, France, and Russia. The population increased more than ten times between 1800 and 1860 and was to double again by 1890. A bitter civil war was fought, and slavery was abolished.

Among the changes were the beginnings of an evolution in the role of women. Winzer (1981) makes a convincing case that the debate on communication divided temporarily into opposing factors based on gender. She reports that when women were first hired by the male-dominated teaching profession, it was because of their "comparative cheapness" (p. 125). Although A. G. Bell was the most influential advocate, Winzer argues that oralism achieved dominance through an articulate and dedicated group of women teachers, most of whom taught by speech only and relegated sign language to the status of "ghetto slang" (p. 162). Despite the arguments of male administrators in traditional manual schools that oral schools "simply develop the female mind in the male body," oralism continued to advance. In addition to the Clarke school, leading oral schools in Boston, Chicago, and Providence were staffed and administered completely by hearing women.

As the United States and western Europe became urban, industrialized societies, a change in educational emphasis occurred. Technological societies require universally trained, educated workers. Such societies seek to identify individuals who may not benefit from mass training and educational techniques (Wines, 1888). Within this context, the major thrust of the mental-testing movement, beginning with the work of

Binet in France around the turn of the century, was to identify and remove children of limited intellectual ability from the regular educational program (Kanner, 1967).

In the United States, the situation was compounded by the legacy of slavery and by massive immigration that started with the influx of German and Irish-Catholic groups and continued with waves of immigrants from central, eastern, and southern Europe through the early part of the twentieth century (Dworkin, 1976; Kamin, 1974). The process, of course, has continued to the present, with substantial immigration from Latin America, Asia, and Africa.

In 1840, the majority of Americans were still of English and Scotch-Irish stock. With some variations, there was a commonly shared language, religion, and set of values. Although blacks made up an estimated 20 to 25 percent of the population, they were almost totally subjugated (Dworkin, 1976).

By 1850, the United States had conquered that part of Mexico stretching from Louisiana to California (approximately one-third of the present contiguous United States), with its Native American and Catholic, Spanish-speaking populations. In addition, the Louisiana Territory (stretching from Louisiana north to Minnesota and west to the Pacific) had been acquired from France and the Florida Territory from Spain.

By 1870, blacks theoretically were free, and large numbers of Jewish immigrants had arrived from Poland and Russia. In the 1890s Poles, Czechoslovakians, and Hungarians were working in the mines and factories, and by 1900 Italians had replaced the Irish as the largest ethnic group in many northeastern cities (Dworkin, 1976; Kamin, 1974).

The United States was evolving from a relatively homogeneous society to a society of almost overwhelming ethnic, cultural, racial, linguistic, and religious diversity, a transformation that continues today. Despite confusion, hostility, and frequent bloodshed, the nation survived and prospered, albeit in a form that would be unrecognizable to its founders.

Programs for individuals with disabilities that were developed in the early and middle nineteenth century essentially reflected an optimistic view of the potential benefits of education and training. They were humane and had an educational orientation. The goal was to prepare individuals with disabilities to function in society at large (Kanner, 1967; Kauffman, 1980). The outstanding early educators in this field, such as Thomas Hopkins Gallaudet, Laurent Clerc, Samuel Gridley Howe, and Edouard Seguin, were firm believers in educability. Seguin, who came to the United States after the French Revolution of 1848, was especially instrumental in popularizing this philosophy.

Attitudes began to change during the latter part of the nineteenth century. First, evidence began accumulating that not all people with disabilities could be educated to take their place in society, especially a technical society, using existing methods. Second, the expansion of special schools and institutions was increasingly seen as a drain on the treasuries of the various states. Third, the conviction grew that many individuals with disabilities, especially those with mental retardation, constituted a threat to society. Residential institutions became less educational and more custodial in nature, with the expectation that many individuals would stay in them for their entire lives. This trend was accompanied by a growing tendency to build facilities away from population centers.

Finally, the belief that all children are educable given the appropriate environment and techniques gave way to the belief that heredity is the sole determining factor in human behavior. Studies purported to "prove" that retardation and criminal tendencies passed from generation to generation. This idea was accompanied by a growing fear that the "lower classes" and those of "foreign stock" were outbreeding the original white stock, thus contributing to a degeneration of the U.S. population.

The surge of immigrants to the United States created a public clamor, and limitations on immigration by individuals with retardation were called for (Kamin, 1974). The Immigration Act of 1882 prohibited "idiots" from entering the country (Kanner, 1967). By 1893, James Cattell was advocating the use of mental tests to identify "feebleminded" individuals. A student of Galton in England, Cattell had been influenced by Galton's ideas about eugenics and the heritability of intelligence. The ideas about intelligence testing that Cattell brought to the United States were advanced by eugenics advocates as a means of diagnosing retardation in Americans and would-be immigrants (Kamin, 1974).

At one time or another, members of almost all immigrant groups were considered to be of inferior intelligence. In 1890, Billings reported that immigrant women from Ireland had a larger proportion of children with retardation than did women from England, Wales, Scotland, Germany, Scandinavia, and British North America. By the end of the century, however, a preponderance of immigrants were of Mediterranean and Alpine stock rather than western and northern European origin; thus, the focus of concern shifted. At various times, objections were aired regarding immigrants from Italy, Russia, Poland, Greece, Turkey, and the Slavic and Latin countries. It was argued that people from these areas were markedly less intelligent than western and northern European groups and that the Hebrews ranked far below the average in intelligence (Dworkin, 1976). Other groups also fared poorly, as the following generalizations show:

> Mexicans are flowing into the country [yet] their average intelligence is below that of the Portuguese . . . the increase of French Canadians is alarming. [Their] average intelligence approaches the level of the average Negro.The foreign born have something wrong . . . lips thick, mouth coarse, goose bite noses. (Dworkin, 1976, p. 379)

For the first three-quarters of the nineteenth century, the federal government played a very limited role in immigration. This changed in 1875 with the introduction of federal laws and regulations that increasingly restricted immigration, culminating with the rigid laws of the 1920s. The government set up federal immigration stations to process immigrants. The largest of these facilities was on Ellis Island in New York, where more than one million immigrants per year were processed in peak years (Brownstone, Franck, and Brownstone, 1979).

Requirements for entrance became stricter over time. All immigrants had to pass a physical examination and show no evidence of "mental" problems. Causes for rejection included eye problems, partial blindness, senility, lameness, deafness, general weakness, physical deformity, trachoma, scalp disease, and tuberculosis. After 1917, all adult immigrants had to pass a literacy test either in English or in their native language (Brownstone, Franck, and Brownstone, 1979, p. 10).

Terman (1916) believed that genetically determined differences in intelligence existed across races and that mental subnormality was more common in Spanish-Indian and black populations. He advocated that such children be segregated into special classes. He further believed that from a eugenics point of view those children presented grave problems because of "their unusual prolific breeding" (p. 92).

Terman saw a direct relationship between mental subnormality and moral subnormality. He referred to the well-known studies of poor white family groups such as the Jukes, Kallikaks, and New England Hill people to prove his point. He reported that out of the 496 known descendants of Martin Kallikak and a feebleminded barmaid, 143 were feebleminded, 36 were illegitimate, 33 were sexually immoral, 24 were alcoholic, and 8 ran houses of ill repute (Terman, 1944, pp. 9–11). Of the known descendants of Kallikak and his legal wife, "a respectable girl of good family," none were feebleminded or illegitimate, only one was sexually immoral, and two were alcoholic. Terman interpreted the results as indicating the overwhelming influence of heredity. He buttressed his arguments with reports of the financial strain such families imposed on various states (Terman, 1944, pp. 10–11). The Hill folk, rife with illegitimate offspring, sexual immorality, criminal tendencies, alcoholism, epilepsy, and insanity, had cost Massachusetts more than $500,000. In seventy-five years, the Jukes cost New York $1,300,000 and accounted for 128 prostitutes, 105 illegitimate children, 76 prisoners, 53 poorhouse occupants, and 37 syphilitics. Terman concluded that people with retardation tend to be delinquent and that all such individuals are potential criminals. He did not seriously consider the possibility that adverse environmental conditions affected the behaviors of individuals in these groups.

Segregation of individuals with disabilities into isolated institutions tended to reduce the perceived threat to civilization but brought them into closer contact with one another into adult life. Influenced by the impact of the eugenics movement, Americans became willing not only to segregate but also to sterilize large numbers of individuals judged to be "unfit." In an adumbration of laws, later passed in the 1930s in Nazi Germany, many states passed laws restricting marriage and calling for sterilization of these individuals.

The situation was never as grim for the deaf as it was for people with other conditions, but schools for the deaf increasingly were established away from large cities. At times restrictions on marriage and on procreation of the deaf were seriously considered.

Edward Miner Gallaudet and Alexander Graham Bell

The history of education of the deaf in America from the Civil War to World War I and the success of the combined and oral-only methods may best be illustrated by examining the accomplishments of these methods' respective champions, Edward

Miner Gallaudet (1837–1917) and Alexander Graham Bell (1847–1922). Over a period of decades, these two individuals were the dominant forces in education of the deaf. Originally, their relationship was warm and friendly (Boatner, 1952, 1959a, 1959b; Bruce, 1973), but their increasingly sharp disagreements over methodology led to a bitter antagonism that was at least partly responsible for the dichotomization of educators of the deaf into oral-only and combined oral-manual camps.

The biographies of Bell (Bruce, 1973; Burlingame, 1964; MacKenzie, 1929; Mayne, 1929) and Gallaudet (Boatner, 1952, 1959b) reveal interesting insights into the clash that developed between them. Both were restless, dominating men of genius. Each had a deaf mother and continued the work of a successful father. Each had achieved a full measure of success in his twenties; Gallaudet was appointed president of the first college for the deaf (now Gallaudet University, named in honor of his father) at age twenty-seven, and Bell became world famous at twenty-nine when he received the patent for the telephone. Each made unique contributions to society, Bell through his inventions of the telephone and audiometer and his work on the phonograph and Gallaudet through his book *International Law,* which went through five printings and earned him an honorary doctor of law degree from Yale in 1895 (Boatner, 1959a). McClure (1961), reminiscing at the age of one hundred on the 1890 Convention of American Instructors of the Deaf, referred to Bell as "handsome, brilliant, aggressive" and to Gallaudet as "suave, courteous, at the height of his great powers" (p. 105). After achieving success early in life, both men had continued to be highly acclaimed individuals accustomed to having their own ways. Such individuals do not compromise easily.

Edward Miner Gallaudet

The youngest of twelve children of Thomas Hopkins Gallaudet and Sophie Fowler Gallaudet, Edward Miner Gallaudet not only was a descendant of French Huguenots but also traced his lineage back to Thomas Hooker, the first minister in Hartford in 1635 (Boatner, 1959a). Gallaudet hoped to attend Yale, as had his father, who entered as a sophomore and at age eighteen was the youngest member of his graduating class. Although E. M. Gallaudet's hopes were smashed at age fourteen, when his father died, his early accomplishments were equally impressive. After working for two years as a bank teller to save money for college, he entered Trinity College in Hartford as a junior. He completed his course work while teaching at the American School (full time during the last year) and graduated from Trinity at age nineteen. Some report that Trinity withheld his degree for a while, not because he did not meet the requirements for graduation but because he was able to bypass the first two years of college and then complete the final two years while employed as a teacher, with no noticeable strain. Trinity later awarded him honorary master's and doctorate degrees (Boatner, 1959b).

E. M. Gallaudet was chosen principal of the new Columbia Institution for the Deaf and Dumb in Washington, D.C. Accompanied by his mother, who served as matron, he assumed control of the school in 1857 at the tender age of twenty. His efforts met with considerable success, and in 1864 Congress established a collegiate department, known as the National Deaf Mute College, with Gallaudet as president.

Gallaudet followed the controversy over the establishment of an oral school in Massachusetts with interest, and he kept abreast of work going on in Europe. His father originally had been interested in establishing a school using a combined system, and E. M. Gallaudet was receptive to the idea. Before the establishment of the oral schools in New York and Massachusetts, he made the first of thirteen trips to Europe. In six months he visited forty schools, and in October 1867 he reported to his board. Disagreeing with the reports of previous American educators of the deaf, Gallaudet advocated the introduction of articulation as a branch of instruction in all schools for the deaf in the United States (Boatner, 1937).

In 1868, Gallaudet called a meeting of principals of schools for the deaf, from which grew the present Conference of Educational Administrators of Schools and Programs Serving the Deaf (CEASD). The chief topic was methodology, specifically the place of articulation and lip reading in instruction. The majority of participants proved open-minded and receptive to change. A number had visited the Clarke school during its first year of operation. In a discussion of articulation, Milligan made the following observations:

> I went to Northampton not believing, for physiological reasons, that those who had no audiological nerve could ever learn to speak and articulate; and it is not pleasant for me to find out that they can. (Laughter) I am willing to say that I am disappointed; but it is so that they do talk. We cannot get around it and we have got to put up with it for they won't stop talking for all our resolutions. (Gallaudet, 1868, p. 56)

Gallaudet himself was critical of efforts to teach articulation at the American School, charging that the school did not devote enough attention to oral skills. He claimed to have taught one of his college students, Samuel Greene, to speak and to read lips after Greene had supposedly received two and one-half years of articulation training at the American School (Gallaudet, 1868, p. 70).

The consensus of the conference was not to abandon signs in favor of a pure oral method but to utilize both elements judiciously. It was noted, for example, that the only pupil at the Clarke school who had been observed to read from a printed book was a girl who had previously attended the American School. Turner reflected the majority view: "Dactology and signs, instead of being a hindrance, would, if properly used, be decidedly advantageous" (Gallaudet, 1868, p. 71).

Out of the conference came a resolution stating that all institutions for the deaf had the duty to teach lip reading and articulation to all pupils who might profit from it. Undoubtedly, E. M. Gallaudet played the key role in establishing oral education in schools for the deaf in the United States, and he was instrumental in gaining acceptance of a combined oral-manual philosophy. Jones (1918, p. 16) pictured the young Gallaudet as the single champion of speech and lip reading in U.S. schools in the midst of a number of older superintendents wedded to their philosophies. The proceedings of the meeting suggest that this view is exaggerated, but it is obvious that Gallaudet was forced to use his considerable persuasive powers to win the conference over to this viewpoint. Even then difficulties arose. McClure (1969) reported that for his actions Gallaudet was considered the degenerate son of a noble father. However, his efforts succeeded. Whereas Thomas Hopkins Gallaudet is the co-founder of education of the deaf in the United States, Edward Miner Gallaudet is the founder of oral education. When he was ensuring the future of oral instruction, E. M. Gallaudet was unaware that sign language would later come under strong attack and that a future question would revolve around whether education of the deaf should be a combination of oral and manual methods or oral only.

Thus E. M. Gallaudet, who in 1871 argued that sign language was being used to excess (Gallaudet, 1871), felt constrained to defend sign language in 1887 (Gallaudet, 1887) and, before the end of the century, wrote an article entitled "Must the Sign Language Go?" (Gallaudet, 1899). Jones (1918) pointed out that Gallaudet's position was consistent over the years: in 1868 he was opposed to the prevalent manual-only system, and in 1899 he was denouncing equally strongly the dominance of the oral-only method.

To place this movement in perspective, let us examine the career of Alexander Graham Bell, Gallaudet's contemporary and long-time adversary, whom Deland (1931) inaccurately acclaimed as the person who broke the death grip that the sign method had on Americans.

Alexander Graham Bell

Alexander Graham Bell was born in Edinburgh, Scotland. His father, Alexander Melville Bell, was a noted teacher of diction and elocution whose dreams of fostering a universal language led him to develop the system of Visible Speech, a method of teaching articulation that was used, among others, with the deaf (Bender, 1970; Bruce, 1973, 1974). Alexander Melville had been influenced by his father, Alexander Bell, who started out as a shoemaker (Burlingame, 1964), became an actor, and finally taught speech (Bruce, 1973, 1974). Thus all three generations were dedicated to the teaching of speech. The grandfather is quoted as stating, "Perhaps, in no higher respect has man been created in the image of his Maker, than in his adaptation for speech and the communication of his ideas" (Bruce, 1974, p. 3). Alexander G. Bell's mother had been deaf from scarlet fever since age four, and so he used a manual alphabet to communicate with her (Bender, 1970; Bruce, 1974).

As a teenager, A. G. Bell taught elocution at a boys' school in Scotland (Bruce, 1974). In 1868, he introduced Visible Speech at a private school for the deaf in London (Bender, 1970). Bell moved to Canada with his parents in 1870. Two of his brothers had died of tuberculosis (Mayne, 1929), and his parents were afraid the same fate would befall him if he remained in Great Britain.

In 1871, Bell went to the Boston Day School to teach Visible Speech. The following year, he demonstrated his methods at the Clarke school and at the American School (Bender, 1970). It is reported that he addressed the graduating class of the American School in sign language (Bruce, 1973).

Bell returned to Boston, where he established a school of vocal physiology, taught at Boston University, conducted electrical experiments, and tutored—all at

Alexander Graham Bell (circa 1900). *Founder of the American Association for the Promotion of Teaching Speech to the Deaf.*

the same time. One of his students was Mabel Hubbard, who had been among the first pupils at the Clarke school. A romantic interest developed between Mabel Hubbard and the impoverished young inventor, which caused the Hubbards some concern (MacKenzie, 1929).

Bell also tutored a young deaf boy named George Sanders, with whom he lived in the home of the boy's grandmother, where he conducted his experiments. Thomas Sanders, George's father, along with Gardiner Greene Hubbard, provided Bell with financial support for his experimental work (Burlingame, 1964). Bender (1970) reported that Bell communicated with George Sanders by means of a lettered glove of the type originally recommended by Dalgarno (1680). Despite several years of tutoring, Sanders developed no proficiency in speech or speech reading. In 1882, Bell conceded that Sanders might benefit by enrolling in Gallaudet College, but he was troubled by the college's lack of courses in speech and speech reading (Bruce, 1973, p. 399).

Bell received the patent for the telephone in 1876 at age twenty-nine, where-upon the Hubbards withdrew their opposition to their daughter marrying a still young but no longer impoverished inventor. From then on, although he would continue to think of himself as "a teacher of deaf mutes" (Bruce, 1973), Bell was forced to devote his attention to other matters, the most time consuming and drain-ing being a series of legal actions to verify his claim on the invention of the tele-phone.

In 1879 Bell moved to Washington, D.C., where he met E. M. Gallaudet. Appar-ently, they were brought together by Gardiner Greene Hubbard (Boatner, 1959a). In 1880, Bell received an honorary Ph.D. from Gallaudet College (Boatner, 1959a).

In 1883, Bell established a small private school for the deaf in Washington (Montague, 1940). It had a number of interesting and innovative features. For ex-ample, it used "whiteboards" instead of blackboards and charcoal instead of chalk (Montague, 1940). All objects were labeled. The floors had rugs, and the children clustered around a low table. Hearing as well as deaf children attended the school. Unfortunately, Bell had to turn his attention to rival claimants to the invention of the telephone, and in 1885 he closed the school. After that, he was destined to provide leadership to the cause of education of the deaf in a less direct manner.

The split between Bell and Gallaudet was precipitated by two papers written by Bell: *Memoir upon the Formation of a Deaf Variety of the Human Race* (1883a) and an article entitled "Fallacies Concerning the Deaf" (1884). Bell's basic position was that the U.S. system of education of the deaf tended to isolate deaf people from society and increase the number of intermarriages among the deaf. He stated, "The production of a defective race of human beings would be a tragedy. Before the deaf were educated intermarriage was so rare as to be almost unknown. Intermarriages have been promoted by our methods of instruction" (1884, p. 41). He considered the major contributing factors to be the system of residential schools, which brought the deaf together, and sign language, which Bell believed hindered mastery of English, causing the deaf to associate with and marry one another, thus propagating what he considered to be their physical defect.

Alexander Graham Bell believed that a law forbidding congenitally deaf persons from intermarrying "would go a long way towards dealing with the evil" and that an even more practical step might be to forbid the intermarriage of persons "belonging to families containing more than one deaf-mute" (1884, p. 45). Acknowledging the doubtful advisability of legislative interference, Bell recommended the elimination of (1) educational segregation, (2) the "gesture language," and (3) deaf teachers in programs for the deaf. Bell noted that in 1883, nearly one-third of teachers of the deaf in the United States were themselves deaf. He stated, "This must be considered as another element favorable to the formation of a deaf race—to be therefore avoided" (1884, p. 48).

When Bell's first pupil, George Sanders, made plans to marry Lucy Swett, a deaf woman, Bell attempted to intervene. He warned Swett that because both she and

Sanders had been deaf since birth, the chances of their having deaf children were increased (Bruce, 1973, p. 399).

Gallaudet responded immediately to Bell's opposition to the marriage (Gallaudet, 1884). Gallaudet was answered not by Bell but by Bell's father-in-law, Gardiner Hubbard (1884), who stated that the policy at the Clarke School had always been to prevent marriages between deaf individuals whenever possible. The battle lines had been drawn for a conflict that still rages today.

The Battle Is Joined

On the surface, one would have expected Bell and his supporters to sweep the field with ease. Opposing Gallaudet was an array of seemingly overwhelming forces. Chief among these, of course, was the brilliant, aggressive Bell himself. In addition to his own ability, Bell was able to draw on his well-deserved international reputation and prestige as the inventor of the telephone, and he had at his disposal a personal fortune with which to establish, endow, and support organizations dedicated to pursuing his goals. Outside the field of education of the deaf, Bell enjoyed an unbroken string of victories in his confrontations with rivals, including a smashing defeat of the giant Western Union Telegraph Company, which Bell and his associates drove out of the telephone business (Bruce, 1973; Burlingame, 1964). In addition, the oral-only position had just triumphed in Europe, and the 1880 International Convention in Milan (which Gallaudet attended) represented an overwhelming victory for the "pure oral method." Among the resolutions passed at that convention were those declaring that (1) given the incontestable superiority of speech over signs in restoring deaf mutes to society and in giving them an improved knowledge of language, the oral method ought to be preferred to signs; and (2) considering that the simultaneous use of speech and signs has the disadvantage of hindering speech, lip reading, and grasping of ideas, the pure oral method ought to be preferred.

The conflict was less uneven than it seemed, however, and the pure oral method never achieved the same predominance in the United States that it did in Europe. Bender (1970) reported that the United States was the only real stronghold for the "silent" method after the conference in Milan (p. 168), that "other countries made sincere efforts to incorporate the recommendations of the Congress into their schools" (p. 68), and that the oral method was adopted as the preferred mode in all countries except the United States (p. 167).

Edward Miner Gallaudet was the individual most responsible for the survival of combined oral-manual education, albeit in very reduced circumstances. Although he challenged and defeated the predominant manual-only philosophy in the early stages of his career, he later got involved in a much more difficult struggle to prevent the domination of an oral-only system (Gallaudet, 1907). In this author's opinion, Clerc's pioneering work and Gallaudet's efforts in behalf of combined oral-manual education represent the two most outstanding contributions made by Americans to education of the deaf.

Gallaudet presented Bell with a protagonist at least as determined and single-minded as himself. Gallaudet did not hesitate to confront Bell directly, both in print and in public debate. Bell found these tactics difficult to deal with, preferring to work through organizations or second parties.

In 1887, Bell founded the Volta Bureau in Washington, D.C., with an endowment of $200,000 for the dissemination of knowledge concerning the deaf (Bender, 1970). With Bell's support, a journal called the *Association Review* (now the *Volta Review*) was first published in 1889. In 1890, the establishment of the American Association to Promote the Teaching of Speech to the Deaf was complete, supported by a $25,000 endowment by Bell (Bruce, 1973), who continued to make up for the association's deficit each year (Deland, 1931). In 1909 the association took over the Volta Bureau, and in 1956 its name was changed to the Alexander Graham Bell Association for the Deaf, Incorporated.

Relations between Bell and Gallaudet flared into open hostility in 1890–1891 as a result of Gallaudet's efforts to establish a normal, or teacher-training, component at Gallaudet College aimed at training hearing teachers in the use of the combined method. Gallaudet had mentioned his plans to Bell, who accepted an invitation to lecture the class on the establishment of the program (Boatner, 1959a, p. 132). After the House of Representatives approved a $5,000 appropriation, Bell, without informing Gallaudet, requested a hearing before the Senate Appropriations Committee to oppose the program. He secured petitions from oral-only schools (Boatner, 1959a) and presented to Congress a list of twenty-one oral-school principals who were opposed to appropriations for teacher training at Gallaudet College (Ferreri, 1908, p. 81).

Bell's major expressed fear was that deaf graduates would be admitted to the training department (Bruce, 1973; Ferreri, 1908). Although plans at that time did not call for deaf students in the proposed department, Gallaudet argued that the oral schools could not legitimately oppose the employment of the deaf (Ferreri, 1908, p. 82). The Senate cut the $5,000 appropriation, and Bell wired friends that the manual department had been defeated (Boatner, 1959a), whereupon Gallaudet mounted a counterattack. When Bell modified his position to support an appropriation of $3,000 to be earmarked specifically for oral teaching in the college, Gallaudet noted in his diary, "Bell has heard from the back districts" (Boatner, 1959a, p. 134).

Gallaudet accepted the $3,000 appropriation, set up an articulation schedule, and then set out to raise additional money. Gallaudet's board of directors approved six $500 fellowships to provide training in oral and manual instruction, thus defeating Bell's efforts and setting the foundation for teacher training in the combined method. However, to some extent, Bell was successful. The college did not accept deaf students into its teacher-training program. This policy stayed in effect for more than seventy years, until 1964.

In an apparent response, the Clarke school expanded its training program in 1892 to provide teachers of articulation for other schools (Ferreri, 1908). Bell and the Hubbard family had always kept a close relationship with the Clarke school, which Hubbard had been instrumental in establishing.

The second major source of friction between Gallaudet and Bell was the relationship between the American Association to Promote the Teaching of Speech to the Deaf and the older Convention of American Instructors of the Deaf, established in

1850. Although Bruce (1973) claimed it was Gallaudet's intransigence that led Bell to found a new, independent organization, Boatner (1959a) reported that in 1893 and 1894 Gallaudet made overtures to Bell to merge the two organizations and received what he thought were positive responses. When his suggestion was then rejected, Gallaudet believed Bell had once again misled him. It is logical to conclude, given the strength of mind of the two protagonists, that each was willing to merge only on his own terms. At the 1895 Convention of American Instructors of the Deaf, held in Flint, Michigan, Gallaudet launched a strong attack on Bell that, despite a perfunctory handshake at the end of the convention in response to wild applause (McClure, 1969), spelled the end of attempts to join the two groups. Gallaudet was elected president of the conference and retained this position until 1917 (Boatner, 1952). When Bell attempted to become an active member, in Gallaudet's words, "His money was refused" (Boatner, 1959a, p. 130). As a result, educators of the deaf split into two warring camps, the oral-only and the combined, with each faction having its own professional organization, journal, and parent affiliate. The spirit of excitement and involvement that had prevailed throughout most of the nineteenth century evaporated as the field became increasingly isolated from general education and lost its capacity for growth. In this author's opinion, the split between Gallaudet and Bell precipitated an educational "dark age" that lasted well past the middle of the twentieth century. Although it is wasteful to dwell on missed opportunities, one can only imagine what benefits might have accrued to the education of deaf individuals if Bell and Gallaudet had joined forces and the field had devoted its energies to issues other than the oral-manual controversy.

From 1900 to World War II—Stagnation

The first half of the twentieth century was an undistinguished period in education of the deaf in the United States, indeed the world. After the end of World War I in 1918, the country turned inward, even isolationist; restrictive laws cut immigration to a trickle compared to the massive influx of immigrants in the decades before and after 1900. The depression, which lasted throughout the 1930s, contributed to a hardening of attitudes along, racial, ethnic, and class lines. Teaching of foreign languages, especially German, was opposed. "Americanization" was stressed.

Education of the deaf, of course, was influenced by broad societal forces. The system seemed to congeal into two separate systems—residential and day school, with neither one exhibiting any real creativity or success. There were major differences between the day and residential systems. In the day schools, female white teachers and administrators dominated, with almost no deaf teachers and an exclusively oral approach. To a large degree, students tended to be offspring or grandchildren of immigrants. In the residential schools male white teachers and administrators dominated, although there was a substantial presence of deaf teachers and dormitory personnel in some of the schools. Oralism dominated in the elementary school years, but there was wide variation in modes of instruction at the high-school level across schools. The two systems were similar in their repression.

World War I provided the impetus for an increased emphasis on military-style training and "Americanization." Some residential schools were organized along a military model, with students wearing uniforms. The prevailing philosophy can be summed up by an article by the superintendent of a school for the deaf (Read, 1921; reprinted, 1997), "Americanization in Our Schools for the Deaf." Read (1997, p. 49) quotes Theodore Roosevelt in a message to the American Defense society: "One flag, the American flag; one language, the language of the Declaration of Independence; one loyalty, loyalty to the American people; there must be no sagging back in the fight for Americanism—stalwart, straight-out, thorough-going Americanism." As might be expected, such an environment did not foster acceptance of languages other than English such as American Sign Language.

Deaf African Americans and "Separate but Equal" Education

Within the system of residential schools was a separate subsystem of schools of African-American deaf children that was initiated after Civil War and continued until the 1970s in some states. It is probably an overstatement to refer to the collection of residential schools for deaf African-American children as a system, since their operation was hardly systematic. These schools were underfunded and understaffed and typically were administered by the white superintendent of the school for white children in the state. Because Gallaudet did not accept African-American students until the 1950s, there was no core of deaf African-American teachers to provide role models and cultural leadership. Very little was written about these schools, and what is known about them may be lost as former teachers and students grow older. Some enterprising scholars could provide invaluable information by interviewing as many of these individuals as possible in the near future.

One notable exception to this dearth of information is a book by Mary Herring Wright (1999), "Sounds Like Home: Growing Up Black and Deaf in the South." Wright attended the North Carolina School for the Blind and Deaf in Raleigh from nine years old in 1935 to her graduation in 1941 and provides insight into the life of a deaf African-American child at a segregated residential school. Many of her experiences are the same as for all children regardless of race or gender. She writes of a feeling of loneliness and loss at being separated from her family and of her distress in learning she could not even go home for Christmas. On top of that was the inferior food and medical care provided for the African-American students and their bitter awareness that they were not receiving an equal education. Wright (1999, pp. 179–180) writes about a visit to the school for white blind children—the school for white deaf children was in a different city.

> . . . we were given a tour of their campus and the differences between their school and ours were unbelievable. Instead of long rooms with rows of beds, all with white spreads and only shades at the windows, they lived in family type houses with only a few bedrooms to each building and two or three to each room. . . .The auditorium was

beautiful with a sloping floor, comfortable individual seats, and a stage with rich velvet curtains and floodlights, plus a heated swimming pool and gym in another wing. Ours was a level floor with hard wooden benches and no stages or curtains ... seeing such a difference in how the White children were treated and how we were treated at the Black state school left us depressed and angry.... Some of the girls couldn't get over seeing a heated indoor swimming pool while we didn't even have a bathtub in our bathroom.

Contrast Wright's observations with the earlier report of the superintendent of the school for the deaf and blind (Goodwin, 1893, p. 8):

North Carolina was the first state to provide an institution for the colored race..... The institution for the colored is a commodious, well arranged building, more suitable for its purpose than the buildings for the white department. The colored department is under the same general management as the white department, and enjoys the same care and privileges.

Summary

The first American school for the deaf was established in New England during the beginning of the Industrial Revolution, when literacy was a requirement for attaining economic self-sufficiency. The establishment of facilities for the deaf set a precedent for services for individuals with disabilities in the United States. As the nation grew in population, geographic area, and complexity, programs for the deaf grew correspondingly in number, variety, and quality. The major obstacles to progress were oppression of deaf individuals by hearing administrators and intense and often acrimonious disagreement between advocates of oral-only systems of instruction and those of combined oral-manual systems. The original goal of Thomas Hopkins Gallaudet—to combine the best elements of the oral and manual methods—failed to be realized. The legacy of two bitterly hostile camps continued into the twentieth century. Only in recent years has there been a strong movement toward reconciliation and toward addressing other, equally important issues.

CHAPTER

4

Deafness: Causes, Prevention, and Treatment

Introduction

We are undergoing a profound shift in our understanding of the causes of deafness, with important implications for its prevention and treatment. In certain areas, we remain surprisingly ignorant of some of the causes of deafness; in others, tremendous explosions of knowledge have occurred. As we saw in the last two chapters, approaches to medical treatment of deafness extend back at least 3,500 years to the ancient Egyptians. Concern about deafness caused by consanguineous marriages among hearing people was evident by the middle of the nineteenth century, and A. G. Bell asserted that such unions could lead to a deaf variety of the human race. In Chapter 2 we learned how in Nazi Germany concerns about hereditary deafness created an insane cycle of sterilization, abortion, and murder. Some cultures have perceived deafness as an act of God, and some parents believe their sins have been punished through deafness in their children. It is little wonder that faith healing has been among the "cures" sought for deafness.

Although 60 percent or more of early childhood deafness in the United States may be attributed to hereditary factors (Marazita et al., 1993), deafness can result from many causes, each of which may have implications for development. It may be a consequence of environmental factors active before, during, or after birth, or it may be genetic, manifested as either a congenital (present at birth) or a progressive loss (Rose, Conneally, and Nance, 1976). Thus any discussion of the causes of deafness must be considered within a particular time frame and geographical location. Although genetic factors play a major role, the frequency with which deafness occurs is also influenced by disease and the quality of health care. As we will see, improvements in health care may even increase the incidence of deafness in some

86

populations. The most dramatic example of the impact of an outside factor is the rubella epidemic of 1963–1965, which tripled the number of children born deaf in the United States over a period of approximately two years. A rubella vaccine was introduced in 1970, leading to a 97 percent decline in the number of children diagnosed as deaf due to maternal rubella (*Morbidity and Mortality Weekly Report*, 1985). However, the impact of the 1963–1965 rubella epidemic is being felt into the twenty-first century as individuals affected go through the life cycle. Although scientists have been laboring to reduce and even eliminate the threats posed by worldwide epidemics, there is no assurance that the future will not bring another epidemic, which would have dramatic implications for the size and types of educational programs for the deaf. The United States has a good immunization program, but a significant proportion of women of childbearing age remain susceptible to rubella.

Knowledge about both environmental and genetic causes of deafness is incomplete. For example, congenital cytomegalovirus (CMV), a virus that is a major contemporary cause of deafness in the United States (Hanshaw, 1982; Schildroth, 1994), began to receive attention in only 1980. In addition, although more than two hundred kinds of genetic deafness have been identified, the chromosomal location of the genes was known for only a few genetic forms (McKusick, 1992). This means that a specific genetic type of deafness may be identified, often as part of a syndrome, but the chromosome on which the gene resides usually cannot be identified. However, as we have noted, work in the field of molecular genetics and gene mapping has led to exciting new developments, and new information is emerging constantly. Knowledge of chromosomal locations of genes for deafness can be used to determine the likelihood that two people will have deaf offspring. Millions of Americans may carry one or more genes for deafness. For recessive deafness (to be discussed later) to occur, recessive genes from the two parents must be in the same chromosomal location. If the locations of the genes differ, deafness will not result.

Despite recent improvements, parents and professionals frequently are hampered in their efforts to provide adequately for deaf children by a lack of information concerning etiology. This is especially unfortunate because the residual effects of many known causes of deafness, such as maternal rubella, mother-child blood incompatibility, certain genetic causes, and cerebrospinal meningitis, may include heart defects, vision problems, brain damage, and mental retardation in addition to hearing loss.

Vernon (1968) pointed out that gaps in etiological data (1) hinder the development of a constructive approach to the prevention of deafness, (2) leave researchers without knowledge of the base populations with which they are concerned, and (3) in some cases prevent differential diagnosis when factors such as site of lesion and possible central nervous system involvement need to be determined. Significant progress has occurred since Vernon made his observations, but a lack of etiological information remains and is detrimental on both an individual and a programmatic level.

For more than a century, the largest single etiological category for deafness has been "cause unknown," accounting for as much as 30 percent of the deaf population even in recent surveys. One reason for the paucity of information is that the amount of research activity on medical and genetic aspects of deafness has been relatively small until recent years. For example, the relationship between maternal rubella and congenital deafness was not described until 1944 (Bordley et al., 1967), and it was not until 1949 that a group of deaf children were identified as having a common history of erythroblastosis fetalis (a breakdown of the blood cells of the fetus) as a result of Rh-factor incompatibility (Goodhill, 1950, 1956). In the genetic sphere, most of the attention traditionally was devoted to the study of exotic syndromes related to deafness that, however fascinating clinically, account for only a small proportion of the deaf population. This situation has changed as interest in genetic counseling has grown.

A major problem in identifying etiology is that the procedure has typically been retrospective in nature and, as discussed in Chapter 5, usually involves parents who have had little or no previous contact with deafness and for whom the process of diagnosing hearing loss was traumatic. In such a situation, the chances of making an incorrect judgment about etiology are great.

One factor is the tendency of parents to ascribe a child's deafness to external forces beyond their control. Parents often believe that the child had hearing during the early stages of development but lost the ability to hear. This tendency may be reinforced by the absence of any known cases of deafness on either side of the family. Further, since the final diagnosis of deafness is often made when the child is two years old or even older, the mother's recollection of the early stages of her pregnancy may be somewhat blurred. Because a pregnancy commonly entails a certain amount of physical stress, most mothers can vaguely recall discomforts that may have been symptomatic of rubella, flu, or CMV. A misdiagnosis of an environmental etiology is probably made in a significant number of cases in which the actual cause is genetic in nature. The author is aware of several cases in which the parents of a deaf child were told the cause was not genetic, whereupon they had another child who was also deaf. Of course, even when the cause is genetic, the next child will not necessarily be deaf. As we will see, when deafness results from recessive genes, the chances that any one child will be deaf are one in four. Also, in a relatively small number of cases, the deafness may be sex linked, appearing only in male offspring.

Countervailing the tendency to attribute etiology to external factors is the tendency of many professionals to make a diagnosis of genetic etiology when no other cause can be determined. The extent to which this occurs is obviously impossible to ascertain. However, it is probably relatively common, especially in cases involving undiagnosed maternal rubella and CMV. For example, Bordley et al. (1967) worked with a study group of forty-seven children who exhibited positive virus cultures and found that fifteen had no reported history of prenatal rubella or maternal exposure to rubella. The positive virus cultures were proof of prenatal infection, but the mothers had shown no symptoms. Bordley et al. concluded that prenatal rubella can damage a child without giving rise to clinical symptoms in the mother. Although the situation has undoubtedly improved since the this report, difficulties remain.

Obviously, the assignment of etiology is fraught with inaccuracy at present. A substantial number of children classified as deaf by genetic causes probably lost their hearing through disease. On the other hand, many children have been diagnosed with an etiology of disease when the real cause was genetic. There is no way of knowing which misdiagnosis is more common.

Early Investigations of Causality

Evidence suggests that although there has been general awareness throughout history that deafness can result from various kinds of sickness and injury, the causes of early childhood deafness have been poorly understood. Werner (1932) reported that the first reference to familial deafness was made by Johannes Schenk in Germany in the sixteenth century and the first observation of hereditary deafness was made by Felix Platter (1530–1614), a German physician (p. 77). Werner's statements are contradictory in that he also presented evidence that the Velasco family in Spain was acutely aware of familial deafness. Werner reported that Dona Ines de Velasco was the sister of Don Francisco and Don Pedro de Velasco, the deaf boys taught by Pedro Ponce de León. Ines herself had two deaf children and died in 1592 after giving birth to a third child. Werner (1932) quoted the family historian as follows:

> At that period the Count . . . was full of misgivings since he harboured the well-founded fear that his three year old son was deaf. . . . He also harboured the same fear concerning his daughter, Dona Anna, who was one year younger. This fear was all the greater since the Constable, Don Inigo, and his sister, Dona Ines, had two deaf mute brothers and also two deaf mute sisters. (p. 214)

Werner reported that Dona Ines received treatment to prevent the third child from being deaf mute. According to a physician retained as a consultant, Ines's death was caused by the treatments she received. Although medical personnel may have paid little attention to familial deafness, the experience of the Velascos suggests that families in which deafness occurred were well aware of the issue.

From the time of Francis Green's first census of the deaf in Massachusetts (Deland, 1931), educators of the deaf in the United States have been interested in both the prevalence and the causes of deafness in the population. Analyses of the annual reports of the American School for the Deaf reveal consistent early attempts to identify and classify as precisely as possible causes of hearing loss in students at the school. Similar efforts were made at other schools for the deaf in Europe and the United States, especially at the schools in New York City, Philadelphia, and Columbus, Ohio.

In an analysis of the records of 773 former and then current students at the American School from 1817 to 1844, Weld (1844) reported that deafness was congenital, or present at birth, in 341 cases (44 percent) and acquired in 336 cases (44 percent). For ninety-six individuals (12 percent), there was insufficient information on which to make a judgment. Table 4.1 indicates that the two most commonly cited cases in the "acquired" category were a fever of some kind ($N = 140$) and sickness ($N = 84$). Spotted fever was identified as being responsible for deafness in

TABLE 4.1   Causes of Deafness in Students at the American School of the Deaf, 1817–1844

Category	Student Status		
	Former Students	In Attendance in 1844	Total
Acquired			
Fever			
Spotted fever	45	1	46
Scarlet fever	20	22	44 *(sic)*
Fever	29	6	35
Typhus fever	11	1	12
Lung fever	1	1	2
Yellow fever	1	0	1
Sickness	76	8	84
Inflammation in head	24	6	30
Ulcers in head	14	8	22
Accidents	10	12	22
Measles	11	1	12
Whooping cough	8	4	12
Dropsy	5	0	5
Fits	2	2	4
Smallpox	2	0	2
Palsy	2	0	2
Croup	1	0	1
Total Acquired	262	72	336
Congenital	270	71	341
Unknown	87	9	96
Total	619	152	773

Source: Adapted from L. Weld, *Twenty-eighth Annual Report of the American Asylum at Hartford for the Education of the Deaf and Dumb*, 1844, p. 38.

45 of 262 former students with acquired deafness but in only 1 of 72 students with acquired deafness attending in 1844. This is the only category in which great differences appeared between former and current students. Although no data are given concerning age of onset of hearing loss, we may assume the majority of students in the "acquired" category had achieved some level of proficiency in speech and English before losing their hearing. This leads to the conclusion that the composition of the "deaf population" of the American School from 1817 to 1844 differed from that of schools for the deaf today, a large majority of whose students either were born deaf or lost their hearing before they acquired spoken language.

In a follow-up to Weld's report, Turner (1848) presented data on two hundred deaf individuals who had been pupils at the American School, and he speculated on possible causes of deafness. Some overlap probably occurred between Turner's data and the "current" student data Weld presented in 1844, but since the maximum term was six years, it is less than we might expect today. Turner's data indicate that deafness was congenital in 55 percent of the cases ($N = 110$) and acquired, or accidental, in 43 percent ($N = 86$). In four cases, it was unclear whether the loss was congenital or acquired. Scarlet fever accounted for almost half the cases of acquired deafness (forty-one of eighty-six) and more than 20 percent of the entire student population. It is interesting to note that scarlet fever was the named cause of deafness for only 20 of 619 students at the school before 1844 (see Table 4.1).

Turner's discussion of possible causes of deafness contains evidence of great insight as well as some speculation that comes close to superstition. Among the latter is the somewhat diffidently advanced possibility that deafness might be caused by mental impressions of the mother before the birth of her child. In support of this possibility, Turner (1848, p. 28) reported the case of a woman who, upon attending a funeral while pregnant, was frightened by the scream of a deaf girl as the coffin was lowered. The image and sound stayed with the mother, and, as she feared, her child was born deaf. She and her child similarly influenced neighbors, and four families eventually produced eleven deaf children in a neighborhood where no deaf people had lived previously. To buttress his case, Turner pointed out several families with both acquired and congenital* deafness, concluding:

> If then, there be any connection between the accidental deafness of the first child and the congenital deafness of the next, it must be in the way already supposed; and the one event must be regarded as the cause of the other through the impression so sad an occurrence would naturally make upon the mother's mind. (pp. 29–30)

Given Turner's statement, it is quite possible that many of the cases Weld and Turner classified as accidental or acquired were actually familial in nature. Those cases cited in which the first child in a family was judged to have acquired deafness and a later child was born deaf might reflect the fact that, given the presence of one deaf child in a family, parents become sensitive to the possibility of deafness in subsequent children and are more likely to diagnose it at an early age.

Although he believed that in most cases a classification of congenital or accidental could be made with little room for doubt, Turner (1848) acknowledged that it was sometimes impossible to ascertain when or how a child became deaf. He described the process as follows:

> Probably in a majority of instances the attention of parents is first called to the subject by the child's not beginning to articulate at the usual age. It is suggested that deafness

---

*Turner did not use the terms *acquired* and *congenital* as we do today. As noted in the introduction, *congenital* means "present at birth." Congenital deafness could be familial (genetic) or acquired (as in the case of rubella). Turner used *acquired* to mean postnatal, or after birth.

may be the reason for this inability. A series of experiments is instituted, the result of which is a clear conviction, in the minds of the parents, that such is the fact. They next inquire into the cause of deafness in their child; and if they can recall any severe sickness in its infancy, they conclude that this must have been the case, however unlikely to produce such a result. On the other hand, in some cases of accidental deafness, the true cause, having been less noticeable, is overlooked, and the child is said to have been born deaf. (p. 26)

Turner also mentioned the intermarriage of near relations as a possible cause of deafness. Although he suggested that judgment be withheld pending future examination, he reported a widespread impression that a relationship existed between consanguineous marriages and deafness.

The most extensive early analysis of the causes of acquired deafness was performed by a physician, Dudley Peet* (1856), who reported on the assigned causes of acquired deafness in a total of 754 students from thirteen schools for the deaf, nine in Europe and four in the United States (Table 4.2). It is interesting to note that he classified approximately 50 percent of the cases of acquired deafness under the heading "diseases and accidents, unknown," in contrast to Turner, who classified only four cases as unknown. No single cause or group of causes appears to predominate.

Peet also presented information on the age of onset of deafness for 284 of the cases (Table 4.3). If this group was representative of deaf students in general in the nineteenth century, the proportion of students who became deaf after age three was lower than most present-day educators assume. Peet's figures suggest that in more than half of the cases of acquired deafness, the students had lost their hearing by age two, and almost three-quarters had lost their hearing by age three. These data, in combination with those of Turner and Weld, which show that somewhat fewer than half of the students in their studies had acquired deafness, indicate that the postlingual population of nineteenth-century schools for the deaf may have been as small as 20 percent. For the present, we will define *postlingual* as referring to children who were thirty-six months of age or older when they lost their hearing.

Peet discussed in passing the possibility of hereditary transmission of deafness by deaf parents, noting that a certain degree of danger existed but emphasizing that the children of most marriages of deaf individuals had normal hearing. He also mentioned the possibility of a predisposition to deafness resulting either from parental dissipation before gestation or from dissipation in youth.

Peet commented on how a hereditary predisposition might be manifested in what he termed *alternation:* that is, some children will be deaf and others will be hearing. He cited one family in which the second, fourth, sixth, eighth, tenth, twelfth, and fourteenth children were born deaf.

Sharing Turner's concern, Peet (1856) stated that, of all the known causes, marriage among relatives was the most prolific cause of predisposition to deafness:

---

*Dudley Peet is not to be confused with Harvey Peet, the principal of the school for the deaf in New York City.

TABLE 4.2 Reported Causes of Acquired Deafness in Thirteen Schools for the Deaf in Europe and the United States, 1856

Reported Cause	Number
Diseases and accidents, unknown	398
Scarlet fever	44
Fever (not named)	38
Measles	35
Colds	26
Convulsions	24
Inflammation in head	20
Falls	19
Gatherings in head	15
Scrofula	12
Whooping cough	12
Other	111
Total	754

Source: Adapted from D. Peet, "The Remote and Proximate Causes of Deafness," *American Annals of the Deaf,* 8 (1856):129–130.

It has been settled beyond a shadow of a doubt, that intermarriages affected by cousins, and even some second cousins, have given rise to offspring which are generally either of small size, imperfect health, or of imperfect development in some part; they are either idiots, blind, clubfooted, or deaf and dumb. And those offspring of cousins who are not, are rather the exceptions than the rule. (pp. 132-133)

Early Issues of Heredity and Deafness

As previously noted, early investigations into the causes of deafness were greatly concerned with the possible influence of heredity on deafness (or, at least, on the tendency toward deafness). As investigators searched for the causes of deafness, they were swayed by a number of forces operating in society at large. As the nineteenth century unfolded, more and more attention was given to the implications of Darwin's theories for human society. Toward the end of the century, the question of the inheritability of intelligence, or of the relative influences of heredity and environment on human behavior, became a great issue.

The tenor of the times was definitely on the side of heredity, even in the United States, which might have exhibited more of an environmental bent but for the growing influence of Mendelian principles of genetic inheritance. The land-grant colleges started in the United States in the 1860s were introducing principles of scientific experimentation on a widespread basis and, among other things, revolu-

TABLE 4.3   Age of Onset of Deafness in 284 Students, 1856

Age of Onset	Number	Cumulative Percentage
Birth to 12 months	94	33.1
12 to 24 months	73	58.8
24 to 36 months	41	73.2
36 to 48 months	19	79.9
48 to 60 months	27	89.4
60 months and older	30	100.0
Total	284	

Source: Adapted from D. Peet, "The Remote and Proximate Causes of Deafness," *American Annals of the Deaf,* 8 (1856):129–130.

tionizing agriculture across the world. Existing strains of food were being improved, and new, hardier, and more productive strains were being developed. The selective breeding of livestock was also producing continuous and unexpected improvement. It is not surprising, therefore, to observe a growing interest in applying the concept of eugenics to human beings, that is, to improving the human race by influencing its breeding habits.

Consanguinity

The comments about consanguineous marriages made by Turner (1848) and Peet (1856) expressed a general concern about the apparent tendency of marriages among relatives to produce children with disabilities. The most influential mid-nineteenth-century study was conducted by Bemiss (1858), who investigated the extent to which 833 consanguineous marriages in the United States produced children with disabilities. Bemiss found a total of 3,942 children produced from these marriages, of whom 1,134 were "defective" in one way or another, the largest categories being idiotic ($N = 308$), scrofulous ($N = 300$), deaf and dumb ($N = 145$), deformed ($N = 98$), and blind ($N = 85$). The results of his investigations in various state institutions led Bemiss (1858) to state, "Over 10% of the deaf and dumb and over 5% of the blind and near 15% of the idiotic in our State institutions for such subjects of these defects are offspring of kindred parents or of parents themselves the descendants of blood intermarriage" (p. 14).

Morris (1861) argued that marriage of relatives was a violation of natural laws and that blindness, insanity, idiocy, lunacy, and other defects of mind and body were their legitimate consequences. In advocating the elimination of consanguineous marriages, Morris maintained, "In all countries where there is a commingling of races, and where we find residents from every corner of the globe and employment for all, there it is that congenital deafness falls least heavily . . ." (p. 31). Morris quoted from a paper presented by Buxton in 1858 relating to Buxton's investigations in the British Isles:

> As regards the marriage of blood relations, there can be no question now as to the great influences which this cause exercises in the production of congenital deafness, as well as of every other physical and mental defect. In an inquiry which I made some time ago, from a large number of persons, I found that about every tenth case of deafness resulted from the marriage of cousins. (p. 31)

The reaction against consanguineous marriages apparently was influenced by a belief that heterogeneous populations were superior to homogeneous ones; that the more alike parents were genetically, the greater the possibility that they would have affected children. This position was strengthened by investigations showing tremendous differences in incidence figures for various disabilities in the countries of Europe and sometimes even within different parts of the same country.

Peet (1852, 1854) reported an incidence figure of approximately 1 per 1,500 for congenital deafness in Europe, stating that 615 of every 1 million children were born deaf, more than twice the rate in the United States. Peet noted that the range was from 1 per 200 in the isolated Swiss canton of Bern to 1 per 2,180 in Saxony. He pointed out (1854, p. 20) that in areas of Europe with stable populations (and therefore frequent intermarriage), the proportion of children born deaf was high. The more heterogeneous the population, the lower the rate of deafness reported.

In a report to the Paris Academy of Medicine, Maniere is reported as arguing as follows:

> Marriage between near relatives is never met with more frequently, than in the localities where deaf-mutes are born in the greatest numbers; as in some of the valleys of Switzerland, where the inhabitants are almost shut out from communication with the neighboring countries, and present all the conditions favorable to those alliances among relatives. (Morris, 1861, p. 30)

Using 1851 United Kingdom census figures, Buxton (1858) reported that the incidence of congenital deafness in the British Isles was highest in relatively isolated Scotland and lowest in England. Morris (1861) quotes him as having said:

> In Cornwall, Derbyshire, the northern countries of Scotland, among the stationary population of Hartfordshire, in the mountainous parts of Ireland, in remote Norway and Alpine Switzerland, the proportion of children born deaf is very large; for here the native intermarry among each other, age after age; from the cradle to the grave, the same people are found fixed to the same spot, pursuing the same occupations; no enterprise leads them abroad; nothing tempts the native of other locales to come and cast his lot among them; it is a continual process of transmitting the same blood and sinew, from generation to generation, and the lowering of the healthy standard of the race is natural and inevitable. (p. 31)

Despite the great interest in the effects of consanguinity, a relatively large number of deaf children continued to be the products of the unions of blood relatives throughout much of the twentieth century. In a study of the deaf population of New York State, Sank and Kallman (1963) reported that 12 percent of the sample were the offspring of marriages of near relatives. Referring to data collected over more than forty years, Hudgins (1973) reported that approximately 5 percent of the students at the Clarke School for the Deaf were the offspring of consanguineous parents. Powers (1999) reported that the Pakistani/Bengladesh ethnic group accounted for only 2.5 percent of the school-age population in the United Kingdom but about 12 percent of the deaf school population. He noted that 75 percent of deaf children from this ethnic group were the offpsring of cousin marriages.

Marriages Among the Deaf

Although educators of the deaf have long been aware that deaf parents are more likely than hearing parents to produce deaf children, marriages of deaf couples were not treated with the same degree of concern that consanguineous marriages were, at least not during the fifty years following the establishment of the first school for the deaf in 1817. There were probably several reasons for this. First, it was well known that the majority of children produced from marriages of deaf individuals would have normal hearing. The proportion of children with normal hearing produced from such marriages was probably even higher in the nineteenth century than it is today due to the higher proportion of individuals whose deafness was not caused by genetic factors.

There also appeared to be a consensus that marriage of blood relatives, which posed the danger that numerous disabilities would surface in their children, was a far more serious concern. Such a consensus was strengthened by the evidence that in general, the deaf population in the United States in the mid-nineteenth century was a self-sufficient, productive, contributing segment of society (Moores, Harlow, and Fisher, 1974). Turner (1848) summed up the feeling of the times, stating that although it was not surprising for congenitally deaf parents to have deaf children, it was more likely that their children would have normal hearing. Turner believed that the possibility that deaf individuals would have deaf children was so slight that "it need not deter them, when other circumstances render it proper, from entering the married state; especially when the fact is kept in mind that educated deaf-mutes generally manage their affairs judiciously, bring up their children well, and become useful and respectable members of the community" (1848, p. 32).

For hearing educators of the deaf, the presence of large numbers of deaf educators served as a constant reminder that deaf individuals could attain high levels of intellectual achievement. Among educators of the deaf, perhaps no one was held in greater esteem than Laurent Clerc, the first deaf teacher of the deaf in the United States.

The information available seemed to be little cause for alarm. Turner (1848, p. 32) reported that nearly one hundred marriages of former American School students had occurred, and in about half the cases both parents were deaf. However, deaf children appeared in only five families; in the others, even in families with six to eight children, all of the children were hearing. Dudley Peet (1856) reported that there was not enough evidence to form definite conclusions concerning the degree of transmission of hereditary deafness when one or both parents were deaf. He stated (p. 132) that he knew personally of only two families in which both parents were deaf and direct transmission of hereditary deafness occurred, although he acknowledged that he had heard of several other instances.

Harvey Peet (1852) reported that deaf parents were more likely than hearing parents to have deaf children. He found that approximately 5 percent of the children (1 in 20) resulting from marriages of two deaf individuals would be deaf; for marriages of deaf and hearing individuals, the percentage of deaf children was less than 1 percent (1 in 135). Peet also investigated the hearing status of the children of the hearing siblings of his deaf subjects and came to the following conclusion: "The brothers and sisters of a deaf mute are about as liable to have deaf mute children as the deaf mute himself, supposing each to marry into families that have or each into families that have not known a predisposition toward deaf dumbness" (1852, p. 31).

Twenty years after he reported deafness in only five families of married graduates of the American School, Turner (1868) reported a far greater incidence of deafness in the offspring of the school's graduates (Table 4.4). The incidence figures in the latter report probably depict the situation more accurately. Approximately half of the marriages (fifty-six of one hundred) involved a hearing partner, a far higher proportion of marriages of deaf and hearing individuals than is found today. Also, the average family size was smaller than the norm for that period, with a total of 275 children in 110 families, or 2.5 children per family.

The fact that about half the marriages of graduates of the American School involved hearing partners in both 1848 and 1868 is of interest in itself. The school was a residential institution with instruction limited to manual communication and with articulation training provided to only a minority of students. Nonetheless, large

TABLE 4.4   Hearing Status of Children and Graduates of the American School for the Deaf, 1868

Marriage Patterns		Number of Children		
Hearing Status of Parents	Number of Families	Deaf	Hearing	Total
Deaf x deaf	30	15	77	92
Deaf x hearing	56	6	120	126
Congenital deaf x incidental deaf	24	17	40	57
Total	110	38	237	275

Source: Compiled from data collected by W. Turner, "Hereditary Deafness," *Proceedings of the National Conference of Principals of Institutes for the Deaf and Dumb* (Washington, D.C.: 1868), pp. 91–96.

numbers of graduates over the first fifty years of the school's existence had hearing spouses. The rates of deaf/hearing marriages throughout the remainder of the nineteenth century and up to the present time have been much lower, even in schools and programs emphasizing oral-only education and integration. Reasons for the surprisingly high rate of marriage between hearing individuals and graduates of the American School from 1818 to 1868 must remain largely a matter of conjecture. Perhaps a relatively large number of adventitiously deaf graduates retained their oral skills and naturally gravitated toward hearing partners. It is likely that in the first two-thirds of the nineteenth century deafness was less of a hindrance to full participation in society than it is today. It also appears that the concept of a Deaf community did not exist to the extent that it does today. No national organization of deaf people existed at that time, possibly because there was no strongly felt need for an organization to protect the interests of the deaf or serve as their advocate. The National Association of the Deaf was developed later, in 1880, partly in response to the diminishing position of deaf people in society and to attacks on their role in education of the deaf.

Questions about marriage of the deaf were not limited to nineteenth-century America. In classical times and throughout the Middle Ages, there existed laws concerning the right of deaf individuals to marry. Attitudes toward this issue were more flexible in some periods of history than in others. For example, Thomas Sanchez, a Spanish Jesuit, wrote in 1624 that deaf mutes could be excluded from legal business because it would be too easy to take advantage of them, but they had the right to marry because it would be cruel to force them to live a life of continence (Werner, 1932). Even at the beginning of the seventeenth century, however, there was opposition to marriages of the deaf for genetic reasons. Paulus Zacchias, the founder of medical jurisprudence, in a chill, no foreshadowing of Hitler and National Socialism, argued in 1621 that congenitally deaf persons should be forbidden to marry for reasons of national welfare; that is, there was a risk that they would produce deaf children, and it was necessary that the state produce children who were healthy and unimpaired in every respect (Werner, 1932).

It was Alexander Graham Bell who subjected the issue of marriage of the deaf to intense scrutiny in the United States. Given his interest in genetics, Bell was naturally inclined to study the hearing status of the offspring of deaf parents. Because he was also heavily concerned with questions regarding education of the deaf, Bell added a new dimension to the equation. In essence, Bell opposed the prevailing educational philosophy on genetic grounds.

In 1883 Bell published *Memoir upon the Formation of a Deaf Variety of the Human Race,* in which he argued that the educational system for the deaf in the United States was inadvertently contributing to an increase in the incidence of deafness. Among the forces he saw as moving toward the formation of a deaf variety of the human race were the following:

1. Segregation of children into institutional schools for the deaf
2. Reunions of graduates of these institutions and organizations of the deaf into societies, including national associations of the deaf
3. Development by deaf groups of their own periodicals and newspapers

4. Instruction of the deaf by "gesture language," which interferes with English and therefore forces the deaf to associate with one another

5. Widespread employment of deaf teachers

In Bell's opinion (1883a, 1884) these factors increased the chances that deaf people would intermarry and thereby propagate deafness. His arguments relied heavily on data from six schools for the deaf in the United States, with the most extensive data coming from the American School for the Deaf. Bell noted that of 2,106 pupils who had attended the American School, 693 (nearly 33 percent) were known to have had deaf relatives (1883a, p. 9), and of 5,823 pupils from the six schools combined, 1,719 (29 percent) had deaf relatives (p. 11). The percentages were even higher when only those students known to be congenitally deaf were considered.

Bell's interpretation of the data was inconsistent, and he had no justification for his belief that marriages of deaf people would produce "a deaf variety of the human race." A case in point is his treatment of the data on former students of the American School (1883a, p. 9). Although it is true that 693 of 2,106 students had deaf relatives, Bell's own tables indicate that only 2 percent (43 of 2,100) had deaf parents. Of this number only twenty-five had both a deaf mother and a deaf father, and eighteen had one hearing and one deaf parent. Thus the elimination of marriages among deaf people would have reduced the American School's student population by a total of only 25, from 2,106 to 2,081 over more than fifty years.

Bell promoted his ideas forcefully, especially his opposition to sign language, which, according to Bruce (1973, p. 393), he considered to be ideographic, imprecise, inflexible, and lacking in subtlety and power of abstraction—a narrow prison intellectually and socially. In 1887, Bell presented his position in a talk on inheritance to the Gallaudet College Literary Society, during which E. A. Fay provided a running translation in sign language (Bruce, 1973, p. 411). There is no indication that any part of the translation suffered from imprecision, inflexibility, or lack of abstraction.

Bell graciously turned over the data he had accumulated to Fay, who at the time was vice president of Gallaudet College, and helped Fay conduct an expanded and more complete version of his own investigation, the final results of which were published by the Volta Bureau (Fay, 1898). The major conclusions may be summarized as follows:

1. Deaf individuals are less likely to marry than hearing individuals.

2. Those deaf individuals who do marry tend to have fewer children.

3. Deaf people tend to marry deaf people.

4. When both parents are deaf, the marriage is more likely to be a happy one, with a lower incidence of divorce or separation.

5. Despite Bell's arguments for integration and elimination of sign language, those who attend day schools and exclusively oral schools still tend to marry deaf people. This is true even of those who attend no program for the deaf.

6. Deaf Americans marry more often than deaf Europeans.

7. The large majority of offspring are hearing, even when both parents are deaf.

Fay's data differed from those reported earlier by Turner in 1848 and 1868 in that Fay reported a tendency among the deaf to marry other deaf individuals. Since Turner's data were limited only to graduates of the American School until 1868, it is possible that marriage patterns were different there than at other institutions. It is more likely, though, that the data reflect a change over time in marriages among the deaf, with decreasing numbers having hearing spouses.

The publication of Fay's findings muted some of the more outspoken objectors to marriages of deaf individuals, although opposition never died completely. Even though Bell was instrumental in disseminating Fay's *Marriages of the Deaf in America,* his own *Memoir* remains more widely known and quoted, perhaps partly because of its provocative title.

Much definitive work on hereditary childhood deafness has grown out of Bell's support of research on hereditary deafness conducted at the Clarke School for the Deaf. In summing up what is known concerning the effects of marriages of deaf individuals on the incidence of deafness in the population, Brown, Hopkins, and Hudgins (1967) concluded:

> In evolutionary terms, hundreds of generations, the frequency of genes causing deafness will rise if all other conditions remain the same. In the short run, say the next ten generations, it is to be expected that there will be no noticeable increase in the frequency of identified genetic deafness that cannot be attributed to factors other than increase in gene frequency. The effect of individual decisions about reproduction among the deaf will not be significant in terms of the population because most genetic deafness results from matings of hearing parents. (p. 101)

Contemporary Identified Causes of Deafness

Determining the causes of deafness in children remains a difficult process in many cases. Even today, "etiology unknown" characterizes a sizable proportion of the deaf school-age population. In general, however, a majority of observers have acknowledged a number of factors as major causes of early childhood deafness, even though great diversity of opinion exists about the relative incidence of deafness attributable to the respective causes. The most common presently identified causes of childhood deafness are heredity, maternal rubella, cytomegalovirus, mother-child blood incompatibility, meningitis, and complications of prematurity.*

---

*A note of caution is due at this point. We are dealing with causes of deafness in the present population, which covers a wide age range. Since 1980, rubella and Rh factor have been very infrequent causes of deafness, but they still account for a large portion of prevalent deafness in the adult deaf population.

In a survey of the reported cause of hearing loss among 41,109 students enrolled in programs for the deaf during the 1970–1971 school year, Ries (1973a) reported that causes had been identified for 21,193 students, or only 51.6 percent. The programs reported that the cause had never been determined in 9,784 cases (23.8 percent). In an additional 10,132 cases (24.6 percent), either the information was not available or the schools left the item blank on the reporting form (Ries, 1973a, p. 2). It is probable that in a substantial number of such cases the cause had not been determined. The most commonly reported cause of childhood deafness was maternal rubella, with an incidence of 147.8 per 1,000, or approximately one in every seven students. The only other causes accounting for more than 3 percent of the population were heredity (7.48 percent), prematurity (5.37 percent), meningitis (4.91 percent), and Rh incompatibility (3.41 percent). All except meningitis are prenatal causes. Relatively little fluctuation occurred across age groups, except in the case of rubella, which accounted for 36.19 percent of all cases of deafness in children five to ten years old and only 2.87 percent in children ages fourteen to sixteen. The cyclical nature of rubella is easily observed, and the effects of the 1958–1959 and 1964–1965 epidemics on the groups ages eleven to thirteen and five to seven are apparent.

A survey by Hudgins (1973) was drawn from a smaller sample than Ries's survey was, but was probably more accurate because it relied on a systematic program of data collection and analysis from a single school and therefore did not have to depend on a variety of sources of uneven quality. The survey includes information about students enrolled during the 1972–1973 academic year at the Clarke School for the Deaf, a school that traditionally has devoted more attention to investigations into causes of deafness than any other school in the United States. Hudgins reported that the five major etiologies identified among Clarke students enrolled in 1972–1973 were rubella, blood incompatibility, prematurity, meningitis, and heredity. Approximately one-fourth of the students (48 of 211) had deaf parents and/or siblings. For one-third of the students (68 of 211) etiology was unknown.

In a study of causes of deafness at the California School for the Deaf at Riverside, Vernon (1968) reported that etiology was unknown for 30.4 percent of the students. In a study of seven preschool programs throughout the United States, Moores, Weiss, and Goodwin (1978) reported that etiology was unknown in 32.4 percent of the cases.

Major studies in the late 1960s and the 1970s (Hudgins, 1973; Moores, Weiss, and Goodwin, 1978; Ries, 1973a; Vernon, 1968) consistently identified heredity, maternal rubella, prematurity, blood incompatibility, and meningitis as major causes of deafness. In one-third of the cases, the cause was not known. None of the studies under consideration mentioned cytomegalovirus (CMV).

Of the major identified causes of deafness in the United States today, only heredity and meningitis were cited as major etiological factors during the nineteenth century. This, of course, does not mean that maternal rubella, prematurity, blood incompatibility, and CMV were not major factors; they were simply not yet identified as such.

The fact that CMV did not receive major attention prior to 1980 complicates the situation. It is generally agreed that hereditary deafness accounts for approximately

50 percent or more of early childhood deafness cases in the United States, but it is extremely difficult to ascertain the extent to which the other major etiologies contribute to the deaf population. Thus the "unknown" category remains large, and any figures presented should be considered rough estimates.

A short discussion of each major etiology follows. It is appropriate to begin with hereditary childhood deafness, because it probably accounts for more childhood deafness than any other cause and, being inadequately understood and often difficult to diagnose, is a major source of the discrepancies among future projections.

Hereditary Childhood Deafness

Hereditary deafness is a generic label for a variety of conditions. Konigsmark (1969a, 1969b, 1969c) developed a system for characterizing hereditary hearing loss by type of transmission (dominant, recessive, sex linked), age of onset (congenital, adolescent, adult), type of loss (conductive, sensorineural), and frequencies affected (low frequency, mid frequency, high frequency). Using this categorization, researchers had identified more than sixty kinds of hereditary hearing losses by the early 1970s (Konigsmark, 1972). Within a short time, more than one hundred distinct genetic forms of hearing loss had been described (Bougham and Shaver, 1982). These included hearing loss alone, as well as syndromes that involved characteristics in addition to deafness. By the early 1980s, more than 150 kinds of deafness had been described using Konigsmark's classifications (McKusick, 1983), and in one-third of the cases physical problems existed. Kidney problems were frequent, as were eye, skin, and nervous system conditions. This variability in the etiology of deafness is not surprising, considering the complexity of the human auditory apparatus and the large number of genes that are likely involved in its development (Bougham and Shaver, 1982; Rose, Conneally, and Nance, 1976).

Our discussion will be limited to severe/profound, congenital, and sensorineural losses, since most children enrolled in educational programs for the deaf fall into this category. We will not consider causes of hereditary hearing loss in the teenage years, adulthood, and later life.

DNA (deoxyribonucleic acid), genetic material that is transmitted from parent to child, is packaged within the cells of the body in the form of chromosomes. The genes themselves are located within chromosomes. Each chromosome has thousands of genes, and the nucleus of each human cell contains forty-six chromosomes: twenty-two pairs of autosomal chromosomes and one pair of sex chromosomes. A child receives one member of each pair of chromosomes from the father and one from the mother. All autosomal genes exist in pairs, and, with the exception of the sex chromosomes, every pair of genes has a particular location on a specific pair of chromosomes. The sex chromosomes also exist in pairs, but females have two X chromosomes, whereas males have an X chromosome and a Y chromosome. (We will examine the implications of this difference in the discussion of sex-linked deafness.)

Until the work of the Human Genome Project, to be discussed later, little information was available on the specific locations of genes for deafness. More than two

hundred kinds of genetic deafness have been identified using Konigsmark's classifications. However, the exact chromosomal location of the genes is known for only
some of them.

The three major types of congenital hereditary deafness are dominant, recessive,
and sex linked.

Dominant Congenital Deafness.   Dominant transmission of hereditary deafness
is usually estimated to account for about 10 percent of the cases of early childhood
deafness and 20 percent of the cases of hereditary deafness (Brown et al., 1967;
Konigsmark, 1972). In this situation, a single gene can produce the deafness. For
example, if A is the dominant gene for deafness and a is the gene for hearing, the
heterozygous combination Aa will produce deafness. In a marriage involving a
heterozygous Aa and a homozygous aa, half of the offspring are likely to be deaf
(Aa). The other half aa will have normal hearing, as shown below:

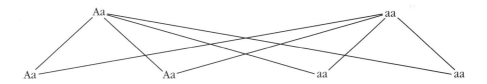

Dominantly inherited hearing loss, as well as other traits caused by dominant
genes, is affected by the penetrance of the gene. *Penetrance,* or *expressivity,* is a
statistical concept referring to the frequency with which a genetic abnormality is
manifested among individuals possessing the genes involved. When people with
the gene exhibit no signs of the condition at all, the gene shows reduced penetrance. Many dominant genetic conditions involve differences in the number or
severity of symptoms. For example, Brown et al. (1967) estimate the penetrance, or
expressivity, of the Waardenburg syndrome in a particular individual to be 80 to 100
percent for dominant genes and 100 percent for recessive genes. Only 20 percent of
those with the dominant gene for the syndrome have that particular manifestation
of deafness. Davis (1970) stated, "With the recognition of the low penetrance of
some genes that produce deafness it becomes reasonable that the majority of cases
of unexplained severe congenital hearing loss and deafness are actually sporadic
hereditary deafness" (p. 26).

Recessive Congenital Deafness.   Recessive deafness typically is transmitted to a
child by clinically normal parents, that is, by parents who themselves have no hearing loss but are carriers of genes for deafness. As a simplified example, suppose H
is the gene for normal hearing and h is the recessive gene for deafness. If each
parent has the gene pair Hh, each will have normal hearing but will be a carrier of
a gene for deafness. For a deaf child to result from a mating between carriers, the
child must receive a double dose of the recessive gene for deafness. The probability
(P) of having a deaf child (hh) is one in four:

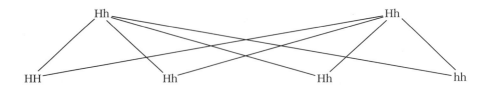

P of HH, homozygous, normal hearing = 0.25
P of Hh, heterozygous, normal hearing, carrier = 0.50
P of hh, homozygous, deaf = 0.25

In this case, there is a 25 percent (one in four) chance that a child will have normal hearing and will carry no genes for deafness; a 50 percent (two in four) chance that he or she will have normal hearing and, like the parents, be a carrier; and a 25 percent (one in four) chance that the child will be deaf. These probabilities apply to each child born from this union. In some such families, all of the children are deaf. In others, all are hearing. In still others, there are deaf children and hearing children.

This type of recessive transmission of deafness accounts for as much as 40 percent of early profound childhood deafness and 80 percent of genetic deafness (Bougham and Shaver, 1982; Brown, 1967; Brown et al., 1967; Konigsmark, 1972). Most types of deafness are caused by one of several recessive genes existing at different genetic loci. From an examination of records, Chung and Brown (1970) concluded that four or five relatively common recessive genes produced most of the cases of congenital deafness in students at the Clarke School. Brown et al. (1967) pointed out that if the deafness of a husband and wife results from different recessive genes, their children will have normal hearing. They reported, "About half of the marriages of hereditary deaf reported at Clarke School are of this type in which both partners are hereditary deaf but due to different genes so that they run no higher risk of having a deaf child than does a couple with normal hearing" (p. 98).

Several investigators (Hudgins, 1973; Konigsmark, 1972; Rose, Conneally, and Nance, 1976; Sank and Kallman, 1963) have noted that the pedigrees for recessively transmitted deafness, as well as for a wide spectrum of diseases, frequently involve the offspring of consanguineous marriages.

Brown et al. (1967, p. 101) postulated that mutation and/or other factors may be maintaining the gene frequency for deafness. They estimated a mutation rate of 4×10^{-5} (0.00004) for both dominant and recessive loci. If correct, this would mean that one out of every six hearing persons in the general population is a carrier for at least one of the recessive genes that causes childhood deafness.

Sex-linked Congenital Deafness.   Males and females differ genetically in that females have two X chromosomes and males have one X and one Y chromosome. The sex of a child is determined by whether the father contributes an X chromosome or a Y chromosome. XX children will be female, and XY children will be male, as follows:

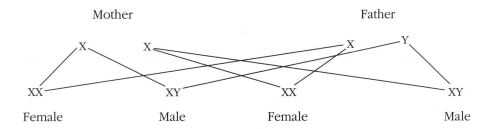

The X chromosomes carry genes that the Y chromosome does not. If one of these genes is abnormal, its effects will depend on the sex of the child. In the XX pairing, the abnormal gene may be recessive, making the daughter normal but a carrier. In the XY pairing, the abnormal gene will not be inhibited, and thus male offspring will be affected. In cases of sex-linked genes, males are affected, but not females. When the mother carries an X-linked gene for deafness and the father has normal hearing, transmission occurs as follows:

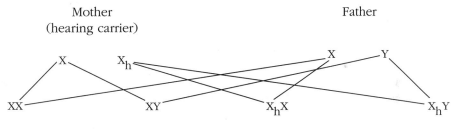

where XX = a hearing daughter
    XY = a hearing son
    X_hY = a hearing daughter but a carrier
    X_hY = a deaf son

The odds are 50 percent that a son will be deaf and 50 percent that he will be hearing. All female children will be hearing, with a 50 percent chance of being carriers.

Sex-linked congenital deafness appears to be a factor in a relatively small number of cases. Konigsmark (1972) quoted studies showing it to be involved in about 3 percent of the cases of early childhood deafness. Brown et al. (1967) reported sex-linked genes or other segregating genes, with the sex factor accounting for fewer than 2 percent of the childhood deafness cases.

Future Projections. The long-term outlook presents an entirely different picture. Advances in the study of genetics and molecular biology seem to occur on a daily basis. This is especially true of the work of the Human Genome Project of the National Institutes of Health and the Department of Energy—as well as some independent organizations—which is involved in mapping the approximately 80,000 to 120,000 human genes. This represents perhaps the most ambitious genetic research in history. The implications are both breathtaking and a cause for concern. For the first time, we will be faced with the ability to genetically change the human "gene line." By altering the composition of sperm and eggs, we have the potential to redirect the course of evolution.

It is one thing to have a new technology. It is quite another thing to decide how to use it appropriately. In a discussion of new medical technology and ethics, Enerstvedt (1999b) explored the relationship between ethics and the scientific method and noted the special problem of the relationship between technology and deafness, especially when some view deafness as a medical pathology and others view it as a cultural condition. Fortunately, this work includes research on the ethical, legal, and social implications of advances in genetic research. In the field of deafness, the Hereditary Hearing Impairment Resource Register at Boys Town National Research Hospital is collecting and sharing information on family hearing loss. One goal of the registry is to disseminate information on genetic hearing loss to primary care physicians and other health care professionals.

Maternal Rubella

Although maternal rubella was not associated with hearing loss until World War II, it was identified as the greatest cause of hearing loss in the middle 1960s and has been recognized as the major nongenetic cause of deafness in school-age children in the 1980s. The effects of the 1964–1965 epidemic will continue to be felt for many years. Rubella is also associated with other handicapping conditions, ranging from blindness to heart defects.

Rubella is a common viral disease that is frequently benign in children and adults and is difficult to diagnose clinically. Approximately 80.9 percent of women of childbearing age have developed an immunity through vaccination or the natural disease (*Morbidity and Mortality Weekly Report,* 1985). If a pregnant woman contracts rubella, particularly during the first trimester (three months) of pregnancy, the virus may cross the placental barrier and attack the developing cells and structures of the fetus, killing or crippling the unborn child. The virus can kill growing cells, and it attacks tissues of the eye, ear, and other organs.

The fact that a rubella epidemic on the scale of the 1964–1965 outbreak (or even that of 1958–1959) has not recurred suggests that prevention procedures have been largely effective. In 1969, the U.S. government approved a rubella vaccine that was given to as many females below childbearing age as possible. Each year since, the number of children reported deaf due to rubella has declined.

The presence of a large number of children rendered deaf through rubella caused major changes in education. The development of preschool programs for the deaf and comprehensive programs for the deaf-blind was spurred by the fact that the epidemic of 1964–1965 left an estimated 3,600 deaf-blind children in its wake.

In addition to vision and hearing impairment, rubella may cause urogenital disorders, cardiovascular defects, and endocrine disorders (Vernon and Hicks, 1980). The population of individuals who are deaf as a result of the rubella epidemic exhibits a wide range of abilities. Large numbers have gone through the regular programs for deaf children with no special difficulty and continued on to postsecondary education and work. Others have severe multiple-handicapping conditions and require much more specialized attention. Programs have been developed and modified as the children have moved through the preschool, elementary, secondary, and college years.

Mother-Child Blood Incompatibility

Although other types of blood incompatibility have been associated with deafness, the type most commonly involved is Rh-factor complications. The difficulty arises when a woman who is Rh– (does not have the factor) carries an Rh+ fetus. The mother's system develops antibodies that may pass into the fetal circulatory system and destroy the Rh+ cells of the fetus. Although little danger exists in the first pregnancy, sufficient antibodies may be developed by the second or third pregnancy to endanger the fetus (Fundenberg et al., 1980). The result is *erythroblastosis fetalis,* a breakdown of fetal blood cells. If the pathology affects the brain in a certain way, the condition is known as *kernicterus.* The mortality rate for this condition is quite high. Among the survivors, the incidence of deafness, cerebral palsy, aphasia, and retardation is high. Vernon (1967a) reports that more than 70 percent of Rh-factor children have multiple disabilities.

Given the widespread residual effects of Rh-factor involvement in addition to deafness, it is heartening to know that we have the means to eliminate Rh-factor complications (Goodhill, 1967, 1968). In the late 1960s, the vaccine Rh immune globulin (Rhogam) was developed to prevent Rh– mothers from developing permanent antibodies (Fundenberg et al., 1980). This vaccine can be administered within seventy-two hours of the birth of an Rh+ baby. However, if a mother has already developed permanent antibodies to Rh+ cells, the vaccine will be ineffective. Prenatal blood transfusion or early induced labor may lessen the damage to a fetus exposed to these antibodies. Transabdominal amniocentesis, a method for sampling the fluid around the fetus, can be used to assess how severely a baby has been injured.

Meningitis

Meningitis is a disease of the central nervous system, specifically, an inflammation of the coverings (meninges) of the brain and its circulating fluid (cerebrospinal fluid). It may extend to other organs, including the brain and the ear. Although most cases of meningitis resulting in hearing loss are caused by bacterial infections, meningitis can also be caused by viruses. It remains the most common cause of postnatal deafness in the school-age population. Best (1943) reported that meningitis accounted for 28 percent of all cases of deafness in 1880 and approximately 15 percent from 1890 to 1920. Later incidence figures (Hudgins, 1973; Ries, 1973b; Vernon, 1967a) range from approximately 5 to 7 percent. More recently, Pappas (1985) estimated the incidence of hearing loss as a result of bacterial meningitis to be 10 percent.

Vernon (1967a) has pointed out that changes in treatment have lowered the age of onset for individuals who do have a residuum of deafness. As an example, he cites the case of tuberculous meningitis, which historically had a 100 percent mortality rate but was reported by Fisch (1964) as the etiology of 106 cases in a British sample of 1,509. Vernon noted five cases in his California sample, among which was a wide variety of disabilities other than deafness. Although the proportional contribution of meningitis to deafness has decreased, those whom it afflicts now tend to have severe neurological impairments in addition to deafness. Current medical research efforts center around the development of vaccines against the major bacterial organisms that cause meningitis.

Prematurity

Evaluation of the impact of prematurity per se on the incidence of deafness is extremely difficult. Although prematurity (defined as birth before thirty-seven weeks or a birthweight of 5 pounds, 8 ounces or less) is more common among the deaf population than among the normal hearing, the degree to which it is a causative factor is debatable. An additional complication is the fact that it occurs in conjunction with other identified major etiologies. For example, in Vernon's data (1967b), 45 percent of the rubella cases and 14 percent of the Rh-factor cases were also premature.

It is reasonable to speculate that the number of children with severe disabilities related to prematurity will increase as improved medical techniques save more premature infants. The lower the birthweight, the greater will be the danger of damage from, for example, intracranial bleeding, anoxia, and ototoxic drugs used to treat infection. Thus an increase in the number of deaf children with additional disabilities is predicted.

Congenital Cytomegalovirus (CMV) Infection

Congenital cytomegalovirus, or CMV, is a herpes virus that infects 1 percent of all newborn babies (Pappas, 1985, Strauss, 1999). It is a major environmental cause of deafness about which very little is known and for which no vaccine exists. CMV can be acquired through the placenta of the mother, during birth if the virus is being shed in cervical secretions, or after birth through transmission of the virus in breast milk. It is present throughout the world and is more prevalent in poverty-ridden areas in countries that lack well-developed sanitation systems (Stagno, 1983).

In the United States, approximately 30,000 infants are born with CMV infection each year (Pappas, 1985). Of these, 4,000 have a hearing impairment ranging from mild to profound hearing loss (Strauss, 1999). In the more severe cases, symptoms may include an enlarged liver and spleen, jaundice, a low blood count, low birthweight, abnormally reduced head size, mental retardation, and sensorineural hearing loss. At present, there is no known treatment.

Unless symptoms are present, most cases of congenital CMV go undiagnosed. Although blood tests are economical and practical, screening tests are rarely done if no symptoms are present. However, tests for CMV are improving, and the number of infants identified as having CMV is increasing. Unfortunately, testing of children from impoverished backgrounds, where the prevalence is greater, lags behind that in more affluent populations.

Schildroth (1994) reports that the severity of CMV is such that of sixteen viruses and six bacteria associated with newborn children infected in the fetal stage, only CMV is linked to *all* of the following: prematurity, intrauterine growth retardation and low birthweight, developmental anomalies, congenital disease, and persistent postnatal infection. He notes that the chief sources of infection in women of child-bearing age are sexual contact with other individuals and close interaction with infected children. Congenital CMV can result in hearing loss, microencephaly, mental retardation, pneumonia, eye lesions, and even death.

Using data on 542 children from the 1991–1992 Annual Survey of Hearing Impaired Children and Youth with an etiology of CMV, Schildroth (1994) reported that mental retardation was present in 19 percent, cerebral palsy in 13 percent, orthopedic problems in 10 percent, learning disabilities in 10 percent, behavior problems in 9 percent, and visual impairment/blindness in 6 percent. Of all the major causes of deafness, only rubella had as many additional serious complications.

Current Developments and Projections

Revolutionary changes have occurred both in the field of genetics and in the development of surgical techniques. Developments are raising serious practical, moral, and ethical issues that will have to be dealt with for generations to come. In the area of genetics, Coucke, Van Camp, and Djoyodiharjo (1994) made a pioneering breakthrough in research on hereditary deafness. Beginning with a large, isolated family in Indonesia with many deaf and hearing members, they were able to localize the gene for a specific type of deafness. They then performed a similar analysis with two other families and in one family established linkage in the same chromosomal area. Although the specific gene had not been isolated at the time of this printing, gene-mapping studies such as this will ultimately lead to the identification of the gene and the determination of its structure and function (Arnos, 1994). Clinical application of this information may eventually include testing of parents-to-be for carrier status, prenatal fetal testing, and earlier diagnosis and treatment.

Since 1984, advances have been made in several countries, including the United States, Great Britain, Israel, and Italy. Steele (1998) reported on research in Great

Britain in detection of a gene related to progressive hearing loss, declaring that detection of such a gene could lead to procedures that would repress properties that cause a progressive hearing loss.

Steele's projections may or may not be accurate, since there are at least two hundred types of hereditary hearing loss, one-third of which are associated with medical, physical, or developmental conditions unrelated to deafness. Success to date is being reported on the more easily identified cases. Implementation of testing, diagnosis, and treatment would be quite complex. However, there is little doubt that the long-term effects of the Human Genome Project will be enormous. Arnos reported in 1999 that twenty genes for syndromic forms of deafness such as Waardenburg syndrome and Ushers syndrome and approximately forty genes for nonsyndromic types of hearing loss had been localized (mapped) on the human chromosomes. Several of these genes have been isolated and the protein products identified.

Arnos (1999) reported that one gene in particular, Connexion 26, has been found to be the most common cause of nonsyndromic recessive hearing loss, accounting for up to 50 percent of childhood deafness in some populations. In a study of mutations in the Connexion 26 gene among Ashkenazi Jews, Morell (1999) reported that this gene accounts for virtually all cases of nonsyndromic recessive deafness in the sample studies.

The most obvious application of genetic engineering is in the eradication of human disorders such as diabetes, sickle-cell anemia, and certain types of cancer. Few people would argue with such efforts to reduce human suffering. This falls within the traditional framework of "negative eugenics," attempts to eliminate negative characteristics of the human race. The second application would involve "positive eugenics," or attempts to improve the characteristics of the race. We all know of the selective breeding of plants and animals to improve or emphasize specific characteristics, and we are all aware of the results of both kinds of genetics when carried to madness in Nazi Germany, which combined efforts to breed "pure Aryans" with efforts to destroy certain groups of "untermenschen" such as Jews, Gypsies, and people with disabilities. The memory of such excesses raises red flags.

Developments in genetics and biology have raised serious practical, moral, and ethical issues that will have to be dealt with. In terms of "negative eugenics," most people would agree that the elimination of cancer and sickle-cell anemia is desirable. The question is, where should it end, where do we draw the line? Rifkin (1998) argues that if cancer can be prevented by altering the genetic codes of individuals, why not proceed to less serious "disorders" such as color blindness, dyslexia, obesity, or short stature? If we spend billions of dollars on Rogaine to restore hair, on psychotropic drugs to alter moods, and on liposuction and chin tucks, many of us would be willing to use gene therapy. Rifkin cites a study in which 43 percent of Americans would approve using gene therapy to improve children's physical characteristics. What, exactly, constitutes an improvement is a debatable point.

Similar issues obviously apply to genetic hearing loss. As we know, in most industrial and postindustrial societies, hereditary hearing loss accounts for approximately half of school-age children with severe to profound hearing loss. The overriding question is whether genetic engineering should be used to reduce the occurrence of hearing loss (Moores, 1998). If the answer is yes, where do we draw the line? Should he concentrate on the one-third of the cases that are associated with medical, physical, or developmental abnormalities? For example 50 percent of children with Jervell and Lange-Nelson syndrome die before age twenty. This would be a logical candidate. On the other hand, once we start, who will have the authority to decide where to stop—the family, the state, or physicians? Who will set the limits?

If we have abortion on demand, will we also have genetic engineering on demand? The genie is already out of the bottle and cannot be put back. The only question now is how our new knowledge will be used. Before long, prospective parents may sit down with a genetic counselor who will provide them with information that we can only imagine. There will be enormous legal and ethical issues. It is not difficult to imagine that many hearing parents will opt for hearing children and that the prevailing public mood will accept the decision. The general public is not aware that at least some deaf parents may opt for a deaf child. If and when such decisions are made, we will be face to face with the question of who, if anyone, should control the genetic constitution of yet-to-be-born children.

Because most hearing people have little or no experience with deafness or understanding of its implications, the potential for complete, clear, and sensitive counseling, which is not available at present, is enormous. Arnos (1994, 1999) points out that genetic evaluation and counseling by qualified clinical geneticists is necessary for diagnosis, treatment, and follow-up. She notes that ignorance about hereditary hearing loss is common not only among families but also among health care professionals. Arnos concludes:

> Much remains to be learned about hereditary hearing loss so that we can provide accurate information and clinical options to these families. Their diversity in terms of degree of hearing loss, age of onset, associated syndromic conditions, and cultural identifications ensures that the debate about research in hereditary hearing loss and its clinical applications will continue to be lively (p. 470).

The study of genetics in general has led to an increasing interest in genetic aspects of deafness and the genetic counseling process. As the information presented in this chapter indicates, identification of a cause of deafness may be quite difficult in some cases. The diagnostic process should include as complete a family pedigree, medical history, and audiological history as possible. Careful physical examination by trained medical geneticists may reveal additional symptoms, permitting diagnosis of a specific syndrome. Establishing an etiology is critical to the counseling process. If, for example, an etiology of recessive deafness is diagnosed, the chance of any future child being deaf is known to be 25 percent. Where the etiology cannot be determined, specific probabilities cannot be predicted. In these cases, empirical risk figures based on population studies may be useful (Bougham and Shaver, 1982).

The purpose of present-day genetic counseling is to inform rather than recommend. It is not the role of the counselor to be directive or to tell prospective parents what they should do. This is especially important in dealing with deaf clients, many of whom are aware of past attempts to limit their choices with respect to reproduction.

Arnos (1999) and Boughan and Shaver (1982) emphasize the necessity that genetic counselors appreciate the viewpoints of people seeking information. They report that some deaf parents believe that having deaf children would be preferable to having hearing children and stress that the counselor must be able to understand and incorporate this position.

Cochlear Implants

In recent years, there has been a great deal of interest in, and controversy over, multichannel cochlear implants (most commonly the Nucleus 22 implant), a surgical procedure that, as the name implies, involves implantation of a permanent device in

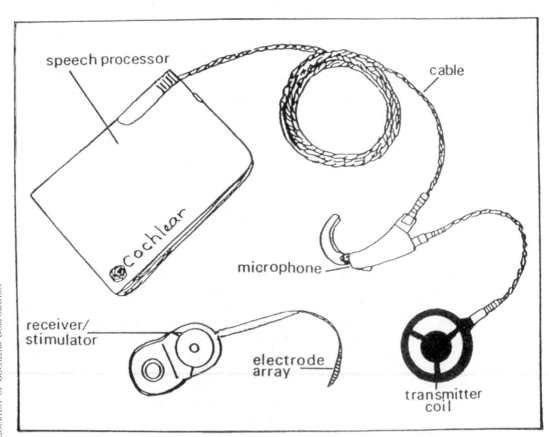

The Cochlear Implant Device.

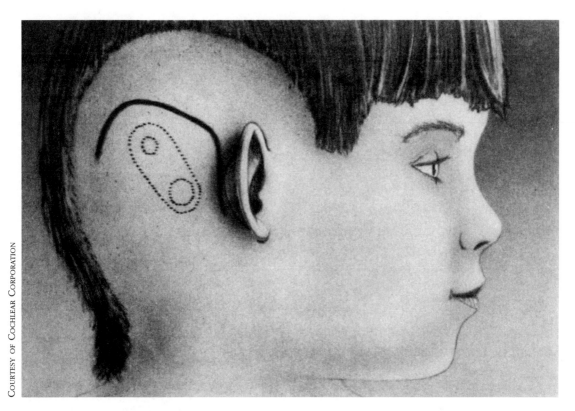

COURTESY OF COCHLEAR CORPORATION

Incision and location of the receiver/stimulator.

the head. Cochlear implant surgery involves opening a skin flap behind one ear, drilling through the skull, removing a section of the mastoid bone, and inserting a wire with an electrode array into the cochlea. General anesthesia is given, the operation requires approximately three hours if no complications arise, and the patient is hospitalized overnight (Balkany, 1993). Cohen, Waltzman, and Fisher (1993) reported complications in almost one-quarter of the eighty cases they studied. Complication risks included infection, respiratory problems, facial nerve paralysis, vertigo, altered taste, cerebrospinal leakage, and tinnitus. Also, the device may fail or require replacement or removal due to a lack of benefit.

Multichannel cochlear implants began to gain attention in the 1980s in Europe, North America, and Australia. At first, they were restricted to adults. In 1990, after a great deal of debate, the U.S. Food and Drug Administration approved the Nucleus 22 multichannel implant for children ages two to seventeen. The approval came in the face of much controversy over the implant's moral and practical implications (Aplin, 1993; Kampfe et al.,1993; Lane, 1992; Vernon and Alles, 1994). The debate has become quite emotional at times and addresses several intricately related issues, including the following:

1. Are implants successful? If so, for what kinds of subjects—in terms of age, nature of hearing loss, extent of loss, and so on—are they appropriate?

2. Do the potential benefits outweigh the risks?

3. Do the advocates of the procedure "oversell" the benefits or fail to provide realistic counseling to recipients or, in the case of children, to parents? For example, professionals may consider the procedure a success if it increases awareness of sound in cases where parents expect their child to process speech in a normal manner.

4. What are the moral and legal issues involving informed consent for invasive surgery on children as young as two years for deafness which is a non-life-threatening condition?

Permanent implantations with children two and three years of age are particularly problematic. Given life expectancies in technologically advanced countries today, such children might be expected to carry foreign objects in their heads for eighty years or more.

In adults, it appears that cochlear implants have generally been more successful with people with late onset of deafness than with people who have been deaf from birth or early childhood (Lane, 1992; Vernon and Alles, 1994). For young children the results have been inconclusive, but they suggest that children with implants may do somewhat better on speech reception than children relying on hearing aids if care is taken to select children for whom an implant is appropriate. Building on previously developed criteria, Hellman et al. (1991) included a minimum age of two years, profound bilateral sensorineural hearing loss, strong family support, absence of additional disabilities, normal intelligence, lack of success in using hearing aids, parental and child expectations, educational environment, availability of support services, and the children's learning styles. If strictly applied, these criteria would exclude most children in programs for the deaf and all children with mild, moderate, and severe hearing losses. Moog and Geers (1991) estimate that only two hundred children per year would be eligible under these criteria. Allen, Rawlings, and Remington (1993) point out that predictions of success are based on availability of postoperative services and the availability of plans to fund them. They conclude that the economics of cochlear implants are crucial and that deaf children with additional disabilities and minority deaf children are most likely to be excluded. The implications are clear: more children from affluent families will receive implants, perhaps inappropriately.

Allen et al. (1993) studied 88 children from Texas who had received implants and compared them to a sample of 4,269 students in attendance at the Texas School for the Deaf and in statewide regional programs for the deaf. The most startling data dealt with ethnic status. Selection for implants was highly biased toward white children: 90 percent of the implant recipients were white, compared to 44 percent of the statewide comparison group. Only one African-American child received an implant, compared to 17 percent of the nonimplant comparison group. Hispanics comprised 8 percent of implants and 36 percent of the comparison group. In a state in which white children comprise a minority of deaf children, they received 90 percent of the cochlear implants. Allen et al. also reported that thirteen of the children with implants had additional disabilities, with two classified with specific learning disabilities and six with mental retardation. The authors note that these data seem to counter established criteria. With respect to etiology, the largest single cause of deafness among the implantees was meningitis (33 percent), followed by cytomegalovirus (12 percent). Only one student was listed as having deafness due to heredity, although there may have been more in an "unknown" category. In the sample of children without implants, meningitis accounted for 12 percent, cytomegalovirus for 2 percent and heredity for 14 percent. Obviously, etiologies differed for the two groups, and there is some evidence that children rendered deaf through meningitis may respond positively to implants. In relation to hearing loss, 85 percent of the children with implants had profound losses, compared to 46 percent of the children without implants. This means that the criterion of a profound hearing loss for a cochlear implant was not followed in 15 percent of the cases.

In the Allen et al. study, children with implants had an unaided threshold of 109.8 dB, which improved to 56.0 dB with the implant. Children without implants had an unaided threshold of 105.1 dB, which improved to 61.8 dB with conventional hearing aids. Allen et al. noted that the standard deviation for the average reduction in threshold for children with implants was greater than for those with hearing aids, suggesting less consistency in improvement for children with implants. It should be stressed that a pure tone hearing threshold of 56.0 dB or 61.8 dB does not mean that a child can process speech at that level; it means only that a child is aware of sound. Obviously, if parents believe cochlear implants with profoundly deaf children will bring clear speech within the normal range, they will be disappointed. If implants represent a gain over conventional hearing aids, as the Allen et al. data seem to indicate, the question is whether the gain might be significant enough to warrant the risks, costs, and commitment to the procedure. Perhaps the answers will be clear-cut in the future, but at present the situation is ambiguous.

Vernon and Alles (1994) raised several issues regarding cochlear implants with young children and noted that much of the research was done in affiliation with the procedure itself and called for independent, unbiased research. They also noted the possibility of surgical complications. In a response to the article, Hanin, Rothschild, and Mueller (1995) replied that many children who are prelingually, profoundly deaf and who receive a cochlear implant at a young age make faster progress and demonstrate higher levels of performance in expressive and receptive oral language. They also responded to the concerns about surgical complications with the statement that some of them never occur and that the rate of others averaged 1 percent.

Another response to Vernon and Alles was made by a parent and educator (Luetke-Stahlman, 1995) who had two children implanted. She reported positive results even though one device failed and a reimplantation was called for. In a different vein, another educator (name withheld, 1995) reported that, as a teacher with three students implanted, she or he reported the following:

...now find myself in the position of picking up the parents' emotional pieces when their expectations disintegrate....

...All this pain and disappointment is for what? Their children are still deaf!

...I've got audiologists telling me that if I *must* sign, I should be using an artificially-based sign system such as Signing Exact English, and that the children should NOT be exposed to ASl at any cost. They are actually discouraging the parents from having anything to do with the deaf community, even to the point of causing an actual fear of deaf adults.

...As far as the physical effects of the surgery itself, all three of my students had balance problems which were not present before the surgery. (p. 5–6)

Rose, Vernon, and Pool (1996) noted that intensive habilitation was necessary over a period of years, and even then the results appears to be "at best, equivocal" (p. 238). They reported on the results of a survey of all private and public residential schools in the United States in which forty-five and sixty-four programs responded. Of the 151 implanted children surveyed, 71 (43 percent) were no longer using the cochlear implant. They also reported that numerous comments indicated despondency over the results of the implants.

Osberger (1996) reported much more positive results, more so for children who receive implants at an early age rather than later, when results tend to be poor. She believes that perhaps half of the children with early implants and training will achieve good results and comprehend speech in single words. Enerstvedt (1999b) raised the issue that if the ability to "comprehend speech is measured in single words, it is debatable if the results can be applied to conversational language."

Enerstvedt (1999b), in a summary of research, concluded that results were good for implantees who had become deaf after age five, but that the picture was not clear for children who were born deaf or became deaf after acquiring a language. He referred to observations of Vestberg (1996, published in Norwegian) of the Central Institute for the Deaf in St. Louis, Missouri, where nearly half the students had received cochlear implants. All children were taught orally, with an hour instruction daily in hearing and speech. Vestberg reported that progress over three years was limited. for two-thirds of the students there was little, if any, benefit over the use of hearing aids.

Enerstvedt argues that in our culture, with strong interests in pathology and profit, a freely made choice is difficult for those with the best interest of the child at heart. Basic choices are often made with little reliance on relevant knowledge and insight. Often the reason for the choice seems to be narrow professional interests, demagoguery, and extremism. He reports that in schools for the deaf in Norway (as in some schools in the United States) teaching is done primarily through sign language and mainly without sound. He notes that for such schools implants will be a threat. He states that it is hard to believe, but the only alternative at present for parents is pure oralism, and he decries this either/or mentality. If parents of children with cochlear implants have only pure oralism as the only available option, this will be nothing but a scandal. Enerstvedt argues for the individualization of instruction so that either/or dichotomies can be avoided.

Of all the controversies surrounding education of the deaf—oral-manual, ASL/English, integration/separation, and so on—none seem to touch the raw nerves that the issue of cochlear implants does. As editor of the *American Annals of the Deaf,* I have been involved in the publication of several articles on cochlear implants with positive, negative, and mixed views. These articles elicit more letters to the editor than any other topic, especially from parents, and invariably generate very different opinions. Personally, as a father, I would be very hesitant to have a foreign object permanently implanted in my child's head to ameliorate a non-life-threatening situation such as deafness. However, none of my children are deaf, and I have never had to make the decision.

Summary

Our understanding of the causes of deafness has always been sketchy, and large gaps in our knowledge still remain. Although the incidence of early childhood deafness has fluctuated greatly due to periodic epidemics and medical advances, approximately 60 percent of early childhood deafness is inherited (up to 50 percent is recessive, 10 percent is dominant, and 1 to 2 percent is sex linked). It appears that the incidence of genetic early childhood deafness will remain stable for the near future, but will eventually decline. In the future, we may have the resources to control environmental causes of deafness to a much greater extent than we can at present. With the development of vaccines and other preventive measures, the incidence of nongenetic early childhood deafness should decrease, but within the afflicted group there will be a higher percentage of individuals with multiple disabilities. However, there is no assurance against sudden and dramatic increases in early childhood deafness at any time given the potential impact of infectious agents such as cytomegalovirus. Current developments in the field of genetics and treatments such as cochlear implants raise issues that are as yet unresolved.

C H A P T E R

5

Deaf Individuals with Additional Conditions

Introduction

Given the evidence presented in Chapter 4, most readers would correctly infer that additional conditions are present to a greater degree in the deaf population than in the population in general. All of the major contemporary known causes of early childhood deafness may be related to other conditions to some extent. These include maternal rubella, prematurity, cytomegalovirus, mother-child blood incompatibility, and meningitis. Even in the case of inherited deafness, whether dominant, recessive, or sex linked, the hearing loss may be only one manifestation of a syndrome that includes a wide range of conditions.

This situation raises several issues with respect to our attempts to understand the impact of deafness on development and functioning. For example, research on the intellectual or cognitive functioning of the deaf must be carefully controlled in a number of aspects, including the selection of subjects. Otherwise, group comparisons might find the functioning of deaf subjects to be inferior to that of hearing subjects when the difference was actually attributable to the presence of other conditions rather than to deafness per se.

On an individual diagnostic basis, even more immediate problems are involved in making educational decisions for a particular child. Consider a deaf child who exhibits the behavioral characteristics of a child with learning disabilities. Hundreds of thousands of children in the general school-age population have been identified as having learning disabilities and receive special educational services. However, the procedures for identifying a hearing child as having learning disabilities are not always appropriate for a deaf child. A hearing child is likely to be referred for

118

evaluation when a discrepancy appears to exist between intellectual potential and academic achievement. Such a gap is common in deaf children for reasons other than learning disabilities (Miller and Moores, 1995): many deaf children have low academic achievement simply because we have not yet developed sufficient skills to teach them effectively. Therefore, an unknown number of deaf children with true learning disabilities are not being identified and served.

The opposite of underidentification of deaf children with learning disabilities is the very real danger of misdiagnosing deaf children as retarded as a result of inappropriate testing. There is always a possibility of misunderstanding artificially low scores. Any psychological test should be administered by a psychologist with training and experience in testing the deaf. The author's experience suggests that this is usually the case in residential schools for the deaf and in most large public school districts with programs serving the deaf. The mandates of PL 94–142 and subsequent laws have provided an impetus for the provision of appropriate testing. Still, in many school districts deaf children are tested by psychologists who lack special training and experience in working with deaf children.

Although research has established that a large proportion of deaf individuals suffer from additional conditions, the nature and extent of this problem have never undergone systematic investigation. A primary obstacle is the lack of agreement over what actually constitutes a disability. Almost all human beings have problems of one kind or another—colorblindness, overbite, curvature of the spine, deviated septum, astigmatism, depression, and so on—that may be bothersome but may not necessarily affect everyday functioning adversely. The major emphasis of this chapter is on disabilities that may have additional implications for educational and psychological functioning.

Although numerous studies have reported incidence figures for various types of disabilities related to deafness, present data must be treated as imprecise estimates. First, the figures primarily represent children enrolled in programs and identified by one means or another as having multiple disabilities. Although the situation has improved, there is no way of knowing how many more such children are not enrolled in programs. This is especially true of children from poor families. Therefore, it is not wise to generalize to the total population on the basis of present incidence figures. Second, categories and definitions tend to be imprecise. Even federal categories and definitions have varied over time. Procedures for classifying deaf children as having retardation, aphasia, learning disabilities, and so on have been inconsistent, and inappropriate labeling has frequently been harmful. Information should be considered illustrative and percentages and incidence figures thought of as only rough estimates. With only a few notable exceptions, studies of the existence of other conditions in deaf populations have provided either incidence data with no definitions or definitions with no incidence data.

We should note that more studies were conducted in the 1960s and 1970s than in ensuing decades. There are several reasons for this. First, federal support for studies of this nature has diminished overall. Second, dissatisfaction with the validity and reliability of past investigations has made researchers reluctant to risk repeating their mistakes. Probably more important, there is no longer the sense of urgency that prevailed in the wake of the rubella epidemic, when the number of children with multiple conditions escalated dramatically and the need to establish new programs and expand existing ones was clear. The aftermath of the rubella epidemic will remain as those affected move through the life cycle. The innovative programs, curricula, and services established during the 1960s and 1970s formed the basis for today's programs for children. Unfortunately, little activity is currently being directed toward development of new curricula or innovative programs.

Changing Terminology

The original wording of Public Law 94–142, which used the term *handicapped* rather than *disability*, caused additional problems because it excluded deaf-blind children. The definition contained in Public Law 94–142 (1975) referred to *multihandicapped* as "concomitant impairments (such as mentally retarded-blind, mentally retarded–orthopedically impaired, etc.), the combination of which causes such severe educational problems that they cannot be accommodated in special education programs solely for one of the impairments." The term did not include deaf-blind. The law was written to exclude deaf-blind children simply because other legislation was written to provide services for them. As a result, the definitions in PL 94–142 were too restrictive. Prior to the enactment of PL 94–142, the term *multihandicapped* was much more inclusive. A series of studies conducted by the erstwhile Office of Demographic Studies (Gentile and McCarthy, 1973; Rawlings and Gentile, 1970; Ries, 1973c), reported a wide range of additional conditions, including visual impairment, health problems, emotional disturbance, perceptual disorders, mental retardation, and cleft lip and palate. Gentile and McCarthy (1973, p. 2) defined an *additional handicapping condition* as "any physical, mental, emotional or behavior disorder that *significantly adds to the complexity* of educating a hearing impaired student" (emphasis added). This approach entailed a completely different philosophy from that suggested by the legal definition. In the PL 94–142 definition, a multi-handicapping condition is one that cannot be accommodated in a program solely for one of the conditions. In Gentile and McCarthy's definition, a multihandicapping condition may increase the complexity of serving a child but does not necessarily demand separate treatment. Such an approach allows a larger number of children to be identified. The same philosophy prevails today, with the qualification that we now refer to *deaf* and *hard-of-hearing children with additional disabilities* rather than *multihandicapped hearing-impaired children*.

Incidence Estimates

General incidence figures suggest that the number of deaf students with additional disabilities is large. Weir (1963) reported that there were 1,069 such students in 1954 and 3,050 in 1960. Using data from the *1968 Annual Survey of Hearing Impaired Children and Youth,* Rawlings and Gentile (1970) reported that more than 7,000 out of a sample of 21,000 deaf students, or one-third, were identified by their programs as having at least one additional condition. When generalized to the total enrollment of deaf students in the United States, this finding suggests that 16,000 to 20,000 such children were enrolled in schools.

Ries (1973b) conducted an analysis of data from the *1971 Annual Survey of Hearing Impaired Children and Youth.* He reported that 23,874 of a total of 41,109 deaf students had no additional conditions, and information was not available for 6,255 individuals (p. 50). The remaining 10,980 had a total of 13,662 other disabilities. Computing the number of deaf students with additional conditions (10,980) in relation to the total in the survey (41,109) suggests that approximately one-fourth of the deaf students might be included in this category. If the 6,266 students for whom information was not available are excluded, the incidence figure rises to approximately one-third, or 10,980 out of 34,843.

In the large-scale surveys (Craig and Craig, 1985; Rawlings and Gentile, 1970; Ries, 1973b), the various programs reported their figures by categories without reference to clear definitions. We can assume that the assignment of children to respective categories varied greatly from program to program.

Conrad (1979) discussed the questionable reliability and validity of the estimates given by both Gentile and McCarthy (1973) and the British Department of Education and Science of the number of deaf children with additional disabilities. Gentile and McCarthy (1973) reported that 32 percent of deaf schoolchildren in the United States had at least one additional educationally significant condition. In a 1972 study of deaf children in England and Wales, the Department of Education and Science (DES) reported that 54 percent of deaf children had additional "handicaps." This population did not include children in two special schools or in one special unit for severely emotionally disturbed and multiply involved children. The Gentile and McCarthy data were gathered through questionnaires. Conrad noted problems with areas such as "emotional or behavioral problems" and "brain damage." He claimed that only half of the diagnoses of brain damage were made by medical practitioners. Conrad argued that there was no evidence for classifying 25 percent of the subjects in the DES study as "emotionally disturbed" and "maladjusted," nor was any reference made to the use of actual tests to label a child as "educationally subnormal." Conrad concluded that the reported estimates of 32 percent by Gentile and McCarthy and 54 percent by the DES were enormously high and that the real incidence of educationally relevant additional conditions is close to 11 percent in both countries.

In a review of the literature, Cohen (1980) reported that several studies had noted that from 20 to 25 percent of hearing students had been indentified as emotionally disturbed. This number is consistent with the DES data on British children. It is likely that the estimates are too high.

It cannot be emphasized too strongly that an unknown number of children may be receiving no education or services. Burns and Stenquist (1960) pointed out that children with multiple disabilities often remain at home or are placed in institutions. Calvert (1970) stated that there might be more such children outside of schools than in them. It is possible that PL 94–142 has reduced this problem, although the greatest increases in the number of children identified and served have been in less severe categories such as learning disabilities and speech pathology (Weiner, 1985). Although the contention is impossible to document (by definition there is no way of knowing how many unidentified children exist), it seems likely that a large number of deaf children are unserved. In the course of doing research on programs for the deaf in large metropolitan areas in California, Texas, and Massachusetts, this author has identified large numbers of poor deaf children in each city. Frequently, their parents are undocumented immigrants who do not speak English and either are not aware that their children are eligible for educational services or do not want to call attention to themselves. In some cases, cultural restraints may prohibit a child with two or more educationally significant conditions from leaving the home.

Using data from the 1992–1993 *Survey of Hearing Impaired Children and Youth* on 42,716 children in four different program types (residential school, day school, local integrated, and local, not integrated), Schildroth and Hotto (1994) found that approximately 25 percent of children overall were reported to have one additional disability and 9 percent to have two or more additional disabilities. Some differences were noted as a function of program type (see Table 5.1), with 13 percent of children in local, not integrated programs reported to be mentally retarded, a much higher percentage than in other types of programs. Conversely, children in local, not integrated programs were less likely to be classified as learning disabled. There may well be a tendency to classify children in nonintegrated settings as mentally retarded and children with similar behaviors in integrated settings as learning disabled. This possibility should be studied.

Table 5.2 presents more complete information from the 1993–1994 *Annual Survey of Deaf and Hard of Hearing Children and Youth* (Schildroth, 1995). Roughly one-third (14,775 of 45,854) of the students had one or more educationally significant additional disabilities; 10,923 had one additional disability, and 3,931 had two

TABLE 5.1   Reported Additional Disabilities Among Children in Four Special Education Program Types, 1992–1993.

	Program Type			
Additional Disabilities	**Residential School**	**Day School**	**Local Integrated**	**Local, Not Integrated**
One	23%	21%	25%	27%
Two or more	9%	6%	13%	—
Type of Additional Disability				
Visual	5%	4%	5%	9%
Mental retardation	7%	5%	7%	13%
Emotional/behavioral	7%	5%	7%	13%
Learning disability	8%	10%	11%	7%

Sources: A. Schildroth and S. Hotto, *American Annals of the Deaf*, 139, no. 2 (1994): 239–243. Data from *Annual Survey of Hearing Impaired Children and Youth*, 1992–1993.

TABLE 5.2   Additional Educationally Relevant Disabilities in 1993–1994 ($N = 45,854$)

Health	Number
Legal blindness	626
Uncorrected visual problems	1,635
Brain damage/injury	512
Epilepsy	463
Orthopedic problems	1,206
Cerebral palsy	1,356
Heart disorder	523
Other health impairment	1,851

Educational	Number
Mental retardation	3,677
Emotional/behavior problems	1,834
Specific learning disability	4,035
Attention deficit disorder	876
Other	1,396

Sources: A. Schildroth, personal communication (Washington, D.C.: Center for Assessment and Demographic Studies, Gallaudet University, April 1995). Data from *Annual Survey of Deaf and Hard of Hearing Children and Youth,* 1993–1994.

or more. The two most common conditions were specific learning disabilities (4,035) and mental retardation (3,677). Note that the numbers in Table 5.2 add up to more than 14,775 because some children had more than one disability.

For some reason the incidence of reported additional conditions among deaf school-age children has been declining since the early 1990s, to the point that the reported incidence rate is closer to one-quarter rather than one-third. The reasons for this are unclear. It is not due to any apparent change in the student population or in the provision of services and may be related to the categories used and their definitions. The 1997 reauthorization of the Individuals with Disabilities Act emphasizes categories less and gives more attention to identifying functional problems without placing labels on a child. Within this context, Karchmer and Allen (1999) reported on the results of data gathered by the 1997–1998 *Annual Survey of Deaf and Hard of Hearing Children and Youth,* which included information on functional assessment as well as traditional categories. The functional questions related to the student's classroom functioning and were clustered into three areas:

Cognitive, behavioral, and social: Thinking/reasoning, maintaining attention to classroom tasks, social interaction/classroom behavior

Communicative: Expressive communication; receptive communication

Physical: vision, use of hands, arms, and legs; balance, overall physical health

Karchmer and Allen reported that 25.8 percent of 36,646 students were classified as having an additional condition, 8.55 percent were reported as having a specific learning disability, 7.8 percent mental retardation, and 4.6 percent attention deficit disorder. Judgments by school personnel for 30,198 of the children in the survey present a far different picture. Two-thirds of the students were reported as having at least a mild functional limitation in one or more areas (Karchmer and Allen, 1999, p. 71). Almost half of the children were rated as having a functional limitation in receptive or expressive communication, and almost half were rated as having a cognitive, behavioral, or social functional limitation. The authors concluded that "the prevalence of limitations in classroom functioning is much greater for children who are deaf or hard of hearing than that predicted by the traditional categorical approach" (p. 76).

The implications of these findings are unclear at present, and much more research is necessary. One question that comes immediately to mind is whether teachers and other professional personnel might tend to overstate the existence of functional limitations in children. Are these limitations more apparent than real?

Karchmer and Allen also reported that most of the children were judged by the schools to have some functional hearing. They state (1999, p. 75), "Specifically, whereas about 36 percent of the students were reported to have unaided hearing leaves exceeding 90 dB in the better ear (i.e., a profound hearing loss), only about 16 percent were estimated to have no functional hearing at all." In the case of functional hearing estimates, Karchmer and Allen state that the estimates must be interpreted carefully because they are subjective.

Major Identified Educational Disabilities Related to Deafness

In discussing other disabilities related to deafness, we need to look separately at the interaction of deafness with a number of other disabilities. Two populations that have received a great deal of attention are individuals with deafness and blindness and those with deafness and mental retardation. Two other groups that recently have received considerable attention but little in the way of services are deaf individuals classified as having learning and behavioral problems.

Mental Retardation

Studies of the incidence of deafness combined with mental retardation generally come from two sources: (1) schools and classes for deaf individuals and (2) schools and institutions for individuals with mental retardation. The trend in most states has been to reduce the institutional populations of individuals with severe retardation while developing programs at local or regional levels. Many state residential schools for the deaf and some large metropolitan school systems have expanded the scope of their services for deaf children to include those with severe mental retardation.

Over a period of years, the percentage of children identified as mentally retarded in programs for the deaf remained fairly stable. Then in the late 1960s, it started to drop. Frisina (1955) reported an incidence of 11 to 12 percent in residential schools for the deaf, and Weir (1963) reported an incidence of up to 11 percent in day and residential programs for the deaf. In a study of educational services available to students with mental retardation in six schools for the deaf, Anderson and Stevens (1969) found that 304 students (19 percent of the total population of the schools) had measured IQs of below 83; of these children, 132 (8 percent) were classified by their schools as retarded. Calvert (1970) stated that 10 to 12 percent of deaf students were either "educable mentally retarded" or "trainable mentally retarded." Rawlings and Gentile (1970) found that 8.05 percent of students were reported as retarded in programs for the deaf participating in the 1968 *Annual Survey of Hearing Impaired Children and Youth*. In the 1971 survey (Ries, 1973c, p. 50), 2,400 of 41,109 students, or approximately 5.9 percent, were reported as retarded. When the students about whom information was not available are excluded, the incidence of reported mental retardation in programs for the deaf rises to approximately 7 percent. Craig and Craig (1985) came up with a total of 2,799 deaf children with retardation out of an enrollment of 49,552 in the United States in 1984. This represents 6 percent of the enrollees, a figure consistent with the 1968 and 1971 surveys and with the 1993–1994 data presented in Table 5.2 (Schildroth, 1995).

Since the late 1960s, a definite decline has occurred in the percentage of deaf children classified as deaf and retarded. The reasons are a matter of speculation, but we should consider a number of factors.

First, the traditional estimates that 10 to 12 percent of deaf students in residential schools also had retardation were probably gross overestimates, including many children who were intellectually normal. Too often deaf children have been classified as retarded by professionals who had no knowledge of the communication problems deaf individuals face and operated under the mistaken assumption that language and speech problems are symptoms of mental retardation. Although such inappropriate diagnoses are still made, the problem is less widespread than in the past.

A second factor has been the growing reluctance of educators to label a child as "retarded." In some cases, the child has merely been assigned a new label, such as "learning disabled." In other cases, teachers may simply work with the child and avoid the use of any label at all, thus leading to a decline in the reported incidence figures.

Still, 6 to 8 percent of students in programs for the deaf continue to be classified as retarded. This incidence rate of retardation is far higher than that for the general population, which is estimated at 3 percent (Kirk and Gallagher, 1993). As previously stated, some reasons for the relatively high rate might be that (1) several of the major etiologies of deafness are also factors in mental retardation (see Chapter 4); (2) intelligence testing of deaf children is often conducted by professionals who cannot communicate with their subjects, and thus the results frequently underestimate the children's intellectual ability (see Chapter 8); and (3) intellectually normal deaf children are sometimes inappropriately labeled "retarded" on the basis of low academic achievement.

Most studies tend to place estimates of hearing loss in institutionalized popula-tions at 25 percent or below. In a survey of 212 facilities for individuals with mental retardation, Brannon (1982) reported that 9.53 percent of the institutionalized popu-lation were also hearing impaired and 2.29 percent were classified as deaf. Lloyd and Reed (1967) found the incidence of hearing impairment to be 15 percent in an institutionalized population with mental retardation. They detected an increased incidence of hearing loss as they moved down the scale of intelligence. This finding implies that the more severely retarded an individual is judged to be, the more likely he or she is to have other disabilities. Lloyd and Moore (1972) concluded that 15 percent of children in schools for children with retardation have educationally significant hearing losses.

Although what is meant by an "educationally significant" hearing loss for an individual with retardation is unclear, and criteria vary from one study to another, the incidence of hearing impairment is obviously greater in institutions for persons with retardation than in the general population. All estimates indicate that large numbers of deaf individuals are enrolled in such institutions.

It is reasonable to assume that many people in these institutions are inappropri-ately classified as "deaf retarded" because they lack well-developed communication skills. On the other hand, the primary disability of large numbers of individuals classified as retarded may be deafness. We may also assume that a large number of deaf individuals with retardation are receiving no services at all, either from pro-grams for people with retardation or from those for deaf individuals. The situation will not improve until precise definitions are developed, accurate incidence figures are obtained, children are appropriately identified, and programs are initiated. Edu-cators of the deaf should be aware of the trend toward reducing institutionalized populations. In the years to come, residential schools and local programs for the deaf likely will have to assume major responsibility for the education of even those deaf individuals with the most severe retardation.

Educational provisions.   Investigations of educational provisions for deaf stu-dents with mental retardation have been conducted both at schools for the deaf (Anderson, Stevens, and Stuckless, 1966) and at schools for individuals with retarda-tion (Mitra, 1970). As we might expect, programs are uneven in extent and quality of services, and criteria for inclusion are inconsistent. For the most part, educational programs for deaf individuals with retardation are low on the list of priorities, are poorly staffed, and receive limited administrative support. This unfortunate state of affairs was highlighted in a study by Anderson and Stevens (1969) of the qualifica-tions of teachers of deaf pupils with mental retardation in residential schools for the deaf. On the basis of responses from 150 teachers, Anderson and Stevens reported the following:

1. Deaf teachers accounted for 43 percent of the respondents, representing a far higher percentage than those employed to teach deaf children with no other disabilities.

2. Fewer than one-fourth of the respondents were teaching deaf children with retardation by choice. The remainder (78 percent) had been placed by administrative assignment.

3. Approximately two-thirds of the teachers of children with retardation stated that they preferred to teach deaf children with no other disability. Of the remainder, 5 percent had no preference and 28 percent preferred to teach deaf children with retardation.

4. Eighty-six percent of the teachers expressed a need for additional training.

In sum, most teachers of deaf students with retardation in residential schools for the deaf are not trained to teach such deaf children, did not choose to teach them, and would prefer not to teach them. We may conclude that the effectiveness of such teachers will be less than ideal.

The paucity of training programs specifically designed for teachers of deaf children with mental retardation has been a major hindrance to the development of effective programs. Apparently, it is not sufficient to take courses in deafness and in mental retardation. The child who has both deafness and retardation presents problems that are qualitatively different from those posed by a child who has either condition alone. Anderson and Stevens (1969) quoted a teacher who had fourteen years' experience teaching children with both deafness and mental retardation:

> If I felt courses for helping the deaf mentally retarded were available, I certainly would take them. In my mind I cannot accept courses for the teaching of the mentally retarded child as being of value for the teaching of mentally retarded deaf children. . . . In other words I see a completely new field in special education, the education of the deaf mentally retarded child. This child requires special techniques, materials, and curriculum to do him justice. . . . The help I need will not come from taking courses on mental retardation or courses on deafness. It will come from courses in the mentally retarded deaf. (p. 31)

The teacher's comments point up an important fact in dealing with deaf individuals who have additional disabilities. The problems of an individual who has both deafness and mental retardation are not additive; that is, they cannot be understood as representing the sum of the problems of deafness plus those of retardation. Instead, the deafness and retardation interact in a multiplicative way, presenting unique, qualitatively different patterns. Just as the problems faced by a deaf individual with retardation differ from those of a deaf person or a person with retardation, the training and qualifications of professionals working with the former must be qualitatively different from those of professionals working with individuals with one or the other disability. Naturally, the same holds true for those working with deaf and blind individuals or with individuals who have multiple disabilities.

Very little improvement has occurred since the Anderson and Stevens study was published in 1969. D'Zamko and Hampton (1985) reported that most educational programs for deaf people with retardation employ teachers of the deaf and try to upgrade their skills through inservice training. In their review of personnel preparation programs, D'Zamko and Hampton identified only one program, at Gallaudet University, that specifically trains teachers of deaf students with additional disabilities.

In a survey of 119 programs serving disabled and hearing-impaired students, Jones and Johnson (1985) found little consistency across programs. The programs reported using sixty-five different commercially available curricula, of which only six were used at four or more programs. Twenty of the programs had developed their own curricula. Of the instructional staff, 9 percent of the teachers and 14 percent of the teachers' aides were deaf. Only 8 percent of the teachers were trained specifically to work with students with additional disabilities, and 15 percent were trained in areas of special education other than deafness. The remainder were trained in education of the deaf. Some professionals in this category also received training in another type of disability.

The data presented by Schildroth and Hotto (1994) and shown in Table 5.1 are cause for concern in that the percentage of children classified as having mental retardation is three times higher in local, not integrated programs (13 percent) than in local integrated programs (7 percent). The biggest concern is whether children in local, not integrated programs are overdiagnosed as having retardation.

Blindness

With a few notable exceptions (such as the program at the Perkins Institute for the Blind), very little effort was made to identify and educate deaf-blind children before the rubella epidemic in the early 1960s. Both deafness and blindness are low-incidence conditions, and combinations of the two are relatively rare. Thus, little motivation existed to develop comprehensive programs. The impetus for the movement grew out of the aftermath of the rubella epidemic and the uncertainty over what its impact would be. The number of children who had been affected was not clear. A sharp rise in the number of children with multiple disabilities was predicted, but just how great the increase might be was uncertain. The United States Senate exhibited considerable foresight by anticipating needs and authorizing the development of comprehensive regional centers for deaf-blind children in January 1968 (Centers and Services for Deaf-Blind Children, 1969). By 1970 ten regional centers serving all fifty states and the U.S. territories had been established and funded through the Bureau of Education for the Handicapped (BEH). The immediate tasks of the centers included the following :

1. Identification of deaf-blind populations
2. Identification of resources available
3. Identification of children served
4. Identification of the population not served
5. Determination of economic cost factors
6. Development and expansion of the number of facilities, programs, and services

7. Development of meaningful inservice training programs

8. Coordination of all community resources

9. Stimulation of the development of teacher-training programs

10. Coordination of all existing federal resources to supplement the program needs of the centers (Dantona, 1970, pp. 4–6)

When the programs began their activities, far more deaf-blind children were identified than had been anticipated. According to data supplied by the BEH (Dantona, 1970), in the 1967–1968 academic year, before the establishment of regional centers for the deaf blind, a total of 256 children nationwide were receiving what might be considered adequate educational services. Of these, 100 children were enrolled in six different residential programs for the deaf blind, and the remaining 156 were in various public and private school programs for the deaf or the blind. By 1970 the surveys had located a total of 2,461 deaf-blind children. Of this number, 802 were enrolled in educational programs—more than a 300 percent increase over the 1967–1968 enrollment in a two-year period, a tremendous stride in a short period of time. Still, even in 1970 fewer than one-third (802 of 2,461) of the children were in adequate educational programs. An additional 347 children, approximately 14 percent, were in institutions for individuals with retardation. The remaining 1,349 children, accounting for more than half of those identified, were at home.

The majority of the children identified by 1970 were under nine years of age, victims of the rubella epidemic. However, more than 1,100 of the children were nine or older, and a large proportion of them had received no educational services at all.

Over the years, the regional centers for deaf-blind children worked effectively to provide educational services for these children, even though the numbers served exceeded original estimates. The ten regional centers reported 4,200 deaf-blind children in 1972 and 5,300 in 1973 (Stewart, 1974); by 1978 a total of 5,872 deaf-blind children were being served (Martin, 1978). As a whole, the efforts of the regional centers stand as an endorsement of the systematic development of regional programs—utilizing local, state, regional, and federal resources—to meet the needs of individuals suffering from severe, low-incidence disabilities. Federal support for regional deaf-blind centers decreased as the number of students dropped and then leveled off. For example, as of 1984, twenty-five state and multistate programs were serving students who were deaf-blind (Craig and Craig, 1985, p. 152), and in 1993 there were twenty-six (Stuckless, 1995, pp. 202–204).

One specific cause of deafness and blindness deserves special mention. This is Usher's syndrome, a recessive genetic condition in which an individual typically grows up deaf or hard of hearing and gradually loses his or her vision over a period of time. Visual problems may begin in childhood, but more commonly start in adolescence or adulthood with night blindness and a narrowing of the visual field. The final outcome may be complete blindness. Although the condition can be diagnosed at an early age, it typically is not. Because it may not occur until a child is older, children now in school may unknowingly have the condition. Data from the *Annual Survey of Deaf and Hard of Hearing Children and Youth* and from state surveys in

Texas and California suggest that Usher's syndrome may be more common among Franco-American populations such as the Cajun population of Louisiana.

This author has worked with college students with Usher's syndrome while their vision was deteriorating and can attest that it is a traumatic experience for those concerned, requiring intensive and sensitive preparation and training.

Special Learning and Behavioral Problems

Although the problems of diagnosing and educating deaf individuals who are classified as mentally retarded or blind are great, they pale in comparison to those of diagnosing and educating deaf individuals who have been identified as having behavioral and/or learning problems. No other field of education has been so abused by specialists, and it will probably take generations to neutralize the effects of their well-intentioned but nevertheless harmful policies. Writing about the term *minimal brain dysfunction,* Anderson (1971) described the situation as follows:

> Minimal brain dysfunction is one of fifty or more terms which describe the same set of symptoms. Experts in the field, representing various professional disciplines, have introduced terminology derived from their own professional orientations; as a result, much confusion has been created. In effect the same behavioral phenomena have been observed from different frames of reference. Terms such as perceptual cripple, interjacent child, developmental dyslexia, hyperkinetic child syndrome, and minimal brain damage have been used. . . .
>
> As communication has increased among the disciplines, there has been an increasing tendency to utilize the term learning disability rather than minimal brain dysfunction or minimal brain damage to describe the syndrome. (pp. 31–32)

Not only are different labels used for the same types of conditions, but sometimes the same label is applied to different types of conditions. For example, children have been labeled "brain damaged" on the basis of poor educational progress and not because of any medical evidence of neurological impairment. In this author's opinion, terms such as *emotional disorder, behavioral disorder,* and *learning disorder* have not been differentiated sufficiently to warrant separate treatment in this chapter.

At present, it is unclear exactly what percentage of deaf children also have educationally significant learning and behavioral problems. Given the major etiologies currently related to deafness, we might predict that a somewhat higher proportion of deaf children than hearing children suffer from additional learning and behavioral problems. Inappropriate educational and counseling procedures would be expected to add to the numbers. The numbers probably could be reduced through appropriate counseling of parents, mental health programs designed to facilitate optimal development in deaf individuals, and more effective educational programs.

Beginning in the late 1970s, the federal government provided substantial support for research in the area of special learning disabilities, including work on diagnosis and definition. The result has been some reduction in the confusion in the field, including a differentiation among some types of learning disabilities and the establishment of special curricula and materials. To date, however, these developments have had little impact on programs for the deaf, and the complexities of adequate diagnosis continue to hamper efforts to provide effective services to deaf children with additional learning or behavioral problems. Because the number of deaf children with emotional, behavioral, and learning problems is relatively small, their needs have received little attention.

Many of the issues surrounding the development of mental health programs to foster positive growth and prevent the development of severe psychological difficulties will be discussed in Chapter 8. It cannot be emphasized too strongly that many serious disturbances can be treated relatively simply when diagnosis is made and treatment is begun in the early stages. Stewart (1974) noted that, as a whole, deaf people with mental illness struggle along without help until the difficulties become so pronounced that they are institutionalized.

In terms of incidence figures, we have already reviewed Conrad's (1979) report that 25 percent of the deaf subjects in a British survey were labeled "emotionally disturbed" or "maladjusted" with no evidence for that classification. We also saw that Cohen (1980) found several studies reporting an incidence of 20 to 25 percent within the deaf population in the United States, but the basis for the classification in most cases was weak. In a study of reports for 41,109 students, Ries (1973c) counted 3,338 children labeled as having emotional and behavioral problems, 8,885 as having perceptual motor disorders, 910 as having learning disabilities, and 168 as being brain damaged. However, since the students were identified by their own educational programs, we can assume that definitions varied and that there was great overlap among categories.

Jensema and Trybus (1975) reported an overall incidence of 7.9 percent of deaf children identified as having "educationally significant emotional/behavioral problems." Differences among the definitions of the terms were highlighted by the fact that the proportion of students reported by their programs as having emotional/behavioral problems varied from 1.6 to 28 percent in schools of comparable size (p. 11). But despite the wide variation, some noteworthy trends appeared. First, the rate was much higher for males (9.8 percent) than for females (5.6 percent). Even the apparently straightforward relationship between sex and reported disturbance is highly complex, however. For example, among students born before 1954, there was essentially no difference: 5.8 percent for males and 5.6 percent for females. However, among those born in 1958–1959 and 1964–1965, the reported incidence of emotional/behavioral problems among males was 11.7 percent and 12 percent, respectively, and for females 6 percent and 6.4 percent, respectively (p. 5). There appears, then, to be much more variability among males as a function of the year of birth, although the figures are highest in the same periods (1958–1959 and 1964–1965) for both groups. Since both periods represent aftermaths of rubella epidemics, it is not surprising to find that maternal rubella is the etiology most frequently associated with reported emotional/behavioral problems, particularly among males, with a reported incidence of 13.9 percent (p. 9).

Craig and Craig (1985) found a total of 3,044 children labeled "learning disabled" and 1,237 labeled "socially/emotionally disturbed" in programs for the deaf—6.1

and 2.5 percent of the total group, respectively. The low reported incidence of emotional problems (2.5 percent) relative to other studies is striking, especially in contrast to the 7.9 percent reported by Jensema and Trybus (1975). For 1993–1994, Table 5.2 lists 4,035 children classified as having specific learning disabilities and 1,834 with emotional/behavior problems—8.9 and 4.0 percent of the total group, respectively. Why the reported percentages increased in a ten-year period is not clear.

In a survey of strategies used to identify deaf and hard-of-hearing with learning disabilities students, Powers, Elliot, and Funderburg (1987) reported that two-thirds of responding programs cited teacher observation as the most common procedure. Forty-nine percent of the respondents reported that no specific criteria were used and a paucity of assessment instruments limited both identification and instruction.

Since that time, aided somewhat by the passage of PL 101–476, the Individuals with Disabilities Education Act of 1990 (IDEA), the situation has improved to some extent. IDEA has promulgated the following basic definition of *learning disabilities:*

> The term "children with specific learning disabilities" means those children who have a disorder in one or more of the basic psychological processes involved in understanding or in using language, spoken or written, which disorder may manifest itself in imperfect ability to listen, think, speak, read, write, spell, or do mathematical calculations. Such disorders include such conditions as perceptual disabilities, brain injury, minimal brain dysfunction, dyslexia, and developmental aphasia.

Papinger and Sikora (1990) have advocated an interdisciplinary diagnostic approach that includes teacher observation, standardized assessment procedures, interpretation, and subsequent recommendations. The proposed sequence follows assessment of visual, auditory, and tactile skills, followed by processing and memory abilities. In a somewhat more complete formulation, Morgan and Vernon (1994) have recommended a battery of tests as a guide for diagnosing learning disabilities in deaf and hard-of-hearing individuals. The recommendations include a thorough case history, an educational history, two measures of intellectual functioning, a measure of academic achievement, neuropsychological screening, assessment of behavioral functioning, audiological and visual testing, and assessment of language and communication skills.

Since major causes of deafness such as prematurity, meningitis, CMV, and genetic predisposition are also primary etiologies of neurological impairment, it is generally accepted that the incidence of learning disabilities is greater among deaf and hard-of-hearing individuals than in the general population (Morgan and Vernon, 1994; Rowell, 1987). Appropriate diagnosis and treatment are only at the beginning stages.

Teacher Morale

One study of teacher morale in a program for deaf and hard-of-hearing children with additional disabilities has special potential significance because of its positive implications. Stedt and Palermo (1983) administered the Purdue Teacher Opinionnaire to forty-six teachers of the deaf and twenty-three teachers of children with multiple disabilities at the California School for the Deaf at Riverside. The responses of teachers of both groups were within the same range as those of teachers of hearing children. Teachers working with children with multiple disabilities had significantly better morale than teachers in the other groups. The most positive factors were teacher rapport with the principal, rapport with other teachers, teaching load, facilities and services, and community expectations. Stedt and Palermo cautioned against generalizing from one study at one school, but they suggested that the characteristics of the teachers and administrative support, rather than the nature of the children taught, are responsible for high morale. They concluded that morale need not be a problem among teachers of deaf students or students with additional disabilities and that the administration of a school plays a vital role in teacher morale.

Modes of Communication

In their survey of programs, Jones and Johnson (1985) noted that eighty-five of the ninety-three respondents reported the use of some form of manual communication, and twenty programs reported employing American Sign Language (ASL). The heavy reliance on manual communication is understandable and is consistent with other findings. However, it is doubtful that ASL was used in its complete language form with most of the children. Most such children would be unable to deal with the expressive and receptive complexities of ASL, and most hearing teachers are not familiar enough with ASL to use it in instruction. It is likely that most programs reporting the use of ASL with MHHI (multihandicapped hearing impaired) children actually used some sign system that draws much of its vocabulary from ASL but is a great deal simpler.

One of the most powerful developments in language intervention and communication training has been the use of nonspeech communication systems, including manual communication (Moores, 1979a), graphic systems (Clark, 1977), and expressive communication aids (McDonald, 1979). Given the variability of the population under consideration, the goals of language and communication training may be quite diverse for different groups. For some children, full language acquisition may be a feasible goal; for others, it may not. Children in the former group may be taught intermediate skills necessary to the natural acquisition of language. The latter group may require setting limited goals; communication skills necessary for everyday functioning and based on the child's needs and interests may have to be taught as ends in themselves.

As a rule, the more severe the set of conditions, the less natural the processes of language acquisition and development of communication skills. The first step is to introduce specific teaching and training techniques to develop carefully defined skills that have been identified as necessary or desirable for everyday functioning. In many cases, goals may be limited. For example, rather than attempting to provide

© Daemmrich/Stock Boston

Communication between deaf individuals.

all children with tools with which they may acquire language primarily through their own efforts, in some cases we may have to strive for the development of functional communication adequacy that is restricted to a narrow set of circumstances. The means used to achieve such a restricted functional adequacy may differ significantly from the means we would employ to foster linguistic mastery in a deaf child with no other disabilities.

In addition to vocal and manual communication, deaf children with multiple disabilities can be exposed to a wide range of input and output systems such as language boards and various nonspeech symbol systems, including Rebus (Clark and Woodcock, 1977), Bliss Symbols (Bliss, 1965; McDonald, 1979) and Non-Slip (Carrier, 1974, 1976). The Rebus system uses ideographic (concept-based) symbols to initiate reading instruction and can be used with a variety of children exhibiting a wide range of communication difficulties. It has also been used with children without disabilities as a mechanism for developing prereading skills while phasing in traditional orthography. The Clark Early Language Program (Clark and Moores, 1980) was developed using speech, a manual mode (signs from ASL), and Rebus symbols. It was field-tested with deaf children, children with mental retardation, and children with developmental delays. Indications are that deaf children with no other disabilities move through it quite rapidly and may not need the structure and sequence, but it is appropriate for many children with additional involvements.

The Bliss System (Clark and Woodcock, 1977) is probably used more than any other nonspeech system at present. Like the Rebus symbols, the Bliss symbols are ideographic, or concept based, but they tend to show less influence of written English. The Non-Speech Language Initiation Program (Non-Slip), developed by Carrier (1974, 1976), is based on many of the principles developed by Premack (1970, 1971) in his research on the teaching of communication systems to chimpanzees. The Non-Slip system, which uses plastic chips as symbols, is designed to teach the child a set of conceptual skills necessary for the acquisition of functional linguistic communication. Using the plastic chips as language constituents, the child may select and arrange units in different ways to convey appropriate messages. The program was developed under the assumption that for many children the complexity of the speech system interferes with language acquisition (Schiefelbusch, Ruder, and Bricker, 1976). Unlike the Rebus and Bliss systems, which use concept-based symbols, the Non-Slip symbols are arbitrary; that is, they do not use ideographics to represent objects.

The results to date suggest that many children who do not exhibit any language or communication ability when vocal responses are required can develop at least some demonstrable expressive and receptive skills when provided with symbols (Moores, 1982). However, progress is usually tedious, and success is limited. The nature of the communication system should depend on the nature of the child's deficits and on the characteristics of the impairments. An alternative communication system might be introduced prior to, in coordination with, or independently of the vocal system, depending on the individual's characteristics and progress. There are several reasons for selecting a nonvocal system:

- An alternative system may be used as part of a diagnostic procedure to determine patterns of functioning. The introduction of the system may be the first step in a clinical program that may later be generalized to other systems or environments.
- A system may be the most effective means for providing factual information, developing a concept, and developing understanding of a relationship.
- A system may provide the individual with a mechanism for expressing needs.
- A system may provide a basis for the establishment of functional communication processes. (Moores, 1979a)

Mild Impairments

One theme emphasized throughout this book is that many deaf children, for a number of reasons, experience impairments and disabilities in addition to deafness.

The scant evidence available suggests that (1) deaf children may have more additional impairments than hearing children and (2) deaf children receive appropriate treatment less frequently, even when their difficulties could be eliminated or ameliorated. Evidence from investigations of the incidence of visual defects provides a clear example of the potential for damage to deaf children when "mild" impairments are not diagnosed and remediated. Presumably, the same would be true for areas other than vision, but unfortunately too little information exists to test this assumption.

Deafness and Vision

In an editorial comment on the importance of vision, McCay Vernon (1977, p. 4) wrote:

> Obviously, sight is a thousand times more important to those who are deaf than to any other group of people. Despite this fact, and despite the threat to vision posed by rubella, Usher's Syndrome, complications of Rh factor, meningitis, and other leading causes of deafness, few educational or rehabilitation facilities and few physicians give adequate attention to visual screening of those with hearing implants. . . .

Given the importance of vision to a deaf child, diagnosis of any type of visual impairment is crucial. The evidence suggests that the deaf population has a relatively high incidence of visual impairment. Braly (1938), Stockwell (1952), and Lawson and Myklebust (1970) reported up to twice as many visual defects among deaf children as among children with normal hearing. Frey and Krause (1971) noted that the prevalence of colorblindness among deaf children was more than twice that among hearing children.

A greater prevalence of colorblindness or a higher incidence of visual defects is not necessarily a cause for alarm. Millions of people with normal hearing are colorblind to varying degrees, but they are not hampered greatly in their everyday functioning. Even more people have a wide range of visual defects, the majority of which are correctable to some extent.

Because the cochlea and retina are formed at the same developmental stage of the embryo, it is not surprising that both hearing and vision frequently show impairment. What is shocking is the evidence that many deaf children have correctable visual defects that have never been diagnosed. Misdiagnosing a deaf child with a correctable visual defect as having a learning disability, mental retardation, distractability, or minimal brain damage is obviously a grave concern and may even constitute a self-fulfilling prophecy. Such a misdiagnosis can destroy a life.

At a program for the deaf, Suchman (1968) tested 103 deaf children ages four to twelve years, nine months. Of this group, forty-three had normal vision and sixty had some visual abnormality. The relatively high incidence of vision problems is consistent with findings of other studies. The disturbing findings relate to diagnosis and treatment. The sixty children identified as having visual impairments constituted 58 percent of the total sample. Of these children, fifty-four, or 90 percent, had visual impairments that medical treatment could have corrected. To the best of the examiner's knowledge, only seven children had received visual correction; the remaining forty-seven with treatable visual defects had never been diagnosed. Of the twenty-five children without other visual problems, who simply had less than normal visual acuity, ranging from 20–30 to 20–70, only one had glasses. The visual acuity defects of the other twenty-four apparently had never been observed!

Obviously, regular and complete physical examinations of deaf children should be mandatory, especially in the area of vision. In many cases, educators will have to convince other professionals that deaf children can be tested efficiently in all areas. Suchman (1968) reported that the ophthalmologists who participated in her study admitted to having misconceptions regarding the feasibility of testing deaf children. After their experiences, they were both surprised and pleased at the ease of testing.

Given the evidence of high rates of visual impairments as far back as Braly (1938) and the ease of testing reported by Suchman (1968), it is disheartening to report a lack of movement over the years to address the problem. Anderson (1971), Vernon and Hicks (1980), and Wolff and Brown (1987) all reported high rates of visual impairment in the deaf and hard-of-hearing population.

Because deaf and hard-of-hearing children are forced to rely on the visual channel for a significant amount of information, the presence of visual defects has enormous implications for development. The lack of early identification and treatment to date is inexcusable.

One exception to this dismal picture is work being done at the National Technical Institute for the Deaf (NTID) Eye and Ear Clinic, which has conducted research on more than 3,000 deaf students since its inception in 1984 (Johnson, 1999). Johnson reports that approximately 55 percent of all entering students at NTID each year have some type of visual anomaly, many of which are directly connected to an etiology of deafness, and are often in need of professional intervention and observation. He concludes that visual problems occur more than twice as often among the deaf than in the general population.

Since NTID students constitute a select population, incidence figures for the general young deaf population may be even higher. The implications are twofold. First, greater attention should be paid to ensuring proper vision for deaf students. Second, it is possible that many deaf students with visual problems may be misclassified as retarded, learning disabled, or with attention deficit disorder, or may engage in inappropriate behavior and be categorized as evincing such behavior.

Training for Academically Low-Achieving Adults

A number of demonstration projects have investigated the feasibility of serving low-achieving school leavers in existing rehabilitation facilities. Lawrence and Vescovi (1967) reported on a program that served 126 deaf clients at the Morgan Memorial Hospital in Boston over a two-year period. Communication difficulties were the biggest problem for clients, and it was concluded that a knowledge of manual communication was imperative for staff members—an interesting conclusion given the fact that at that time, not one school program for the deaf in Massachusetts allowed manual communication. Of the clients, 40 percent achieved full-time employment and an additional 20 percent enrolled in advanced training courses.

In a five-year project conducted by the St. Louis Jewish Vocational Service (Hurwitz, 1971), a total of 265 deaf clients received training in prevocational adjustment and vocational skills. Before training, 85 percent of the clients were financially dependent. A follow-up study indicated that this figure dropped to 24 percent after training. Follow-up also revealed that 64 percent of a random sample were employed, the largest number in semiskilled and unskilled occupations and a relatively small percentage in sheltered workshops.

The Chicago Jewish Vocational Service (CJVS) developed a program of counseling, training, and referral that served 710 clients over a five-year period (CJVS Project, 1972). Follow-up revealed that one-half of the clients who had received substantial services (approximately five hundred) were employed, and an additional 15 percent were in advanced training.

Blake (1970) reported on a project, conducted from 1966 to 1968 by the Hot Springs (Arkansas) Rehabilitation Center that provided services to 131 deaf clients. Despite a dropout rate of 38 percent, follow-up investigations revealed that 41 percent of all clients were employed full time. It was estimated that 85 percent of all clients received some observable benefit from their training.

The results of these four projects suggest that at least one-half of low-achieving deaf adults can be rehabilitated with a core program of vocational and social services, but a substantial number require more extensive services (Rice, 1973, p. 8).

From 1968 to 1973, a project that grew out of the pilot project summarized by Blake (1970) was conducted at the Hot Springs Rehabilitation Center to provide comprehensive medical, social, psychological, and vocational services to low-achieving deaf adults (Rice, 1973). The center provided extensive services to 212 deaf individuals from twenty-nine states, the District of Columbia, and the Virgin Islands. Most clients were within the normal range of intelligence. The most commonly noted problem was impoverished communication (Stewart, 1971). Motivation tended to be low, and clients frequently exhibited inappropriate, ineffective, and impulsive behavior. Stewart noted that such behavior apparently had been accepted in the school programs the students had attended and therefore recommended a restructuring of such programs. Despite a past history of academic failure, poor communication, and low motivation, 55 percent of the clients served by the center completed training. The most common areas of training were printing and laundry work. Rice (1973) reported that more than 60 percent of the clients were gainfully employed as a result of the training they received. He noted that although the center served clients from more than half of the states, the majority were from Arkansas and adjacent states. He concluded that to serve low-achieving adult deaf clients effectively, comprehensive rehabilitation services for the deaf should be provided on a regional basis.

At the present time, up-to-date information on recent school leavers, especially those with an etiology of rubella, is lacking. Less information on low-achieving school leavers is available now than in the 1970s, and the situation may become critical. For the first time, the majority of deaf students leaving schools in the United States have been enrolled in public school programs. It appears that, for the most part, the public schools have failed to develop the working relationships with local and state rehabilitation agencies that evolved along with residential schools for the deaf over a period of decades. Although little information is available on the role of counseling services, we may speculate that large numbers of low-achieving students leaving public schools will not be guided to the appropriate supporting agencies and services.

Summary

Examination of the situations of deaf individuals who have additional conditions leads to some grim conclusions. First, evidence exists that large numbers of deaf individuals are incorrectly classified as having mental retardation, learning disabilities, brain damage, and so forth. Frequently, the classification is based on factors such as poor communication skills and low academic achievement, conditions that would more appropriately be attributed to poor training and inadequate education. Evidence also exists that many deaf individuals suffer from minor, easily correctable visual defects. Inadequate or nonexistent diagnostic procedures place additional burdens on deaf individuals. Due to a lack of identification procedures for mild conditions, a substantial number of deaf students with additional conditions such as learning disabilities may remain undiagnosed.

The presence of a condition in addition to deafness does not merely add to an individual's problems; it compounds them exponentially. Thus experience and training in work with the deaf and with the blind does not prepare one to deal with deaf-blind individuals. Their special needs are qualitatively different and demand skills that training in the separate areas of deafness and blindness does not provide.

With only a few exceptions, teacher training programs do not train people to work with deaf individuals with additional conditions. The majority of teachers of deaf children with mental retardation not only are trained inadequately but would also prefer not to teach such children. However, the morale of teachers of deaf children with additional conditions can be quite high given appropriate resources and administrative support.

Curriculum methods and materials specifically designed for deaf children with additional disabilities are needed. More adequate counseling techniques must be developed to help the parents of these children and to facilitate optimal development of deaf children.

Prevention programs can and should be developed to reduce the number of deaf individuals with additional conditions. These would include activities in such diverse areas as basic research on medical and psychological causes, development and initiation of mental health curricula for deaf students, genetic counseling, widespread vaccination programs, and counseling for parents. Last, but far from least, educational programs for deaf children, from preschool to postsecondary levels, must be improved. This step alone would probably reduce the incidence of multiple conditions among deaf individuals.

6

Families with Deaf Members: Interpersonal Relations from Diagnosis to Adulthood

Introduction

Unquestionably, the family has always been of primary importance in the social, emotional, linguistic, and cognitive development of deaf children, even when the majority of deaf children spend the entire school year, with only perhaps a winter and spring break, at a residential school. During the school year, the schools, of necessity, have functional and in loco parentis (in place of parents) duties and have assumed responsibility for moral training, health care, and even religious instruction. Over the past two generations, the role of parents has grown for families with deaf children because of federal regulations and changing school attendance patterns. As we have learned, most deaf children now commute to school on a daily basis, and children residing in residential schools typically go home on weekends or twice a month. Because parents are important throughout the educational process, it might be possible to consider families within the context of related chapters. However, it seems preferable to consider families as a separate subject, even at the risk of overlapping with other sections.

As we know, most deaf children have hearing parents. More than 90 percent of the time, a deaf child is born into a family in which both the mother and the father are hearing and have had little exposure to deaf individuals. Most commonly, deafness is not present among siblings, grandparents, cousins, or other members of the extended family. Because of this phenomenon, most professionals in the field tend to think in terms of "a deaf child in a hearing family." This concept is inaccurate and potentially harmful. It implies that the child is different and is an outsider rather than a completely integrated part of the family constellation. Actually, once a deaf child enters a family, a "hearing" family no longer exists; by definition, it is now a family with both deaf and hearing members. The process is not just the simple integration of the child into an existing structure. The birth of any child, whether hearing or deaf, changes a family in fundamental ways. The entry of a deaf child into a family with hearing parents represents an additional element, but the basic principles of growth and development are the same.

Although child development researchers and other professionals have traditionally acknowledged the importance of the family as a whole, many intervention programs have been either child centered or parent centered, with the primary focus on the mother. In the field of deafness, Greenberg (1983) reported that a family-oriented approach resulted in more effective communication, lower stress, and better interactions in families with deaf children. Since that time, there has been a growing focus on a "family-centered" approach, which has evolved into the concept of *family-systems theory* (Roush and McWilliam, 1994). Quite simply, a deaf child is an integral member of a complex system—a family—and anything that affects one member of the family affects all members. In essence, the family represents the first social system to which most children belong, and for these children the family is the first and most important means of socialization and enculturation. Thus, among other things, clear and consistent communication is mandatory.

Fortunately, federal legislation and professional awareness have come to focus on the importance of the family for children with disabilities. A brief review of the relevant federal legislation since 1975 illustrates this development. As we have seen, Public Law 94–142, the Education of All Handicapped Children Act of 1975, mandated a free, appropriate public education for all children with disabilities over age five and stipulated that each child must have an individualized educational plan (IEP). In 1986, the law was reauthorized as Public Law 99–457 and mandated services to children from three to five years of age. PL 99–457 also provided support to states for provision of services to children below age three and their families. However, it did not require state participation in this aspect of the law. PL 99–457 called for an individualized family service plan (IFSP), instead of an IEP, for infants and their families, and in this way changed the focus to the family, at least for very young children. In 1990 the law was reauthorized as PL 101–476, the Individuals with Disabilities Education Act (IDEA). The latest modification to date occurred in 1997.

The legislation reveals three major changes in emphasis since 1975. The first was a movement away from the concept of *handicap* per se toward thinking in terms of disability. The second was the expansion of the law to include children of younger ages, with the family system as the focus. The third was the continual lowering of the age of eligibility for services from time of birth, or time of identification. McConigel (1994) argues that the IFSP is the core of the recent family-centered approaches to early interventions for children and their families; it ensures "that their strengths will be recognized and built on, their beliefs and values will be respected, that their choices will be honored, and that their hopes and aspirations will be encouraged and enabled" (p. 1).

In most cases, the family into which a deaf child is born and the family to which he or she belongs as an adult differ significantly. In childhood there is a deaf child–hearing parents relationship, and in adulthood there is a deaf parent–hearing child relationship. In the more than 90 percent of families of deaf children in which parents are hearing, the parents typically have had no experience in interacting with deaf individuals and have no firsthand knowledge of deafness. When the deaf child matures into adulthood and marries, which a majority do, the spouse is usually deaf as well. The evidence suggests that the percentage of deaf people who marry other deaf people is very high (Reagan, 1990). As we saw in Chapter 4, studies in the United States in the nineteenth and twentieth centuries have consistently shown that most of the children of deaf parents are hearing.

In some ways, deaf Americans may be said to constitute an identifiable ethnic group given their distinct language, American Sign Language (ASL), and their tendency toward in-group marriage (Reagan, 1985, 1990). Of course, not all deaf Americans use ASL or marry other deaf Americans, just as not all Hispanic-Americans speak Spanish or marry other Hispanic-Americans. Nevertheless, marriage patterns and language usage may be defining characteristics of an ethnic group in general. This ethnolinguistic identification is mitigated by the fact that most or all relatives across three or more generations may be hearing, with the exception of the spouse. The necessity for close relationships with hearing relatives within the family circle suggests that presently accepted definitions of ethnicity and minority status are too simplistic to capture the complexities of the real-life situation of deaf Americans (Reagan, 1990).

As we saw in Chapter 1, deaf children are born into every cultural situation in the United States. Families vary by race, ethnic identification, socioeconomic status, home language, parental hearing status, and myriad other characteristics. Each family is thus unique, as is its perception of disability.

The manner in which any person develops into a socialized member of a society is a complex process that involves ongoing interaction with a wide range of individuals and situations. In our society, the nuclear family unit—a mother, a father, and children—traditionally has been considered the primary socializing unit for the young child. However, this "norm" does not reflect the reality of many family situations. Many children are raised by single parents, usually the mother, sometimes with the help of extended family members and sometimes not. To some extent, this situation has always existed. At the beginning of the twentieth century, life expectancy for both men and women was around fifty years, and one or both parents often died before all of the children had grown to maturity. Today single parenthood may be due more frequently to divorce or to the parents never marrying, but the lack of two parents in the home per se is not a new phenomenon. In a pluralistic culture such as ours, the key is to be sensitive to the fact that any individualized family service plan must take tremendous diversity into account.

The role of the family is continually evolving. Increases in life expectancy are improving the chances that both parents will live until their children reach adulthood. At the same time, more children are being raised either by a single parent or in a family in which one parent is not the biological father or mother. The proportion of single-parent families in which fathers have sole responsibility for child care will probably continue to rise. Thus, although this chapter deals primarily with the concept of a nuclear family, readers are again cautioned to remember that numerous variations on the traditional model exist. Even within the traditional model, changes are occurring. Birthrates have been falling for generations. Families with six or more children are no longer common, suggesting that children may receive more individual attention. This development, however, is offset by the increasing number of mothers of even young children entering the labor market.

Changes in the role of the family have tremendous implications for early education programs for the deaf. Many programs were established in the 1960s under federal support with the concept of mother-as-teacher. In many cases, the mother was required to come to a school or clinic several times a week for training with her child, under the supervision of a speech/language pathologist or a teacher of the deaf. Usually, the training involved interacting with the child in a homelike setting, with many activities centered around the kitchen.

The approach was satisfactory for families in which the father worked, the mother stayed home, and transportation to and from the training facility was available. It was never viable for poor families that lacked access to transportation. With the increase in single-parent families and families in which both parents work, the model became even less feasible. Citing her experiences as the parent of a deaf child, Frederickson (1985) provided a strong critique of such a program from a feminist perspective. Beginning with PL 99–457, many early intervention programs now have home visitation components; one or more professionals go into the home to provide support, thus meeting the needs of a wider variety of families.

Nuclear family units may be viewed as organisms with relatively uniform life cycles consisting of identifiable periods of growth, change, and decline. Typically, these family units may be viewed as moving from the original dyadic unit—the husband and wife alone—through the bearing of children, the education of children, and the preparation of adolescents and young adults for independent existence. Finally, the process comes full circle, ending with the aging family, in which the original family members—the husband and wife—once again constitute the nuclear family unit.

The following family stages, based on Duvall's (1970) criteria, have been identified for the purposes of this chapter:

1. The childless married couple
2. The childbearing family
3. The family with preschool children
4. The family with school-age children
5. The family with adolescent children
6. The family launching young adults
7. The aging family

When a family moves from one stage to another, the roles and functions of its members are subject to change. Periods of change bring greater tension and an increased possibility of role conflict and family disintegration. Available evidence suggests that the presence of a child with a disability tends to exacerbate normal family strains and frequently hinders a smooth transition from one stage to another. In this chapter, we will examine what is known about the dynamics of families with a child who has a disability and what this information implies about the conditions necessary for the sound development and functioning of families with one or more deaf children.

To provide a framework from which to study families and their individual members, we will make the following assumptions:

1. Family behavior is the result of family members' past experiences incorporated into the present, as well as their goals and expectations for the future.

2. Families develop and change over time in a similar and consistent fashion.

3. Individuals initiate actions as a result of maturational and social development as well as in reaction to environmental pressures.

4. The family and its members must perform time-specific tasks set by associations in the broader society as well as those tasks they set for themselves.

5. The individual in a social setting is the basic autonomous unit. (Aldous, 1969, p. 709)

Although all of these assumptions are important, the implications of the first assumption are predominant and should constantly be borne in mind. If family behavior is a result of past experience and future expectations of family members, the presence of a deaf child is likely to be accompanied by at least some trauma because (1) most parents of deaf children have had minimal prior exposure to deafness and (2) the presence of a deaf child raises uncertainty and calls into question goals and expectations about the future, not only for the deaf child but also for the mother, father, and siblings.

Schlesinger (1978), drawing on the work of Erikson (1963, 1964, 1968, 1969), stated that the whole life cycle can be seen as an integrated psychological development in a series of critical stages. Successful negotiation of each stage enables the individual to grow psychologically and to prepare for the next stage. Failure at any level impedes the individual's development at all subsequent states. Schlesinger argued that professionals should concentrate on creating mechanisms that allow deaf children to meet the challenges of developing successfully through all critical stages of the life cycle.

It is imperative that professionals study the impact of deafness on the family as well as on the child (Moores, 1995a). Much more than just a loss of hearing is involved. The family's whole world changes, and feelings of guilt, confusion, and helplessness are both common and natural. Professionals must develop ways to deal effectively with these feelings if the whole family is to be helped.

In this context, it is of limited benefit to consider either the deaf child or the family as a separate entity. The reciprocal nature of parent-child and child-child interactions cannot be overemphasized. The deaf child is a member of a social group and as such exerts considerable influence on the role and function of each member of the group. In turn, as a participating member, the deaf child is influenced by the group as a whole and by its individual members. We cannot ignore the complex interactions operative in the overall family constellation if we are to gain insight into the developmental process as it involves deaf children and their families.

The Impact of a Deaf Child on a Family

For most families, the greatest adjustment usually involves moving from the childless married couple dyad into the childbearing family stage. Parents typically remember the period before childbearing as the happiest time of their marriage (Hill et al., 1970). The immediate impact of the first child is to disrupt previous family routines and modify parents' values. Frequently, the family had two sources of income in the childless stage and enjoyed relative freedom of movement. The birth of the first child may remove the wife/mother from the labor market, at least temporarily, and place her in a more dependent financial position relative to the husband/father. Her freedom of movement is constrained, and the demands of motherhood are both physically and emotionally tiring. A husband who for the first time faces sole responsibility for the financial well-being of the family may have reservations about his ability to function as provider. Both husband and wife may have some difficulty accepting the fact that the child is receiving a great deal of attention that previously was devoted to the spouse.

Most families adjust adequately to the birth of the first child, and the family enters a new stage of functioning. The birth of additional children usually is perceived as less traumatic than that of the first child. Since changes in role and function are the major sources of the stress that the birth of a child brings, it is logical to assume that the strain increases when the child is identified as being deaf. Effects of the strain, in turn, will affect the child. The deaf child presents the family with specific problems that may result in shame, guilt, parental recriminations, and restricted communication if adequate counseling is not received.

An excellent resource for parents of deaf children is a book entitled *Can't Your Child Hear?*, written specifically for deaf parents by Freeman, Boese, and Carbin (1981). The text was developed with the help of professionals in areas related to deafness; deaf individuals and parents of deaf children around the world also contributed. The book contains concise information on such topics as causes of deafness, the process of diagnosis, and educational options and issues related to the establishment of communication at an early age. All topics are addressed within the context of the needs of deaf children and their families.

Greenberg and Kusché (1993) have developed the PATHS curriculum, a school-based mental health program that can be integrated into a family orientation. This approach is treated in Chapter 8.

Periods of Stress

Although there is great variation, families appear to go through four periods of stress during their deaf child's development:

1. The process of identification of hearing loss
2. Entrance into the school situation
3. Beginning adolescence
4. Early adulthood (Moores, 1973, p. 115)

These periods may be perceived as corresponding to Duvall's (1970) family stages 3 through 6.

Identification of Hearing Loss

The final identification of deafness generally represents the culmination of a long, emotionally draining process. Typically, the mother has known for some time that something is wrong with the child, but she is not exactly sure what it is. Frequently, a pediatrician has offered assurances that the mother is overly concerned and that the child is merely a "late bloomer" (Meadow-Orlans, 1967, 1990).

In studying deaf children and their families in British Columbia, Freeman (1977) reported an average time lag of about a year between the first parental suspicion and the professional confirmation of a hearing loss. About one-third of the physicians refused to refer the parents to a specialist. Meadow (1967) reported similar findings in California; more than 60 percent of the parents had at least four medical consultations before a diagnosis was made. One-third of the parents stated that the first doctor consulted assured them the child was not deaf.

Despite the increased interest in early identification and service, as exemplified in PL 99–457 and subsequent legislation, identification of hearing loss still commonly occurs much later than it should. The Joint Committee on Infant Hearing (1991) has recommended that diagnosis of hearing loss and initiation of treatment be under way by the time a child is six months of age. As noted by Diefendorf and Weber (1994) and documented in Chapter 10 which discusses early intervention programs, the age of diagnosis and the implementation of services far exceed this goal. The result is months of unnecessary uncertainty and frustration for parents, other family members, and especially the deaf child.

At first, the final diagnosis may bring a feeling of relief—at least the parents now know what is wrong—but this feeling is quickly followed by overwhelming

GALLAUDET UNIVERSITY DEPARTMENT OF PUBLICATIONS AND PRODUCTION

Effective parent/child communication.

worries. Parents may wonder whose fault it is, the father's or the mother's. Even today, some interpret a child's deafness as God's way of punishing the parents for past sins.

On a somewhat different plane, other practical considerations quickly emerge. Because the parents lack knowledge about deafness, they may question whether the child will ever become self-sufficient and assume a productive role in society. They may assume the child will be a lifelong burden, draining the family's emotional and financial resources. The immediate financial problem faced by families with young deaf children should not be minimized. Medical care, consultations, and the almost mandatory immediate fitting of the child with a hearing aid, which may cost hundreds of dollars, can quickly erode a young family's financial resources. Parents must react to and cope with the shock right away. The child needs their attention, and usually no professionals are available to help them work through their grief.

Finally, reflecting on their desire for the child to be an idealized extension of themselves, parents ask, "Will our child be normal? Above all, will speech be possible?" Often it is at this point that professionals first fail deaf children and their families. If parents receive inaccurate and misleading advice at this time, the negative effects may never be overcome. It is only natural for parents to think that the basic problem of the deaf child is an inability to speak, when in reality it is an inability to hear. Professionals are responsible for ensuring, as gently but firmly as possible, that parents understand this fact.

The following comment comes from a deaf individual who fathered two deaf children and had been a professional in the area of deafness for twenty years:

> A disconcerting trend in special education today is what I feel is a deliberate "normalization" of the deaf person. The implicit goal is to eliminate differences and thereby eliminate discrimination. To my mind this is another attempt toward encouraging the denial of deafness or disability. It is not going to help the total person if normalization means infringement upon self-identity and whatever cultural pride may be derived from the deaf subculture. Blacks, Jews, and Hispanics are not told to forget their color, religion, or ethnic connections. So why should children with special needs be encouraged to forget or deny their specific disabilities? (Thompson, Thompson, and Murphy, 1979, p. 349)

Another fact of life that is difficult for parents to accept is the irreversibility of deafness (Meadow, 1968). For most deaf children no cures exist, and none are projected over the foreseeable future. Parents, however, are not aware of this fact. Once the deafness has been diagnosed, they expect remedial medical treatment. Raised in a society that tends to regard differentness as a "disease," parents naturally assume that deafness can be treated in much the same way as appendicitis, tonsillitis, pneumonia, or the common cold—surely there must be some medicine or surgical technique to help the child. The realization that the child and the family must prepare for a lifetime of deafness requires a great deal of adjustment.

Parents who never work through the trauma to achieve a mature acceptance of deafness are forced to assume a double burden of unacknowledged (and therefore unrelieved) grief and pretense. For some, the word *deafness* itself is anathema and is replaced by more euphemistic terms such as *auditorily handicapped, hearing handicapped,* and *soft of hearing.* Schlesinger (1992) noted that some parents abhor any suggestion of difference between a hearing child and a deaf child. They may forgo the use of hearing aids and prohibit their deaf children from using gestures and vocalizing.

Some organizations in the field of deafness function primarily to facilitate the development of speech in deaf children. This is a commendable undertaking, but certainly not the only, or even the most important, goal for young children. Fixation on speaking alone may prevent parents from working through their grief to the mature acceptance of deafness that is a prerequisite for adequate psychological and social development. Without such acceptance, parents will fail to develop healthy mechanisms to cope with the outer reality of bringing up a child with a hearing loss and the inner reality of desiring a normal child.

As they work through the outer and inner realities of having a deaf child, most parents feel considerable ambivalence. Family equilibrium cannot be achieved in a vacuum. Parents cannot plan for the needs of one member of the family without considering the needs of the family as a whole. For example, should the entire family move to a community that has a school or program for the deaf child? In a multichild family, concentrating on one child alone is disruptive. In research on families with children with mental retardation, Farber (1957) reported that nonretarded sisters are frequently expected to assume responsibilities for the sibling with the disability that they are not prepared to handle. This may lead to personality problems for these children. According to Powell and Galladino (1993), results of more recent work have been mixed. McHale and Gamble (1989) reported that both older sisters and older brothers of children with mental retardation showed somewhat poorer adjustment than did siblings of children without retardation. Grossman (1972) reported that some college students without disabilities felt guilty about being in good health but neglected because of their parents' preoccupation with the sibling with a disability. They also expressed concerns about their own future children. On the other hand, Lobato (1990) found that extra caregiving responsibilities do not necessarily lead to negative adjustment. Unfortunately, we do not have comparable data on hearing siblings of deaf children, but we should be aware of the potential for disruption.

Because the presence of a child with a disability can create additional stress on the family, many professionals have assumed that separation and divorce are more common among parents of deaf children. However, Freeman, Malkin, and Hastings (1975) reported no differences in divorce rates between families with deaf children and those with no deaf children.

The effects of deafness or of communication limitations arising from deafness have an early and profound impact on families and on parent-child communication. Schlesinger and Meadow (1971, 1972a) noted that compared to mothers of young hearing children, hearing mothers of young deaf children were rated as being more controlling, more intrusive, more didactic, less flexible, and less approving or encouraging. Goss (1970) found that mothers of deaf children were less likely to show verbal antagonism. Collins (1969) reported that 40 percent of the behavior of mothers of preschool deaf children was "directing." Thirteen of the sixteen mothers in his study could communicate with their children only about things or events that were present in time and/or space. Gregory (1976) noted that mothers made more concessions to their deaf children than to hearing siblings and that the siblings of deaf children reported more feelings of jealousy than did siblings of children with normal hearing.

Schlesinger and Meadow (1972a) noted that parents of deaf children reported a constant concern about whether they were being overprotective or underprotective. These parents used a narrower range of discipline techniques, with greater reliance on spanking, and exhibited more frustration with respect to their children. Meadow (1980) concluded that the protectiveness most families exhibit toward their deaf children probably inhibits the children's social development.

In some cases, what appears to be overprotective concern on the part of parents may be a reaction to a history of health problems. Evidence (Freeman, 1977; Freeman, Boese, and Carbin, 1981) suggests that deaf children have a higher rate of illness and hospitalization than hearing children, particularly in the first two years of life. This situation may result from a number of factors, including health problems related to the cause of deafness and heightened sensitivity of parents and physicians to the deaf child's physical well-being.

An issue that has received little or no consideration in the literature is the role of the extended family unit in times of stress. Hill et al. (1970, p. 304) reported that for help in times of trouble families turn predominantly to the vertical kinship network of three generations (child-parent-grandparent) rather than to the horizontal networks of siblings and cousins, of friends and neighbors, and of helping agencies. Each generation turns to the network for help in solving problems it cannot solve itself. It would be logical to assume, then, that the occurrence of a disability would lead to an increase in vertical, or cross-generation, involvement. Although little hard evidence is available in this area, Vernon and Andrews (1990) commented on the influence of grandparents on families with deaf children. They noted that mothers who were frustrated by their children's inability to communicate often refrained from using manual communication because of grandparents' opposition. If possible, grandparents as well as siblings should be involved in helping families adjust to the presence of a deaf member.

Meadow (1980) reported that because the deaf child's problem has been viewed as an educational problem, educators train the mother to become a teacher. Thus, to the strain of poor communication is added the pressure of extended demands on the mother's time and attention. In discussing the dangers of placing too great a strain on parents, Meadow (1976) said:

> The press from educators who begin to work with deaf children and their parents very early leads to over-expectations for verbal achievement and over-emphasis on the training that may or may not lead to verbal competence. This encourages in some mothers a didactic, intrusive, over-anxious surveillance of the deaf child's oral progress, with accompanying reduction in the relaxed, playful, creative, happy interaction that may be necessary for normal growth and development. (p. 432)

The following concurring opinion comes from a different perspective: that of a deaf mother with a master's degree in education of the hearing impaired and six years' experience as a teacher of the deaf before the birth of her two deaf children:

> Educators, especially when the children are young, tend to encourage parents of hearing impaired children to be educators, to teach communication. I soon found I had a conflict of roles. It revolved around the question: What is more important, to be a teacher or to be a mother? Where deafness is involved, teaching is not a natural function. I found I could not do both. I chose mothering. Many parents find they have to make a choice. (Thompson, Thompson, and Murphy, 1979, p. 334)

One interesting question is whether the use of manual communication by hearing parents of young deaf children facilitates family communication and adjustment of these children. Because the use of signs by hearing parents with young deaf children is a recent phenomenon, relatively little information is available, but the indications to date are promising. Greenberg (1980) compared fourteen deaf children of hearing parents who used oral-only communication to fourteen deaf children of hearing parents who used simultaneous oral-manual communication. He reported that the children in the simultaneous-communication category had a significantly higher percentage of spontaneous communication with their mothers and demonstrated more sociable and cooperative behaviors with them, as well as more compliance with their requests. More physical contact with mothers and less gaze avoidance occurred. Overall, the simultaneous mother-child dyads had longer and more complex interactions and spent more time interacting.

In a subsequent related study, Meadow, Greenberg, Erting, and Carmichael (1981) compared four groups: fourteen oral-only deaf children with hearing parents, fourteen simultaneous-communication deaf children with hearing parents, seven deaf children with deaf parents, and fourteen hearing children with hearing parents. No significant differences were observed between the deaf child–deaf mother and hearing child–hearing mother dyads. Child-mother interactions in these two groups had the most complex and most frequent interactions. The oral-only deaf child–hearing mother dyads had the least complex and least frequent interactions. The simultaneous-communication deaf child–hearing mother dyads were intermediate in the ranking: the quality of interaction was better than that in the oral-only deaf child–hearing parent dyads, but lagged behind that in the deaf mother–deaf child and hearing mother–hearing child pairs. The issues of parent-child interaction and the use of manual communication are treated in greater detail in later sections of this chapter.

Entrance into the Formal School Situation

The next period of potential stress begins when the child is five or six years old and about to enter kindergarten. The life cycle of a family involves changes in family relations and in individual roles over a long period of time. Although the deaf child generally has received some preschool training, parents perceive entrance into the formal elementary school years as a critical point. In essence, this constitutes the first substantive change in roles of the deaf child. Successful development of the family life cycle entails managing status changes in such a way that all of the family's several careers mutually support the style of life the family is seeking to achieve (Griffin, 1993; Hill et al., 1970). Farber (1957, 1958) claims that family integration depends heavily on an absence of role tension in interpersonal relationships among family members.

The choice of educational program that parents make for the child at this juncture is critical. It is essential for family integration that the child make a successful adjustment to the new role as a student. Failure may arrest part of the family life cycle and may alter individual and familial expectations for later groups.

Goals and expectations at this time probably are greatly influenced by the advice of outside professionals as well as by direct experience. Moores, McIntyre, and Weiss (1972, p. 72) found attitudinal differences in parents of deaf children as young as four years of age as a function of the type of preschool program the child was attending. For example, parents of deaf children in oral-only programs believed the primary function of an educational program for hearing-impaired children was to develop speech and speech-reading skills. Parents of children in programs using both oral and manual communication believed the primary function was to provide appropriate instruction in academic skills such as reading, language, and writing.

Historically, the majority of deaf children not living in large cities were enrolled in public or private residential schools for the deaf. This marked the beginning of their integration into the Deaf community. Now that most deaf children, including a substantial number of those who attend "residential" schools, live at home, it is imperative that information be gathered on the family dynamics of deaf school-age children. At present, very little exists.

Beginning Adolescence

When an American child enters adolescence, the likelihood of role tension in the family increases. Frequently, beginning adolescence is a time of uncertainty for the youth, who is undergoing physical and emotional changes and is no longer a child and not yet an adult. The strain greatly intensifies for a deaf child, who may experience greater difficulty in establishing a personal position within the family structure. Schlesinger and Meadow (1971) reported that adolescence is a time of particular stress for deaf children and their parents. In many ways, the gap between the deaf child and the hearing child widens at this point. A deaf child's socialization patterns may differ from those of siblings with normal hearing. The deaf child's speech has probably not come along as well as parents expected or were led to expect. Parents who were told their child would develop normal speech if only they would talk to the child now realize that this has not happened and will not happen. As different patterns of boy-girl interaction develop, the parents notice that the child has fewer hearing friends than he or she once did and that the friends are less patient than they used to be. If the child is not in school with other deaf students, he or she begins to search them out in church or social groups. Concerning the family, Koester and Meadow-Orlans (1990) reported that parents of older deaf children rated their relationships with professionals less positively than parents of younger children.

Stinson (1972) reported that mothers of adolescent hearing boys tended to react to task pressures by increasing demands on children, whereas mothers of adolescent deaf boys reacted to the same conditions by relaxing demands.

It is at this time that many parents see their hopes for "normality" crushed (Mindel and Vernon, 1972). For parents who were not helped to work through the conflict when the child was young, the final realization may unleash a tide of frustration, resentment, and hostility, which the parents vent on the system of professionals that has misguided them and has failed to prepare them for reality.

While this is happening, the position of the deaf child relative to hearing siblings may be eroding. Jenne and Farber (1957) reported that children with retardation come to be treated as more immature than even younger brothers and sisters, and the deaf child may be treated similarly. Parents may believe the deaf adolescent is generally less mature than a younger sibling. They are unaware that the immaturity may be a result of their own failure to help the child develop to full potential. They may forget that the hearing sibling has had more leeway in dating, driving, and staying out late, as well as more responsibility for household chores. Meadow (1967) provided an example of the different expectations parents may have, taken from an interview with a mother of two adolescent boys, one hearing and one deaf:

> They tell us he [the deaf boy] has the potential but we've always been told he doesn't apply himself. His younger brother is a straight A student. This makes it hard for the others because we expect the same from all of them. [How does he get along with his brother?] All right. Though there's a little conflict. His younger brother is given more privileges, that makes a little tension. We let his brother take the car anywhere. Fred being deaf, I felt he wouldn't be quite as capable, not as responsible. Careless. We wouldn't let Fred stay out as late. (p. 145)

Mendelsohn (Mendelsohn and Fairchild, 1984) summed up the situation as follows:

> What happens in adolescence is that the realization hits—no magic, no miracles are going to happen. . . . there *is* a future and that future involves deafness. It is a period of time when parents begin to think of life after family—life after hearing family. Life as a deaf person. It is as big a shock for many families as the original diagnosis of deafness. (p. 113)

Adulthood

The final point of stress we will consider comes when the deaf individual prepares to leave the nuclear family and begin an independent existence. This step may well be more traumatic for deaf persons and their families than for their hearing counterparts. The evidence presented earlier in this chapter suggests that parents of deaf children are generally more overprotective and that deaf children are more dependent. However, no research exists to provide insight into what, if any, special challenges deaf individuals face as they mature into adulthood. This may be largely because funding for research on deafness has concentrated on educational and communication issues. In these areas, early intervention and preschool programs have received the greatest attention, with the allocation of resources for research usually decreasing progressively as the focus shifts from elementary to secondary to postsecondary education. Research, which should encompass the entire life span of its subjects, concentrates disproportionally on infancy and childhood. Very little objective data are available on age ranges past adolescence.

Deaf people tend to marry at somewhat later ages than hearing people do, and most of the marriages are with other deaf individuals. The great majority of their offspring are hearing. An area in need of study is the development of hearing children of deaf parents and the types of adjustments such families make. For example, do hearing grandparents perceive the situation as a continuing crisis? Are they more involved (or involved in different ways) in the families of their deaf children than in the families of their hearing children? Do deaf parents expect their hearing children to assume adult roles at an early age? If the hearing children act as go-betweens on the telephone and as interpreters in face-to-face situations, how does this affect the roles, functions, and expectations of the family and its individual members? The answers to these important questions must remain largely conjectural at present because of a lack of information. Substantial federal funds have been available for more than a generation for research on children with disabilities, including deaf children. However, there has not been a similar mechanism of support to investigate families in which the parents are deaf and the children are hearing.

In a survey of 229 adult hearing offspring of deaf parents, Bunde (1979) found that 95 percent of the respondents had as children interpreted for their parents, most commonly on the phone and in medical and shopping situations. When asked about their feelings toward interpreting for parents, 65 percent did not respond and 19 percent expressed no feelings. Royster (1981), a hearing daughter of deaf parents, reported that she sometimes resented always having to interpret and always knowing about the family's financial affairs and problems. Hoffmeister (1985), a hearing son of deaf parents, commented on the problems deaf parents may face because of the ignorance of some hearing professionals. Medical personnel may make inappropriate referrals to social agencies simply because the parents are deaf. Efforts may even be made to remove hearing children from the family because of unfounded fears that the children will fail to develop adequate speech and English skills. Lack of access to support services may prove detrimental to deaf parents and their hearing children. For example, in a report on deafness and mental health, Schlesinger and Meadow (1972a) stated:

> The findings regarding hearing children with deaf parents are of sufficient interest to merit further investigation. Since guidance clinics sometimes appear to be at a loss when dealing with deaf parents, this group of hearing children suffers as much from the lack of appropriate mental health services as do the deaf themselves. (p. 188)

Facilitating Satisfactory Growth and Development

The life span of deaf individuals is generally considered from one of three perspectives. The first may be thought of as a medical/pathological model, which regards deafness as a disease. This approach seeks to cure or prevent deafness or, when this is not possible, to "normalize" the deaf individual, that is, to make him or her function as much like a hearing person as possible. This mindset can lead to a devaluation and dehumanization of the individual and can inhibit his or her development.

One reaction against this medical model has been the development of the Deaf community, which has its own language (American Sign Language) and cultural attributes and provides deaf individuals with a support system and a sense of pride. In Chapter 8, we will consider the Deaf community (as opposed to a *deaf* community); for now, we will only note its positive influence on the lives of deaf people.

The second perspective, a separatist model, is an overreaction to the misunderstanding and mistreatment of deaf individuals by the hearing majority. To some extent, the Deaf community may be considered an ethnic-linguistic minority (Reagan, 1990; Janesick and Moores, 1992) in a multicultural society. However, advocates of the second model tend to think of this community as an isolated group, out of contact with the rest of society. Practically speaking, this is untenable for most deaf people if only because of the hearing status of their parents, children, and other relatives. It is to the credit of deaf people that they have resisted a simplistic separatist model far more successfully than hearing people have resisted a simplistic medical/pathological model of deafness.

The third and most practical model views deafness as having very serious life-long implications involving hearing impairment and disability, but not necessarily a handicap. A profound hearing loss raises obstacles in a society in which early childhood deafness occurs in only one person per thousand. It is a fact of life that deaf people have to deal with a world in which everyday functioning is made more difficult by a lack of sensitivity on the part of most of the hearing people they meet. As a result, deaf individuals must develop special coping skills. However, it is as unrealistic to paint an overly pessimistic picture as it is to paint an overly optimistic one. The majority of deaf people make an adequate adjustment to the world despite the fact that they usually receive inadequate instruction in language, speech, and school subjects, their parents are miscounseled and misled, and they face prejudice, distrust, and discrimination. Most of their problems stem from the dominant society. But even in the face of an indifferent world that they must deal with daily, deaf people survive and endure. They marry, raise children, pay taxes, contribute to the good of the community, quarrel, watch television, and entertain themselves in much the same way everyone else does.

Instead of approaching the topic with an eye to what is deviant, wrong, or pathological about families with deaf children, one might ask, "What are the characteristics of families with deaf children that are making satisfactory adjustments?" Although we might assume that factors such as age and sex of the deaf child, ages and sex of siblings, hearing status of other family members, religious affiliation, and familial socioeconomic status would affect family integration, we know very little about the impact of any of these factors other than the hearing status of parents.

The Need for Observational Data in Naturalistic Settings

In the 1960s, educational programs for deaf children began to extend services to younger children. Today some types of educational services for deaf children and their families are mandated from the time of identification of a hearing loss. Educational interventions for deaf children, then, must be perceived as extending into the home and involving not only the deaf individual but also the complete family unit. However, few researchers have attempted to observe systematically the impact of deafness on a child and his or her family.

Because of a lack of information about the interaction of deaf children and their environment, interpretation of differences found between deaf and hearing children or among various categories of deaf children must be tentative. The most obvious case would be research in the 1960s and 1970s suggesting that deaf children of deaf parents are superior to deaf children of hearing parents in social-emotional adjustment, academic achievement, and English language abilities (Brasel, 1975; Meadow, 1968; Moores, 1976, 1979a; Stuckless and Birch, 1966; Vernon and Koh, 1970).

The documented superiority in social-emotional development of deaf children of deaf parents over deaf children of hearing parents does not suggest that the presence of deaf children does not cause strain for deaf parents. In an interview about their reactions (Thompson, Thompson, and Murphy, 1979), two deaf parents noted that after the diagnosis of deafness in their children they became increasingly aware that they themselves had never completely accepted their own deafness. In fact, because both had believed their deafness did not result from genetic factors, they were shocked when their first child's hearing loss was diagnosed. The mother commented, "We've gone through what all parents go through—shock, helplessness, guilt, the whole gamut. We're no different in our reactions from hearing parents." The father added, "People assume we have an advantage. But greater awareness of the way the world is built brings more frustration. We know what our children will have to deal with; that can be painful" (p. 341).

Careful, detailed observation of the behavior of deaf children in naturalistic settings is needed to determine whether the environmental challenges they face differ from those faced by hearing children and, if so, the extent to which such differences require different modes of adaptation. Not only must we study deaf individuals to understand the nature of their abilities and how they use them, but we must also have a better understanding of what the environment requires of them.

Hinde (1966) argued that if a species appears to be deficient in some faculty, as defined by a particular type of test, one must refer to the natural situation to assess the extent to which the development of other faculties compensates for this condition. By extending such reasoning to research in the area of deafness, it should be possible to (1) identify those environments that facilitate maximum development in deaf children and (2) identify those areas, if any, in which deafness per se has implications for the individual's development. The most important theoretical and practical issue, which lies at the base of the oral-manual (now oral–total communication) controversy, is the nature of human communication and language. In its simplest terms, the question may be put as follows: Is the core of human language auditory-vocal, or does it lie deeper, with the auditory-vocal channel being merely the most convenient and most common mode of communication? Phylogenetically, we have acquired elaborate acoustic and articulatory mechanisms that have enabled our species to develop spoken language. We remain uncertain about the extent to which a nonfunctioning or partially functioning acoustic mechanism blocks children from realizing the linguistic competence that is theirs by nature of genetic inheritance. The use of observational techniques in naturalistic settings could help resolve this issue.

Applications of ethological principles might help us to identify what factors in the deaf child's environment require adaptation by means of cognitive skills and to determine how frequently such demands occur. Such an approach would be tedious and time consuming, involving minute categorical and episodic observations that, only after much trial and error, would lead to the construction of ecologically valid test items or situations capable of tapping basic skills. However, we must move beyond the laboratory and consider how individuals function in nontest situations if we wish to identify basic cognitive skills and fundamental problem-solving processes that are significantly related to successful adaptation. The potential benefits to be realized justify a major commitment to this approach.

Deaf Children and Their Families

Fortunately, the field is now beginning to develop a body of literature about deaf children and their families, partly because of the influence of federal legislation and funding. With some exceptions, this does not include research on very young children. Yoshinaga-Itano and Apuzzo (1998) reported that severe to profound hearing losses are typically identified at an average age of 18 months to 2.5 years. Even when hearing loss was identified at 2.5 years of age, on average the children were not enrolled in intervention programs until a year later, around 3.5 years of age. Regrettably, this is the same gap between identification and service reported by Freeman (1977) more than twenty years previously. There still is a lacuna for information on the early lives of most deaf children. This is probably most true for children from poor families, in which identification may be even later.

Evans (1995) reported on a case study of a family of ten members with eight children from ages two to fourteen, one of whom was a deaf seven-year-old girl who attended a state-supported school for the deaf on a commuter basis. Evans commented on the complexities of the interactions, with various members of the family using signs, speech, and gesture to communicate. Family members reported an ambivalence about their sister's and daughter's deafness, and she did not always have access to communication to the same extent as other family members. However, she was a competent communicator, with mastery of the pragmatic dimensions of conversation. She used language appropriately in different situations. Evans interpreted the results as contradicting the opinions of many educators that deaf children's exposure to language is largely tutorial, with emphasis on correct English grammar. In this family the emphasis was on meaning and getting things done. The family engaged in the kinds of everyday activities that facilitate deaf children's language development.

Calderon, Bargones, and Sidman (1998) conducted a follow-up study of twenty-eight sets of hearing parents and their deaf or hard-of-hearing children who had participated in an early intervention program (zero to three months of age). The children entered programs at an average age of twenty-one months, and the average time within the program was fifteen months. The authors reported that the families received fewer than three visits per month, with each visit usually lasting between one to two hours. Communication skills of mothers were quite variable, ranging from highly skilled to having a significant difficulty in communication. Twenty eight percent of the families reported changing residences to be nearer services for their deaf or hard-of-hearing child. The authors concluded:

> The consistent theme of our investigation is the striking heterogeneity among deaf and hard of hearing children and their hearing families. Even within the same intervention program, any attempt to create a "typical profile" of a child with hearing loss and his or her family or the services that child receives is quickly defeated. . . . Findings derived from the present study demonstrate the high level of sensitivity needed by early interventionists to work with a diverse population in which ethnic minority family members are disproportionately represented.
>
> The average age of entry into early intervention continues to be troubling. . . . The average for the present study suggests almost two years of auditory and language deprivation. Furthermore, more than half the sample lived in rural areas, which might present them with a number of obstacles, including less accessibility to intervention, fewer professional resources, less parent-to-parent support, less developed local education programs for children with hearing loss, higher rates of unemployment and financial stress, and less accessibility to deaf adult role models or qualified interpreters. (p. 354)

Mapp and Hudson (1997) reported on stress and coping among African-American and Hispanic parents of deaf children. The sample was taken from a group of parents or caretakers of ninety-eight children attending a school for the deaf, of whom sixty-six were Hispanic and twenty were African-American. Fifty-one percent of the respondents had a high school diploma or higher, and 74 percent had yearly incomes of $20,000 or below. In general, the respondents reported low levels of stress overall. There were no differences related to marital status, age of children, income, education, or gender of the child. Parents who attended church frequently reported less stress than those who did not. Hispanics reported using more coping strategies such as confrontation, self-control, and positive reappraisal than did African-Americans and other racial/ethnic groups.

Calderon and Low (1998) investigated the effect of father presence or absence in the home for a group of elementary-school-age deaf and hard-of-hearing children who had previously enrolled in an early intervention program. Observation of direct interaction between mothers and children revealed no significant differences between father-present and father-absent families. However, children in families in which fathers were present had significantly better academic achievement and language development, with the differences persisting over time. Possibly, father absence did not influence the mother-child interaction per se but the mother might have also had to assume multiple roles, which would not have been the case of another adult were present.

Fisiloglu and Fisiloglu (1996) assessed the family functioning of three sets of 120 Turkish parents; 40 hearing parents of deaf children who had participated in a parent workshop, forty hearing parents of deaf children who had not participated, and 40 hearing parents of hearing children. There were no differences reported in communication, roles, affective responses, affective involvement, behavior control, and general functioning. Problem-solving families with hearing children tended to be more dysfunctional than families with deaf children. The authors conclude that families with deaf children may be special families but not necessarily dysfunctional families, and that stress can be an occasion for growth. They state (p. 234), "These findings clearly support the argument that parents of deaf and hard-of-hearing children have adjusted quite well to the stresses associated with raising a child with hearing loss." The authors caution that the data were gathered from parents of children who attended special schools for the deaf and may not be representative of parents of deaf and hard-of-hearing children who attended regular schools.

Lampropoulou and Konstantareas (1998) investigated parent involvement and stress in 42 Greek hearing mothers of deaf children. They reported more stress with younger children and with boys. Involvement with boys was longer in such caregiving activities as bedtime routines, bathing, and play. Mothers with greater stress were also more likely to rate the affective tone of their involvement as neutral or chorelike. Mothers reported little support from their extended families.

Obviously, no clear pattern emerges from this sampling of studies. This may be due to the different instruments used or to the cultural variability represented in the research. As Calderon, Bargones, and Sidman noted, the heterogeneity of families of deaf children makes it extremely difficult to arrive at generally applicable decisions.

The important thing to note for the purposes of this chapter is the evidence that families with deaf parents provide rich stimulation for infants through voice, manual communication, and physical contact, regardless of the hearing status of the child. Thus the foundation is laid for the development of effective communication with other members of the family, whether or not the child has a hearing loss. The situation differs for deaf children from families with hearing parents, in which the establishment of effective communication is hindered by a lack of familiarity with deafness and by inexperience in dealing with its impact.

Summary

The growth of a healthy personality and the maintenance of family integrity depend on complex actions, reactions, and interactions of family members. The development of a healthy concept of self is contingent on the ability to express wants, needs, and desires (Mead, 1934). As the family moves through different cycles and members take on different roles, strains are placed on the family. These strains may be intensified by the presence of a child with a disability such as deafness, particularly if the child has hearing parents with little or no prior exposure to deafness or understanding of its implications.

Despite the very real problems of communication, understanding, and acceptance, most deaf children and their families apparently make better adjustments than they have been credited for. Studies suggest that deaf adults function in much the same way that hearing adults in our society do. Without minimizing the profound impact of a deaf child on a family, it seems that in one way or another the parents turn away from unrealistic expectations of a cure or of "normalization" and accept, at least to some degree, the implications of deafness as a lifelong condition for their child. We do not know how far most hearing parents go toward completely accepting the realities of deafness, but the success of their children makes it clear that many do go a long way.

C H A P T E R

Deafness and Cognitive Functioning

Introduction

In his influential book, *How the Mind Works,* Pinker (1997) argues that the mind is a system of organs of computation designed by natural selection to solve the problems faced by our evolutionary ancestors in their foraging way of life. This implies that all of the human senses, especially the tele-senses, or "far" senses of vision and hearing, have been involved in the evolution of the human brain and—by extension—the mind. If one accepts this basic premise, as many scientists do, it is understandable that there has been so much attention to the cognitive development and functioning of deaf individuals by researchers and theorists outside of our field. If one of the "organs of computation" does not function, what are the implications for the development of a deaf child? Is human intellectual potential so plastic, as I believe, that other organs can take over the functioning of a missing element, or does its lack place limitations on development?

Many of the basic issues concerning the development of cognitive and intellectual skills in deaf individuals are subject to ongoing debate in various disciplines. Two distinct but related controversies are receiving particular attention. The first has been referred to as the "nature-nurture" controversy. The overriding question is the extent, if any, to which the functional lack of a major sense, in this case hearing, affects the way people develop and use their intellectual skills. Obviously, the environment of a deaf person is qualitatively different from that of a hearing person, even if the two individuals grow up in the same household. If we could determine that no differences of either a qualitative or a quantitative nature exist between deaf

162

and hearing people, we could argue that human intelligence is not controlled by the environment but unfolds as dictated by biology. On the other hand, if we could document great differences of a qualitative and/or quantitative nature, the environmentalist position would be strengthened.

The second area, which some consider to be an offshoot of the nature-nurture controversy, concerns what is referred to as the "linguistic relativity" or Whorfian hypothesis (Whorf, 1956). Basically, this theory holds that the language an individual uses will influence the way he or she perceives and organizes the environment. One test of this hypothesis is to investigate whether deaf individuals who use ASL do in fact differ in their perceptions of the world from standard English users.

Over the past generation, the most powerful theories of cognition have been stage theories, which hold that humans go through universal stages of cognitive development before achieving adult levels of functioning. Each stage is more sophisticated and qualitatively different from the one preceding it. The most influential work of this type has been that of Piaget (1926, 1952, 1970; Inhelder and Piaget, 1958; Piaget and Inhelder, 1969) and Vygotsky (1989; Knox and Stevens, 1993). Stage theories have influenced investigation of questions such as the following:

1. Do deaf children go through the same stages of cognitive development that hearing children do, or do the sequences differ?

2. Do deaf children develop cognitive abilities at the same rate as hearing children—that is, do they go through the same stages, but at a slower rate?

3. Are the final levels of abstract abilities achieved by deaf adolescents and adults equivalent to those of hearing adolescents and adults?

Related to these investigations of cognition is the equally long but quite distinct tradition of intelligence testing. Whereas the stage theorists investigated qualitative commonalities of development, the intelligence-testing movement grew out of efforts to establish and quantify individual differences and to assign people ratings by which they could be characterized relative to a population. The best-known procedures are the Stanford-Binet and the various Wechsler tests of intelligence, in which the "average" or norm score is 100 and approximately two-thirds of the population score between 85 and 115. Because many of the tests assume fluency in a standard language and at least some shared cultural experiences, their validity for many populations, including the deaf, has been a matter of sometimes acrimonious debate. Research has addressed questions such as the following:

1. Are IQ tests valid for the deaf? Do they really test what they are designed to test?

2. Does deafness per se influence intelligence as measured by IQ tests?

3. Can parts of IQ tests—for example, those that do not rely on standard English skills—be used or modified for use with the deaf?

A great deal of confusion has arisen out of the tendency to subsume within one area two quite different sets of activities: (1) the investigation of cognitive development and functioning and (2) the IQ (intelligence quotient) testing movement. Each has different goals, procedures, and even terminology.

Intelligence testing was originally a product of special education. It grew out of efforts in France to identify for special class placement those children who would have difficulty competing in the regular academic program. Although prior researchers had done much exploratory work, Alfred Binet has been acclaimed as the creator of a legitimate intelligence test (Kanner, 1967). Binet was motivated in his work by a desire to serve individuals with intellectual disabilities. A commission in France had charged him with studying measures for providing the benefits of instruction to children with disabilities. According to Binet (1916), the purpose of the commission was to ensure that "no child suspected of retardation should be eliminated from the ordinary school and admitted to a special class, without first being subjected to a pedagogical and medical examination from which it could be certified that because of the state of his intelligence he was unable to profit, in an average measure, from the instruction given in the ordinary schools" (p. 9).

It is interesting that Binet's position regarding placement in the Paris public schools anticipated the "least restrictive environment" requirements of PL 94–142 and other legislation in the United States approximately sixty years later: that is, children should be retained in a regular setting unless it can be certified that they would not benefit from such placement. According to Binet, the scale he developed focused on eleven distinct faculties: attention, comprehension, imagery, imagination, memory, suggestibility, aesthetic appreciation, moral sentiment, strength of will, motor skill, and judgment of visual space.

Binet (1916) acknowledged that his scale was not a theoretical work but a combination of psychological questions. He reported:

> This scale properly speaking does not permit the measure of intelligence because intellectual qualities are not supposable, and therefore cannot be measured as linear surfaces are measured, but are, on the contrary, a classification, a hierarchy among diverse intelligences. (p. 41)

The leading scientists engaged in the study of child development have not been concerned with the categorization of children. Rather, they have tended to address the complex interactions between child and environment and between nature and nurture, as well as the intricate processes involved in the development and acquisition of cognitive, linguistic, motor, and social skills. In the area of cognitive development, the search for general, universal attributes of development emphasizes the specification of behavior common to children in the developmental process.

Psychologists in the United States have played leading roles in the creation of IQ tests but have devoted relatively little attention to cognitive development and functioning. It is not surprising that the greatest impact has come from the work of Europeans, such as Vygotsky in the former USSR and Piaget in Switzerland. Now that the utility of IQ tests is under severe attack in the United States and nonbiased assessment of children with disabilities is mandated, attention is increasingly turning to the assessment of children within a diagnostic/prescriptive model, that is, assessment that facilitates the development of appropriate educational programs. In other words, less attention will be devoted to norm-referenced tests, including IQ tests, and more to criterion-referenced measures of how a child functions on particular tasks.* Consequently, this chapter concentrates not on the history of IQ testing of the deaf but on the identification of relevant developmental and functional variables.

Regardless of the orientation of their educational programs, most school psychologists are not prepared to test deaf children (Vernon and Andrews, 1990; Sullivan and Vernon, 1979). Levine (1974) found that fewer than 20 of 172 school psychologists working with hearing-impaired children were able to communicate in sign language and 83 percent had no special preparation to work with these children. Data from a longitudinal study of public high school programs for the deaf (Moores, Kluwin, and Mertens, 1985) suggest that there continues to be a lack of school psychologists with special training in the area of deafness. Sullivan and Vernon (1979) note that school psychologists almost universally rely on standard spoken English alone in assessment procedures and frequently administer tests that presuppose standard language skills. Too frequently, the result has been the erroneous labeling of deaf children as mentally retarded or emotionally disturbed (Donoghue, 1968; Rosen, 1959; Vernon, 1976). There is no way of knowing how many deaf children have been saddled with such labels by school psychologists with limited communication skills. Conversely, we cannot know how many deaf children have additional disabilities that school psychologists have not identified. No indication exists that the situation has improved since the passage of PL 94–142 with its mandate for nonbiased testing. The *American Annals of the Deaf* 1999 reference issue lists only *one* graduate-level program in school psychology in the United States and Canada with an emphasis on deafness (Carew, 1999, p. 174).

Much research concerning the cognitive development of deaf children has been conducted by psychologists, linguists, psycholinguists, and others interested in pursuing basic research questions of human cognition and communication (Vernon, 1967d). These scientists often perceive deafness as an "experiment of nature." In some cases, the concern has been for investigating development in the absence of a distal sense: hearing. In others, the focus has been on the effects of limited communication between parent and child. In yet others, attention has been devoted primarily to what might be termed an "experiential deficit," that is, the effects of what some perceive as a reduced opportunity to interact with the environment.

Unfortunately, as Conrad (1979) pointed out, much of the work has been conducted with the expectation that deaf children would manifest a variety of deficiencies in addition to hearing loss. This generalized deficiency hypothesis has prompted

---

*A norm-referenced test is scored to permit comparison with a certain sample or population. Criterion-referenced tests are more functional in that they refer not to norms but to how a child performs on a particular task.

numerous studies of perception, learning, and memory. Given the reliance on tests developed for hearing children, the limited ability of experimenters to communicate with deaf children, and the implicit and explicit expectations of failure held by the investigators, we would expect an unbroken string of experiments documenting low performance among deaf children. This has not been the case, however. A majority of studies have found no differences between hearing and deaf children, an astonishing result considering the prejudiced nature of such investigations.

Because so much of the research has consisted of "theory testing" by scientists with no practical concern for the everyday functioning of deaf people, the results have had relatively little impact on practitioners in the field such as teachers, counselors, and school psychologists. Professionals who have extensive contact with deaf children and adults tend to rely more heavily on their own experiences and insights than on the reports of scientists who assess a limited range of behaviors and then publish their results without bothering to acquaint themselves with the field or to acquire the communication skills necessary to interact fluently with deaf children and adults.

In addition to being skeptical about the validity of many of the studies, teachers, counselors, and psychologists often disagree with the priorities and world views of the scientists. The teachers' responsibility is to work with the children at their present level of functioning and knowledge and help them acquire more skills and more knowledge. For practitioners, important questions include the following:

1. Are there "discrepancies in growth" in deaf children that have implications for the teaching/learning process?
2. If there are lags, can they be remediated by instructional programs designed for other populations, such as "disadvantaged" children?
3. If remedial programs are developed, should they emphasize cognition or strategy?

Some discussion is called for to put these questions into context. First, if deaf individuals vary cognitively from some norm, do they vary in the same way as do other groups of individuals? This leads to the question of whether cognitive remediation procedures developed for other populations would be applicable for deaf students. In this author's opinion, the most pressing issue relates to functional cognition. As defined by Pressley and Levin (1983), the area of functional cognition is concerned not only with cognitive abilities but also with the individual's knowledge of when to apply certain knowledge or strategies. The fact that children do not spontaneously use strategies does not necessarily mean that they cannot use them; it might mean that the children do not know under what circumstances they are expected to use them (Moores, 1985a). For example, in a study of short-term memory, Karchmer and Belmont (1976) found that deaf students performed at a lower level than hearing students. However, after teaching appropriate strategies to deaf subjects, Karchmer and Belmont found that the deaf children could function at the same level as hearing children. They concluded that the lower initial performance of the deaf subjects was due not to a cognitive deficit but to not knowing which strategy to apply. Extrapolating from this research to the classroom, we can see that much of the academic difficulty observed in schools should be interpreted as relating to what the children *do not* do rather than what they *cannot* do.

The Development of Thought and Language

Many investigators have conducted research on the development of deaf children as a means of examining the developmental relationships between thought and language. A brief overview of basic trends will provide some insight into the evolution of the fundamental issues.

Interest in and speculation about the essence of humanity and the nature of human intellectual processes traces back through the writings of antiquity, which (assuming ancient oral traditions are reliable) provided part of the framework for our legal, moral, and cultural codes. The basic philosophical issue may be expressed by this question: In what ways, if any, do human beings differ from (other) animals? The topic probably has been a subject of discussion since human beings first demonstrated the ability to communicate with one another using an abstract symbol system, that is, language.

The present supremacy of the human race obviously cannot be explained in purely physical terms. Although human beings are relatively large, powerful, and swift, several larger, more powerful, and swifter animals come readily to mind. Although specialized developments such as the thumb (or opposable digit) undoubtedly have provided us with unique capabilities for advancement, it is clear that we differ most markedly from animals in our intellectual abilities and our use of language.

The acknowledgment of differences does not adequately resolve the issue of whether the differences are quantitative or qualitative. One possibility is that we are like other animals, only more highly advanced. Are our brains merely more complex versions of those of other primates? Are the presence of language and the development of religion, culture, and science a logical outgrowth of an evolutionary process that may be operating on other members of the animal kingdom? The other possibility is that human beings are qualitatively different from all other beings. Do different laws apply to us to the extent that language and at least some types of mental functioning represent characteristics limited to one species?

This issue will probably continue to occupy the human race for centuries. The notion that human beings are unique can never be proved conclusively; it can only be disproved. It is possible that chimpanzees have religious beliefs (or the potential to have them), dolphins have fully developed linguistic systems, and earthworms have rich fantasy lives. However, until it is demonstrated that animals are capable of functioning at the "human" level, most people will continue to believe that humans are in some way unique. This is the position taken by Lenneberg (1973), who noted that what differentiates us from animals is not the size of the human brain, nor is it general cognitive ability, since even individuals with severe retardation show signs of language development. Lenneberg (1973) stated:

> Thus our capacity for learning language is not due to special brain connections between sight and hearing; nor is it due to a simple increase in the size of the brain or in general intelligence. Something must be going on in our brain that is just lacking in the brains of other species. (p. 54)

A substantial number of psychologists, especially American psychologists, do not subscribe to the position that human communication and thought are qualitatively different from animal communication and thought. This stance reflects the influences of behaviorism, which, as exemplified by Watson (1924) and later by Skinner (1957), had a profound effect on twentieth-century American psychology. The advent of behaviorism represented a break with the European tradition, in which psychology was closely related to philosophy, and reflected a conscious attempt to pattern psychology after the "hard" sciences such as chemistry and physics. With the advent of behaviorism, the emphasis of psychology in the United States shifted from the study of the mind to the study of behavior. "Mentalistic" approaches were rejected, and the domain of problems deemed amenable to investigation was limited to the observable and quantifiable. The search for powerful, encompassing laws of behavior led psychologists to concentrate on more and more tightly conceived and rigidly conducted experiments. This, in turn, led to an increased emphasis on animal experimentation, especially concerning basic paradigms of learning involving operant conditioning. Special attention was devoted to the differential effects on learning of positive reinforcement, negative reinforcement, and punishment.

The underlying assumption is that we may generalize from the behavior of mice in contrived laboratory situations to the complex behavior of human beings in social situations. The same factors that control bar-pressing and maze-running behavior are seen as controlling linguistic functioning. Manipulation of contingencies of reinforcement is viewed as developing and maintaining the strength of verbal behavior as well as other behaviors. Skinner presented this school of thought in its strongest form in his book *Verbal Behavior* (1957).

Thought and Language

The existence of human language obviously complicates the study of human thought. When we ask people how they think and they respond, our interchange takes place through words; that is, we think and then translate our thoughts into language. The essence of thought remains unknown. It is possible that we think in words, that language raises thought to new heights, or that language distorts thought. The limitations of present research techniques and the unreliability of introspection prevent us from reaching any definitive conclusions. Chomsky (1968) stated that perhaps the one thing the human mind is incapable of comprehending is the human mind.

In the past, there was some optimism that the evolution of language might be studied by first investigating its nature in "primitive" societies and then following its development in presumably more complex cultures, culminating in its full realization in industrial society. However, the languages of so-called primitive cultures are every bit as complex as those of other cultures (Brown, 1958). No society has ever been found that lacks a fully developed language. Therefore, it is impossible to rank languages on a scale of complexity or along a concrete-abstract continuum.

The concept that intellectual development is unfolding as human beings live in increasingly technical environments is also being challenged by the growing awareness that all societies are organized into extremely complex structures and that the individual members of these societies function in a highly complex manner. For a comprehensive treatment of the subject, interested readers are referred to the writings of French anthropologist Claude Levi-Strauss, especially his book *The Savage Mind* (1966).

Linguistic Relativity

Related to the question of the evolution of language is speculation about linguistic relativity. On one hand is the Whorfian hypothesis (Whorf, 1956), which suggests that the structure of the language one habitually uses influences one's *Weltanschauung* (world view). This implies that language either determines thought or greatly influences the manner in which an individual perceives and organizes the environment. Whorf developed this hypothesis as a result of his investigations of American Indian languages and their apparent lack of congruence with traditionally studied Indo-European languages.

Although languages undeniably vary in numerous ways, linguists tend to reject the Whorfian hypothesis, at least in its strong form, and to contend that superficial differences mask a remarkable uniformity across languages in the deep structure (Chomsky, 1965, 1968). Despite their many differences, all languages exhibit certain basic psychological and linguistic commonalities. Greenberg (1963) stated, "Underlying the endless and fascinating idiosyncrasies of the world's languages there are uniformities of universal scope. Amidst infinite diversity, all languages are, as it were, cut from the same pattern" (p. 255).

In the period following World War II, there was widespread interest in the possible influence of language on thought. By themselves and in collaboration with scholars across the world, Osgood, Suci, and Tannenbaum (1957) conducted a wide-ranging series of cross-cultural studies using what are called *semantic differential techniques*. The results showed remarkably consistent underlying meaning systems across cultures and languages. The researchers concluded that although people who speak different languages may vary in their reactions to specific concepts, human beings share a common framework for the process of differentiating meaning.

In a review of the literature on childhood language acquisition, in which a total of forty languages were considered, Slobin (1973) reported that the initial processes were consistent across such apparently diverse languages as Japanese, Russian, Yarabu, and English. These results, supported by Chomsky's theoretical arguments, lead to the conclusion that great similarities exist across languages and that these similarities result from cognitive processes and experiences that all human groups share. This conclusion finds additional support in the work of Piaget, who, after extensive studies of the development of children, concluded that language depends more on cognition than cognition depends on language (Piaget, 1926, 1952, 1970).

Nineteenth-Century Views on Deafness and Thought

Given the fact that deaf people do not acquire language primarily through the auditory-vocal channel, as well as the common belief that deaf people are linguistically deficient, it is not surprising that considerable interest has been expressed in the nature of intellectual processes in deaf people. As Braudel's (1981, 1982) model of histories of events, cycles, and long-term duration predicts, many of the positions being argued today were also points of discussion in the past, whereas other issues that were important to previous generations are of less immediacy to us. Among the latter group of issues is the quality of thought in deaf children prior to instruction.

Nineteenth-century educators of the deaf were particularly interested in the nature of deaf children's thought before instruction (Ballard, 1881; Peet, 1855). Such a concern was natural, since a large number of deaf children did not begin their education until age ten or later. Before that age, the major sources of information for most deaf children were their own observations and participation in the environment. Communication usually occurred through a primitive gesture system developed by the children and their families.

Since the emphasis in the schools at that time was on moral and religious training, a great amount of attention was given to whatever value systems or religious insights children developed in the absence of instruction. Several schools made attempts to encourage students to recall through introspection the nature and extent of their experiences and thoughts before their education began.

In an intriguing treatise on the notions deaf children held before instruction, Peet (1855) dealt with human nature, the origin of language, and the relationship between language and thought in a highly insightful way. Beginning with Humboldt's statement "Man is man only by means of speech, but in order to invent speech he must be already man" (p. 8), Peet developed the position that the first language consisted of gestures intermingled with instinctive cries. Arguing that "the possession or capacity of acquiring a language is one of the surest tests of humanity" (p. 19), he noted that all human languages, including those of primitive tribes, are fully developed and that languages are not at different stages of development—an insight ahead of its time. In a discussion of the similarities found among the languages of Europe, Peet rejected the idea that one of those languages constituted the original language. He suggested instead that "a primitive language may have provided the stem from which all languages of the Caucasian race have branched" (p. 19). Although Peet does not make specific reference, he must have been familiar with the work of William Jones, who in 1786 related Sanskrit, Greek, Latin, Gothic, Celtic, and Persian and postulated a common descent from an earlier language no longer in existence (Waterman, 1970).

Peet reported that without instruction deaf children have no conception of God, the Creation, or the soul and that they have a terror of death. He concluded that no religious thought is possible without instruction.

In an earlier investigation, Ray (1848) noted that before instruction deaf children tend to interpret parts of their environment in anthropomorphic terms. For example, the sun and the moon are frequently personified. This notion, in one form or another, is not unknown in modern society or even in modern religion.

The American psychologist William James (1890) and the French psychologists Binet and Simon (1910) argued that thought processes develop before language in deaf persons. Referring to two deaf individuals' reports concerning their thoughts before instruction, James noted the presence of abstract and metaphysical concepts, even when the only language was that of pantomime.

Booth (1878) argued that concern over the relation between thought and language is misdirected. He took the position not only that thought is independent of the various modes of expression but also that thought and language are separate and distinct processes. Thus it is possible to employ one or the other alone and independently. According to Booth (p. 224), the point is not whether deaf people think in words or in gestures but which, words or gestures, come first to mind when thought seeks expression.

The writings of Peet, Ray, James, Booth, and Binet and Simon appear to be in accord with many of the positions currently in favor. To a large degree, they anticipate present-day attitudes toward language and thought, some of which are widely regarded as recent breakthroughs. From a long-range perspective, we may be witnessing a cyclical phenomenon.

The Assessment of Cognitive Abilities

The assessment of cognitive abilities, whether accomplished through traditional IQ tests, aptitude tests, or Piagetian-based measures, is commonly accepted to be an inexact science. The problem lies in the necessity of "measuring" small incidences of behavior over a short period of time in a contrived situation and then making generalizations about how an individual will function in the real world. Even assuming assessment instruments are adequate—an overoptimistic assumption—results should be considered valid and reliable only to the extent that the motivation and experience of the test subject match those of the population on which the test was standardized.

Dissatisfaction with psychometric practices in the schools, especially the use of IQ scores to decide placement in classes for children with retardation, is widespread. Evidence suggests that children who do not speak standard English are likely to be discriminated against by such tests and placed in special classes in disproportionate numbers.

The disadvantage for deaf children can be even more severe. In many cases, they possess minimal speech skills and have difficulty understanding what is expected of them unless the psychometrist is experienced in dealing with deaf children. As a rule, the scores of deaf children tend to be depressed if a test requires proficiency in speech or speech reading or in knowledge of standard English. Communication difficulties may also depress scores in timed tests. It is advisable to suspect low scores in the testing of all individuals, but it is particularly important when the subjects are deaf. For a discussion of the most appropriate tests to use with deaf individuals, see Vernon and Andrews (1990).

An adequate presentation of trends in research and theory on the cognitive development and functioning of deaf individuals would fill a book in itself. In such a presentation, we might review hundreds of investigations under such discrete topics as perception, short-term memory, and classification. However, the goal here is simply to illustrate how perceptions of the intellectual functioning of deaf people have changed over the years. To get an idea of how we arrived at our present position on cognition and deafness, we will examine the work of researchers who have studied the issues and reviewed the literature (Myklebust and Brutton, 1953; Ottem, 1980; Pintner, Eisenson, and Stanton, 1941; Rosenstein, 1961; Vernon, 1967d) at different periods of time.

Stage 1: The Deaf as Inferior

The work of Pintner in the first part of the twentieth century greatly influenced perceptions of the cognitive abilities of deaf individuals. In a widely quoted early study of visual memory, Pintner and Patterson (1917) noted a lower digit-span memory in deaf children than in hearing children and concluded that deaf children lag behind hearing children. Over the years, Pintner, his associates, and other researchers reported similar findings.

As a culmination of his own decades of research in deafness, Pintner (Pintner, Eisenson, and Stanton, 1941) reviewed and summarized all available data on the intelligence of deaf people. Although the results of different investigations were confusing and even contradictory, Pintner and his colleagues reported a relatively small variation across different types of tests and concluded that deaf children are inferior in intelligence (pp. 126–128). In the case of tests using IQ scores, they set the average retardation at 10 points.

State 2: The Deaf as Concrete

Reviewing the work done since the time of Pintner's summary, Myklebust and Brutton (1953, p. 351) concluded that the evidence indicated that deaf children are not generally inferior in intelligence. However, Myklebust qualified his stand by arguing that even if deaf children are quantitatively (in terms of IQ points) equal to hearing children on some tests, they are not necessarily qualitatively equal. He went on to claim that the qualitative aspects of perceptual and conceptual functioning of deaf individuals and their reasoning seem to be different. Myklebust concluded that it is difficult for the deaf child to function "in as broad and in as subtle and abstract a manner as the hearing child" (p. 35).

Myklebust's interpretation of the results of research led him to make the following statement:

> Deafness causes the individual to behave differently. The entire organism functions in an entirely different manner. This shift in behavior and adjustment is compensatory in nature. . . . Deafness does not simply cause an inability in human communication. It causes the individual to see differently, to smell differently, to use tactile and kinesthetic sensation differently. And perhaps more important than all of these, but because of them, the deaf person perceives differently. As a result of all these shifts in functioning, his personality adjustment and behavior are also different. To say that the deaf person is like the hearing person except that he cannot hear is to oversimplify and to do an injustice to the deaf child. His deafness is not only in the ears, it pervades his entire being. (1953, p. 347)

Although Myklebust's opinion is a welcome improvement over Pintner's summary, in essence Myklebust perceives deaf individuals as being quantitatively equal to hearing persons but qualitatively inferior. He attributes the qualitative inferiority to the more "concrete," and therefore less "abstract," nature of the intelligence of deaf people. Myklebust and Brutton (1953) commented on the "overall concreteness which has been attributed to the deaf" and stated that deafness "restricts the child functionally to a world of concrete objects and things" (p. 93). Unfortunately, largely because of the influence of Myklebust, the idea that deaf children are more "concrete" has become accepted among educators of the deaf. It is doubly unfortunate because of the somewhat pejorative nature of the term and because neither *concrete* nor *abstract* is ever defined. Brown (1958) treated this subject in detail, especially the tendency to use *concrete* to categorize without explaining or defining terms. Brown remarked:

> There is a beautiful simplicity in the notion that all departures from ourselves are basically the same kind of departure. Abstract is the word that has been chosen to name the special quality of our mind and concrete the word for all other minds. The words have been used to maintain the master preconception rather than with referential consistency. The result is that concrete and abstract name all sorts of behaviors having no clear common properties. These unwitting shifts in reference are responsible for the general agreement that all kinds of subhuman minds are concrete, as opposed to the abstract mind of the healthy, civilized adult. (p. 297)

Stage 3: The Deaf as Intellectually Normal

In a review of the literature on perception, cognition, and language in deaf children, Rosenstein (1961) remarked on the lack of agreement in terminology. He noted, for example, that the label *abstract ability* has been used to refer to a visual memory task, a test of nonverbal reasoning by analogy, and an arithmetic reasoning task (p. 276). Conversely, the same task has been assigned different labels; for example, one writer interpreted a figure-ground relations test as representing a perceptual ability and another as representing a conceptual ability (p. 276).

After reviewing several studies conducted with deaf subjects, Rosenstein reported that no differences had been found between deaf and hearing subjects in conceptual performance when the linguistic factors presented were within the language experience of the samples of deaf children. He concluded that the sphere of abstract thought is not closed to the deaf. In a survey of the literature on language and cognition, Furth (1964) reached essentially the same conclusions and reasoned that the poorer performance of deaf individuals on some tasks may be explained simply either by a lack of general experience that is no longer manifested in adulthood or by specific task conditions that favor linguistic habits.

Using a somewhat different approach, Vernon (1967d) reviewed a total of thirty-one research studies, all studies of intelligence of deaf individuals conducted from 1930 to 1966 that Vernon could locate. These studies, conducted on more than eight thousand deaf children ranging in age from three to nineteen, involved sixteen different performance tests of intelligence. Vernon reported (p. 330) that in thirteen of the experiments, the deaf subjects had mean or median scores superior to either test norms or control group scores, whichever were used. In seven studies the scores did not differ significantly, and in the remaining eleven studies the deaf subjects' scores were inferior. Vernon (1967a) summarized the results as follows:

> When one examines the high mass of data and the comparisons made with it, keeping in mind the aforementioned higher incidence of neurological impairment of the lower socioeconomic background of the deaf group, it is clear that these language-impoverished [sic] youths do as well in a wide variety of tasks that measure thinking as do youngsters of normal language development. (p. 331)

Thus, by the 1960s, leading researchers had concluded that deaf people are not intellectually deficient. Obviously, however, the consensus remained, based on many deaf individuals' poor skills in standard English, that deaf people are language deficient or linguistically impoverished. The following section challenges this consensus.

The Relationship Among Thought, Language, and Deafness

The concept of deafness as an experiment of nature appeals to scientists who wish to investigate basic questions about the development of intellectual and communication skills. As a result, research with deaf subjects has been designed more within the framework of a particular psychological or linguistic school of thought than with the idea of generating knowledge that could facilitate optimal development. The use of deaf subjects has contributed significantly to knowledge in the fields of

Valid individualized assessment is the key to educational planning.

psychology and linguistics. Unfortunately, deaf children and adults have not benefited to an equal degree from research in these fields.

Many researchers are not aware that reliance on deaf subjects to investigate basic research questions does not ensure a "clean" experiment. Three basic problems that immediately arise have been ignored by many investigators. First, the major causes of deafness are frequently related to other conditions, including visual problems, neurological impairment, and a wide range of health limitations. Even a carefully screened group of deaf children may be assumed to have a greater number of other disabling conditions than a matched group of hearing children. Any group differences that favor hearing subjects should thus be suspect; there is no way to decide how much of the difference is attributable to deafness per se and how much to secondary conditions.

The second mistake many researchers make is to assume that deafness is complete. Deaf individuals and people who work with the deaf are aware that although the reception of sound may be incomplete and the input degraded, great variability exists in the reception of speech and environmental noise. Therefore, deaf subjects cannot be assumed to lack auditory input entirely.

The third and perhaps biggest problem relates to research conducted to investigate relationships between language and thought. Deaf subjects have been used in such studies under the assumption that the deaf lack language—an assumption with which this author disagrees. Much of the research has been excellent and has contributed toward an understanding of the cognitive functioning of deaf individuals. Where the work fails, ironically, is in its basic goal of investigating language-thought relationships with deaf subjects believed to lack language. That is simply not the case.

The activities of Furth (1964, 1966, 1969a, 1971, 1973, 1974) made educators of the deaf aware of Piaget's work and helped to modify educators' perceptions of language, thought, and deafness. Perhaps of greatest impact was Furth's assertion that the majority of deaf children make an adequate adjustment to the world despite the fact that they receive inadequate instruction in English, speech, and school subjects; that their parents are miscounseled and misled; and that they face prejudice, distrust, and discrimination.

Furth, among others, contributed to a movement away from the tendency to view deafness and deaf individuals on the basis of deviancy, deficiency, or pathology and toward the much healthier and more positive approach of searching for strengths and fostering optimal development. He advocated reordering priorities in education of the deaf (as well as in general education) to give learning to think priority over language instruction. Without denying the importance of language, especially for the developed mind, Furth (1971) argued that the appropriate medium for helping the developing mind is not verbal language but experience in concrete situations.

In his writing, however, Furth made several debatable statements, some of which seem contradictory. The following direct quotes provide some examples:

> The simple fact is that Piaget is the one great psychologist who holds a theory of thinking that makes sense of the fact that deaf children can grow up into thinking human beings even though they do not know much language. (1971, p. 9)

> The inferior performance of the deaf on some tasks is parsimoniously attributed to either lack of general experience which is no longer manifested by adulthood or to specific task conditions which favor linguistic habits. (1964, p. 145)

> Language refers to the living language as heard and spoken in our society. (1964, p. 147)

> We use the term experiential deficiency to describe the intellectual poverty in which deaf children grow up. (1973, p. 259)

> Sign language is the natural language of the deaf. (1974, p. 267)

> Language is a principal and preferred medium of thinking for a developed mind, for a mind that has reached, as Piaget calls it, the formal operative stage. (1971, p. 11)

> Where deaf persons in general fall short is at the formal operative level. More precisely what happens is that they barely reach formal operative thinking, and then they cannot develop their minds much further because they do not have the tool of language. (1971, p. 12)

Furth's belief, implicit and explicit, that deaf individuals typically know little language is an unquestioned assumption that should be challenged. Furth referred to the extensive literature regarding low levels of reading achievement to justify his position that deaf individuals tend to be linguistically deficient. However, reading achievement scores do not necessarily reflect linguistic functioning. Given Furth's comment that sign language is the "natural language of the deaf," it would seem that his statements about deaf individuals' lack of language should be qualified pending intensive investigations into the nature and functioning of sign language. It has been my experience that sign language is a highly effective language. When I was a classroom teacher beginning to learn to sign and to teach through the use of simultaneous signs and speech, I found that if one deaf student was able to grasp a concept that I was having difficulty communicating, that student could convey it easily and efficiently through sign language, no matter how complex it seemed.

Furth's position that deaf persons fall short at the formal operative level is similarly unproven. After reading studies of intellectual functioning of the deaf, I have concluded that in cases where the deaf have shown inferior performance, the simplest explanation may be neither lack of language nor experiential deficiency but the very real possibility that the experimenters were unable to communicate effectively with the deaf subjects.

It should also be pointed out that despite Furth's claims, Piaget is not the only theorist who does not consider intelligence to be based on language. As Furth himself acknowledged (1964, p. 145), William James in 1890 and Binet and Simon in 1904 suggested that in a deaf person thought processes develop before language does. A review of articles in the *American Annals of the Deaf* suggests a consistent interest in the relationships between thought and language, beginning with an article in the first volume by Ray (1848) entitled "Thoughts of the Deaf and Dumb Before Instruction." As we might expect, opinions were diverse, and frequently very active exchanges occurred, sometimes running over several issues of the *Annals*. The most ambitious undertaking was a translation from the German of Schneider's "The Thought and Language of the Deaf-Mute," which was published in nine installments of the *Annals* from 1908 to 1911.

In his survey of cognition in children with disabilities, Suppes (1972, p. 41) commented that Furth failed to make a strong theoretical point because his analysis concerned only the command of a standard natural language. Noting Furth's acknowledgment that the processes deaf children use are not clear, Suppes pointed out that process-oriented approaches to cognitive skills seem to argue strongly that these children use some sort of language internally, even if the language is not that of the society in which they live.

Suppes went on to state that the experiments on logical reasoning, on which Furth based his conclusions, are all extremely elementary. Suppes (1972) summarized his position as follows:

> It seems to me that the real test will not be successful efforts to transform more sophisticated forms of inference into nonverbal contexts, because this seems prima facie impossible, but rather to test the ability to communicate and handle such inferences in sign language. The more developed forms of inference are not primarily auditory in nature but visual; for example, there is very little development of mathematical proofs in purely auditory fashion. (p. 41)

Blank (1965) criticized Furth for using deaf subjects as nonlanguage control groups, noting the oral preschool experiences of many of the children at that time. Furth (1966) defended his position by pointing to the failure of oral preschool programs to teach English to the deaf. Spence (1973) argued that deaf children who learned sign language in infancy and deaf adults who are fluent signers are not linguistically deficient. She asserted that Furth's view of older deaf children and adolescents as lacking in language was incorrect but the question becomes more complicated when one considers younger children with no access to manual communication. Back when Furth was conducting his major work in the area of deafness, almost all young deaf children with hearing parents fell into the latter category.

Liben (1978) suggested that a Piagetian perspective be used in investigating the possible existence of experiential deficiencies in the development of deaf children. Since in Piagetian theory (Piaget, 1926, 1952, 1970; Piaget and Inhelder, 1969), sensorimotor actions are the basis for the development of logical thought, it should be beneficial to study the interactions of the deaf child with the physical world during the process of development.

Liben recommended that four factors Piaget identified as causal agents of development be studied: maturation, experience with objects, social experience, and equilibrium. Liben argued that many deaf children grow up in an overprotected and restricted home environment. The tendency for parents to overprotect their deaf children, thereby limiting the children's social experiences as well as the range of experiences and objects available for manipulation, could have implications for development. According to Liben, such limiting may affect equilibration (a process by which the child compensates for external disturbances to a current cognitive structure) by diminishing opportunities for external disturbances.

Watts (1979) worked with deaf, hard-of-hearing, and hearing children in tests of conservation, spatial thinking, and social thinking. On conservation tasks, the hearing children scored highest and the hard-of-hearing subjects scored lowest; the deaf children scored in between. The reasons for this ranking are unclear, since both the hearing and the hard-of-hearing subjects possessed better speech and English language skills than did the deaf subjects. The tests of spatial thinking (understanding of position in space and horizontality) produced no differences across the three groups, although within each group boys performed better than girls. Social thinking was assessed through arrangement of pictures to make a story in comic-strip form. No differences were found across the groups, although the deaf and the hard-of-hearing children tended to score higher than the hearing children. Watts concluded that, to a great extent, young children acquire knowledge through skills that are active upon and interactive with the environment. Within this context, the cognitive development of deaf children is similar to that of hearing children.

Since research investigations have begun to reflect a more sophisticated understanding of procedural difficulties and the need for clear communication of the task
requirements, the results have tended to show little or no differences between deaf
and hearing subjects. When differences do appear, they usually may be attributed to
factors not related to basic cognitive functioning. Rittenhouse, Morreau, and Iran-
Nejad (1981) presented four Piagetian conservation problems to matched groups of
deaf and hearing children under two instructional conditions. Under standard Piagetian
procedures, they found a significant difference in favor of the hearing subjects. In
an alternative condition, which they termed "attribute specific," Rittenhouse et al.
modified the instructions by substituting new phraseology. They found no significant performance differences, either qualitative or quantitative, between the two
groups. Rittenhouse et al. concluded that previous research showing a cognitive
deficit in deaf children was likely marked by instructional problems, particularly
problems of a linguistic nature.

Hoeman and Briga (1980) commented that although many studies have reported
that deaf children lagged behind hearing children at early ages, the lags often were
not observed at older ages. If we accepted proficiency in standard English as a
criterion for language ability, this "catch-up" effect would be difficult to reconcile,
because over the course of childhood deaf children exhibit an increasing deficit
relative to hearing children with respect to ability in English. For similar reasons, it
is difficult to accept the idea that an experiential deficit operates to impede the
development of deaf children.

In a review of fifty-one cognitive studies with deaf subjects, Ottem (1980) found
that deaf and hearing subjects performed equally well when required to refer to one
set of data, but deaf students functioned poorly when the task required reference to
two sets of data. In trying to explain the reasons for the difference, Ottem speculated:

> The only reasonable explanation the author can find is that deaf people have been
> particularly trained or taught to communicate about single events. This may have its
> roots in that we, as hearing individuals, have imposed upon the deaf a requirement
> about simple and unambiguous communication, and that this type of communication
> is best obtained by referring to single events. (p. 568)

In a study that used sign language in the testing situation, McDaniel (1980) reported that deaf and hearing children are comparable over a wide range of visual
memory tasks. This equivalence applies even to temporal order, an area in which
previous studies had reported deficiencies among the deaf subjects.

Rittenhouse and Spiro (1979) presented Piagetian conservation problems of number, weight, and volume to deaf and hearing students. Unlike previous investigators, they included an interrogation phase in the study; that is, after giving a response, the subject was asked to explain why he or she made that particular response.
Furth (1973) contended that conservation interrogation is unusually difficult for deaf
subjects and is, in effect, a test of language, not cognition. The principal investigator
in this particular experiment was proficient in oral and manual communication and
could communicate equally well with both deaf and hearing subjects, a relatively

rare phenomenon until recently. Rittenhouse and Spiro classified responses into three categories: compensation, invariant quantity, and reversibility. Among both deaf and hearing subjects, 83 percent of the explanations were of the invariant-quantity type (for example, "You did not add or subtract anything"; "They were the same before, and you really did not change them"). Of a total of 408 conservation responses, in only seven instances was a subject unable to give an adequate explanation; five of these instances involved three deaf subjects, and the other two one hearing subject. The total sample included forty-one deaf and thirty-four hearing children. The investigators concluded that the deaf children not only were able to rationalize their conservation decisions verbally but also provided rationales identical to those of the hearing subjects.

The findings of Rittenhouse and Spiro cast a somewhat different light on discussions of the language-thought controversy as it relates to deafness. It was found that once fluent communication was established between the investigator and deaf subjects, not only the responses but also the explanations provided by deaf and hearing children were the same. Previously reported low performance in other studies probably was due not to lower cognitive skills or to a lack of language but to limitations in standard English vocabulary and grammar and in oral English skills. Traditionally, one justification for categorizing deaf children as "concrete" has been their difficulties in dealing with multiple meanings of English words. Because they have reduced exposure to English words and because vocabulary is frequently taught as though each word had one meaning, American deaf children have not been exposed to the nuances of English. It takes years to sort out the variations on so many of the language's short words (*can* do, tin *can, can* it; *run* fast, mill *run, run* on a bank), let alone the differences between a literal statement and a figurative statement (*the sky is blue; he feels blue*). Rittenhouse, Morreau, and Iran-Nejad (1981) referred to the difficulty that the figurative statement "I am a rock" may cause deaf children. Deaf children may also have problems mastering slang, which is constantly changing, and idioms. M. Boatner (1966) edited the *Dictionary of Idioms for the Deaf,* which has been widely used in programs for the deaf. The problem is that to use the dictionary a child has to realize that a particular phrase, clause, or sentence contains an idiom. A child is likely to interpret a phrase such as "The material is over my head" or "Mary was in a stew" literally, without suspecting the presence of an idiom.

Rittenhouse, Morreau, and Iran-Nejad (1981) investigated the ability of hard-of-hearing and deaf students to comprehend metaphor, which is a form of figurative language. Each child was presented with twelve metaphor items, each consisting of a short story of fewer than fifty words, along with four possible interpretations. For example, a boy being confined to his room for taking cookies might be related by analogy to a prisoner going to jail. For the first four items, the students were given feedback on the correctness of their responses. The authors found that both hard-of-hearing (27 dB to 85 dB loss) and deaf (greater than 90 dB loss) subjects were able to comprehend metaphor by using analogical reasoning. They concluded that a deaf child "may fail to realize the language *can* [sic] be used metaphorically, a problem which would have nothing to do with his ability to comprehend metaphors once he understands they are permissible" (p. 452). Rittenhouse, Morreau, and Iran-Nejad postulated that well-meaning teachers may not expose deaf children to metaphors becasue of the mistaken assumption that the children can't understand them. The authors suggested using classroom activities in which analogies can be drawn.

Recent Developments

Whereas in many related areas the levels of interest and research have sunk below those of the 1960s and 1970s, in the area of cognition and deafness work has steadily continued. Two symposia held at Gallaudet University resulted in the publication of summaries of work on cognition, education, and deafness (Martin, 1985, 1991).

The reports covered a range of topics. In general, the results supported the idea that deaf individuals have normal intellectual capabilities, although performance deficits may sometimes appear. In a review, Wolff (1985) claimed that the supposed cognitive deficits alluded to in the traditional literature are usually attributable to factors such as secondary disabilities and/or problems of communication. He concluded that deaf children have an "intact cognitive machinery" (p. 78). Zweibel and Mertens (1985) reported that young deaf children seemed to lag behind hearing children in some Piagetian tasks but that no differences were observed in older children. They suggested that some tests may not be appropriate for use with deaf children, at least those at young ages.

In the United States the most frequently used intelligence test for children has been the Wechsler Intelligence Scale for Children (WISC). In 1974 a revised form of the WISC, the WISC-R, was published (Wechsler, 1974) and norms for deaf children were developed for the Performance Scale but not for the Verbal Scale. Reporting on factor analytic studies of 324 investigations of scores of 21,307 deaf children on performance tests (mostly the Wechsler Intelligence Scale for Children–Revised), Braden (1991) noted patterns of cognitive skills "virtually identical" to those of hearing children. The average performance IQ score for deaf children was 99.95, almost identical to the hearing children's norm of 100. Braden addressed the issue of using instructional programs designed to improve the cognitive functioning of culturally different children and concluded that they were not directly appropriate for deaf children because these children exhibit no cognitive deficits relative to hearing children.

A third edition of the WISC, the WISC III, was published in 1991 (Wechsler, 1991) and since that time has replaced the WISC-R in general usage. A little noted fact is that scores on the later editions of the WISC are lower than on the previous ones. This point needs some clarification. If a group of 100 or 1,000 children were to take the WISC and obtain average IQ scores of 100, and then take the WISC-R, their average IQ scores would be somewhat lower than 100; if they were to then take the WISC III, their average IQ scores would be below both their WISC and WISC-R scores. Obviously, the children have not changed, but the tests and the scoring have. This might be due to a number of factors. Perhaps previous tests inflated IQ scores. Perhaps the present WISC III falsely lowers scores. Perhaps children today are more intelligent than a generation or two ago. Because the concept of IQ is an artificial construct, there is no clear answer. However, since an IQ score may be used in assessing whether a child may be classified as retarded, it is important for school psychologists to be aware of the differences.

Slate and Fawcett (1995) investigated the validity of the WISC III for forty-seven hard-of-hearing children. They found that over a three-year period the relationship between the WISC-R and WISC III was high ($r = +.93$) but that the average scores for the same children were 3.8 points higher on the WISC-R than on the WISC III.

In a later analysis of the same date, Slate (1996) investigated the performance scores of deaf males and females. Previous research on various samples of children in the United States and other countries have consistently reported that boys score higher than girls on performance tests and subtests. From their sample of twenty-one boys and twenty-six girls, Slate reported that boys scored approximately fifteen points higher than girls on both the WISC-R and WISC III Performance IQ scales. However, there were no gender differences between boys and girls in academic achievement, as measured by the Wide Range Achievement Test–Revised. This raises some serious questions. It is not logical for children with significantly different IQ scores to have essentially the same academic achievement. They must be bringing similar intellectual capacities to the task, capacities that are not adequately measured by the WISC-R and WISC III Performance Scales. My reaction is to question the utility of relying only on performance tests for predicting school achievement, especially for girls, when verbally loaded measures predict academic achievement better than performance measures (Braden, 1994).

One area that has received attention recently is the use of verbal IQ scales in the assessment of deaf children. Traditionally, such measures have not been used because of the low scores attained by deaf subjects relative to performance scales and the acknowledgment that they do not adequately reflect the intellectual capacity of deaf children. However, it is undeniable that reliance on the performance scales of tests such as the WISC-R or WISC III in effect produces half a test, with implications of lowered reliability and validity. Both Braden (1991) and Moores (1990b) reported that scores of deaf subjects on verbal subtests of the WISC-R and WAIS (Wechsler Adult Intelligence Scale) were lower than scores on performance subtests; however, scores on the verbal subtests correlated *more highly* with measures of academic achievement. This finding illustrates the paradox that, for deaf children, performance IQ measures may validly assess intellectual capacity but have little correlation with academic achievement. Verbal measures predict (correlate with) school achievement at a higher level but underestimate intellectual capacity.

Mackinson, Leigh, Blennerhassett, and Anthony (1997) investigated the validity of the Test of Nonverbal Intelligence, 2nd Edition (TONI-2) with deaf and hard-of-hearing children. The TONI-2 (Brown, Sherbonou, and Johnson, 1990) is nonverbally administered, requires only pointing or motor responses, and is relatively culture-free. Mackinson et al. reported moderate correlations of the TONI-2 with the WISC III and concluded that the results supported its validity as a quick measure of intellectual functioning for deaf and hard-of-hearing children.

Following principles of test construction theory, Miller (1985) reported on some promising procedures for administering the verbal subtests of the WISC-R and WISC III involving the use of signs by a test administrator with fluency in various communication systems and the ability to code-switch between ASL and English-based manual codes on English. The approach appears to be effective with all verbal subtests, with the exception of vocabulary. Miller has cautioned against the use of the verbal subtests until norms for deaf students have been developed. An effort to establish such norms is currently under way.

Miller (1991) investigated the issue of test validity and nonbiased assessment of deaf students, using signs for vocabulary tests. In an analysis of the items on the Peabody Picture Vocabulary Test–Revised (PPVT-R), Form L (Dunn and Dunn, 1981), Miller reported that the practice of finger-spelling the items turns the test into one of reading comprehension, thus invalidating it as a measure of receptive vocabulary. In addition, many of the ASL signs for more advanced English words are the same signs used for developmentally easier words with similar meanings. Significantly, many of the ASL signs used with the PPVT-R were iconic, in that the action of the sign itself gave a clue to its meaning. Miller reported that nonsigning hearing college students were able to respond correctly at the 80 percent level to PPVT-R items when chance responding would have been at the 25 percent rate (selecting the correct response from four alternatives). The introduction of alternative choices reduced scores significantly, but scores remained above chance level. Signs for words such as *drum, typing,* and *sewing* were so iconic that all hearing subjects responded correctly.

The reader must remain sensitive to the fact that the development of appropriate receptive sign tests is a highly complex process, given the iconic nature of sign languages. Assumptions upon which spoken tests are based do not always hold for sign tests. In a test such as the PPVT-R, it is not simply a matter of changing a spoken stimulus to a sign and retaining the same alternate response choices. The highly iconic nature of many ASL signs, as demonstrated in the Miller study, precludes this. Using the American Manual Alphabet and finger-spelling each stimulus word, as some testers have advocated, distorts the task and turns it into an English reading test. Also, there is no one-to-one relationship between a spoken English word and an ASL sign. For example, a person may use the same sign for the spoken words *dig* and *excavate* in certain contexts. Scores of a deaf-signing child in some cases, then, may be spuriously inflated, not only on the basis of visual perceptual matching, but because ASL may not distinguish between vocabulary in the same way that spoken English does.

In his role of respondent from a researcher's perspective to the 1984 International Symposium on Cognition, Education and Deafness, Moores (1985c) noted, "Probably the biggest discrepancy in relation to theory and its applications was the rare reference to the work of Vygotsky" (p. 225). The only exception was a treatment by Miller (1985). The lack of attention was noted because, unlike Piaget, Vygotsky had proposed a stage theory of development that placed a great emphasis on socialization. Also, Vygotsky had been assigned to what was then known as the Moscow Institute of Defectology in the 1930s, and his work had provided the foundation for much of the curriculum in education of the deaf in the former Soviet

Union (Moores, 1972b). At the Second International Symposium on Cognition, Education and Deafness, Bonkowski, Gavelek, and Akamatsu (1992) responded with a presentation on education and the social construction of mind from a Vygotskian perspective. They emphasized Vygotsky's position that social factors fulfill a facilitative function in bringing out qualities that already exist in the individual. Vygotsky believed that the development of higher psychological processes is environmentally driven and is made possible through acquisition of communicative systems, especially language. Bonkowski et al. (1991) state, "Misconceptions concerning deaf individuals as intellectually inferior or limited to concrete forms of thinking may result from a failure to understand the extent to which the development of higher intellectual processes results from the communicative use of language" (p. 187). In 1993, Knox and Stevens published the English translation of Volume 2 of the six-volume *Collected Works of L. S. Vygotsky,* entitled *The Fundamentals of Defectology.* This volume covers work from the end of World War I into the 1930s and should be of interest to all special educators. We will briefly consider some applications of Vygotsky's work to educating deaf children in a later chapter.

Summary

The available evidence suggests that the condition of deafness imposes no limitations on the cognitive capabilities of individuals. There is no evidence to suggest that deaf people think in more "concrete" ways than hearing individuals or that their intellectual functioning is in any way less sophisticated. As a group, deaf people function within the normal range of intelligence, and deaf individuals exhibit the same wide variability that the hearing population does. As Rittenhouse and Spiro (1979) demonstrated, deaf children apparently reason through cognitive-type problems using strategies like those children with normal hearing use.

The evidence with respect to "experiential deficits" is less clear-cut. Studies have documented that the majority of parents with no prior exposure to deafness tend to restrict their deaf children's social and physical experiences. This may cause lags in the development of deaf children. In this case, deficits would be attributable not to deafness itself but to inappropriate responses to deafness.

Growing numbers of studies are being conducted in which deaf subjects who clearly understand the tasks are being tested by experimenters fluent in oral-manual communication. These studies tend to show great similarity between the performances of deaf and hearing subjects on tests of conservation, social thinking, spatial thinking, and memory. Given the present state of knowledge, the most parsimonious conclusion to draw from the evidence is that deaf and hearing children are similar across a wide range of areas traditionally related to the study of cognitive and intellectual abilities. The great difficulties deaf children encounter in academic subject matter most likely are not caused by cognitive deficiencies. In fact, it is safe to say that educators of the deaf have not capitalized on the cognitive strengths of deaf children in the academic environment.

8

Deafness and Social-Emotional Adjustment

Introduction

Perhaps one way to address the issues involved in the social-emotional development and mental health of deaf individuals is to consider the question "Is there a psychology of deafness?" It might come as a surprise to learn that the question has generated some considerable controversy. On the one hand, we know that the sensory inputs of a deaf individual are different from those of the general population and that therefore the world may be experienced in different ways. Several books have been published on psychology and deafness; in fact, three well-known texts bear the title *The Psychology of Deafness* (Levine, 1960; Myklebust, 1964; Vernon and Andrews, 1990). The concept of a separate psychology of deafness has been challenged, particularly in the area of psychotherapy, as presenting a stereotypical view of deafness and Deaf culture. For example, Sussman (1988) has argued that many deaf individuals of various economic, educational, social-cultural, and communication backgrounds respond to and benefit from the various forms of psychotherapy used with hearing people when conditions for effective psychotherapy are present.

Part of the reaction against the concept of a psychology of deafness is due to the belief that its proponents, especially some of its early ones such as Levine and Myklebust, held a pathological perspective on deafness and therefore viewed it in terms of a deficiency model. Vernon, on the other hand, has demonstrated the cognitive normalcy of deaf individuals and is concerned with environmental impacts of deafness on the deaf child and adult. Vernon and Andrews (1990) argue that the effects of a hearing loss can be pervasive and can create psychological stress. If there is a lack of communication because of the inability or unwillingness of significant others to sign, there may be an isolation from other people and from knowledge. The result can be a severe form of deprivation and an alteration of interpersonal relationships. Vernon and Andrews assert, "We take the view that deafness is a psychological variable which influences the behavior of deaf persons such that their life experience differs in significant ways from that of those who are not deaf" (p. xiii).

Interest in the mental health of deaf people has been quite variable through the years. For a period of time, approximately equal amounts of work were being done in the area of mental health and deafness and in the area of cognition and deafness. For a period of about fifteen years, roughly 1975 to 1990, much more research appeared to be devoted to cognition than to mental health. This was at least partially a result of the increased emphasis on academic achievement as more and more deaf children attended classes with hearing students and there was a press for adaptation to the general curriculum. Since the late 1980s, interest in the social-emotional adjustment of deaf children has increased. Two major factors may have influenced this trend. First, the emphasis on families of PL 99–457, at least on families with infants, gives major attention to facilitating social-emotional adjustment. Second, as the least restrictive environment, mainstreaming, and full inclusion movements gathered momentum, concern has grown about the psychological effects on deaf children, especially profoundly deaf children, who are totally submerged in a hearing environment and isolated from significant contact with deaf adults and deaf peers. Although much work needs to be done, at present many gaps in our knowledge remain concerning both the overall development and adjustment of deaf children and adults in general and the implications of various types of educational placement for psychosocial development in particular.

In previous chapters, we noted that professionals have tended to view the development and functioning of deaf individuals from two different perspectives. The first and traditionally dominant view concentrates on the lack of hearing, sometimes with implicit and explicit assumptions about the inferior development of deaf individuals. (See the discussion in Chapter 7 of approaches to the study of cognitive abilities of deaf individuals.) The second view, which has grown in popularity among professionals, focuses on the development of effective, well-integrated, and well-adjusted deaf individuals.

The first view assumes what is called a "deviance model." This model emphasizes identifying ways in which deaf persons differ from a norm or standard established for a hearing population. *Difference* is equated with *deviance*, with all of its negative connotations, and *deviance* comes to be used interchangeably with *deficiency*. The deviance model has been the basis for various "psychologies of deafness" that have been promulgated over the last several generations. Implicit in the term *psychology of deafness* is a belief that the impact of deafness is so overwhelming that general psychological principles are inadequate to deal with the condition.

The second approach, which is healthier and more realistic, is beginning to receive attention and support from professionals concerned with the social-emotional development of deaf individuals. Rather than searching for what is different, deviant, or deficient, these professionals emphasize the conditions necessary for the development of a healthy, whole, well-integrated person. Implicit in this approach is the assumption that the basic needs of all human beings, hearing or deaf, are essentially similar and that the development of a healthy personality is based on meeting those needs satisfactorily. The presence and growing influence of deaf professionals in the field have contributed greatly to the general change in attitude.

The trend toward a more positive model of human nature, held by those concerned with the impact of deafness on development, reflects a general movement away from the deviance models, especially those based on Freudian principles, which dominated psychology in the nineteenth century and most of the twentieth century. The developmental theories of Maslow (1954) and Erikson (1963, 1964, 1968) have been especially instrumental in laying the foundation for perceiving the growth of the individual within a more balanced framework.

Schlesinger and Meadow (1972a) placed the issue in perspective as follows:

> Does the absence of early auditory stimulation, feedback and communication in itself create a propensity toward a particular adaptive pattern? Or, alternatively, does early profound deafness elicit particular responses from parents, teachers, siblings and peers that contribute to developmental problems referred to above? These are questions that are difficult to resolve in an either/or way, since the concomitants of organic deafness and the social expectations it arouses in others are intertwined from the very beginning. Rather than belaboring the nature/nurture controversy, it is more fruitful to look instead at the entire life cycle, examining instances of optimal and minimal adjustment and seeking out the antecedents, correlates and consequences of these patterns. (pp. 2-3)

Sussman and Brauer (1999) note the heterogeneous nature of the deaf population and maintain that current rational, cognitive, client-centered approaches are as applicable to deaf as to hearing individuals. They advocate the "depathologizing" of deafness and the embracing of a wellness model based on sociocultural components that enhance the psychological integrity of deaf people. They argue that the implementation of psychological services for deaf people may differ, as in the use of sign communication, but that the process itself is consistent with that undergone by other populations.

An example of the application of this philosophy may be seen in research on the application of narrative therapy with deaf children who have good oral language. Furlinger (1999) characterizes narrative therapy as a special kind of conversation that elicits a client's strengths, competencies, and solutions and in which the child becomes better able to assume control of the problem. He reports success in two case studies with children with good oral skills, and suggests that further research be done with children who use sign as a preferred mode of communication.

Although the therapeutic process may be similar, Sussman and Brauer do not argue that assessment instruments should necessarily be the same or that there are not cultural issues that must be taken into consideration. It seems to me that a completely separate psychology of deafness does not exist but that certainly some factors must be taken into consideration. This was illustrated most clearly by Lala (1998) in his treatment of the fourth edition of the *Diagnostic and Statistical Manual of Mental Disorders,* or DSM (American Psychiatric Association, 1994). The DSM has been revised to reflect advances in knowledge regarding differential diagnosis associated with variances in age, gender, and culture. From his review of the literature, Lala concludes that the next revision of the DSM should include information on Deaf culture to give care providers a better understanding of the needs of deaf clients. He reasons that deaf people have the same psychological and psychiatric behaviors and needs as hearing people and that they deserve to have their needs addressed accurately and precisely, without irrelevancies clouding the issue. He quotes Vernon and Andrews (1990, p. 161): "One must note that society usually responds inappropriately to the needs of deaf people and to the reality of deafness. Such response is a cause for a significant amount of the psychopathology seen in deaf people. Furthermore, certain normal coping responses by deaf persons are misconstrued as abnormal by the general public."

Limitations of Research on Social-Emotional Development of Deaf Individuals

Before addressing representative research, we need to establish an appropriate background for interpreting results. Two overriding factors cannot be ignored. First is the extremely difficult nature of the task of assessing what we will call *personality.* Second is the fact that the impact of deafness per se on an individual can never be measured in isolation but only within the context of complex social variables.

If the measurement of intelligence is an inexact science, the measurement of personality is an inexact art. For despite the difficulties that the field of intelligence testing has faced, a wide variety of reliable and empirically validated tests have been developed and used extensively. Examiners have at their disposal individual and group tests, verbal and performance tests, oral and paper-and-pencil tests, and tests that provide either quantitative or qualitative results. With only a few notable exceptions—for example, the Minnesota Multi-Phasic Inventory (MMPI)—similarly reliable and valid measures of personality do not exist. The process is much more subjective, and interpretation of results is susceptible to a much greater degree of interpreter bias. Because most of the more commonly used measures either require a relatively high level of reading (for example, the MMPI) or involve substantial communication between tester and testee (for example, the Rorschach Inkblot Test and the Thematic Apperception Test, or TAT), their applicability to deaf individuals may be limited. An exceptional degree of caution must be used in interpreting results obtained through procedures such as those used in the Rorschach or the TAT. It is essential that the examiner have experience in communicating with deaf people with a wide range of oral and written English skills, including some who rely completely on manual communication.

Results of investigations of social-emotional adjustment of deaf individuals may be influenced by factors only incidentally related to deafness itself. The most obvious example of such a factor is the commonly observed familial stress caused by inadequate adjustment to the presence of a deaf child. As detailed in Chapter 6, the presence of a deaf child in a family can be a traumatic, emotionally draining experience. Feelings of guilt, recrimination, and hostility are common. Because the majority of parents of deaf children have normal hearing and have had little contact with deaf individuals, deafness constitutes a mysterious, threatening force that is difficult to confront. Communication with the child is often minimal, and normal two-way communication between parent and child may not exist.

In such a situation, a deaf child, reacting to a lack of effective communication and to other negative aspects of the environment, may develop patterns of behavior that are classified as "immature," "hyperkinetic," "autistic," "egocentric," and so on. However, to attribute this behavior to deafness per se is to miss the point entirely. It is more appropriately attributed to unsatisfactory environmental conditions that developed because the child's parents were not helped to adjust to the fact of deafness and therefore did not provide the child with sufficient environmental support to develop to his or her full potential.

Another factor that is commonly overlooked, and is of special concern in evaluating studies that compare groups of deaf individuals with groups of hearing individuals, is the possibility that some major causes of deafness, such as rubella, meningitis, and mother-child blood incompatibility, involve harmful residual effects in addition to hearing loss. To take a hypothetical example, suppose researchers compared a group of deaf people and a group of hearing people born in the early 1960s on a number of variables and found that the hearing children were more robust, better coordinated, and less impulsive. Unless the researchers controlled for etiology, the extent to which they could generalize their findings would be severely limited. Lower group scores might be explained by the presence of substantial numbers of deaf children with an etiology of rubella with involvements, however mild, in addition to deafness. Low scores also might result in part from a tendency of some mothers of deaf children to restrict the children's activities, preventing them from developing physical skills to the same degree as their hearing siblings.

A useful rule of thumb in evaluating research of this nature is to examine the upper range of scores of the respective groups. If the highest scores obtained by individuals in the deaf group are similar to the highest scores in the hearing group on a particular measure, it will be a mistake to conclude that deafness itself influences functioning in that area, even if group mean scores are lower for the deaf group.

Summarizing results of investigations of social-emotional adjustment of deaf individuals, Levine (1960) reported:

1. Many of the instruments used assume a level of communicative interaction that may not exist between hearing testers and some deaf testees.

2. Adequate development of a deaf individual may be inhibited not by deafness itself but by inadequate coping behaviors of significant others in the environment.

3. The residual effects of some of the major etiologies of deafness may involve impairments in addition to hearing loss. (pp. 51–52)

Levine's findings apply today as documented by Lala (1998), Sussman and Brauer (1999), and Vernon and Andrews (1990).

In addition, A. Harris (1978, p. 224) pointed out that a deaf child may be a limited or atypical participant in social exchanges with the parents. She suggested that parent-child interaction may be out of phase long before an appropriate diagnosis is made. In a similar vein, R. Harris (1978, p. 145) argued that the side effects of hearing loss, rather than the hearing loss itself, may account for what has been perceived as poor self-control of rage in deaf people. He included among these side effects factors such as inappropriate rearing practices, negative parental attitudes toward disability in general and deafness in particular, poor parental coping with unexpected crises and stresses, and the inability of hearing parents to communicate manually to meet the needs of their deaf child.

R. Harris (1978) called attention to the work of Klein (1962) in the area of blindness to illustrate the importance of appropriate parental response. Klein argued that a specific sensory deficit such as blindness (or deafness) may be considered a form of deprivation not because the sensory deficit per se involves isolation from the environment but because it often engenders an interpersonal isolation that may influence the child's personality development.

A final cautionary note is in order. In the behavioral sciences, it is a common failing among practitioners to neglect to define their terms. One widespread phenomenon is the recourse to *nominalism,* equating the naming of a behavior or characteristic with a description or definition of the behavior or characteristic. Although terms such as *schizophrenic, aphasic, autistic,* or *learning disabled* may be useful in the proper context, their abuse is much more frequent than their proper use. Gross examples of nominalism appear in the literature concerning social-emotional functioning of the deaf; terms like *submissive, dependent, neurotic,* and *rigid* are almost never defined appropriately.

Research on Personality Characteristics of Deaf Individuals

In an early review of personality studies conducted with deaf groups, Donoghue (1968) presented the major issue in the following manner:

> Psychological research indicates, as is so often the case in our discipline, that over the years professional opinions concerning the effects of auditory failure on the adjustment pattern of the deaf have polarized to some extent. In one division of this dichotomy of opinion there are those who maintain the loss of hearing, whether fully or partially, leads to an increasing number of atypical behavioral symptoms which suggest at least a graduated degree of emotional maladjustment probably is present. At some variance with this form of ontological metaphysics, there are those who

maintain that functional loss of any part of the physique, be it motor, sensorineural, or some other variety, need not necessarily be pinpointed as a probable etiological source of observed abnormalities. (pp. 39–40)

As shown earlier in this chapter the polarization continues to this date. Although the predominant position has shifted to thinking of deafness more in cultural than pathological terms.

One disturbing trend should be noted. It appears that much more research on the social-emotional development and psychological adjustment of deaf individuals was reported prior to and including the 1970s than in the ensuing decades. It is not clear why this is so. Perhaps much of the early work was done by researchers who considered deafness as a pathology or experiment of nature and who wanted to test theories with deaf subjects. Perhaps, with the growing consensus concerning the essential normalcy of the deaf population, there is less motivation now for research into differences. For whatever reason, the literature is more sparse in recent times than previously. On the positive side, more of the work is being conducted by deaf professionals themselves and by hearing and deaf scientists who have better communication skills and who typically do not approach their tasks with some of the prejudices that marked their predecessors.

A reading of the most commonly cited studies of personality characteristics of deaf individuals from the 1930s to the 1970s would suggest, incorrectly in this author's opinion, that the loss of hearing leads to atypical behavior symptoms. The references immediately following present a consistently negative view of the adjustment of deaf individuals. The studies are of questionable validity, because typically they were not developed for deaf subjects and did not take into account difficulties in reading standard English sentences out of context. Thus it is debatable whether they should be referenced. However, they represent forty years of personality research in the area of deafness, and they indicate the mindset of professionals in the field during that period. It should be noted that reservations were frequently expressed about the findings, sometimes by the researchers themselves, and that more recent work has suggested satisfactory adjustment by deaf individuals.

In one of the earliest studies, using mailed responses to the Bernreuter Personality Inventory, Pintner (1933) reported that deaf adults were more emotionally unstable, more introverted, and more submissive than hearing adults. No differences were found in self-sufficiency. Using a revised form of the test, Pintner, Fusfeld, and Brunswig (1937) reported that the deaf subjects were more neurotic, more introverted, and less dominant than the hearing individuals. Soloman (1943) reported deaf subjects to be immature, submissive, and dependent. Deaf subjects also tended to be more insecure, apathetic, anxious, and suspicious. In a study of deaf teenage girls using the Wechsler Adult Intelligence Scale (WAIS) and the Rorschach Inkblot Test, Levine (1956) reported that the deaf subjects were egocentric, irritable, impulsive, and suggestible and that for them controls were external. Myklebust (1964) noted an immaturity in caring about others and stated that responses of deaf subjects to the Minnesota Multi-Phasic Inventory suggested psychotic reactions. Springer and Roslow (1938) reported a higher incidence of neurotic tendencies among deaf subjects as well as a greater degree of repressive behavior. In comparing deaf and hard-of-hearing male and female adults to normative data on the MMPI, Myklebust (1964) reported that deaf males were significantly different from hearing males on all ten scales of the test and hard-of-hearing males were different on nine of the ten scales. Deaf and hard-of-hearing females were significantly different from the hearing female norms on seven and five of the ten scales, respectively. Rosen (1959) administered the MMPI to a sample of deaf college students and noted that the results suggested the existence of aberrant personality functioning in the deaf subjects.

Goetzinger et al. (1966) reported that deaf adolescent males and females were more aggressive and less cooperative than hearing adolescents. These researchers characterized the deaf subjects as emotionally immature, rigid, and possessing restricted interests. In a study of the 16 Personality Factor (16PF) Questionnaire, Trybus (1973) concluded that deaf males were more divergent from hearing norms than were deaf females. In a study that administered the 16PF to more than eight hundred Gallaudet students, Jensema (1975a, 1975b) reported that deaf females were found to be more outgoing, more emotionally stable, more conscientious, and less suspicious than deaf males. They were also considered to be less assertive and venturesome and more apprehensive and tense than their male counterparts.

Baroff (1955) stated that deaf individuals exhibited a lack of anxiety, introspection, and impulse control. Levine (1948) reported similar findings, but suggested that such behaviors reflect normal adjustment mechanisms given the environment deaf individuals face. Altshuler (1962, 1963) characterized the behavior of deaf subjects using terms such as *egocentric, lack of empathy, gross coercive dependency, impulsivity,* and *absence of thoughtful introspection.*

In summarizing research results obtained using projective techniques with deaf individuals, Levine (1960, pp. 61–62) reported that all studies found the following characteristics: emotional immaturity, personality constriction, and deficient emotional adaptability. More than a decade later, Schlesinger and Meadow (1972a) arrived at the same conclusion: "Psychologically, the most frequently stated conclusion about deaf individuals is that they seem to reflect a high degree of 'emotional immaturity' " (p. 2).

However, the situation is less clear-cut than a summary of the literature might suggest. Almost every one of the above researchers felt constrained to qualify his or her findings. The lack of confidence in the results, or at least the reluctance to generalize from the findings, may be attributed to a number of factors. First is the questionable suitability of the instruments used. Heider and Heider (1941), for example, decried the practice of studying deaf individuals primarily by means of instruments developed for individuals with normal hearing. They expressed particularly strong reservations about the comparison of deaf and hearing groups based on tests designed to measure adjustment to the life normally hearing individuals face. Grinker (1967) advocated the development of instruments directly devised for and applicable to deaf subjects and suggested that a thematic apperception test could be devised to elicit the specific emotional problems of the deaf.

Although Myklebust (1964) reported that scores on the MMPI deviated from hearing norms, he also pointed out the extroverted social feelings of deaf individuals, a condition that is not common in individuals who exhibit psychotic behavior. Therefore, the usual psychopathological categories delineated by the MMPI were considered inappropriate for his subjects. Similarly, Rosen (1959) concluded that the language and idiomatic expressions used in the MMPI are not appropriate for deaf subjects and that the results obtained from deaf individuals should not be compared to hearing norms. Jensema (1975b) concluded that the 16PF is of low reliability and questionable validity when used with deaf subjects. Best (1943) commented on the gregariousness of deaf people as a group and expressed admiration for their optimism and ability to cope with an indifferent and sometimes hostile world.

Another factor that should be emphasized is that behavior considered to be maladaptive, neurotic, or psychotic in one situation might be deemed healthy and realistic in another. In many cases, deaf persons have faced rejection and hostility from their families. Their sense of worth has been denigrated because of unclear speech patterns. People do talk about them, and they do face social and economic discrimination. Within this context, Knapp (1968) and Zeckel (1953) challenged the negative conclusions of many of the studies on personality adjustment of deaf individuals, arguing that because deaf people have good reason to be aware of the derogatory behavior of others toward them, a feeling of mistrust is a healthy, not a psychopathological, reaction.

In addition, the testing situation must seem a threatening situation to many deaf subjects. In all of the above studies except those by Jensema and R. Harris, the testers had normal hearing. The vocabulary frequently was unfamiliar, and the deaf subjects usually had to rely completely on oral communication. Even when manual communication was employed, the situation tended to be artificial. In a review of the literature, Mangan (1963) noted that Levine's (1956) investigation of responses of deaf girls to the Rorschach Inkblot Test involved manual as well as oral communication, and he concluded that the study provided for excellent communication between examiner and subjects. However, there is reason to question this conclusion. All of the subjects were students at a school that did not allow signs in the classroom at that time. Although it has been reported that the students used signs as their preferred mode of communication outside the school grounds (Kohl, 1966), they probably were reluctant to do so with hearing adults. Also, in the research study under consideration, manual communication was a one-way street. The examiner never resorted to signs but relied completely on speech. Only the subjects were free to respond by speech, signs, and gestures. In discussing the use of projective techniques, Donoghue (1968) stated:

> Language is not an insurmountable barrier to a test such as the Rorschach; it can be given in English, German, Urdu or the language of signs used by deaf persons. The only really important criterion, aside from the examiner's professional proficiency, is the determination of whether the language employed is the one the client and examiner can adequately use in discussing the precept seen. This is a most important consideration where the deaf are concerned. (p. 43)

Instead of using projective techniques or language-based tests, Freedman (1971) observed six deaf girls from two to five years of age in a variety of situations. He reported that they were friendly, outgoing children whose behaviors and interests were typical of girls their age. The internal regulation of their behavior was normal. Freedman concluded that spoken language was not a prerequisite or even a significant factor in early personality development.

Garrison, Tesch, and DeLaro (1978) reported a low self-concept among deaf adolescents, but concluded that their finding resulted more from a limited understanding of the text itself than from actual feelings of low self-esteem. Farrugia and Austin (1980) noted no differences in the social-emotional adjustment of deaf adolescents in residential schools and that of hearing adolescents in public schools. A third group, deaf adolescents in public schools, scored significantly lower than the other two groups. If future studies indeed also indicate more mature behavior in deaf residential school students than in deaf public school students, the implications for the goals and impact of PL 94–142 will be profound.

Unfortunately, there is little additional evidence against which to check the Farrugia and Austin results. In a review of research, Hummel and Schimer (1984) noted that the least-restrictive-environment stipulation of PL 94–142 should have led to increased interest in the study of the social skills of deaf children. However, these researchers reported, "There has been a tendency to overfocus on cognitive and linguistic factors, sometimes to the exclusion of affective factors. Because of this, there is an unfortunate gap in our knowledge of the social adjustment of deaf children in different educational settings" (p. 259).

To fill the need for instruments to assess the social-emotional adjustment of deaf children, Meadow developed the Meadow/Kendall Social-Emotional Assessment Inventory, or SEAI (Meadow, Karchmer, Peterson, and Rudner, 1980). The original form was based on teachers' ratings of more than two thousand deaf children from seven to twenty-one years of age. A second inventory designed for preschool children, ages three to six, was subsequently developed with norms from ratings of more than eight hundred hearing-impaired children. Using the SEAI, Meadow (1984) compared teachers' ratings of four groups of preschool children: deaf children with additional conditions, deaf children without additional conditions, hearing children with disabilities, and hearing children without disabilities. The deaf children without additional conditions and the hearing children without disabilities received similar ratings. Both groups received significantly more favorable ratings than did hearing children with disabilities and deaf children with additional conditions. Concerning the similar ratings of deaf and hearing children, Meadow concluded:

> It may be that deafness is *not* as great a detriment to social development as clinicians, researchers and educators have assumed. Perhaps we have based our ideas too frequently on and generalized too broadly from experience with groups of children referred for treatment of behavior problems. Perhaps we tend to assume that problems of social adjustment in deaf children are related to their auditory loss rather than to other causes. (p. 39)

After considering all the obstacles deaf individuals face in their development, Altshuler (1974) noted that, despite difficulties, most develop along predictable lines.

He observed, "It is nothing short of miraculous that the majority of deaf children develop to be normal neurotics like the rest of us" (p. 370).

Briccetti (1994) highlighted the potential for misdiagnosis of deaf children when using a test such as the Draw-A-Person Screening Procedure for Emotional Disturbance (DAP:SPED), which has no deaf norms. Since human figure drawing tests are the most frequently used measures of the social-emotional status of deaf and hard-of-hearing children by school psychologists in the United States (Gibbins, 1989), the danger for the inappropriate use of the DAP:SPED is significant. Briccetti administered the DAP:SPED to two samples of deaf children. One had been clinically diagnosed as emotionally disturbed or behavior disordered, and the other was judged to have no disturbance. She reported no differences in the DAP:SPED between the two groups. Sixty percent of the "not disturbed" group were misclassified. In fact, the most severely misclassified subjects were four children determined to be free of emotional disturbance by a social-emotional inventory normed on deaf children, a teacher rating questionnaire, and psychological documentation. Briccetti concluded that the DAP:SPED is not a valid screening device for deaf children because there are differences in the drawings of deaf children and those of hearing children and separate normative data for deaf children are needed.

Murdoch (1996) investigated the existence of stereotyped behavior in 390 residential school deaf children in the United Kingdom. Stereotyped behaviors included socially unacceptable repetitiveness, immaturity, inconsistency, and unresponsiveness to environmental change related to diminished functioning. Murdoch noted that the sample was not representative of the school-age deaf and hard-of-hearing population of the United Kingdom and contained a relatively large proportion of children with additional disabilities, 79 percent. The children without disabilities did not show stereotypical behavior, whereas 35 percent of those with one or more disabilities showed stereotyped behaviors. Such behavior was commonly reported for children with visual impairment and learning difficulties.

In sum, it appears that efforts to assess personality variables among deaf individuals are at about the same level today as intelligence testing of the deaf was thirty years ago. For the most part, inappropriate tests have been administered under unsatisfactory conditions, and results have been compared with unrealistic norms. An impressive number of competent researchers with experience in the area of deafness (Briccetti, 1994; Donoghue, 1968; Heider and Heider, 1941; Jensema, 1975b; Levine, 1948; Myklebust, 1964; Schlesinger and Meadow, 1972a; Sussman and Brauer, 1999; Trybus, 1973) have questioned the results obtained and/or the extent to which the findings reflect actual deviancies in the deaf population. When a test standardized on deaf subjects was employed (Meadow, 1984), no differences were found between deaf and hearing children.

Self-Concept

As we might expect, research on the self-concept of elementary and secondary school-age deaf students is limited. The Tennessee Self-Concept Scale (TSCS) has been the instrument of choice in the few studies reported in the literature, and it has been usually administered to young adult and adult deaf subjects. For example, Sussman (1988) found self-concept among deaf adults, as measured by the TSCS, to be significantly lower than for the general population. Randall (1969) used the TSCS with a sample of forty-nine students at a residential school for the deaf with an average age of eighteen years and reported scores significantly below hearing norms. Garrison, et al. (1978) reported that 109 deaf students at the National Technical Institute for the Deaf scored lower than the published norms for the TSCS. They concluded, however, that low self-concept scores may not reflect valid low levels of self-concept among deaf people but may be determined by the English language level of some of the items.

Koelle and Convey (1982) used several measures of self-concept and locus of control with ninety deaf students from thirteen to nineteen years of age in four residential schools. They reported that the sample of deaf children in general scored lower than hearing norms, but not as low as in studies that had used the TSCS. They concluded that the English language difficulties of the TSCS depressed the scores of deaf students, in contrast to the Piers-Harris Children's Self-Concept Scale (PHCSCS), on which the scores of the deaf subjects were close to hearing norms. Koelle and Convey argued that the easier readability of the PHCSCS led to higher and more valid scores among deaf students.

The Piers-Harris Children's Self-Concept Scale (Piers and Harris, 1969; Piers, 1984) may be appropriate for use with deaf children because it appears not to artificially depress self-ratings. It is a group test of eighty yes/no questions that can be administered in less than thirty minutes. Items are written at the third-grade level, and word meanings are clarified where the explanations will not influence the answers. The questions deal with six attributes:

1. Behavior
2. Intellectual and school status
3. Physical appearance and attributes
4. Anxiety
5. Popularity
6. Happiness and satisfaction

Scoring consists of one (1) point for each positive response, with a maximum possible score of 80. The mean for the Piers-Harris test among children without disabilities is 54, with a standard deviation of 13.

Moores (1995b) reported on a three-year study of school placement in which the Piers-Harris was administered to 920 deaf students: 529 from residential schools, 356 from large local public school programs, and 35 from small local public school programs. The overall mean score for the subjects was 55.2. The performance indicated no functional difference from the score of 54 for the fiftieth percentile for the norm sample. Within each category, the mean scores of deaf subjects in residential schools (55.9), large local public school programs (54.1), and small local public school programs (57.0) were also quite similar. The average total score for deaf subjects was well within the normal range of expressed self-concept, with little variation across different placements.

The results for all programs participating in the study differ from those reported in previous research using other measures that indicated that deaf subjects had lower self-concepts than hearing subjects. The subjects within the sample reported by Moores (1995b) showed no variation in total scores from the hearing norm. If future research establishes the reliability and validity of the Piers-Harris for use with deaf subjects, the results suggest that previous research using instruments such as the Tennessee Self-Concept Scale produced spuriously low measures of self-concept among deaf subjects because it demanded English language skills.

The scores of deaf students of both genders and in different placements were similar to those of hearing children. The data did not confirm concerns about possible low self-esteem among children in public school settings. They also did not confirm concerns about possible low self-esteem among deaf female students. Given the evidence, it seems that both hearing and deaf parents are fostering healthy self-esteem in their deaf children. Most deaf individuals appear to cope well with the strains imposed by deafness.

One study had a puzzling outcome. In a 2 x 2 x 2 analysis of the Moores data by race (white, African-American), gender (male, female), and placement (residential school, local program), Hairston (1994) reported that African-American residential school males scored *highest* and African-American local school males scored *lowest* of the eight groups. This variability did not show up in white or female students, and it is unclear whether the environment for African-American males was more different in the two kinds of setting or whether there were demographic differences such as socioeconomic status between African-American males in the two kinds of setting.

The Establishment of Psychiatric and Mental Health Services for Deaf Persons

Major initial advances in research and provision of services to deaf individuals in the fields of psychiatry and mental health have been made essentially by professionals in four institutes: the New York State Psychiatric Institute; the Michael Reese Medical Center Psychiatric and Psychosomatic Institute in Chicago; St. Elizabeth's Hospital in Washington, D.C.; and the Langley-Porter Neuropsychiatric Institute in San Francisco. Although the objectives of these institutes vary somewhat, their combined efforts have had a profound impact on educational, rehabilitative, and social programs for the deaf throughout the world. They have made contributions in the development of models for the provision of services to deaf individuals on inpatient and outpatient bases, in clinical and incidence research, in parent counseling, and in the training of professional personnel to work with deaf individuals. Each program has also begun to study techniques to facilitate optimal development of deaf individuals. With their involvement in training, research, and service, these institutes form a unique group.

The New York program, which began in 1955, preceded the other three by approximately ten years. New York State took a leading role in making commitments to the development of mental health programs for the deaf, and the statewide system of services is a model that other areas should emulate. A short description of the evolution of the New York system may provide some insight into the conditions and procedures necessary for the development of mental health services on a state or regional basis. For complete details on the system, readers are referred to the reports written on the various projects connected with the system (Altshuler and Rainer, 1968; Rainer and Altshuler, 1966, 1967, 1970; Rainer, Altshuler, and Kallman, 1963).

The first major activity involved a statewide census of deaf individuals, gathering basic statistics, and interviewing randomly selected deaf individuals and their families. All deaf patients in New York State mental hospitals were identified and tracked, and a psychiatric outpatient clinic for the deaf was established. Although little publicized and open only two days per week, the outpatient clinic served more than two hundred patients (Rainer, Altshuler, and Kallman, 1963). Information gathered about the deaf patients scattered throughout the state's twenty-one mental hospitals suggested that they were frequently isolated, misdiagnosed, poorly evaluated, and virtually untreated. For example, original figures suggested that the incidence of schizophrenia among deaf individuals was higher than would be predicted on the basis of population figures. However, closer examination revealed that schizophrenia was no more common among deaf admissions than among hearing admissions. The discrepancies were traced to the fact that hearing patients received treatment and were released, whereas deaf patients more frequently went untreated and were institutionalized longer. Because of the lack of trained professional personnel capable of communicating with them, deaf patients often became custodial cases.

The first phase, gathering data and establishing outpatient services, extended from 1955 to 1962. The second phase, from 1963 to 1966, involved development of a special inpatient unit for deaf persons at Rockland State Hospital as a demonstration project (Rainer and Altshuler, 1966). The outpatient services were expanded, and consultative relationships were established with the New York School for the Deaf in White Plains.

The third phase, from 1966 to 1970 (Rainer and Altshuler, 1970), had a number of objectives. First was the development of a halfway house to facilitate reintegration of deaf patients into the community. A related goal was a renewed effort to establish close cooperation between the overall state psychiatric program and the various state rehabilitation agencies. A new aspect of the system was the development of a program of preventive psychiatry in the New York City metropolitan area. In somewhat of a departure from the focus of previous activities, this effort encompassed a wide age range, from early school age through the adult years. Services included group therapy for students, group counseling for parents, and discussions with teachers and cottage personnel at a school for the deaf.

Relying on the knowledge and experience gathered from their efforts from 1955 to 1970, Rainer and Altshuler (1970) advanced the following recommendations and observations:

1. Mental illness and emotional difficulty are no less prevalent among the deaf than among the hearing. Diagnosis and treatment are more difficult and take longer.

2. Experienced mental health personnel (psychiatrist, psychologist, social worker, rehabilitation worker, nurse) must and can be recruited and trained in manual communication and special problems of the deaf. A teacher of sign language is an early and prime requisite.

3. Psychiatric treatment methods (individual and group psychotherapy and pharmacotherapy) can be adapted and applied to the deaf patient.

4. A clinic can be established once the personnel are available and will draw referrals from schools, rehabilitation agencies, families, physicians, and the deaf themselves.

5. The Deaf community can be made aware of the value of mental health facilities and will give aid to educational and volunteer programs, once the stigma of mental illness is removed.

6. For the acute or more seriously mentally ill deaf person, inpatient hospital facilities are the most efficient means for concentrating therapeutic efforts. A ward for patients of both sexes, with a specially trained staff, is most effective, and 30 beds have been found adequate to deal with the needs of the adult deaf population of a state as large as New York. Patients with illness of recent onset have the best prognosis, but chronic patients transferred from other hospitals to such a special ward often do strikingly well.

7. Such a ward ought to offer, as a minimum, medical and nursing care, individual and group psychotherapy, drug and other somatic treatments, and an occupational therapy workshop. Group therapy is particularly effective in fostering deaf patients' insight into their own behavior.

8. For the most effective results of a comprehensive treatment program, it has to be supplemented by a rehabilitation approach as described in the present report. Psychiatric case findings, diagnosis, and treatment of the deaf patient only bear full results when a rehabilitation team paves the way back to the outside world. This is especially important for the deaf where many needed facilities must be built or strengthened.

9. The rehabilitation counselor can function best as part of the mental health team, working in regular liaison with state agencies to open case files while patients are still under treatment. Exploration of patients' vocational skills and interests must begin before discharge and the lag between discharge and placement kept to a minimum.

10. Through occupational therapy workshops and other vocational training shops, new skills can be developed. Group and individual teaching in the hospital can improve patients' abilities in the 3R's; for this an experienced teacher of the deaf is essential.

11. Housing is of prime importance; by adding an experienced social worker who knows the problems of the deaf and can communicate well, it is possible to arrange for such placement (family, individual, home, foster care, as the case may be) and to teach the patients how to go to and from work and organize their lives in the most healthy way.

12. Halfway house facilities in the community can be used for an interim housing and reintegration of the deaf hospital [sic] into the community. A social worker at the halfway house specifically assigned to the group of deaf persons can effectively show them the upward path of increasing independence. Deaf and hearing ex-patients work together well at this halfway house level.

13. Turning to prevention of psychiatric disturbance, schools for the deaf can make effective use of a mental health team—psychiatrist, psychologist, and social worker. Trouble shooting with early psychiatric intervention is but one approach. Group therapy with adolescent students encourages greater awareness of interpersonal relations and forestalls problems in this area. Discussions with teachers and cottage personnel alert them to difficulties and assist them in proper handling of their pupils.

14. Since mental health begins at home, early contact with parents of deaf children and counseling, individually and in groups, can help these parents to overcome their guilt and shame, avoid the extremes of overprotection and rejection, and encourage them to communicate with the children by all means available. Social worker and psychiatrist can both work in bringing parents together for this purpose.

15. Deaf professional personnel can be of great value at all levels and should be recruited or trained whenever possible. (Rainer and Altshuler, 1970, pp. iii–iv)

The comprehensive recommendations of Rainer and Altshuler provide the foundation for effective state and regional programs. With only a few notable exceptions, however, these suggestions have yet to be utilized systematically. At the present time, they are ideals to be pursued. In fact, curtailment of federal funds and constraints on state budgets have made staying at present levels a major achievement.

Although a number of laudable programs exist to serve adults, there is an appalling lack of inpatient services for deaf children. This author knows of no psychiatric hospital with a unit for inpatient treatment of deaf children. In assessing the situation, Schlesinger (1977) wrote:

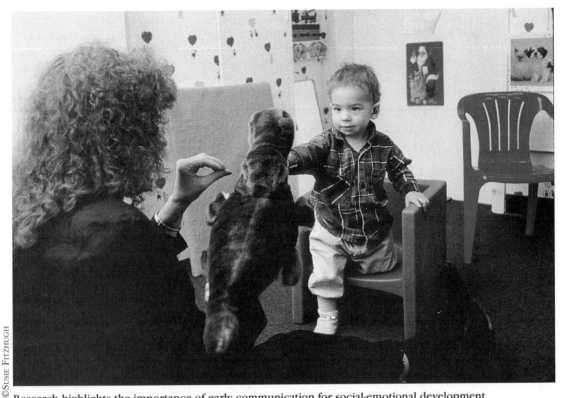

©SUSIE FITZHUGH

Research highlights the importance of early communication for social-emotional development.

Deaf children who have the additional burden of emotional disturbance have fallen between the slots of the bureaucratic funding system. Furthermore, federal demonstration projects cease and state budgets are tight. . . . It would appear that unless a more clear-cut funding pattern emerges, mental health services for the deaf will remain a stepchild in the psychiatric and mental health fields. (p. 102)

Raifman and Vernon (1997) reported that there have been improvements in services for deaf patients since the enactment of the Americans with Disabilities Act of 1990, but class action suits are often necessary to obtain appropriate services. Vernon and Daigle-King (1999) provided a historical overview of inpatient care for deaf mental patients beginning with the work of Hansen (1929) in Norway. Some consistencies were reported over time and across countries. In general, deaf patients have longer hospital stays, possibly because of the inadequate communication skills of care providers. Characteristics symptoms leading to hospitalization of deaf patients tend to be different from those of hearing patients. Over a seventy-year period all investigators found frequent misdiagnosis of deaf patients. Finally, for both deaf and hearing patients, dual diagnoses, such as mental illness and alcohol abuse, are far more common today than in the past. Vernon and Daigle-King commented that there has been a paucity of research in the area over the past two decades compared to earlier times.

The Facilitation of Optimal Development

Most professionals have emphasized that the incidence of emotional disturbance in deaf adults would be much lower if effective programs were established to reach parents of deaf children and help them deal with their children in more effective ways. In discussing the Michael Reese program, Stein, Merrill, and Dahlberg (1974) stated:

> Many of the mental health problems of the adult deaf can be traced to inadequacies of early parent-child relationships, unrealistic expectations on the parts of parents, and the inability of parents to ever accept the fact that their growing child is different and to a certain extent always will be different. Basically we were interested in developing programs to prevent or at least moderate the occurrence of mental health problems in the adult deaf population by fostering a more healthy early parent-child relationship. With this in mind, staff child psychiatrists, clinical psychologists, and psychiatric social workers established individual and group psychotherapy sessions to explore the feelings of parents who enrolled in our preschool program. (p. 3)

Robinson developed the first program of this type in 1963, when he initiated a group psychotherapy class for six deaf patients with mental illness at St. Elizabeth's Hospital in Washington, D.C. (Bowe, 1971). The first full-time staff member was added in 1968, and the hospital now serves individuals on both an inpatient and outpatient basis.

Meadow, a sociologist, and Schlesinger, a psychiatrist, also stressed the importance of the early years for satisfactory development (Schlesinger, 1978; Schlesinger and Meadow, 1971, 1972b). In their work at the Langley-Porter Institute, they have devoted great effort to facilitating parents' realistic acceptance of deafness in their children.

Meadow and Schlesinger utilized the developmental approach of Erikson (1963, 1964, 1968, 1969), who perceived the development of the individual as progressing through a sequence of critical stages or phases. Each stage presents the individual with a crisis, or task, that must be met successfully. The individual has parental and societal resources at his or her disposal. Erikson identified the following eight phases in the life cycle of the individual:

1. Basic trust versus mistrust: infancy
2. Autonomy versus shame and doubt: early childhood

3. Initiative versus guilt: childhood

4. Industry versus inferiority: school age

5. Identity versus identity confusion: adolescence

6. Intimacy versus isolation: young adulthood

7. Generativity versus stagnation: parenthood

8. Integrity versus despair: old age

The outcome of each phase is usually some balance between the extremes. From an Eriksonian perspective, Schlesinger and Meadow (1972b) examined influences on the deaf child's development at each of the eight stages in an attempt to understand how parents might help their deaf children develop in spontaneous and joyful ways. Schlesinger and Meadow noted that successful passages through the life cycle were found most often in deaf children of deaf parents. Since the majority of deaf children have hearing parents, Schlesinger and Meadow presented their account in the "hope that it will help hearing parents to ponder, to increase the acceptance of deafness in their children, and with this acceptance help their children to meet and master the challenges of each life crisis" (p. 29).

Schlesinger (1978) devoted particular attention to the importance of the first three phases in the development of the deaf child. She emphasized that the development of trust in infancy (birth to eighteen months) leads to later feelings of hope about oneself and the world. She stressed that in order to thrive, infants' cognitive and affective as well as physiological needs must be met effectively. In early childhood (ages eighteen to thirty-six months), the child should develop a sense of autonomy whereby he or she becomes aware of being a separate human being with some control over the environment. In later childhood (ages three to six years), the child should develop a sense of initiative and of the purposefulness of life.

Schlesinger reported that the typical deaf child of hearing parents suffered in the resolution of each of the three early phases; deaf children of deaf parents who used American Sign Language demonstrated better overall functioning. Schlesinger found that when deaf children and hearing parents communicated with each other through a combination of speech and signs, the communication was "more meaningful, joyful and reciprocal" (p. 169) and that the children negotiated the first three stages more successfully.

One significant outcome of the interest in facilitation of optimal psychosocial development was the establishment of the PATHS (*Promoting Alternative THinking Strategies*) curriculum over a period of more than ten years (Greenberg and Kusché, 1993; Kusché and Greenberg, 1993). Dismayed by an absence of quality research and the neglect of psychosocial development in education of the deaf, the authors produced a school-based curriculum with a focus on interpersonal development that emphasizes the role of family and school environments in personal, social, communicative, and cognitive development.

PATHS was developed to facilitate development in three areas: (1) self-control, (2) emotional understanding, and (3) social problem solving. These areas comprise the major elements of the curriculum, with a total of 130 lessons. Results have been quite positive. Although there is no separate parent curriculum, the material can be adapted easily for use by parents. At the time of this writing, PATHS was being used in the United States, Canada, Belgium, and the Netherlands.

Group Counseling and the Use of Interpreters

For any deaf individual whose primary mode of communication is through ASL, it is preferable that the therapist or counselor be a fluent signer. Given the scarcity of professionals with sign skills, well-trained professional interpreters might be used. In all cases, the preferences of the deaf client should be paramount. Other issues that must be approached with sensitivity are group counseling with deaf individuals, the role of interpreters in counseling sessions, and the question of whether deaf and hearing clients should be members of the same group. Again there is great variation in how these areas are viewed. Miller and Moores (1990) have addressed in some detail applications of group counseling principles for deaf clients.

Summary

Approaches to the study of cognition and mental health among deaf populations have demonstrated a certain consistency. In each case, two perspectives seem to be at work, one that regards deaf people as deviant and inferior and one that concentrates on facilitating optimal growth. Fortunately, recent trends have been toward acceptance of the second perspective.

The assessment of the personality or mental health of a group or an individual is a matter of great uncertainty. The problems are magnified when dealing with individuals who have a condition such as deafness, especially when most of the testers are hearing. Tests standardized only for the hearing are of questionable validity because of assumptions about the experiences of the subjects and the possibility of breakdowns in communication. In investigating group differences, great care should be taken to account for the effects of additional disabilities in the deaf subjects.

Recent research using material developed for use with deaf subjects and employing deaf and hearing testers who are fluent in manual communication indicates that no fundamental differences exist between deaf and hearing individuals. The evidence suggests that the social-emotional adjustment of deaf persons is similar to that of hearing persons, with great individual variation. Most deaf individuals cope with the reality of deafness as a lifelong condition and lead normal, productive lives. This fact supports the contention that deafness itself has no direct impact, either negative or positive, on the development of a mentally healthy individual.

CHAPTER

American Sign Language and Manual Communication

Introduction

Because most hearing Americans are not familiar with American Sign Language (ASL), many think it is some kind of esoteric, mystical system, and there is much confusion about its nature and function. Hearing people often ask if ASL is a universal language and sometimes are surprised to learn that there is as much variation in signed languages as in spoken languages. Others assume it is a picture language that relies on imagery and iconicity, lacking the abstract nature of spoken languages. This has led to the common perception, especially among people who have taken one or two classes, that ASL is easy to learn. It is not. Kemp (1998), the director of the American Sign Language, Linguistics, and Interpretation Department at Gallaudet University, argues that the misconception is due partly to the fact that some of the first basic signs learned may be thought of as iconic (e.g., signs for *eat, sleep,* and *drink*), but that mastery beyond a basic level requires extensive exposure and practice over a substantial period of time. He notes that some hearing people, after only one or two classes, actually *teach* classes in ASL.

There has been no research on the relative difficulty of learning ASL for a native English user, but there have been some estimates using the American Foreign Service Institute and the Defense Language Institute categories of difficulty for a native user of English. Category 1, the easiest, includes Spanish, German, French, and Italian; Category 2 includes Swahili and Indonesian; Category 3 includes Greek, Czech, and Hebrew; and Category 4 includes Arabic and Korean. Francis (1980), a hearing man, proposed that ASL should fall within Category 2. Jacobs (1996), a deaf

205

woman, placed ASL in Category 4. If correct, this means that an average English speaker should take 1,320 hours of instruction to reach a limited working proficiency level, meaning that the person would be able to handle limited work requirements and routine social demands. General proficiency and native proficiency would require a much longer period of time. Regardless of where ASL falls in relation to other languages, it is clear that it should be approached with respect and a sense of commitment.

In addition to misconceptions about the complexity of ASL, there are also several "creation myths"—mostly written by hearing persons—about its origin. We do know that one root was provided by Laurent Clerc when he modified the French instructional system to accommodate it to English. We also know that the largest early concentration of deaf Americans was at Martha's Vineyard and that signs were used by both deaf and hearing islanders. However, there is no information about the system or language, so it is difficult to gauge its influence on the development of ASL. There were no cities the size of London or Paris in colonial times or in the early years of the republic, but we may assume there were populations of deaf people in towns such as New York, Philadelphia, and Baltimore and that they developed and used sign languages. However, to the best of my knowledge, there are no descriptions of these languages.

Each year, several books are published on the form and function of ASL. This book contends that ASL is a full, legitimate language in its own right. Specifically:

1. ASL is a complete verbal language.
2. ASL is independent of English.
3. ASL is a defining characteristic of the American Deaf community.

Simple as they are, these statements require some explanation. First, ASL is clearly not a *vocal* language, but it is a *verbal* one; that is, it possesses all of the complexity, sophistication, and power of a spoken language. ASL does not have a commonly accepted graphic or written system—the written system of most deaf Americans is the same as that of most hearing Americans, English—but many spoken languages also lack a written system.

Second, ASL has developed within the context of a larger culture that is overwhelmingly English using; thus it is not surprising that English has influenced ASL. The use of finger spelling, some hand configurations, and, to a lesser extent, word order show an English influence. This does not detract from the linguistic nature of ASL. By the same token, English is a Germanic language with a heavy French influence, but certainly it is neither German nor French.

Third, ASL may be seen as the language of a distinct cultural or ethnic group, the American Deaf community. However, there are some problems in applying the commonly accepted concept of ethnicity to the deaf population. We are accustomed to thinking of a child as sharing the ethnic status of his or her family. If parents and siblings use a language other than English in the home, that ethnic language is also the child's home language. Since most deaf children have hearing parents, the home language is English or some other spoken language, and they learn ASL at school, typically from deaf individuals who are not biologically related. In fact, since it has been documented for more than a century that deaf parents have far more hearing children than deaf children, most children who learn ASL as a home language are hearing children of deaf parents. Identification of oneself as deaf or as a member of the Deaf community requires a psychological adoption of the cultural values and behaviors of that community. Within the Deaf community, *deafness* is not a disability; rather, it refers to an attitude and a community within which ASL plays a significant role. Unfortunately, even today few hearing parents are aware of this community, and fewer still have any proficiency in ASL.

Many deaf children have no home language in that the speech of parents and other relatives is inaccessible to them. This gives rise to great frustration. This frustration, along with the seemingly intractable nature of the problem, has added to the bitterness of the oral-manual controversy. Even if the decision is made to use signs with the child, this divisive controversy remains. We may think of this dispute as the "manual-manual" or American Sign Language (ASL)/Manual Codes on English (MCE) controversy. Opinions on this vary widely. Some educators advocate using MCEs (sign systems designed to represent English word order, grammar, and vocabulary) along with speech and auditory training. Others advocate ASL only, with English to be learned later through reading and writing. Opponents of Manual Codes on English argue as follows:

1. The systems are awkward and cannot reflect English adequately.
2. Parents and teachers cannot master them, and therefore they do not provide a complete English model.
3. Because MCEs are speech based rather than content based, they are not intelligible.
4. Signs and speech cannot be coordinated well.

Arguments for Manual Codes on English include the following:

1. The systems *do* reflect English word order perfectly, as well as the most common grammatical structures of English.
2. Hearing parents and teachers can learn MCEs more easily than ASL, which is a separate language.
3. English print is speech based and is a *graphic* code on English; therefore, it is intelligible. By the same reasoning, a Manual Code on English can be intelligible.
4. Substantial research indicates that signs and speech *can* be coordinated.
5. A Manual Code on English, with the incorporation of the manual alphabet, easily leads into English print, which is a graphic code on English.

Arguments against ASL-only instruction include the following:

1. Hearing parents cannot learn a new language quickly enough to facilitate language development in their deaf children.
2. Because English is the home language, it would be easier to learn a Manual Code on English.
3. ASL has no relationship to reading and writing.
4. ASL-only communication fails to take advantage of the residual hearing that most deaf children possess.

Advocates of ASL argue as follows:

1. ASL is a natural language; it is not an incomplete, invented artificial system.
2. ASL has evolved to make efficient use of space, movement, and vision.
3. Being a natural language, ASL is more easily learned than an artificial system.
4. ASL is an integral part of the Deaf community. It is a source of identification and pride.

Most professionals, including this author, take an intermediate position. There is strong evidence that ASL and Manual Codes on English can be complementary aspects of the lives of deaf individuals. However, there is vehement opposition to this position.

Human language in general, and any language in particular, can be approached from any number of perspectives. Even major disciplines such as linguistics, psychology, sociology, and anthropology have diverse and sometimes conflicting conceptions of language. Attempts to establish collaborative work at intersections such as sociolinguistics, psycholinguistics, and neurolinguistics have not been particularly fruitful. Although language is a defining human characteristic and its use permeates our existence, little consensus exists on its exact nature and whether a language per se can be said to exist in reality. We may all agree that there is a "language," such as English, Chinese, or ASL, but not on whether that language is an abstract, ideal competence or is characterized by human everyday performance replete with grammatical, semantic, situational, and motivational limitations.

Clearly the question of language can be quite emotional from an individual viewpoint. A person's language is part of his or her essence, and an attack on that language may be interpreted as an attack on the individual as well as on the cultural group itself.

The reader should bear in mind as we proceed through this chapter that, despite grammatical and vocabulary similarities, ASL and the Manual Codes on English have some fundamental differences. ASL is a full language, and Manual Codes on English are invented systems. There is little doubt in my mind that ASL is more powerful and efficient. The questions that arise are how to develop English skills and how to bridge the gap between ASL and English. I believe that it is within this context that Manual Codes on English should be approached.

This chapter provides the necessary background for the consideration of linguistic systems that apparently meet all criteria deemed necessary for human languages, with one exception: These systems employ the visual-motor channel rather than the auditory-vocal channel as the primary means of communication. Manual sign languages such as ASL and other languages used by deaf individuals around the world do indeed constitute legitimate language systems. This chapter discusses the nature and uses of sign languages and presents a brief overview of ASL. It provides background information on the Deaf community, of which ASL is an integral part. The chapter also examines the educational use of manual communication and attempts to dispel some common misunderstandings. For example, it emphasizes that English-based manual communication systems currently in use in the classroom rely heavily on ASL for their vocabularies but have some fundamentally different structures and therefore are not simply variations of ASL.

The material in this chapter is essential to educational practice. Teachers and other professionals who work with deaf students need to understand the world of deaf adults and to realize that ASL and English-based manual communication systems need not be in conflict. This chapter highlights the early advantages that deaf children with deaf parents enjoy and reinforces the importance of having deaf teachers. For more complete background information, readers are referred to reviews by Moores (1992b) and Wilbur (1979). Comprehensive resources include *American Sign Language and Sign Systems: Research and Applications* (Wilbur, 1979), *Sign Language Research: Theoretical Issues* (Lucas, 1990), and *Theoretical Issues in Sign Language Research* (Siple and Fischer, 1991). Although our knowledge of ASL and other sign languages has increased significantly over the past generation, further generations will be needed to establish a satisfactory knowledge base.

As we have noted, ASL has many unique features and characteristics. Two of these features cannot be overemphasized. First, ASL is a complete and legitimate language in every sense of the word, not a representation of English. Second, although ASL may be a natural language for deaf individuals, it is usually not the *home* language. As we have noted, more than 90 percent of deaf children have hearing parents who have had little previous exposure to deafness or to ASL. These parents use English or some other spoken language in the home. Historically, most deaf children learned ASL from other deaf children in residential schools outside the classroom or from deaf adults later in life. Hearing parents were discouraged from learning either ASL or any of the Manual Codes on English. Most bilingual programs for hearing children in the United States are designed to serve children who enter school with an already developed language that is not English and to use the home language to facilitate a transition into English. For deaf children, access to the home language is partly or fully restricted by lack of hearing unless they have deaf parents who use ASL. A bilingual ASL/English program entails teaching *two* languages to the child rather than using the natural home language to develop proficiency in English.

One obvious answer to the problem is to have hearing parents use ASL with their deaf children. On further examination, however, this is a naive solution. ASL is a separate, complex language and is acquired no more easily by English-speaking adults than is French, Chinese, or Lao. To illustrate the complexity, tenure at Gallaudet

University requires faculty members to achieve a certain level of proficiency in sign communication within six years. Even though they work in an environment with numerous highly skilled signers, some hearing Gallaudet faculty members fail to obtain the required sign skills within the mandated six years. Therefore, it is unreasonable to expect hearing parents, especially those who work and/or have other children, to acquire ASL in a shorter period of time. Rather, they may do so over a period of years, after the child has passed the optimal age for language acquisition. The situation would be similar to that of monolingual English-speaking parents who must communicate with a hearing child in another language. We will return to this issue later in this and the following chapter.

Although a majority of deaf adults in the United States and Canada probably use some variety of ASL, ASL remains in many ways an exotic language. Historically, ASL has been subject to less scientific analysis than some languages spoken by isolated groups in inaccessible areas. One reason for the neglect of ASL has been the tendency of many educators of the deaf to treat any form of manual communication as behavior that must be repressed. Until the 1970s, almost all programs followed an oral-only philosophy of education, at least until students reached eleven or twelve years of age. After students reached this age, some programs allowed their "oral failures" to be exposed to signs in the classroom. Children were considered failures if they did not meet the single criterion for success: speaking well enough to become part of the hearing world. Because the goal of education of the deaf was "normalcy"—that is, speaking—a prejudice developed against signs; they were considered to be alinguistic, concrete, and inflexible. Some educators confused signs with "natural" gestures, reflecting their ignorance of the arbitrary, learned nature of a true language of signs. Silverman and Davis (1970) expressed the dominant view of sign language: "It is generally agreed that sign language is bound to the concrete and is rather limited with respect to abstraction, however, and subtleties such as figures of speech which enrich expression" (p. 390).

A factor that inhibited the study of manual communication systems was the assumption among many linguists, especially those influenced by Bloomfield (1933), that all languages are primarily spoken and other forms of communication—for example, writing—are imperfect outgrowths of a basic spoken system. Developments in the 1960s and 1970s worked directly and indirectly to focus interest on the biological bases of language rather than on output modes. If one believes language is a product of the human mind, it is relatively easy to accept the argument that it can be expressed manually as well as vocally.

American Sign Language

For a period of time, the journal *Sign Language Studies* was a source of information on ASL and other sign languages. The journal ceased publishing, and as a result there has been some decrease in the literature about ASL in recent years. There has been some discussion about reconstituting the journal, and it is hoped that it will resume publication shortly after the appearance of this text.

Dealing with any language presents numerous difficulties. For example, researchers attempting to develop a comprehensive definition of the English language would have to come to terms with the wide variety of dialects spoken in England, the United States, South Africa, and Australia. They would have to decide at which point two dialects of a language differ so much that they become two separate languages. Pushing further, they would find differences in English usage not only among countries but also among regions of the same country. To further complicate matters, they would observe that class differences in the use of English cut across regional and national lines. Finally, they would find that individuals move easily from one dialect to another, depending on the circumstances.

In earlier eras, the problem of definition would have been resolved by reference to a standard dialect. For a number of reasons, mostly political, the English that was spoken around London assumed a dominant status. Questions of correct usage were decided by the prescriptions of the King's English. Since most early English-speaking settlers of the American colonies came from the midlands and from the north of England, they spoke different, and therefore "inferior," dialects. The tendency today, however, is to treat dialects as equals. There is no reason to perceive London English as being more correct than any other dialect. Its ascendancy reflected political and economic, not linguistic, supremacy in much the same way as that of Parisian French and Castilian Spanish.

The fact that dialects have become "respectable" makes the problem of definition much more difficult. English must be redefined to encompass enormous diversity, an almost impossible task. Most people eventually would be satisfied to conclude that although they cannot define and describe English, they do have the ability to recognize it and to understand and use it when circumstances require.

The difficulties inherent in dealing with the term *sign language,* or even *American Sign Language,* are still more complex. Deaf children and adults across the United States and Canada use a variety of visual-motor communication systems. At the lowest level, a system might consist of homemade gestures invented and understood by perhaps only six or seven students in a classroom; parents, teachers, and even other deaf students in the same program might be excluded. At the other end of the continuum might be an arbitrary, abstract, somewhat standardized system capable of expressing all levels and nuances as well as any spoken system can. A complicating factor is that signs usually have not been passed down from parents to children; rather, they have been suppressed by most adults with whom the children have had contact. Although ASL is not suppressed today, most deaf children do not attend residential schools and typically are now first exposed to a Manual Code on English by hearing teachers before encountering ASL. A growing minority of deaf children are exposed to ASL at early ages, but the numbers are still small.

At one time it was believed that the standard of correctness for sign language was the relatively formal system used in classroom instruction at Gallaudet University, the world's only university for the deaf. Gallaudet Sign was, and is, to American Sign Language as London English was, and is, to the English language. As a hearing

Thomas Hopkins Gallaudet with
Alice Cogswell, the first student
at the American School for the
Deaf.

GALLAUDET UNIVERSITY ARCHIVES

graduate student at Gallaudet, this author learned formal sign language in a class-room situation. However, attempts to use the newly learned skills in informal situations quickly demonstrated the differences between how some concepts "should" be signed and how they actually are signed. Although deaf students recognized the formal signs for words such as *animal, father,* and *mother,* they seldom, if ever, used those signs themselves.

Manual Alphabets and Signs

Manual communication can be used in two different ways to present a word. One involves *finger spelling,* or spelling the word letter by letter using a manual alphabet that consists of twenty-six letters with a one-to-one correspondence with traditional orthography. In finger spelling, the hand is held in front of the chest and letters are represented by different hand configurations. The rate of presentation is equivalent to a comfortable rate of speech, somewhat faster than the rate of an accomplished typist.

The one-handed American manual alphabet has been traced back to the work of Bonet in Spain in 1620, and at least one educator believed it was in use in Italy a century earlier (Best, 1943, p. 518). Farrar (1923, p. 39) reported that a manual alphabet was in common use in the Middle Ages, and Best (1943, p. 518) noted that pictures of dactylology appear in twelfth-century Latin bibles. These alphabets apparently were used by individuals with normal hearing rather than for instruction of deaf individuals.

Bonet's one-handed alphabet is essentially the same as that currently used in Europe and North and South America. The Spanish manual alphabet was introduced in France by Pereire, who modified it somewhat to conform to French orthography and, like Bonet, used it as a means of teaching speech (Abernathy, 1959).

The Abbé de l'Epée, and later Sicard, adopted Pereire's alphabet for use with signs rather than as a means of teaching speech. With minor modification, it was brought to the United States by Gallaudet and Clerc in 1817 (Abernathy, 1959). Figures 9.1 and 9.2 illustrate the manual alphabets in use in the United States and Russia, respectively. The similarity between them is striking.

Other manual alphabets have been developed but have never achieved as wide acceptance as the one-handed Spanish alphabet. Alexander Graham Bell (1883a, 1883b) used a manual alphabet that traces back to the work of Dalgarno (1680). Farrar (1923) reported that although many alphabets of a phonetic or syllabic nature have been developed, none of them ever achieved any degree of permanence.

The second way to present a word or a concept is through a *sign,* which represents a complete idea. Each sign has three elements: (1) the position of the hands, (2) the configuration of the hands, and (3) the movements of the hands to different positions.

Proficient practitioners of manual communication, then, have a variety of options. They may communicate through signs, without using spelling, or they may communicate through finger spelling. Communication through finger spelling alone, of course, represents English and would not be considered part of ASL. As a general rule, the more informal a situation, the more signs tend to dominate; as the situation becomes more formal and "Englishlike," the tendency is to use spelling to a greater extent.

The United States and English-speaking parts of Canada use one distinct sign language, ASL, and a variety of separate systems, which rely heavily on ASL vocabulary, that have been developed to represent English manually. Confusing the situation is an array of titles such as Signed English, Manual English, Siglish, Linguistics of Visual English (LOVE), Seeing Essential English (SEE 1), Signing Exact English

FIGURE 9.1   American Manual Alphabet

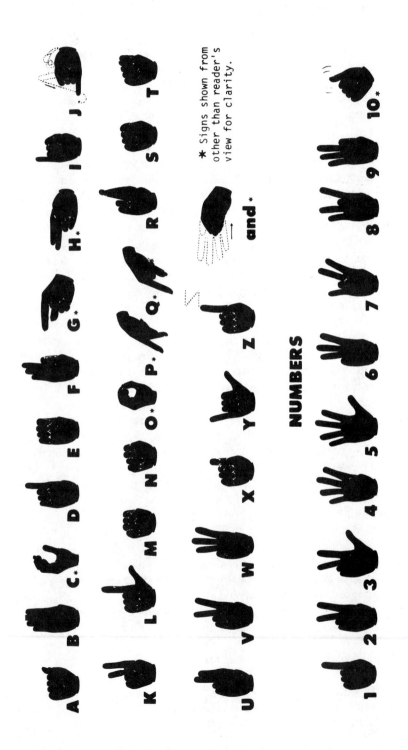

Source: Gallaudet University

FIGURE 9.2   The Russian Language Alphabet

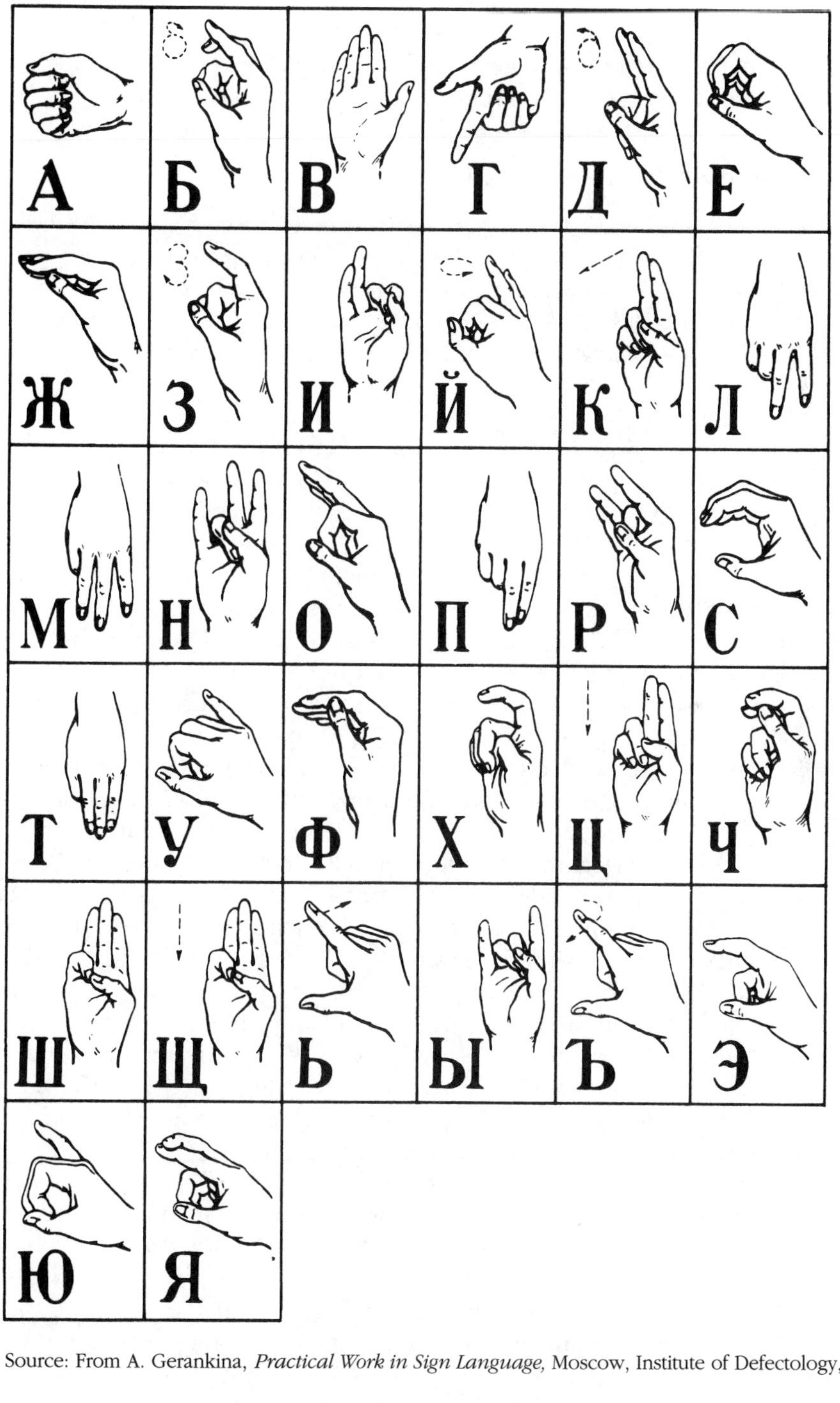

Source: From A. Gerankina, *Practical Work in Sign Language,* Moscow, Institute of Defectology, 1972.

(SEE 2), and Pidgin Sign English. Although each of these systems relies heavily on ASL vocabulary, each has been designed to represent English word order and syntax. Therefore, they may be considered Manual Codes on English, not variations of ASL.

Before we discuss Manual Codes on English, we will review some background information on the development of ASL and the Deaf community.

The Development of ASL

Many of the signs the Abbé de l'Epée invented were actually based on Latin or Greek etymology, reflecting his orientation toward classical languages (Stedt and Moores, 1990). Relying on classical bases sometimes changed the signs' meanings. Three examples are de l'Epée's signs for *comprendre* (to understand), *satisfaire* (to satisfy), and *introduire* (to introduce).

French	Latin Base	English Equivalent
comprendre	*prendre + cum*	to take with
satisfaire	*facere + statis*	to do enough
introduire	*ducere + intro*	to leap into

In English it would be similar, without going back to Latin, to sign *understand* using two morphemes *stand + under* instead of the commonly accepted sign, which is completely different. De l'Epée's system of "methodical signs" was too clumsy, and five or more signs might be used to represent all elements of one verb. De l'Epée's system was streamlined by his successor, Sicard, but it remained "prescriptive," that is, designed to teach a rather formal, "correct," literate French. It was not concerned with dialects or everyday communication (Stedt and Moores, 1990).

The catalyst for the growth of ASL undoubtedly was Laurent Clerc, who assumed responsibility for the development of a manual instructional system at the American School for the Deaf in 1817. Clerc himself had been instructed in Paris in a modified form of the system originally developed by de l'Epée. De l'Epée took an existing sign language and altered it to reflect French, making use of the Spanish manual alphabet and new signs he invented to illustrate aspects of grammar.

Relying heavily on the Spanish/French manual alphabet, Clerc used the French instructional sign system as the basis for an American system. For example, the American sign for *green* was the same as the French sign for *verte,* except for the hand configuration, which was changed from *v* to *g.* Clerc developed signs for Monday through Saturday by changing the hand configuration to represent the first letter of the word: *m* for *Monday, t* for *Tuesday* (*h* was used for *Thursday*). For some reason, the original hand configuration was retained in some cases. Even today, in ASL we find the French influence in hand configurations, such as *b* (*bon*) for *good, c* (*chercher*) for *search,* and *m* (*mille*) for *thousand.* Of course, this sharing across languages is not restricted to ASL. Thousands of spoken English words have been borrowed from French, Spanish, Italian, and other languages. Although many basic American signs remain cognates with the original French ones, French and

American Sign Languages have evolved separately and are two distinct sign languages.

How Clerc himself became proficient in standard English so rapidly is not known. It has been said that Clerc learned English from Thomas Hopkins Gallaudet while coming over on the boat from France. Even for someone as obviously talented as Clerc, this seems a bit unbelievable. However, according to all indications (Lane, 1984), Clerc did master English in a short period of time and developed a high level of literacy in the language very quickly.

From the beginnings of the American School in 1817, indications existed that the signing students used in class differed in at least some ways from the communication system they used outside of class. Of course, this is also true for spoken languages. Students use a different speech code of the same language when they are in class from what they use outside of class. The differences in sign language seem to go deeper than this, however. Obviously, a system designed to *teach* English would have some characteristics that would not be found in a system geared to ease of communication on a daily basis. It is also likely that the system first developed by Clerc, who was neither a linguist nor a native user of English, had some weaknesses that were modified by use over time. Throughout most of the nineteenth century, disagreement reigned over whether class instruction should rely on "methodical" or "natural" sign systems. The methodical systems followed English word order and used signs for English grammatical markers. In short, they were designed for much the same purpose as the Manual Codes of English in use today. The "natural" sign system was the ancestor of present-day ASL.

The existence of basic structural differences between ASL and French Sign Language, as well as between ASL and English, has led to speculation that one or more sign languages were in use in the United States prior to the establishment of the first schools. No description of any such sign language exists; however, there is some circumstantial evidence to support such a hypothesis. Special interest has been focused on the community of Martha's Vineyard, an island off the coast of Massachusetts that had a large deaf population due to generations of inbreeding among a homogeneous population with a pool of recessive genes for deafness (Groce, 1981, 1985). The population of deaf islanders peaked around the middle of the nineteenth century and then rapidly declined due to an influx of "mainlanders" and Portuguese fishermen and an outmigration of the island population to the mainland.

When Groce conducted her research in the late 1970s, no deaf people remained on the island. She gathered most of her information through oral histories by means of interviews with elderly hearing natives of the island, who recollected experiences from their early lives with the few remaining deaf islanders. From her work, Groce concluded that the hearing population of Martha's Vineyard, at least those in communities with large numbers of deaf people, maintained bilingual communication based on spoken English and a sign language. She concluded that the deaf residents had no communication barriers to overcome and participated in all aspects of the community, sometimes even as leaders.

No description of the sign language used on Martha's Vineyard exists, and Groce (1980, p. 154) concluded that it may be impossible to reconstruct it. The dearth of information about the sign language itself during the peak of the deaf population in the 1840s prevents us from ascertaining to what extent, if any, it influenced the development of ASL.

Groce (1981) reported that deaf residents of Martha's Vineyard were sent to the American School for the Deaf in the 1820s and 1830s. Since islanders were sent to the American School at Hartford, it is here that we should find any evidence of the influence of indigenous signs on the development of ASL. However, it wasn't until the tenth Annual Report of the American School for the Deaf (T. Gallaudet, 1826) that the enrollment of three students from Chilmark was noted. According to the twenty-seventh Annual Report of the American School for the Deaf (Weld, 1844), which listed all students enrolled from 1817 to 1843 and their hometowns, only two additional students from the island were enrolled in the 1830s, one in 1832 and one in 1834. Only 6 of 619 individuals who had attended the school during the twenty-seven-year period were identified as being from Martha's Vineyard, and all of them were from Chilmark. It is unlikely that a sign system used by 1 percent of the school's students would have had a major impact on the signing behavior of the student body as a whole.

The First Methods Controversy: Methodical Signs Versus Natural Signs

The system of instruction formulated by Clerc contained four modes of communication: (1) the natural language of signs of the deaf, (2) the natural language of signs as methodized by d l'Epée and Sicard, (3) the manual alphabet, and (4) writing.

As in the Paris institution, the major emphasis was on the acquisition of literacy. For example, a subject might be introduced and discussed in "natural" signs, then followed by a presentation by means of "methodical" signs, and ending in a lesson with the manual alphabet and drill-and-practice in writing.

Clerc instructed all teachers at the American School in his system of instruction, as well as in the use of methodical signs. Many of these teachers went on to found and teach in other schools for deaf children. In addition, several men (only male educators of the deaf existed at this time) were trained by Clerc before establishing schools on their own. As a result, the system of instruction developed at the American School extended throughout the country by 1828 (T. Gallaudet, 1828).

Apparently, the first American school for the deaf to move away from reliance on methodical signs was the New York Institution for the Instruction of the Deaf and Dumb. The institution's sixteenth annual report (Peet, 1834) claimed that deaf students never used methodical signs on a daily basis outside the classroom and that the system was meaningless rote repetition. In other words, the emphasis was on the structure of English and not on content.

Debate raged regarding the best method of educating deaf children. The consensus among educators was that deaf students must be educated using some form of sign language or sign system. The form of the sign language was hotly debated, however. One group supported the use of methodical signs (i.e., signs presented in English morphology and syntax), whereas the other group thought natural or colloquial signs (i.e., the forerunner of ASL) were superior.

Communicating in ASL.

Burnet (1854) reported that "in this country . . . their [methodical signs'] use was once universal or nearly so, they have been discarded wholly in some schools, partially in others, and in some cases, after being denounced, again taken in partial favor. . . . The prevailing opinion among the more experienced American teachers is that these signs are useful, at least to some extent and in the earlier lessons" (pp. 1–2). This quote clearly indicates that methodical signs were widely accepted in the first half of the nineteenth century. In fact, they were highly refined. For example, signs had been invented for even the function words, such as *the* and *to be* (Jacobs, 1856).

John Carlin, a deaf educator, was a particularly strong advocate of the manual alphabet and methodical signs and an opponent of natural or colloquial signs. In discussing relative merits of the different systems, Carlin (1851) wrote:

> That the American system, adapted after the Abbés de l'Epée and Sicard's, has proved itself superior to any already known, except the French, none can have reason to deny; nor can he ever disagree with me that the manual alphabet, being the principal branch of our system, is the best and surest channel of knowledge and communication for the deaf and dumb; nor can he offer any dissent to the fact that the language of signs, properly used is indispensable to their mental improvement in the schoolroom and chapel. (p. 51)

Cochrane (1871) stated that methodical signs should be used during the first years of instruction, with more finger spelling used later. He thought that the main job of the teacher was to be a facilitator of language (English), not a facilitator of knowledge, and the best way to facilitate language was through the use of methodical signs. Similarly, Valentine (1872) claimed that natural signs must be discouraged so that deaf children would learn the syntax of English.

The support for methodical signs was by no means unanimous. Numerous educators of the deaf had a strong antipathy toward the use of methodical signs, which they viewed as stilted and unnatural. Stone (1851) argued that "methodical signs are too artificial and stiff to be used in conversations and they are never used for this purpose. The only use to which they are applied is to teach language by means of dictation" (p. 189). In one of the strongest condemnations on record, Ray (1851) claimed that "Sicard's system of methodical signs [is] charlatanry, from beginning to end . . . time will come and at not distant day, when all our American schools . . . will discard methodical signs" (p. 187).

The confusion over the most appropriate methods of instructing deaf children and the conflicting claims of proponents of different approaches probably masked deep frustrations among nineteenth-century educators of the deaf over the enormous difficulties in helping deaf children master the language of the dominant community. These difficulties remain today. E. A. Fay (1869) best summed up the dilemma as follows:

> We are none of us satisfied in the attainments in language ordinarily made by the deaf and dumb. The great majority of pupils born deaf graduate from our institutions without the ability to express their ideas in correct idiomatic language, or to understand readily the language of books. . . . Even the students who enter college and who represent the greatest intelligence and highest attainments of the deaf and dumb of this country encounter no little difficulty in the concise and often technical phraseology of college textbooks. In all the writer's acquaintance with deaf mutes, which includes many of the most accomplished graduates of the high classes at Hartford and White Plains, and the students of the College at Washington, he does not know one deaf person who uses language with the freedom and accuracy of an educated hearing and speaking man. (p. 194)

Fay's comments reflect the difficulties faced by educators of the deaf over generations, and they were consonant with the opinions of many of his contemporaries. For example, the following year, in a treatment of language and deafness, Gillett (1870) documented that the acquisition of English—which is what educators meant by the term *language*—has always presented severe obstacles for deaf American children.

In the mid-nineteenth century, educators of the deaf were bitterly divided over the issue of what kinds of signs to use, despite the fact that neither side had any type of data to support their arguments—a situation uncomfortably like that of today.

The controversy disappeared around 1880 with the "final" victory of oralism. In effect, ASL disappeared from education of the deaf and went underground for approximately one hundred years. It was kept alive by the Deaf community, for which it became a symbol. In recent years, ASL has been accepted, albeit belatedly, as a legitimate language.

The Growth of the Deaf Community

It is beyond the scope of this text to discuss the Deaf community in detail. The subject would require, and in fact has received, book-length treatment. For background information, several valuable resources include *Deaf Heritage: A Narrative History of Deaf America* (Gannon, 1981), *Deaf in America: Voices from a Culture* (Padden and Humphries, 1988), *A Place of Their Own: Creating the Deaf Community in America* (Van Cleve and Crouch, 1989), and *Outsiders in a Hearing World: A Sociology of Deafness* (Higgins, 1980). This section is intended to inform the reader of the existence of the Deaf community. Many teachers and other professionals working with deaf children are unaware of the role the Deaf community plays in the lives of deaf people and of the resources it offers. At this point, we will consider not the Deaf community as it exists today but some of the factors influencing its development.

Judging from the available evidence, the Deaf community as we know it today was slow to develop. Although paternalism and evidence of discrimination existed, the pressure to establish a separate Deaf culture or subculture was not apparent. For example, large numbers of students at the American School remained in Hartford after graduation and worked in a variety of professions (Lane, 1984). Turner (1848) reported that about half of the marriages of graduates of the school involved hearing partners. In a similar study twenty years later, Turner (1868) again found that half of the marriages of graduates of the school involved a hearing spouse. These figures were much higher than they would be by 1900 and throughout the twentieth century. Although there were separate schools for the deaf, as well as religious missions, it appears that the deaf were mainstreamed into the fabric of everyday life. In the mid-nineteenth century, no large, separate organizations of the deaf existed. These would come later, partly in response to threats to the well-being of deaf individuals.

The establishment of the Deaf community as a self-conscious entity may be traced to a growing awareness among deaf people of burgeoning threats to their position within society in general and within education of the deaf in particular. Laurent Clerc, a deaf man, unquestionably was the dominant figure in education of the deaf in the United States for its first forty years. In addition, deaf people had established many schools, and a substantial number of the faculty members in most schools were deaf, although, as we saw in Chapter 3, true equality was denied deaf professionals. However, the situation was better than the outright repression that began in the late nineteenth century and persisted for more than one hundred years.

The scope and rapidity of the change are difficult to comprehend from our present perspective. The push for oral-only education, coupled with repression of signs in the school setting and concern about the establishment of a deaf variety of the human race, had long-lasting effects. In 1880 the Congress of Milan voted overwhelmingly against the use of signs in the classroom. Deaf delegates were not allowed to participate in the general discussions and were prohibited from voting on the proposals.

In 1880 the National Association of the Deaf (NAD) was established to serve as an advocate of the deaf in the United States. This association was established at a time when the influence of deaf professionals was steadily declining, and to a larger extent its organization reflected a general feeling that the majority of hearing educators would not allow deaf individuals any significant role in education of the deaf. It is likely, however, that a Deaf community would have developed even had there not been a significant threat. The shared experience of deafness itself would be ample reason for such an organization. However, the process was speeded up (to say the least) by the changing spirit of the late nineteenth century.

Of course, the development of the Deaf community occurred within the context of a very complicated environment, not merely as a response to one issue. In an examination of one state organization of the deaf that was established toward the end of the nineteenth century, the Pennsylvania Society for the Advancement of the Deaf (PSAD), Boyd and Van Cleve (1994) reported that the leadership of PSAD was quite sophisticated in its effort to advance the interests of deaf people. Hearing administrators dominated the schools and controlled middle-class employment at that time. This sometimes caused deaf leaders to remain silent on some of the areas of controversy while concentrating on philanthropy and lobbying for the general good of deaf Pennsylvanians. Boyd and Van Cleve argued that a simplistic focus on the actions of hearing "oppressors" might obscure the creativity, persistence, and sophistication of America's deaf leaders.

Although it remained aloof from the debates over pedagogical methods in deaf education, during its first twenty-five years the PSAD created a benevolent home for elderly deaf persons, lobbied against laws that stigmatized deaf people, raised money for an important memorial, and worked toward the education of all deaf children. The historical lives of deaf Americans, the PSAD experience suggests, were richer, more complex, and more meaningful than our current focus on communication would lead us to believe. Dependence and autonomy coexisted in an uneasy struggle as deaf people, like other contemporary minorities, tested the meaning and limits of self-determination.

Over a period of decades, the elements of the Deaf community were formed. State and local organizations of the deaf, many affiliated with NAD, were established. The clubs became a focus of social and athletic activities, frequently interacting with other clubs on a state or regional basis. A national journal of and for the deaf, *The Silent Workers,* was established in 1892. This was the forerunner of *The Deaf American,* which is published by NAD. Prior to the turn of the century, when deaf individuals had difficulties obtaining insurance, the National Fraternal Society of the Deaf (NFSD) was organized. Another source of support was various religious groups, whose programs for deaf people had both religious and cultural components. Catholic, Protestant, and Jewish deaf associations existed, in many cases at local, state, and national levels. Although until recently few, if any, of the ministers, rabbis, and priests serving deaf congregations were deaf themselves, they typically were supportive of the Deaf community and ASL.

Ironically, the core element of the Deaf community was the residential school for the deaf, an environment that was dominated by hearing educators who were opposed to the use of sign language. It was at the residential schools that deaf children, 95 percent of whom had hearing parents, were enculturated into the Deaf community and learned ASL (Padden, 1980; Padden and Humphries, 1988).

At the adult level, the Deaf community can be identified by networks of religious, social, and cultural organizations at local, state, national, and even international levels. The source of enculturation has traditionally been the residential school, and ASL has been the operating language. In the face of continuing pressures, the Deaf community has maintained its identity and cohesiveness for more than a century. Despite the absence of a deaf superintendent of a school for the deaf from 1900 to the 1970s, NAD and other organizations of the deaf continued in their advocacy role. ASL is seen as an integral part of the Deaf community, and it was defended as such when hearing educators denigrated it as being concrete and not a "legitimate" language. To a large degree, an attack on ASL is an attack on the Deaf community.

The Boundaries of ASL and English

At this point in the text, the reader may have the idea that because disagreement abounds over every important issue in the education of deaf children, there is probably disagreement over a definition of ASL. The reader would be right! As we noted at the beginning of this chapter, problems of definition for any language are compounded by the special nature of ASL. Most deaf children and adults learn ASL outside of the home, after they have been exposed, however imperfectly, to some form of English. One of the roots of ASL was a system of "methodical" signs modified from the French by the deaf educator Clerc to represent English. Although the etymology may not be apparent to many signers, the hand configurations for many signs show the relationship between the manual alphabet and written English. In addition, English is the written system for deaf Americans. Print permeates their lives, probably more so today than ever before, because of the general availability of closed-captioned TV decoders, telecommunication devices for the deaf, and various forms of E-mail, including Internet. Finally, so many English-based manual systems that draw heavily from ASL vocabulary have been developed that the lines may become blurred. Clearly there is a "pure" ASL and there are somewhat less "pure" Manual Codes on English. In the past, some people conceived of a continuum from ASL to English, but the situation is far more complex than that. Too many variations exist to make a continuum possible.

For a time, interest was devoted to the concept of a Pidgin Sign English (PSE), a term used by Woodward (1980, 1973) to refer to a kind of signing in English word order, with reduced redundancy and a mixture of ASL and English structure. Later Reilly and McIntire (1990) defined PSE as a dialect of ASL frequently used by hearing people when interacting with deaf people. However, Woodward (1973), Reilly and McIntyre (1990), and others, such as Lucas (1990) and Stewart (1990), have noted the complexities of the interactions, and the term *contact signing* has been replacing PSE.

In highlighting the complexity, Lucas and Valli (1990) provide a "partial" list of possible contact situations:

1. Deaf bilinguals with hearing bilinguals
2. Deaf bilinguals with deaf bilinguals
3. Deaf bilinguals with hearing spoken-English monolinguals
4. Hearing bilinguals with deaf English signers
5. Deaf bilinguals with deaf English signers
6. Deaf English signers with hearing spoken monolinguals
7. Deaf English signers with hearing bilinguals
8. Deaf English signers with deaf ASL monolinguals
9. Deaf bilinguals with deaf ASL monolinguals
10. Deaf ASL monolinguals with hearing bilinguals (p. 289)

Lucas and Valli acknowledge that even this list is incomplete. They define deaf bilinguals as people who learned ASL natively, either from parents or at an early age from their peers in residential school settings, and who have been exposed to spoken and written English all their lives. This may have represented a majority of the deaf population prior to 1970, but changing enrollment patterns now indicate that most signing deaf children first learn an English sign system from hearing teachers and/or parents and later learn ASL from deaf teachers and peers. From my perspective, these individuals would also be bilingual, but with different linguistic experiences. Also, Lucas and Valli (1990) define hearing bilinguals as "native English speakers who learned to sign as adults, both through formal instruction and through interaction with deaf people, and who, while not being native ASL signers, *do not use manual codes for English either*" (p. 290). Their definitions apparently preclude English signers from being bilingual. A deaf person who learned ASL natively and was exposed to written or spoken English is bilingual. A deaf person who learned ASL and English signing natively and who was always exposed to signed, spoken, and written English is *not* bilingual according to Lucas and Valli. I believe that Lucas and Valli's definitions are too narrow and that both individuals are bilingual in reality. It seems unnecessarily restrictive to consider a hearing native English user who learns ASL to be bilingual but a hearing native English user who later uses ASL and Manual Code on English not to be bilingual. In essence, it argues that a hearing or deaf person who uses ASL and spoken or written English stops being bilingual if she or he also uses a third, manual, code on English (in addition to speech and writing).

During the late 1980s and early 1990s, there was a movement to restrict sign communication to ASL and prohibit the use of Manual Codes on English or Sim-

Com (combined use of signs and speech). Within the educational context, we will discuss this movement along with the development of bilingual-bicultural programs. At present, we are addressing it in a somewhat broader context. In 1989 Valli, Thumann-Prezioso, Lucas, Liddell, and Johnson presented in an open letter to the Gallaudet community the goal to develop a policy that would ban the use of simultaneous communication from the campus. They unequivocally stated:

> There may be times when either written or spoken English is appropriate, and there will be many times when ASL is appropriate. *At no time will simcom be appropriate* [emphasis added]. (p. 6)

Such attempts at violating First Amendment freedom of speech (or sign) are doomed to failure, and the proposal was rejected by the Faculty Senate. Gallaudet now has a written policy stating that it is a bilingual, multicultural community and encouraging mutual sensitivity, acceptance, and respect for all communication variations. Interestingly, the opposition to the proposal was led by deaf leaders who saw the proposal as being led by hearing people who oversimplified the situation. Writing in the National Association of the Deaf (NAD) *Broadcaster,* Merv Garretson (1990) commented:

> This paper turns into a polemic against the use of English as a means of communication among deaf people, as well as among deaf and hearing people—suggesting that they should communicate only in ASL, and relegating English to a reading/writing role. Historically deaf people have long used both English and ASL. . . . Personally, I believe the time has come for linguists to face the reality of how deaf persons actually communicate. . . . As a teacher of deaf youth for at least 15 years, I tended to use both ASL and English in my communication approach. I do not buy the idea that a bilingual deaf person must communicate in ASL and use English only in reading and writing. To achieve fluency in any language, one must use it constantly in day to day communicating situations. (p. 3)

In a similar vein, Goodstein (1990) argued for a more inclusive atmosphere. He noted that it is a nuisance to deal with different labels for some variations of ASL "however useful they might be to the linguistics." He continued:

> Recently a couple of deaf colleagues jokingly remarked that they had to face an "identity crisis" every time they were asked as to which sign language they were using; ASL, PSE (a taboo?), Sign English, a combination thereof, or what? . . . As for the rest of us daily users of sign communication, if we take the view that ASL is all-inclusive, as discussed above, then each of us will be able to proclaim with pride, "I AM USING ASL." . . . . It is time for us to relive the old days and once again refer to our sign communication as American Sign Language." (p. 49)

Bernard Bragg (1990), a Gallaudet faculty member and noted deaf actor, also argued that the definitions of ASL developed within the linguistics field were too narrow and that we should consider a more generic alternative:

> This more generic ASL includes all of the variety of language that American deaf people employ when they sign. Some of the varieties of ASL are heavily influenced by English, the majority language of the United States. Other varieties, especially the variety I call "traditional ASL," are hardly influenced by English at all. I believe that the linguistic study of ASL has been too narrowly focused on the variety of sign language and not on the full spectrum of American Deaf signing. . . . Evidently, ASL is all inclusive and adaptable, depending on the person one comes in contact with and also on the subject one wishes to communicate. (p. 9)

Bragg (1990) proposed that deaf children and their hearing parents could use and progress through three different types of ASL, which he labeled Traditional ASL, Modern ASL (somewhat like the previously mentioned PSE), and "Englished" ASL. He argued that ASL should embrace all dialects and stated, "It is only through communication/usage that differences in the language would be diminished—certainly *not* through control by any dominant purist/extremist group, such as linguists who wish to decide what language Deaf people should communicate in or which language to change" (p. 12).

Larry Stewart, a psychologist and board member of the National Association of the Deaf, responded with great emotion and humor and urged people to respect differences in means of communication that others use. He stated, "One of the claims opponents of SimCom often make is that it is impossible to use two languages at once (which they would have us believe is the case with SimCom). This criticism is superficial and entirely unfounded; SimCom in fact uses only one language—English" (Stewart, 1990, p. 121). Stating that he was not a prescriptive linguist, Stewart wrote:

> Somehow, plain deaf folks have discovered a simple truth: That is, in the great trenches of life, where daily battles are fought and won or lost, linguistic theory—and all other academic theory for that matter—counts about as much in that great scheme of things as a flea on a leaf floating down the Mississippi River at spring flood. The reality is that most Deaf folk have had to use whatever was at hand at the time, reality be damned, including SEE1, SEE2, SEE-Heinz 57, Siglish, the Rochester method, Cued Speech, gestures, flipped birdies, demonstrations, pointing, eye blinking, face twitching, head nodding, ear wiggling, and just about everything else that might possibly bridge the vast gulf that separates us deaf people from one another. (p. 121)

Stewart concluded:

> Consistent with the thinking of my deaf colleagues, Bernard Bragg and Harvey Goodstein, it is proposed that from now on we of the deaf community put aside current orthodoxy regarding the labeling of sign language . . . let us now open our arms to any and all forms of sign communication that are used in this great nation as they seek to communicate with one another and with the larger world. (p. 123)

Summary

ASL has a long and proud history. The role of manual communication in the education of the deaf and in the everyday functioning of deaf individuals has been a subject of controversy for centuries. Even the supporters of manual communication are divided. Some support a sign system based on a spoken language, and some identify a separate language such as ASL as a mark of distinction and a source of pride.

Fortunately, the effects of clashing opinions among predominantly hearing educators, psychologists, counselors, and other professionals serving the deaf have been limited. The languages used by deaf individuals have long thrived in the face of prejudice, hostility, and attempts to repress them.

For more than two hundred years, educators have argued that the teaching of speech and lip reading (speech reading) would spell the doom of signs and that the system would fade away and die unmourned as deaf children acquired oral skills. Over the years, enthusiasm has developed for panaceas in the guise of auditory training, integration, early intervention, and parent training. For some reason, each of these trends, though worthy in itself, has been viewed as obviating the need for manual communication. This simply has not proven to be the case.

Experience with deaf children and adults confirms that ASL and other language systems have shown great resilience and durability because they are meeting a need. Particularly impressive is the number of highly educated deaf adults who use ASL in daily activities, yet have excellent receptive and expressive oral skills. As long as ASL retains its power of expression and utility, it will survive the attacks of its detractors. In all probability, the increasing exposure of manual communication on television, in public school systems, and in the theater will greatly extend its use.

Debates over the relative benefits of ASL and Manual Codes on English also appear to be subsiding. Deaf professionals have provided leadership in making the term *ASL* more inclusive and in embracing varieties of signing within a common core. In the coming chapters, we will explore the implications of ASL for education.

CHAPTER

10

Early Intervention, Infant, and Preschool Programs

Introduction

Before beginning this chapter, the reader might wish to review Chapter 6: "Families with Deaf Members." An effort has been made to keep redundancy to a minimum, but federal initiatives for family-centered services can blur the distinction between where services end and families begin. The author and reviewers decided to have separate chapters with the realization that there would be quite a bit of overlap.

Given the present situation, many educators assume that federal legislation has mandated early identification of hearing loss and provision of services to deaf children and their families since the passage of Public law 94–142, the Education for All Handicapped Children Act of 1975. This represents a misunderstanding of PL 94–142 and its revisions over time and of the relationship of the federal government to the states in regard to education. At the beginning of 1999 only eleven states had enacted legislation concerning universal newborn screening. Although the number doubled in that year, by the beginning of the year 2000 still less than half the states had universal newborn hearing legislation (Boswell, 2000). Many of the states projected that implementation would require several years to meet their goals. To some extent the delay may be due to a lack of initiative at the state level. Because of the level of state control of education in the United States, there is a difference between what the federal government can mandate and what it can encourage. Still, there is little doubt that the federal government wasted time in establishing a leadership role in early identification. Passage of the act took nine years from the time legislation for universal newborn screening was first introduced in 1991 but not passed because of funding concerns (Boswell, 2000). Success was finally achieved in the Newborn Infant Screening and Intervention Act of 1999, which was incorporated into the Omnibus Budget Reconciliation Act of 1999 (HR 3194). The law calls for funding for state grants to develop infant screening and intervention programs, with support from the Centers for Disease Control, the National Institute on Deafness and Other Communication Disorders, and the Health, Resources and Services Administration. Participation is not mandatory.

The importance of universal newborn screening cannot be overemphasized. Traditionally, some states have used a "high-risk" registry to identify hearing loss in children, selecting only children with certain characteristics for testing. Such an approach apparently misses approximately 50 percent of all children with congenital sensorineural hearing losses. Yoshinaga-Itano and Apuzzo (1998) reported that the use of a high-risk registry was more likely, in a Colorado population, to identify infants with noticeable syndromes (e.g., Waardenburg, Treacher Collins) and with lesser degrees of hearing loss than it was to identify individuals with more profound hearing losses but without secondary disabilities. As a result, since 1997 Colorado has used universal infant screening.

Originally, then, PL 94–142 had little impact on very young deaf children and their families. Federal and state legislation has lagged behind public recognition of the need for early intervention, and state and local programs have lagged behind legislation. However, progress has been substantial since 1975, as the following brief outline documents.

Public Law 94–142 did not apply to children with disabilities below three years of age. The age range specified was from three to twenty-one. Even within that range, exceptions existed. In a review of the impact of PL94–142, Weiner (1985) noted that the requirement to provide special education to children ages three to five and ages eighteen to twenty-one did not apply if the rule "would be inconsistent with state law or practice" (p. 99). She stated that this "political trade-off" was necessary to get the law passed. As a result, the parts of the law dealing with ages three to five and eighteen to twenty-one were not mandatory but "permissive." It was up to the various states to decide whether to provide public educational programs for children with disabilities below age six. If they did, the federal government paid part of the cost for children ages three to five but did not reimburse states for educational services to children below age three. According to Weiner (1985, p. 100), services to all three-to-five-year-olds with disabilities were mandated in only nineteen states.

The reader should exercise caution regarding the term *early intervention*. Technically, the term today refers to ages from birth to three, or what would be considered infancy. Traditionally, the term has been used for children up to six years of age. This book will use the second, broader range to accommodate the literature.

An example of the traditional use of the term *early intervention* is provided by two publications, *Early Intervention for Hearing Impaired Children: Oral Options* (Ling, 1984a) and *Early Intervention for Hearing Impaired Children: Total Communication Options* (Ling, 1984b). Of the eight programs classified, only one, the Kendall Demonstration School Parent Infant Program (Somers, 1984), served children from birth to age three. The others provided services for children as old as twelve.

The enactment in 1986 of PL99–457, subsequently reauthorized under PL101–476, effectively replaced the child-centered orientation of PL94–142 with a family-centered focus. Bailey et al. (1990) have applauded this move toward involving parents more closely in decision making and enhancing family support systems. This orientation requires a redefinition of the roles of parents. In a survey of 204 professionals involved in providing early intervention services to deaf and hard-of-hearing children, Roush, Harrison, and Palsha (1991) reported strong support for family-centered services and interdisciplinary cooperation. Some respondents noted formidable barriers to family-centered intervention related to single-parent families, low-income families, families in which English is a second language, and others with difficult life situations. Because most professionals are not from minority backgrounds, there was an expressed need for multicultural sensitivity in general. A number of respondents expressed a need to expose hearing parents to the cultural aspects of deafness.

Roush et al. report that when conflicts arise, some professionals are reluctant to defer to family priorities. They note that it is not surprising that professionals find it difficult to remain supportive when they feel that parental choices are inconsistent with what they believe to be best for the child. They conclude that when opinions differ about matters such as educational placement or the selection of a communication system, conscientious parent-professional collaboration is required.

The passage of Public Law 99–457, then, was designed to increase support for early intervention programs, extend the focus from individualized educational plans (IEPs) to individualized family service plans (IFSPs), and provide for statewide coordinating councils. Bernstein and Morrison (1992) sent questionnaires to the departments of education of the fifty states and the District of Columbia concerning available programs for deaf infant and preschool children and the characteristics of the programs. Responses from sixteen states and the District of Columbia identified 340 programs. Only 134 of the 340 programs responded to the questionnaire. Of these, only 76 percent offered preschool services of any kind to deaf and hard-of-hearing children. The *youngest* average age allowed to enter programs was thirty months. Only three of the early intervention programs were residential. Twenty-five percent of the programs reported parental involvement only five times a year or less.

Of the 134 responding programs, 69 percent were school based and 41 percent were home based; that is, professionals went into the homes. (The numbers add to more than 100 percent because some programs had both school-based and home-based services.) As we might expect, activities in the two types of settings varied. As Table 10.1 shows, more than 90 percent of school-based programs emphasized language, speech, listening, and motor development, as well as academic readiness, and 89.2 percent offered sign language instruction. Clearly, when the authors used the term *language,* they meant *English*. The term *sign language* probably referred predominantly to Manual Codes on English, since only 24.7 percent offered instruction in ASL. In general, then, the school-based programs emphasized oral, written, and signed English development and academic readiness.

The home-based programs (see Table 10.1) presented a different picture, with the greatest emphasis on language/English development (100 percent of the pro-

TABLE 10.1 Types of Activities Reported by School- and Home-Based Early Intervention Programs

Type of Activity	Percent of Programs Using Activity	
	School-Based	Home-Based
Language development	100.0	100.0
Speech development	98.9	68.4
Motor development	94.6	50.0
Auditory training	93.5	81.6
Social skills	93.5	60.5
Math readiness	92.5	21.1
Reading readiness	91.4	21.1
Experiential/cognitive enrichment	91.4	73.7
Sign language instruction	89.2	78.9
Music/rhythm	83.9	21.1
Sensory stimulation	74.2	60.5
Speech reading	73.1	44.7
Physical therapy	66.7	0
Finger spelling	62.0	21.1
Instruction in ASL	24.7	10.5

Source: M. Bernstein, and M. Morrison, "Are We Ready for PL99–457?" *American Annals of the Deaf,* 137, (1992): 11.

grams), auditory training (81.6 percent), sign language (78.9 percent), and experiential/cognitive enrichment (73.7 percent). Again, since ASL instruction was provided in only 10.5 percent of the programs, the term *sign language* in essence referred to Manual Codes on English. The greatest overall emphasis reported for home training entailed suggestions for speech and auditory activities (p. 12). Involvement of fathers and siblings in home-based training was low.

The results do not present a reassuring picture. Almost one-quarter of responding programs had no services for deaf preschool-age children. Of those that had programs, the average minimum age for acceptance was thirty months. Bernstein and Morrison reported that the information provided by state agencies with federal mandates to monitor and coordinate services was *inaccurate* in at least 27 percent of the cases reported, suggesting that state agencies may not understand what is going on in the field. Clearly the ideal of family-based early intervention services has not been realized. If anything, the situation in the thirty-four states that did not respond is probably worse.

The Bernstein and Morrison findings suggest that high levels of stress may be present in families. In an investigation of parental stress and support services for families with deaf and hard-of-hearing infants, Meadow-Orlans (1995) administered the Parenting Stress Inventory (PSI) (Abidin, 1986) and the Scale to Measure the Stress of Life (SLE) (Thoits, 1983) to hearing parents of nine-month-old deaf and hard of hearing infants and parents of hearing infants. Overall scores on the PSI did not differ for parents by infants' hearing status, although there were subscale differences; mothers in both groups reported more stress related to "restrictions of role" and to "relations with spouse" than did their husbands.

The major differences surfaced in the total scores on the SLE measures. With a score of 12 representing high stress, the breakdown was as follows:

Group	Score
Mothers	
Deaf and hard-of-hearing infants	10
Hearing infants	8
Fathers	
Deaf and hard-of-hearing infants	7
Hearing infants	7

Reported stress among mothers of deaf and hard-of-hearing infants was significantly higher than for fathers in either group. Much of the stress among mothers of deaf infants, according to Meadow-Orlans (1995) related to a need for additional personal emotional support and to serious concerns about finances and work, as illustrated by the following quotes:

"Financially, we're struggling. It's really a strain. I can't decide if I should sacrifice the signing and go back to work, or if I should continue to stay at home so they can have the sign communication. . . . My husband's working constantly and I'm feeling guilty that I'm not working and helping him to support us." (p. 95)

"While [my husband] wasn't as outwardly grievous, there was no question that he was miserable too. But I think he allowed me to be more expressive, while he was more supportive." (p. 95)

"I felt like I didn't want to live. My husband was with me and he said something like, 'Why was I so upset, I already have one deaf child.' . . . Oh, he was shocked, but he accepts easier than I do." (p. 95)

"There are always extra expenses connected with deafness. We put special lights in the house, that was a nice $409. The TTY cost $300. . . . Lots of expenses for doctors." (p. 95)

Despite these issues, Meadow-Orlans reported that professional support services can be quite effective, as exemplified by the following comments from mothers:

"Our therapist. She's a marriage counselor and family therapist. Basically, she deals with the deaf. She had deaf parents, so she knows the deaf way, the deaf world." (p. 95)

"[My older daughter's teacher] helps us to find out our rights regarding schooling and the options that are available." (p. 95)

"Everyone I've dealt with, I've never met a group of more committed, caring professionals. They're what's made this whole experience [coping with the diagnosis of
deafness] bearable." (p. 95)

To be truly effective, an early intervention program—one that serves deaf children and their families from time of identification of a hearing loss—should have
several related components. Services to parents and other family members should
be provided across several domains—knowledge, adjustment, and skill—and each
domain should be addressed as quickly as possible. Parents should receive information about deafness in general and about the immediate and long-term implications
for their child and other family members. At the same time, parents should receive
counseling and support as they work through their own adjustment to the presence
of deafness in their child. Simultaneously, they should be developing skills related
to the proper fitting and care of hearing aids, the provision of intellectually and
socially stimulating environments, and perhaps the addition of a manual form of
communication to the family's repertoire.

Within the family plan, the child's needs can also be seen as tripartite. First, of
course, is the need for a system of early identification and appropriate referral. The
next step is the development of an individualized plan for the child, involving a
team of professionals and the parents. After that comes implementation of the program and monitoring of the child's and family's progress.

Deaf and hearing professionals who work with families must demonstrate great
sensitivity and understanding to hearing parents. Those of us who think of deafness
as having a strong cultural component must remember that such thinking may distress some parents who want to consider their deaf children as part of their own
cultural, ethnic, religious, and social identity and not as part of a Deaf culture that
will be transmitted by people outside of the family structure. Parents must be helped
to understand that such an identity can supplement rather than conflict with the
family's identification. Miller (1992) has noted that deaf professionals can be especially effective in this area.

This text is intended to provide an overview of education of the deaf for prospective teachers of the deaf, other professionals, and parents. It is expected that those
who are in training to become teachers will go on to take methods courses where
they will master specific techniques and curricula relevant to their area. Unfortunately, in the area of early intervention, no validated comprehensive curriculum is
available that, in this author's opinion, addresses all of the needs of deaf children
and their families. Perhaps this is to be expected, because an ideal curriculum
would have to cover a variety of competencies, including counseling, child development, linguistics, speech and hearing, and instruction. Many excellent early intervention programs exist, but there is no curriculum that can stand alone.

The expense of providing services, even federally mandated ones, clearly has inhibited the development of programs for young deaf children, especially in large cities
with shrinking tax bases and escalating costs in education and other areas. Bernstein
and Morrison (1992) reported that almost 25 percent of respondent programs that did
not offer services to deaf preschool children and their families listed lack of funding as

a major factor. Many state and local agencies are quick to point out that since the enactment of PL94–142 in 1975 and its evolution into the Individuals with Disabilities Education Act (IDEA), the U.S. Congress has never appropriated the money that it authorized to meet its mandates. Congress established a formula in which by 1982, for each child with a disability educated, the federal government would reimburse the states 40 percent of the excess cost per year above that required to educate a child without a disability. In reality, by 1985 Congress had never appropriated more than 12 percent of the excess cost (Weiner, 1985), and the percentage has probably decreased since then. This, of course, is only one of many partially funded mandates that expect states to pick up the extra costs.

Despite fiscal restraints, some states have recognized the need to quickly provide support to parents and educational services to children diagnosed as deaf. In many states today, early intervention programs may begin as soon as a hearing loss is identified in a young child. The programs involve a much wider range of services than those traditionally associated with education. In addition to language, speech, and pre-academic training, services include parent and family counseling, provision of factual information about deafness and its implications, and training in communication techniques. Thus a strong relationship exists between the material in this chapter and that in the chapter on family dynamics (Chapter 6). Readers might want to refer to that chapter to integrate the information.

To avoid confusion in discussing programs for deaf children under the traditional age of entrance into a formal educational program—which may be placed at age six—we must establish some operational definitions of terms. As more and more programs have been created to serve children at increasingly younger ages, terms have proliferated. Thus, we may read about preschool, nursery, kindergarten, prekindergarten, pre-preschool, and infant programs. Although infant programs are usually designed for children up to age three and kindergarten commonly serves children just before entrance into elementary school, much overlap exists. For example, the terms *preschool, pre-preschool, nursery, prekindergarten,* and *infant* have all been applied to programs serving three-year-old children. The use of different terms would be justifiable if the terms actually represented different programmatic efforts, but in most cases they do not. This chapter, as noted, will use the term *early intervention* to refer to programs designed to serve deaf children from birth, or time of identification of hearing loss, to age six; within this range, *infancy* covers birth to age three.

Thus, early intervention incorporates services to children as well as those programmatic activities designed for parents of young deaf children. The latter include educating parents about causes of deafness, individual and group counseling and therapy sessions, and training parents to work with their deaf children in the home. In some cases, siblings and other relatives also are involved.

Historically, a number of factors have hampered the development of effective early intervention programs for deaf children. The two major obstacles to the organization of comprehensive services have been the facts that (1) deafness is a low-incidence condition and (2) deafness poses such severe communication limitations that specially trained personnel are required to work with the program.

Most residential schools, being cognizant of the importance of the home during a child's early years, have hesitated to extend the residential components of their programs below age four. Until the late 1960s, public school programs typically did not offer services to children below age five or six because of restrictive state laws. In cases where lower age limits were set, the legislation was usually permissive, not mandatory; that is, school systems were permitted to establish programs for younger children, but they were not mandated to do so, and no funds were appropriated.

As a result, most early intervention programs for deaf children were established within the context of private schools, university clinics, and speech and hearing centers. Frequently, a lack of coordination and even of communication existed between these programs and the public and residential schools in which the children would eventually enroll, and the differences in orientation and goals proved to be detrimental to the children and parents involved. Although the situation has improved in recent years, in many cases these problems continue to impede the development of comprehensive, well-integrated programs.

Meeting the Problems of Early Intervention: The Nineteenth Century

Despite the self-conscious tendency of many recent programs to label themselves "exemplary," "innovative," "model," and so on, few—if any—elements of these programs were not employed, or at least considered, generations ago. Meier's (1961) proposal to train mothers to use the manual alphabet with deaf children as young as eighteen months was anticipated by Dalgarno (1680), who drew up the outlines of a training program for young children in the home and advocated that adults fingerspell to children in the cradle. The supposedly new concept of integrating young deaf children and hearing children was advocated in England by Arrowsmith (1819) and was widespread in Germany in the late nineteenth century (Gordon, 1885a). Although a Santa Ana, California, program has rightfully been acknowledged as the first public school program to teach manual communication to hearing children (Holcomb, 1970), neither the idea nor the practice is new. In nineteenth-century Germany, signs were used along with speech in many of the common schools that integrated deaf and hearing children.

The first program designed for the young deaf child in the United States, established by Bartlett in New York City in 1852, possessed many of the elements of recent "innovative" programs. After more than twenty years' experience teaching in a residential school, Bartlett established a "family" school "adapted to the physical, mental and moral wants of children of an early and tender age" (1852, p. 32). He proposed:

> not so much to confine the little ones to a regular routine of exercises in school hours, as to teach them and accustom them at the table, in their little plays, walks

and amusements, and in the ordinary every-day occurring incidents of juvenile life, to express their thoughts and learn to think in alphabetic language, thus making the acquisition of language a matter of early imitation, practice and habit, as nature plainly indicates it should be. (p. 35)

Bartlett also accepted hearing children, usually siblings of deaf children, into his family school. The hearing children acquired facility in the language of signs and the manual alphabet. Bartlett believed the system was mutually beneficial to deaf and hearing children. Echoing Dalgarno and Thomas Hopkins Gallaudet, both of whom believed the manual alphabet would help hearing children master English orthography, Bartlett argued:

We find this beneficial to both classes—to the deaf mutes in enlarging their scope of thought by bringing their minds into contact with those of their more favored companions; beneficial yet more variously to those who hear and speak, quickening their perception and improving their mental development by presenting to their minds language under entirely new forms; by the use of the manual alphabet in spelling words; and also by no means inconsiderable advantage of improved ease and expressiveness of manner, induced by practice in the use of gesture language. (Gordon, 1885b, p. 249)

Bartlett's program, then, was modeled along the lines of a family unit. It integrated deaf and hearing children. Language learning occurred by a natural process, and all modes of communication were used by both deaf and hearing children. The program apparently was a success (Gordon, 1885b), but it did not survive its founder. Many of its innovative features were lost, only to be "reinvented" in the latter part of the twentieth century.

One other early intervention program deserves mention: the Sarah Fuller Home for Little Children Who Cannot Hear. This program was established in West Medford, Massachusetts, in 1888 to serve very young children before entrance into school programs (Adams, 1928). The home was closed in 1925 because of rising expenses. As an alternative, a home visitation program was established in cooperation with the Horace Mann School for the Deaf in Boston. A trained teacher of the deaf visited the homes of deaf children to train mothers and to teach children the oral method. A mother, an aunt, or a grandmother would be present at each lesson and would be given instructions in procedures to follow with the child until the next visit.

The home visitation program could have been a prototype for the home visitation components of many contemporary programs. However, most of these programs were actually modeled after family-oriented programs developed in Great Britain and Scandinavia. As is the case with Barlett's family school, no direct line of progression can be traced from the Fuller home visitation program to present early intervention programs for deaf children in the United States.

Except for the students who attended a few privately financed programs such as those mentioned above, early education for deaf children was limited to those whose parents had the financial means to retain tutors. Although they were unable to initiate early intervention programs, educators in residential and day school programs were acutely conscious of the importance of early education and the development of communication between deaf children and their families. The first issues of *American Annals of the Deaf* contained articles about early instruction and suggestions for parents of young deaf children (Ayres, 1849; Woodruff, 1848). This topic appeared consistently throughout the nineteenth century (for example, see Crouter, 1885; Gordon, 1885b; Hirsch, 1887; Peet, 1886; Pettengill, 1874; Ray, 1852; Waldo, 1859). Many schools developed instructions and procedures for parents to use with their young children (Gordon, 1885b). Signs, the manual alphabet, and pictures for instruction were common components.

For the most part, educators emphasized the advantages of having very young deaf children live at home. Pettengill (1874) stated:

> The very best way, in my opinion, to educate a deaf-mute, is for the parents of the child, as soon as they discover he cannot hear, to commence to make efforts to open and enlighten his mind by means of natural signs, and at the same time to endeavor to make him utter sounds and read from the lips. (p. 1)

Pettengill noted that deaf individuals originally were educated by their parents or by private tutors, with instruction and training being addressed directly to the individual. Pettengill contended that only tutoring could yield optimal results and that schools, which through necessity deal with groups of children, could only hope to approach this ideal. To maximize the effectiveness of schools, Pettengill supported the following approach:

> A school for young children, in my opinion, is rightly constituted and likely to subserve the end of its establishment just in proportion as it conforms to its prototype—the well ordered family. If we accept the family as the model school, it settles some disputed questions in education, and establishes the principles, first that both male and female teachers should be employed—females especially—in the more tender years; second, that boys and girls should be trained together; third, that the monitor system is a good one, the elder pupils assisting in the education of the younger; and fourth, that each individual pupil should receive special instruction according to his personal requirements, peculiar deficiencies, particular gifts and prospective work, and not be taught in large classes. (1874, pp. 6–7)

Pettengill's approach at the first stage was similar to that of Ayres, an earlier educator who also had addressed himself to techniques of early home training. Ayres, however, saw the processes as being more complex, especially in their consideration of the role of natural signs during children's development. Asserting that education, to be complete, must begin and end at home, Ayres attempted to show parents how to begin the intellectual training of deaf children before they entered school. He believed that communication is the child's primary need and the natural language of signs is the foundation of all language. About these natural signs, Ayres (1849) stated:

> This language of signs—and we shall not be understood here to speak of the systematized language of signs used in our Asylums for the deaf and dumb, or as they are

> called by the French, signs of reduction—is the foundation of all language. It is just as
> necessary to the child who hears, as to the child who is deaf. It is the first vehicle of
> thought, the first means of intellectual or soul communication. But its range is limited,
> its capacity small, and its use, but for a brief period. Upon this stock is grafted,
> in the case of the child who can hear, language or speech. . . . Yet the first lessons in
> language, provided by nature, are the same for the deaf and dumb child and the child
> who enjoys the faculty of hearing. (p. 180)

It is interesting to note that Ayres's position concerning the foundation of language is consistent with Piaget's, especially as it relates to sensorimotor operations as prerequisites to language acquisition. During the Piagetian sensorimotor period (approximately from birth to eighteen months), children begin to coordinate various sensorimotor acts (for example, what they hear, they look at; what they touch, they taste; and so on). Thus, infants act on their immediate environment. Piaget considered infants to be completely "earthbound" during this stage in that "life" is what exists in the present moment and within the perceptual environment. The hallmark achievement of this stage, object permanence, unbinds sensorimotor infants. As a function of the various complex interactions they have experienced, infants come to realize that "out of sight" does not mean "out of mind." They now understand that things and people have permanency, which can be represented cognitively. For Piaget and others, this knowledge is prerequisite to language development, for in order to talk about things, children must be able to represent or know them.

Ayres argued that the utility of natural signs is limited for the most part to the very early stages of development and that deaf children will cease to progress past a certain point if the signs continue to be the major mode of communication. To unfold for children "the mystery of speech in the home" (1849, p. 181), Ayres suggested that parents use the manual alphabet, which he claimed could be learned in one or two hours. For young children, Ayres preferred the use of the manual alphabet over that of systematic signs because he believed it to be superior in helping deaf children acquire an initial knowledge of English.

Ayres's approach was consistent with that of his contemporary, Bartlett (1852). Both emphasized the manual alphabet in early instruction and were convinced that the acquisition of language should develop along natural lines. Ayres (1849) exhorted parents:

> The great secret of success is practice. Teach the child to talk at all times. Talk to him
> and talk with him. Let all the household do the same. It is not by lessons; it is not by
> systematic instruction that any child learns language well. It is by conversation, here a
> little and there a little, as his necessities, his inclinations, or his circumstances prompt.
> (p. 183)

An article by an unidentified author ("The Kindergarten Method," 1875) argued for the desirability of the kindergarten method, based on Froebel's concepts of early education with orderly, "unstructured" activities designed for children ages three to seven. The use of the manual alphabet was seen as providing a means of communication. Using reasoning consistent with that of the previously mentioned educators of the time, "The Kindergarten Method" emphasized the primacy of the home influence:

> There can be no doubt that the most favorable circumstances for the development of a deaf-mute child would be a training at home, according to the Froebel method, conducted by the mother, or by a competent kindergartner, with six or eight hearing and speaking children at the same age as companions. (p. 123)

Acknowledging that realistically such a program could not be developed for the majority of young deaf children, the author suggested alternative plans, the most preferable being a system by which a kindergarten would be established for deaf children in every large city. The kindergartens, although physically separate, would be affiliated with state residential schools for deaf children and would enroll children between two and three years of age. The proposed system was never developed.

Substantial evidence exists that nineteenth-century educators of the deaf in the United States and Europe were aware of the ways in which even slight amounts of residual hearing facilitated speech development (Gallaudet, 1868), of the difficulties parents encountered in the diagnostic process, and of the initial tendency of parents to regard the child's inability to speak as the major problem instead of the child's inability to hear. Describing the difficulties in ascertaining deafness in a young child, Hill (1868) wrote:

> The child gives the father the hand asked for, goes to him at his call, looks at the striking clock, turns about when the door is shut hard, notices the ball rolling behind it. Are these not unmistakable signs of the ability to hear? The father thinks so and the mother will cherish this belief. That a deaf mute child could do all this they have no idea. The deaf mute child does it all, but with this distinction—it does not obey the spoken order or the call, but the outstretched hand of the father and the nod; it turns its eye to the clock because it sees its brother look in that direction; the shut door, the rolling ball, the passing wagon, the clapping of the hands act upon the child's sense of feeling. The father and the mother moreover, easily and willingly allow themselves to be deceived. (p. 72)

A sensitive article printed in a report of the Royal Wurtemburg Institution for the Deaf and Dumb ("Early Home Training," 1869; trans. 1879) stressed that the cause of speechlessness lies not in the organs of speech but in the lack of hearing. Reporting on parents' difficulty in understanding this, the article noted:

> That the dumbness of the child, which in many cases is discovered first, is only the consequence of deafness, they seldom take into consideration. They regard the dumbness as the real infirmity, and instead of getting at the root of the evil, instead of attacking the cause (the deafness) with which the effect (the dumbness) would cease, they try to cure the dumbness. (p. 15)

The article from the Royal Wurtemburg Institution reveals an attitude similar in several respects to the one prevalent at that time in the United States. These similarities, of course, reflect the influence of prominent German educators of the time on American educational thought rather than that of Americans on German educators. The desirability of initiating training at birth, or at the time of identification of deafness, was emphasized. Parents were encouraged to use signs along with speech in communicating with their child, and a liberal use of pictures for instructional purposes was advocated. The article stated that deaf children should be sent to the village schools for little children and that the teacher and the pastor had a moral obligation to meet their special needs to prepare them for entrance into formal programs for deaf children around age eight or nine.

In summary, although nineteenth-century educators of the deaf lacked the means to implement widespread early intervention programs, they were united in their conviction that early communication between the child and the family was important and that facilitation of intellectual development should begin as early as possible. The recommendations of various educators were highly consistent and contained progressive components that until recently were lacking in most twentieth-century early intervention programs. Some of these components are as follows:

1. Use of the family unit as the organizational model
2. Use of natural signs and gestures to establish a basis for communication
3. Reliance on simultaneous oral-manual communication
4. Reliance on the manual alphabet
5. Early introduction of reading and writing in the education of the deaf child
6. Commitment to a natural, informal, relaxed atmosphere to facilitate the development of speech and language
7. Early integration of deaf and hearing children for the mutual benefit of both

Early Intervention, Infant, and Preschool Programs in the Twentieth Century

As previously noted, most programs for young deaf children before the 1960s were not affiliated with either public school programs or state-supported residential schools for the deaf. They were supported primarily through private means, and they did not reach the general population of deaf children. Typically, they were conducted under the leadership of otologists and audiologists, and speech therapists were responsible for working with the children. Teachers of deaf children were not involved. In such programs, educational considerations received low priority. The

Large group activities in an early intervention program.

problems of deafness were perceived as either falling within a medical/pathological framework or involving an inability to speak, which could be remediated simply by proper fitting of hearing aids and training in articulation. The problems this naiveté caused were compounded by the fact that those affiliated with such programs usually had no knowledge of the programs for deaf individuals in which the children would eventually be enrolled. They did not know what had happened to their former pupils, and had no social or professional contacts with deaf adults. This situation did not change until the late 1960s, when there emerged a new generation of audiologists and speech pathologists who were much more attuned to problems of language and communication (as well as of speech) than their predecessors had been.

The situation changed again, but not necessarily for the better, in the early 1970s, when educators of the deaf "took over" to a large degree. During that period, teachers in many programs for the deaf assumed the responsibilities of parental counselors, social workers, child development specialists, educational audiologists, and psychologists—roles they were inadequately qualified to assume.

The few residential and public day schools that did establish programs for the most part simply extended their minimum age requirement down to age four or five. They seldom dealt systematically with the special needs of younger children or with family dynamics. Although some programs were housed in separate buildings or were "off campus," the actual practices represented no major departures from tradition; instead, they usually consisted of watered-down versions of activities originally designed for six- and seven-year-old deaf children. These programs shared with private clinics and centers a fixation on the development of articulation and oral-aural receptive skills to the exclusion of social, cognitive, and linguistic factors. They were usually less successful than their private counterparts in utilizing residual hearing, probably because they (1) did not have the same sophisticated equipment, (2) lacked trained specialists, and (3) worked with fewer children who had mild and moderate hearing losses. Before the methods revolution in the 1960s, only one early intervention program in the United States allowed the use of any form of manual communication along with oral communication. This was the New Mexico School for the Deaf, which employed the Rochester Method (Hester, 1963).

The impetus for the development of early intervention programs during this period came from several sources. First, widespread dissatisfaction with the results obtained by educational programs for the deaf yielded a consensus that sweeping changes of some sort were necessary. Evidence had accumulated that, according to standardized tests, intellectually normal deaf adolescents and adults in North America and Europe were unable to read at the fifth-grade level (Furth, 1969a; Norden, 1970; Wrightstone, Aranow, and Moskowitz, 1963); lacked skills in the language of the hearing community (Moores, 1970b; Simmons, 1962; Tervoort, 1961); and were incapable of receiving and expressing oral communication on anything but a primitive level despite the commitment of most schools to exclusively oral instruction (*Education of the Deaf,* 1968; Montgomery, 1966). One position held that the educational retardation of deaf students who left school could be reduced by establishing early intervention programs.

A second major impetus for early intervention programs was the influence of the movement in general education toward "compensatory" education and an increasing emphasis on the impact of the early years on later functioning, which resulted in the federally sponsored Head Start system. In the same way that many idealists perceived Head Start as compensating for all the handicaps of poverty, malnutrition, and discrimination suffered by politically and economically disadvantaged segments of the population, some educators of the deaf saw the early intervention programs as overcoming all the linguistic, social, and academic difficulties with which deafness is so frequently associated.

The rubella epidemic of the early 1960s, the worst recorded rubella epidemic to hit the United States, also played a major role in the establishment of early intervention programs. In its aftermath, educators of the deaf nervously anticipated a wave of deaf children inundating elementary school programs and taxing existing facilities beyond their capacities. Estimates of the number of children varied widely. All that was known for certain was that the group of deaf children entering school would be the largest in the nation's history and would include many who suffered from additional conditions. Early intervention programs were established across the country not only to prepare these children for eventual entrance into school programs but also to allow program developers to understand and plan for the needs of these children.

Research on the Effectiveness of Programs

Unfortunately, few models existed on which to base the new early intervention programs. Individuals interested in the development of new programs or in the modification of ongoing ones quickly discovered that although such programs had been available for generations, almost no educational guidelines existed for effective intervention programs for deaf children. Most of the literature cited as research involves a description, a defense, and praise of a program by someone who developed it or was closely associated with it in some way. With the exception of a possible audiogram or tape accompanying a lecture, no data are presented.

The lack of data may be traced to two factors. First, it is extremely difficult to evaluate the effectiveness of early intervention programs, not only because the low incidence of deafness reduces the efficacy of the usual statistical procedures but also because communication is frequently lacking between child and evaluator. Second, and perhaps even more inhibiting, is the highly emotional nature of the question regarding the methodology to be used with deaf children, especially young deaf children. Some educators firmly believe that the use of any kind of manual communication will prevent children from developing speech and language and will doom them to a lifelong existence in a mute subculture. Others equally firmly believe that depriving children of such a system will cause them irreparable linguistic, educational, and emotional damage. Given such a climate, most researchers prefer to investigate other questions. None of these factors, however, should be sufficient to deter a search for objective analysis. Educational decisions must be made daily. If no information exists, the decisions will be made on the basis of other, less desirable factors, as has typically been the case in education of the deaf.

One of the mysteries confronting the professional with an interest in research is the lack of research on early education programs, especially of a comparative nature, relative to the 1960s and 1970s. Beginning in the 1960s, several studies documented the shortcomings of oral-only preschool programs. These were followed by comparisons of oral-only preschool programs with programs employing the Rochester Method or total communication. Today, despite much debate over the use of ASL-only, oral-only, and oral-manual communication, there is a dearth of material with which to make an informed decision. One reason may be that more options are available to parents and children. Most critics of oral-only programs acknowledged that they were effective for some children; however, they were not appropriate for other children. Now that individual options are open to children and their families, it is more difficult to match children with similar characteristics receiving different treatments.

Drawing on subjects from six schools for deaf children, Phillips (1963) compared children receiving preschool training from age three on with others receiving no preschool training. By the time the children were nine years old, no differences were found between experimental and control groups in terms of language arts, arithmetic, and socialization. Drawing on subjects from two schools for deaf children, Craig (1964) matched children who had preschool training (over age three) with those who had no preschool training; no differences were reported in lip reading or reading skills.

McCroskey (1967, 1968) evaluated the effectiveness of a home-centered preschool program with an auditory emphasis by comparing children who had gone through the program with children who had received no training. The few differences found between the groups tended to favor the children who had received no preschool training. McCroskey postulated that perhaps the children who received early training had more severe problems and thus were identified at an earlier age. Since no pretreatment data were gathered for these children, this hypothesis must remain speculation.

Vernon and Koh (1970) matched sixty-nine children at the California School for the Deaf at Riverside who had graduated from the Tracy Clinic's three-year preschool program from 1944 to 1968 on the basis of age, IQ, and gender with children who had received no preschool training. They found no differences between the children trained at the Tracy Clinic and those without preschool training in speech, speech reading, academic achievement, or reading. A third group, consisting of deaf children of deaf parents, was found to be superior in academic achievement and reading. No differences in speech or speech reading were found between the children of deaf parents and either of the other two groups.

A Longitudinal Evaluation

Moores and associates conducted a longitudinal evaluation based on the modification of Cronbach's (1957) characteristics-by-treatment interaction model in cooperation with seven early education programs (Moores, 1985a; Moores, Weiss, and Goodwin, 1978). The programs were selected to represent a number of important components of various early intervention systems. The programs differed in methodology (auditory, oral-aural, Rochester Method, total communication); setting (day, residential); orientation (traditional nursery, academic, cognitive); emphasis (parent-centered, child-centered); and placement (integrated, self-contained). Each participating program was considered to be a strong representative of a particular early intervention model.

The evaluation was designed to avoid what had been perceived as weaknesses in previous evaluations. Among the steps taken were the following:

1. To be involved, programs had to provide services from time of identification of a hearing loss and had to serve complete rather than select populations.

2. Programs were given no role in the evaluation.

3. Measures of the use of residual hearing were employed.

4. Decisions about inclusion of pupils in the study were made by an audiologist on a "blind" basis; that is, data presented to the audiologist did not identify the program from which a child came.

5. Investigators were able to follow children who entered neighborhood schools—in other words, those who were mainstreamed.

6. Measures of expressive and receptive communication abilities were developed and administered in addition to tests measuring articulation and receptive vocabulary.

Subjects were tested every spring for four successive years. By the final testing, the average age was seven years, with a range from six to eight years. Basic findings are summarized in the following paragraphs. For complete results, readers are referred to the original sources.

Academic achievement.   As measured by the Metropolitan Achievement Test (MAT), Primer Battery, achievement of the sample was comparable to that of hearing children of the same age in reading and below that of hearing children of the same age in arithmetic. The relatively poor achievement in arithmetic was noted in the last two years of the evaluation, suggesting a general weakness in all programs involved; reading was apparently emphasized to the detriment of computational skills. The high reading scores suggest that the programs provided children with the skills for basic reading. However, since evidence indicates that the children lacked knowledge of more complex English linguistic structures (such as passives, interrogatives, verb tenses, and negatives), it was considered probable that over the years the children would show less progress in reading than would the standardization hearing population.

Regarding program comparisons, average scores for reading, arithmetic, and overall academic achievement were highest in the program that used the Rochester Method and emphasized cognitive and academic skills. A traditional auditory program with emphasis on integration had the lowest average score in each category.

Illinois Test of Psycholinguistic Abilities (ITPA).   In the second, third, and fourth years, the average scores of the subjects on the five visual-motor subtests of the ITPA were almost identical to norms established for children with normal hearing, suggesting normal functioning in these areas. The deaf subjects consistently exhibited superiority on one subtest, Manual Expression. The ITPA scores with this population do not correlate with scores on expressive and receptive communication, suggesting that for young deaf children, visual-motor tests of the ITPA may assess underlying cognitive abilities rather than psycholinguistic abilities per se.

In the beginning years of the study, mean scores were quite sensitive to the amount of structure and academic orientation of a program. These differences seemed to disappear by the fourth year, indicating that previous differences on the ITPA among programs were spurious.

Receptive communication.   The subjects' receptive abilities were assessed across five modes: printed messages; sound alone; sound and speech reading; sound, speech reading, and finger spelling; and sound, speech reading, and signs. Children from programs that did not use finger spelling and/or signs were not tested under these conditions. The receptive tasks varied in difficulty from simple two-word phrases (for example, *red ball*) to complete sentences involving verb tense, negation, and passives. In each case, the child was given four possible choices and had to point to the drawing representing the correct answer. As Table 10.2 indicates, the least efficient mode was sound alone. Understanding increased with the addition of each element—speech reading, finger spelling, and signs—and the combined use of sound, speech reading, and signs was the single most effective means of communication. Scores on the printed-word subtest increased dramatically from the third to the fourth year as a function of increased attention to reading in all programs.

Scores on understanding of passives, negatives, and verb tenses suggest that the deaf students tended to process all sentences as simple, active declaratives and to ignore indications of tense, mood, and negation, regardless of the mode of communication. Only when dealing with the printed word did they perform somewhat better.

Cognitive development.   Tests of classification, conservation, and seriation revealed no differences among programs on any of the measures in the last year. Previous differences in favor of a "Piagetian" preschool program disappeared, indicating that the activities themselves had no lasting effect on cognitive development as measured in these three areas.

Communication patterns.   Classroom observation consistently showed that the least communication occurred in oral-aural classes and the most took place in total communication classes. To a large extent, teachers and children in oral-aural classes relied on gestures, apparently unconsciously; this tendency was so strong that one program could properly have been classified as oral-gestural. Similarly, in some total communication classes, only a small proportion of the spoken words was

TABLE 10.2   Percent Correct for All Subjects on Receptive Communication Scale (Core Items) in Second, Third, and Fourth Years of Testing

Subtest	Year 2	Year 3	Year 4
Printed word	38	56	76
Sound alone	34	43	44
Sound and speech reading	56	63	68
Sound, speech reading, and finger spelling	61	72	75
Sound, speech reading, and signs	72	86	88
Average correct	50	62	69

signed. This was especially true in programs that had recently switched methodologies.

Parental attitudes.   At the beginning of the evaluation, parents of children in oral-aural programs saw the goals of early intervention programs to be the development of speech and speech-reading skills, whereas parents of children in combined oral-manual programs placed greater emphasis on academic skills such as reading and mathematics. By the fourth year, the attitudes of parents with children in oral-aural programs had become essentially the same as those of parents with children in combined programs.

A Survey of Support Services

Meadow-Orlans et al. (1997) conducted a national survey of parents of deaf and hard-of-hearing children and the early services they had received. Hearing loss was confirmed at a mean age of 14.5 months for the deaf group and at 28.6 months for the hard-of-hearing group. Identification tended to be around five months after a hearing loss was suspected. The gap between diagnosis and intervention tended to be large. According to parental reports, children waited eight months on the average for hearing aids, ten months for speech and auditory training, and eleven months for introduction to signs or sign language. Children with deaf mothers were identified earlier and began speech training and received hearing aids at later ages. Diagnosis of deafness in a child, as might be expected, had less of an impact on deaf mothers than on hearing mothers. Parents rated the early services they received highly. Because white mothers were more positive about services than parents of non-white or mixed race children, the authors noted the need for sensitivity to diversity.

The Methodology Issue

In recent years, the debate between oralists and manualists has lessened substantially. The evidence suggests that the use of manual communication does not impede the development of oral skills in young deaf children and can facilitate growth in English and academic subject matter. Most contemporary programs exhibit a laudable flexibility, reacting to a child's individual needs at any point in time. Confusion still exists over what to do, in terms of modes of communication, with the child who has been diagnosed recently. The crux of the methodology issue for the very young child is: What type of communication should be recommended for newly identified deaf children? Diagnosing very young children is difficult, and in many cases it is uncertain how much sound they receive and how they process that sound. This is especially true of children with etiologies of rubella, meningitis, and prematurity, which may include other complicating factors. For children whose potential for developing language auditorially is difficult to predict, educators have two alternatives. If they believe the base of language lies in the auditory mode and that visual presentation inhibits development of this mode, they will recommend a straight auditory emphasis. The auditory failures will later be programmed into multisensory systems. If the professionals believe the base of language lies deeper, they will consider modality to be relatively unimportant and, when in doubt, will provide simultaneous auditory-visual presentation.

If the base of language really is auditory, the first approach will serve the auditory children educationally and lose the others, whereas the second approach will lose all the children. If the base of language goes deeper, the first alternative will save all the auditory children and lose the others, whereas the second alternative will save all the children. Given the present state of knowledge, educators must make decisions regarding methodology in the face of great uncertainty. In thinking through the problem, they must be aware that if their orientation is wrong, their decisions will have lasting detrimental effects on these children.

After considering practical and theoretical issues and reviewing the extensive literature on the topic, this author has come to the following position: If there is any chance that sole reliance on auditory-vocal communication will create difficulty for a child, oral-manual communication should be initiated immediately, since the use of oral and manual communication can facilitate development. Withholding manual communication until a child "fails" orally is a disservice to the child. In my opinion, too many early intervention programs in public schools still follow this procedure.

ASL and Early Intervention

As previously discussed, Bernstein and Morrison (1992) reported that 78.9 percent of home-based early intervention programs provided instruction in sign language, but only 10.5 percent offered ASL instruction (see Table 10.1). Meadow-Orlans et al. (1997) reported that only 5 percent of children in their sample had sign-alone in their initial program. Obviously, the emphasis has been on Manual Codes on English, a logical emphasis given the skills and orientation of hearing parents. In my view, however, deaf children should be exposed to ASL as early as possible and have the opportunity to become truly bilingual and to participate in the Deaf community. This can come about only through interaction with deaf adults and requires a complete reorientation of early intervention programs, from which deaf professionals traditionally have been excluded. Some programs now involve teams of deaf and hearing professionals in home-based programs. This practice should become more widespread. Miller (1991) has proposed intensive, ASL-oriented, total immersion programs based on the concept of "family learning vacations" in which hearing parents can gain exposure to linguistic, cultural, and social aspects of the Deaf community.

Summary

Interest in the education of very young deaf children traces back to the nineteenth century. The development of early education programs was greatly influenced by the rubella epidemic in the early 1960s and federal legislation passed since then. The majority of programs are now supported by public school districts and residential schools for deaf individuals. This has represented a change from the traditional provision of services by clinics and speech and hearing centers.

The most recent federal legislation mandates early identification and services, along with individualized family service plans. Dramatic changes in American family life—smaller families, more children raised in single-parent homes, more mothers working outside of the home—call for creative early intervention programs. One crucial element continues to be missing from early intervention programs: the participation of deaf professionals. The situation is changing, but slowly.

C H A P T E R

11

The Acquisition of English: Teaching and Training Techniques

Introduction

Before beginning this chapter and the following two chapters, it would be helpful to explicate some of the assumptions about deafness and education of deaf children that have been presented in this book. We come back to the three basic issues: What do we teach deaf children? How do we teach deaf children? Where do we teach deaf children? The questions are simple on the surface, but they hide an underlying complexity. The answers depend on an individual's philosophy. One major thrust in education of deaf children has been what may be called "normalization," the idea that deafness is a pathology and the primary goal is to make the deaf child as close to a hearing child as possible. Since speech is typically the most obvious difference between deaf and hearing children, many educators have concentrated on the development of articulate speech as the sine qua non of education of the deaf. One need not question the importance of speech in our society to disagree strongly with this orientation. If we agree on the essential normalcy of the deaf child, then the goal of "normalization" is self-defeating and, to a great extent, denigrates the self-worth of a deaf child. The real goal should be to help all children achieve their potential and develop emotionally, socially, and intellectually into productive adults.

Another major thrust has been the search for a "key" that will open up the world of communication to the deaf child. In fact, one of the systems we will examine is called the Fitzgerald Key. The assumption is that, once effective communication and mastery are established, the deaf child will develop normally academically. This

250

represents an improvement over the pathological model in that it establishes the deaf child as normal and instead concentrates on modifying the communication environment to enhance growth. It is to be hoped that such an approach is becoming dominant in our field. However, in its extreme form, it is somewhat naive, at least for the majority of deaf children who have hearing parents. If we had identification of hearing loss at birth, with immediate provision of appropriate services and counseling and training of parents, then there would be no problem. It would simply be a matter of turning the key and getting with the program. As we know, even with recent improvements, deafness often is not diagnosed and services are not provided until precious months and even years have been lost. This is especially true of children from poor families. In large city programs, I have seen children ten, twelve, or fourteen years of age—frequently recent immigrants—who have never been in an educational environment before. As we learned in Chapter 6, even some of the more comprehensive family-oriented programs provide only a few hours a month of home visitation. I have heard early childhood educators say that a child who begins receiving services at age two, three, or four has a learning age (or, in the case of auditory-based programs, a listening age) of zero. This is a serious misconception. A three-year-old child is physically, neurologically, socially, and experientially different from a newborn. It stands to reason that the process of language acquisition beginning at three years of age does not recapitulate the process that begins at birth. It is more difficult. To assume otherwise constitutes a disservice to the child.

There is a general consensus that, to the greatest extent possible, the curriculum for deaf children should be the same as that for hearing children. This is the case in residential schools as well as in local public schools. The reader should be thinking about how we can best balance general educational needs with the special educational needs of each deaf child.

This chapter and the following three chapters provide background information on the ways education of the deaf is similar to and different from education in general. This chapter investigates past and present practices in areas that have received special attention from educators of the deaf: the expression and reception of through-the-air communication and the teaching of English grammar. Through-the-air communication includes ASL manual speech, speech reading, and use of residual hearing. Chapter 12 deals with literacy, which, of course, includes reading and writing. Chapter 13 considers program or-ganization and instruction in the basic academic areas: mathematics, science, social studies, and English.

In this chapter, we look at techniques designed to foster the development of English skills in through-the-air modes of communication. English skills include knowledge of English grammar. Unfortunately, very little work in semantic and pragmatic aspects of English has been documented in the literature on the instruction of deaf children. Thus there is little information on which techniques are most effective in fostering the development of pragmatic and semantic skills. All of the techniques described in this chapter were designed specifically for deaf children and are not part of the general education curriculum.

Developments in the teaching of English grammar and through-the-air communication to deaf children have probably been fewer than in any other area in the field. Significant improvements have occurred in the development of sophisticated hearing aids and medical technology. But the instructional techniques themselves differ little from those used generations ago. There are probably several reasons for this. First, as more and more deaf children have been integrated into regular classrooms, emphasis on specialized training has lessened to some extent. Also, with the exception of a relatively few oral schools, there has been a shift away from oral communication to a focus on literacy. In my opinion, in some instances the pendulum has swung too far in the opposite direction, and some programs have failed to take advantage of the potential for good oral communication that many children possess.

The presentation of reading and writing separately from grammar and speech may cause some confusion. However, reading is not really an academic subject; rather, it is a tool for gathering information. There is a cliché in education that during the first four years of school we learn to read, and after that we read to learn. Throughout most of our school years, English classes are devoted to subjects such as Elizabethan authors or the American novel, but not to reading per se.

Traditionally, educators of the deaf, including this author, have dealt with material on literacy and oral communication separately. This distinction is somewhat artificial, however; we should think of all components of communication as related. To this end, the next chapter presents an instructional approach that has been labeled an *interactive compensatory model*. This model was developed in the field of reading but applies to all aspects of communication.

This chapter suffers from a lack of information on instructional techniques for developing expressive and receptive manual communication skills in deaf children. Unfortunately, this is not an oversight. Reviews of the literature have turned up few viable curricula for teaching manual communication to deaf children. Many schools endorse and use a manual communication system and/or ASl but do not have a curriculum for teaching the individual signs or the communication system. Apparently, they assume that the children will learn to understand and use the system essentially through exposure. Although the majority of deaf children are taught by means of signs and speech, direct instruction in the use of a sign system is not normally part of the school curriculum. Ironically, ASL is now taught for credit to hearing students in many high schools in the United States and Canada.

Some exceptions to this rule do exist, and their numbers should grow. This is especially apparent in some of the Bi Bi programs that first establish communication through ASL and then teach English through reading. At this point one important observation by Schimmel et al. (1999) should be mentioned. Many people not familiar with ASL assume that it is an easy language to master and that somehow deaf children learn it even without extensive exposure and use. The authors pointed out that the deaf children in their program had to receive instruction in ASL and that development of ASL fluency had to be an integral component of the system. Many children in the school at the beginning of the study were proficient neither in ASL or in English. This, of course, is consistent with Kemp's (1998) position on the difficulty of true ASL mastery.

It should be pointed out that many deaf individuals do not learn to sign until later in life, if then. For example, at Gallaudet University and the National Technical Institute for the Deaf, entering deaf students with little or no prior experience with signs go through instructional programs to develop signing skills. The Model Secondary School for the Deaf, on the campus of Gallaudet University, enrolls many students whose prior education was in integrated oral-only public schools or in private oral schools for the deaf. These students are also taught to sign. However, the programs mentioned here are the exception and are not designed for younger children.

As in many other chapters of this text, each topic in this chapter deserves book-length treatment. In some cases, pertinent books do exist and will be identified. In other areas, information is scarce. Interested readers are encouraged to investigate all areas as completely as possible through additional reading. In doing further reading, the reader should be alert to differences in the usage of terms such as *language, English,* and *grammar.* Many educators of the deaf refer to the language problems of deaf children when they really mean the English problems. A deaf person may have difficulty with the standard English language, yet be fluent in American Sign Language or vice versa. Educators may even use a broad term such as *language* or *English* when referring to specific aspects of English grammar, such as subject-verb agreement or understanding of the passive voice. The tendency to overgeneralize or to be overly inclusive can lead to an underestimation of the English abilities or language skills of a deaf child. For example, a child's writing or speech may show deficiencies in subject-verb agreement, such as producing *She go* instead of *She goes.* In reading an isolated sentence, a child may misinterpret *The girl was hit by the boy* as *The girl hit the boy.* However, neither of these mistakes is necessarily a valid indication of the child's overall abilities. Many deaf children are able to utilize their general knowledge of the world and the context of a message or story to obtain a clear understanding of its meaning or intent. Our usual testing techniques, which are restricted predominantly to multiple-choice or short-answer questions, may not be valid measures of the real abilities of deaf children.

Basically, two approaches have been employed in helping deaf children master the language of society. The first, known as the *natural method,* is concerned with helping children acquire idiomatic usage of a language. This type of approach has also been labeled variously as the *synthetic,* the *informal,* and the *mother's method.* As the names imply, an effort is made to follow the "normal" course of language acquisition as closely as possible. The term *method* in this context has nothing to do with the controversy over oral, manual, combined, or total communication methods.

The second approach, originally known as the *grammatical method* (Nelson, 1949), has also been referred to as the *scientific,* the *philosophical,* the *logical,* the *systematic,* the *formal,* the *analytical,* and the *artificial method.* The major aim of this approach is to provide students with simple and correct oral and graphic language structures. This chapter will use the terms *natural* and *analytical* to identify the two philosophical approaches.

Both approaches have long and respectable historical antecedents. (See the discussion in Chapter 2 of the origins of education of the deaf in Europe.) The techniques developed in sixteenth- and seventeenth-century Spain by Bonet and de Leon represent analytical approaches to the teaching of language. Dalgarno's (1680) contention that children would develop language normally if their mothers would finger-spell to them in the crib presaged the development of the natural method.

Most teachers and programs are, for practical reasons, somewhat eclectic in their approaches. Although they may lean toward one or the other approach, they usually incorporate both to some extent. The issue was highlighted in 1876 in the course of an exchange between Pettengill and Fay (the editor of *American Annals of the Deaf*) in an article entitled "The Natural Method of Teaching Language" (Pettengill, 1876). Pettengill took exception to an earlier statement by Fay that "nature's method" was attractive in theory but had never really been practiced in any institution for the deaf. Pettengill claimed that he had put the theory into practice with good results. Fay responded:

> We are very glad to learn that the experiment in question has been tried by Mr. Pettengill and Mr. McWhorter with satisfactory results. The article in the *Annals* was written for the purpose of urging teachers to follow the methods of nature more closely than had generally been done. But then, as now, we believed that in this attempt to follow nature, the average teacher, especially when charged, as in the case of most of our institutions, with the instruction of a large class, needs the guidance of some prearranged plan, system and order. (Pettengill, 1876, p. 1)

Thus advocates of both the natural and analytical methods acknowledged the desirability of a natural type of language acquisition process. Disagreement remains over the extent to which this is possible without conscious "artificial" techniques, as well as the extent to which the natural method becomes unnatural in a clinical or classroom situation. This author leans more toward a natural approach, but is aware of the need for structure, drill, and specific teaching activities.

Instruction for the Development of Grammatical Structure

We will use the term *grammar* here in the traditional educational sense to include word order and word forms and their changes, such as those used to show number (*boy-boys, woman-women*), tense (*walk-walked, fall-fell*), comparison (*big-bigger-biggest, bad-worse-worst*), adverbials (*quick-quickly*), and so on. It is helpful to think of word order as referring to syntax and word form as referring to morphology, but the reader should be aware that the term *syntax* is frequently used in much the same way that *grammar* is employed here, that is, to include both word order and word form.

Analytical Methods

Table 11.1 lists the major analytical systems used in the United States. The analytical method was brought to the United States from France by Laurent Clerc and Thomas Hopkins Gallaudet and was established in this country before the introduction of the natural method (Farrar, 1923). Originally, instruction was based on the system of de l'Epée in France (Gallaudet, 1871), in which complete sentences were learned at the outset, with signs associated with printed words. Signs were employed for function words as well as content words and for bound morphemes such as those that signify person, number, and tense (Peet, 1859). Emphasis was on memorization rather than on original composition. Sicard, de l'Epée's successor, believed that deaf children could learn to construct sentences by means of a grammatical system, and he developed his theory of ciphers (Clerc, 1851; Wing, 1887). Sicard divided the sentence into five basic parts—nominative case, verb, objective case, preposition, and object of preposition—and used them to develop basic "correct" word order. At one time, the system was in wide use in the United States. It probably was the model for the Barry five-slate system developed later (Nelson, 1949).

Frederick Barnard, a teacher at both the American and White Plains schools and later president of Columbia University, developed a comprehensive system of grammatical symbols based on notions of being, assertion, attribution, and influence (Barnard, 1836). Although well developed on a firm theoretical base, the system never achieved popularity because it was complex and difficult to use with young children (Wing, 1887).

A course of instruction that was the model for primary training in schools for the deaf for several years was introduced by Harvey Peet (1868), who believed that ideas should precede words and that difficulties should be presented to children one step at a time. Lessons were developed as a series of carefully designed progressions through increasingly difficult grammatical principles.

TABLE 11.1 Major Analytical Systems Used to Teach English to Deaf Children in the United States

System	Year Introduced
Sicard's theory of ciphers	Developed in France in early 1800s; demonstrated in the United States by Clerc
Barnard's symbols	1836
Peet's language system	1844
Hartford (Storrs) symbols	1860
Wing's symbols	1883
Barry five-slate system	1893
Fitzgerald Key	1926
Streng's applied linguistics	1972
Rhode Island curriculum	1978

Hartford, or Storrs, symbols (Porter, 1868, 1869; Storrs, 1880) were developed by Storrs in the belief that the natural method was confusing to deaf children. Storrs contended that for deaf children, language should involve a step-by-step process of principle construction. He claimed that through use of the analytical method ("scientific method" in his terms), children could memorize three hundred conversational formulas that would serve their everyday needs.

Storrs symbols were designed to provide visual representations of grammatical relations. Sentence "pictures" were presented in boxlike form. Figure 11.1 presents examples of three sentences: *Birds fly, Cows eat grass,* and *John's books lie on the table.* The complexity of the symbols Storrs developed to represent English probably accounts in part for the decline of the analytical method relative to the natural method at that time.

The next major analytical system was Wing's symbols, developed in 1883 by George Wing, a deaf teacher at the Minnesota School for the Deaf (*Minnesota Course of Study,* 1918). The symbols consist of numbers and letters placed over words, phrases, or clauses. The system differs from others in that it is designed to show forms, functions, and positions of parts of sentences rather than being limited to

FIGURE 11.1   Sentence Representations Used in the Storrs System

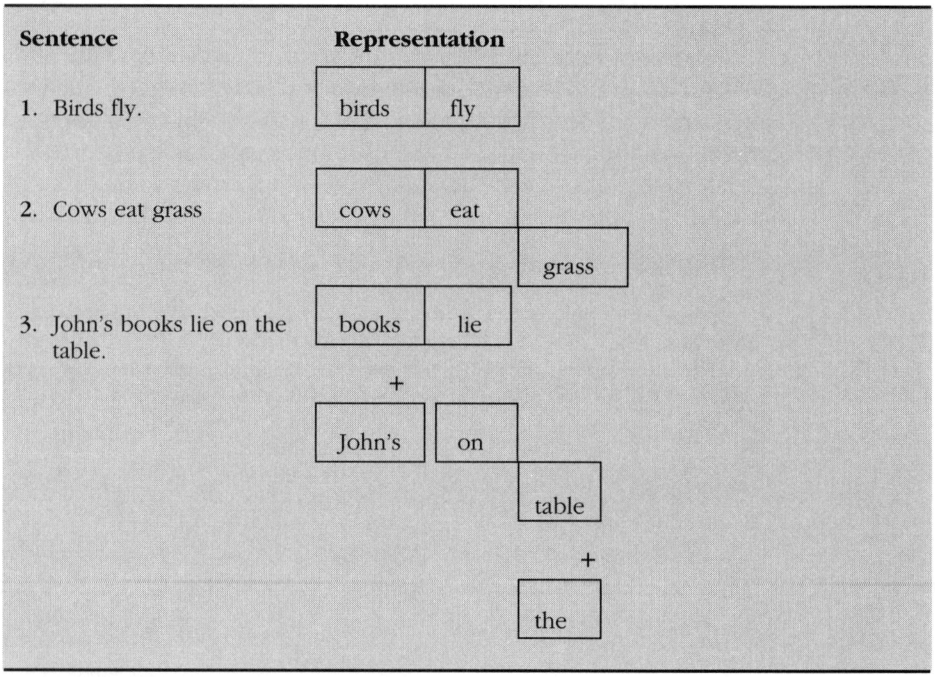

Source: Adapted from S. Porter, "Professor Porter's Paper on Grammar," *Proceedings of the Sixth Convention of the American Instructors of the Deaf* (Washington, D.C.: U.S. Government Printing Office, 1868), p. 145.

traditional parts of speech. The symbols are grouped into four categories: essentials, modifying forms, correctives, and special symbols.

Barry developed a five-slate system (Barry, 1899; Pope, 1938) that apparently was based on Sicard's theory of ciphers (Nelson, 1949). As its name implies, the system used five slates, reserved for five categories: subject, verb, object, preposition, and object of preposition. The blackboard was divided into five large slates, and the children had small slates similarly divided. Great attention was paid to careful analysis of sentences and their component parts. The system was quite popular. According to Long (1918), it was in use in every school for the deaf in the United States by 1918.

The Barry five-slate system was supplanted by the Fitzgerald Key, developed by Edith Fitzgerald, a deaf teacher. The Key, as it is commonly known, was developed to provide children with rules by which they could generate correct English sentences as well as find and correct their own errors in compositions (Fitzgerald, 1931). Usually, the first step in instruction in the Key is to have students place individual words under appropriate headings, such as *who, what,* and *where.* The systems employ the following six visible symbols:

$$====$$ verb

$$===\!\!\!\!>$$ infinitive

$$\Leftarrow\!\!==$$ present participle

$$\bigtriangledown$$ connective

$$\sqcap$$ pronoun

$$\sqcap$$ adjective

After first combining words in a simple manner under appropriate headings (such as *who* or *what*), students practice proper word order. For example, the sequence of modifiers preceding nouns is presented as *how many, what kind, what color, what.*

The complexity of the utterances is increased gradually to include transitive verbs and objects, possession, phrases of place and time, and so on, following definite procedures, until the children are able to work with the complete Key, which still may be found along a wall in many classrooms for deaf children. In some schools, children also work exercises in their seats with "Key paper" containing the various elements of the Key. Table 11.2 presents some simple sentences organized according to one version of the Key.

In a comparison of the Barry five-slate system and the Fitzgerald Key, Buell (1931) argued that the Key was more comprehensive, flexible, and grammatically oriented. A majority of educators of deaf students apparently shared her opinion. In an investigation of language methods used with deaf students in the United States and Canada, Nelson (1949) reported that the Fitzgerald Key was used in 84 of 132 schools and programs surveyed. In fifty-five cases it was employed exclusively, and in twenty-nine it was used in combination with another method. The Barry five-

TABLE 11.2 Sample of Exercises Using the Fitzgerald Key

Whose:	Who: What:	What did ___ do?	What: Whom: Whose:	Whom: What:	Where:	From:___: For:___: With:___: How:	How far: How often: Why: How long: How much: When:
	Mary	went			home		often
	Bob	rode	his	bike			
	Sue	threw	her dog	a bone			
	Molly	played				with Sally	
Bill's	mother	drove			to St. Paul		
	He	walked			outside		last night

slate system was used exclusively in twelve programs and in combination with other methods in an additional thirteen programs, eleven of which involved some use of the Fitzgerald Key. Since Nelson's survey, the popularity of the five-slate system has eroded further, and the Key continues to be by far the most widely used analytical approach.

Streng (1972) developed an approach based on principles of generative-transformational grammar that represents significant advances over previous analytical methods. The more sophisticated approaches—such as the Barry five-slate system, the Wing symbols, and the Fitzgerald Key—may appropriately be classified as generative grammar systems because they provide the tools with which to generate most of the most commonly used English structures. However, they are limited in that they produce essentially linear, left-to-right strings and cannot illustrate some logical relations between utterances that would be intuitively obvious to a native user of a language. An example is the relationships between active and passive transformations such as *The girl pushed the boy* and *The boy was pushed by the girl.* A generative-transformational grammar is more efficient for a number of reasons, including its ability to demonstrate logical and syntactic relations between utterances.

The most comprehensive analytical system currently in use is a generative-transformational grammar program developed at the Rhode Island School for the Deaf by Blackwell et al. (1978). The curriculum was designed to integrate principles of language development with Piagetian developmental psychology. Emphasis is first placed on the development of five basic sentence patterns: (1) noun phrase + verb *(The baby cries)*; (2) noun phrase + verb + noun phrase *(The baby drinks milk)*; (3) noun phrase + linking verb + adjective *(The baby is cute)*; (4) noun phrase + linking verb + noun phrase *(The baby is a boy)*; (5) noun phrase + linking verb + adverbial phrase *(The baby is in the crib).* More complex patterns are then taught as transformations of these five simple patterns.

The availability of a carefully constructed curriculum based on principles of generative-transformational grammar represents a major improvement. However, no analytical approach by itself will provide all deaf children with a knowledge of standard English. Analytical methods are necessary where "natural" approaches have failed to provide breakthroughs. In discussing the limitations of our understanding of language as it relates to teaching language to deaf children, Lenneberg (1967a) stated:

> From these examples it is clear that the construction of proper sentences is not facilitated by telling a child how to do it. It must be admitted that no one knows how it is done. . . . No grammar, old or new, furnishes us with a recipe of how to speak grammatically. There is no grammatical system available that could be used to help an essentially language-deficient person to put words together to form good sentences. So far, grammars merely specify the underlying structure of sentences and explain how sentences of different structure are related to each other. (p. 324)

The most sophisticated grammars now in existence are models of a language, not of a user. Constraints imposed by factors such as memory limitations, situational variance, motivation, and distortion of the communication channel are not considered in dealing with a model of a language, but they certainly influence a user of a language. The fact that a user is subject to constraints not placed on a language model of competence must be acknowledged in considering the teaching of language or the language functioning of an individual.

Natural Methods

The major impetus for the introduction and spread of the natural method in education of the deaf was provided by the German educator Frederick Maritz Hill, a follower of Pestolozzi (Nelson, 1949; Schmitt, 1966). Hill believed that natural language could be developed in deaf children just as it was in hearing children. In his "mother's method," Hill placed great emphasis on children's experiences, and teaching of grammar was delayed until a relatively late age.

Interest in the natural method grew in the United States after the Civil War, apparently because of widespread dissatisfaction with results obtained through adherence to strictly analytical approaches. Pettengill (1876, 1882) argued that a natural method was theoretically sound and could be employed in schools for the deaf. In his initiation of the Rochester Method (simultaneous use of speech and the manual alphabet) at the Rochester School for the Deaf in 1878, Westervelt (Scouten, 1942; Westervelt and Peet, 1880) embraced the natural method, putting special emphasis on "instruction" during play situations.

Another powerful advocate of the natural method during the same period was Greenberger, principal of the Lexington School for the Deaf, who argued (1879) that so long as deaf children were taught language in an artificial manner, they would never transfer their knowledge into use. He advocated supplying words to deaf children on the basis of need; that is, rather than teaching vocabulary in any systematic way, one should introduce words in natural situations. Ever since then, the Lexington School has been known as a leading exponent of the natural method. At one time, the natural method was sometimes referred to as the Lexington method (Nelson, 1949).

A final factor in the spread of the natural method was the influence of Alexander Graham Bell, in particular his publication of the methods he employed in tutoring young George Sanders (Bell, 1883b). Following Froebel, Bell utilized play to a great extent, organizing lessons around toys and games. He combined this idea with those of Dalgarno (1680) concerning the early introduction of reading and writing, which Bell attempted to carry out in a "conversational" manner. Bell's approach seemed to be a reasonable combination of natural and analytical systems as well as of oral and manual methods. To enable a child to communicate ideas to others, Bell once again resorted to Dalgarno's work, using a finger alphabet in which the letters were written on a glove. Messages were spelled by pointing to the appropriate spot on the hand with the index finger of the other hand. By six years of age, Sanders had mastered English sufficiently to be able to communicate effectively with hearing persons by writing.

Despite the claims of proponents of the natural method and its unquestioned advantages, at least in theory, it has not become the predominant method in the

© Monkmeyer/Forsyth

Practice in English grammar.

United States. Before the turn of the century, two influential analytical systems, Wing's symbols and the Barry five-slate system, had been developed. These were used in programs for the deaf in the United States until they were replaced by another analytical system, the Fitzgerald Key. In her survey of methods, Nelson (1949) reported that the natural method was used exclusively in only 10 of 132 programs surveyed. In 9 other programs, it was used in combination with an analytical method.

In the past few decades, the use of the natural method, or at least of natural methods, has increased. The work of Groht (1933, 1958), who, like Greenberger, was a principal at the Lexington School for the Deaf, has been particularly influential in this area. Groht argued that language principles are best taught in natural situations and then practiced through games and stories; drill and textbook exercises are far less effective than repetition in meaningful situations.

Results suggest that a pure natural method has not been more effective than a pure analytical method in meeting the needs of deaf children. The similarities between this controversy and the oral-manual debate, in which the evidence suggests limited benefits from either a "pure" oral or a "pure" manualist system, are obvious, although the level of intensity has been lower.

Teaching Speech

Given the lip service paid to the development of speech by all educators of the deaf and the century-long dominance of the field by oral-only proponents (a dominance that has only recently been overturned), one might expect that the teaching of speech to deaf children would be a well-researched, empirically based, systematic process. In fact, more research and development may have been done in the 1930s and 1940s. Except for an excellent presentation of techniques used to develop speech at the Lexington School for the Deaf by Vorce (1974), an overview of speech and deafness by Calvert and Silverman (1975), and a text by Ling (1988), the literature since that time has been scarce. None of these three publications is research based or data based in such a way as to support one particular approach to teaching speech over another. Teaching speech to deaf individuals is like the weather: everyone talks about it, but very few seem to do much about it.

Although some people use the terms *speech* and *articulation* interchangeably, technically articulation is only one of a number of complex processes incorporated in human speech. *Articulation* involves the generation of speech sounds by modifications of the vocal tract, which consists basically of the mouth and the nasal and pharyngeal cavities. Changes in placement and manner of articulators such as the lips, teeth, tongue, palate, and pharynx cause changes in speech sounds. *Respiration,* which provides the air stream from which speech develops, depends on the lungs and various muscular and skeletal elements. *Phonation,* or vocal tone production, depends on the larynx, which produces a vibrating air stream.

All of the mechanisms involved in speech production originally were developed in human beings to serve biological functions. The most obvious cases are the mechanisms involved in breathing, such as the lungs and larynx, as well as the nose, mouth, and pharynx.

A complete treatment of the anatomy and physiology of the human speech and hearing mechanism is provided by Zemlin (1988) in *Speech and Hearing Science: Anatomy and Physiology*. Readers interested in pursuing the subject of speech more fully might begin with Pickett's *The Sounds of Speech* (1980) and Ling's *Foundations of Spoken Language for Hearing Impaired Children* (1988).

Techniques and methods for teaching speech currently in use in the United States have existed for fifty years or more. This fact in itself would not be cause for alarm if the evidence suggested that the approaches had met with consistent success, but that is not the case. Although most program directors view their approaches to the teaching of speech as eclectic, a better descriptor might be haphazard. The state of the art may be summarized as follows:

1. Knowledge about the processes by which deaf children acquire speech is virtually nonexistent.
2. Information about the use of speech by deaf individuals in natural situations is almost completely anecdotal.

3. Educators of the deaf, with a few notable exceptions, make no distinction between speech development and speech remediation.

4. No valid, reliable diagnostic speech tests have been developed for deaf individuals. Those most commonly used have been designed for hearing individuals.

5. Understanding, in qualitative and quantitative terms, of the speech of deaf children is inadequate. The classic study of speech intelligibility (Hudgins and Numbers) was reported in 1942, and results are based on the reading of ten simple sentences.

6. To the best of this author's knowledge, no study has ever been conducted comparing the effects of different techniques or methods of teaching speech to deaf individuals.

7. As a general rule, methods of teaching speech to deaf individuals in the United States have neither a theoretical nor a pragmatic base.

Hudgins and Numbers (1942) analyzed the speech of 192 deaf pupils from two schools for the deaf. Each subject read ten unrelated simple sentences, and intelligibility was rated by testers familiar with the speech of deaf individuals. Two major types of errors were identified: articulatory and rhythmic. Within the area of articulation, seven categories were developed for consonant errors and five for incorrectly articulated vowels. However, articulation per se was found to be less important than other aspects of speech in determining the intelligibility of the deaf subjects' speech. For example, sentences spoken with correct rhythm were understood correctly four times more frequently than those with incorrect rhythm. In general, the speech of the subjects was characterized by arrhythmic patterns, poor phrasing, monotonic expression, and lack of pitch.

Various aspects of the speech of deaf children and adults have been studied over a long period of time. Although individual variation is great, the results consistently reveal major deficiencies in vocal production. In general, the speech of deaf individuals may be characterized as high pitched (Boone, 1966), monotonic (Calvert, 1962), relatively slow in rate (Nickerson et al., 1975; Voelker, 1938), and possessing poor rhythm and timing (Bell, 1906; Hudgins and Numbers, 1942; Nickerson, 1975a). In addition, the speech is more labored, requires the use of more breath, and is marked by inadequate breath control (Hudgins, 1934, 1936, 1937). Related to these difficulties is the problem of poor velar control (Brehm, 1922). The velum, or soft palate, regulates the passage of sound between the oral and nasal cavities. Poor velar control tends to give the speech of some deaf individuals a nasal quality. Because the raising and lowering of the velum is not detectable through lip reading and because the activity itself provides very little proprioceptive feedback, proper velar control is especially difficult to develop in deaf speakers (Nickerson, 1975a).

With respect to articulation, deaf people tend to have more difficulty producing vowels than consonants (Angelocci, Kopp, and Holbrook, 1964; Boone, 1966). Although consonants tend to be produced more clearly (Joiner, 1922; Jones, 1967), some consonants are omitted and others are confused. The most common manifestation may be a lack of differentiation between voiced and unvoiced consonants—for example, between /b/ and /p/ or between /d/ and /t/ (Calvert, 1962).

In a review of the status of speech curricula in programs for the deaf in the United States, Vorce (1971, pp. 223–224) stated that little or no experimentation has been related to speech content and methodologies and that few models exist from which a curriculum might be adapted. She acknowledged the existence of a substantial amount of literature dealing with various aspects of speech teaching, such as voice quality, pitch variations, breath support, durational aspects, abutting consonants, color coding for breath-nasal-voice contrast, speech charts, orthographic systems, spectrographic analyses, and so on. However, she pointed out that not one well-controlled study of deaf speech had been conducted over large populations between the time of the Hudgins and Numbers study in 1942 and the publication of her overview in 1971. She further noted that only a few books are relevant to the planning of speech programs. A case in point is the monograph in which the Vorce chapter appears, *Speech for the Deaf Child: Knowledge and Use* (Connor, 1971). Although many interesting and useful background chapters, overviews, and descriptions of speech aids are presented, in this author's opinion only the chapters by Vorce and Magner have direct applicability to the classroom.

Vorce concluded that, given the paucity of materials, the responsibility for initiating changes rests on the coordinators and teachers of individual programs. This reliance on local sources has led to a high degree of inconsistency. Vorce received responses from twenty-one programs to a questionnaire designed to elicit information about speech curricula. The results gave little indication of agreement, and Vorce reported that philosophy and/or methods varied not only from program to program but often within programs themselves. Vorce (1971) summarized her findings as follows:

> Most include systematic or routine teaching of speech skills (although speech methods and content vary with the age and individual needs of the children and many indicate that skills "are taught only as needed"); most children of elementary school age have daily speech periods, but at other levels specific daily work is often not provided in the overall plan; most speech work is group work at least some of the time, with a few programs providing individual tutoring at specific levels; less than half employ special speech teachers (the majority of these being at the upper levels where pupils "rotate" among subject matter specialists); no consistent system for planning speech work emerges (some decisions are made jointly by the classroom teacher and the departmental or speech supervisor, others by the teacher or the supervisor without reference to other personnel). (pp. 224–225)

These results are based on conditions in the twenty-one programs that responded to the questionnaire. It is likely that conditions in other programs are not as good.

Nickerson (1975b) conducted an extensive review of speech training and speech reception aids for deaf individuals, including auditory aids, instantaneous visual displays, visual displays with time history, multifeature visual displays, display systems, and tactile displays. He concluded that communications science and engineering have done little to benefit people with disabling communications problems (p. 97), stating:

> It is well known that the speech of the deaf tends not to be very intelligible, and it is possible to list a variety of things that are wrong with it . . . but nobody can yet say very precisely how much each of these deficiencies contributes to its overall lack of intelligibility or its generally poor quality. (pp. 98–99)

If anything, the situation regarding speech training has deteriorated since the reports of Vorce and Nickerson. A few private clinics emphasize speech development, but they are exceptions. Although I have no data to support it, I believe that in my career the field has gone from an unthinking dedication to speech development as the *only* goal of educating the deaf to the point where it is sometimes undervalued and ignored. The more means of communication at a deaf child's disposal, the more access to information is available.

Methods of Teaching Speech

Although at present few programs follow exclusively one identifiable method of teaching speech, it is helpful to be aware of how the more widely used techniques and systems developed and how they fit into a broader perspective. To label the methods, we might use such categories as *analytic* (or *elemental*) versus *whole word, formal* versus *informal* (or *natural*), and *unisensory* versus *multisensory*.

Perhaps one of the most effective treatments for teaching speech to deaf individuals appears in the first book ever published on education of the deaf, by Bonet (Bonet, 1620; Peet, 1850). Among other things, it deals with the relationships among speech, language, and reading, and it contains specific techniques for their development. However, the foundations for the teaching of speech to deaf people were established principally in the nineteenth century. To a large degree, they did not involve incorporation of the techniques developed in Germany by "German" or "oral method" teachers; rather, they represented relatively independent systems. The following sections present short treatments of Visible Speech and the element method, the babbling method, the acoustic method, the concentric method, and the TVA method.

Visible Speech and the Element Method.   Visible Speech, a system designed to represent any sound the human mouth can utter, was developed by Alexander Melville Bell out of his work as a phonetician. Bell started work on the system in the 1840s and developed it over a period of years; some of his writings have been published in several editions (1898, 1904, 1932). The system was based not on sounds but on the actions of the vocal organs in producing them. Visible Speech was first used with deaf individuals by Bell's son, Alexander Graham Bell, in London in 1869. The younger Bell claimed that his four students, ranging in age from seven to twelve, learned nearly all of the elementary English sounds in a few days (Bell, 1872, p. 5). When he taught the system to teachers in Boston in 1871, he commented that a group of adult deaf mutes had acquired all of the sounds of English in ten lessons of Visible Speech (p. 6). Bell contended that perfect articulation could be obtained through Visible Speech. He made no claims for its effect on rhythm and modulation, viewing these attributes as separate branches of training (p. 19).

Alexander Graham Bell introduced his father's system at a time when the majority of educators of the deaf in the United States were committing themselves for the
first time to the teaching of speech. His ideas were enthusiastically accepted
because they were advanced as being applicable to both oral-only and oral-manual
programs. Bell (1872) stated:

> The system takes no part in the contest between articulation, on the one hand, and
> signs and manual alphabets on the other. In presenting this system for adoption all the
> inventory means to say is this: Here is a means by which you can obtain perfect
> articulation from deaf mutes; make what use of it you choose." (p. 9)

The principles on which Visible Speech was based have had a general effect on
the teaching of speech up to the present. Alexander Melville Bell's books on the
subject all enjoyed multiple editions, a few over periods of fifty years or more. The
influence of Visible Speech is so strong that more than a century after its conception
by Bell senior, it could be claimed that "the system of Visible Speech . . . is even
today the basis for the method used in teaching the deaf to talk" (Streng et al., 1955,
p. 5).

Although Visible Speech is not employed in the classroom today, its influence is
still evident. The work of the Bells had a great impact on the development of methods of teaching speech to deaf students at the Clarke School for the Deaf. In turn, the
methods developed at Clarke have been adopted, or adapted, by many programs in
the United States. The single most influential work was Yale's *Formation and Development of Elementary English Sounds* (1939). Yale, principal of the Clarke School for
many years, incorporated the genius of the Bells' system into her work. Although
other educators may have drawn up more complete sets of exercises (for example,
Joiner, 1936) utilizing the element method, Yale set the foundation. The Northampton
charts of vowel and consonant sounds (see Tables 11.3 and 11.4), also known as the
Yale charts, are still commonly used by teachers of deaf pupils.

The Babbling Method.   The babbling method was developed by Avondino (1918,
1919, 1924) on the basis of what she believed to be the natural order of speech
acquisition for children with normal hearing. It is essentially a system of syllable
drills that stresses voice, rhythm, and breath control as opposed to isolated elements.

The system relies on constant repetition until fluency is obtained. There are three
stages. The first entails drills of single syllables in groups of three, spoken with
rapidity. In the second stage, words of two syllables are combined, with the accent
on the second syllable. In the third stage, two syllables—each beginning with a
consonant—are combined, and the accent may fall on either syllable.

Although this method is advanced as following "natural" patterns of development, little evidence suggests that hearing children develop speech by constantly
repeating meaningless syllables. As with other methods of teaching speech, the
effectiveness of the babbling method must remain a matter of conjecture because
empirical evidence is lacking.

TABLE 11.3 Northampton Chart: Consonant Sounds

Consonant Sounds

h__				
wh	w__			
p	b	m		
t	d	n	l	r__
		ng		
k	^{1}g	n(k)		
c				
ck				
f	v			
ph				
th^1	th^2			
s	z			
c(e)	s^2			
c(i)				
c(y)				
sh	zh		y	
	s^3		x = ks	
	z^2		qu = kwh	
ch	j			
tch	g^2__			
	__ge			
	dge			

Source: Reproduced with permission of the Clarke School for the Deaf, Northampton, Mass.

The Acoustic Method. The acoustic method was introduced by Goldstein at St. Joseph's School for the Deaf in St. Louis. It was incorporated into the curriculum of the Central Institute for the Deaf upon the institute's founding in 1914 and has been the basis, at least in part, for most of the acoustic methods used in the United States. Within his definition of the acoustic method, Goldstein (1939) included voice and musical sounds; sound vibration as sensed by tactile impression to interpret pitch, rhythm, accent, volume, and inflection; analysis of speech sounds by tactile differentiation; synthesis and speech construction by tactile impression; and sound waves and their significance as appreciated by visual perception.

The method concentrates on developing the auditory sense within the context of the speech program. Training is conducted daily and includes instrumental as well as vocal stimulation. The program may be perceived as having two parts: passive education and active education. *Passive education* does not involve conscious effort on the part of students. Musical instruments and sustained amplified tone

TABLE 11.4   Northampton Chart: Vowel Sounds

Vowel Sounds

$\overset{1}{oo}$	$\overset{2}{oo}$	o--e	aw	-o-
(r)u-e		oa	au	
(r)ew		-o	o(r)	
		$\overset{2}{ow}$		
ee	-i-	a--e	-e-	-a-
-e	-y	ai	$\overset{2}{ea}$	
$\overset{1}{ea}$		ay		
e-e				
	a(r)	--u--	ur	
		-a	er	
		-ar	ir	
		-er		
		-ir		
		-or		
		-ur		
		-re		

a--e	i--e	o--e	ou	oi	u--e
ai	igh	oa	$\overset{1}{ow}$	oy	ew
ay	-y	-o			
		$\overset{2}{ow}$			

Source: Reproduced with permission of the Clarke School for the Deaf, Northampton, Mass.

frequencies are used. *Active education* involves "analytic" exercises (which concentrate on interpretation of vowels, consonants, and syllables independently of ideas or words) and "synthetic" exercises (which are concerned with actual speech or language).

The Concentric Method.   The concentric method, developed by Rau (Moores, 1972b), was the official method of teaching speech in the Soviet Union. Unlike the dominant American methods, it incorporates the use of finger spelling into the teaching of speech. The central principle is to begin the speech development of children with a limited number of phonemes. The method is based on the premise that normally hearing children use an abbreviated phoneme system; that is, they use a limited number of sounds to express the phonemes of their language.

At the beginning of instruction, children are expected to master only seventeen of the forty-two Russian phonemes. These consist of twelve voiceless consonants and five vowels. At this stage, difficulty in understanding due to poor speech reading—or difficulty in expression due to poor speech—is reduced by the simultaneous use of finger spelling. Thus, children who have difficulty articulating the initial distinctions between *pat, bat,* and *mat* (to use an English analogue) would make themselves understood by means of finger spelling.

At first an approximated pronunciation of sounds is allowed. Then the related sounds are introduced. The teaching of pronunciation has three phases:

1. A preparatory period involving development of imitative processes, breathing habits, phonation, and articulation
2. A second stage involving systematic work in sound production
3. A final stage involving perfection of pronunciation skills and correction of deficiencies

By age nine, children are expected to have mastered all forty-two phonemes and to be able to use them appropriately. A description of and rationale for the concentric method appears in Korsunskaya (1969) and Rau (1960).

The TVA method. The TVA (tactile-visual-auditory) method is a multisensory, "natural" approach to the development of speech. In the United States, it is closely associated with the speech program of the Lexington School for the Deaf. The approach might be more accurately called a philosophy than a strict method. Children are encouraged to use speech spontaneously at all times, and a whole-word approach is employed. The approach is both synthetic and analytic, but the analytic aspects are not primary. For example, articulation is seen as an outgrowth of the speech process, not a foundation for it. The emphasis is on meaningful, interesting, and relevant communication as opposed to meaningless drill in elements or syllables. Rhythm and voice qualities receive a great deal of attention.

The speech program is obviously highly coordinated with the natural language program at the Lexington School. Children are bombarded with natural, informal spoken language and are expected to develop it in a manner approximating that of normally hearing children.

Present Status

Ling (1976, 1988) has proposed what he describes as a model of speech acquisition in teaching deaf individuals; however, his model is not concerned primarily with grammar, sentence structure, or pragmatic usage. The teaching of speech is viewed as an elemental activity carried out mainly at the phonetic level. Seven major stages are identified, each of which has a variety of speech target behaviors that are founded on a set of criterion-referenced subskills. Children are expected to progress from one stage to another in invariant order. Cumulative acquisition of subskills is seen as leading to mastery of target behaviors. The seven stages are divided into three broad categories: vocalization, teaching of vowels, and teaching of consonants. The vocalization stages involve vocalization on demand and development of supra-segmental patterns. In the third stage, diphthongs and vowels are taught. Stages 4 through 7 address the teaching of consonants, beginning with manner (Stage 4) and then adding place (Stage 5) and voicing (Stage 6). The teaching of consonant blends comprises the final stage.

Although Ling presents the system as being appropriate for either a natural or an analytic approach, the emphasis on developing specific skills in the same order with all children and the building up of elements on a serial component basis would seem to make it more applicable to an analytic framework. The order of acquisition differs from that of some other approaches, and Ling concentrates first on vowels. However, he presents no research evidence to support his sequence, and therefore its effectiveness, like that of other approaches to teaching speech, is unknown.

The past decades apparently have brought no improvements in techniques of teaching speech to deaf individuals. Ironically, progress seems to have ended at the same time the oral-only philosophy became dominant. Some breakthroughs obvi-ously are needed, especially in techniques appropriate to combined oral-manual approaches.

Personal Observation

From my observations in both residential schools and local public schools, attention to speech training varies more now than in the past, although the old cliché that every teacher of the deaf is a teacher of speech no longer holds and there is prob-ably less direct instruction in speech now than there was throughout the twentieth century. With the exception of the few remaining private oral schools, speech thera-pists tend to have more responsibility for speech training than teachers of the deaf. This "pull-out" model has its drawbacks. It separates vocal communication from the everyday life of the classroom and from ongoing communication, sometimes mak-ing it an artificial exercise. Moreover, I have observed that it can remove the child from sorely needed academic instruction. However, my subjective opinion is that young deaf adults in settings such as Gallaudet, The National Technical Institute for the Deaf, and California State University, Northridge, have much clearer speech than previous generations. This is regardless of whether their customary form of communication is speech, signs plus speech, ASL, or, as is typically the case, a combination of all three, depending on the situation.

The Utilization of Residual Hearing

Acoupedics

An approach to language and speech development that has been limited to very young children deserves special mention. This technique or series of procedures, which has been variously termed the *aural method,* the *acoustic method,* the *unisensory method,* the *auditory method,* and *acoupedics,* received wide attention during the 1960s. Some advocates (Griffiths, 1967a, 1967b; Pollack, 1964, 1970, 1976; Stewart, Pollack, and Downs, 1964) viewed this method as the final breakthrough in education of the deaf. In fact, Griffiths (1967a, pp. 42–50) claimed that her procedures may cure deafness if instituted before a child is eight months of age.

Acoupedics represents a departure from other techniques in that it emphasizes the primacy of audition over vision. The major base for this approach in the United States may be traced to Goldstein (1939) and his acoustic method. Goldstein argued that children should focus attention on sound, without the diversion of watching the face or hands. The role of vision is deemphasized for even the most profoundly deaf child on the basis that the child, if allowed, will become too dependent on vision and will fail to develop auditory-vocal proficiency. Advocates of acoupedics are critical not only of combined oral-aural-manual methods but also of the most common oral-aural approaches, which employ multisensory (auditory-visual-tactile) techniques. For example, emphasis on lip reading with young children is considered to be a hindrance to the development of hearing. According to Pollack (1970), children taught using lip reading or signs will continue to rely on visual skills and may ignore sound. Acoupedics, then, does not represent merely an improvement in techniques of auditory training. According to its purest advocates, it cannot be incorporated into an oral-aural or oral-aural-manual program. It is unisensory and must stand alone.

Acoupedics grew out of work in Europe during and shortly after World War II. In 1943, a program was initiated in Holland to provide hearing aids to rural deaf children under three years of age to prepare them for subsequent entrance into residential schools. It was discovered that with early fitting and guidance many children did not have to enter the residential programs. Some could be integrated into regular classes, and others could attend classes for hard-of-hearing students (Huizing, 1959). A few years later, reports of work in Sweden (Wedenberg, 1951, 1954) and in England (Fry and Whetnall, 1954) indicated great benefits from the utilization of residual hearing with young children. Related work in the United States was reported by Griffiths (1967a, 1967b); McCroskey (1968); Pollack (1964, 1970, 1976); Simmons (1962); and Stewart, Pollack, and Downs (1964).

More than two generations later, it is difficult to appreciate the impact of these findings. The widespread use of powerful hearing aids was only beginning, and with few exceptions the methods employed—oral, manual, or combined—assigned little importance to hearing. With the evidence that reliance on vision alone was not satisfactory for all children, it was only a matter of time before the pendulum would swing to the other extreme and some educators would advocate the use of audition alone with all deaf children.

Acoupedics is not restricted to early auditory training. It is a "comprehensive habilitation program for the hearing impaired infant and his family which includes an emphasis upon auditory training without lipreading instruction" (Pollack, 1970, p. 13). It is based on the development of an auditory function and is made possible by (1) early detection; (2) fitting of powerful hearing aids; (3) intensive and systematic training; (4) heavy parental involvement, especially by mothers; and (5) deemphasis of nonauditory cues.

The focus on early identification and fitting of hearing aids is related to the idea of a critical period for the development of the use of hearing. Griffiths (1975) reported on a child who received a hearing aid at twenty-one days of age. Downs (1967) suggested that a decision be made at a very early age:

> If by the time a child is a year and a half old, we have determined that no auditory perceptions can be developed, the visual orientation program is clearly laid out for us—whether by lip reading and oral approaches, fingerspelling and manual techniques or a combination of both of these. (p. 749)

Children are expected to wear their hearing aids at least during all waking hours. Most programs use binaural, as opposed to bilateral, aids; that is, the child is fitted with two microphones, two power controls, and two receivers.

The demands on the mother are great. In the foreword to Pollack's book on acoupedics (1970), Wedenberg stated, "My wife gave up her profession which will determine if the work will succeed or not." Pollack also places the major responsibility on the role of the mother, with very little concern for the father and his obligations. She claims that the clinician working with the program should be a mother herself and that all children under age three are more naturally drawn to a woman than to a man.

Although the developers of acoupedic programs continually stress its unisensory nature, examination of their procedures clearly illustrates that they also rely heavily on visual and tactile modalities. In reality, human beings, including very young ones, function as integrated organisms. The young child relies on sensorimotor experience. Because hearing, vision, and touch constantly interact with and complement one another, it appears almost impossible to place total emphasis first on audition. Examination of descriptions of techniques employed in acoupedic programs seems to support this conclusion.

Objective research on the effectiveness of acoupedic programs relative to that of other types of programs reveals more modest results. As previously noted, McCroskey (1968) found few differences between children trained in an auditory-based preschool and children with no preschool training. Two auditory-based programs were involved in a longitudinal evaluation of eight early intervention programs for deaf children (Moores, 1985a). One of the two auditory-based programs withdrew from the study after the first year's data were published. When testers' mouths were uncovered, scores of the children from the remaining program fell below the average of children in the other six programs. Overall, children from this program scored sixth (out of seven) in receptive communication; fifth in expression communication; and seventh in reading, arithmetic achievement, amount of classroom interaction, quality of classroom interaction, and academic achievement.

In recent years, enthusiasm for an exclusive unisensory method has waned. Despite the position of its strongest advocates, many of the techniques have been incorporated into admittedly multisensory programs; for example, see Hartbrauer

(1975) and Sanders (1971). In at least two major areas, educators of the deaf owe a debt to workers in acoupedics. First is the emphasis placed on early detection and intervention and on the role of the parents, or at least the mother. Second is the demonstration that even severe and profound hearing loss does not preclude the utilization of residual hearing as part of everyday functioning.

The Auditory Global Method

Calvert and Silverman (1975) developed the label *auditory global method* to characterize the techniques incorporated under the terms *acoupedic, unisensory, auditory, aural,* and so on. Table 11.5 lists the essential characteristics of the method. Calvert and Silverman believed that the primary, though not always the exclusive, channel for speech development is auditory and that the input should consist of fluent, connected speech (p. 148).

Calvert and Silverman recommended using the auditory global method as the initial method for all children (pp. 156, 168) but acknowledged that it would not be satisfactory for all children. They recommended specific procedures for assessing children's progress in making decisions about alternative approaches. In evaluating developments, Calvert (1976) commented:

> Although there are reports of profoundly deaf children who make surprisingly good use of aural language, there has been no demonstration that the primarily auditory approach works well with all or most profoundly deaf children or even that it works well with many severely hearing impaired children. (p. 78)

Speech Reading

Speech reading, traditionally known as *lip reading,* involves visual interpretation of a speaker's communication. It is a highly complex process in which a speech reader must utilize situational and motivational variables as well as a mastery of the gram-

TABLE 11.5   Essential Characteristics of the Auditory Global Method

1. Maximum emphasis on use of hearing
   a. Early use of amplification
   b. Periodic reexamination of hearing
   c. Selection of optimal amplification systems
   d. Periodic examination of hearing aid
   e. Constant usage
2. Comprehensive intervention
3. Emphasis on connected speech

Source: Adapted from D. Calvert and R. Silverman, *Speech and Deafness* (Washington, D.C.: A. G. Bell Association, 1975), pp. 148–156. Reprinted with permission from "Essential Characteristics of the Auditory Global Method," in *Speech and Deafness* by D. Calvert and R. Silverman. Copyright © 1975 by the Alexander Graham Bell Association for the Deaf, 3417 Volta Place N.W., Washington, D.C. 20007.

mar of a language. The speaker must decode messages containing elements that are not visible or are of low visibility (for example, sounds made in the back of the throat, such as the italicized components of the words *key*, st*ing,* and *g*un, as well as elements that may sound different but appear similar on the lips (homophones). Since the usual sounds for the phonemes /p/, /b/, /m/, /t/, /d/, and /n/ are homophonous—that is, they are articulated in a similar way and look similar on the lips—in isolation the following nine words would look similar to a speech reader:

bat	mat	pat
bad	mad	pad
ban	man	pan

Bruhn (1949) noted that about 50 percent of the words in the English language have some other word or words homophonous to them. She listed the following homophonous sounds:

1. f—v—ph—(gh as in cough or laugh)
2. m—b—p—mb—mp
3. w—wh—(qu)
4. s—z—soft c
5. sh—ch—j—soft g
6. d—t—n—nt—nd
7. k—hard c—hard g—ng—nk
8. (l has no sound homophonous to it) (p. 13)

In a review of the literature on speech reading, Farwell (1976) pointed out that no commonly accepted definition of the term *speech reading* exists. Some researchers argued that it is entirely dependent on vision, whereas others saw it as complementing audition, at least to some extent.

Although speech reading was incorporated into programs developed to educate deaf children as early as the seventeenth century, as noted in Chapters 2 and 3, the methods used in the twentieth century have reflected different goals and techniques. Of the various approaches to speech reading, four deserve further consideration: the Jena, the Mueller-Walle, the Nitchie, and the Kinzie methods.

The Jena Method

Developed in Jena, Germany, by Brauckmann (Deland, 1931), the Jena method incorporates basic principles of kinesthesis, imitation, and rhythm. Although Brauckmann directed a school for deaf children, the method was originally developed for hard-of-hearing and deafened adults. Procedures attempt to integrate speech, speech reading, reading, and writing, and involve memorization and practice in analytic drills initially of a syllabic nature. The Jena method was introduced into the

United States in the 1870s. The most complete English treatment of the method is provided by Bunger (1961).

The Mueller-Walle Method

Mueller-Walle, like Brauckmann, had been a teacher of the deaf. When he began teaching speech reading to hard-of-hearing adults, he found the need for different instructional techniques and therefore developed a six-week course that relies on rapid syllable drill and rhythmic speech (Bruhn, 1949; Deland, 1931). At first the most visible sounds are introduced; then less visible elements are added gradually. The system was introduced in the United States in 1902 by Bruhn, a teacher of French and German in Massachusetts who went to Germany to be trained by Mueller-Walle after she lost her hearing. Bruhn translated Mueller-Walle's work and adapted it to English. By 1949, her book on the Mueller-Walle method was in its seventh edition (Bruhn, 1949).

The Nitchie Method

Although he lost his hearing at age fourteen and had no training in speech reading, Edward Nitchie graduated Phi Beta Kappa from Amherst College. After graduation he was trained by Lillie Warren, an early teacher of lip reading who had developed a method of "expression reading" (Deland, 1931). Building on Warren's work, Nitchie developed an analytic system using a set of symbols by which speech reading ability could be developed through mirror practice. Nitchie gradually moved from an analytic to a synthetic approach to speech reading and came to emphasize training the individual to grasp thoughts as wholes (Nitchie, 1912). Nitchie was the first educator to consciously utilize psychological principles in a method of speech reading.

The Kinzie Method

The Kinzie method was developed by Cora Kinzie, who lost her hearing while training to become a medical missionary, and her sister Rose, who joined Cora to develop a school of speech reading. After losing her hearing, Cora Kinzie was trained by Bruhn; she then established her own Mueller-Walle school of lip reading. While running her school, she studied under Nitchie. Kinzie and Kinzie (1931) utilized Nitchie's psychological principles and the Mueller-Walle classification of introductory sounds to develop a graded series of speech reading exercises.

Speech Reading and Deaf Children

Two factors should be considered in evaluating the most popular approaches to speech reading in the United States. First, most of the methods were developed for hard-of-hearing or deafened adults who already had acquired a mastery over spoken language and could use it to acquire skills in speech reading. Even many of the

American leaders in the field, including Nitchie, Kinzie, and Bruhn, had lost their hearing after acquiring speech and language. Although intensive efforts were devoted to applying the techniques to deaf children, the methods had been grounded in work with hard-of-hearing adults. The speech reading task is far different for deaf children, who have no foundation of oral language to draw from, than for adult native users of a language.

Second, as is true in so many other parts of the field, no objective data are available about the various approaches. Miller, Ramsey, and Goetzinger (1958) and Farwell (1976) remarked on the lack of experimental evidence in the area of speech reading. Methods employed in the education of deaf children, especially those of preschool age, in the United States in recent years have tended to minimize the importance of speech reading. Advocates of the acoupedic (auditory global) approach tend to deemphasize the visual channel and discourage formal training in speech reading. Although the concept of total communication encompasses speech reading, for some reason speech reading tends to receive less emphasis than other components such as signs, speech, auditory training, finger spelling, and writing.

The review of research by Farwell (1976) presents some discouraging results. Although it has been well established that most deaf individuals are not good speech readers, no evidence suggests that they cannot *become* good speech readers. The lack of innovation in teaching speech reading is as severe as the previously mentioned lack of innovation in teaching speech. Aside from the use of film in teaching speech reading (Morkovin, 1960), no new methods have been developed since 1930 (O'Neill and Oyer, 1961). What seem like new techniques are really just combinations of old methods.

What is needed is the development of a series of activities designed for use with young deaf children from time of identification of a hearing loss. The activities should be based on principles of child development, visual and auditory perception, linguistics, and learning, and they should be designed specifically for young children with severe or profound hearing loss, not adapted from a series of drills for hard-of-hearing adults.

Speech-reading ability is an invaluable tool for any deaf individual. Why processes for developing speech reading—and speech—have received so little attention over the past fifty years from both oralists and combined oral-manual proponents remains a mystery.

Summary

Most of the methods used today to help deaf children acquire grammatical proficiency and expressive and receptive communication skills were developed generations ago. It is disturbing that despite the ascendancy of the oral method during most of the twentieth century, few advances were made in the development of speech, speech reading, and listening skills. Educators continue to draw on the legacy of work done thirty or more years ago, without making substantial improvements. The field cries out for theoretical and applied investigations into the acquisition of speech, grammar, speech reading, and listening skills as developmental processes.

At present, we do have the means to significantly improve the communicative functioning of deaf children. Two quite different sources of potential improvement that have been utilized inefficiently are improved hearing aids and manual communication. Large numbers of deaf children who could benefit from effective aids often are not appropriately diagnosed and fitted, and those aids that are fitted often are not properly monitored or maintained. Partly because of a traditional separation of speech from signs and finger spelling, almost no work has been done to develop techniques involving manual communication in programs for the training of speech, speech reading, and use of residual hearing. Finger spelling, in particular, could be an effective tool in the development of oral-aural expressive and receptive skills. Most programs do set aside time during the school day for training in expressive and receptive oral skills and for the teaching of English grammar; no such attention has been devoted to the development of manual communication skills. This may be one reason the signing used by teachers and students seems quite variant.

Educators using combined oral-manual communication for instructional purposes have not addressed the issue of the extent to which signs should be used to convey academic subject matter. Under aural or oral-aural conditions, deaf children tend to miss bound morphemes (involving tense, number, and gender) and function words (articles, prepositions, and pronouns) in addition to having the obvious difficulties in learning to speech read content words. Many teachers leave out bound morphemes and function words when signing—the very elements most difficult to pick up through audition and speech reading. Such an approach may convey academic subject matter more clearly, since content words (nouns, verbs, adjectives, and adverbs) are clearest when spoken and signed. However, the benefits in terms of English usage may be only somewhat greater than the minimal results achieved through oral-only instruction.

A major problem is that many teachers—and, perhaps more important, many trainers of teachers—have not been prepared to take advantage of the potential benefits that both improved technology for speech reception and manual communication offer when properly used in instructional programs. The efforts of innovative and creative minds must be brought to bear on these challenges if we are to make advances in linguistics and in speech and hearing science.

12

Literacy: The Development of Reading and Writing

Introduction

For most people, learning to read and write seems to be a relatively straightforward process, although writing might seem to be more difficult than reading. Fluent writing seems to follow fluent reading. Reading has been characterized as simply training the eye to do the work of the ear. By extension, we might think of writing as training the hand and fingers to do the work of the tongue. We know that most children acquire the basics of their native language by three years of age and that they have impressive conversational capabilities. By the time they start formal reading instruction, they have developed prereading skills. Typically, they know that English print proceeds from left to right and top to bottom. They can decode environmental signs (McDonald's, Coke, etc.) at an early age. Adults have read to them, and they know that print can tell stories. Despite this, learning to read a language that one has already mastered conversationally is a relatively long process. The first years of schooling are devoted to learning the principles of reading and mastering imperfect relationships, at least in English, between sound and spelling. The child must learn, for example, that print does not have intonation and that elements such as commas, colons, periods, question marks, quotation marks, and exclamation points are used to roughly convey aspects of spoken communication. It has been said that for the first four years of school we learn to read and only after that we can read to learn. However, we are all aware that many children who are fluent in a language still can have difficulty in learning to read it. The field of education is cyclical: holistic approaches to reading are in the ascendancy for a time, only to come into question and be replaced by "back to basics" phonics approaches. Sooner or later, the phonics approach comes under criticism. To be replaced by a more "natural" whole-world or holistic approach. Advocates at the extremes of each position seem to believe that the solution is simple—just use the right approach.

The reality is much more complicated. If it were not, we would have settled on the "correct" approach long ago. The syndicated columnist William Raspberry has suggested that anyone who claims to have the solution to improving reading should be required to spend a year in a classroom before disseminating his or her theory. This rule would at least reduce the number of self-proclaimed experts.

Effective functioning in a complex, literate society demands that one be able to read and to express oneself in writing. The fact that reading and writing have been cornerstones of American education from its beginnings attests to the importance of literacy. In many ways, reading may be considered more important for deaf individuals than for hearing individuals. Limited in the amount of general information obtainable through word of mouth, a deaf person's access to the larger culture often depends on whether she or he has developed fluency in reading. Similarly, a deaf person's ability to communicate with hearing individuals may rely heavily on his or her fluency in writing.

In the United States, the development of telecommunication devices for the deaf (TDDs), the accessibility of electronic mail and systems such as Internet, and the general availability of closed-captioned television programming give deaf individuals access to communication and information approaching that available to hearing individuals. To take advantage of these unprecedented opportunities, however, a deaf person must be literate in English.

Most school programs, those for both deaf and hearing children, usually give reading more attention than writing. For example, in the United States prior to the Industrial Revolution, a major goal of education was to teach children to read the Bible; writing was of secondary importance. Reading is seen as a tool for acquiring knowledge. It is also a means of inculcating in children the mores and beliefs of the society or culture. The more centralized and uniform a national system of education is, the more likely it is that reading will be used as a means of indoctrination. Systems that emphasize reading to the exclusion of writing imply that the individual has little of importance to express. A truly literate person can both receive and express information.

Relatively little attention has been paid to the development of writing skills in deaf children. One exception is a comprehensive special issue of the *Volta Review* entitled "Learning to Write and Writing to Learn" (Kretschmer, 1985). Moores (1990b) has argued that the neglect of writing has had a more negative impact than reading limitations.

At first glance, deaf children do not seem to face the same disadvantage in reading and writing that they do in expressive and receptive oral communication. Hearing children enter school with fully developed oral skills, but, like deaf children, they have to be taught to read and write as part of the educational process. Closer examination, however, shows that learning to read and write is a more difficult task for most deaf children than for the typical hearing child. The hearing child can learn the graphic system on the basis of a fully developed phonemic system, because although English has many inconsistencies (for example, *ough* is pronounced differently in *though, through,* and *rough*), a basic phoneme-grapheme, or sound-spelling, correspondence exists. The deaf child, on the other hand, usually lacks the acquired mastery of the English sound system needed to develop literacy; to a large degree, the sound system must be bypassed. Deaf children thus face a double barrier to acquiring literacy. First, most deaf children have not achieved fluency in standard English in any form by the beginning of instruction in reading and writing. Second, many of the reading curricula currently in use with hearing children assume a knowledge of spoken English and are therefore of limited utility with deaf students.

It is not logical to talk about having the eye do the work of the ear. Even for children with significant residual hearing, we are dealing with a situation in which greater reliance must be placed on vision. By this I mean that a deaf child may develop a conversational language through vision, regardless of whether the mechanism is signs, speech reading, or some combination of the two. The child then uses vision in a different way to decode English or some other print language. In fact, conversational and print language may be developed in tandem.

Deaf children may have one potential advantage in learning to read and write: their knowledge of the American Manual Alphabet. Each of the twenty-six letters of the English alphabet has a counterpart in the American Manual Alphabet. This one-to-one correspondence is much more efficient than the phoneme-grapheme correspondence between spoken and written English. Because the manual alphabet is a direct representation of written English, transfer between finger spelling and graphic modes should be relatively easy to accomplish. Because the use of finger spelling and signs with younger children was restricted in the past, little information is currently available on this subject. Work should be forthcoming, however.

As we might expect, approaches to the teaching of reading can be divided into those favoring an elemental, analytic approach and those favoring a holistic, functional approach. The differences are similar to those previously identified in our discussion of the teaching of speech and of English grammar, although different terminology is used in the field of reading. The reading literature makes frequent references to bottom-up and top-down models of reading and reading instruction. The *bottom-up models* are sequential and hierarchical, building up elements on a step-by-step basis. These models emphasize learning small units and then joining them together in a constructive way. Word and letter recognition skills and, in general education, phonic skills constitute the building blocks. *Top-down models* are more dependent on the use of context, semantics, and background knowledge. More attention is devoted to obtaining meaning from text than to training in separate skills. The role of prediction is important to the extent that the reader is expected to anticipate what will happen in the text.

Bottom-up models of reading, then, incorporate analytical, elemental procedures, whereas top-down models rely more on holistic, functional approaches. In practice, teachers use elements of both approaches. There is little disagreement that, among skilled readers, reading is under the control of higher-level cognitive processes and involves an interaction between the reader and the text. Comprehension of text, like comprehension of speech, may be seen as a constructive process. Meaning is generated as the reader mediates the text through his or her prior knowledge by means of a confluence of situational, motivational, semantic, and syntactic variables. The disagreement lies in how the reader can be helped to achieve this level of functioning. Is the bottom-up model too simplistic for a process as complex as reading? Does the top-down model ignore some of the necessary fundamental skills? Is there a middle way or an alternative or eclectic approach that can be applied?

Many observers have written about the perceived failure of education for the deaf, pointing to low reading levels as support. It is true that the measured reading of deaf children, on the average, is far below that of hearing peers and that we must increase our efforts to facilitate literacy—both reading and writing. There are several obvious reasons for the gap. First, as stated, our graphic system of English is based on a phonemic system that deaf children cannot hear. Second, many deaf children are not identified for years, and there is often a lag from the time of identification to the provision of services to the child and the family. We know that the earlier the child receives services, the greater the possibility for developing literacy.

My experience with postsecondary undergraduate- and graduate-level deaf students leads me to believe that unprecedented numbers of deaf children are now acquiring high levels of literacy, both in reading and writing fluency. However, my observations of children in early intervention, elementary, and secondary programs make it clear that we face major obstacles in closing the literacy gap. Unfortunately, many of the critics seem to believe that there are easy answers. As anyone who has spent time as a teacher knows, there is no royal road to literacy for deaf children. Improvement is incremental and requires hard work, creativity, and the cooperation of children, parents, and teachers.

In this chapter, we will review research on the reading and writing skills of deaf individuals. Let the reader be forewarned that the statistics are grim. The literature is not complete, but it is sufficient to establish that deaf children have encountered great difficulty in mastering the graphic English system. However, reason for some optimism exists, particularly with respect to reading. There is now strong evidence to indicate that standardized tests of reading underestimate the ability of deaf readers to process text. This finding suggests that, for generations, deaf readers have not received full credit for their reading skills. If this is true, as I believe it is, then although the difficulties deaf students face in learning to read are fundamental, they are not as severe as is commonly assumed. Problems in the development of writing skills may be somewhat more difficult to overcome. When one has not mastered all of the grammatical complexities of a language, it is probably easier to understand a message or a story in context than to express oneself clearly. Still, some promising developments in the field have the potential to alleviate the situation.

Reading

Investigations into the Reading Skills of Deaf Children

Many studies of the reading skills of deaf students have focused on these children's lower reading achievement relative to hearing students (Ewoldt, 1981). Most of these studies have obtained scores for deaf subjects on standardized tests of achievement and have compared them either to national norms for the hearing population or to scores of hearing subjects matched on specific variables such as age, sex, and IQ. In a somewhat smaller but still substantial body of work, deaf and hearing subjects have been matched on standardized reading achievement scores and then compared on other variables such as grammatical skills and vocabulary. Both types of research are informative only to the extent that they provide comparisons with hearing norms or to matched hearing subjects. Unfortunately, they offer no insight into what deaf children *can* do but instead present an unbroken, and perhaps invalid, picture of failure and underachievement. It was not until about 1980 that some researchers began to examine the processes that deaf children use in their reading. From this examination has come the beginnings of an appreciation of deaf children's skills, which had not been identified previously.

Standardized Tests of Reading.   Investigations into the performance of deaf children on standardized tests of reading comprehension suggest that the students encounter great difficulty in processing standard English in print. In an investigation of the performance of more than five thousand deaf students in the United States and Canada on the elementary-level reading subtest of the Metropolitan Achievement Test, Wrightstone, Aranow, and Moskowitz (1963) reported that fewer than 10 percent of the children over ten years of age read at the fourth-grade level. In commenting on these findings, Furth (1966) emphasized that between ages eleven and sixteen the average reading score of the deaf students increased only from grade 2.6 to grade 3.4—less than one year of growth over a period of five years.

Pugh (1946) examined scores earned by children at fifty-four day and residential schools for deaf children on the Iowa Silent Reading Test. No groups scored above the sixth-grade level on any subtest. Pugh reported very little improvement in reading achievement scores between the seventh and thirteenth year of schooling.

Myklebust (1964) compared the reading vocabularies of deaf and hearing students at ages nine, eleven, thirteen, and fifteen and reported higher scores for the nine-year-old hearing subjects (21.37) than for the fifteen-year-old deaf subjects (11.32). Scores for the deaf students tended to plateau around age thirteen, enabling hearing students to increase their relative advantage in adolescence.

Goetzinger and Rousey (1959) obtained similar results from a study of 101 students at a residential school for deaf students. They noted that scores in the Vocabulary and Paragraph Meaning subtests of the Stanford Achievement Test (SAT) tended to level off between ages fourteen and twenty-one.

Gentile (1972, 1973) reported on scores of 16,908 deaf students who had taken one of five batteries of the Stanford Achievement Test. Scores in Paragraph Meaning increased from an average grade equivalent of 1.61 at age six to 4.36 at age nineteen. Scores of students older than nineteen were somewhat lower, leading Gentile to postulate that those students still in school at age twenty or older tend to be lower achievers. Gentile (1973) compared the mean grade equivalents by sex at four age levels (eight, eleven, fourteen, and seventeen) and found essentially no differences. Females scored slightly higher at each age, but in no case did the

© SUZIE FITZHUGH

The joy of reading.

differences exceed two-tenths of a grade. SAT scores of deaf males and females were much closer than those of hearing males and females, with females consistently achieving at higher levels on Paragraph Meaning (Kelley et al., 1966).

Results of the investigations by Pugh, Goetzinger and Rousey, Wrightstone et al., and Gentile all highlight an apparent leveling off of achievement in adolescence, at least as measured by standardized reading achievement tests. It should be pointed out that the research reported was cross-sectional rather than longitudinal in nature. In other words, children were not identified, followed, and tested over a long period of time; rather, children of different ages were tested at the same time. Because older adolescent deaf students did not score higher than younger adolescent deaf students, it was concluded that a plateau in reading achievement occurs. Other possible explanations exist for this apparent plateau, however. Because the deaf population in the United States is heterogeneous, one age group may have a different proportion of children with additional conditions due to etiological factors such as rubella. Another possibility is that many higher-achieving deaf adolescents may transfer to integrated settings and not appear in the testing program for hearing-impaired students. If so, what appears to be a plateau may to some extent reflect changing placement patterns. A study by Allen (1986) addressed some of the major issues concerning reading achievement by deaf students, including achievement trends over time and the establishment of norms for deaf students on standardized tests. Although the standardizations have covered a range of subject matter, at this point we will consider only reading.

Trends in Reading Achievement.   Although for deaf students achievement in reading, as well as in other areas, is low compared to hearing standards, there appears to have been improvement since the middle 1970s. In 1974, the sixth edition of the Stanford Achievement Test was published. It was the first such test for which norms had been developed for deaf and hard-of-hearing students. The Stanford Achievement Test, Hearing Impaired (SAT-HI) battery was normed from a representative sample of more than six thousand students from eight to eighteen years of age. The representation was identified on the basis of geographic area, ethnic status, sex, and school placement. The development of the SAT-HI was a significant advance. For the first time, the performance of a deaf child could be compared to two points of reference: hearing norms and deaf and hard-of-hearing norms. Norms for the Stanford Achievement Test were developed for the seventh edition in 1983 and for the eighth edition in 1990 (Holt, Traxler, and Allen, 1992).

Allen (1986) analyzed data from the first two norming projects for hearing-impaired children to ascertain whether levels of achievement had changed from 1974 to 1983 and to identify factors that might account for achievement. Although he investigated performance in reading comprehension and mathematics computation, this section will deal only with findings in reading comprehension.

The most notable finding was that for every age from eight to eighteen, scores on reading comprehension were higher in 1983 than in 1974. A score that would have put a twelve-year-old deaf or hard-of-hearing student at the fiftieth percentile in 1974 (above 50 percent of deaf and hard-of-hearing children of the same age) would have put the child at only the thirtieth percentile in 1983. The trend in reading achievement among deaf children from 1974 to 1983, then, appears to have been similar to that among hearing children from 1970–1971 to 1983–1984 as reported in the national assessments of educational progress (*Reading Report Card,* 1985). The reading achievement of both deaf and hearing children apparently improved from the 1970s to the 1980s. As we might expect, hearing students in the 1983 norming of the SAT scored higher than hearing students in the 1974 norming (Allen, 1986). Patterns in the reading achievement of deaf subgroups noted in the 1983 SAT-HI were similar to those of hearing subgroups noted in the national assessments of educational progress. Females tended to score higher than males, and whites tended to score higher than blacks or Hispanics. Regional patterns were more difficult to identify, but the average sixteen-year-old in the Northeast (*average* is defined as being at the fiftieth percentile) scored higher than the average sixteen-year-old in the north central, southern, and western regions.

The results point to a dilemma first mentioned in Chapter 1. Because of the increased emphasis on academic achievement in education in general, deaf children must improve achievement merely to remain in the same position relative to hearing children. Allen noted that deaf students as a group acquired reading comprehension skills more rapidly in 1983 than in 1974, but they showed little or no gain relative to their hearing cohorts.

Holt, Traxler, and Allen (1992) reported similar improvements from 1983 to 1990 in the scores of deaf and hard-of-hearing children. Thus these children's scores were higher in 1990 than in 1983, which in turn were higher than in 1974. A ten-year-old in 1990 was roughly equivalent to a twelve-year-old in 1974 in reading achievement.

As we might expect, patterns of achievement have differed. Holt et al. (1992) reported median reading comprehension grade equivalent scores at age seventeen of 3.8 among children with profound losses, 4.5 among children with severe losses, and 5.4 among those with less than severe losses. In terms of ethnicity, at age seventeen, white deaf and hard-of-hearing children had median reading comprehension grade equivalents of 5.4, and black children's scores at age eighteen (grade 3.6) were higher than at seventeen. This was not true for white and Hispanic children, suggesting different retention patterns. In terms of school placement, seventeen-year-old children in local, integrated settings read at grade 5.7, compared to grade 3.8 in day and residential school settings and 2.8 in local, nonintegrated settings. Holt et al. were careful to point out that the higher achievement of children in integrated settings could not be attributed to placement per se, because most of these children had less than severe hearing losses and tended to come from families of higher socioeconomic status.

Studies of Reading and Grammatical Structure.   In considering the preceding studies of performance, we must remember that reading achievement scores are not a measure of the grammatical ability of deaf students (or any other students). Reading tests measure skills commonly acquired during the educational process. Children—or adults—may possess strong language skills but still be unable to read, as Cooper and Rosenstein (1966) pointed out.

Interpretation of reading scores of children with normal hearing and proficiency in standard English is relatively straightforward. Interpretation of scores of children whose primary language is different from that used in the classroom (say, Spanish-speaking children tested in English) is much harder. The difficulty is even greater when the scores are those of deaf children. The tests assume the presence of a common English usage. By an early age, children with normal hearing have mastered the basic principles of their language and can handle most common structures automatically. Linguistic proficiency in the standard language is established before reading instruction. With deaf children, mastery of standard English cannot be assumed at the beginning of reading instruction; most deaf children have not internalized the rules of English at this point.

Moores (1970b) used the cloze procedure (filling in words deleted from passages) to compare thirty-seven deaf students with an average age of sixteen years nine months and thirty-seven hearing students with an average age of nine to ten years. The mean grade reading level of the deaf group on the Metropolitan Achievement Test was 4.77, compared with 4.84 for the hearing group. The performance of the hearing students on the cloze task was superior on passages at three different levels of difficulty. Analysis indicated that the lower performance of the deaf students resulted from a lower level of English grammatical skills and limited vocabulary.

In a partial replication of the Moores study, Marshall (1970) used cloze procedures to compare twenty-four deaf students whose mean grade reading level was 4.5 with twenty-four hearing students with a mean grade reading level of 4.4. Marshall reported that the hearing students' performance was superior on measures of grammar and vocabulary. When grammatical differences were taken into account, there were no significant differences in vocabulary.

Schmitt (1968) reported that eight- and eleven-year-old hearing children understood passives, negatives, and verb tenses better than did deaf children eight, eleven, fourteen, and seventeen years old. Schmitt interpreted the results as indicating that in their reading deaf children ignore markers signifying negation, passive voice, and verb tense, and thereby read sentences as simple active constructions.

Tervoort (1970) investigated the ability of deaf children in the Netherlands to understand passive sentences. On a task on which two hearing six-year-olds and two hearing twelve-year-olds obtained perfect scores, deaf children under age thirteen scored 27.5 percent correct (chance was 20 percent) and those over thirteen scored 74 percent correct. The higher scores for the older children reflected more effective processing of nonreversible passives than of reversible passives.* Like Schmitt, Tervoort concluded that deaf children master the simple active declarative sentence first and use it predominantly thereafter.

The results of the studies of various written English and Dutch grammatical structures of deaf children of elementary and secondary school age are consistent with those reported for younger children by Moores (1985a), who found that deaf children tend to first learn a simple subject-verb-object order and then process sentences within that framework.

It must be emphasized, however, that the research by Marshall, Moores, Schmitt, and Tervoort reported in this section concentrated primarily on grammatical components of reading and was not designed to investigate reading proficiency per se. These studies did not address the possibility that deaf readers are able to utilize context and prior knowledge in their everyday reading. In other words, these readers might apply their cognitive abilities and past experiences to compensate for difficulties with English grammar. If so, their actual functional reading ability would be higher than that suggested by reading achievement tests based on subjects with normal hearing.

Reading Fluency of Deaf Students.   Ewoldt (1981) studied the reading of four deaf students by means of the cloze procedure, miscue analysis, and story retellings. She found that the reading process for deaf students appeared to be remarkably

---

*An example of a reversible passive is *The boy was pushed by the girl*. Compare this with the nonreversible passive *The house was painted by the girl*. Understanding the first sentence obviously requires more grammatical knowledge than is needed to understand the second.

similar to that for hearing students as delineated in Goodman's (1967, 1973) theoretical model. Ewoldt noted that deaf readers have more options than do hearing readers, for example, speech, finger spelling, pantomime, and a variety of sign systems. The major difference between the strategies of deaf and hearing readers is that deaf readers tend to finger-spell a difficult or unknown word, whereas hearing readers might produce a nonword.

Ewoldt noted that when given whole, meaningful, interesting, and predictable stories, the students read with proficiency even when the stories were many grade levels above their measured achievement. She concluded that providing deaf students with more content than an isolated sentence or paragraph usually contains gave them more opportunity to read for meaning. Ewoldt stressed the benefits of allowing children to use any communication mode available to them.

In a similar vein, Pehrssen (1978) argued that most approaches to teaching reading to deaf children rely on techniques that are more appropriate for children who have mastered the English spoken system and English grammar. In other words, instruction in reading is dependent on those areas in which deaf children have the greatest difficulty and fails to take advantage of their cognitive strengths. Pehrssen advocated that curricula with a cognitive/semantic emphasis be developed for deaf children.

McGill-Franzen and Gormley (1980) found that deaf students could understand a grammatically complex structure better when it appeared in a familiar fairy tale than when it was presented in an isolated sentence. These researchers concluded that it is easier for deaf students to read material about which they have prior knowledge. Gormley (1981) assessed prior knowledge of fifteen deaf students and then tested their reading of three familiar and three unfamiliar paragraphs through retellings and probes. (A familiar paragraph might be on baseball and an unfamiliar one on curling.) Even though the paragraphs were written at the same level of difficulty, recall of paragraphs on familiar topics was significantly better than recall of unfamiliar paragraphs. Gormley concluded that prior knowledge facilitates deaf readers' understanding of written text.

The recommendations of Ewoldt and Pehrssen and the implications of the work of McGill-Franzen and Gormley could provide the basis for the development of reading programs for deaf children. Surprisingly, reading (like other academic subjects) has received relatively little attention in education of the deaf. Coley and Bockmiller (1980) pointed out that the standards used by the Council on Education of the Deaf do not list reading as one of the eight areas of communication in which teachers should have knowledge and understanding. LaSasso (1978) reported that teachers of deaf students had a lack of course work in reading during their training. They tended to use basal readers—which, of course, were developed for hearing children—in their instruction. Coley and Bockmiller (1980) reported similar findings from questionnaire responses of 395 teachers of reading in programs for hearing-impaired children. Although these teachers were responsible for reading instruction, only 35 percent had taken even one course in reading. Like LaSasso, Coley and Bockmiller (1980) found that teachers relied predominantly on basal readers. They concluded:

> There is nothing wrong with a basal reader as one instructional technique, but it certainly has shortcomings as a method of teaching reading to hearing impaired children. If teachers are relying solely, or even mainly, on basal readers because they are unaware of alternative approaches, then we as educators need to insist on training to acquire the necessary skills to employ a variety of techniques for reading instruction. (p. 913)

Although no hard evidence exists, the situation appears to be changing for the better. With the push for academic achievement in the schools, teacher training programs seem to be devoting more attention to reading. At least one institution of higher education, Gallaudet University, has established a specialized, graduate-level program in reading and deafness.

Teaching Reading to Deaf Students

There is general agreement that for the fluent reader the act of reading is an active, constructive process. Such a reader has an unconscious mastery of English grammar and vocabulary and approaches the material with a wealth of background information and expectations. She or he has a range of skills and strategies to adapt to the characteristics of the material. For example, in the course of a day, a college student may read part of a textbook, a weekly magazine, a technical article, and the editorial page and comics in a daily newspaper. Each of these items represents a different kind of "reading," but the fluent reader handles the requirements without conscious effort.

For the literate person, then, reading is a highly complex process composed of several interrelated subprocesses. To some extent, the reader processes print at the graphemic, word, sentence, and story levels. Syntax and meaning interact in complex ways. The reader actively brings to the process past knowledge and expectations and makes predictions about what will be encountered in the text—predictions that may be modified through the course of the reading.

The traditional approach to developing adult reading fluency is to provide an elemental, step-by-step program of instruction. Recently, however, interest has been growing in a more holistic, natural, semantic approach to developing reading. Although the use of terminology such as *top-down* and *bottom-up* models tends to obscure the issue, the split is between advocates of an elemental approach and advocates of a holistic approach, just as in the teaching of speech and grammar. As we might expect, little evidence exists to support either approach so far, although work done to date seems to favor the use of a holistic approach. In practice, most teachers do not adopt an either-or position but use a pragmatic mix of elements. The question is what kind of a mix would be most productive.

Fundamental disagreement exists between those who believe that weakness in English grammar is the primary block to reading for the deaf child and those who believe that the deaf child's semantic strengths can be used to minimize the impact of grammar on developing reading skills. The efforts of those emphasizing grammar are based on work we have already reviewed on grammatical abilities of deaf individuals and their difficulties in understanding many grammatical structures. In many cases, the result has been what might be considered a "textual control," or simplified, bottom-up model. Materials written for fluent hearing readers may be written for deaf readers, or new material may be developed specifically for deaf children. Syntactically complex structures are withheld in the hope that the materials will be more readable for deaf students (Shulman and Decker, 1980). King and Quigley (1985) developed a series of basal readers, *Reading Milestones,* for deaf children that introduced grammatical structures in a controlled manner, one at a time.

King and Quigley (1985) developed syntactically controlled reading materials specifically for deaf students on the basis of two arguments. First was their position that a mismatch exists between a deaf child's linguistic, inferential, and experiential background and the background assumed by regular reading materials. Second was their belief that beginning deaf readers need special help in decoding words.

Dissatisfaction with an elemental approach was raised by several investigators who argued for what has become known as a "whole language" approach. Yurkowski and Ewoldt (1986) claim that a step-by-step approach is unnecessary because deaf readers use a strategy of bypassing syntax and processing print on the basis of meaning. They argue that the research on which the controlled grammar approach is based used sentences in isolation rather than in a connected discourse, which would more closely simulate a real-life reading task. Yurkowski and Ewoldt concluded that grammar is not unimportant but is secondary to pragmatic and semantic components in a top-down model of the reading process such as that developed by Goodman (1967). According to Yurkowski and Ewoldt, reading depends on bringing sufficient background knowledge to the text and, given this background knowledge, the deaf reader may be able to handle the complexities of English grammar without having to go through a simplified, step-by-step process. For this reason, these authors see no benefit in the use of simplified text or controlled introduction to grammar. Yurkowski and Ewoldt (1986) stated, "Preparing the reader to meet the text is the focus of instruction in the whole language instructional model based on Goodman's work. Unfortunately, current instruction often focuses on *preparing the text to meet the reader"* (p. 245).

The whole language approach was incorporated in the *Kendall Demonstration Elementary School Language Arts Curriculum* (1981). This curriculum was based on the belief that readers construct meaning from print based on their language and world knowledge as well as on semantic and syntactic cues presented in the text. Reading is taught in the context of meaningful prose. Instead of focusing on developing isolated skills, the teacher fosters a learning environment that allows simultaneous use of all available cues.

Through the dissemination of the Kendall School Curriculum and the efforts of its advocates, the whole language approach gained a growing number of supporters throughout the 1980s and early 1990s. In 1992, *Perspectives in Education and Deafness,* a journal published by the Gallaudet University Pre-College Programs, began a whole language annual issue, published in the January/February issue each year. The 1995 annual issue was entitled "Whole Language: Great Expectations, Impressive Results." Unfortunately, little data have been presented and, as we might expect in our sometimes contentious field, there is some disagreement over the benefits of a whole language approach.

In an article entitled "Some Concerns about Using Whole Language Approaches with Deaf Children," Dolman (1993) argued that many of the practices are beneficial for deaf and hearing children, but because many deaf children have difficulty acquiring literacy in English, a more direct approach to instruction may be warranted, at least for some children. Dolman's main premise was that the field of education of the deaf moves from one trend in general education to another when it should be developing a knowledge base consisting of the most effective practices for fostering literacy in deaf children. Dolman contended that research had failed to show that practices consistent with the whole language philosophy were any more effective in promoting literacy in hearing children than traditional practices and that, in fact, such methods may have a deleterious effect on reading abilities in disadvantaged children. Dolman (1993) concluded:

> In the early 1980s, *Reading Milestones* basals (Quigley and King, 1981, 1982, 1983, 1984) were a familiar sight in almost any classroom in which reading was taught to deaf students, elementary age through high school. . . . Educators of the deaf should not make the same mistake of imposing whole language on deaf children, regardless of its appropriateness, in the same way that *Reading Milestones* was imposed a few years back. (p. 281)

Ewoldt (1993) responded to this position with the argument that whole language is not an approach but a philosophy and that, being a philosophy, whole language will not mesh with other approaches or materials. Ewoldt also stated, "Dolman draws, in part, upon the ethnocentric assumptions of King and Quigley (1985), which are typical of most hearing researchers" (p. 10). Ewoldt concluded, "Rather, whole language presents to children the complete vast rich array of language in all its forms, in all its uses, and trusts each child to choose from that array what the child needs to work on" (p. 12).

Dolman (1993) responded:

> Rather than viewing whole language as the embodiment of Truth that must be defended, it is more useful to evaluate the effectiveness of the many practices resulting from this philosophy and to compare these practices to those of more traditional approaches used in the education of deaf children. (p. 13)

Kelly (1995) investigated reading competence in deaf readers by comparing the cognitive processes used by skilled deaf readers with those of average-ability deaf readers. He studied the bottom-up and top-down processing of text of the two groups and the implications for whole language instruction. The average reading group consisted of nine high school–age students in a metropolitan secondary school for deaf students with an average SAT-HI reading achievement of grade three. The skilled reading group consisted of nine deaf students from the same school with an average reading achievement of grade twelve. The school had a whole language program. Kelly reported that both groups of readers employed similar top-down processes in their reading. The average readers were like the skilled readers in that they used world knowledge and prior text in constructing meaning from text. Statistically, neither group engaged more than the other in top-down processing. Kelly found that the discrepancies between the two groups occurred primarily in the visual information processing of text, that is, bottom-up processing. He stated that the average deaf readers were vulnerable to a variety of obstructions to comprehension that could be exacerbated by texts appropriate for secondary-level students. These obstructions included longer processing time, a greater burden on working memory, more difficulty in retrieving word meaning, and perhaps inaccurate lexical construction of meaning. Kelly (1995) reached three conclusions from the results:

> First, a logical theoretical basis for expecting that whole language practices will lead to fluency requires explication; second, methods for monitoring effective development of bottom-up fluency need to be developed; and third, the criticisms of whole language that cite insufficient amounts of direct and systematic instruction in basic, bottom-up skills need to be answered. (p. 331)

Schimmel, Edwards, and Prickett (1999) reported on a comprehensive innovative reading program at a residential school for the deaf. The authors alluded to the widely stated belief that ASL is the first language of deaf children and English is the second language. It was noted that, although ASL was accessible to the students in school, their ASL skills remained low. A reading program was developed consisting of five components:

1. **Phonemic awareness.** Relying on research indicating that successful deaf readers make use of phonological information, a system was developed to teach basic phonemic awareness.

2. **Adapted Dolch word lists.** These are commonly used words found in the majority of basal readers. Videotapes and decks of cards were developed to demonstrate multiple meanings of words such as *can* or *run* and their meanings in context.

3. **Bridging lists and bridging.** Lists were developed to bridge some of the differences between print and sign and the training provided for teachers and children. For example, the written words *put out* would be signed differently in the sentences, "Put out the fire" and "Put out the dog."

4. **Reading series.** A commercially available series, Multiple Skills Series, was used.

5. **ASL development/language experiences stories.** Language experience approaches were used, with the children signing stories and the teacher retelling stores and providing appropriate language models. Resigning, writing, and videotaping followed.

Data analysis has revealed dramatic gains in reading levels and academic behavior. One interesting outcome was the amazement expressed by the researchers that initially many children did not know what ASL or English meant, even though manual English codes and ASL were used in the classrooms and the terms were used with the children daily (Schimmel et al., 1999, p. 301). The researchers developed a diagram to demonstrate the English/ASL continuum to the students, and teachers gave the students clues as to which type of signing was being used during a specific instructional time. Schimmel et al. also found that when teachers actually had to point on the continuum to the type of communication they were using, the teachers' own awareness of the input they were providing was heightened.

An Interactive Compensatory Model of Reading

Stanovich (1980) developed an interactive compensatory model of reading designed to address the development of reading proficiency by taking individual differences into account. Stanovich claimed that bottom-up, serial-stage models of reading and reading development run into difficulty because they contain no mechanism whereby higher-level processes, such as semantics, can affect lower-level processes. In other words, an elemental, incremental approach to reading does not take the influence of semantics into account. Stanovich was also critical of top-down models in which higher-level processes are seen as directing the flow of information through lower-level processes. In a top-down model, reading is seen as being semantically driven; that is, meaning is the most important element. Stanovich argued that reading is neither bottom-up nor top-down but is in reality *interactive:* it involves a synthesis of simultaneous processes at several different levels. Levels are more independent in an interactive model than in a top-down model, in which semantic processes direct lower-level processes. Stanovich claimed that an interactive model provides a more accurate description of how a fluent reader functions than does any other paradigm.

Stanovich proposed combining an interactive model with a theory of compensatory processing to improve understanding of reading and its development. He argued, in brief, that a deficit in any process will result in a greater reliance on other knowledge sources, regardless of their level in the processing hierarchy. Other knowledge sources will compensate for the deficit. Stanovich thus took an interactive model of reading and combined it with the assumption that the various component subskills of reading can interact in a compensatory manner; hence the term *interactive compensatory*. Stanovich thought it was possible that "given a deficit in a lower-level process, poor readers might actually rely *more* on higher-level contextual factors" (p. 30). In his treatment of reading, Stanovich did not directly address the case of the deaf reader, but his conclusions were close to those of Pehrsson (1978), Yurkowski and Ewoldt (1986), and others who have advocated greater reliance on the deaf child's semantic abilities to compensate for grammatical deficiencies. Stanovich (1980) and Ewoldt (1981) agree that good readers appear to have superior strategies for comprehending and remembering large units of text. The major issue on which these researchers would probably differ is the role of context-free word recognition, an area to which Ewoldt assigns less importance than does Stanovich. Although Stanovich maintained that an interactive compensatory model is distinct from both bottom-up and top-down approaches, in practice it would seem to have much in common with the better-known top-down theories. It would be interesting to see a reading curriculum developed on Stanovich's principles and tested with deaf children.

Reading in the Home and in Residential Schools

Although the fact is infrequently mentioned in the literature, there is an implicit understanding that for most children reading begins at home, not in school. In our society, literacy has social and cultural bases whose roots are established early. The first stage in becoming a reader begins as soon as the child is exposed to and becomes aware of books and other artifacts of a literate tradition (Taylor, 1983). Children are exposed to print through television, through the environment (street signs, food labels, advertisements, etc.), and through reading aloud by parents and others. Exposure to literacy events provides children with a metalinguistic awareness.

In education in general, there is considerable interest in what might be called the "alterable" curriculum of the home. Factors such as parental monitoring of homework, the presence of reading materials in the home, and parental limiting of access to television may all have a positive effect on school achievement. In the case of the deaf child, some fundamental improvements in literacy might be accomplished with relatively little effort. Parents of young deaf children are painfully aware of their children's difficulties in using oral communication expressively and receptively, since they witness the children's problems in mastering the speech and grammatical systems of English. It is less obvious to parents than to teachers that deaf children do not approach reading with the same base that hearing children do, even if they have equivalent intellectual potential. Parents naturally tend to view person-to-person communication as a much more immediate concern than literacy. Either because they are not aware of the benefits of reading for their deaf children or because they do not understand how to approach the study of reading, parents may fail to provide their deaf children with reading materials in the home. As a result, many deaf children experience fewer literacy events in the home than do their hearing brothers and sisters. A sensitive teacher can emphasize the importance of parents' reading to their children and provide some practical advice on how to introduce the child to print. One good resource is the Signed English Series, developed by Bornstein, Saulnier, and Hamilton (1972–1994), which consists of fifty-seven sets of booklets of nursery rhymes and fairy tales printed in illustrated form and accompanied by print and representations of signs. Such materials can help the young deaf child understand that a relationship exists among speech, signs, finger spelling, and print.

Gillespie and Twardosz (1996) reported that residential schools for the deaf regularly made reading and writing material available to students in residence and that counselors read to students regularly and supervised homework. However, in most schools time was not set aside for group storybook reading. The authors later (Gillespie and Twardosz, 1997) investigated the effects of group storybook reading intervention with children in one residential school.. They found the children to be highly engaged in the process. Children in the experiment performed more independently on an emergent reading task than children who did not participate in group storybook reading.

Several lists of books appropriate for use in classrooms with deaf children have been developed. Two deserve special mention here. One is a list developed by Cerra, Watts-Taffe, and Rose (1997) for the elementary grades to help teachers select books to match their instructional goals. The other is an annotated bibliography of children's literature featuring deaf and hard-of-hearing children for use in inclusive classrooms (Turner and Traxler, 1997).

Writing

The evidence suggests that the problems deaf children face in mastering written English are more formidable than those they encounter in developing reading skills. A deaf person can resort to compensatory strategies to understand a message when grammar and vocabulary skills are limited. It is much more difficult to express oneself clearly in writing in the face of such limitations. Although its benefit may not be as immediately obvious as that of a compensatory approach to reading, a compensatory approach to writing is called for. One problem is that research on writing in deaf children has lagged significantly behind research on reading. Much of the work was conducted decades ago and reflects primarily a concern with grammar and vocabulary, much as the traditional research on reading did. Whereas recent research on reading has addressed meaning and comprehension of narrative, there is still a paucity of work investigating how deaf writers express meaning. To some extent, we are still constrained by the legacy of the elemental, analytic approach, which held that children should be taught mechanical skills of writing before being allowed to begin the process of writing. The development of holistic, meaning-based approaches has been somewhat slower in the field of writing than in speech and reading, so some of our projections will have to be tentative. In the past generation, however, most research conducted on the teaching of writing to deaf children has had a functional, semantic orientation, suggesting that in all aspects of communication, both written and person to person, the trend in education of the deaf is clearly toward an acceptance of the primacy of meaning and away from the importance of mechanics per se.

Investigations into the Writing of Deaf Children

Over the years, numerous studies have been conducted on the writing of deaf students; in fact, there have been more studies of written language than of spoken language. Because of the difficulty of comprehending the speech of many deaf children, most studies concerned with assessing expressive language proficiency have been limited to written compositions. Such studies have indicated that on standard English grammatical usage deaf children lag significantly behind children with normal hearing.

Heider and Heider (1940a) analyzed compositions describing a short motion picture written by deaf students ages eleven to seventeen and by hearing students ages eight to fourteen. Results indicated that deaf students used relatively rigid, immature, and simple writing patterns. The investigators stated that the differences between the deaf and hearing children could not be described completely in quantitative terms. The differences were seen as resulting not only from different skills in the use of language but also from dissimilar thought processes. These results contrast with those obtained by the same authors in four experiments on color sorting with young deaf and hearing children (Heider and Heider, 1940b): the performance of the deaf children on the color-sorting tasks was similar to that of younger hearing children. These findings suggest a quantitative rather than a qualitative difference in intellectual functioning. Heider and Heider concluded that the thought process deaf children use in color sorting is essentially similar to that used by hearing children and is not distorted by inadequate or imperfect concepts.

Walter (1955) noted a lack of flexibility and an absence of sentence complexity in the written sentence construction of 102 children between ages six years and twelve years eleven months at a school for deaf students in Australia. In a later study of three Australian and four English schools for deaf children, Walter (1959) analyzed the written work of a total of fifty-eight children between ages nine years eleven months and twelve years eleven months. She noted similar patterns of language development and usage, although the level of the sentences was somewhat higher and the sentence structure somewhat more complex than in the original study.

In an investigation of the written language of eight hundred students, Thompson (1936) reported an average of 104 mistakes per 1,000 words. Thirty years later, in a study employing similar techniques, Birch and Stuckless (1963) reported a total of 5,044 grammatical errors from a corpus of 50,050 words, or slightly more than 100 errors per 1,000 words.

Myklebust (1964) developed a syntax score to measure written language. Using the syntax score, he compared deaf and hearing children between ages seven and fifteen and reported statistically significant differences at every level in favor of the hearing children. The mean score for seven-year-old hearing children (86.8) was similar to that for fifteen-year-old deaf children (86.2). Myklebust noted that in the hearing children significant differences appeared between seven-year-olds and nine-year-olds and between nine-year-olds and eleven-year-olds, but differences did not occur after eleven years of age. He concluded that the structure of written language conforms closely to the spoken form and that maturity in the syntax of written English is based on previously developed maturity in spoken language. It would be interesting to investigate whether the reported maturity of hearing children in written language syntax would be evident at an even younger age if errors of punctuation were not included in the syntax score.

Wells (1942) attempted to identify differences between deaf and hearing children in development of what he identified as abstract and concrete forms. He concluded that deaf children were equal to hearing children in the use and understanding of concrete words but were four to five years behind in their understanding of abstract terms. However, he did not clearly define the terms *abstract* and *concrete*. Without behavioral definitions, such terms tell us little about processes of understanding.

Simmons (1959) investigated word usage of 54 students at the Central Institute for the Deaf and 112 hearing students attending public schools by means of a type-token ratio, a measure of vocabulary diversity. Analyzing five written compositions and one spoken composition by each subject, Simmons reported that the deaf children tended to use more stereotyped, rigid, and redundant structures and vocabularies. Even grammatically correct and understandable sentences were marked by a lack of richness and spontaneity, as the following example illustrates:

> A girl threw a ball to a boy. The boy bat a ball. The boy bat the ball to a window and the window was broken. The mother heard the boy broke the window. The mother saw a boy broke the window. She went to see the ball game. (p. 35)

Whereas hearing children would vary their reference to a boy in a picture with terms such as *kid, boy, urchin, friend, him, Tom,* and so on, deaf children would repeatedly use the noun *boy*. Four verbs tended to be used by the deaf children: *have, be, go,* and *feel.* Also, compared to the hearing children, the deaf children tended to underuse possessives and definite articles such as *these, that,* and *those.*

It is apparent from the work of Myklebust, Simmons, Thompson, Wells, and Walter that deaf children have had limited success in written expression of English vocabulary and grammar. However, none of the studies addressed the children's ability to express content or get ideas across in writing. Yoshinaga-Itano and Snyder (1985) noted that research has not gone past the sentence level. We may assume that deaf children do have significant problems, but the nature and extent of these problems have yet to be documented.

A shift in paradigm has taken place. A reading of the special issue of the *Volta Review*, "Learning to Write and Writing to Learn" (Kretschmer, 1985), forcefully illustrates the fact that meaning is receiving much more attention than it has in the past and that formal structure (such as grammar) is no longer viewed as the principal area of concentration. In the following section, we consider the shift to a focus on meaning and its implications for teaching deaf children to write.

Writing as a Communicative Process

The final goal of a writing curriculum is to help the individual develop written expressive skills that may be applied across a variety of situations. Just as the fluent reader is able to apply different strategies according to the demands of different texts, the competent writer can satisfy a number of requirements, from developing grocery lists, writing personal notes, filling in the myriad forms our society requires, ordering by mail and internet, and writing formal correspondence to employing the writing skills specific to a profession. Any limitations on the number of areas in which an individual has written skills can translate into limitations on participation in society and in social and economic mobility. Once again, it is easy for us to define the goals but difficult to determine how to achieve them.

Dahl (1985) and Laine and Schultz (1985) argued that a shift in education has occurred from the teaching of writing as a product toward the teaching of writing as a process. In the past, emphasis at the beginning stages of instruction was on establishing the mechanical aspects of writing. The idea that mastery of mechanical aspects of writing may occur as part of the communicative effort and need not be a prerequisite for it is gaining a growing acceptance. The emphasis is on writing as a creative activity rather than as a goal to be achieved through a series of incremental steps involving specific subskills as building blocks.

Taylor (1983) conducted an ethnographic study of the development of literacy at home. She documented the complex interaction of reading and writing among preschool-age hearing children. The results suggest that the literacy process should be approached as a whole rather than being segmented into reading and writing components. Reading and writing are seen not as separate entities but as components of a larger and more complex process involving production, mediation, and reception. By extension, this larger and more complex process—which we term *literacy*—may be viewed as a component of an even more inclusive process—*communication*—which also encompasses oral and manual person-to-person exchanges.

Ewoldt (1985) reported on an investigation of literacy development in which ten deaf children from 4.2 to 5.5 years of age were selected for observation over a period of three years. Nine of the ten children had deaf parents. Naturalistic measures included writing samples, live observations, and parent interviews. Children were also videotaped performing various tasks and were given cloze procedures to perform. Ewoldt predominantly used deaf children of deaf parents for this study because they represented a "linguistically advantaged" group of deaf children whose swifter progress allowed more information to be gained in a shorter period of time (p. 124). She reported that the children demonstrated the ability to develop literacy naturally and that the patterns and strategies they employed were similar to those reported for hearing children. She concluded that the children learned the major goal of the study—that writing signifies. In discussing the instructional implications, Ewoldt concluded:

> The role of the teacher in this setting was that of facilitator. Rather than predetermining and directing the daily activities, the teachers provided (a) extensive input about how written language works (through reading to the children and taking their dictation); (b) a framework within which the children could establish and work toward their own goals (the free-writing period); and (c) a climate that encouraged risk-taking while at the same time allowing the child to relinquish the risk whenever the pressure became too great.
>
> This type of teaching is not easy. The teacher must be willing to abandon long-held notions of what a teacher's role should be. There are no manuals with step-by-step

procedures to help the teacher become adept at observing the child and recognizing when to move forward or step back. Even with the conceptual growth the children demonstrated almost daily, at times the teachers needed reassuring that they were indeed doing their job. However, as they witnessed the gains made by the children in the first year, their enthusiasm and expectations grew. As a result of this experiment the teachers have become even more positive in their attitude toward hearing impaired children and more accomplished in their ability to perceive the strength of each child. (p. 123)

In the most ambitious effort to date to improve the writing skills of deaf students, Kluwin and Kelly (1992) worked for two years on a project involving ten public school programs for deaf children, including 325 students in grades four through ten and 52 teachers. In the first year, teacher workshops focused on developing a rationale for writing instruction, teaching writing as a process rather than as a product, and promoting writing through dialogue journal writing. The writing process was presented as a four-phase (prewriting–writing–revision–publishing) cycle. The second-year teacher workshops concentrated on expressing nonjudgmental acceptance of the content of students' writing while discussing revisions to the form and creating classroom dialogue about form as a means of conveying content in a specific fashion. Teacher self-reports indicated widespread adoption of the process approach, and direct student evaluation showed dramatic improvement in students' writing, particularly in grammatical skills.

Literacy and Predictive Factors

Moores and associates (Moores et al., 1987; Moores and Sweet, 1990a, 1990b) reported on two separate groups of deaf adolescents who had been educated through combined oral-manual instruction (classified by the schools as "total communication") from age four or earlier with the purposes of identifying for each group factors predictive of and related to reading and writing skills. One group consisted of sixteen- and seventeen-year-old deaf students with deaf parents who used ASL in home communication. The second group consisted of sixteen- and seventeen-year-old deaf students with hearing parents. All subjects were students at residential schools for deaf students. As specified by the government funding agency, the subjects in the two groups were not compared; differences occurred in socioeconomic status, racial-ethnic composition, and parental education. Also, the acquisition of reading and writing skills by deaf children whose deaf parents had signed to them from birth may have been very different from that of deaf children of hearing parents, even when both groups of children were educated in total communication programs. Also, a deliberate effort was made to obtain samples with large ranges of achievement to investigate factors within groups. The areas comprising the study were as follows:

1. Levels of literacy
   a. Reading
   b. Writing

2. Intellectual functioning and world knowledge
   a. Verbal
   b. Performance

3. Academic achievement

4. Knowledge of English

5. Person-to-person communication
   a. American Sign Language
   b. Simultaneous communication/English-based signing
   c. Oral-aural communication

6. Hearing and speech
   a. Audiological
   b. Articulation

7. Background variables
   a. Student characteristics
   b. Family characteristics

Over the course of a year, a test battery was developed to assess the areas of study. The final test battery is presented in Table 12.1. The study was unique in that it conducted more than eleven hours of testing on each subject in a wide range of areas. One component was the inclusion of the verbal subtests of the Wechsler Adult Intelligence Scale (WAIS) as well as the performance subtests. As we noted previously, the work of Miller (1991) has indicated that verbal subtests can be given in a valid and reliable manner. The evidence from pilot testing that verbal measures might correlate more highly than performance measures with reading and writing among deaf students led to their inclusion.

Most of the tests listed in Table 12.1 are documented in the literature, and the reader should be familiar with many of them. Two measures, the Manual English Morphology Test and Language Proficiency Interviews, do not fall into this category and will be described only briefly.

The *Manual English Morphology Test* is based on studies conducted by Gaustad (1986) on the development of imitation, comprehension, and production (ICP) measures of English-based signing. The Manual English Morphology Test is administered individually and consists of a total of forty-four sentences presented on videotape. The subject views each sentence and then repeats it. Responses are videotaped.

The tester in this study was an adventitiously deaf research assistant skilled in English-based signing who had experience with the development of the Gaustad assessment scales. Within the forty-four sentences, seventy-seven bound morphemes and ninety-six function words were identified as follows:

TABLE 12.1   Predictive Factors Study: Final Test Battery

I. Literacy
   A. Reading
       1. Stanford Achievement Test–Hearing Impaired, Reading Comprehension
       2. Narrative Comprehension—"Space Pet"
       3. Cloze Task—"Devil's Trick"
       4. Peabody Individual Achievement Test, Reading Comprehension
       5. Gates-MacGinitie Reading Test
           a. Comprehension
           b. Speed and Accuracy
   B. Writing
       1. Educational Testing Service Written Language Tests
           a. Descriptive Narrative
           b. Business Letter

II. Other Measures
   A. Related Measures of Achievement
       1. California Achievement Test, Vocabulary
       2. Stanford Achievement Test, Hearing Impaired, Spelling
       3. Peabody Picture Vocabulary Test
       4. Clinical Evaluation of Language Function, Producing Word Associations
       5. Expressive One-Word Picture Vocabulary Test
   B. English Grammar/Structure
       1. Test of Syntactic Abilities
       2. Rhode Island Test of Language Structure
       3. Manual English Morphology Test
   C. Communicative Fluency
       1. Language Proficiency Interviews
           a. American Sign Language
           b. English-based Signing
           c. Oral

Bound Morphemes (77)		**Function Words (96)**	
_____ S (Pl)	16	Pronoun	31
_____ LY	16	Auxiliary Verb/Copula	30
_____ ED	13	Preposition	20
_____ ING	12	Article	15
_____ EST	12		
_____ FUL	3		
_____ ER	3		
_____ NESS	2		

The score is presented as the number of correct morphemes reproduced out of a possible total score of 173. Scoring was based on the subjects' ability to use English-based signing rather than ASL features.

D. Cognition/World Knowledge
  1. Wechsler Adult Intelligence Scale, Verbal
    a. Information
    b. Comprehension
    c. Arithmetic
    d. Similarities
    e. Digit Span
    f. Vocabulary
    g. Verbal Scale Score
  2. Wechsler Adult Intelligence Scale, Performance
    a. Digit Symbol
    b. Picture Completion
    c. Block Design
    d. Picture Arrangement
    e. Object Assembly
    f. Performance Scale Score
E. Speech Production
  1. Speech Intelligibility (SPINE) Test
  2. CID Phonetic Evaluation of Speech
  3. Woodcock Reading Mastery Test, Word Attack
F. Hearing
  1. Hearing Sensitivity
    a. Unaided Thresholds
    b. Aided Articulation Index
  2. Speech Perception
    a. Monosyllable, Trochee, Spondee Test
    b. Minimal Auditory Capabilities Test, Visual Enhancement
G. Questionnaires
  1. Parent
  2. Student

The Language Proficiency Interview (LPI) procedure is an adaptation of the Oral Proficiency Interview, a procedure developed by the Foreign Service Institute and now widely used to obtain rapid, valid, and reliable estimates of proficiency in the use of spoken language (Clark, 1975; Jones, 1979; Liskin-Gasparro, 1979). Several groups of researchers have applied the LPI to the assessment of sign language proficiency. For example, the National Institute for the Deaf and Gallaudet University use it in the assessment of students, faculty, and staff.

The procedures call for the interviewers to conduct a series of "probe and check" techniques in which they attempt to guide the subject to his or her maximum level of proficiency. In this project, the LPI was used to determine levels of proficiency for each subject in each of the three language varieties: fluent American Sign Language without voice, fluent English signing with the simultaneous use of spoken English by the interviewer, and spoken English with no signing. Under each condition, an interviewer talked with the student using the variety of language being assessed. Using information derived from the student interview and several standard topics for discussion, the interviewers determined a global rating of proficiency for that language variety. Levels of proficiency were reported on a five-point scale, with the lowest value representing no skill in the language variety in question and the highest value representing a high level of proficiency.

A different interviewer was used for each language variety assessed. In each case, the interviewer customarily used the variety under consideration. Accordingly, the American Sign Language fluency assessment was conducted by a fluent native signer who was able to use all signing varieties typically employed by deaf children of this age group; the assessment of English signing with simultaneous voice was administered by two hearing persons skilled at and accustomed to using this variety; and the spoken English interview was conducted by two hearing persons accustomed to communicating orally with deaf people. Each interview required approximately fifteen minutes and was videotaped for later review. The five functional levels were as follows:

0 = No functionally useful proficiency

1 = Limited practical proficiency; no school proficiency

2 = Basic practical proficiency; limited school proficiency

3 = Full practical proficiency; basic school proficiency

4 = Full practical proficiency

Each functional level was described in terms of an intersection of formal, structural criteria (vocabulary, pronunciation, grammar, fluency, and comprehension) and topical, content criteria related to the ease or sophistication with which a person can talk about topics at various levels of social and technical complexity. Concurrent with the development of the scale, a checklist of diagnostic performance factors was designed for each of the three varieties assessed. The tool of analysis is multiple regression, a multivariate method of analyzing the collective and separate contributions of two or more independent variables to the variation of a dependent variable. This study used two separate dependent variables—reading and writing—with independent variables clustered into seven categories as shown below. For details, the reader is referred to the original sources (Moores et al., 1987; Moores and Sweet, 1990a).

Dependent Variables	Independent Variables
Reading	Related measures of achievement
Writing	English grammar/structure
	Communicative fluency
	WAIS—Verbal
	WAIS—Performance
	Speech production
	Hearing

In sum, there were seven categories of independent variables with a total of thirty-one measures (see Table 12.1). The analysis was conducted to identify those measures from each category that would be important in the prediction of reading and writing competence of deaf adolescents with deaf parents. Because large numbers of prediction variables relative to the number of subjects reduce the replicability of the results, the goal is to identify from the comprehensive battery of thirty-one tests a small number of measures that can efficiently predict achievement in reading and writing. Factor analyses were conducted separately on the outcome measures of the two sets of dependent variables, reading and writing.

The thirty-one predictors were individually correlated with the two dependent outcome variables to establish covariation with the dependent variables. Table 12.2 shows the correlations of each of the thirty-one measures with factor scores for reading and writing achievement in deaf children of deaf parents. The higher the correlation, the stronger the relationship. For purposes of this study, a probability of less than .01 was set to indicate statistical significance. For example, for the tests of language proficiency in Table 12.2, oral proficiency ($p = .009$) and English-based sign proficiency ($p = .001$) correlate with reading achievement in deaf children of deaf parents, but ASL ($p = .32$) does not. Notice, however, that even though English-based sign proficiency and oral proficiency may correlate with measures of reading, they are not among the measures with the highest correlations. Very briefly, five measures have correlations of .50 or above for both reading and writing proficiency in deaf children with deaf parents. Three of these measures are from the WAIS verbal scales (vocabulary, information, arithmetic), and two are tests of English grammar, the Test of Syntactic Abilities (TSA) and the Manual English Morphology Test.

		Correlation	
Category	**Measures**	**Reading**	**Writing**
WAIS Verbal	Vocabulary	.66	.67
	Information	.65	.57
	Arithmetic	.61	.57
English grammar	TSA	.76	.61
	Manual English Morphology	.64	.51

Some readers may be surprised that ASL does not correlate with English reading and writing, but remember that we are dealing with two separate languages. Although the subjects were quite fluent in ASL, no apparent correlation with literacy existed. It appears that world knowledge, as measured by the WAIS verbal tests, and scores on English syntax and English sign morphology are the best predictors of literacy.

Table 12.3 shows the correlations of each of the thirty-one measures for factor scores for reading and writing for deaf children of hearing parents. As with deaf children of deaf parents, ASL fluency was not correlated with reading and writing. Again, correlations on the verbal scale of the WAIS and measures of English grammar tended to be higher for reading and writing than for hearing, language profi-

TABLE 12.2   Deaf Children of Deaf Parents: Bivariate Correlations of Predictors with Factor Scores for Reading and Writing

Measure	Reading		Writing	
	Correlation	Probability	Correlation	Probability
Hearing				
Better ear loss	−.24	.03	−.12	.17
Articulation index	.01	.46	.04	.39
MTS recognition	.23	.04	.09	.24
MTS categories	.11	.20	.005	.484
MAC aided	.46	.000	.44	.000
MAC unaided	.41	.000	.35	.002
Verbal scale				
Information	.65	.000	.57	.000
Comprehension	.35	.002	.45	.000
Arithmetic	.61	.000	.57	.000
Similarities	.50	.000	.39	.001
Digit span	.40	.001	.34	.003
Vocabulary	.66	.000	.67	.000
Performance IQ				
Digit symbol	.36	.002	.52	.000
Picture completion	.44	.000	.21	.05
Block design	.32	.005	.34	.003
Picture arrangement	.27	.02	.38	.001
Object assembly	.15	.12	.10	.20
Language proficiency				
ASL	−.06	.320	−.02	.424
Oral	.30	.009	−.22	.04
English-based sign	.41	.001	.23	.04
Speech production				
SPINE	.26	.02	.15	.115
CIDPES	.19	.075	.13	.15
Related achievement				
CAT vocabulary	.56	.000	.43	.000
SAT spelling	.48	.000	.37	.000
PPVT	.52	.000	.45	.000
CELF	.37	.000	.20	.000
One-word PVT	.51	.000	.46	.000
Woodcock	.43	.000	.33	.000
English grammar				
TSA	.70	.000	.61	.000
Rhode Island	.43	.000	.42	.000
Manual English				
Morphology	.64	.000	.51	.000

TABLE 12.3 Deaf Children of Hearing Parents: Bivariate Correlations of Predictors with Factor Scores for Reading and Writing

	Reading		Writing	
Measure	**Correlation**	**Probability**	**Correlation**	**Probability**
Hearing				
Better ear loss	−.02	.225	−.09	.236
Articulation index	.007	.482	−.083	.258
MTS recognition	.25	.05	.20	.06
MTS categories	.22	.08	.07	.30
MAC aided	.38	.006	.36	.003
MAC unaided	.47	.001	.25	.026
Verbal scale				
Information	.54	.000	.27	.015
Comprehension	.48	.000	.37	.001
Arithmetic	.52	.000	.44	.006
Similarities	.57	.000	.39	.001
Digit span	.43	.002	.40	.001
Vocabulary	.70	.000	.62	.000
Performance Scale				
Digit symbol	.34	.01	.36	.002
Picture completion	.27	.04	.25	.02
Block design	.18	.111	.22	.04
Picture arrangement	.38	.006	.20	.06
Object assembly	.31	.02	.23	.04
Language proficiency				
ASL	.04	.402	-.10	.230
Oral	.42	.002	-.21	.05
English-based sign	.41	.003	.16	.122
Speech production				
SPINE	.18	.119	.26	.019
CIDPES	.37	.007	.21	.05
Related achievement				
CAT vocabulary	.69	.000	.46	.000
SAT spelling	.34	.019	.28	.018
PPVT	.61	.000	.37	.002
CELF	.24	.000	.18	.107
One-word PVT	.75	.000	.56	.000
Woodcock	.48	.001	.33	.004
English grammar				
TSA	.70	.000	.66	.000
Rhode island	.37	.008	.20	.07
Manual English				
Morphology	.55	.000	.35	.005

ciently, or speech production. Three of the thirty-one independent measures correlated at .50 or higher with factor scores for both reading and writing for deaf children with deaf parents.

Category	Measures	Correlation Reading	Writing
WAIS Verbal	Vocabulary	.66	.67
English Grammar	TSA	.70	.61
Related Achievement	One-Word PVT	.75	.56

The WAIS vocabulary measure and the Test of Syntactic Abilities (TSA) also correlated higher than .50 for reading and writing for deaf children of deaf parents.

In general, then, it appears that world knowledge, as measured by various subscales of the WAIS Verbal Scale, and measures of English grammar are the highest predictors of literacy in deaf adolescents in total communication programs. At the time of testing, there were not enough deaf adolescents in public schools who had been educated through total communication since preschool to test. Therefore, generalizations should be made with caution. However, given the correlations reported, it seems reasonable to conclude that both top-down (e.g., world knowledge, vocabulary) and bottom-up skills (English syntax, English morphology) make substantial contributions to the development of literacy in deaf children and that both should be emphasized in schools.

Summary

Literacy consists of two highly interrelated components: reading and writing. Literacy itself is a subcomponent of a higher-order category that also includes direct person-to-person oral and manual communication. Traditionally, research on the reading and writing of deaf individuals has focused on areas of perceived weaknesses, especially grammar, and has concentrated on the word, phrase, or sentence level. More recent investigations suggest that the functional reading ability of deaf children is much higher than scores on standardized achievement tests suggest. When reading, deaf children and adults are able to employ their intact cognitive abilities and knowledge of the world to compensate for grammatical difficulties. In the area of writing, some recent developments suggest that approaches emphasizing function (meaning) over form (syntax) may be more beneficial.

Some clear trends in the development of literacy skills are emerging. A shift appears to be taking place from an elemental, step-by-step process toward more holistic, functional, semantic-based instruction. The final outcome may be a pragmatic blend of analytic and holistic techniques to develop literacy, somewhat akin to the interactive compensatory model advocated by Stanovich (1980).

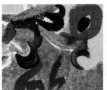

13

Elementary and Secondary Education

Introduction

Of all of the important changes and developments in elementary and secondary education for deaf children, the gradual absorption of deaf education within the framework of general education has had perhaps the most profound influence in recent years. Whether or not the change in focus has been positive or negative is debatable, but the impact is undeniable. As we learned in earlier parts of the text, the move toward attendance in local public schools has been going on since the end of World War II, and the mandates of the original Education of all Handicapped Children Act of 1975 and its evolution into the Individuals with Disabilities Education Act, which both emphasized the least restrictive environment, have been major factors. Now, every movement, controversy, and fad in general education has an impact on education of the deaf, ranging from competency testing for teachers and standards of learning for students, to changes in the teaching of math and reading, to technology in the classroom. These trends have major implications for teachers of the deaf. A growing number of our teachers are employed as itinerant teachers, traveling from school to school to provide services to children attending regular classes. There appears to be a smaller but similar growth in coteaching classrooms, where a teacher of the deaf and a general education teacher share a class of both deaf and hearing students. Charter schools for deaf children have been established in some metropolitan areas under the jurisdiction of public school districts, and more are projected to come into existence. The influence of general education is also felt in residential schools, which more and more are incorporating general education curricula, partly to accommodate children transferring in from local public schools and partly because of a consensus that the traditional curricular offerings in programs for the deaf have not been sufficiently challenging. In recognition of the changing roles of teachers of the deaf, the Council for Exceptional Children (CEC) and the Council on Education of the Deaf (CED) published a "Joint Knowledge and Skills Statement for All Becoming Teachers of Students Who Are Deaf or Hard of Hearing" (Joint Standards Committee, 1996). The goal was to create standards for the establishment and maintenance of credible teacher preparation programs; the publication also assumes that colleges and universities that train teachers of the deaf are committed to a full continuum of options for students.

A survey of administrators of 145 residential and local public school programs for deaf students by Lytle and Rovins (1997) illustrates the change in focus toward general education curricula and procedures. Ninety-six percent of the respondents believed that teachers of the deaf should be knowledgeable about the effective teaching strategies used with *hearing* students, 95 percent believed that they should have the same subject matter competency as teachers of hearing students, and 90 percent believed that teachers of the deaf should pass national teacher exams in reading, writing, and mathematics skills. I do not have similar data from early years, but I believe that this represents a fundamental shift in emphasis. Lytle and Rovins suggested that the findings represented a paradigm shift away from how to teach (such a the mode of communication) toward what to teach in the curriculum, with particular emphasis on upgrading the knowledge and skills of teachers of the deaf in content areas.

In 1986 Congress passed the Education of the Deaf Act (EDA), which has been reauthorized in ensuing years. The act addressed a number of issues, including the authorization of Gallaudet College to become Gallaudet University. Congressional concern over a lack of information on education of the deaf led to the inclusion in EDA of a mandate to establish the Commission on Education of the Deaf, which would examine the state of the field and submit recommendations to Congress. The commission was chaired by Dr. Frank Bowe.

The report of the commission (1988), "Toward Equality: Education of the Deaf," concluded that education of deaf individuals suffered from inappropriate priorities and inadequate resources. The report stated, "Parents, deaf consumers, and professional personnel of all persuasions have, with almost total unanimity, cited Least Restrictive Environment (LRE) as the issue that most thwarts their attempts to provide an appropriate education for children who are deaf" (p. x). The report itself contained a large number of recommendations. The issue of academic placement, with eight recommendations, represented the largest single topic. Those recommendations (pp. xvi–xvii) were as follows:

1. The Department of Education should provide guidelines and technical assistance to state and local educational agencies and parents to ensure that an individualized education program for a child who is deaf takes into consideration the following: severity of hearing loss and the potential for using residual hearing; academic level and learning style;

communicative needs and the preferred mode of communication; linguistic, cultural, social, and emotional needs; placement preference; individual motivation; and family support.

2. The Department of Education should refocus the least restrictive environment concept by emphasizing appropriateness over least restrictive environment.

3. The Department of Education should issue a policy statement to permit consideration in placement decisions of curriculum content and methods of curricular delivery required by the nature or severity of the child's handicapping conditions.

4. The Department of Education should issue guidelines and standards by which school officials and parents can, in selecting the least restrictive environment, consider potential harmful effects on the child or on the quality of services the child needs.

5. The Department of Education should publish in the *Federal Register* a policy interpretation that removal from the regular classroom does not require compelling evidence.

6. The Department of Education should monitor states to ensure that they maintain and nurture center schools (day or residential schools with only deaf students) as placement options as required by law.

7. The Department of Education should monitor states to ensure the availability and appropriateness of integrative programs for students in center schools.

8. The Department of Education should issue a policy statement requiring that school personnel inform parents of all options in the continuum of alternative placements during each individualized education program conference.

In their entirety, the recommendations of the commission challenge the philosophical premise that LRE is the "core value" of special education. DuBow (1989) has argued that the U.S. Department of Education, with its primary emphasis on LRE, turned a congressional preference into a requirement and that the emphasis is contrary to both legislative intent and judicial interpretations of EDA. The commission's report emphasized appropriateness over LRE, expressed support for center schools, demanded individualized educational programs, and argued that removal from the regular classroom should *not* require compelling evidence. All of this implies a refocus of the least restrictive environment concept.

It appears, then, that the issue of educational placement has taken on paramount importance in the field and has supplanted communication modes as the primary area of contention. Throughout much of this chapter, we will examine placement from several angles. First, we will consider the results of a unique study conducted in the 1920s. Then we will examine the impact of general education on the field.

An Early Survey

Until the 1970s, only one comprehensive in situ (on site) study of school placement had ever been conducted. *A Survey of American Schools for the Deaf: 1924–25* (Day, Fusfeld, and Pinter, 1928) analyzed the governance structure, physical facilities, teacher background, student characteristics, and student achievement scores of twenty-nine public residential schools for the deaf and thirteen public day schools. The survey demonstrated that in the first quarter of the twentieth century children in day and residential schools differed so widely in demographic characteristics that it was difficult to compare the relative effectiveness of different programs. Several more recent studies have reached the same conclusion.

In the residential schools, one-quarter of the academic teachers and more than half of the industrial teachers were deaf. Males made up one-quarter of the academic teachers and almost one-half of the industrial teachers. In the public day schools, the teaching staff "consisted practically entirely of women" (Day et al., 1928, p. 17), and there was not one deaf teacher in the thirteen schools.

The day schools tended to have hard-of-hearing students and more students with late onset of hearing loss. Average loss was reported at 65 to 70 percent, with 43 percent of students having acquired their hearing loss after age two. Average hearing loss for residential school students was 75 to 80 percent, with 25 percent having experienced the loss after age two. Day students had higher IQ scores and higher academic achievement. They also began school at earlier ages.

The day school children were representative of immigration into large cities; 70 percent had at least one foreign-born parent, and for 57 percent both parents were foreign born. Thirty percent of the residential students had at least one foreign-born parent. A language other than English was spoken in the homes of one-third of the day students, with Yiddish (12.4 percent) and Italian (12.1 percent) being the most common. In fewer than 19 percent of homes of residential school students, a language other than English was spoken, with Italian (5.3 percent) and Yiddish (2.9 percent) again being the most common. The residential schools also represented a multicultural population with significant numbers of children whose parents were born outside of the United States, although not as many as in the day school population.

Modes of instruction also differed. In day schools, 97 percent of the children were taught through oral-only instruction. Only one school allowed manual communication with any students. The residential schools were more variable; 38 percent of students were taught using some form of manual communication, and 62 percent received oral-only instruction. Generally, students started off in oral-only classes. At a specified age, those children classified as "oral failures" were reassigned to either manual-only instruction or combined oral-manual instruction. We may think of manual-only instruction in terms of ASL and combined oral-manual instruction as being similar to simultaneous speech and an English-based sign system. Some residential schools with large numbers of hard-of-hearing children also had "auricular" classes that concentrated on the use of residual hearing.

There was one other significant difference between the two types of settings. The residential schools clearly functioned *in loco parentis*. All twenty-nine schools had courses in moral training, and twenty-six had Sunday school classes taught by teachers, usually male. The day schools left religious and moral issues to the families. Only four had moral or ethical training courses, and religious training and attendance were considered to be family matters.

A quick review of the tables in Chapter 1 allows us to make some comparisons between 1925 and the present. Children in today's programs for deaf students tend to have greater hearing losses and a much smaller number of students who became deaf after age two than the earlier programs. Although the teaching staffs still tend to be predominantly female and hearing, the day schools have both deaf teachers and male teachers. Readers who believe multiculturalism is a recent development may be surprised to learn that a larger percentage of deaf students had foreign-born parents in 1925 than is the case today, but we have always been a nation of immigrants and children of immigrants.

The two greatest differences between 1925 and the present concern communication and placement. Undeniably, signs are used much more extensively in both settings today. It would no doubt shock day school teachers of the 1920s to learn that a majority of students today use some kind of sign communication. Even more shocking would be the fact that today's residential schools and day schools for deaf children combined account for a minority of enrollment in programs for deaf students. Many of the day schools have been closed and children dispersed throughout the cities. Relatively few residential schools have been closed, but many have been substantially reduced and function much less in place of parents. The situation today is much more complicated, and it is imperative that we try to understand it if we are to serve children effectively.

Equity and Excellence

Two somewhat incompatible themes have permeated U.S. education for more than 150 years. Simply put, the conflict may be viewed as equity versus excellence. A powerful force in American life has been the push for equality of opportunity. An equally powerful force has been the belief that outstanding achievement should be highly rewarded. The terms *equity* and *excellence* are constantly being redefined and mean different things to different people.

Prior to the Industrial Revolution, relatively little attention was paid to education in the United States (Alden, 1984). There was no American university in the eighteenth century, and only eight small colleges existed: three in New England (Harvard, Yale, Brown), four in the Mid-Atlantic area (Columbia, Princeton, Rutgers, Pennsylvania), and one in the South (William and Mary). Most of these schools had religious affiliations, and no academic admission standards existed. Admission was to an economic and social, not an intellectual, elite. As Chapter 1 noted, the greatest push to extend education to a broader segment of the population came from the demands of the Industrial Revolution for a literate, skilled mass of workers. Public education first emerged in New England in the early part of the nineteenth century and eventually spread to other parts of the country. Successive waves of immigration throughout the nineteenth century and into the twentieth century caused politicians and educators to look at the public schools as a means of educating and

"Americanizing" the newcomers, especially those with different religious, cultural, and linguistic backgrounds. These ideas tied in with both Jefferson's concept of an informed citizenry and Mann's goals of education and enculturation. Gradually, education came to be accepted as a right of all and not a privilege intended for only a few. Some of the more basic issues involved in equality of access to education were not resolved until the second half of the twentieth century. For example, the practice of educational segregation by race was long upheld by the argument that education for blacks was "separate but equal." Racial segregation in education was discontinued only when the system proved to be inherently unequal. An even more recent development was the passage of PL94–142, which guarantees access to a free, appropriate public education to all children with disabilities.

The benefits of education have gradually been made available to more and more Americans, and today a free public education is available to all. This means that equity of access is guaranteed; it does not imply that equity of opportunity exists. We will return to this point shortly.

The case for excellence in American education is much more difficult to make, especially historically. If we think of excellence in terms of educating an elite, we can identify two distinct movements, one related to private school education and one to public school education.

Throughout most of their history, private colleges drew their student bodies primarily from among graduates of private preparatory schools for men. Although they always had distinguished faculty members, the colleges frequently had anti-intellectual atmospheres, and the formal and informal quotas based on religious affiliation, race, and ethnic status discriminated against capable students. Today entrance into prestigious private colleges and universities in America is highly competitive. After allowing for a healthy mix of left tackles, forwards, tuba players, and children of alumni, these institutions may be said to accept and train an intellectual elite, whereas in the past many of them trained a social elite.

In the public schools, a system of tracking and of special junior and senior high schools has been used to separate out and educate children with high academic potential. This approach, which was always more common in the eastern part of the country, continues to exist in some school systems today. Tracking implies that at some point in their school careers (usually by the end of elementary school) children are assigned to a type of educational training. For example, the choice may be among vocational, business, general, or academic tracks. In some districts, students must apply to special schools and pass their entrance exams; well-known examples are the Boston Latin School and the Bronx High School of Science.

To some extent, the different concepts of equity and excellence represent different world views, and thus conflict is inevitable. Those people concerned primarily with equity have addressed access to educational services and not necessarily outcomes. Over the twenty-five-year period from 1960 to 1985, the advocates of equity were quite successful. Since then the emphasis has changed. Critics argued that improvements were made at the expense of quality; hence the present emphasis on academic achievement. The question to be decided over the next generation is the extent to which the term *excellence* will be applied to an identifiable group of students who might be considered an elite and the extent to which there will be a commitment to excellence in education in general. The resolution of this question will have profound implications for education of the deaf.

Strike (1985) maintained that the perceived conflict between the pursuit of equity and the pursuit of excellence is related to a fundamental conflict between the economic and political goals of education. Strike argued that there is a tendency to view excellence in relation to the performances of others, including the economic performances of nations. Such a definition of excellence may be considered norm-referenced, because one person's or nation's performance is evaluated by comparing it to those of others rather than to a particular standard. In Strike's view, this concept of excellence is presented in reports such as *A Nation at Risk* by the National Commission on Excellence in Education (1983), in which economic competitiveness with other nations is the issue. Strike believed that such a view leads to the perception of excellence versus equity as a problem of resource management and causes the issue to be stated misleadingly in questions such as the following: "Shall we spend our educational dollars on the education of the poor or on our future scientists and engineers?" (p. 402). This view regards individuals as "human capital," reducing them to a resource to be used to make a nation as competitive as possible. Those considered to be unable to make a contribution to strengthening our competitive position are regarded as being less important and hence receive fewer resources.

Strike proposed that we should frame our concepts of excellence more in terms of the Jeffersonian ideal, which he saw as more political than economic. He characterized excellence this way: "Here the purpose is to achieve a relatively wide, indeed, if possible, a universal, distribution of those skills that provide for full and meaningful participation in the political institutions of a democratic society" (p. 411). Strike obviously did not limit his definition of excellence to a select few. He stated:

> . . . if excellence is "criterion-referenced"—if it is defined in relation to a standard that is formulated independently of others' performance—then it is, in principle, achievable by everyone, and people are not in competition for it. It does not follow, of course, that everyone can or will achieve excellence. Indeed, it is possible to set standards sufficiently high so that only a very few can be excellent. Nevertheless, here the fact that not everyone can be excellent is a point of fact, not a point of logic. More importantly, being excellent is a matter of achieving at a given level of proficiency, not of doing better than others. (p. 110)

In this chapter, we will think of excellence and equity as compatible goals of education and will operate under the belief that excellence is attainable by most students, hearing and deaf. Given the basic premise of this book that deaf children are normal, it follows that much of the research on the academic achievement of hearing children can be generalized to deaf children if allowances are made for differences in experiences and in modes of communication.

The Influence of Regular Education

In the early 1970s, for the first time in history, more deaf children were enrolled in local public school programs than in residential schools. Since then, the number of deaf children enrolled in residential schools has dropped from one out of every two to about one in every five. Inevitably, general education has come to exert a profound and growing influence on education of deaf children. This influence has been both beneficial and detrimental. Perhaps the best example of a positive effect has been the continuing emphasis on improving academic achievement and maintaining academic standards on a worldwide level. Every decision by a state or local education agency to introduce a longer school day, an expanded school year, additional academic course work requirements for promotion and graduation, districtwide or statewide testing, evaluation of teacher competency, or foreign language requirements is of immediate concern to public school programs for deaf children. These decisions also have an indirect impact on residential schools for deaf children, where demographics have been changing. Many schools now enroll a high proportion of students of junior and senior high school age who attend local public school programs through the elementary school years and then transfer to residential schools. These schools must structure their educational programs to accommodate the needs of children transferring in. Although the changes may be less immediate in residential schools than in public school programs, they are nonetheless substantial.

The situation today is far different from that of the late 1950s, when the cycle of American education brought a similar press for academic achievement. The launch of the Soviet *Sputnik* fueled the concern that the United States was falling behind its foreign competitors in technology. The response was a surge in emphasis at the federal, state, and local levels on expanding the quality and quantity of training in the hard sciences. Funded by federal monies, new curricula were developed in subject matter such as physics and chemistry, and course requirements were upgraded. This push had little or no discernible influence on residential schools for deaf children, where the majority of deaf children were educated, or on training programs for teachers of deaf students. In the residential schools, few of which were subject to state education requirements, the emphasis continued to be on the traditional mainstays of education of the deaf: speech, speech reading, and English grammar.

The public school influence has a negative side as well. Being a low-incidence condition with very special implications for the use of spoken language, deafness is a mystery to most hearing people. One deaf child in a school with one thousand hearing children may get lost in the shuffle. In fact, thirty deaf children from a widely dispersed geographic area in five classes for deaf students may get overlooked in a school with one thousand children from a relatively small neighborhood.

Perhaps of greater concern, but less obvious, is the existence of much greater diversity among deaf children in local public school programs than in residential schools. There is also greater diversity among deaf children than among hearing children in public schools. First, we will look at the residential/public differences. Then we will examine the different experiences of deaf and hearing students within local public schools. Finally, we will consider issues of academic placement and implications for academic achievement and socialization.

Prior to 1965, essentially two separate systems of educating deaf children existed in the United States: a nationwide system of residential schools that were mostly state supported and that included a regional, racially segregated system of residential schools for African-American children in the southern and some midwestern states; and day schools for deaf children in large cities serving first- and second-generation American children and/or poor children. Both systems were oppressive, including the residential schools. This statement may come as a shock to some readers who have read that residential schools of the past were the core of Deaf culture. That is true, but the culture developed in spite of, not because of, the prevailing attitudes. With the exception of a few private schools, the residential schools were quite similar. Classes were oral-only, at least up to age twelve. The curriculum was interchangeable: the Yale or Northampton Charts for speech, the Fitzgerald Key for grammar, and little attention to academic subjects prior to junior high school age. Deaf teachers, predominantly Gallaudet graduates and themselves products of residential schools, were restricted to vocational training and teaching older children. The influence of education in general was minimal. Reference points were other residential schools for deaf children, and interaction was maintained through regional athletic competitions and nationwide associations of teachers and educators who were predominantly from residential schools for the deaf. The *American Annals of the Deaf* was a major source for dissemination of information within this system.

It would be an overstatement to refer to the collection of residential schools for deaf African-American children as a system, since their operation was hardly systematic. These schools were underfunded and understaffed and typically were administered by the superintendent of the school for white deaf children in the state. Because Gallaudet did not accept African-American students until the 1950s, there was no core of educated deaf African-American teachers to provide role models and cultural leadership. Because of segregation and discrimination in general, very few hearing African-American teachers had been trained as teachers of deaf students. In some states, perhaps as few as one-third of all deaf African-American children had any education at all. Very little was written about these schools, and what is known about them may be lost as former teachers and students grow older. Some enterprising scholars could provide invaluable information by interviewing as many of these individuals as possible in the near future.

The contrast between the official descriptions of the segregated schools and programs for African-American deaf children and the reality of the experiences of the deaf children in those schools is stark. For example, in Chapter 3 we presented information from a book by Mary Herring Wright (1999) about her experiences attending a segregated state school for deaf children and the anger and depression felt by the African-American children over what Wright called the "unbelievable differences between her school and the school for white children" (p. 179). Contrast her experience with the official history of the North Carolina Institution for the Deaf and the Dumb and the Blind. Goodwin (1893, p. 6) wrote: "The institution for the colored is a commodious, well-arranged building, more suitable for its purpose than the buildings for the white department. The Colored department is under the same general management as the white department and enjoys the same care and privileges." It is possible that Goodwin deluded himself and really believed that the Colored department received the same care and privilege. It is also possible that he was lying.

The day schools for deaf children provided another model. Located in large cities, they served an urban population of students who commuted to the school from throughout the city. The schools were oppressive in that none allowed signs in the classroom. Because students commuted, they had no opportunity to learn ASL in dormitories. Also, because the schools hired no deaf teachers, students had no exposure to deaf adults or Deaf culture. As part of a city school system, each day school for deaf students was oriented toward local educational models, and, except for the AG Bell Association, little collaboration or communication existed on a national basis.

At the present time, the differences between residential school and local public school programs remain significant. The curricula of residential schools throughout the country tend to be similar. Most schools have a core group of fluent signers, both hearing and deaf. Contact with other residential schools for deaf students occurs by means of social events and athletic competition. Residential school staff and administrators constitute majorities in the Convention of American Instructors of the Deaf (CAID) and the Conference of Educational Administrators of Schools and Programs Serving the Deaf. Local public school programs present a different picture. Students live within commuting distance of the schools, but the trip may still be time consuming. Local and state priorities have more importance, leading to greater diversity. There is somewhat more commitment to state associations such as the California Association of Teachers of the Deaf and Hearing and similar organizations in states across the country that hold their own annual conventions. The local public school programs tend to have fewer fluent signers and fewer deaf teachers and administrators, although the situation is improving.

Finally, the differences among public school programs are incredible. They reflect not only state and regional differences but also great discrepancies within states. It is common to find large-city programs for deaf children with inadequate facilities, inappropriate curricula, and few or no options for placement or mode of communication. All too often, programs in affluent suburbs with up-to-date facilities, placement options from complete integration to self-contained classes, oral and sign options, well-trained interpreters, and a complete program of after-class activities exist just a few miles away.

In the next section, we will continue to examine issues of academic placement.

Educational Programs for Deaf Children

Chapter 1 and the preceding section in this chapter briefly discussed school placement alternatives and patterns in school placement. This section provides more information about the different educational settings and the children they serve. Much of the information was acquired in the process of establishing networks of research on residential and public school programs throughout the United States.

We have stressed several themes in this text. Among them is the variation in educational programs across the United States due to the concept of local and state control of education. Further differences in communication modes of instruction and educational placement options have increased this variation in programs for deaf students. Although PL94–142 and subsequent legislation have been important, each state has its own set of unique laws and regulations governing education of the deaf. In fact, as Chapter 1 pointed out, the defining of *deaf* and *hard of hearing* is not consistent. The variation is evident in patterns of education in California, New York, and Texas. Not only is each state as large as a moderate-size nation, but the differences in the ways deaf children are educated might be said to reflect different countries.

Publicly Supported Residential Schools

The term *publicly supported school* is more precise than *public school,* because the line between public and private residential schools for deaf students is hazy in some northeastern states. Historically, many publicly supported schools functioned autonomously even though they received state support in the form of tuition payments. Today they function as part of public state systems of education and thus will be included under the term *public residential school.*

As we have noted, education is primarily a state and local responsibility in the United States, and great diversity exists. Each state has its own set of unique laws and regulations regarding education of the deaf. Again, let us consider California and New York, two of the most populous states in the country. As of 1999, California had approximately 6,700 children in programs for deaf and hard-of-hearing students, of whom 1,000 (15 percent) attended the two state-supported residential schools. New York State had 4,200, with 1,000 (almost 25 percent) in six state-supported residential schools (*American Annals of the Deaf,* 2000). We might expect California, with its much larger geographic area, to have more children in residential schools, but for historical reasons this is not the case. Western states tend to have fewer residential schools than northeastern ones. However, the two schools in California each enroll five hundred or more children. In New York, only one school had more than 165 students, the Lexington School for the Deaf (389 students).

California and New York, with the two largest cities in the United States, have the two largest public school programs in the country. New York City public schools, with almost 2,300 children, have more than half of the state enrollment in programs for deaf and hard-of-hearing children. Los Angeles, with 2,500 children, has more than one-third of children in such programs. In Texas, by comparison, only Dallas (305) and Houston (360) enroll more than 200 deaf and hard-of-hearing children in public school programs. In the more sparsely populated states, there can be even greater variation in service provision. As we briefly discuss "prototypical" settings, bear the variation in mind.

Keeping in mind the diversity in real-world schools, for purposes of comparison let us consider the characteristics of the prototypical residential school for deaf students in the United States. It enrolls 150 to 200 deaf students from preschool through high school. It has an outreach program on a day basis for children who live within commuting distance. At the elementary and secondary levels, all students living within a thirty-mile radius of the school (approximately 40 percent of the school population) commute daily. A majority of elementary students commute. Enrollment is higher at the secondary level than at the elementary level because of an influx of students from public school programs. The secondary-level student population, which comes from a wider geographic area than does the elementary-level population, is predominantly residential.

In the residential schools, there is a common perception that the public day schools are not doing their job. This perception stems in large part from the fact that many students transferring into residential schools tell "horror stories" of alienation, lack of communication, and rejection. All too often these stories are true, but they do not reflect the complete situation. Although many local school programs, especially those with small to moderate-size populations, do not offer appropriate services and some have exhibited shocking neglect, these programs fortunately are in the minority. Also, in some states public school programs may refer lower-achieving or difficult-to-manage students to the residential schools. As a result, some residential schools receive a disproportionate number of children who have encountered difficulties in public day programs and have had little contact with students who have experienced success.

The prototypical residential school endorses a system of total communication, which entails the use of speech and a manual code based on English. Growing numbers are also using ASL. Prior to 1975, instruction was oral through the elementary grades; simultaneous sign and speech was used only in the high school, and deaf teachers were restricted to the secondary level. Today some deaf teachers work in the elementary program, but they are still rarely involved in preschool. The teachers believe education has improved in the school since the introduction of total communication, but they are not sure the improvement would show up in achievement scores because their school now enrolls more students with multiple disabilities and fewer highly talented students.

Approximately one-half of superintendents of schools for deaf children are themselves deaf or hard of hearing. This is a tremendous change. As recently as the late 1960s, not one superintendent was deaf.

The school offers a full range of athletic opportunities for boys and girls; students compete with teams from small schools for hearing students. The student population is less cohesive than it was twenty years ago, because most elementary students go home every day and many high school students have recently transferred in from public schools. Although the signing system the students use among themselves clearly differs from that used in the classroom, the disparity is less significant than it was when the school employed the oral method for students up to age twelve. The English-based signing system used by hearing preschool and elementary teachers, some parents, and transfer students from public day schools is having an impact on the signing students use out of class. Although the implications for the future of the Deaf community of English-based signing, students who live at home, and students who transfer in from day programs are not clear, they are a cause of concern among some of the teachers, both deaf and hearing.

Support services at this school are excellent. There are trained, full-time audio-logical, counseling, and psychological personnel, and the school works with the state's department of vocational rehabilitation to plan for the students' transition to work, training, or postsecondary education. Students with the highest academic achievement are counseled to apply for admission to Gallaudet University or to the National Technical Institute for the Deaf (NTID).

Day Programs

The diversity found in residential schools is not nearly as great as that encountered in public day class programs. In general, three major types of public day class programs may be identified: metropolitan programs, suburban programs, and programs serving moderately or sparsely populated areas.

Metropolitan Programs.   Based in large cities, metropolitan programs have early intervention/preschool, elementary, and secondary programs. Typically, most deaf children in these programs are of "minority" status, suggesting that the term *minority* is rapidly becoming a misnomer. For example, Hispanics constitute the majority in the San Antonio program for deaf students; blacks are the majority in Philadelphia; and Hispanics, blacks, and Anglos are approximately equally represented in the Boston public school program. As in the case of residential schools, no comments about a prototypical metropolitan program for deaf students will apply to all programs.

The prototypical day class program follows a total communication philosophy, having made the change from oral-only education in 1977. The early intervention program has a home visitation component; teachers go into the home to work with parents. After age three, children are bussed into a nursery program three days a week.

The elementary-level deaf children are bussed to three different elementary schools across the city. Each school has a hearing student population of about six hundred and has from four to eight classes for deaf children. About 35 percent of the deaf students are integrated with hearing students for one or more classes, sometimes with manual sign language interpreters.

Because of the need for a greater concentration of support services and subject matter specialists, the high school program for deaf students is located in one school near a freeway, to which all students are bussed. The high school enrollment is smaller than the elementary enrollment because some of the more academically able students are integrated into their neighborhood schools, others drop out, and others transfer to residential schools.

Support services are concentrated at the high school; the elementary programs are served more by part-time personnel. The program has recently begun hiring deaf teachers, but as of now they employ relatively few. There is concern that some students spend too much time on the bus and have restricted social lives. The program has just established an affiliation with the Junior National Association of the Deaf.

Accompanied by manual interpreters, approximately 45 percent of the high school students in the prototypical day class program are integrated with hearing students for one or more academic classes, most commonly math. The regular classroom teachers are enthusiastic about the performance of the deaf students. All school assemblies are interpreted, and there is discussion about offering sign language for credit to hearing students. The more academically able students are counseled to apply to NTID and to Gallaudet; local and regional vocational/technical programs for deaf individuals are recommended to others.

Suburban Programs.   The suburban programs are much more homogeneous than the residential schools and metropolitan programs, probably because suburbs across the United States have much in common. Therefore, we can generalize more about these programs than about others. First, there is usually an intensive infant/early education program. Children with hearing losses are identified and fitted with appropriate hearing aids, and training is initiated at an early age. Under the auspices of the infant program, professionals go into the home and offer suggestions; children and their mothers are also invited to attend a school with a simulated home environment for training. These programs typically offer instruction through both oral-only and total communication modes. Parents are given recommendations, but the decision as to mode of instruction ultimately rests with the parents. Throughout the elementary and secondary school years, the emphasis is on flexibility and individualization of instruction. In addition to a choice between oral and total communication classes, parents are given placement options, including self-contained classes, partial integration, and full-time integration with the services of an itinerant teacher and interpreter, if needed. Usually, the parents in these situations are sophisticated, know their rights, and get the type of communication, placement, and support they want. Some teachers think the administration is too accommodating and should present its professional opinion more forcefully to parents, but these teachers are a minority.

The self-contained classes tend to enroll a relatively small portion of the students in the program because the extent and quality of individual support services enable many children to attend neighborhood schools. School achievement is relatively high, as it is among hearing children in the district. Large numbers of the deaf students are expected to attend college. In addition to those at Gallaudet and NTID, parents may investigate services at state universities and private colleges. As we might expect, support services are usually good. Teachers, psychologists, audiologists, counselors, interpreters, and therapists tend to be well trained and present in sufficient numbers.

Programs in Moderately or Sparsely Populated Areas.   Programs in less populated areas often face unique problems. Because of the low incidence of deafness, they frequently lack the critical mass of students needed to ensure proper grade-level placement. Often a shortage of qualified personnel exists. Because of low population density and the need to provide services to a wide geographic area, transportation may be a problem in terms of time and the costs of gas, drivers, and vehicles.

The prototypical rural program primarily enrolls children through the elementary grades, serving a total of thirty children in three schools distributed across two counties. One school has twenty students and three teachers; the other two have six and four students, respectively, each with one teacher. In the latter two schools, each teacher has students of different grades in a resource room, and the students are integrated into age-appropriate classes part time. Of the thirty students, some of the younger ones have profound hearing losses but most have losses in the moderate-to-severe range. Children with profound losses are usually referred to a residential school before completion of the elementary years. At the high school level, there are no teachers of deaf children. Students still in the program may receive therapy from a speech/language therapist. Professional support services are provided by the regular school staff.

Itinerant Teachers.   Itinerant teachers may be employed in large cities, suburban programs, or rural areas, each of which has different demands. However, all itinerant teachers have common experiences. Yarger and Luckner (1999) reported that itinerant teachers in the course of a week often work with students of all ages from preschool to high school; they have little influence over what will be taught in the regular classroom; and they do not have their own classrooms and may have to work in inadequate locations such as hallways, gyms, libraries, closets, and lunchrooms. Furthermore the very nature of itinerant teaching—that is, traveling between schools, cities, towns, and districts in order to provide services—is isolating, and often the teacher feels distanced from other professionals. On the positive side are variety, autonomy, time for reflection, and a diversity of students to work with. Yarger and Luckner concluded that it was critical that itinerant teachers understand the opportunity they have to empower others to make an impact on the education of deaf students. This, of course, is different from the traditional role of teachers of the deaf, and the authors emphasized that our teacher preparation programs must train personnel for the growing number of itinerant teaching jobs.

Coteaching Classrooms.   "Coteaching" refers to cooperative efforts of two or more teachers to coordinate their instruction in classroom settings. The procedure has been around for years and has gone under different names. The first time I observed it with mixed classes of deaf and hearing children was in St. Paul, Minnesota, in the 1970s, when it was referred to as team teaching.

At present, little is known about the effectiveness of coteaching classes involving deaf and hearing children, but two studies should be mentioned. Luckner (1999) studied two coteaching classrooms. One enrolled eighteen hearing and four deaf students in grades one to two, and the other enrolled twenty-five hearing students and eight deaf students in grades two to four. Every student, teacher, parent, and administrator who was interviewed expressed positive feelings about the coteaching model. Benefits included (a) high expectations and exposure to content, (b) opportunities for social interaction, (c) availability of language and speech models, (d) the opportunity for hearing students to learn sign, and (e) the sense of shared responsibility and collegial support. Several concerns were also raised. It was reported that coteaching was quite time consuming, that it increased work demands, and that it could be difficult and stressful. Strong interpersonal communication skills and a willingness to change teaching styles are required.

Kluwin (1999) investigated the social integration of deaf children who had been in coteaching situations. He reported that there were no negative social consequences of coteaching for deaf students, and suggested that coteaching may alleviate some of the feelings of social isolation encountered by some deaf students in integrated environments. Consistent with Luckner, Kluwin noted that coteaching situations required increased planning time.

Academic Achievement

As in other areas, the academic problems of deaf children have been documented much more extensively than those of hard-of-hearing children. In general, deaf children of normal intelligence suffer from severe academic retardation caused primarily by difficulties in understanding and expressing standard English. Achievement, then, tends to be highest in the areas that rely relatively little on English skills and lowest in areas that depend heavily on English. Thus, in typical achievement test batteries, scores on subtests like arithmetic computation, spelling, and punctuation are relatively high. On the other hand, scores on subtests requiring proficiency in English (e.g., reading comprehension, science, and word meaning) are relatively low.

Although arithmetic computation scores are high relative to scores on paragraph meaning, they are far below what they should be. An average seventeen-year-old should achieve at the twelfth-grade level. Thus deaf and hard-of-hearing seventeen-year-olds are up to eight years behind in reading and five years behind in math.

Although academic achievement is low compared to hearing standards, there are some indications of improvement over time. Norms for deaf and hearing children were developed on the sixth edition of the Stanford Achievement Test in 1974, on the seventh edition in 1983, and on the eighth edition in 1990 (Holt, Traxler, and Allen, 1992). Achievement on the average seems to peak around the fourth-grade level in reading comprehension and the seventh-grade level in math computation. As previously noted, achievement levels of deaf and hard-of-hearing children in 1990 appear to have been higher than those in 1983, which in turn were higher than those in 1974. A ten-year-old was roughly at the same level of achievement in 1990 as a twelve-year-old in 1974. Despite tremendous and continuing problems, improvements have been made.

As we might expect, patterns of achievement have varied. Holt (1993) reported median reading comprehension grade-equivalent scores at age seventeen of 3.8 for children with profound hearing losses, 4.5 for those with severe losses, and 5.4 for those with less than severe losses. In terms of ethnicity, white deaf and hard-of-hearing children had median reading comprehension grade equivalents of 5.4 at age seventeen, and black children's scores at age eighteen (grade 3.6) were higher than at seventeen. In terms of school placement, seventeen-year-old children in local, integrated settings read at grade 5.7 compared to 3.8 in day and residential school settings and 2.8 in local, nonintegrated settings. Holt et al. reported that differences could not be attributed to placement per se because a majority of these children had less than severe hearing losses and tended to come from families of higher socioeconomic status.

Educational Programs and Academic Placement

Debate over educational placement—which began almost two generations ago, well before the passage of PL94–142—has surpassed the "method war" as the major conflict in education of the deaf. Various terms, such as *integration, mainstreaming, least restrictive environment (LRE), regular education initiative, inclusion,* and *zero-reject models,* have been used with a variety of meanings, but overall they indicate a movement toward educating children with disabilities alongside nondisabled children to the greatest extent possible. Many educators of deaf children, including this author, have taken strong exception to the implication that the least restrictive environment for a deaf child is placement with hearing children, interpreting this position as reflecting a pathological view of deafness and ignoring the need for individually developed educational plans.

Reporting in 1975, the year of the enactment of Public Law 94–142, Jensema compared the academic achievement of deaf and hard-of-hearing children in three general settings: integrated with itinerant services, residential placement, and resource rooms and self-contained classes in public schools. He found that children in itinerant settings achieved highest on the average, followed by those in resource rooms and self-contained classes, and finally children in residential schools. However, as we might expect from the data presented in Chapter 1, the groups exhibited differences in terms of degree of hearing loss, age of onset, number of additional conditions, presence of mental retardation, and ethnicity. When Jensema statistically accounted for the difference among groups, he found no differences in achievement. The implication was that school placement per se had little or no effect on academic achievement. Allen and Osborne (1984) examined demographic and achievement data for 1,465 deaf and hearing students and found higher achievement among children in integrated settings. They reported that student ability was the major factor in achievement, but integration did have a positive effect.

In a text on effective public school programs for deaf students, Kluwin (1992) presents a "vision of a complex and fractured field." He continues:

> The question seems to have become, "Does mainstreaming work?" This book answers that the question itself is too simplistic. Programs are varied; students are selected for placement for specific reasons; success can be defined in a variety of ways and can occur in supposedly competing environments. The answer, from this book, is, "It depends." (p. 5)

Of course, the same answer might apply to the questions "Do residential schools work?" and "Do day schools work?" In 1982 Moores, Kluwin, and colleagues began a program of research that would expand the knowledge of the field to include public school programs and integrate it with ongoing research on residential schools. Work began with large urban programs for deaf students in Boston, Dallas, Philadelphia, and San Antonio and expanded over the years to include more than forty residential schools and urban, suburban, county, and regional programs. Much of the information presented here was developed in that program of research. For more complete details, the reader is referred to Kluwin, Moores, and Gaustad (1992) and Kluwin and Stinson (1993).

Kluwin, Moores, and Gaustad (1992) investigated communication of 260 deaf adolescents in twelve schools across the United States. Ninety-four percent of the respondents were categorized into the following four groups: 10.4 percent spoke orally with both deaf and hearing students, 35.8 percent spoke orally with hearing students and signed with deaf students, 30.45 percent signed to both deaf and hearing students, and 16.9 percent reported no communication with hearing students and signing with deaf friends. The responses represented a good amount of diversity. Placement (integrated, resource room, self-contained classes) apparently was a bigger factor than speech skills alone. Also, a substantial number of hearing students appeared to be motivated to learn at least some signs. Interestingly, there were important differences among programs. Communication was greater in programs that had sign language instruction and encouraged its use by hearing students.

Moores, Kluwin, and Mertens (1985) reported that deaf students in these programs who attended regular math class accompanied by sign interpreters showed greater gains in achievement than did similar students in the same schools who were in self-contained math classes for deaf students. This was not a comparison of day versus residential programs but a comparison of achievement of public school children in integrated versus self-contained classes. Further analysis (Kluwin and Moores, 1985) suggested that the differences were related not to class placement per se but to instructional variables. In the integrated classes, there was a higher level of expectation as well as more exposure to a greater quantity of demanding material. Also, the regular classroom teachers were content area specialists; everyone interviewed had at least a master's degree in mathematics or mathematics education. Not one teacher of deaf students who taught math in self-contained classes in the same school had received special training in mathematics or mathematics education. Kluwin and Moores (1985) concluded:

> The prerequisites for success, then, do not appear to be limited to an integrated versus a self contained classroom or to a day versus a residential setting. The major components appear to be teachers trained in academic content areas, high expectations, presentation of large amounts of content, individual attention, and assignment and monitoring of relevant homework. All of these components can be provided in self-contained public school classrooms and in residential settings. Honors programs and demanding homework should be part of all programs, not only for integrated

children. If we are to maximize academic achievement of deaf children in all settings, we must supply them with the best possible learning environment within each setting. (p. 159)

Kluwin and Moores (1989) followed up with a process-product study of seventy classrooms to investigate the influence of placement on mathematics computation and mathematics concepts. After accounting for race, gender, and prior ability, they reported that academic placement was not a factor. Individual child characteristics and the quality of instruction were far more important. Higher achievement was related to the level of content covered, regardless of placement.

Kluwin and Stinson (1993) reported on a longitudinal study of 451 deaf students from grades nine through twelve in fifteen public school programs for deaf students. Forty-nine percent of the sample was white, 27 percent black, 17 percent Hispanic, and 7 percent Asian. English was the primary language in 75 percent of the homes, Spanish in 15 percent, an Asian language in 6 percent, and ASL in 4 percent. It is interesting to note that a non-English home language was more common among deaf children in city day schools in the 1920s (Day, Fusfeld, and Pintner, 1928), with Italian and Yiddish predominating, than in the Kluwin and Stinson study.

Kluwin and Stinson reported that 57 percent of the parents were currently married, and in 43 percent of the cases the child lived with a divorced, separated, widowed, or never-married parent. Socially, 16 percent of the deaf students reported that they associated primarily with hearing students, 29 percent associated mainly with deaf students, and 41 percent associated mostly with both deaf and hearing students. The remainder had few friends, either hearing or deaf.

Academically, group differences existed but the results were not straightforward. For example, white students tended to have higher achievement levels and Hispanic groups lower achievement levels than other groups, but the differences were due largely to income level and other family variables. Social class was also a factor in achievement, but interacted in complex ways with other variables. There was one instance of a change in relative achievement. On the average, girls achieved higher than boys in ninth grade but lower in twelfth grade, a finding similar to those reported in general education.

In a later analysis of the data, Kluwin (1994) stated that the concept of race in relation to education of deaf students is ambiguous and needs to be considered in light of other factors. He argued for the removal of institutionalized bigotry and concluded that "while race is a nebulous construct in educational research, racism is a fact in American society" (p. 470).

Moores (Moores, 1990a; 1995b) provided information on seven residential schools, seventeen large local public school programs, and four small (thirty students or fewer) public school programs for deaf students. Information was gathered on 1,059 students, 660 families, 213 teachers, and 71 interpreters. Consistent with previously reported research, children in residential schools tended to have greater hearing losses. Also, only 2 percent of parents of children in local public schools were deaf or hard of hearing compared to 17 percent in residential schools. Ethnic status was reported for 808 students: 69 percent were white, 19 percent black, 8 percent

Hispanic, and 4 percent Asian. It appears that the number of Hispanic students was underreported. One program that is prohibited by regulation from reporting ethnic status appeared to have a majority of Hispanic students. More than 80 percent of children in residential and small local public schools were white compared with 45 percent in the large public schools, where black, Hispanic, and other "minority" children constituted the majority.

As noted in Chapter 8, the results indicated that the self-concepts of deaf children in all three settings as measured by the Piers-Harris Children's Self-Concept Scale (1969) were comparable to hearing norms. There was little variation by gender, placement, or race, with one exception. Black deaf residential school males had the highest average self-concept scores of all groups, and black deaf public school males had the lowest scores. Although one may speculate, there is no obvious reason why the difference would show up for black males but not for females or for black residential students but not for white residential students. Clearly, this area needs further study.

Overall, the positive self-concepts of deaf students in all settings are encouraging. Parental adjustment also appears to be satisfactory, with a majority of respondents reporting that they sign with their children and that understanding is good. Children's reports substantiate this finding. On the other hand, morale of teachers in all three settings was found to be low, with special problems related to workload and to feeling pressured by community expectations.

Large urban programs were under great financial pressure and were experiencing lower enrollments in general, due in some cases to the development of suburban programs that no longer sent children into center programs. Options for placement were more limited in the large urban programs. A trend among residential schools toward expanding their roles to serve as state resource centers was identified as a part of an effective model for residential schools.

Educational programs were found to be much more flexible and to have moved past the federal interpretation of the least restrictive environment mandate, which had pressed for placement of deaf students contiguous to hearing peers. The educational programs had evolved to the point where social factors were considered to be part of the appropriateness component of the individualized education plan. Consistent with the recommendations of the Commission on Education of the Deaf (1988), Moores (1990b) concluded that the Department of Education should liberalize its regulations concerning LRE to reflect actual developments in education of the deaf.

Educational Interpreters

As noted, Moores included seventy-one interpreters in his study. The presence of skilled sign interpreters has been a significant benefit for the American deaf population. Federal legislation up to the Americans with Disabilities Act (ADA) has been an impetus to ensuring equal access to information and services by mandating the provision of interpreters for deaf people in medical and legal settings as well as in the work environment. Numerous interpreter training programs have been estab-

Gallaudet University Department of Publications and Production

A deaf student integrated into a high school class with the services of an interpreter.

lished throughout the country, and the Registry of Interpreters for the Deaf (RID) has played a leadership role. The development of a profession of interpreters for deaf individuals is relatively recent and has made substantial progress.

The increasing placement of deaf children in regular classroom settings, along with the growing acceptance of sign instruction, has greatly increased the demand for educational interpreters for deaf children in elementary and secondary schools. The 1995 reference issue of the *American Annals of the Deaf* lists more than five hundred programs that employ interpreters. Utilizing responses from seventy-one educational interpreters and subsequent discussions with interpreters and administrators, Moores (1995b) concluded that the role of educational interpreters has not been defined and that in many programs, interpreters' expectations and the professional standards of RID conflict. RID has established and promulgated categories and levels of certification and developed a professional code of ethics for interpreters (Hunt and Marshall, 1994). Much of the curriculum in interpreter training programs has concentrated on training in the areas of medical and legal interpreting, with an emphasis on maintaining confidentiality. Unfortunately, no uniform set of requirements exists in educational programs for deaf children. Perhaps the most common approach is to hire an individual under the category of tutor/aide, with the expectation that only part of the time will be devoted to interpreting. In a few instances, a teacher of deaf students may interpret for one or more students in an integrated class and use another period to tutor the students on the materials.

The interpreter may be seen as part of the educational team and, as such, may be expected to take part in planning for the child. This, of course, conflicts with the code of confidentiality, which was developed to preserve confidentiality in interpreting for adults. In many, if not most, of the programs, the general classroom teacher has more contact with the interpreter than any other person associated with the program. In many cases, the general classroom teacher will turn to the interpreter for advice and information.

In a study of fifty-nine regular classroom teachers working with educational interpreters, Beaver, Hayes, and Luetke-Stahlman (1995) reported that only nineteen of the teachers had ever attended an inservice training session on using educational interpreters with deaf children in educational environments. The greatest single need that teachers identified was for more information on the teacher's role with the educational interpreter. Of the forty teachers who received no inservice training, seventeen reported that they received most of their information from the educational interpreter and sixteen reported that a teacher of deaf students or a special education teacher was the main source of information.

Moores (1995b) reported that some states have established a category of educational interpreter, but most have not. In most schools, interpreting is treated not as a professional function but as a paraprofessional position. The importance of the interpreter calls for a much more systematic approach. The lack of research on effective interpreting provides no base on which to build a model for implementation with children who themselves may not have developed fluency in either ASL or an English-based sign system. The establishment and adoption of a code of ethics for educational interpreters would be an important first step in defining the role of interpreters in the schools.

Research on Academic Achievement

Dissatisfaction with American education probably began in 1635, when some members of the first class of what is now the Boston Latin School were unable to master Cicero and Livy! With only a few exceptions, education was a concern for an elite group or for a particular religious group for almost two hundred years. Before the Industrial Revolution, changes usually reflected political or demographic developments. In Massachusetts, for example, education was under Puritan control until 1728, when Episcopalians, Quakers, and Baptists were allowed to establish schools. In New Amsterdam, education was the domain of Dutch Calvinists. When the colony became New York and the school leaders refused to switch to English over Dutch, they lost the franchise. In Pennsylvania in 1715, all Protestant (but not Catholic or Jewish) bodies were authorized to establish schools. All of these changes provoked controversy (Graves, 1917). As we are aware, controversy has permeated American education since colonial times.

Concern about American education reached a high point just before 1960, when technological advances in the Soviet Union had led to a restructuring of some elements of general education, and then slowly declined. The cycle returned in the mid-1980s with the general feeling that American children could not compete academically with their peers in Western Europe and Eastern Asia. Motivated by suggestions of steady declines in high school achievement, which may or may not have been accurate, several reports were disseminated. Among the most influential were *A Nation at Risk: The Imperative for Educational Reform* (National Commission for Excellence in Education, 1983), *The Troubled Crusade: American Education, 1945–1980* (Ravitch, 1983), and *High School: A Report on Secondary Education in America* (Boyer, 1983). At the same time, preliminary results of Coleman's studies (Coleman and Hoffer, 1987), which suggested that academic achievement was higher in parochial schools than in public schools, were being disseminated. Concern over education has remained high since that time, with the growing emphasis on the need for a highly educated population to compete economically at the global level.

Howe (1984) pointed out some limitations of the reports, stating that classroom teachers had little input in their preparation. Duckworth (1984) noted that none of the reports gave attention to qualities we might wish to develop in young people for their lives outside the marketplace and the university. Nevertheless, the simultaneous appearance of so many reports sounding a theme of failure contributed to a feeling of crisis. The result was the introduction of educational reforms in most states. In one way, the feeling of crisis was ironic. Achievement had already started to improve well before 1983, the "year of reports." Declines in scores of graduating seniors in the 1970s reflected the achievement of students who had entered the public schools in the 1960s. As we saw in Chapter 12, reading achievement in the schools improved from the 1970s to the present. Overall, achievement has been improving and probably will continue to do so.

Research has already provided us with sufficient information to identify the most important factors influencing school learning and academic achievement. The real problem is how to put the existing knowledge to use to improve instruction and learning. Walberg (1984) synthesized the results of thousands of research studies to identify the most important factors influencing learning. The analysis yielded several practical recommendations for improving the efficiency of instruction. Walberg concluded that three groups of factors were consistently powerful across countries, social class, age, and gender. He categorized these groups as student aptitude factors, instructional factors, and environmental factors and identified a total of nine factors under the three groupings:

Student Aptitude Factors

1. Ability or prior achievement, as measured by the usual standardized tests

2. Development, as indexed by chronological age or maturation

3. Motivation, or self-concept, as indicated by personality tests or the students' willingness to concentrate intensively on learning tasks

Instructional Factors

4. The amount of time students engage in learning

5. The quality of the instructional experience

Environmental Factors

6. The home

7. The classroom social group

8. The peer groups outside the school

9. Use of out-of-school time (specifically the amount of leisure time spent watching television) (p. 20)

In their search for pragmatic implications of the thousands of studies that had been conducted over half a century, Walberg and his associates concentrated on what is termed the "alterable" curriculum. The fact that socioeconomic status is related to school achievement, for example, is of little benefit to educators per se. More important is how the home environment might be structured, regardless of family income, to facilitate learning.

The key, then, is not only to identify the most important factors for learning but also to ascertain the extent to which each factor is alterable. Walberg concluded that although the first five factors listed—those related to student aptitude and instruction—are all important, they are only partly alterable by educators. To achieve truly significant breakthroughs, educators must focus on creating educationally stimulating psychological climates in the environments of the home, the classroom social groups, and the peer groups outside the school. Students learn from these factors directly and also benefit indirectly from increased ability, motivation, and responsiveness to instruction. Walberg and Shanahan (1983) suggested that the mere four or five hours per week that American high school students devote to homework might be supplemented by some of the twenty-eight hours per week they spend watching television.

Of the three sets of factors, student aptitude factors are least alterable and environmental factors are most alterable. Thus IQ, although probably influenced by the home environment and by instruction, is not seen as being particularly alterable. Walberg has identified some of the instructional efforts that have had the most significant effects:

1. **Reinforcement**—reward for correct performance, instructional cues, engagement, and corrective feedback

2. **Acceleration programs**—advanced activities provided for elementary and high school students with outstanding test scores

3. **Reading training**—training to coach learners in adjusting reading speed and techniques to such purposes as reading, skimming, and finding answers to questions

Several other, less powerful factors have also been identified. One is instruction time, or time on task. *A Nation at Risk* (National Commission for Excellence in

Education, 1983) pointed out that both the school day and the school year are longer in Western Europe and Japan than in the United States. Since then the school day has been expanded. Walberg noted that the special science and math curricula developed in the decade after *Sputnik* had moderate positive effects on learning, but many schools no longer use them.

Some instructional variables that have little or no effect have also been identified. Reduced class size has been shown to have little impact on learning. The documented impact of computer-aided instruction (CAI) has been quite low. Walberg speculated that this may be due to the limited nature of the CAI programs in use to date. He thought that future programs would have better results but predicted that we would probably have to wait a decade or two for any substantial payoff.

Environmental factors, which are most amenable to alteration and can have a significant impact on learning, have not received adequate attention in recent studies. Walberg reported the foremost environmental effects as follows:

1. **Graded homework**—homework that is graded or commented on (such homework has been found to have three times the effect of homework that is merely assigned)
2. **Class morale**—psychosocial properties of the classroom as perceived by the students
3. **Home interventions**—school-parent programs to improve academic conditions in the home

The effects of these environmental factors are quite strong and seem to have much greater potential impact than other factors that have been assumed to play paramount roles in achievement. For example, the effects of graded homework appear to be three times as great as the effects of socioeconomic status, and class morale has more than twice the influence of the peer group outside the class. Of particular promise is the finding that cooperative efforts by parents and educators to modify alterable academic conditions in the home have strong beneficial effects. In a review of twenty-nine controlled studies, Walberg (1984) reported that 91 percent of the comparisons favored children in such programs over nonparticipant control groups. In addition to increasing their supervision of homework and limiting children's leisure-time television watching to twelve hours or less a week, parents can alter the home curriculum by engaging in informed parent-child conversations about school, encouraging leisure reading, expressing affection, and showing interest in the child's academic and other progress as a person.

Conventional Instruction, Mastery Learning, and Tutoring

Bloom (1984) contrasted alterable educational variables with stable variables over a period of years. Among the stable variables he included teacher characteristics, intelligence measures, and family socioeconomic status. He concentrated on six classes of alterable variables: (1) quality of teaching, (2) use of time, (3) cognitive and affective characteristics of students, (4) formative testing, (5) rate of learning, and (6) the home environment (Bloom, 1980).

Bloom (1984) reported on comparisons of results of three different types of instruction on student learning: conventional instruction, mastery learning (ML), and tutoring. Conventional instruction involves class instruction with periodic testing to mark students. Mastery learning involves the same instruction as in the conventional class, using the formative tests to provide feedback, followed by corrective procedures and additional tests to determine mastery of subject matter. Tutoring, of course, involves learning the subject matter with an individual tutor.

The results for different age levels and subject matter show that tutoring has a consistent and wide advantage over conventional instruction and that mastery learning has a smaller but still substantial advantage. The size of the differences is staggering. Bloom took the average scores of students in the conventional conditions and computed the standard deviation, or sigma (σ). He then compared scores of students under mastery learning and tutorial conditions to the distribution of scores under conventional instruction. Across the studies he found that the average student under mastery learning was about one standard deviation (1 sigma) above the average of the conventional class. This means the average mastery learning student (the student at the fiftieth percentile) was above 84 percent of the students in the conventional class. The most striking finding was that the average student under tutoring was about two standard deviations (2 sigmas) above the average student under conventional instruction. In other words, the average tutored student was above 98 percent of the students taught under typical conditions!

The results lead to two overriding conclusions. First, most students have the potential to reach high levels of learning—to achieve excellence—when instructed under optimal or ideal conditions. Second, these "ideal" conditions are not some abstract set of procedures or hypothetical constructs; they represent documented tutorial procedures. Unfortunately, we simply lack the resources to provide the tutorial one-to-one instruction that would enable the average child to improve achievement two standard deviations (2 sigmas) over today's norms. Approximately 45 million tutors would be needed to serve the current school-age population of the United States. Bloom (1984) labeled this dilemma the "2-sigma" problem and asked, "Can researchers and teachers devise teaching-learning conditions that will enable the majority of students under *group instruction* to attain levels of achievement that can at present be reached only under good tutoring conditions?" (pp. 4–5).

Bloom and his colleagues argued that none of the alterable variables alone can make up this 2-sigma difference, and they are investigating combinations of two or three variables to ascertain whether combined they contribute to greater increases in learning. Because of their success with the mastery learning feedback-corrective process, which has been shown to increase learning by one standard deviation, these researchers have been using ML as one of the variables in their studies. Table 13.1 lists the ten most powerful variables as adapted by Bloom (1984) from the work of Walberg (1984). Note that the norm for conventional instruction represents the fiftieth percentile. An effect size of 2.00 sigma would place the child in the ninety-eighth percentile, and an effect size of 0.60 sigma would result in placement at the seventy-third percentile.

TABLE 13.1   Effect Size of the Ten Most Powerful Alterable Variables on Student Achievement

Variable	Effect Size in Standard Deviation	Percentile Equivalent
Tutorial instruction	2.00	98
Reinforcement	1.20	88
Mastery learning	1.00	84
Cues and explanations	1.00	84
Student classroom participation	1.00	84
Student time on task	1.00	84
Improved reading/study skills	1.00	84
Cooperative learning	0.80	79
Graded homework	0.80	79
Classroom morale	0.60	73

Source: Adapted from B. Bloom, "The 2-Sigma Problem," *Educational Researcher* (1984), 13, no. 6:6.

Implications for Education of the Deaf

The research in general education on the alterable curriculum has obvious and immediate implications for training programs for teachers of deaf students, programs for deaf children, teachers, and parents. Although responsibilities overlap, the foremost obligation rests with the teacher training programs, which must prepare teachers by giving them the general skills of an excellent regular class teacher as well as those skills specific to teaching deaf children. At the programmatic and direct-service level, a number of instructor, program, and home variables lead to enhanced learning.

Instructor Variables.   Here the teacher is the key. In addition to knowledge of subject matter and skill in communicating with deaf children, the following instructional variables enhance the teaching/learning process:

1. **Reinforcement**. The teacher should provide appropriate reinforcement and positive feedback.
2. **Mastery learning.** The addition of teaching and feedback procedures to conventional instruction enhances learning.
3. **Graded homework.** Meaningful homework that is assigned, graded, and responded to will result in increased learning.
4. **Time on task.** There is a positive correlation between the time spent on a subject and the amount learned. This may seem a rather simplistic statement, but many teachers, particularly teachers of deaf students in academic content areas, spend surprisingly little time on task.
5. **Class morale.** Teachers should strive to maintain cohesiveness, satisfaction, and goal direction in the classroom.

Program Variables.   Program variables are instruction variables that fall under the domain of a program rather than an individual teacher. In addition to fostering the teacher's individual efforts, programs should concentrate on the following components:

1. **Reading training**. Over and above conventional reading instruction, there should be a special program to train deaf students in adjusting reading strategies for various purposes.
2. **Special programs.** Deaf students with high potential should be identified and receive accelerated training.
3. **Tutoring.** Although the ideal one-to-one situation cannot be attained, with careful planning the low student-teacher ratio in programs for deaf children can significantly enhance one-to-one and small-group instruction.
4. **Cooperative parent programs.** The alterable curriculum of the home can be manipulated to foster school achievement.

Home Variables.   The idea behind the use of the alterable home curriculum is not to place the responsibility for teaching on parents but to encourage academic achievement. The results have been excellent. Parents are asked to do the following basic things:

1. Keep television viewing to moderate levels, that is, twelve hours a week or less
2. Monitor homework to see that it is completed
3. Encourage leisure reading
4. Discuss school with the child
5. Express interest in the child's progress

Many parents do these things as a matter of course. Others do them with their hearing children but not with their deaf children. Most parents, with guidance and support from their schools, are able to substantially improve the academic environment of the home by following a few relatively simple procedures.

The same principles apply for children residing in schools for deaf students. School personnel can monitor television viewing and homework, encourage leisure reading, discuss school with the child, and express interest in progress. Since many residential students spend their weekends at home and all spend their vacations away from school, even during the course of the year they are away from the school more than they are in it. Therefore, a cooperative home/school program is desirable for all children.

No research specifically addresses the alterable curriculum for deaf students. However, interest in the concept is growing, and some investigators are initiating activities in this area.

Special Curricular Methods

Although much of the lay public—and, unfortunately, many practitioners—view education of the deaf as an esoteric, somewhat mystical process, very little has been done to develop special curricula outside of language-and-speech teaching and auditory training. In other areas, especially those involving traditional academic subjects, the tendency is to rely on texts, courses of study, syllabi, and curricula designed for students with normal hearing. Sometimes the material is adopted without change, and sometimes it is modified, which typically involves a simplification of the vocabulary used.

The first comprehensive compilation of information about curricular materials for deaf students was the monograph *Curriculum: Cognition and Content,* edited by Kopp (1968). It is divided into eight sections: natural sciences, social science, mathematics, learning theory, resources, art, language, and social and physical development. Although the publication contains a wealth of information, a reading of the various sections highlights the lack of development or modification of curricula specifically suited for deaf students. For example, in the area of social studies, Behrens and Meisegeier (1968) noted:

> A review of the literature on curricula for social studies for deaf children published in the two American periodicals on education for deaf children can be quite a shock. From the paucity of articles on this subject, one might conclude that social studies is not considered important for our children. If the number of publications listed under each category in the Bibliography on Deafness [Fellendorf, 1966] were rank ordered, papers on general educational issues would seem to be most important followed by articles on language, speech, speechreading and psychology. These categories have received six to nine times as much written attention as social studies. The other content areas of arithmetic and science would appear to have been considered as low, or perhaps even lower, in their importance to the field of education of deaf children.

The situation has not changed noticeably since Behrens and Meisegeier wrote their report. For example, when the *Volta Review* published a special issue entitled *Curriculum: Content and Change,* not one of the fourteen articles specifically addressed a curriculum for an academic subject such as math, science, social studies, or history (Kirby, 1980).

Most professionals involved in training teachers of deaf students are aware of the need for more training in content areas (Lytle and Rovins, 1997). However, satisfying this need is not a simple matter. There is also a need for training in special techniques, and training programs impose time constraints. The issue of time on task is not limited to elementary and secondary school classrooms; it is equally important in postsecondary education at the undergraduate and graduate levels.

Another factor that must be taken into account is the certification requirements for teachers of deaf students in various states. These requirements have evolved over a period of time and cannot be modified quickly or easily. The present requirements in many states do not show a great concern for training teachers of deaf students in academic content areas. Garber, Garne, and Testut (1984) surveyed certification requirements for teachers of hearing-impaired children in the fifty states and identified the most common "hearing-impaired specific curricula" requirements. Table 13.2 lists the five topics most commonly required.

Almost two-thirds of the states require training in aural habilitation to be certified as a teacher of deaf students, more than one-half require audiology, and more than one-third require speech pathology. Only fourteen states require course work in teaching academic content to deaf children to be certified as a teacher of deaf students.

Because training in speech and in hearing has been seen as the major need of deaf children, content areas such as mathematics, science, and social studies have received insufficient attention. Since teachers of deaf students have traditionally been expected to be teachers of grammar and speech, even class time intended for academic subjects has often been devoted entirely to speech and grammar remediation. The fact that most teachers of deaf students have not been trained in specific academic areas increases the tendency to sacrifice content. This neglect of the intellect is the basis for much of Furth's criticism of education of deaf students and for his plea for more cognitively based learning experiences in education (Furth, 1973).

Lack of instruction in the area of mathematics exemplifies the lack of attention given to academic subject matter in programs for deaf children. Broadbent and Daniele (1980) argued that the priority given to language development in education of deaf students limits early mathematics training. The evaluation of early intervention programs conducted by Moores (1985a) supports the contention that mathematics receives relatively little attention in programs for young deaf children. The results of a survey by Johnson (1977) of fifty-eight programs for deaf students provided further corroboration: the time allocated to mathematics was found to be minimal, particularly in the early grades. These findings, along with the paucity of materials or techniques specifically designed to meet the needs of deaf children in mathematics, indicate that teachers of deaf students tend to underestimate the need for mathematics instruction. The evidence that the achievement of deaf children in areas such as arithmetic computation is higher than it is in reading—even though

TABLE 13.2   State Certification Requirements

Topic	Number of States Requiring Topic for Certification
Aural habilitation	32
Audiology	27
Speech pathology	17
Audiometry and hearing aids	15
Teaching academic subjects	14

they receive less instruction in all areas of mathematics than do hearing children—suggests that their achievement is probably far below what it should be.

Summary

As growing numbers of deaf children are being taught in public school settings, education of deaf students is increasingly coming under the influence of general education. Educational trends, such as the push for greater attention to academic achievement, are having a significant impact on education of deaf students. Interest in applying the results of work with hearing children to education of deaf children is growing. Improvements in academic achievement have already been documented, although the gap between scores of deaf and hearing children is still unacceptably large. Work is beginning on modifying the alterable curriculum of the home, developing effective procedures for assigning homework, and increasing time on task for academic subject matter. These developments will require educators of deaf students to examine their priorities. They must make explicit decisions on how much attention programs should give to areas traditionally emphasized in the field, such as auditory training, speech therapy, and English grammar, and still meet the demands for higher academic standards. There are no simple answers and no easy trade-offs. The directions in which the field goes in the next several years may shape the nature of education of deaf students for generations to come.

CHAPTER

14

Postsecondary Education and the Economic Status of Deaf Individuals

Introduction

Theoretically, deaf students have the same access to higher education as hearing students, with the same options they enjoyed in elementary and secondary school years—from complete educational inclusion to separate programs developed specifically for deaf students. Reasons for the development of the present situation, which evolved over the last third of the twentieth century, are quite complex and include changing cultural perspectives, federal legislation, an appreciation of diversity, a growing awareness of human potential, and a consensus that access to opportunity for qualified individuals should not be restricted by considerations of race, ethnic identity, gender, or physical condition. Now that we live in a society in which so many opportunities are available, it is incumbent on us to redouble our efforts to help deaf students acquire the knowledge and skills to take advantage of them. Access to advanced work in mathematics or chemistry is worthless if the basics have not been mastered.

A convincing argument can be made that the growth in the number and quality of postsecondary opportunities represents perhaps the greatest success story in education of the deaf. Beginning with federal support for a natural technical institute and for regional vocational technical programs for the deaf in the mid-1960s, we have witnessed an incredible explosion of opportunities. Deaf students now have access to vocational training, technical education, and undergraduate and graduate degree programs of all kinds, with support services guaranteed by federal legislation, most notably the Americans with Disabilities Act of 1990. Career opportunities also have opened up from the trades to the professions.

338

Still, it would be hasty to claim that parity has been achieved. Quite clearly, equal access does not guarantee equal success or equal outcomes. Many deaf students are hampered by limited skills in reading and writing English. As many as 50 percent may not get a high school diploma. Those who do begin secondary education tend to drop out at a higher rate than hearing students. Finally, those who do earn degrees will, on the average, make less money than their hearing counterparts. In short, despite significant improvements, an economic cost of deafness is paid at every educational level. In this chapter we will review the situation, appreciating the improvements that have been made but acknowledging the obstacles.

At the time of their establishment in the early nineteenth century, the first schools for deaf students in the United States were designed to provide students with all the skills necessary for success in the world of work. No thought was given to the establishment of college or advanced technical training programs. In fact, for the first fifty years of education of the deaf in America, only two schools offered any high school-level training. However, schools for deaf students in the United States were among the leaders in the provision of vocational training. For example, the American School for the Deaf introduced industrial training in 1822, five years after its founding (Jones, 1918). As noted previously, the introduction of vocational training at the school coincided with the beginning of the Industrial Revolution in New England. Historically, schools for deaf individuals organized their programs to provide the majority of students with technical/vocational skills. Usually, the students spent an increasing portion of their day on vocational training as they progressed through school; thus, by the time they reached their last few years, a relatively small percentage of their time was devoted to academic subjects. Considering that the majority of students entering these schools were adolescents or young adults and that the total number of years of schooling they received was small, the system functioned relatively effectively.

Such a situation was not surprising in the nineteenth century and even in the early twentieth century, when high school graduates constituted only a small proportion of the general U.S. population. But as the country evolved from a rural, agrarian economy into an increasingly urban, suburban, and industrial society, the type of training provided by the schools for deaf students could no longer meet the increasingly complex technical demands of the working world. What had once been adequate vocational preparation could now be considered only prevocational.

The years following World War I produced a great increase in the proportion of the hearing population that received secondary and postsecondary education. An even greater increase occurred after World War II, when postsecondary opportunities were expanded, especially for males, through the aid of the GI bill. By the 1960s, a majority of students graduating from American high schools could look forward to some type of postsecondary training.

Educational opportunities for deaf individuals did not keep pace. Except for those at Gallaudet College, established specifically for deaf students in 1864, no postsecondary programs for deaf individuals existed before World War II. In essence, no postsecondary vocational or technical training opportunities were available for deaf students because Gallaudet was a liberal arts college. Partly because of the lack of adequate training programs to meet the increasing demands of industry, deaf individuals saw their position deteriorate from general economic parity with the hearing population in the nineteenth century to economic inferiority by the middle of the twentieth century (Moores, Fisher, and Harlow, 1974). The deaf population did not share in the expansion of educational opportunities that occurred after World War II. With a few notable exceptions, such as the Riverside (California) program, which was established through the cooperation of the Riverside School for the Deaf and Riverside Community College, no new programs were established until the mid-1960s.

Thus postsecondary opportunities for deaf students in general remained static from 1864 to 1964. Deaf students could either attend a liberal arts college for deaf individuals (Gallaudet) or attempt to succeed in a regular college, university, or technical school with no supportive services. Because Gallaudet was not accredited until 1955, students attending before that date faced additional obstacles because they had difficulty transferring credits to other institutions of higher learning. Frequently, they were unable to gain admittance to graduate schools on the basis of undergraduate study at Gallaudet College.

Early Efforts Toward Postsecondary Education

From 1864 to 1964, Gallaudet College was the only postsecondary program in the world specifically developed for deaf individuals. Its special nature is illustrated by the facts that (1) no other liberal arts college for deaf students has ever been established in the United States or any other country and (2) no comparable postsecondary agricultural, vocational, or technical schools for deaf students have ever been established.

The establishment of the college can be attributed to a fortuitous set of circumstances that, unfortunately, was never duplicated. The two protagonists were Edward Miner Gallaudet and Amos Kendall (Boatner, 1959b). Gallaudet had been hired in 1857 at age nineteen by Kendall to head the Columbia Institution for the Deaf (now the Laurent Clerc National Deaf Education Center) in Washington, D.C., and he wished to develop advanced programs for qualified deaf students. Kendall supported Gallaudet's plans, and the two brought to bear an impressive array of talents in their efforts. Gallaudet was young, brilliant, persuasive, and aggressive. Kendall was older, highly successful, philanthropic, well connected, and equally aggressive. Still, it is unlikely that they would have succeeded in a location other than Washington, D.C., or at a time other than the decade of the 1860s. The United States was engaged in a bloody civil war, and the nation was divided. The establishment of a national college in the federal capital was one of many ways the federal government emphasized its concern with national interests in the midst of a war that threatened to split the country in two permanently. It was not by accident that the school was first established as the National Deaf Mute College. The name was changed later in honor of Thomas Hopkins Gallaudet, the father of Edward Miner

Gallaudet. For a full treatment of the establishment of the college, see Boatner's (1959a) definitive biography of E. M. Gallaudet.

Gallaudet was—and, to a somewhat lesser degree, still is—the primary source of Deaf leadership in the United States. Its graduates not only have become deaf teachers of deaf students in residential schools but have also gone on to success in a wide variety of professions. The teacher training program established by the college in 1892 to train individuals with normal hearing to be teachers of deaf students has also had a profound impact on education of the deaf in the United States. Historically, a large number of leading educators of the deaf have been products of the Gallaudet training program. Even today, a large proportion of school administrators, teacher training personnel in colleges and universities, and researchers received their first training in the area of deafness or received their Ph.D. at Gallaudet University.

In the area of vocational/technical education of deaf individuals, our contemporary concerns echo those of late-nineteenth-century educators. Speaking at a meeting of the Eleventh Convention of American Instructors of the Deaf in 1886, F. D. Clarke declared, "The high honor of establishing the first schools in the country where any persistent attempt was made to teach trades belongs to the institution of the deaf. But, though we began first, I hardly think we are keeping abreast of those who started later in the race."

A review of topics in the *American Annals of the Deaf* over its more than 150 years of existence provides ample evidence of the importance educators of deaf students have accorded vocational, technical, and agricultural, as well as academic, education. Wilkinson (1885) recommended the establishment of mechanical arts schools to train deaf students ages twelve to nineteen. Even the idea of postsecondary technical training for deaf students was expressed in the nineteenth century. Arguing that deaf students require more special preparation than hearing students, Rogers (1888) recommended that a national polytechnical institute for deaf students be established to provide the comprehensive vocational preparation that individual schools could not supply.

Several educators supported the expansion of Gallaudet College to provide technical and agricultural education in addition to liberal arts. The college actually did establish an agricultural department in the early 1900s (Jones, 1918, p. 23), but it was short-lived. Representing a committee on technical education, Fay (1893) recommended that a technical department equivalent to the liberal arts department be established at Gallaudet. Fay's recommendations were later echoed by Morrison (1920), who advocated the addition of industrial training to the basically liberal arts program at Gallaudet. Morrison urged:

> Add to the National College for the Deaf more industrial teaching with the idea of giving more technical training than is possible in the state and other schools. Let it in great measure set the standard for attainment for the deaf along industrial as well as academic and scientific lines. (p. 223)

Morrison recommended that secondary programs (1) drop training in obsolete fields, (2) emphasize machine skills, (3) intensify efforts in a few trades, (4) anticipate trades with growing demand, (5) foster close cooperation between shop and classroom, and (6) pay more attention to placement. Before the United States entered World War II, Barnes (1940a, 1940b) proposed the separation of academic and vocational education of deaf students through the creation of job training centers in urban areas. He also urged the establishment of a nonprofessional national school of trades, agriculture, and vocational training for deaf students ages eighteen and older.

Investigations of the Vocational Status of Deaf Individuals

The first comprehensive study of the vocational status of deaf individuals that this author has been able to find concerned the employment of 422 employed graduates of the American School for the Deaf. In the school's seventieth annual report, Superintendent J. Williams (1886) stated that more than 50 percent of the employed men were clustered in seven occupations: seventy farmers, twenty-seven shoe factory operators, twenty-one mill operators, twenty shoemakers, twenty mechanics, seventeen carpenters, and fifteen teachers. Of the fifty-four employed women, twenty-seven were mill operators. One male graduate had established his own insurance company; it had flourished, and he continued to be a major shareholder. He was listed as a capitalist. The graduates also included three ordained members of the clergy, one patent lawyer, and one artist. Williams noted that the wages of the 422 employed men and women were equivalent to general wages in New England. There was no indication that the economic status of the school's graduates was below that of hearing graduates. Although some of the success may be attributable to the higher proportion of adventitiously deafened individuals at that time, late-nineteenth-century schools for deaf students apparently were better able than today's schools to prepare their students to compete effectively in the economic marketplace.

Robinson, Park, and Axling (1906) reported the responses of fourteen employers of sixty-four deaf workers to questionnaires concerning the industrial status of deaf individuals. The deaf individuals were considered good workers. Difficulties of communication presented the major problem. Like Williams, these researchers found that deaf workers invariably received the same wages hearing workers did for the same class of work.

Fusfeld (1926) investigated the occupations of graduates of twenty-nine schools for deaf students in relation to the vocational training they had received. Evidence from the schools' reports suggested that approximately 50 percent of the graduates entered occupations for which they were trained. Printing, carpentry, farming, shoe repair, and dressmaking were the most commonly reported occupations. Only one school reported cooperation with state and local rehabilitation agencies, and only two schools employed placement workers.

Deaf employee using a telecommunications device.

Lunde and Bigman (1959) reported the responses of more than ten thousand deaf men and women to a questionnaire. Of the men, approximately 10 percent reported no training; 40 percent had been trained in the printing trades; 20 percent in carpentry; 15 percent in shoemaking; 10 percent in woodworking, cabinetmaking, and baking; and 5 percent in other areas. Of the women, 15 percent had been taught clerical skills and others had studied sewing, cooking, and domestic science. Major areas of employment were printing, tailoring, and shoemaking. Lunde and Bigman reported a median income of $3,465, well above the reported national average income of $2,818 at that time. The discrepancy in favor of deaf workers was attributed to the nonrepresentativeness of the samples. Minorities, women, very young children, and very old people—groups that traditionally have faced economic discrimination—were all underrepresented.

Rosenstein and Lerman (1963) investigated the vocational status of 121 women graduates of the Lexington School for the Deaf. With respect to their positions at the time of the investigation, 25 percent responded that no specific skills were required, 12 percent had received the necessary training at the Lexington School, 15 percent had received training in other schools, 10 percent had received on-the-job training, and 36 percent had acquired their skills in previous, similar jobs. (Percentages do not add up to 100 due to rounding.)

Impetus for establishment of postsecondary programs for hearing-impaired individuals came from the publication of studies by Boatner, Stuckless, and Moores (1964) and Moores (1969) on the occupational status of young deaf adults in New England. The results were interpreted as demonstrating the need for regional, postsecondary, vocational/technical training centers. Among the major findings were the following:

1. Young deaf adults were underemployed; the majority were engaged in semiskilled or unskilled positions (see Williams, 1886).

2. The wages of young deaf adults were 22 percent below those of their hearing siblings (see Williams, 1886).

3. Training provided by the programs for deaf individuals in New England was in reality prevocational training and failed to provide the students with the necessary competitive skills.

4. The unemployment rate of 20 percent was approximately four times that of the New England region.

5. Of 840 specific occupations rated as to necessary aptitude levels, 753 were seen as suitable for one or more students. Among the general fields were

library science	artistic arranging
managerial and industrial	quantity cooking
routine recording	bench work
mechanical repair	electrical repair
complex machine operation	structural arts
typing and stenographic	graphic arts
food serving	inspecting and testing (Moores, 1969)

6. Deafness itself precluded relatively few skilled occupations. However, most of the positions were not available to deaf students because they lacked appropriate training.

7. Deaf students and young deaf adults received insufficient vocational counseling and placement services (see Morrison, 1920). Friends and relatives helped in obtaining jobs in 59 percent of the cases.

8. Of the employed adults, 95 percent were rated average or better in job performance by their immediate supervisors.

9. The greatest problems noted by supervisors related to difficulties in communication (see Robinson, Park, and Axling, 1906).

10. More than 90 percent of the parents of current and former students of schools for deaf individuals and 73 percent of the young deaf adults approved of the concept of regional technical/vocational centers at the postsecondary level. (Moores, 1969, pp. 101–102)

These results, the authors concluded, supported the position that vocational education for deaf students could be best conducted on a regional basis, under a faculty of vocational educators specially prepared to provide instruction and ancillary services to deaf individuals.

The study was replicated in seven southern and southwestern states by Kronenberg and Blake (1966). The purpose was the same as that of the New England study: to assess the occupational status of and opportunities for young deaf adults. The results, which were essentially similar, also supported the concept of preparation programs for postschool employment. The authors reported the following:

1. With respect to unemployment, occupational level, wage earnings, and opportunities for advancement, in all groups deaf individuals fared worse than the general United States population.

2. The favorable reports of most supervisors regarding their deaf employees' job performance indicated that employed young deaf adults performed well in their jobs. The supervisors' expressed willingness to have more deaf subordinates and to advance them if they received further training.

3. The vocational preparation resources for deaf individuals were limited.

4. Opportunities for young deaf adults to advance were limited. Despite their employers' ratings of "average" or "above average" in the performance of their jobs, only a few of the employed young deaf adults could advance beyond their present occupational levels without retraining and/or relocation.

5. An updating and upgrading of vocational training and ancillary services for young deaf adults appeared to be long overdue.

6. A majority of current students, former students, and parents perceived a need for postsecondary training and indicated they would support such programs if the opportunity were available. A majority of parents preferred that postschool training for young deaf adults be provided in a facility for hearing students, with modifications, including additional staff, introduced to serve deaf trainees. Approximately 40 percent of the young deaf adults preferred to be trained with deaf peers.

The two studies, conducted in different parts of the United States, documented the difficulties deaf individuals faced in acquiring appropriate postsecondary training and obtaining employment commensurate with their abilities. It appears that the economic status of deaf individuals, which was equivalent to that of the hearing population throughout the nineteenth century, deteriorated significantly over the first two-thirds of the twentieth century.

Deaf Students in Colleges for Hearing Students

Every generation has included some deaf people who have managed to attend and graduate from institutions of higher learning. For example, Ferreri (1908) mentioned that in 1901 he interviewed four deaf students at Harvard who appeared to be adjusting and achieving quite satisfactorily. However, except for anecdotal reports, little information has been available about those deaf individuals who successfully negotiated the demands of colleges and universities for hearing students. Although we might assume that these individuals tended to have adventitious hearing losses and more residual hearing than the general deaf population, these assumptions can be neither verified nor disproved with respect to past generations.

Except for studies by Bigman (1961) and Breunig (1965), most information about students who attended colleges for hearing students before 1965 came from efforts by some of the private schools for deaf students to follow up on their graduates and from the Alexander Graham Bell Association's annual survey of deaf graduates of schools and colleges for hearing students. Unfortunately, the annual listings provided little more than an enumeration of individuals, most of whom were attending high schools rather than colleges and many of whom were in day programs for deaf students and receiving supportive services.

With the cooperation of several groups and associations, Quigley, Jenne, and Phillips (1968) attempted a survey of deaf individuals who had attended colleges for hearing students. The Alexander Graham Bell Association was the major initial source of information and was granted funds to fill in the gaps for the ten years in which the surveys were not conducted (p. 14). Also involved in the project were the National Association of the Deaf, Gallaudet College, and various state vocational rehabilitation agencies.

Results of the survey were based on questionnaire responses of 653 individuals who had attended an institution of higher learning between 1910 and 1965. The responses indicated far more diversity than had been anticipated in terms of extent of hearing loss, age of onset of loss, and type of education received. Five distinct groups were identified:

1. **Group A:** Deaf or hard-of-hearing individuals with at least a four-year undergraduate degree from a regular institution of higher education ($N = 224$)

2. **Group B:** Deaf or hard-of-hearing individuals who attended a regular institution of higher education but had not graduated ($N = 131$)

3. **Group C:** Deaf or hard-of-hearing individuals who were enrolled in a regular institution and were working toward an undergraduate degree at the time of the investigation ($N = 161$)

4. **Group D:** Deaf or hard-of-hearing individuals who transferred to Gallaudet College from other institutions of higher learning, most of whom were in attendance in the first semester of the 1964–1965 academic year ($N = 39$)

5. **Group E:** Deaf or hard-of-hearing individuals who graduated from Gallaudet College and later attended graduate school at other colleges and universities ($N = 92$). (Quigley, Jenne, and Phillips, 1968, p. 24)

Quigley et al. classified individuals with losses of more than 64 dB as deaf and those with losses of up to 64 dB as hard of hearing. Defining prelingual deafness as a loss of 65 dB or more before age four, the researchers classified fewer than one-half (281 of 653) of the respondents as prelingually deaf. Only 113 prelingually deaf individuals were identified as having graduated from regular colleges and universities from 1910 to 1965, a period of more than fifty years. This number would be even lower if the criteria were changed to reflect today's definition of deafness as a loss greater than 90 dB.

The study suffered from a number of difficulties, and one must agree with the investigators' conclusions that their results are underestimates (p. 159). It is disquieting to note that the combined efforts of the Alexander Graham Bell Association, the National Association of the Deaf, the United States Vocational Rehabilitation Administration, state vocational rehabilitation agencies, and the University of Illinois Institute for Research on Exceptional Children could not yield more accurate results.

Crammatte (1968) interviewed eighty-seven individuals identified as leading deaf professionals and reported that their backgrounds essentially were similar to those of hearing professionals; they tended to come from upper-middle-class and upper-class families with highly educated parents. Of the eighty-seven interviewees, eighty-two had attended college and seventy had graduated. Seventeen had master's degrees, and five had doctorates.

Approximately two-thirds (fifty-six of eighty-seven) had been educated primarily in programs for deaf students: thirty in public residential schools, fifteen in day programs, ten in private residential schools, and one who spent equal time in a private residential school and in a day school for deaf students (p. 36). Those who attended schools for hearing students represented a predominantly postlingually deaf population. Only seven of the thirty-one had lost their hearing before age six, and fewer than one-half (fifteen of thirty-one) had lost their hearing before age twelve (p. 36). Of the entire group, forty-three had lost their hearing before age three, and forty-four had lost it after age three.

The individuals in Crammatte's sample showed great flexibility in their methods of communication. More than 90 percent relied on oral communication to some extent at work, where their colleagues had normal hearing, and more than 80 percent used manual communication with their deaf friends (p. 28). Skill in speech generally was acquired without training; that is, two-thirds of those with the best speech had lost their hearing after age six.

Development of Programs for Deaf Individuals at Postsecondary Institutions for Hearing Students

Research has established that without some type of supportive services, relatively few prelingually deaf people are able to matriculate at colleges designed for students with normal hearing. The majority of individuals identified as graduates of such programs have been hard of hearing or adventitiously deaf. Although no comparable studies have been conducted on the attendance of deaf students at vocational and technical schools for students with normal hearing, studies of the vocational status of young deaf adults in New England and the Southwest (Boatner, Stuckless, and Moores, 1964; Kronenberg and Blake, 1966) suggest that the majority of them were unable to obtain adequate postsecondary vocational/technical training prior to 1965. The major development in postsecondary education of deaf individuals has been the establishment of programs within existing facilities for students with normal hearing. The impetus for such development has come from three federal actions that have affected national, regional, and state programming.

At the national level, Congress authorized the establishment of the National Technical Institute for the Deaf (NTID) in 1965. Following submission of proposals by several leading technical schools, the Rochester Institute of Technology (RIT) was chosen as the host facility. The first NTID class opened in 1968, and by 1972 enrollment had grown to 389 full-time deaf students out of a total RIT enrollment of 5,942 (Stuckless and Delgado, 1973). The majority of beginning students enter a vestibule (preparatory) program that offers career sampling, technical mathematics, science, English, and personal social and cultural development programs. Training may lead to a certificate program or to an associate or a baccalaureate degree. Support services include manual interpreting and note taking; tutoring; vocational, personal, and social counseling; training in speech, hearing, and manual communication; supervised housing; and vocational placement. The NTID program is viewed as the technical counterpart of Gallaudet University, that is, as a national program serving highly qualified deaf students.

The second thrust was the establishment of three federally funded, regional, model vocational/technical programs for deaf students, which also were set up within existing facilities for students with normal hearing. The programs were located at Delgado Vocational Technical Junior College in New Orleans (Louisiana), at Seattle (Washington) Community College, and at St. Paul (Minnesota) Technical Vocational Institute. The Delgado program began in 1968, and the Seattle and St. Paul programs opened the following year.

Each of the three programs offers preparatory training, including instruction in mathematics and English, job sampling, and orientation. Like the NTID program, these programs offer a number of support services, including manual interpreting and note taking; vocational, personal, and social counseling; manual communication training; and vocational placement. The duration of the training programs varies according to individual needs, but it tends to be somewhat shorter than that of programs offered at NTID.

Another cluster of programs developed out of federal legislation specifying that states were obligated to spend significant portions of federal money to provide vocational training for students with disabilities. Several states elected to invest funds in the vocational education of deaf students at the postsecondary level. A large number of new postsecondary programs emerged after 1969: 27 programs were identified in 1972 (Stuckless and Delgado, 1973), 40 programs in 1975 (Rawlings et al., 1975), 77 programs in 1978 (Rawlings, Trybus, and Biser, 1978), 86 programs in 1980 (Rawlings, Trybus, and Biser, 1981), and 102 programs in 1983 (Rawlings, Karchmer, and DeCaro, 1983).

Most of the programs have been in the vocational/technical area, but there have been some exceptions. The most notable was at California State University at Northridge (CSUN), which in 1964 accepted deaf graduate students into its National Leadership Training Program in the Area of the Deaf for the first time. Before then, all students in the program had normal hearing. With the help of note taking and manual interpretation services, the students successfully completed requirements for master's degrees, and since that time the program has accepted deaf students regularly (Jones, 1972).

In 1969, CSUN initiated a graduate program to train teachers of deaf students and encouraged applications from deaf individuals. Educational and support services for deaf students were broadened to include all undergraduate and graduate programs in the university. The impact of the programs for deaf students at CSUN has led the federal government to provide support similar to that given to the three regional vocational/technical programs.

An important development in the 1980s was the establishment in 1983 of the Postsecondary Education Consortium (PEC), which may serve as a model for cooperative programs in a multistate region. A federally funded project, PEC serves postsecondary institutions in thirteen southeastern states and Puerto Rico. By means of consultation and technical assistance, program evaluation, inservice training, and an information network for deaf individuals, it provides support to affiliated institutions serving deaf students in the area. PEC publishes a quarterly newsletter. The entire program is administered through the University of Tennessee at Knoxville.

Postsecondary Programs

The Postsecondary Education Programs Network (PEPNet) is a collaborative organization of four regional postsecondary centers around the United States that have been established to provide technical assistance to postsecondary programs that enroll students who are deaf and hard of hearing and that provide workshops, written materials, conferences, informational guides, and consultation (Rawlings, Karchmer, DeCaro, and Allen, 1999). PEPNet's objectives are as follows:

1. To improve postsecondary access and transition opportunities for individuals who are deaf and hard of hearing
2. To develop a national design for technical assistance and outreach service delivery
3. To expand the knowledge and skill of postsecondary institutions related to the provision of services to students who are deaf and hard of hearing
4. To increase networking among postsecondary educational institutions
5. To increase the postsecondary enrollment, retention, graduation, and employment rate of students who are deaf and hard of hearing

PEPNet serves programs in the fifty states, the District of Columbia, Puerto Rico, and American possessions in the Pacific. The regional centers are all based in institutions that have had a history of service to deaf students. In addition to the University of Tennessee Postsecondary Education Consortium (PEC), they are the following:

1. The Midwest Center for Postsecondary Outreach (MCPO) at the St. Paul, Minnesota Technical College
2. The Northeast Technical Assistance Center (NETAC) at the Rochester, New York, Institute of Technology
3. The Western Region Outreach Center and Consortia (WROCC) at the California State University, Northridge

These regional centers help provide a consistency and level of service that were missing during the initial development of postsecondary services for deaf students.

Prior to the establishment of PEPNet, the proliferation of postsecondary programs for deaf individuals proceeded in an unsystematic way. Because of the absence of standards, guidelines, and established procedures, services varied widely in extent and quality. Since postsecondary programs for deaf students, with the exception of those at Gallaudet University, are a recent phenomenon, research concerning the students and the quality of such programs has been sparse. Craig, Newman, and Burrows (1972) discussed the characteristics of the deaf students in the three model postsecondary programs (the Delgado, Seattle, and St. Paul programs) to draw a composite profile. They reported the following:

1. The students tend to come from states closest to the regional program; to come from a variety of high school backgrounds, though most frequently from residential schools; and to have brought with them the handicaps imposed by being deaf throughout most of their lives.
2. The students enroll in a wide range of courses, though more than half follow career lines in office work, graphic arts, and data processing. However, the selection of vocational areas appeared to be restricted unnecessarily.
3. Two-thirds of the students who left before graduation did so by individual choice. Through counseling and career guidance, the number of those cases might be reduced. Test scores taken from the evaluation reports strongly suggest that deaf students should succeed in schools that provide special tutoring and supportive services.

Examination of the information provided about the 27 postsecondary programs identified in 1972 (Stuckless and Delgado, 1973) and the 153 programs in 1998 (Rawlings, et al., 1999) gives insights into their nature and functions. The 27 programs enrolled a total of 2,271 deaf students, with Gallaudet and NTID accounting for more than half of them.

The fourteen programs identified as having been established between 1969 and 1972 (excluding the three model programs) enrolled a total of 287 students. Only one program had more than twenty-five deaf students: La Puente (California) Valley

Vocational Adult School, with ninety students. Four programs had ten or fewer students. Geographic distribution was uneven. In the South, the only program east of Louisiana was at St. Petersburg (Florida) Junior College, with twenty one students. The only program in the entire Northeast was the Community College of Philadelphia, with five deaf students.

By 1975, the number of programs had grown to forty-three, with a student population of 2,903 (Rawlings et al., 1975). As of 1980, fifty-two postsecondary programs in the United States had a minimum of 15 full-time deaf students, for a total of 4,236 full-time deaf students. Twenty-nine other programs each enrolled from 1 to 14 deaf full-time students. In addition, 166 full-time deaf students were identified in five postsecondary programs in Canada (Rawlings, Trybus, and Biser, 1981).

By 1982, the number of programs identified had grown to 104 (Rawlings et al., 1983); 61 programs with 15 or more deaf full-time students had a total enrollment of 4,310, and 41 other programs, each with up to 14 students, had a total of 253 students. In short, a total of 4,563 deaf postsecondary students were reported as receiving services.

Rawlings et al. (1999) found a different pattern in 1998. The survey reported a total of 4,535 students in 153 programs, a somewhat smaller enrollment than in 1982 but many more programs. The enrollment may be due to a larger pool of deaf Americans of college age in 1982 as a result of the rubella epidemic of the early and middle 1960s. The real change was in the number and size of programs. Only 32 programs were identified with 15 or more full-time deaf students, for a total enrollment of 3,722 students. The rest were attending the 98 programs with fewer than 15 deaf full-time students. The reasons for the changes must remain speculative, but they may have been influenced by the work of PEPNet as well as by more openness on the part of institutions of higher education.

Most of the programs were relatively small, and most offered training leading to a certificate or diploma rather than to an academic degree. As we might expect, the federally established national programs had the largest enrollments; Gallaudet had 1,188 full-time deaf students, and NTID had 960. Both served somewhat less than half of the full-time deaf postsecondary students identified in the United States. Only two other programs enrolled more than 100 deaf full-time students. Ohlone College in Fremont, California, reported 280 deaf students, or 12 percent of a full-time enrollment of 2,387. California State University, Northridge, reported 155 deaf full-time students out of a student population of 15,662.

It is interesting to note that, although numbers changed substantially from 1972 (Stuckless and Delgado, 1973) to 1998 (Rawlings et al., 1999), the relative influence of Gallaudet and NTID remained constant. Because of enrollment increases, the combined enrollment at both institutions served almost half of the 2,271 students in 1972 and almost half of the 4,535 students in 1998.

Despite the enormous growth in the postsecondary enrollment of deaf students, it appears that relatively few complete four-year educational programs to receive a bachelor's degree. In a preliminary report on a multiyear study of higher education for deaf students, Ouellette (1985) reported that one-third of deaf postsecondary students surveyed intended to pursue a bachelor's degree, but only 5 percent actually received one. The rest of the students surveyed received degrees or certificates at or below the associate of arts level. These results are consistent with information provided by Rawlings, et al., (1983). The implication is that although deaf students today may have equal access to higher education in general, relatively few receive the support they need to complete the requirements for a full four-year bachelor's degree.

Perhaps because of the pragmatic nature of postsecondary education, the issues that are so hotly debated in the early intervention, elementary, and secondary years have been resolved with a refreshing lack of emotion and recrimination. The lack of controversy over the acceptance of manual communication and mainstreaming in postsecondary programs is especially noteworthy. In 1972, use of manual communication was reported by all 27 programs, 26 of which had been established within facilities for students with normal hearing. In 1982, 100 of the 102 programs utilized manual communication. Interpreters were provided for integrated classes in all but 2 programs. Those programs—at Lexington Technical Institute and at Washington University—reported a total of four full-time students (Rawlings et al., 1983). At Gallaudet University, all classes are taught through simultaneous oral-manual communication, and proficiency is required of the entire faculty.

There has been concern, however, about the rapid increase of small programs unable to offer the range of services needed by postsecondary vocational/technical deaf students. The three model demonstration programs in New Orleans, St. Paul, and Seattle were studied with the following objectives:

1. To provide postsecondary programs with guidelines for developing programs for deaf students

2. To determine as precisely as possible the nature of the three demonstration programs in relation to
   a. Population served
   b. Courses of study offered
   c. Supportive services provided
   d. Cost of services

3. To determine the effectiveness of the type of postsecondary programming offered by the three demonstration programs in
   a. Course success
   b. Employment success
   c. Attrition
   d. Comparison of student and nonstudent success

4. To consider student characteristics to derive implications for specific vocational instructional procedures (Moores, Fisher, and Harlow, 1974, p. 3)

The objectives were carried out in two stages. First, a formative evaluation of three federally funded demonstration programs was conducted in an attempt to improve their effectiveness. The results were reported in a series of research monographs (Fisher, Harlow, and Moores, 1974; Fisher, Moores, and Harlow, 1974; Harlow,

Fisher, and Moores, 1974; Harlow, Moores, and Fisher, 1974; Moores, Harlow, and Fisher, 1974). Then a summative evaluation of the demonstration programs led to a summary of findings and the establishment of guidelines for new programs (Moores, Fisher, and Harlow, 1974). Readers are referred to the original sources for complete details. Some of the major findings and implications of the study were as follows:

1. A majority of former students (73 percent) approved of the idea of technical/vocational programs for deaf individuals, were positive toward their programs, and appreciated the training and supportive services they received.

2. A comparison of the occupational status of young deaf adults ten years previously (Boatner et al., 1964; Kronenberg and Blake, 1966) and the occupational status of former students of the three postsecondary programs under study provided evidence that the programs facilitated upward movement of their students in the job market.

3. The upward movement reflected no major shifts in occupations or any breakthroughs in terms of new types of jobs; it merely reflected a general upward trend among positions traditionally held by deaf people. There was a tendency to cluster in certain occupations, such as general office work for females and printing for males.

4. Training, placement opportunities, salaries, and chances for advancement were much more restricted for deaf females than for deaf males.

5. Former students reported greater job satisfaction than had been found in previous studies.

6. Comparative figures suggested that the young deaf adults interviewed earned higher salaries than did hearing adults of equivalent ages. This advantage tended to disappear as interviewees got older.

7. As in previous studies, deaf workers identified communication difficulties as the major on-the-job barrier to advancement.

8. Despite the counseling and placement services the programs provided, a substantial proportion of jobs were located through the aid of parents, friends, and relatives.

9. Immediate supervisors regarded deaf workers as desirable employees and were willing to hire more deaf workers.

10. However, supervisors believed deaf workers had limited opportunities for advancement, even with further training.

11. The majority of parents favored postsecondary programs for deaf individuals within ongoing programs for students with normal hearing.

12. Most parents expressed satisfaction with their children's vocational/technical training.

13. The majority of vocational rehabilitation counselors believed that the training their deaf clients received in postsecondary programs was adequate.

14. Vocational rehabilitation counselors tended to be more critical of the education their clients had received prior to their vocational/technical training.

15. Nearly 90 percent of the current students interviewed were satisfied with the training they were receiving. Most approved of the idea of vocational/technical programs for hearing-impaired individuals, and most preferred to attend school with both hearing and hearing-impaired peers.

16. Occupational choices tended to fall along traditional and gender-based lines. Nearly 40 percent of the males chose graphic arts/printing or cabinetmaking/carpentry as their future occupations. Sixty percent of the females' choices came under the category of general office work.

17. The educational training of the preparatory program teachers was not geared toward the postsecondary level.

18. Courses offered in the preparatory programs were heavily remedial in nature, stressing math and English.

19. Preparatory program teachers believed deaf students had not been 9provided with basic academic skills.

20. Regular classroom teachers expressed nearly unanimous support for interpreters and regarded them as the catalyst permitting deaf students to receive vocational/technical training with hearing students.

21. Regular classroom teachers were supportive of and enthusiastic about the programs for deaf students. Many expressed a need for more background information concerning deafness.

22. Analysis of the scores of deaf subjects on the Stanford Achievement Test, the General Aptitude Test Battery, and the Wechsler Adult Intelligence Scale indicated that deaf adults are equal intellectually to hearing adults and may be superior in areas demanding spatial and perceptual skills. Therefore, deaf individuals should have no more difficulty than anyone else in meeting the cognitive demands of any job. The high ratings supervisors and regular classroom teachers gave to deaf workers and students support this position.

23. Due to the underemployment of deaf people, a deaf person is more often than not intellectually superior to a hearing person employed in the same type of work.

24. Problems arise not from the cognitive demands of a job but from difficulties in communication, especially insufficient command of the English language.

25. The effectiveness of well-run secondary vocational/technical programs for deaf students has been documented. However, these programs are

hampered by the inadequate education students generally receive prior to the postsecondary level. (Moores, Fisher, and Harlow, 1974, pp. 16–29)

Attrition of Deaf Students

One obstacle to benefiting from improved educational opportunities is the high rate of attrition at every level for deaf students relative to hearing students. In a study of 6,196 deaf school leavers ages sixteen to twenty-two, Allen, Rawlings, and Schildroth (1989) reported a dropout rate of 29 percent, with females (33 percent) being more likely than males (25 percent) to drop out of secondary programs. Only 52 percent of deaf school leavers received high school diplomas, and 19 percent received certificates of attendance.

In the states requiring competency testing for high school diplomas, only 39 percent of deaf school leavers received diplomas. Among deaf students, 59 percent of white students received diplomas compared to 38 percent of black students and 36 percent of Hispanic students. In a review of literature, Nash (1992) concluded that deaf and hard-of-hearing youth are at risk for dropping out of high school. The pool of potential postsecondary students is reduced by 25 to 30 percent due simply to dropouts and an additional 10 to 20 percent because many students with certificates of attendance would not be qualified.

Stinson and Walter (1992) estimated a dropout rate of 70 percent for deaf students in postsecondary programs, a much higher rate than that for their hearing counterparts. They report that, similarly to individuals in other groups, many deaf students regard contacts with members of their own group as the best opportunities for friendship, dating, and interaction. In terms of academic preparation, Stinson and Walter (1992) conclude that many deaf students "do not possess the mathematics, science, and reading skills to function effectively in 'traditional' classes designed primarily for hearing students even if sign language, interpreting, and notetaking services are available" (p. 58). Earlier, Foster and Elliot (1986) noted the importance of social factors in postsecondary education of deaf students. From interviews with deaf students who had transferred to the National Technical Institute for the Deaf from other institutions, they concluded that the three primary factors were an inability to communicate with teachers, inadequate support services, and limited social interactions.

The Economic Cost of Deafness

Higher levels of unemployment and underemployment among deaf individuals have created a significant and long-standing gap between the earnings of deaf and hearing workers. As noted earlier, Boatner et al. reported in 1964 that wages of young deaf adults were 22 percent below those of hearing siblings. Weinrich (1972) estimated the cost of deafness in terms of lost lifetime wages at more than $260,000 (much more in today's dollars due to inflation) and attributed the gap to the fact that far more hearing people than deaf people attend college. Later research by Welsh and associates (Welsh and MacLeod-Gallinger, 1991; Welsh, Walter, and Riley, 1989) suggests that Weinrich's conclusion may be only partially true. Using information from alumni and school leavers from five postsecondary programs for deaf individuals,* they demonstrated that deaf people earn less than hearing people at each of four educational levels, but the discrepancy decreases significantly at higher levels. Over forty years of work, a deaf high school graduate was projected (using inflation-adjusted figures) to earn $609,705 less than a hearing high school graduate ($1,316,111 versus $1,925,816) and a deaf person with a master's degree was projected to earn $356,404 less than a hearing person with more than four years of college ($2,782,958 versus $3,139,362). For example, a deaf person with a master's degree who earned $22,783 in 1985 is projected to earn $2,782,958 over a forty-year career given inflation estimates and reasonable expectations for career advancement.

General access to postsecondary education should improve the economic status of deaf Americans provided only that they have the academic skills to take advantage of equal access. Since only about 50 percent of deaf students receive high school diplomas, this is not an easy task. Reporting on a survey of twenty-seven secondary programs for deaf students for the period 1985 to 1990, Welsh and MacLeod-Gallinger (1991) offer this sobering conclusion: "The employment picture for the latter part of the 1980s is not much better than it has been traditionally. The overall unemployment rates for the respondents ages twenty and older average about 20 per cent. This is equivalent to what was reported by Boatner, Stuckless, and Moores in 1964."

Gallaudet University 1993 Alumni Survey

Rawlings et al. (1993) reported on the responses of 4,278 Gallaudet alumni ages twenty-five to ninety-five from the classes of 1923 to 1991. Of these individuals, 2,415 held undergraduate degrees, 885 held graduate degrees, and 978 were nondegreed alumni. The results provide information about a relatively well-educated and affluent population as well as an indication of change over time in educational emphasis and employment trends. First, we find the familiar relationship between educational attainment and income. Median annual income was $26,000 for nondegreed alumni, $31,000 for alumni with undergraduate degrees, and $34,000 for those with graduate degrees. We also find the familiar gender difference. For males, median income was $35,000 for undergraduate degree holders and $44,000 for graduate degree holders. For females, median income was $28,000 and $32,000 for undergraduate and graduate degree holders, respectively. The pattern did *not* hold for hearing status for graduate degree holders where 70 percent of the respondents were hearing and 30 percent were deaf. Median income for deaf graduate degree holders was $37,000, and for hearing graduate degree holders it was $34,000.

---

*National Technical Institute for the Deaf, California State University at Northridge, University of Tennessee Consortium, St. Paul Technical Vocational Institute, and Seattle Community College.

In 1992 total annual income for all Gallaudet degree holders was over $50,000 for 45 percent of families, over $75,000 for 17 percent, and more than $100,000 for 5 percent. Rawlings et al. noted that in many families both spouses were employed Gallaudet alumni. Although encouraging, these data are still somewhat below what we would expect for comparably educated families in 1992, when 17 percent of U.S. families had incomes in excess of $100,000 (Rawlings et al., 1993, p. 41).

Among undergraduate alumni, majors have changed significantly over the years. Prior to 1952, 28 percent of undergraduates majored in education, 19 percent in home economics, and 17 percent in English. From 1952 to 1961, 31 percent majored in education, 12 percent in math, and 10 percent in computer science. By 1982–1991, almost one-third of graduates had majored in either psychology (16 percent) or business administration (15 percent).

Ironically, education had the largest concentration of majors until 1961, before which time the undergraduate program was not accredited and deaf students were not allowed into the graduate program in education. Many deaf undergraduates were hired as teachers and dormitory supervisors at residential schools for deaf students but were not eligible for public school employment. As we might expect, a relatively large number of undergraduate degree holders (45 percent) work in educational settings, but the numbers have decreased over time, from 54 percent in 1952–1961 to 36 percent in 1982–1991. As training continues to emphasize areas such as business administration, it is projected that the careers of graduates will continue to diversify.

It is interesting to note that Gallaudet undergraduate degree holders are quite successful in graduate education, with more than half earning advanced degrees. Since 1982, 82 percent of master's degrees and 95 percent of doctoral degrees were earned at institutions other than Gallaudet.

Summary

With the exception of programs at Gallaudet University—the world's only university for deaf students, established in 1864—postsecondary education used to be available only to those individuals who were able to enroll in colleges and universities for students with normal hearing. Evidence suggests that few deaf individuals have graduated from such institutions over the years and that the majority of those who have were in reality hard of hearing or postlingually deaf.

The economic status of deaf American workers in the nineteenth and early twentieth centuries was comparable to that of hearing workers, but it deteriorated as industry demanded more and more specialized workers and training opportunities for deaf individuals did not keep pace with those for hearing workers. By 1965 deaf workers were an economically depressed group, with high rates of unemployment, low wages, and little chance for advancement.

The establishment of the National Technical Institute for the Deaf on the campus of the Rochester (New York) Institute of Technology and of three regional model vocational/technical programs in New Orleans, St. Paul, and Seattle in 1968 and 1969 provided the major thrust for the growth of postsecondary programs for deaf students. All were affiliated with existing host facilities serving students with normal hearing. Later federal support for the Postsecondary Education Consortium, based at the University of Tennessee at Knoxville, and for the California State University at Northridge program for deaf individuals further expanded opportunities. The passage of the Americans with Disabilities Act of 1990 ensures that qualified deaf students have equal access to postsecondary education.

During the 1970s, the number of deaf students in postsecondary programs more than doubled. Today an impressive array of options are available to deaf students, ranging from vocational training to graduate school. Developments in programs from 1965 to the present constitute a literal revolution in postsecondary education, a revolution that has not received the attention it deserves. This progress has been realized through the cooperation of institutions of higher education and the provision of a pragmatic mix of support services, including sign language interpreting, note taking, and counseling.

Evidence suggests that deaf students are as intellectually capable as hearing students and can handle the cognitive demands of a work situation with relative ease. Research over several generations has shown that deaf individuals tend to be rated as good or even superior workers. The major obstacle they face on the job is difficulty in communication, which has restricted job mobility and advancement.

Evaluation of the regional model vocational/technical programs indicates that the programs have helped their students achieve upward job mobility. However, no major breakthroughs have been made, and the number of fields in which deaf students, especially female deaf students, have been trained and found jobs remains limited.

Despite unquestioned improvements and advances, problems remain. Although an unprecedented number of postsecondary training opportunities for deaf individuals are now available, many deaf students are unable to take advantage of them. Almost one-half of deaf high school students either drop out or receive only a certificate of attendance. Of those with high school diplomas who go on to postsecondary education, the attrition rate is high. Those who do receive degrees earn less money over their careers than do their hearing counterparts. By every measure, the economic cost of deafness is steep.

Epilogue

Introduction

I try to approach the development of each new edition of this text in a systematic way. As soon as the previous edition is completed, I begin to develop notes and file material for each of the fourteen chapters. I also try to discuss developments in our field with a range of colleagues, seeking out a range of perspectives and philosophies. Also, since I teach a class on educational aspects of deafness (the reason why I originally developed the text), I have the benefit of immediate candid and useful feedback from the main intended audience. Finally, during the initial phase of development, the publisher, Houghton Mifflin, asks several respected leaders in the field to review the previous text and my plans for revision and make recommendations for additions, deletions, and modifications.

One issue we face is the question of whether there have been substantial changes, developments, or trends since the publication of the previous edition as well as since the publication of the first edition in 1978. I am always amazed at how much change—usually for the better—has occurred in the intervening years. But I am also struck with the staying power of both some of our most enduring realities and some of our misconceptions. This is when I turn to the work of Braudel (1981) and his conception of short-term, middle-term, and enduring realities (my choice of words). We have spoken for generations about how many parents believe that speech is the main problem of deaf children and that articulate speech is the only way in which a deaf child can achieve "normalcy." This belief has led many parents to avoid sign language, deaf adults, and educational programs in which there were other deaf children. Today, we have earlier identification, and most parents receive balanced information from professionals. Sign language is accepted, if not embraced, by the

359

general culture. Unquestionably, the situation has improved over the past five, ten, and twenty-five years. However, one thing that many of us tend to forget is that, for most (hearing) parents of deaf children, deafness is a new experience. It is immediate and usually unexpected, and some parents have difficulty working through the issues. This is as true today as it was a century ago.

I recently interacted with the parents of a twelve-year-old deaf girl who was in a completely inclusive sixth-grade class and was the only deaf child in the school. The parents were determined that the child would be "normal," which they defined as having good oral communication skills, attending school and socializing with only hearing children, and competing academically at grade level. Support services were much more extensive than this girl would have received in the past. A comprehensive IEP was in place, she wore a sophisticated hearing aid, and a sign interpreter was available for some classes and for participation on an athletic team; the parents requested this interpreter even though neither of them was fluent in sign or used it extensively at home.

However, from the perspective of observers and, to some extent, the parents, problems were beginning to arise. Despite extensive time spent on homework, the girl was falling behind in class and was beginning to ask why she was "dumb" compared to her classmates. She had trouble following class discussions, a common situation for children as they begin to move into larger classes with more academic content. Her friendships were not as close as they had been at younger ages, and concern was expressed about what would happen as the children started dating. The issues faced by this child and her family are similar to those faced by thousands of deaf children and their families for almost two hundred years in this country. The old saying that the more things change the more they remain the same is true for deaf children, their families, and the professionals who interact with them. I have tried to make this a theme of the book.

In writing the fifth edition of *Educating the Deaf: Psychology, Principles, and Practices,* I reviewed the development of the first four editions over a period of more than twenty-five years. Revolutionary changes in the field are reflected in dramatic changes in the content and organization of the text. Some truly startling developments have occurred since a generation ago. Among the most notable changes is evidence that the number of deaf children, at least in the United States and other industrial countries, has declined and continues to fall. Several factors explain this phenomenon. First, because of immunizations, no worldwide rubella epidemic has occurred since the 1960s. Medical advances and improved care have also reduced the incidence of deafness related to mother-child blood incompatibility, meningitis, prematurity, and even chronic middle ear infection. Qualitative improvements in hearing aids have enabled some children, who a generation ago would have been rendered deaf, to function as hard of hearing; in fact, some children now function as hearing rather than hard of hearing. Cochlear implants have clearly been effective with deafened adults, and the outlook for congenitally deaf individuals appears to be brightening. The Human Genome Project is yielding insights into human genetics that were only dreamed about in the not-too-distant past. Charter schools are starting to develop.

Federal legislation has also had a significant impact. Deaf and hard-of-hearing Americans have benefited from an impressive array of laws, including the Education of All Handicapped Children Act and its evolution into the Individuals with Disabilities Education Act, the Americans with Disabilities Act, and the Education of the Deaf Act. Mandated access to telephone services through statewide relay services and to television through closed-caption features on all television sets have brought tremendous benefits.

Legislation has influenced, and been influenced by, public perceptions of deafness and deaf individuals. A growing segment of the general population is becoming aware of American Sign Language (ASL) and accepting the concept of a Deaf community and a Deaf culture. Increasing numbers of deaf people are entering the professions, business, and the entertainment field. Deaf educators, psychologists, counselors, researchers, and administrators are now having a profound influence on education of deaf children.

In education, from birth through adulthood deaf individuals have an impressive variety of placement, communication, and curricular options, many tailored to individual preferences and needs. Placement may range from complete integration with hearing peers to total integration with deaf peers. Communication may range from English exclusively to ASL. Specialized curricula, including Deaf Studies, are available.

On the other hand, seemingly intractable problems and conflicts persist. The Balkanization of education of the deaf is greater than ever before. Communication across the battle lines is sadly lacking in a field that has committed itself predominantly to communication. Differences of opinion and philosophy quickly degenerate into ad hominem disputes. Despite surgical, technical, and scientific advancements, the final "cure" for deafness is not imminent. Given the complexity of the process of hearing, the range of causes, and the physical mechanisms involved, any technique or device will be limited to certain kinds of hearing loss. We remain nowhere near the point where implants, vibrotactile devices, or computers will resolve the problems deaf individuals face in our society.

Despite overall improvement, the academic achievement of deaf children remains unacceptably low. Limitations on literacy—reading and writing English—continue to block achievement of full potential for a majority of deaf students. Equal access to education is of little benefit to individuals who lack the academic skills needed to take advantage of them. Opportunities for poor deaf children, many of whom live in large cities and are of minority status, are abysmally lacking. For these children, equal access has not been a reality.

In trying to reconcile this paradox of apparent change along with a lack of progress, it may be helpful to keep in mind Braudel's concept of the event, cycle, and long-term components of history, as discussed in Chapter 1. Significant changes and improvements *have* occurred, as attested to by events such as the Deaf President Now movement and the selection of a deaf Miss America. Over the past generation, there *has* been a cycle of improvement in educational programs and academic achievement for deaf students. Still, problems in communication, literacy, and acceptance persist that are similar to those deaf Americans faced 150 years ago. Most deaf children are born to parents with little or no prior exposure to deafness.

One problem encountered by deaf people and by the professionals, both hearing and deaf, who serve them is the persistent ignorance about the condition of deafness that is displayed in the popular press. Proclamations of new "cures" for deafness imply that deafness will soon be a thing of the past. First came elaborate promises that more advanced hearing aids would bring the "gift of sound" to all deaf people. Later the press lauded the benefits of acupuncture, with anecdotal reports of restoration of hearing. Other reports have proclaimed that special eyeglasses will help deaf people to decode speech and that devices worn on the wrist will provide vibrotactile analogs to vocal communication.

Largely because newspapers and television rarely discuss deafness other than to report unrealistic projections of dramatic breakthroughs in the near future, the general public still has a distorted view of deafness. Deaf people and professionals in the field frequently develop a sense of resignation and cynicism concerning popular misconceptions. In reality, the number of deaf children with additional conditions has been growing, not decreasing, partly because of medical advances. Quite simply, medical advances have increased the survivability of infants with multiple disabilities. However, the popular media do not mention this trend, which is too complex to describe in a 30-second TV shot or a 500-word blurb in the Sunday supplement of a newspaper.

This epilogue will make projections covering a relatively short period of time—approximately a generation, or twenty-five years. Some projections will be made with a measure of confidence. For example, if we know the demographic characteristics of deaf ten-year-olds today, we can project what deaf twenty-five-year-olds will be like in fifteen years. On the other hand, we have no way to determine whether an epidemic of some indeterminant nature will substantially increase the incidence of deafness in newborn babies. In Chapter 1, I contend that education of the deaf has faced three fundamental questions since its inception:

1. Where should we teach deaf children?
2. How should we teach deaf children?
3. What should we teach deaf children?

We will return to these three general but crucial topics of placement, instruction, and curriculum and then close with a brief consideration of the Deaf community.

School Achievement and Classroom Placement

The trend toward education in public school settings on a commuting basis is likely to continue for the foreseeable future. This trend has existed since World War II and shows no evidence of abating. It was initiated by two factors, one general and one specific to deafness. The first was the post–World War II baby boom, which lasted from 1946 to around 1960. The second was the rubella epidemic of the mid-1960s.

The unprecedented number of children born during the baby boom set off large-scale construction of elementary and later secondary schools throughout the country. The need for new schools was especially pronounced because few schools had been constructed during the Depression and war years, when the U.S. birthrate had dropped to an all-time low.

Following the rubella epidemic of the mid-1960s, there developed a consensus that preschool programs should be offered to deaf children and their families. Many residential schools were already operating at close to capacity, since construction of residential schools for deaf students had not kept pace with the increasing number of deaf children born during the baby boom. Coincidentally, in the late 1960s public schools were experiencing the beginning of a decline in early elementary school enrollment. For the first time in more than a generation, elementary schools had empty classrooms and unused space. In the 1970s, the effects of reduced enrollment reached the high schools. Given the availability of space in public schools, state legislatures were reluctant to commit large sums of money to establish new residential schools for deaf students or to expand existing ones to serve a one-time-only group of children. These children, born in 1964–1965, had moved through elementary and secondary school by 1984. This situation set the stage for steadily increasing public school participation in education of deaf students, a participation that has received added impetus from the mandates of Public Law 94–142 and subsequent legislation.

Although I believe that public schools will continue to serve the majority of deaf children, it is difficult to estimate what proportion will be in self-contained classes for deaf students and what proportion will be integrated with the help of interpreters. The mandates for individualized educational programs will facilitate the provision of placement options, and the availability of interpreters will allow many deaf students to participate in classes with hearing students. However, the Supreme Court's decision in *Rowley* v. *Hudson School District* that a school does not have to provide an individual interpreter makes unclear the extent to which schools will continue to provide extensive interpreter support, especially in the face of increasing costs of education in general.

There has been a good deal of speculation on the future, if any, of residential schools for deaf students. These schools have been unfairly stigmatized by some professionals outside of the field who have inaccurately equated them with some of the more repressive institutions for individuals with severe or profound disabilities. In fact, residential schools for deaf students, both public and private, have an exemplary record of service to deaf children and adults and have provided the foundations for the Deaf community and Deaf culture.

To approach the issue from an objective position, I looked at enrollment in residential schools for deaf students from 1994 back to the middle of the nineteenth century. Enrollment in residential schools passed ten thousand in 1904 and generally remained at that level, despite a threefold increase in the American population. Two periods of increase occurred. The first was in 1934. It appears that during the worst part of the Depression in the 1930s, many state schools for deaf individuals served a welfare as well as an educational function. Many children who had mild and moderate hearing losses and came from destitute families were enrolled in residential schools, and the facilities were stretched to their limits. The other increase in residential school enrollment was in 1974, reflecting the impact of the rubella epidemic, which again put unusual demands on facilities. By 1994 residential school enrollment had declined to less than ten thousand. This figure is somewhat lower than the ten thousand residential school students reported for 1904. Improvements in transportation increased these schools' commuter populations, and the residential enrollment has declined substantially.

Relatively few new schools were constructed throughout the twentieth century. What little construction has occurred since 1960 has primarily been to replace existing facilities, not to establish entirely new programs. Given the high cost of construction, it is possible that no new residential schools for deaf students will be built in the intermediate future, although new buildings may be constructed at existing schools. If so, residential school enrollment may continue to decline as physical plants age and are closed down. In my opinion, such an erosion would have a serious negative impact on education of the deaf, especially at the high school level. As noted in Chapter 1, residential schools educate a disproportionate number of high school students and account for a majority of high school graduates. In addition, as pointed out in Chapter 13, rural areas and metropolitan regions of moderate population have neither the critical mass of students nor the concentration of resources to provide comprehensive services to a wide range of students. The option of placement in a residential school for deaf students is necessary to meet the requirements of a free, appropriate public school education. Aggressive and persuasive campaigns of support will be needed if residential schools are to continue to play their crucial role in education of the deaf.

Instruction and Curriculum

The push for academic achievement is likely to continue for a considerable period of time. It is projected that although the achievement of deaf children will continue to improve, it will still lag somewhat behind hearing norms. As attempts are made to close the gaps between potential and actual performance, research and practices in general education will have increased influence on educators of deaf individuals. The alterable curriculum of the home and school will be accorded greater importance, with more emphasis on variables such as time on task, level of material, regular and graded homework, encouragement of leisure reading, and monitoring of television viewing. In general, the atmosphere will be more academically demanding and challenging.

Changes in expectations will result in a reevaluation of procedures used in personnel preparation programs. These programs will have to reach a middle ground between providing training in the skills traditionally required of teachers of deaf students and meeting the demands for academic achievement. The final resolution is unclear.

The Deaf Community and ASL

Over the past several generations, most members of the Deaf community have shared two sets of reference: education in a residential school and the use of American Sign Language (ASL). Because educational programs themselves were oral (at least through the elementary grades) and deaf teachers were not employed with younger students, children typically learned signing from one another, often in violation of the rules of the school. It was a rare parent who learned to sign after being told that signs inhibited acquisition of English and speech. Frustration over the inability to communicate at home during weekends, vacations, and summers strengthened the identification of most deaf children with the Deaf community and with ASL. Today most deaf children live at home, and their exposure to signs comes predominantly from hearing teachers and perhaps hearing relatives, who typically use a manual code based on English, frequently in coordination with speech. First exposure to manual communication is through hearing adults using an English-based mode rather than through deaf children using a mode separate from English. The educational placement of deaf children, their residence at home, and the type of manual communication to which they are first exposed will have a great impact on the future composition of the Deaf community and on the nature of ASL.

Fears that public school education will lead to the demise of the Deaf community appear to be groundless. In our research on public school programs (Kluwin et al., 1992), we have found little evidence of isolation of deaf students from one another. The students seem to have a strong sense of themselves as deaf and to identify with deaf peers. Although the situation may be different in smaller school districts with fewer deaf students, the number of deaf teachers in such schools is growing and there seems to be a general acknowledgment by the hearing staff of the existence of a Deaf community, although relatively few have had contact with it.

A general movement is occurring among American public schools to recruit and retain deaf teachers and other deaf professionals. This should help to provide role models for the students. Many of the schools have also expressed an interest in having course work and curriculum materials on Deaf awareness and Deaf culture incorporated into their programs. Several public school programs have established affiliates of the Junior National Association of the Deaf (Jr. NAD), which has long existed in residential schools. Expansion into public school programs has given the National Association of the Deaf the opportunity to build lasting, fruitful relationships with public school programs, which now enroll the majority of deaf students. Thus, NAD can ensure the identification of deaf students in public schools with the Deaf community.

It seems likely that as today's students mature into adults, their backgrounds, values, and experiences will modify the Deaf community and ASL in ways not presently understood. Because the point of reference for their first signing is generally English-, not ASL-based, I predict that deaf children in public schools will operate on English-based systems, perhaps developing more efficient and sophisticated creolelike language systems among themselves outside the classroom. As programs incorporate both ASL and English-based signs, ASL may undergo several modifications as these children join the adult Deaf community. However, ASL, like other languages, is robust and will survive. The Deaf community will also probably undergo significant modification, but it too is robust and will thrive.

Conclusion

This text has tried to project an attitude of tempered optimism concerning the educational and developmental aspects of deafness. Without underestimating the difficulties deaf individuals face in society, we must also acknowledge the dedication of professionals in the field and the successes of deaf people themselves. I believe we are at the threshold of exciting breakthroughs.

Appendix: World Wide Web Resources

This section provides a variety of Internet resources relating to education, advocacy, literacy, and the Deaf community in general.

Alexander Graham Bell Association for the Deaf, Inc.
http://www.agbell.org
The nonprofit membership organization works to promote awareness of deaf issues, strives to get more children tested for hearing loss, and gives scholarships and financial aid to qualifying children. Up-to-date news on political decisions that affect deaf and hard-of-hearing people can be found here.

American Annals of the Deaf
http://www.gallaudet.edu/~pcnmpaad/index.html
The *American Annals of the Deaf* is a professional journal devoted to quality in education and related services for deaf and hard-of-hearing children and adults. First published in 1847, the *Annals* has the distinction of being the oldest educational journal in the United States—as well as the oldest and most widely read English language journal in the world—dealing with deafness and the education of deaf persons. The *Annals* is the official organ of the Convention of American Instructors of the Deaf (CAID) and the Conference of Educational Administrators of Schools and Programs for the Deaf (CEASD).

American Speech-Language Hearing Association
http://www.asha.org
The ASHA is an organization/community of speech-language pathologists, audiologists, and scientists whose work relates to hearing loss. This site contains an abundance of useful medical and scientific information and news.

Association of Late-Deafened Adults
http://www.alda.org
The Association of Late-Deafened Adults works to create a community between people who have lost their hearing as adults by sponsoring a yearly conference and several regional meetings. Information on upcoming and past events, as well as membership, can be found here.

The Deafened People Page
http://home.golden.net/~deafened
Stories, links, and resources for adults who lose their hearing abilities later in life can be found here. Catherine Woodcock, the site's creator and the first deaf woman to receive a Ph.D. in engineering, shares information (not advice, the page stresses) with understanding and humor.

Deaf Nation
http://www.deafnation.com
This is the online version of the newspaper *Deaf Nation,* which, like the Internet solutions provider that created this site (WebbyNation), was founded and published by and for deaf individuals. Numerous job listings, as well as technology updates and deaf community–related sports news, can be found here.

Deaf Source
http://home.earthlink.net/~drblood/index.html
A number of health- and medical-related articles for people working with the deaf can be found at this site. It features information on mental health, substance abuse, and HIV/AIDS, as well as various links.

Deaf World Web
http://www.deafworldweb.org
This enormous and multilingual site contains resources, international news, and numerous interactive pages where members of the Deaf community share their stores. Post and/or read anything from thoughts on deaf education to a humorous anecdote about day-to-day life.

ERIC Clearinghouse on Disabilities and Gifted Education
http://ericec.org
ERIC—the Educational Resources Information Center Clearinghouse on Disabilities and Gifted Education—has created this enormous federally funded information network of academic writing, information, and resources.

The Federal Resource for Special Education—Deafness and Hardness-of-Hearing
http://www.dssc.org/frc/deaf.htm
http://www.dssc.org/frc.hi.htm
These two sites contain several links to schools, research centers, and other web sites that are devoted to using technology to help the deaf and hard of hearing communicate.

Gallaudet University
http://www.gallaudet.edu
World-renowned Gallaudet University in Washington, D.C., specializes in the education of deaf and hard-of-hearing individuals. Various centers there, including the

National Information Center on Deafness and the Laurent Clerc National Deaf Education Center, provide a wealth of online information and resources.

Gallaudet University Laurent Clerc National Deaf Education Center
http://www.gallaudet.edu:80/~precpweb/
Formerly known as Pre-College National Mission Programs (PCNMP), the Clerc Center is composed of two federally funded schools devoted to teaching deaf children from birth to twenty-one. It also has a large national outreach mission.

Health Care Information Resources—Deafness Links
http://www-hsl.mcmaster.ca/tomflem/deaf.html
Various links that provide health-related information for deaf and hard-of-hearing individuals, including information on cochlear implants as well as sign language, can be found on this page.

National Association of the Deaf
http://www.nad.org
The official web site of the National Association of the Deaf, the oldest and largest nonprofit advocacy group in America for deaf and hard-of-hearing people, offers information on various publications, conferences, youth camps, and organization membership.

National Information Center of Deafness at Gallaudet University
http://www.gallaudet.edu:80/~nicd/
This site, dubbed "Info To Go," has a number of links and resources for parents and for children from birth to twenty-one who are deaf or hard of hearing. A few of the many issues featured include health, technology, cultural issues, and social resources for children and teenagers.

National Institute on Deafness and Other Communication Disorders Clearinghouse
http://www.nih.gov/nidcd
As a branch of the National Institutes of Health (NIH), the National Institute on Deafness strives to encourage and fund research on deafness and hardness of hearing. This site has an abundance of research funding information, as well as health and technology news.

National Technical Institute for the Deaf
http://www.rit.edu/~418www/new/NTID.html
The National Technical Institute for the Deaf (NTID) is one of seven colleges of the Rochester Institute of Technology. The mission of NTID is to provide deaf students with outstanding state-of-the-art technical and professional education programs that prepare them to live and work in the mainstream of a rapidly changing global community.

SIGNhea Communication Center
http://library.advanced.org/10202
This user-friendly site, created by three high school students, is devoted to teaching ASL online. The contents include the ASL alphabet, numbers, various useful phrases, a dictionary, and helpful hints. According to the site, the Spanish version is coming soon.

Volta Review
http://www.agbell.org/publications/periodicals.html
The *Volta Review* is a professional journal dealing with issues in education, audiology, speech and language science, and psychology related to deaf and hard-of-hearing children and adults. It has been published for more than one hundred years and is the official organ of the Alexander Graham Bell Association.

Where Do We Go from Hear?
http://www.gohear.org
Parents and educators can find much useful information on, and resources for, children recently diagnosed with deafness or hardness of hearing. Multimedia, technological news, and visitors' stories combined with short cartoons make this site a great resource for parents and children alike.

World Federation of the Deaf
http://www.wfdnews.org
Human rights and education (preferably through sign language) for deaf and hard-of-hearing individuals, especially in developing countries, are the main goals of this worldwide advocacy group. Their site contains global news and membership information.

References

Abernathy, E. 1959. "An Historical Sketch of the Manual Alphabets." *American Annals of the Deaf,* 104, no. 3: 232–240.

Abeson, A. 1972. "Movement and Momentum: Government and the Education of Handicapped Children." *Exceptional Children,* 39, no. 1: 63–66.

———. 1974. "Movement and Momentum: Government and the Education of Handicapped Children." *Exceptional Children,* 41, no. 2: 109–115.

Abidin, R. 1986. *Parenting Stress Index—Manual (PSI).* 2d ed. Charlottesville, Va.: Pediatric Psychology Press.

Adams, M. 1928. "A Preschool Experiment." *American Annals of the Deaf,* 73, no. 2: 169–171.

Alden, J. 1984. *George Washington: A Biography.* Baton Rouge: Louisiana State University Press.

Aldous, J. 1969. "Occupational Characteristics and Males' Role Preference in the Family." *Journal of Marriage and the Family,* 31, no. 7: 707–712.

Alford, H. 1972. *The Proud People.* New York: Mentor.

Allen, T. 1986. "A Study of the Achievement Patterns of Hearing-Impaired Students: 1974–1983." In *Deaf Children in America.* Edited by A. Schildroth and M. Karchmer. San Diego: College-Hill Press, 161–206.

Allen, T., and T. Osborne. 1984. "Academic Integration of Hearing Impaired Students." *American Annals of the Deaf,* 129: 100–113.

Allen, T., B. Rawlings, and A. Schildroth. 1989. *Deaf Students and the School-to-Work Transition.* Baltimore, Md.: Paul H. Brooks.

Allen, T. E., B. W. Rawlings, and E. Remington. 1993. "Demographic and Audiological Profiles of Children with Cochlear Implants." *American Annals of the Deaf,* 138, no. 3: 260–266.

Altshuler, K. 1962. "Psychiatric Consideration in the Adult Deaf." *American Annals of the Deaf,* 107, no. 4: 560–561.

———. 1963. "Sexual Patterns and Family Relationships." In *Family and Mental Health Problems in a Deaf Population*. Edited by J. Rainer, K. Altshuler, and F. Kallman. New York: New York State Psychiatric Institute, 187–204.

———. 1974. "The Social and Psychological Development of the Deaf Child: Problems and Treatment." In *Deafness in Infancy and Early Childhood*. Edited by P. Fine. New York: Medcom Press.

Altshuler, K., and J. Rainer. 1968. *Mental Health and the Deaf: Approaches and Prospects*. Washington, D.C.: U.S. Department of Health, Education and Welfare, Social and Rehabilitation Services.

American Annals of the Deaf. 2000. "Reference Issue." *American Annals of the Deaf,* 145, no. 2.

American Psychiatric Association. 1994. *Diagnostic and Statistical Manual of Mental Disorders 4th ed.*. Washington, D.C.: Author.

Anderson, L. 1980. "Sign Language Number Systems and the Numerical Alphabet." Paper presented at NATO Advanced Institute on Sign Language and Cognition, Copenhagen.

Anderson, R. 1971. "Minimal Brain Dysfunction and the Rehabilitation Process." In *Toward More Effective Rehabilitation Services for the Severely Handicapped Deaf Client*. Edited by L. Stewart. Hot Springs: Arkansas Rehabilitation Research and Training Center, 31–49.

Anderson, R., and G. Stevens. 1969. "Qualifications of Teachers of Mentally Retarded Deaf Pupils in Residential Schools for the Deaf." *Special Education in Canada,* 43, no. 1: 23–32.

Anderson, R., G. Stevens, and E. Stuckless. 1966. *Provisions for the Education of Mentally Retarded Deaf Students in Residential Schools for the Deaf*. Pittsburgh: University of Pittsburgh.

Andrews, J. F., and D. Jordan. 1993. "Minority and Minority Deaf Professionals." *American Annals of the Deaf,* 138, no. 5: 388–396.

Angelocci, A., G. Kopp, and A. Holbrook. 1964. "The Vowel Formants of Deaf and Hearing 11- to 14-Year-Old Boys." *Journal of Speech and Hearing Disorders,* 29, no. 2: 156–170.

Aplin, Y. 1993. "Psychological Evaluation of Adults in a Cochlear Implant Program." *American Annals of the Deaf,* 138, no. 5: 415–420.

Arnold, T. 1879. *Aures Surdis: The Education of the Deaf and Dumb*. London: Eliot Stock.

Arnos, K. 1994. "Hereditary Hearing Loss." *New England Journal of Medicine*, 331: 469–470.

———. 1997. "Genetic Counseling for Hearing Loss." *Volta Review,* 99, no. 5: 85–96.

Arrowsmith, J. 1819. *The Art of Instructing the Infant Deaf and Dumb*. London: Taylor and Hessex.

Assessment of Educational Progress, Report No. 15-R-01. Princeton, N.J.: Educational Testing Service.

Avondino, J. 1918. "The Babbling Method." *Volta Review,* 20, no. 7: 667–671.

———. 1919. "The Babbling Method." *Volta Review,* 21, no. 3: 237–282.

———. 1924. *The Babbling Method: A System of Syllabic Drills for Natural Development of Speech*. Washington, D.C.: Volta Bureau.

Ayres, J. 1849. "Home Instruction for the Deaf and Dumb." *American Annals of the Deaf,* 2, no. 2: 177–187.

Bailey, D., P. Winton, J. Rouse, and A. Turnbull. 1990. "Family Goals and Infant Intervention." *Journal of Early Intervention*, 14, no. 1: 15–26.

Baker, C., and R. Battison. 1980. *Sign Language of the Deaf Community*. Silver Spring, Md.: National Association of the Deaf.

Balkany, T. 1993. "A Brief Perspective on Cochlear Implants." *New England Journal of Medicine*, 328, no. 4: 281–282.

Ballard, M. 1881. "Reflections of the Deaf Mute Before Instruction." *American Annals of the Deaf*, 26, no. 1: 34–41.

Barker, J. 1966. *Justinian and the Later Roman Empire*. Madison: University of Wisconsin Press.

Barnard, F. 1836. *Analytic Grammar with Symbolic Illustrations*. New York: E. French Company.

Barnes, H. 1940a. "A Cooperative Job Training Center for the Deaf—If." *American Annals of the Deaf*, 85, no. 5: 347–350.

———. 1940b. "The Need for Separating Advanced Vocational Training from the Elementary School Atmosphere." *American Annals of the Deaf*, 85, no. 6: 449–451.

Baroff, G. 1955. "A Psychomotor, Psychometric and Projective Study of Mentally Defective Twins." Ph.D. diss., New York University.

Barry, K. 1899. *The Five Slate System: A System of Objective Language Teaching*. Philadelphia: Sherman.

Bartlett, D. 1852. "Family Education for Young Deaf-Mute Children." *American Annals of the Deaf*, 5, no. 1: 32–35.

Beaver, D., P. Hayes, and B. Luetke-Stahlman. 1995. "In-Service Trends: General Education on Teachers Working with Educational Interpreters." *American Annals of the Deaf*, 140, no. 1: 38–46.

Behrens, T., and R. Meisegeier. 1968. "Social Studies in the Education of Deaf Children." In *Curriculum: Cognition and Content*. Edited by H. Kopp. Washington, D.C.: A. G. Bell Association, 44–48.

Bell, A. G. 1872. "Visible Speech as a Means of Communicating Articulation to Deaf Mutes." *American Annals of the Deaf*, 17, no. 1: 1–21.

———. 1883a. *Memoir upon the Formation of a Deaf Variety of the Human Race*. Washington, D.C.: National Academy of Science.

———. 1883b. "Upon a Method of Teaching Language to a Very Young Congenitally Deaf Child." *American Annals of the Deaf*, 28, no. 2: 124–139.

———. 1884. "Fallacies Concerning the Deaf." *American Annals of the Deaf*, 28, no. 2, 124–139.

———. 1906. *The Mechanism of Speech*. New York: Funk & Wagnalls.

Bell, A. M. 1898. *The Faults of Speech: A Self-Corrector*. Washington, D.C.: Volta Bureau.

———. 1904. *Popular Manual of Vocal Physiology and Visible Speech*. 3d ed. Washington, D.C.: Gibson Brothers.

———. 1932. *English Visible Speech in Twelve Lessons*. 6th ed. Revised by C. Yale. Washington, D.C.: Volta Bureau.

Bemiss, S. 1858. *Report of the Influences of Marriages of Consanguinity*. Philadelphia: Collins.

Bender, R. 1970. *The Conquest of Deafness*. Cleveland: Case Western Reserve.

Bernstein, M., and M. Morrison. 1992. "Are we ready for PL99-457?" *American Annals of the Deaf*, 137, no. 1: 7–13.

Bersoff, D., and E. Voltman. 1979. "Public Law 94-142: Legal Implications for the Education of Handicapped Children." *Journal of Research and Development in Special Education*, 12, no. 1: 10–22.

Best, H. 1943. *Deafness and the Deaf in the United States*. New York: Macmillan.

Bienenstock, M.A., and M. Vernon. 1994. "Classification by the States of Deaf and Hard of Hearing." *American Annals of the Deaf*, 139, no. 2: 80–85.

Biesold, H. 1999. *Crying Hands: Eugenics and Deaf People in Nazi Germany*. Translated by William Sayers. Washington, D.C.: Gallaudet University Press.

Bigman, S. 1961. "The Deaf in American Institutions of Higher Learning." *Personnel and Guidance Journal,* 39, no. 6: 743–749.

Binet, A. 1916. *The Development of Intelligence in Children.* New York: Arno Press.

Binet, A., and T. Simon. 1910. "An Investigation Concerning the Value of the Oral Method." *American Annals of the Deaf,* 55, no. 1: 4–33.

Birch, J., and E. Stuckless. 1963. *Programmed Instruction as a Device for the Correction of Written Language in Deaf Adolescents.* Pittsburgh: University of Pittsburgh.

Blackwell, P., E. Engen, J. Fischgrund, and C. Zarcadoolis. 1978. *Sentences and Other Systems.* Washington, D.C.: A. G. Bell Association.

Blake, G. 1970. *An Experiment in Serving Deaf Adults in a Comprehensive Rehabilitation Center.* Little Rock: Arkansas State Board for Vocational Rehabilitation.

Blank, M. 1965. "Use of the Deaf in Language Studies: A Reply to Furth." *Psychological Bulletin,* 63, no. 3: 442–444.

Bliss, C. 1965. *Semantography.* Sydney, Australia: Semantography Publications.

Bloom, B. 1980. "The New Direction in Educational Research: Alterable Variables." *Phi Delta Kappan,* 61, no. 6: 382–385.

_____. 1984. "The 2 Sigma Problem: The Search for Methods of Group Instruction as Effective as One-to-One Tutoring." *Educational Researcher,* 13, no. 6: 4–16.

Bloomfield, L. 1933. *Language.* New York: Holt.

Boatner, E. 1937. "Articulation at the American School." *New Era,* 23, no. 3: 50–57.

Boatner, E., E. Stuckless, and D. Moores. 1964. *Occupational Status of Young Deaf Adults of New England and the Need and Demand for a Regional Technical-Vocational Training Center.* West Hartford, Conn.: American School for the Deaf.

Boatner, M. 1952. "The Educational Psychology of Edward Miner Gallaudet." Ph.D. diss., Yale University.

_____. 1959a. *Edward Miner Gallaudet: The Voice of the Deaf.* Washington, D.C.: Public Affairs Press.

_____. 1959b. "The Gallaudet Papers." *Library of Congress Journal of Current Acquisitions,* 17, no. 1: 1–12.

_____. 1966. *A Dictionary of Idioms for the Deaf.* West Hartford, Conn.: American School for the Deaf.

Bonet, J. 1620. *Reducción de las Letras y Arte Para Enseñar a Hablar los Mudos.* Madrid: Par Fracisco Arbaco de Angelo.

Bonkowski, N., J. Gavelek, and T. Akamatsu. 1991. "Education and the Social Construct of Mind: Vygotskian Perspectives in the Cognitive Development of Deaf Children." In *Advances in Cognition, Education and Deafness.* Edited by D. Martin. Washington, D.C.: Gallaudet University Press, 185–194.

Boone, D. 1966. "Modification of the Voice of Deaf Children." *Volta Review,* 68, no. 7: 686–694.

Booth, E. 1878. "Thinking in Words and Gestures." *American Annals of the Deaf,* 23, no. 4: 223–225.

Bordley, J., P. Brookhauser, J. Hardy, and W. Hardy. 1967. "Observations on the Effect of Prenatal Rubella on Hearing." In *Deafness in Childhood.* Edited by F. McConnell and P. Ward. Nashville: Vanderbilt University Press, 123–141.

Bornstein, H., and K. Saulnier. 1981. "Signed English: A Brief Follow-Up to the First Evaluation." *American Annals of the Deaf,* 126, no. 1: 69–72.

_____. 1984. *The Signed English Starter.* Washington, D.C.: Gallaudet College Press.

Bornstein, H., K. Saulnier, and L. Hamilton. 1980. "Signed English: A First Evaluation." *American Annals of the Deaf,* 125, no. 3: 468–481.

———. 1983. *The Comprehensive Signed English Dictionary*. Washington, D.C.: Gallaudet College Press.

———. 1972–1984. *The Signed English Series*. Washington, D.C.: Gallaudet College Press. (Level I, 12 Beginning Books; Level II, 18 Growing-Up Books; Level III, 20 Advanced Stories and Poems; One Record; and Three Posters.)

Boswell, S. 2000. "Congress Funds Newborn Hearing Screening." *ASHA Leader,* 5, no. 1: 1, 15–16.

Bougham, J., and K. Shaver. 1982. "Genetic Aspects of Deafness." *American Annals of the Deaf,* 127, no. 3: 393–400.

Bowe, F. 1971. "Dr. Luther Robinson and Mental Health Care for Deaf Persons." *Deaf American,* 23, no. 1: 3–6.

———. 1992. "Radicalism vs. Reason: Directions in the Educational Use of ASL." *A Free Hand: Enfranchising the Education of Deaf Children*. Edited by M. Walworth, D. Moores, and T. J. O'Rourke. Silver Spring, Md.: T. J. Publishers, 170–181.

Bowen, J. 1972. *A History of Western Education: Volume I: The Ancient World*. London: Methune.

———. 1975. *A History of Western Education: Volume II: Civilization of Europe*. New York: St. Martin's Press.

Boyd, R., and J. Van Cleve. 1994. "Deaf Autonomy and Deaf Dependence." *American Annals of the Deaf,* 139, no. 4: 438–447.

Boyd, W. 1966. *The History of Western Education*. 8th ed. New York: Barnes & Noble.

Boyer, E. 1983. *High School: A Report on Secondary Education in America*. New York: Harper and Row.

Braden, J. 1991. "A Meta-analytic Review of IQ Research with Deaf Persons." In *Advances in Cognition, Education and Deafness*. Edited by D. Martin. Washington, D.C.: Gallaudet University Press, 56–61.

———. 1994. *Deafness, Deprivation, and IQ*. New York: Plenum Press.

———. In press. "The Factorial Similarity of the WISC-R Performance Scale in Deaf and Hearing Samples." *Journal of Personality and Individual Differences*.

Bragg, B. 1990. "Communication and the Deaf Community." In M. Garretson, ed., *Communication Issues Among Deaf People*. Edited by M. Garretson. Silver Spring, Md.: National Association of the Deaf, 9–14.

Braly, K. 1938. "A Study of Defective Vision Among Deaf Children." *American Annals of the Deaf,* 83, no. 3: 192–193.

Brannon, C. 1982. "Programs and Services to Hearing Impaired Mentally Retarded Children: State of the Art." In *The Multihandicapped Hearing Impaired Student: Population, Instruction and Communication*. Edited by D. Tweedie and E. Shroyer. Washington, D.C.: Gallaudet College Press, 29–36.

Brasel, K. 1975. "The Influence of Early Language and Communication Environments on the Development of Language in Deaf Children." Ph.D. diss., University of Illinois.

Braudel, F. 1981. *Civilization and Capitalism, 15th–18th Century: Volume I: The Structures of Everyday Life* (translated from French by S. Reynolds). New York: Harper and Row.

———. 1982. *Civilization and Capitalism, 15th–18th Century: Volume II: The Wheels of Commerce* (translated from French by S. Reynolds). New York: Harper and Row.

Brehm, F. 1922. "Speech Correction." *American Annals of the Deaf,* 67, no. 4: 361–370.

Breunig, L. 1965. "An Analysis of a Group of Deaf Students in Colleges for the Hearing." *Volta Review,* 67, no. 1: 17–27.

Briccetti, J. K. A. 1994. "Emotional Indicators of Deaf Children on the Draw-A-Person Test." *American Annals of the Deaf,* 137, no. 5: 500–505.

Broadbent, F., and V. Daniele. 1980. "A Review of Research on Mathematics and the Deaf." Unpublished manuscript, Syracuse University.

Brown, K. 1967. "The Genetics of Childhood Deafness." In *Deafness in Childhood.* Edited by F. McConnell and P. Ward. Nashville: Vanderbilt University Press, 177–203.

Brown, K., L. Hopkins, and M. Hudgins. 1967. "Causes of Childhood Deafness." *Proceedings of the International Conference on Oral Education of the Deaf.* Washington, D.C.: A. G. Bell Association, 77–107.

Brown, L., J. R. Sherbenou, and S. K. Johnson. 1990. *Test of Nonverbal Intelligence (2nd ed.): Examiner's Manual.* Austin, Tex.: Pro-Ed.

Brown, R. 1958. *Words and Things.* New York: Free Press.

Brownstone, D., I. Franck, and D. Brownstone. 1979. *Island of Hope, Island of Tears.* New York: Rawson, Wade.

Bruce, R. 1973. *Bell. Alexander Graham Bell and the Conquest of Solitude.* Boston: Little, Brown.

_____. 1974. *Alexander Graham Bell: Teacher of the Deaf.* Northampton, Mass.: Clarke School for the Deaf.

Bruhn, M. 1949. *The Mueller-Walle Method of Lipreading for the Hard of Hearing.* Washington, D.C.: Volta Bureau.

Buell, E. 1931. *A Comparison of the Barry Five Slate System and the Fitzgerald Key.* Washington, D.C.: Volta Bureau.

Bunde, L. 1979. *Deaf Parents—Hearing Children.* Washington, D.C.: Registry of Interpreters for the Deaf.

Bunger, A. 1961. *Speech Reading: Jena Method.* 4th ed. Danville, Ill.: Interstate Press.

Burlingame, R. 1964. *Out of Silence into Sound: The Life of Alexander Graham Bell.* New York: Macmillan.

Burnet, J. 1854. "The Necessity of Methodical Signs Considered." *American Annals of the Deaf,* 8: 1–15.

Burns, D., and G. Stenquist. 1960. "The Deaf-Blind in the United States: Their Care, Education and Guidance." *Rehabilitation Literature,* 21, no. 3: 334–344.

Buxton, 1858. *An Inquiry into the Causes of Deaf-Dumbness; Congenital and Acquired.* Liverpool, England: Brakell.

Calderon, R., J. Bargones, and S. Sidman. 1998. "Characteristics of Hearing Families and Their Young Deaf and Hard of Hearing Children." *American Annals of the Deaf,* 143, no. 4: 296–305.

Calderon, R. J., and S. Low. 1998. "Early Social-Emotional Development in Children with Hearing Loss: Families with and without Fathers." *American Annals of the Deaf,* 143, no. 3: 225–234.

Calvert, D. 1962. "Speech Sound Duration and the Surdsonant Error." *Volta Review,* 78, no. 1: 76–81.

_____. 1970. "Multi-Handicapped Deaf Children: Problems and Responses." *Proceedings of the 1969 Conference of American Instructors of the Deaf.* Washington, D.C.: U.S. Government Printing Office, 58–66.

_____. 1976. "Communication Practices: Aural/Oral and Visual/Oral." *Volta Review,* 78, no. 1: 76–81.

Calvert, D., and R. Silverman. 1975. *Speech and Deafness.* Washington, D.C.: A. G. Bell Association.

Carew, M. 1999. "Programs and Services for the Deaf." *American Annals of the Deaf,* 144, no. 2.

Carlin, J. 1851. "Advantages and Disadvantages of the Use of Signs." *American Annals of the Deaf,* 4: 49–57.

Carrier, J. 1974. *Application of Functional Analysis and a Nonspeech Response Mode to Teaching Language*. Washington, D.C.: American Speech and Hearing Association, Monograph no. 18.

———. 1976. "Application of Nonspeech Language Systems with the Severely Language Handicapped." In *Communication Assessment and Intervention Strategies*. Edited by L. Lloyd. Baltimore: University Park Press, 523–548.

Carton, L. 1883. *L'Education de Sourds-Muets (in Miscelleae)*. Paris: Dubrano & Dupont.

Centers and Services for Deaf-Blind Children. 1969. Washington, D.C.: Bureau of Education for the Handicapped.

Cerra, K., S. Watts-Taffe, and S. Rose. 1997. "Fostering Reader Response and Developing Comprehension Strategies in Deaf and Hard of Hearing Children." *American Annals of the Deaf*, 142, no. 5: 379–386.

Chaves, T., and J. Solar. 1974. "Pedro Ponce de Leon: First Teacher of the Deaf." *Sign Language Studies*, 5, no. 1: 48–63.

Chicago Jewish Vocational Service (CJVS) Project for the Deaf. 1972. Chicago: Chicago Jewish Vocational Service.

Chomsky, N. 1965. *Aspects of the Theory of Syntax*. Cambridge, Mass.: M.I.T. Press.

———. 1967. "The Formal Nature of Language." In *Biological Foundations of Language*. New York: Wiley, 397–442.

———. 1968. *Language and Mind*. New York: Harcourt Brace Jovanovich.

Chung, C., and K. Brown. 1970. "Family Studies of Early Childhood Deafness." *American Journal of Human Genetics*, 22, no. 4: 630–644.

Clark, C. 1977. "A Comparative Study of Young Children's Ease of Learning Words Represented in the Graphic Systems of Rebus, Bliss, Carrier-Peak, and Traditional Orthography." Ph.D. diss., University of Minnesota.

Clark, C., and D. Moores. 1980. *Clark Early Language Program*. Hingham, Mass.: Teaching Resources Corporation.

Clark, C., and R. Woodcock. 1977. "Graphic Systems of Communication." In *Communication Assessment and Intervention Strategies*. Edited by L. Lloyd. Baltimore: University Park Press, 549–606.

Clark, J., 1975. "Theoretical and Technical Considerations in Oral Proficiency Testing." In *Testing Language Proficiency*. Edited by R. Jones and B. Spolsky. Washington, D.C.: Center for Applied Linguistics, 47–71.

Clerc, L. 1851. "Some Hints to Teaching the Deaf." *Proceedings of Second Convention of American Instructors of the Deaf and Dumb*. Hartford, Conn.: Case, Tiffany & Company, 64–75.

Cochrane, W. 1871. "Methodical Signs Instead of Colloquial." *American Annals of the Deaf*, 16: 11–17.

Cohen, B. 1980. "Emotionally Disturbed Hearing Impaired Children: A Review of the Literature." *American Annals of the Deaf*, 125, no. 9: 1040–1048.

Cohen, N. L., S. B. Waltzman, and S. G. Fisher. 1993. "Complications Related to Cochlear Implants." *New England Journal of Medicine*, 328, no. 4: 233–237.

Coleman, J., and T. Hoffer. 1987. *Public and Private High Schools*. New York: Basic Books.

Coley, J., and P. Bockmiller. 1980. "Teaching Reading to the Deaf: An Examination of Teacher Preparedness and Practices." *American Annals of the Deaf*, 125, no. 7: 909–915.

Collins, J. 1969. "Communication Between Deaf Children of Preschool Age and Their Mothers." Ph.D. diss., University of Pittsburgh.

Commission on Education of the Deaf. 1988. *Toward Equality: Education of the Deaf*. Washington, D.C.: U.S. Government Printing Office.

Connor, L. 1971. *Speech for the Deaf Child: Knowledge and Use*. Washington, D.C.: A. G. Bell Association.

Conrad, R. 1979. *The Deaf School Child*. New York: Harper and Row.

Cooper, R., and J. Rosenstein. 1966. "Language Acquisition of Young Deaf Children." *Volta Review,* 68, no. 1: 58–67.

Corbett, E., and C. Jensema. 1981. *Teachers of the Hearing Impaired: Descriptive Profiles*. Washington, D.C.: Gallaudet College Press.

Corson, H. 1973. "Comparing Deaf Children of Oral Deaf Parents and Deaf Children Using Manual Communication with Deaf Children of Hearing Parents on Academic, Social, and Communicative Functioning." Ph.D. diss, University of Cincinnati.

Corson, H., and E. R. Stuckless. 1994. "Programs and Services for the Deaf." *American Annals of the Deaf,* 139.

Coucke, P., G. Van Camp, and B. Djoyodiharjo. 1994. "Linkage of Autosomal Dominant Hearing Loss to the Short Arm of Chromosome 1 in Two Families." *New England Journal of Medicine,* 331: 425–431.

Craig, W. 1964. "Effects of Preschool Training on the Development of Reading and Lipreading Skills of Deaf Children." *American Annals of the Deaf,* 109, no. 3: 280–296.

Craig, W., and H. Craig. 1975. "Directory of Services for the Deaf." *American Annals of the Deaf,* 120.

_____. 1985. "Directory of Services for the Deaf." *American Annals of the Deaf,* 130.

Craig, W., J. Newman, and N. Burrows. 1972. "An Experiment in Post Secondary Education for Deaf People." *American Annals of the Deaf,* 117, no. 5: 606–611.

Crammatte, A. 1968. *Deaf Persons in Professional Employment*. Springfield, Ill.: Charles C Thomas.

Cronbach, L. 1957. "The Two Disciplines of Scientific Psychology." *American Psychologist,* 12: 671–684.

Crouter, A. 1885. "Preliminary Home Training." *American Annals of the Deaf,* 30, no. 3: 225–228.

Cusick, P. 1983. *The American High School and the Egalitarian Model*. New York: Longmans.

Dahl, K. 1985. "Research on Writing Development." *Volta Review,* 87: 35–46.

Dalgarno, G. 1680. *Didascopholus; or the Deaf and Dumb Man's Tutor*. Oxford: Timothy Halton (reprinted in *American Annals of the Deaf,* 1857, no. 9: 14–64).

Dantona, R. 1970. *Centers for the Deaf-Blind*. Washington, D.C.: Bureau of Education for the Handicapped.

Davis, H. 1970. "Abnormal Hearing and Deafness." In *Hearing and Deafness*. Edited by H. Davis and R. Silverman. New York: Holt, 83–139.

Day, H., I. Fusfeld, and P. Pintner. 1928. *A Survey of American Schools for the Deaf, 1924–25*. Washington, D.C.: National Research Council.

Degerando, J. 1827. *De l'Education des Sourds-Muets de Naissance*. Paris: Chez Meguignon L'Aire Père, ed.

DeLadsbut, L. 1815. *A Collection of the Most Remarkable Definitions and Answers of Massieu and Clerc, Deaf and Dumb, to the Various Questions Put to Them of Public Lectures of the Abbé Sicard in London*. London: Cox and Baylis.

Deland, F. 1931. *The Story of Lipreading*. Washington, D.C.: Volta Bureau.

Delgado, G., ed. 1984. *The Hispanic Deaf*. Washington, D.C.: Gallaudet College Press.

Diefendorf, A., and B. Weber. 1994. "Identification of Hearing Loss." In *Infants and Toddlers with Hearing Loss*. Edited by J. Roush and N. Matkin. Baltimore: York Press, 43–64.

Dietz, C. H. 1995. *Moving Towards the Standards: A National Action Plan for Mathematics Education Reform for the Deaf*. Washington, D.C.: Pre-College Programs, Gallaudet University.

Dobbert, M. 1974. "Education, Schools and Cultural Mapping." In *Education and Cultural Process: Toward an Anthropology of Education*. Edited by G. Spindler. New York: Holt, 204–218.

Doctor, P., ed. 1962. "Directory of Services for the Deaf." *American Annals of the Deaf,* 107.

Dolman, D. 1992. "Some Concerns About Using Whole Language Approaches with Deaf Children." *American Annals of the Deaf,* 137, no. 3: 278–287.

———. 1993. "In Response to Carolyn Ewoldt." *American Annals of the Deaf,* 138, no. 1: 12–13.

Donoghue, R. 1968. "The Deaf Personality: A Study in Contrasts." *Journal of Rehabilitation of the Deaf,* 2, no. 1: 35–51.

Downs, M. 1967. "Early Identification and Principles of Management." *Proceedings of the International Conference on Oral Education of the Deaf.* Washington, D.C.: A. G. Bell Association, 746–757.

Doyle, J. 1893. *Histories of the American Schools for the Deaf and Dumb.* Hartford, Conn.: American School for the Deaf.

Drouot, E. 1932. Prologo de Seguin, E. *Jacobo Rodriguez Pereira, Primer Maestro de Sordomudos en Francia.* Madrid: Francisco Beltran, 5–21.

DuBow, S. 1989. *Legal Rights of Hearing Impaired People.* Washington, D.C.: Gallaudet University Press.

Duckworth, E. 1984. "What Teachers Know: The Best Knowledge Base." *Harvard Educational Review,* 54, no. 1: 15–20.

Dunn, L. 1968. "Special Education for the Mildly Retarded: Is Much of It Justified?" *Exceptional Children,* 35, no. 1: 13–20.

Dunn, L., and L. Dunn. 1981. *Peabody Picture Vocabulary Test-Revised.* Circle Pines, Minn.: American Guidance Service.

Duvall, E. 1970. *Family Development.* 4th ed. Philadelphia: Lippincott.

Dworkin, G., ed. 1976. *The IQ Controversy: Critical Readings.* New York: Pantheon Books.

D'Zamko, M., and I. Hampton. 1985. "Personnel Preparation for Multihandicapped Hearing Impaired Students." *American Annals of the Deaf,* 130, no. 1: 9–14.

"Early Home Training of Deaf Mute Children." 1879. *American Annals of the Deaf,* 24, no. 1: 9–36 (translated from 1869 Reprint of the Royal Wurtemburg Institute for the Deaf).

Education of the Deaf: The Possible Place of Fingerspelling and Signing. 1968. London: Her Majesty's Stationery Office.

Enerstvedt, R. T. 1999. *Legacy of the Past: Those Who Are Gone But Have Not Left.* Dronning, Denmark: Forlaget Nord-Press.

Enerstvedt, T. 1999. "New Technology: To What Does It Lead?" *American Annals of the Deaf,* 144, no. 3: 242–249.

Erikson, E. 1963. *Childhood and Society.* New York: Norton.

———. 1964. *Insight and Responsibility.* New York: Norton.

———. 1968. *Identity, Youth and Crisis.* New York: Norton.

———. 1969. *Identity and the Life Cycle.* New York: International University Press.

Erting, C. 1983. "The Development of Communication Skills and the Construction of Social Identity by Preschool Deaf Children Through Interaction with Deaf and Hearing Adults." Ph.D. diss., American University, Washington, D.C.

Evans, J. F. 1995. "Conversations at Home: A Case Study of a Young Deaf Child's Experiences in a Family in Which All Others Can Hear." *American Annals of the Deaf,* 140, no. 4: 324–332.

Ewoldt, C. 1981. "A Psycholinguistic Description of Selected Deaf Children Reading in Sign Language." *Reading Research Quarterly,* 13, no. 1: 58–59.

_____. 1985. "A Descriptive Study of the Developing Literacy of Young Hearing Impaired Children." *Volta Review,* 87: 109–126.

_____. 1993. "Whole Language." *American Annals of the Deaf,* 138, no. 1: 10–12.

Farber, B. 1957. "An Index of Marital Integration." *Sociometry,* 20: 117–134.

_____. 1958. *Effects of a Severely Retarded Child on Family Integration.* Chicago: Society for Research on Child Development, Monograph 24, no. 3.

_____. 1960. *Family Organization and Crisis.* Chicago: Society for Research on Child Development, Monograph, 25, no. 1.

Farrar, D. 1923. *Arnold on the Education of the Deaf.* London: Francis Carter.

Farrugia, D., and G. Austin. 1980. "A Study of Social-Emotional Adjustment Patterns of Hearing Impaired Students in Different Educational Settings." *American Annals of the Deaf,* 125, no. 5: 535–541.

Farwell, R. 1976. "Speech Reading: A Research Review." *American Annals of the Deaf,* 121, no. 2: 13–30.

Fay, E. 1869. "Acquisition of Language." *American Annals of the Deaf,* 14: 193–204.

_____. 1893. "Report of the Committee on a Technical School." *American Annals of the Deaf,* 38, no. 3: 279–280.

_____. 1898. *Marriages of the Deaf in America.* Washington, D.C.: Gibson Brothers.

_____. 1912. "What Did Lucretius Say?" *American Annals of the Deaf,* 57, no. 3: 213.

Feldman, H. 1970. *A History of Audiology.* New York: Columbia University.

Fellendorf, G. 1966. *Bibliography on Deafness.* Washington, D.C.: A.G. Bell Association.

Ferreri, G. 1908. *The American Institutions for Education for the Deaf.* Philadelphia: Pennsylvania School for the Deaf.

Fisch, L., ed. 1964. *Research in Deafness in Children.* London: Billing and Sons.

Fischer, L., and D. de Lorenzo, eds. 1983. *History of the College for the Deaf, 1857–1907, by Edward Miner Gallaudet.* Washington, D.C.: Gallaudet College Press.

Fischer, R. 1993. "Abbé de l'Epee and the Living Dictionary." In *Deaf History Unveiled: Interpretations from the New Scholarship.* Edited by J. Van Cleve. Washington, D.C.: Gallaudet University Press, 13–26.

Fisher, S., M. Harlow, and D. Moores. 1974. *Postsecondary Programs for the Deaf: Monograph II: External Views.* Minneapolis: University of Minnesota Research and Demonstration Center in Education of Handicapped Children, Research Report No. 61.

Fisher, S., D. Moores, and M. Harlow. 1974. *Postsecondary Programs for the Deaf: Monograph III: Internal Views.* Minneapolis: University of Minnesota Research and Demonstration Center in Education of Handicapped Children, Research Report No. 67.

Fisiloglu, A. C., and H. Fisiloglu. 1996. "Turkish Families with Deaf and Hard of Hearing Children: A Systems Approach." *American Annals of the Deaf,* 141, no. 3: 231–235.

Fitzgerald, E. 1931. *Straight Language for the Deaf.* Staunton, Va.: McClure Company.

Foster, S., and L. Elliot. 1986. *The Best of Both Worlds: Interviews with NTID Transfer Students.* Technical Report. Rochester, N.Y.: Rochester Institute of Technology.

Francis, J. 1980. *The Evaluation of Language Proficiency.* Washington, D.C.: Gallaudet College.

Frederick v. *Thomas,* 419 F. Supp. 960 E.D. Pa. 1976, Aff'd 557 F.2d 373, 3d Cir., 1977.

Frederickson, J. 1985. *Life After Deaf: Impact of Deafness on a Family.* Silver Spring, Md.: National Association of the Deaf.

Freedman, D. 1971. "Congenital and Prenatal Sensory Deprivation: Some Studies in Early Development." *American Journal of Psychiatry,* 127, no. 7: 1539–1545.

Freeman, R. 1977. "Psychiatric Aspects of Sensory Disorders and Interpretation." In *Epidemiological Approaches in Child Psychiatry.* Edited by P. Graham. New York: Academic Press, 275–304.

Freeman, R., R. Boese, and C. Carbin. 1981. *Can't Your Child Hear?* Baltimore: University Park Press.

Freeman, R., S. Malkin, and J. Hastings. 1975. "Psychosocial Problems of Deaf Children and Their Families: A Comparative Study." *American Annals of the Deaf,* 120, no. 4: 391–401.

Frey, R., and I. Krause. 1971. "The Incidence of Color Blindness Among Deaf Children." *Exceptional Children,* 38, no. 5: 393–394.

Frisina, R. 1955. "A Psychological Study of the Mentally Retarded Deaf Child." Ph.D. diss., Northwestern University.

_____. 1974. *Report of the Committee to Redefine Deaf and Hard of Hearing for Educational Purposes,* Washington, D.C.

Frost, S. 1947. *History of Education.* Woodbury, N.Y.: Barrons.

Fry, D., and E. Whetnall. 1954. "The Auditory Approach in the Training of Deaf Children." *Lancet,* 266, no. 4: 584–587.

Fundenberg, H., D. Sytes, J. Caldwell, and J. Wells. 1980. *Basic and Clinical Immunology.* Los Altos, Calif.: Lange Medical Publications.

Furlinger, E. 1999. "Narrative Therapy and Children with Hearing Impairments." *American Annals of the Deaf,* 144, no. 1: 51–61.

Furth, H. 1964. "Research with the Deaf: Implications for Language and Cognition." *Psychological Bulletin,* 62, no. 2: 145–162.

_____. 1966. "A Comparison of Reading Test Norms for Deaf and Hearing Children." *American Annals of the Deaf,* 111, no. 5: 461–462.

_____. 1969a. *Thinking Without Language.* New York: Free Press.

_____. 1969b. *A Thinking Laboratory for Deaf Children.* Washington, D.C.: Catholic University Press.

_____. 1971. "Education for Thinking." *Journal of Rehabilitation of the Deaf,* 5, no. 1: 7–71.

_____. 1973. *Deafness and Learning: A Psychological Approach.* Belmont, Calif.: Wadsworth.

_____. 1974. "The Role of Language in the Child's Development." *Proceedings of the 1973 Convention of American Instructors of the Deaf.* Washington, D.C.: U.S. Government Printing Office, 258–261.

Fusfeld, I. 1926. "National Research Council Committee on the Survey of Schools for the Deaf." *American Annals of the Deaf,* 71, no. 1: 97–135.

_____. 1934a. "Discontinuation of Blatter fur Taubstummenbildung." *American Annals of the Deaf,* 79, no. 4: 356–358.

_____. 1934b. "The Sterilization Law in Germany." *American Annals of the Deaf,* 79, no. 2: 181–182.

Gallaudet, E., chairman. 1868. "Panel Discussion on Articulation." *Proceedings of the National Conference of Principals of Institutions for the Deaf and Dumb.* Washington, D.C., 60–90.

_____. 1871. "Is the Sign Language Used to Excess in Teaching Deaf Mutes?" *American Annals of the Deaf,* 16, no. 1: 26–33.

_____. 1884. "Response to Dr. Bell." *American Annals of the Deaf,* 29, no. 2: 64–67.

_____. 1886. "History of the Education of the Deaf in the United States." *American Annals of the Deaf,* 32, no. 3: 110–147.

_____. 1887. "The Values of Sign Language for the Deaf." *American Annals of the Deaf,* 32, no. 2: 141–147.

_____. 1888. *The Life of Thomas Hopkins Gallaudet.* New York: Holt.

_____. 1899. "Must the Sign Language Go?" *American Annals of the Deaf,* 44, no. 5: 225–229.

_____. 1907. *The Present State of Deaf Mute Education in America.* Report of the International Congress on Education of the Deaf. Edinburgh, Scotland: Darwin Press, 18–24.

Gallaudet, T. 1826. *Tenth Annual Report of the American Asylum at Hartford for the Education of the Deaf and Dumb.* Hartford, Conn.

———. 1828. *Twelfth Annual Report of the American Asylum at Hartford for the Education of the Deaf and Dumb.* Hartford, Conn.

Gamble, H. 1984. "A National Survey of Programs for Intellectually and Academically Gifted Hearing-Impaired Students." Ph.D. diss., University of Maryland.

———. 1985. "A National Survey of Programs for Intellectually and Academically Gifted Hearing-Impaired Students." *American Annals of the Deaf,* 130, no. 6: 508–513.

Gannon, J. 1981. *Deaf Heritage: A Narrative History of Deaf America.* Silver Spring, Md.: National Association of the Deaf.

———. 1988. *The Week the World Heard Gallaudet.* Washington, D.C.: Gallaudet University Press.

Garber, C., G. Garne, and E. Testut. 1984. "A Survey of Certification Requirements for Teachers of the Hearing Impaired." *Volta Review,* 86, no. 4: 342–346.

Garnett, C. 1968. *The Exchange of Letters Between Samuel Heinicke and Abbé Charles Michel de l'Epée.* New York: Vantage.

Garretson, M. 1990. "Communication Parameters." *The NAD Broadcaster,* January, 12, no. 5: 3.

Garrison, M., and D. Hamil. 1971. "Who Are the Retarded?" *Exceptional Children,* 38, no. 1: 13–20.

Garrison, W., S. Tesch, and P. DeLaro. 1978. "An Assessment of Self Concept Levels Among Post Secondary Deaf Adolescents." *American Annals of the Deaf,* 123, no. 8: 968–975.

Gaustad, M. 1986. "Longitudinal Effects of Manual English Instruction on Deaf Children's Morphological Skills." *Applied Linguistics,* 7, no. 2: 101–127.

Geanakoplos, D. 1976. *Interaction of the Sibling Byzantine and Western Cultures in the Middle Ages and Renaissance Italy.* New Haven: Yale University Press.

Gentile, A. 1972. *Academic Achievement Test Results of a National Testing Program for Hearing Impaired Students: 1971.* Washington, D.C.: Gallaudet College Office of Demographic Studies, Ser. D., No. 9.

———. 1973. *Further Studies in Achievement Testing of Hearing Impaired Students: Spring, 1971.* Washington, D.C.: Gallaudet College Office of Demographic Studies, Ser. D, No. 14.

Gentile, A., and B. McCarthy. 1973. *Additional Handicapping Conditions Among Hearing Impaired Students, United States: 1971–72.* Washington, D.C.: Gallaudet College Office of Demographic Studies, Ser. D, No. 14.

Gibbins, S. 1989. "The Provision of School Psychological Services for the Hearing Impaired: A National Survey." *Volta Review,* 91: 95–103.

Gillespie, C., and S. Twardosz. 1996. "Survey of Literacy Environments and Practices in Residences at Schools for the Deaf." *American Annals of the Deaf,* 141, no. 3: 224–230.

———. 1997. "A Group Storybook Reading Intervention with Children at a Residential School for the Deaf." *American Annals of the Deaf,* 142, no. 4: 320–332.

Gillett, H. 1870. "Language." *American Annals of the Deaf,* 152: 232–244.

Goetzinger, C., J. Ortiz, B. Bellerose, and L. Buchan. 1966. "A Study of the Rorschach with Deaf and Hearing Adolescents." *American Annals of the Deaf,* 111, no. 5: 510–522.

Goetzinger, C., and E. Rousey. 1959. "Educational Achievement of Deaf Children." *American Annals of the Deaf,* 105, no. 2: 221–224.

Goldin-Meadow, S., and H. Feldman. 1975. "The Creation of a Communication System: A Study of Deaf Children of Hearing Parents." *Sign Language Studies,* 8: 225–234.

Goldstein, M. 1939. *The Acoustic Method for the Training of the Deaf and Hard of Hearing.* St. Louis: Laryngoscope Press.

Goodhill, V. 1950. "Nuclear Deafness and the Nerve-Deaf Child: The Importance of the Rh Factor." *Transactions of the American Academy of Ophthalmology and Otolaryngology,* 54: 671–687.

_____. 1956. "Rh Child: Deaf or Aphasic?" *Journal of Speech and Hearing Disorders,* 21, no. 4: 407–410.

_____. 1967. "Auditory Pathway Lesions Resulting from Rh Incompatibility." In *Deafness in Childhood.* Edited by F. McConnell and P. Ward. Nashville, Tenn.: Vanderbilt University Press, 215–228.

_____. 1968. "Deafness Research." *Volta Review,* 70, no. 8: 620–629.

Goodlad, J. 1983. *A Place Called School.* New York: McGraw-Hill.

Goodman, K. 1967. "Reading: A Psycholinguistic Guessing Game." *Journal of the Reading Specialist,* 6, no. 2: 126–135.

_____. 1973. "The Goodman Taxonomy of Reading Miscues." In *Findings of Research in Miscue Analysis: Classroom Implications.* Edited by D. Allen and D. Watson. Urbana, Ill.: National Council of Teachers of English.

Goodstein, H. 1990. "American Sign Language." In *Communication Issues Among Deaf People.* Edited by M. Garretson. Silver Spring, Md.: National Association of the Deaf, 47–50.

Goodwin, E. M. 1893. "The North Carolina Institution for the Deaf and Dumb and Blind." In *Histories of American Schools for the Deaf: Volume 1, Public Schools Established 1817–1854.* Edited by E. A. Fay. Washington, D.C.: Volta Bureau, 1–8.

Gordon, J. 1885a. "Deaf Mutes and the Public Schools from 1815 to the Present Day." *American Annals of the Deaf,* 30, no. 2: 121–143.

_____. 1885b. "Hints to Parents." *American Annals of the Deaf,* 30, no. 4: 241–250.

Gormley, K. 1981. "On the Influence of Familiarity on Deaf Students' Text Recall." *American Annals of the Deaf,* 129, no. 9: 1024–1030.

Goss, R. 1970. "Language Used by Mothers of Deaf Children and Mothers of Hearing Children." *American Annals of the Deaf,* 115, no. 2: 93–96.

Graves, F. 1917. *A History of Education in Modern Times.* New York: Macmillan.

_____. 1918. *A History of Education During Middle Ages and the Transition to Modern Times.* New York: Macmillan.

Greeley, A. 1981. *The Irish Americans.* New York: Harper and Row.

Greenberg, J. 1963. *Universals of Language.* Cambridge, Mass.: M.I.T. Press.

Greenberg, M. 1978. "Attachment Behavior, Communicative Competence and Parental Attitudes in Preschool Deaf Children." Ph.D. diss., University of Virginia.

_____. 1980. "Social Integration Between Deaf Preschoolers and Their Mothers: The Effects of Communication Method and Communicative Competence." *Developmental Psychology,* 16, no. 4: 465–474.

_____. 1983. "Family Stress and Child Competence." *American Annals of the Deaf,* 128, no. 5: 407–417.

Greenberg, M., and C. Kusché. 1993. *Promoting Social and Emotional Growth in Deaf Children: The PATHS Project.* Seattle: University of Washington Press.

Greenberger, D. 1879. "The Natural Method." *American Annals of the Deaf,* 24, no. 1: 33–38.

Gregory, S. 1976. *The Deaf Child and His Family.* London: George Allen.

Griffin, A. W. 1993. *Family Therapy: Fundamentals of Theory and Practice.* New York: Bruner/Mazel.

Griffiths, C. 1967a. *Conquering Childhood Deafness.* New York: Exposition Press.

_____. 1967b. "Auditory Training in the First Year of Life." *Proceedings of International Conference on Oral Education of the Deaf.* Washington, D.C.: A. G. Bell Association, 1758–1772.

_____. 1975. "The Auditory Approach: Its Rationale, Techniques and Results." *Audiology and Hearing Education,* 1, no. 1: 35–39.

Grinker, R. 1967. "Conference Summary." In *Psychiatry and the Deaf.* Edited by J. Rainer and K. Altshuler. Washington, D.C.: U.S. Department of Health, Education and Welfare, Social and Rehabilitation Services, 147–154.

Groce, N. 1980. "Everyone Here Spoke Sign Language." *Natural History,* 89, no. 6: 10–19.

_____. 1981. "Hereditary Deafness on the Island of Martha's Vineyard." Ph.D. diss., Brown University, Providence, R.I.

_____. 1985. *Everyone Here Spoke Sign Language.* Cambridge, Mass.: Harvard University Press.

Groht, M. 1933. "Language as Taught at the Lexington Street School." *American Annals of the Deaf,* 78, no. 4: 280–281.

_____. 1958. *Natural Language for Deaf Children.* Washington, D.C.: A.G. Bell Association.

Grossman, F. K. 1972. *Brothers and Sisters of Retarded Children: An Exploratory Study.* Syracuse, N.Y.: Syracuse University Press.

Gustason, G. 1983. *Teaching and Learning Signing Exact English: An Idea Book.* Rossmoor, Calif.: Modern Signs Press.

Gustason, G., D. Pfetzing, and E. Zawolkow. 1972. *Signing Exact English.* Rossmoor, Calif.: Modern Signs Press.

Hairston, E. 1994. "A Comparative Analysis of Deaf Students' Self-concept by Race, Gender, and Placement." Ph.D. diss., Gallaudet University, Washington, D.C.

Haj, F. 1970. *Disability in Antiquity.* New York: Philosophical Library.

Hanin, L., P. Rothschild, and K. D. Mueller. 1995. "Cochlear Implants Benefit Children." *American Annals of the Deaf,* 140, no. 3: 247.

Hansen, V. C. 1929. *Beretning um Sindslidelse Blandt Damarks Dovstumme.* Copenhagen, Denmark.

Hanshaw, J. 1982. "On Deafness, Cytomegalovirus, and Neonatal Screening." *American Journal of Diseases of Children,* 136: 886–887.

Harlow, M., S. Fisher, and D. Moores. 1974. *Postsecondary Programs for the Deaf: Monograph V: Follow-Up Data.* Minneapolis: University of Minnesota Research and Demonstration Center in Education of Handicapped Children, Research Report No. 75.

Harlow, M., D. Moores, and S. Fisher. 1974. *Postsecondary Programs for the Deaf: Monograph IV: Empirical Data Analysis.* Minneapolis: University of Minnesota Research and Demonstration Center in Education of Handicapped Children, Research Report No. 72.

Harris, A. 1978. "The Development of the Deaf Individual and the Deaf Community." In *Deaf Children: Developmental Perspectives.* Edited by L. Liben. New York: Academic Press, 217–233.

Harris, R. 1978. "Impulse Control in Deaf Children." In *Deaf Children: Developmental Perspectives.* Edited by L. Liben. New York: Academic Press, 137–156.

Hartbrauer, R. 1975. *Aural Rehabilitation.* Springfield, Ill.: Charles C Thomas.

Harvey, J., and J. Siantz. 1979. "Public Education and the Handicapped." *Journal of Research and Development in Education,* 12, no. 1: 1–9.

Hatfield, N., F. Caccamise, and P. Siple. 1978. "Deaf Students' Language Competence: A Bilingual Perspective." *American Annals of the Deaf,* 123, no. 1: 8–47.

Heath, S. 1981. "English in Our Language Heritage." In *Language in the USA.* Edited by A. Ferguson and S. Heath. Cambridge: Cambridge University Press, 6–20.

Heider, F., and G. Heider. 1940a. "A Comparison of Sentence Structure of Deaf and Hearing Children." *Psychological Monographs,* 52, no. 1 (Whole No. 232): 42–103.

_____. 1940b. "A Comparison of Color Sorting Behavior of Deaf and Hearing Children." *Psychological Monographs,* 52, no. 1 (Whole No. 232): 6–22.

_____. 1941. "Studies in the Psychology of the Deaf." *Psychological Monographs,* Vol. VIII. Evanston, Ill.: American Psychological Association.

Hellman, S., P. Chute, R. Kretschmer, M. Nevins, S. Parisier, and L. Thurston. 1991. "The Development of a Children's Implant Profile." *American Annals of the Deaf,* 136, no. 2: 77–81.

Hester, M. 1963. "Manual Communication." *Proceedings of International Congress on Education of the Deaf.* Washington, D.C.: U.S. Government Printing Office, 211–222.

Higgins, P. 1980. *Outsiders in a Hearing World: A Sociology of Deafness.* Beverly Hills, Calif.: Sage.

Hill, M. 1868. *Die Giestlichen und Scholleber im Dionste der Traubstrummen (Pastors and Preachers in the Service of Deaf Mutes).* Wiemar, Germany: Bohlin.

Hill, R., N. Foote, J. Aldous, R. Carlson, and R. MacDonald. 1970. *Family Development in Three Generations.* Cambridge, Mass.: Shenkman Publishing Company.

Hinde, R. 1966. *Animal Behavior.* New York: McGraw-Hill.

Hirsch, D. 1887. "Advice to Parents." *American Annals of the Deaf,* 22, no. 2: 93–103.

Hoeman, H., and J. Briga. 1980. "Hearing Impairment." In *Handbook of Special Education.* Edited by J. Kauffman and D. Hallahan. Englewood Cliffs, N.J.: Prentice-Hall, 222–248.

Hoffmeister, R. 1985. "Families with Deaf Parents: A Functional Perspective." In *Children of Handicapped Parents.* Edited by K. Thurman. New York: Academic Press, 111–130.

Holcomb, R. 1970. "The Total Approach." *Proceedings of International Congress on Education of the Deaf,* Stockholm, 104–107.

Holt, J. 1993. "Stanford Achievement Test—8th Edition: Reading Comprehension Subgroup Results." *American Annals of the Deaf,* 138: 172–175.

Holt, J., C. Traxler, and T. Allen. 1992. *Interpreting the Scores: A User's Guide to the 8th Edition, Stanford Achievement Test for Educators of Deaf and Hard of Hearing Students.* Technical Report 92-1. Washington, D.C.: Gallaudet Research Institute.

Howe, H. 1984. "Introduction: Symposium on the Year of the Reports." *Harvard Educational Review,* 54, no. 1: 1–3.

Hubbard, G. 1868. *The First Annual Report of the Clarke Institution for Deaf Mutes.* Boston: Wright & Potter.

_____. 1884. "Response to Gallaudet." *American Annals of the Deaf,* 29, no. 2: 64–67.

Hudgins, C. 1934. "A Comparative Study of Intelligibility of Speech of Deaf and Hearing Subjects." *Journal of Genetic Psychology,* 54, no. 1, 64–76.

_____. 1936. "A Study of Respiration and Speech." *Volta Review,* 38, no. 6: 341–343, 347.

_____. 1937. "Voice Production and Breath Control in the Speech of the Deaf." *American Annals of the Deaf,* 83, no. 4: 338–363.

Hudgins, C., and M. Numbers. 1942. "An Investigation of Intelligibility of Speech of the Deaf." *Genetic Psychology Monographs,* 25: 289–392.

Hudgins, R. 1973. "Causes of Deafness Among Students at the Clarke School for the Deaf." *Clarke School for the Deaf, 106th Annual Report.* Northampton, Mass., 59–60.

Huervas y Panduro, L. 1795. *Escuela Española de Sordo-Mudos o'Arte para Enseñarlos a Escribir y Hablar el Idioma Español.* Madrid: En La Imprinta Real.

Huizing, H. 1959. "Deaf Mutism: Modern Trends, Treatment and Prevention." *Advances in Otolaryngology,* 7, no. 1: 74–106.

Hummel, J., and B. Schimer. 1984. "Review of Research and Description of Programs for the Social Development of the Hearing Impaired." *Volta Review,* 86, no. 2: 259–266.

Humphries, T., and C. Padden. 1992. *Learning American Sign Language*. Englewood Cliffs, N.J.: Prentice-Hall.

Hunt, J., and W. Marshall. 1994. *Code of Ethics for Interpreters for the Deaf*. Silver Spring, Md.: Registry of Interpreters for the Deaf.

Hurwitz, S. 1971. *Habilitation of Deaf Adults: Final Report*. St. Louis: Jewish Employment and Vocational Service.

Inhelder, B., and J. Piaget. 1958. *The Growth of Logical Thinking from Childhood to Adolescence*. New York: Basic Books.

Jacobs, J. 1856. "The Methodical Signs for AND and the Verb TO BE." *American Annals of the Deaf*, 8: 185–186.

Jacobs, L. 1996. "Just How Hard Is It to Learn ASL? The Case for ASL as a Truly Foreign Language." In *Multicultural Aspects of Sociolinguistics in Deaf Communities, Vol. 3*. Edited by C. Lucas. Washington, D.C.: Gallaudet University Press, pp. 183–226.

James, W. 1890. "Thought Before Language: A Deaf Mute's Recollections." *American Annals of the Deaf*, 34, no. 2: 135–145.

Janesick, V., and D. Moores. 1992. "Ethnic and Cultural Considerations." In *Toward Effective Public School Programs for Deaf Students*. Edited by T. Kluwin, D. Moores, and M. Gaustad. New York: Teachers College Press, 49–65.

Jenne, W., and B. Farber. 1957. "Interactions Between Severely Retarded Children and Their Normal Siblings." Paper presented at Institute for Research on Exceptional Children Conference, Allerton Park, Ill.

Jensema, C. 1975a. "Reliability of the KPF, Form E, for Hearing Impaired College Students." *Journal of Rehabilitation of the Deaf*, 8: 14–18.

———. 1975b. "A Statistical Investigation of the KPF, Form E, as Applied to Hearing Impaired College Students." *Journal of Rehabilitation of the Deaf*, 9: 21–29.

Jensema, C., and R. Trybus. 1975. *Reported Emotional/Behavioral Problems Among Hearing Impaired Students in Special Education Programs*. Washington, D.C.: Gallaudet College Office of Demographic Studies, Ser. R, No. 1.

Johnson, D. 1999. *Deafness and Vision Disorders*. Springfield, Ill.: Charles C. Thomas.

Johnson, D., and R. Whitehead. 1989. "Effect of Maternal Rubella on Hearing and Vision." *American Annals of the Deaf*, 134, no. 3: 232–242.

Johnson, K. 1977. "A Survey of Mathematics Programs, Materials, and Methods in Schools for the Deaf." *American Annals of the Deaf*, 122, no. 1: 19–25.

Johnson, R., and C. Erting. 1984. *Linguistic Socialization in the Context of Emergent Deaf Ethnicity*. New York: Wenner-Gren Foundation Working Papers in Anthropology.

Joiner, E. 1922. "Teaching of Speech." *American Annals of the Deaf*, 72, no. 4: 397–404.

———. 1936. *Graded Lessons in Speech*. Morganton: North Carolina School for the Deaf.

Joint Committee on Infant Hearing. 1991. "1990 Position Statement." *ASHA*, 33 (Suppl. 5): 3–6.

Joint Committee on Infant-Hearing Screening. 1983. "1982 Position Statement." *Ear and Hearing*, 4: 3–4.

Joint Standards Committee. 1996. "CEC-CED Joint Knowledge and Skills Statement for All Becoming Teachers of Students Who Are Deaf or Hard of Hearing." *American Annals of the Deaf*, 141, no. 3: 220–230.

Jones, C. 1967. "Deaf Voice: A Description Derived from the Literature." *Volta Review*, 69, no. 8: 507–508.

Jones, J. 1918. "One Hundred Years of History in the Education of the Deaf in America and Its Present Status." *American Annals of the Deaf*, 63, no. 1: 1–43.

Jones, R. 1972. "The Northridge Plan." *American Annals of the Deaf*, 117, no. 5: 612–616.

_____. 1979. "The FSI Oral Interview." In *Advances in Language Testing*. Edited by D. Spolsky. Washington, D.C.: Center for Applied Linguistics, 62–87.

Jones, T., and J. Johnson. 1985. "Characteristics of Programs for Multihandicapped Hearing Impaired Students." Paper presented at Convention of American Instructors of the Deaf, St. Augustine, Fla.

Jordan, I., G. Gustason, and R. Rosen. 1976. "Current Communication Trends at Programs for the Deaf." *American Annals of the Deaf,* 121, no. 5: 527–531.

_____. 1979. "An Update on Communication Trends in Programs for the Deaf." *American Annals of the Deaf,* 124, no. 3: 350–357.

Kamin, L. 1974. *The History and Politics of IQ.* New York: Halstead Press.

Kampfe, C., M. Harrison, T. Oettinger, J. Luddington, C. McDonald-Bell, and H. C. Pillsbury III. 1993. "Parental Expectations as a Factor in Evaluating Children in the Multichannel Cochlear Implant." *American Annals of the Deaf,* 138, no. 3: 297–303.

Kanner, L. 1967. *A History of the Care and Study of the Mentally Retarded.* Springfield, Ill.: Charles C Thomas.

Karchmer, M., and T. Allen. 1999. "The Functional Assessment of Deaf and Hard of Hearing Students." *American Annals of the Deaf,* 144, no. 2: 68–77.

Karchmer, M., and J. Belmont. 1976. "On Assessing and Improving Deaf Performance in the Cognitive Laboratory." Paper presented at the American Speech and Hearing Association Annual Convention, Houston.

Kauffman, J. 1980. "Historical Trends and Contemporary Issues in Special Education in the United States." In *Handbook of Special Education.* Edited by J. Kauffman and D. Hallahan. New York: Prentice-Hall, 3–23.

Kelley, T., R. Madden, E. Gardner, and H. Rudman. 1966. *Stanford Achievement Test.* New York: Harcourt Brace Jovanovich.

Kelly, L. 1995. "Encouraging Faculty to Use Writing as a Tool to Foster Learning Through Writing Across the Curriculum." *American Annals of the Deaf,* 140, no. 1: 16–22.

Kemp, M. 1998. "Why Is Learning American Sign Language a Challenge?" *American Annals of the Deaf,* 143, no. 3: 255–259.

Kendall Demonstration Elementary School Language Arts Curriculum. 1981. Washington, D.C.: Gallaudet College, Pre-College Programs.

"The Kindergarten Method." 1875. *American Annals of the Deaf,* 20, no. 2: 120–124.

King, C., and S. Quigley. 1985. *Reading and Deafness.* San Diego: College Hill Press.

Kinzie, C., and R. Kinzie. 1931. *Lipreading for the Deafened Adult.* Chicago: Winston.

Kirby, A., ed. 1980. "Curriculum: Content and Change." *Volta Review,* 82: 6.

Kirk, S. 1975. "Labeling, Categorizing and Mainstreaming." Paper presented at the International Congress of Special Education, Kent, England.

Kirk, S., and J. Gallagher. 1979 (rev. 1993). *Educating Exceptional Children.* Boston: Houghton Mifflin.

Klein, G. 1962. "Blindness and Isolation." *Psychoanalytic Study of the Child,* 17, no. 1: 82–93.

Klopping, H. 1972. "Language Understanding of Deaf Students Under Three Auditory-Visual Conditions." *American Annals of the Deaf,* 117, no. 3: 389–396.

Kluwin, T. 1981a. "The Grammaticality of Manual Representations of English in Classroom Settings." *American Annals of the Deaf,* 125, no. 3: 417–421.

_____. 1981b. A Rationale for Modifying Classroom Signing Systems." *Sign Language Studies,* 31: 179–188.

_____. 1994. "The Interaction of Race Gender and Social Class Effects in the Education of Deaf Children." *American Annals of the Deaf,* 139, no. 5: 465–471.

_____. 1999. "Coteaching Deaf and Hearing Students: Research and Social Integration." *American Annals of the Deaf,* 144, no. 4: 339–344.

Kluwin, T., and A. Kelly. 1992. "Deaf Adolescents Who Drop Out of Local Public Schools." *American Annals of the Deaf,* 137, no. 3: 293–301.

Kluwin, T., and D. Moores. 1985. "The Effects of Integration on the Mathematics Achievement of Hearing Impaired Adolescents." *Exceptional Children,* 52, no. 2: 153–160.

———. 1989. "Mathematics Achievement of Deaf Adolescents in Different Placements." *Exceptional Children,* 55, no. 4: 327–335.

Kluwin, T., D. Moores, and M. Gaustad, eds. 1992. *Toward Effective Public School Programs for Deaf Students.* New York: Teachers College Press.

Kluwin, T., and M. Stinson. 1993. *Deaf Students in Local Public Schools.* Springfield, Ill.: Charles C Thomas.

Knapp, P. 1968. "Emotional Aspects of Hearing Loss." *Psychosomatic Medicine,* 10, no. 2: 203–310.

Knox, J. E., and C. B. Stevens, trans. 1993. *The Collected Works of L. S. Vygotsky: Volume 2: The Fundamentals of Defectology.* New York: Plenum Press. (R. W. Ries and A.S. Carton, Editors of English Translation.)

Koelle, W., and J. Convey. 1982. "The Prediction of the Achievement of Deaf Adolescents from Self-Concept and Locus of Control Measures." *American Annals of the Deaf,* 127, no. 6: 769–779.

Koester, L., and K. Meadow-Orlans. 1990. "Parenting a Deaf Child: Stress, Strength, and Support." In *Educational and Developmental Aspects of Deafness.* Edited by D. Moores and K. Meadow-Orlans. Washington, D.C.: Gallaudet University Press, 299–320.

Kohl, H. 1966. *Language and Education of the Deaf.* New York: Center for Urban Studies.

Konigsmark, B. 1969a. "Hereditary Deafness in Man, Part 1." *New England Journal of Medicine,* 281: 713–720.

———. 1969b. "Hereditary Deafness in Man, Part 2." *New England Journal of Medicine,* 281: 774–778.

———. 1969c. "Hereditary Deafness in Man, Part 3." *New England Journal of Medicine,* 281: 827–832.

———. 1972. *Genetic Hearing Loss with No Associated Abnormalities.* Chicago: Maico Audiological Library Series, Vol. 11, Report 6.

Kopp, H. 1968. *Curriculum: Cognition and Content.* Washington, D.C.: A. G. Bell Association.

Korsunskaya, E. 1969. *A Method of Teaching Speech to Preschool Deaf Children.* Moscow: Institute of Defectology.

Kretschmer, R., ed. 1985. "Learning to Write and Writing to Learn." *Volta Review,* 87: 5.

Kronenberg, H., and G. Blake. 1966. *Young Deaf Adults: An Occupational Survey.* Hot Springs: Arkansas Rehabilitation Service.

Kuntze, M. 1992. "Blueprints for the Future." In *A Free Hand.* Edited by M. Walworth, D. Moores, and T. J. O'Rourke. Silver Spring, Md.: T. J. Publishers, 3–19.

Kuriloff, P., R. True, D. Kirp, and W. Buss. 1974. "Legal Reform and Educational Change." *Exceptional Children,* 41, no. 1: 35–42.

Kusché, C., and M. Greenberg. 1993. *The PATHS Curriculum.* Seattle: Developmental Research and Programs.

Lala, F. S. 1998. "Is There Room in the DSM for Consideration of Deaf People?" *American Annals of the Deaf,* 143, no. 4: 314–317.

Laine, C., and L. Schultz. 1985. "Composition Theory and Practice: The Paradigm Shift." *Volta Review,* 87, no. 5: 9–20.

Lampropoulou, V., and M. M. Konstantareas. 1998. "Child Involvement and Stress in Greek Mothers of Deaf Children." *American Annals of the Deaf,* 143, no. 4: 296–305.

Lamson, M. 1878. *Life and Education of Laura Dewey Bridgeman, the Deaf, Dumb, and Blind Girl*. Boston: New England Publishing Company.

Lane, H. 1976. *The Wild Boy of Aveyron*. Cambridge, Mass.: Harvard University Press.

———. 1984. *When the Mind Hears*. New York: Random House.

———. 1992. *The Mask of Benevolence: Disabling the Deaf Community*. New York: Alfred A. Knopf.

———. 1993. "The Mask of Irrelevance." *American Annals of the Deaf*, 138, no. 4: 315–319.

Lappe, M. 1973. "Genetic Knowledge and the Concept of Health." *Hastings Center Reports*, 3: 1–3.

LaSasso, C. 1978. "National Survey of Materials and Procedures Used to Teach Reading to Hearing Impaired Children." *American Annals of the Deaf*, 123, no. 1: 22–30.

Laurie, S. 1907. *Historical Survey of Pre-Christian Education*. London: Longmans.

Lawrence, C., and G. Vescovi. 1967. *Deaf Adults in New England: An Exploratory Service Program*. Boston: Morgan Memorial.

Lawrence, E. 1970. *The Origins and Growth of Modern Education*. Baltimore: Penguin Books.

Lawson, L., and H. Myklebust. 1970. "Ophthalmological Deficiencies in Deaf Children." *Exceptional Children*, 37, no. 1: 17–20.

Lee, S., and E. Stevens. 1981. *The Rise of Literacy and the Common School in the United States: Socioeconomic Analysis to 1870*. Chicago: University of Chicago Press.

Lenneberg, E. 1964. "The Capacity for Language Acquisition." In *The Structure of Language*. Edited by J. Fodor and J. Katz. Engelwood Cliffs, N.J.: Prentice-Hall, 579–603.

———. 1967a. *Biological Foundations of Language*. New York: Wiley.

———. 1967b. "Prerequisites for Language Acquisition." *Proceedings of the International Congress on Oral Education of the Deaf*. Washington, D.C.: A. G. Bell Association, 1302–1362.

———. 1973. "Biological Aspects of Language." In *Communication, Language and Meaning*. Edited by G. Miller. New York: Basic Books, 49–60.

Leutke-Stahlman, B. 1995. "On Deciding to Implant." *American Annals of the Deaf*, 140, no. 1: 4–5.

Levine, E. 1948. "An Investigation into the Personality of Normal and Deaf Adolescent Girls." Ph.D. diss., New York University.

———. 1956. *Youth in a Soundless World*. New York: New York University Press.

———. 1960. *The Psychology of Deafness*. New York: Columbia University Press.

———. 1974. "Psychological Tests and Practices with the Deaf." *Volta Review*, 76, no. 5: 298–319.

Levinson, R., ed. 1967. *A Plato Reader*. Boston: Houghton Mifflin.

Levi-Strauss, C. 1966. *The Savage Mind*. Chicago: University of Chicago Press.

Lewis, B. 1966. *The Arabs in History*. New York: Harper and Row.

Liben, L., ed. 1978. *Deaf Children: Developmental Perspectives*. New York: Academic Press.

Ling, D. 1976. *Speech for the Hearing Impaired Child*. Washington, D.C.: A. G. Bell Association.

———. 1984a. *Early Intervention for Hearing Impaired Children: Oral Options*. San Diego: College Hill Press.

———. 1984b. *Early Intervention for Hearing Impaired Children: Total Communication Options*. San Diego: College Hill Press.

———. 1988. *Foundations of Spoken Language for Hearing Impaired Children*. Washington, D.C.: A.G. Bell Association.

Liskin-Gasparro, J., ed. 1979. *Foreign Language and Proficiency Assessment*. Princeton, N.J.: Educational Testing Service.

Lloyd, L., and E. Moore, 1972. "Audiology." In *Mental Retardation, Vol. IV.* Edited by J. Wortis. New York: Grune and Stratton, 374–398.

Lloyd, L., and M. Reed. 1967. "The Incidence of Hearing Impairment in an Institutionalized Mentally Retarded Population." *American Journal of Mental Deficiency,* 72, no. 5: 746–763.

Lobato, D. 1990. *Brothers, Sisters and Special Needs.* Baltimore: Brookes.

Long, D. 1918. *Speech for the Hearing Impaired Child.* Washington, D.C.: A. G. Bell Association.

Lucas, C. 1990. *Sign Language Research: Theoretical Issues.* Washington, D.C.: Gallaudet University Press.

Lucas, C., and C. Valli. 1990. "ASL, English and Contact Signing." In *Sign Language Research: Theoretical Issues.* Washington, D.C.: Gallaudet University Press, 288–307.

Luckner, J. 1999. "An Examination of Two Coteaching Classrooms." *American Annals of the Deaf,* 144, no. 1: 24–34.

Lunde, A., and S. Bigman. 1959. *Occupational Conditions Among the Deaf.* Washington, D.C.: Gallaudet College Press.

Lytle, R., and M. Rovins. 1997. "Reforming Deaf Education: A Paradigm Shift from How to Teach to What to Teach." *American Annals of the Deaf,* 142, no. 1: 7–15.

MacKenzie, C. 1929. *Alexander Graham Bell: The Man Who Conquered Silence.* Boston: Houghton Mifflin.

Mackinson, J. A., I. Leigh, L. Blennerhassett, and S. Anthony. 1997. "Validity of the TONI-2 with Deaf and Hard of Hearing Children." *American Annals of the Deaf,* 42, no. 4: 294–299.

Mallory, G. 1880. *Introduction to the Sign Language Among North American Indians as Illustrating the Gesture Speech of Mankind.* Washington, D.C.: Smithsonian Institute, Bureau of Ethnology.

Mallowan, M. 1965. *Early Mesopotamia and Iran.* New York: McGraw-Hill.

Mangan, K. 1963. "The Deaf." In *Behavioral Research on Exceptional Children.* Edited by S. Kirk and B. Weiner. Washington, D.C.: Council for Exceptional Children, 183–229.

Mann, L. 1974. "Giacobbo Rodrigues Pereire." *Journal of Special Education,* 8, no. 4: 294–295.

Mapp, I., and R. Hudson. 1997. "Stress and Coping Among African American and Latino Parents of Deaf Children." *American Annals of the Deaf,* 142, no. 1: 48–56.

Marazita, M. L., L. M. Ploughman, B. Rawlings, E. Remington, K. Arnos, and W. E. Nance. 1993. "Genetics." *American Journal of Medicine,* 46: 486–491.

Marshall, W. 1970. "Quantitative and Qualitative Analysis of the Language of Deaf Children." Ph.D. diss., University of Illinois.

Martin, D., ed. 1985. *Cognition, Education and Deafness: Implications for Research and Instruction.* Washington, D.C.: Gallaudet College Press.

_____. ed. 1991. *Advances in Cognition, Education, and Deafness.* Washington, D.C.: Gallaudet University Press.

Martin, E. 1978. "Full Cooperation to Support Full Services to Deaf-Blind Children and Youth." *Proceedings of the National Conference for Deaf-Blind Children and Youth.* Washington, D.C.: Bureau of Education for the Handicapped, 1–2.

Martsinovskaya, E. 1961. "The Influence of Fingerspelling on the Reproduction of the Sound-Syllable Structure of a Word." *Spetsial Skola,* 102, no. 1: 22–28.

Maslow, A. 1954. *Motivation and Personality.* New York: Harper and Row.

Mayne, R. 1929. "The Bell Family and Visible Speech." *Volta Review,* 31, no. 5: 453–456.

McCarthy, M. 1985. "Religion and Public Schools: Emerging Legal Standards and Unresolved Issues." *Harvard Educational Review,* 55, no. 3: 278–317.

McClure, G. 1961. "The History of LPF." *Proceedings of the 1961 Convention of American Instructors of the Deaf.* Washington, D.C.: U.S. Government Printing Office, 103–108.

McClure, W. 1969. "Historical Perspectives on Education of the Deaf." In *Persons with Hearing Loss.* Edited by J. Griffith. Springfield, Ill.: Charles C Thomas.

McConigel, M. 1994. "The Individualized Family Service Program." In *Infants and Toddlers with Hearing Loss.* Edited by J. Roush and N. Matkin. Baltimore: York Press, 99–112.

McCroskey, R. 1967. "Early Education of Infants with Severe Auditory Impairments." *Proceedings of the International Conference on Oral Education of the Deaf.* Washington, D.C.: A.G. Bell Association, 1891–1905.

_____. 1968. "Final Report of a Four Year Home Training Program." Paper presented at the A.G. Bell National Convention, San Francisco.

McDaniel, E. 1980. "Visual Memory in the Deaf." *American Annals of the Deaf,* 125, no. 1: 17–20.

McDonald, E. 1979. "Early Identification and Treatment of Children at Risk for Development of Intelligible Speech." In *Nonspeech Language and Communication: Analysis and Intervention.* Edited by R. Schiefelbusch. Baltimore: University Park Press, 321–374.

McGill-Franzen, A., and A. Gormley. 1980. "The Influence of Context on Deaf Readers' Understanding of Passive Sentences." *American Annals of the Deaf,* 125, no. 7: 937–942.

McHale, S. M., and W. C. Gamble. 1989. "Sibling Relationships of Children with Disabled and Nondisabled Brothers and Sisters." *Developmental Psychology,* 25, no. 3: 421–429.

McKusick, V. 1983. *Mendelian Inheritance in Man.* 6th ed. Baltimore: Johns Hopkins Press.

_____. 1992. *Mendelian Inheritance in Man.* 10th ed. Baltimore: Johns Hopkins University Press.

Mead, G. 1934. *Mind, Self and Society.* Chicago: University of Chicago Press.

Meadow, K. 1967. "The Effect of Early Manual Communication and Family Climate on the Deaf Child's Environment." Ph.D. diss., University of California, Berkeley.

_____. 1968. "Parental Responses to the Medical Ambiguities of Deafness." *Journal of Health and Social Behavior,* 94: 299–309.

_____. 1969. "Self-Image, Family Climate and Deafness." *Social Forces,* 47, no. 5: 428–438.

_____. 1976. "The Development of Deaf Children." In *Review of Child Development Research,* Vol. 5. Edited by E. Hetherington, J. Hagen, R. Kroon, and A. Stein. Chicago: University of Chicago Press, 429–506.

_____. 1980. *Deafness and Child Development.* Berkeley: University of California Press.

_____. 1984. "Social Adjustment of Preschool Children: Deaf and Hearing: With and Without Other Handicaps." *Topics in Early Childhood Special Education,* 3, no. 4: 27–40.

Meadow, K., and B. Dyssegaard. 1983. "Teachers' Ratings of Deaf Children: An American-Danish Comparison." *American Annals of the Deaf,* 128: 900–908.

Meadow, K., M. Greenberg, C. Erting, and H. Carmichael. 1981. "Interactions of Deaf Mothers and Deaf Preschool Children." *American Annals of the Deaf,* 126, no. 4: 454–468.

Meadow, K., M. Karchmer, L. Peterson, and L. Rudner. 1980. *Meadow/Kendall Social-Emotional Assessment Inventory for Deaf Students: Manual.* Washington, D.C.: Gallaudet College, Pre-College Programs.

Meadow-Orlans, K. 1987. "Understanding Deafness: Socialization of Children and Youth." In *Understanding Deafness Socially.* Edited by P. Higgins and J. Nash. Springfield, Ill.: Charles C Thomas, 29–58.

_____. 1990. "Research on Developmental Aspects of Deafness. In *Educational and Developmental Aspects of Deafness.* Edited by D. Moores and K. Meadow-Orlans. Washington, D.C.: Gallaudet University Press, 283–298.

_____. 1995. "Sources of Stress for Mothers and Fathers of Deaf Infants." *American Annals of the Deaf,* 140, no. 4: 352–357.

Meadow-Orlans, K. D. Mertens, M. Sass-Lehrer, and K. Scott-Olson. 1997. "Support Services for Parents and Their Children Who Are Deaf or Hard of Hearing." *American Annals of the Deaf,* 142, no. 4: 278–293.

Meier, M. 1961. "Role of Non-Verbal Signals in Education of the Deaf." *Proceedings of the 1961 Convention of American Instructors of the Deaf.* Washington, D.C.: U.S. Government Printing Office, 148.

Meisegeier, R. 1985. "Talented and Gifted Programs: The Need for Dialogue." Paper presented at the American Instructors of the Deaf National Convention, St. Augustine, Fla.

Mendelsohn, J., and B. Fairchild. 1984. "Years of Challenge." In *The Habilitation and Rehabilitation of Deaf Adolescents.* Edited by G. Anderson and D. Watson. Proceedings of the National Conference on the Habilitation and Rehabilitation of Deaf Adolescents. April, Wagoner, Okla.

Mercer, J. 1973. *Labeling the Mentally Retarded.* Riverside: University of California Press.

Meyer, F. 1966. *Bases of Ancient Education: Volume I: Great Ideas of Education.* New Haven: College and University Press.

Miller, J., C. Ramsey, and C. Goetzinger. 1958. "An Exploration and Investigation of a Method of Improving Speechreading." *American Annals of the Deaf,* 103, no. 3: 473–478.

Miller, M. 1985. "Experimental Use of Signed Presentations of the Verbal Scale of the WISCR with Profoundly Deaf Children." In *Cognition, Education, and Deafness.* Edited by D. Martin. Washington, D.C.: Gallaudet University Press, 187–192.

_____. 1991. "Sign Language Iconicity and Test Construction Theory for Deaf Individuals." Ph.D. diss., Georgetown University, Washington, D.C.

_____. 1992. *Effects of Early Intervention Programs Upon Sign Skills of Parents with Deaf Children.* Washington, D.C.: Gallaudet University Family Life Program.

Miller, M., and D. Moores. 1990. "Principles of Group Counseling and Their Applications for Deaf Clients." *Journal of the American Deafness and Rehabilitation Association,* 23: 82–87.

_____. In Press. "Bilingual Education for Deaf Students." In *Defining Special Education into the 21st Century.* Ed. M.A. Winzer and K. Mazurak. Washington, D.C.: Gallaudet University Press.

Mills v. *Board of Education of the District of Columbia,* 348, F. Supp. 866, 868, 875, D.D.C. 1972.

Mindel, E., and M. Vernon. 1972. *They Grow in Silence.* Silver Spring, Md.: National Association of the Deaf.

Minnesota Course of Study: A Brief Exposition of the Wing's Symbols. 1918. Faribault, Minn.: Minnesota School for the Deaf.

Mitra, S. 1970. "Educational Provisions for Mentally Retarded Deaf Students in Residential Institutions for the Retarded." *Volta Review,* 72, no. 3: 225–236.

Montague, H. 1940. "Mr. Bell's Private School." *Volta Review,* 5: 325–326, 395.

Montessori, M. 1912. *The Montessori Method.* Trans. A. George. New York: Stokes.

Montgomery, G. 1966. "The Relationship of Oral Skills to Manual Communication in Profoundly Deaf Adolescents." *American Annals of the Deaf,* 111, no. 5: 557–565.

Montgomery, G., and A. Lines. 1976. "Comparison of Several Single and Combined Methods of Communicating with Deaf Children." In *Changing Attitudes to Communication.* Carlisle: British Deaf News, Supplementum.

Moog, J., and A. Geers. 1991. "Educational Management of Children with Cochlear Implants." *American Annals of the Deaf,* 136, no. 2: 69–76.

Moores, D. 1969. "The Vocational Status of Young Deaf Adults in New England." *Journal of Rehabilitation of the Deaf,* 2, no. 1: 29–41.

_____. 1970a. "Evaluation of Preschool Programs." *Proceedings of International Congress on Education of the Deaf,* Stockholm, 1964–1968.

_____. 1970b. "Investigation of Psycholinguistic Abilities of Deaf Adolescents." *Exceptional Children,* 36: 645–654.

_____. 1972a. "Mental Health and the Hearing Impaired." *Deaf American,* 23, no. 1: 7–12.

_____. 1972b. "Neo-Oralism and Education of the Deaf in the Soviet Union." *Exceptional Children,* 38, no. 5: 377–384.

_____. 1973. "Families and Deafness." In *Deafness Annual.* Edited by A. Norris. Silver Spring, Md.: Professional Rehabilitation Workers with the Adult Deaf, 115–130.

_____. 1976. "A Review of Education of the Deaf." In *Third Review of Special Education.* Edited by L. Mann and D. Sabatino. New York: Grune and Stratton, 19–52.

_____. 1977. "Issues in the Utilization of Manual Communication." *Proceedings of the National Symposium on Sign Language Research and Teaching.* Edited by W. Stokoe. Silver Spring, Md.: National Association of the Deaf, 85–92.

_____. 1979a. "Alternate Communication Modes: Visual Motor Systems." In *Nonspeech Language and Communication: Analysis and Intervention.* Edited by R. Schiefelbusch. Baltimore: University Park Press, 27–41.

_____. 1979b. "Review of B. Tervoort, Developmental Features of Visual Communication." *Studies in Language,* 3, no. 2: 294–297.

_____. 1980a. "American Sign Language." In *Nonspeech Language and Communication: Analysis and Intervention.* Edited by R. Schiefelbusch. Baltimore: University Park Press, 93–100.

_____. 1980b. "Manual Communication." Paper presented at the Nonspeech Communication Conference of the Ontario Institute for Studies in Education, Toronto.

_____. 1982. "The Language of Hearing Impaired Mentally Retarded Children." In *The Multihandicapped Hearing Impaired: Identification and Instruction.* Edited by D. Tweedie and E. Shroyer. Washington, D.C.: Gallaudet College Press, 201–210.

_____. 1985a. "Early Intervention Programs for Hearing Impaired Children: A Longitudinal Assessment." In *Children's Language: Volume V.* Edited by K. Nelson. Hillsdale, N.J.: Erlbaum, 159–195.

_____. 1985b. "Educational Programs and Services for Hearing Impaired Children: Issues and Options." In *Education of the Hearing Impaired Child.* Edited by F. Powell, T. Finitzo-Hieber, S. Friez-Patti, and D. Henderson. San Diego: College Hill Press, 5–22.

_____. 1985c. "A Synthesis: Reactions from the Researcher's Point of View." In *Cognition, Education and Deafness: Directions for Research and Instruction.* Edited by D. Martin. Washington, D.C.: Gallaudet College Press, 224–228.

_____. 1986. "Educational Keynote: Life and Work in the 21st Century: The Deaf Person of Tomorrow." Paper presented at the National Association of the Deaf Forum, Las Vegas.

_____. 1990a. "Keynote Address." International Congress on Education of the Deaf. June, Rochester, N.Y.

_____. 1990b. *Dissemination of a Model to Create Least Restrictive Environments for Deaf Students.* Final Report to National Institute on Disability and Rehabilitation Research. Project No. 84133, Grant No. G008720128, Washington, D.C.

_____. 1991. "The Great Debates: Where, How, and What to Teach Deaf Children." *American Annals of the Deaf,* 136, no. 1: 35–37.

_____. 1992a. "An Historical Perspective on School Placement." In *Toward Effective Public School Programs for Deaf Students*. Edited by T. Kluwin, D. Moores, and M. Gaustad. New York: Teachers College Press, 7–29.

_____. 1992b. "What Do We Know and When Did We Know It?" In *A Free Hand: Enfranchising the Education of Deaf Children*. Edited by M. Walworth, D. Moores, and T. J. O'Rourke. Silver Spring, Md.: T. J. Publishers, 67–88.

_____. 1993a. "Review of H. Lane, The Mask of Benevolence." *American Annals of the Deaf*, 138, no. 1: 4–9.

_____. 1993b. "The Mask of Confusion." *American Annals of the Deaf*, 138, no. 4: 319–321.

_____. 1995a. *Free Appropriate Public Education: A Reinterpretation for Deaf Students*. Washington, D.C.: Gallaudet Research Institute Monograph.

_____. 1995b. *Placement of Deaf Children in the Most Appropriate Environment*. Washington, D.C.: Gallaudet Research Institute.

_____. 1998a. "Genetic Engineering and Our Brave New World." *American Annals of the Deaf*, 143, no. 3: 223–224.

_____. 1998b. "Race, Ethnicity, and Minority Status." *American Annals of the Deaf*, 143, no. 4: 291–292.

_____. 1999. "Total Communication and Bi-Bi." *American Annals of the Deaf*, 144, no. 1: 3–4.

Moores, D., B. Cerney, and M. Garcia. 1990. "School Placement and Least Restrictive Environment." In *Educational and Developmental Aspects of Deafness*. Edited by D. Moores and K. Meadow-Orlans. Washington, D.C.: Gallaudet University Press, 115–136.

Moores, D., S. Fisher, and M. Harlow. 1974. *Postsecondary Programs for the Deaf: Monograph VI: Summary and Overview*. Minneapolis: University of Minnesota Research and Demonstration Center in Education of Handicapped Children, Research Report No. 80.

Moores, D., M. Harlow, and S. Fisher. 1974. *Postsecondary Programs for the Deaf: Monograph I: Introduction and Overview*. Minneapolis: University of Minnesota Research and Demonstration Center in Education of Handicapped Children, Research Report No. 60.

Moores, D., T. Kluwin, R. Johnson, P. Cox, L. Blennerhassett, L. Kelly, C. Ewoldt, C. Sweet, and L. Fields. 1987. *Factors Predictive of Literacy in Deaf Adolescents*. Project No. NIH-NINCDS-83-19. Final Report to National Institute on Neurological and Communicative Disorders and Stroke.

Moores, D., T. Kluwin, and D. Mertens. 1985. *High School Programs for the Deaf in Metropolitan Areas*. Washington, D.C.: Gallaudet College Research Monograph No. 3.

Moores, D., C. McIntyre, and K. Weiss. 1972. *Evaluation of Programs for Hearing Impaired Children: Report of 1971–1972*. Minneapolis: University of Minnesota Research Development and Demonstration Center in Education of Handicapped Children, Research Report No. 39.

Moores, D., and C. Oden. 1978. "Educational Needs of Black Deaf Children." *American Annals of the Deaf*, 122, no. 3: 313–318.

Moores, D., and C. Sweet. 1990a. "Factors Predictive of School Achievement." In *Educational and Developmental Aspects of Deafness*. Edited by D. Moores and K. Meadow-Orlans. Washington, D.C.: Gallaudet University Press, 54–201.

_____. 1990b. "Reading and Writing Skills in Deaf Adolescents." *International Journal of Rehabilitation*, 13, no. 1: 66–67.

Moores, D., K. Weiss, and M. Goodwin. 1978. "Early Intervention Programs for Hearing Impaired Children." *American Annals of the Deaf*, 123, no. 8: 925–936.

Morbidity and Mortality Weekly Report (MMWR). 1985. 34, no. 5: February 8.

Moreva, N. 1964. "Learning Dactyl Reading by Various Age Groups." Ph.D. diss., Moscow Institute of Defectology.

Morgan, A., and M. Vernon. 1994. "A Guide to the Diagnosis of Learning Disabilities in Deaf and Hard of Hearing Children and Adults." *American Annals of the Deaf*, 139, no. 3: 358–370.

Morkovin, B. 1960. "Experiment in Teaching Deaf Preschool Children in the Soviet Union." *Volta Review,* 62, no. 4: 260–268.

Morozova, N. 1954. *Development of the Theory of Preschool Education of the Deaf*. Moscow: Moscow Institute of Defectology.

Morrell, R. J., H. J. Kim, L. J. Hood, L. Goforth, K. Friderice, R. Fisher, G. Van Camp, C. I. Berlin, C. Oddoux, H. Ostrer, B. Keats, and T. B. Friedman. 1999. "Mutations in the Connexion 26 Gene (GJB2) Among Askenazi Jews with Nonsyndromic Deafness." *New England Journal of Medicine,* 339: 1500–1505.

Morris, O. 1861. "Consanguineous Marriages and Their Results in Respect to Deaf Dumbness." *American Annals of the Deaf,* 65, no. 3: 213–224.

Morrison, J. 1920. "Industrial Training." *American Annals of the Deaf,* 65, no. 3: 213–224.

Murdoch, H. 1996. "Stereotyped Behavior in Deaf and Hard of Hearing Children." *American Annals of the Deaf*, 141, no. 5: 379–386.

Myklebust, H. 1964. *The Psychology of Deafness*. New York: Grune and Stratton.

Myklebust, H., and M. Brutton. 1953. "A Study of Visual Perception in Deaf Children." *Acta Oto-Laryngologica,* Supplementum, 105.

Name withheld. 1995. "Cochlear Fallout." *American Annals of the Deaf,* 140, no. 1: 5–6.

Nance, J. 1975. *The Gentle Tasaday*. New York: Harcourt Brace Jovanovich.

Nash, K. 1992. "The Changing Population: A Challenge for Postsecondary Education." In *Deaf Students in Postsecondary Education*. Edited by S. Foster and G. Walter. New York and London: Routledge, 3–23.

National Commission on Excellence in Education. 1983. *A Nation at Risk: The Imperative for Educational Reform*. Washington, D.C.: U.S. Department of Education.

National Council of Teachers of Mathematics. 1998. *U.S. Showing in Twelfth Grade International Math Study Unacceptable but Not Unexpected*. [On-line]. Available: http://www.nctm.org/publications/releases/1998/02/timss.12.reaction/press.release.html

National Education Goals Panel. 1997. *National Education Goals Report*. Washington, D.C.: National Education Goals Panel.

Nelson, M. 1949. "The Evolutionary Process of Teaching Language to the Deaf." *American Annals of the Deaf,* 95: 230–294, 354–396, 491–511.

Nickerson, R. 1975a. "Characteristics of the Speech of Deaf Persons." *Volta Review,* 77, no. 5: 342–362.

_____. 1975b. *Speech Training and Speech Reception Aids for the Deaf*. Cambridge, Mass.: Bolt, Beranek, & Newman, Report No. 2980.

Nickerson, R., K. Stevens, A. Boothroyd, and A. Rollins. 1975. *Some Observations of Timing in the Speech of Deaf and Hard of Hearing Speakers*. Cambridge, Mass.: Bolt, Beranek, & Newman, Report No. 2905.

Nitchie, E. 1912. *Lipreading: Principles and Practices*. New York: Stokes.

Nober, E. 1968. *The Audiometric Assessment of Mentally Retarded Persons*. Syracuse, N.Y.: Syracuse University.

Norden, K. 1970. "The Structure of Abilities in a Group of Deaf Adolescents." *Proceedings of International Congress on Education of the Deaf,* Stockholm, 238–251.

O'Neill, J., and H. Oyer. 1961. *Visual Communication for the Hard of Hearing*. Englewood Cliffs, N.J.: Prentice-Hall.

Osberger, M. J. 1996. "Speech Production and Receptive Skills in Children with Cochlear Implants." In *Profound Deafness and Speech Communication*. Ed. G. Plant and D. E. Spens. London: Whurr.

Osgood, C., G. Suci, and P. Tannenbaum. 1957. *The Measurement of Meaning*. Urbana: University of Illinois Press.

Ottem, E. 1980. "An Analysis of Cognitive Studies with Deaf Subjects." *American Annals of the Deaf,* 125: 564–575.

Ouellette, S. 1985. "National Project on Higher Education for Deaf Students." Paper presented at a meeting of the Association on Handicapped Student Service Programs in Post-Secondary Education, Atlanta.

Padden, C. 1980. "The Deaf Community and the Culture of Deaf People." In *Sign Language and the Deaf Community: Essays in Honor of William Stokoe*. Edited by C. Baker and R. Battison. Silver Spring, Md.: National Association of the Deaf, 89–103.

Padden, C., and T. Humphries. 1988. *Deaf in America: Voices from a Culture*. Cambridge, Mass.: Harvard University Press.

Pagliaro, C. M. 1998a. "Mathematics Preparation and Professional Development of Deaf Education Teachers." *American Annals of the Deaf,* 143, no. 5: 373–379.

_____. 1998b. "Mathematics Reform in the Education of Deaf and Hard of Hearing Students." *American Annals of the Deaf,* 143, no. 1: 22–28.

Papinger, D., and D. Sikora. 1990. "Diagnosing a Learning Disability in a Hearing-Impaired Child." *American Annals of the Deaf,* 135, no. 4: 285–292.

Pappas, D. 1985. *Diagnosis and Treatment of Hearing Impairment in Children*. San Diego: College Hill Press.

Peet, H. 1834. *Sixteenth Annual Report of the New York Institution for the Instruction of the Deaf and Dumb*. New York.

_____. 1850. "Analysis of Bonet's Treatise on the Art of Teaching the Dumb to Speak." *American Annals of the Deaf,* 3, no. 3: 200–211.

_____. 1851. "Memoir on the Origin and Early History of the Art of Educating the Deaf and Dumb." *American Annals of the Deaf,* 4, no. 2: 129–161.

_____. 1852. *Statistics of the Deaf and Dumb*. New York: Egbert.

_____. 1854. *Thirty-Fifth Annual Report of the New York Institution for the Instruction of the Deaf and Dumb*. New York.

_____. 1855. "Notions of the Deaf and Dumb Before Instruction." *American Annals of the Deaf,* 8, no. 1: 1–44.

_____. 1856. "The Remote and Proximate Causes of Deafness." *American Annals of the Deaf,* 8, no. 3: 129–158.

_____. 1859. "Memoir on the History of the Art of Instructing the Deaf and Dumb." *Proceedings of the Fifth Convention of American Instructors of the Deaf*. Washington, D.C.: U.S. Government Printing Office, 19–26.

_____. 1868. "The Order of the First Lessons in Language for a Class of Deaf Mutes." *Proceedings of the Sixth Convention of American Instructors of the Deaf*. Washington, D.C.: U.S. Government Printing Office, 19–26.

_____. 1886. "Family Instruction." *American Annals of the Deaf,* 31, no. 4: 260–271.

Pehrsson, R. 1978. "Semantic Organization: An Approach to Teaching Deaf Children How to Process Written Language." Ph.D. diss., Hofstra University.

Pettengill, B. 1874. "Home Education for Deaf Mutes." *American Annals of the Deaf,* 19, no. 1: 1–10.

_____. 1876. "The Natural Method of Teaching Language." *American Annals of the Deaf,* 21, no. 1: 1–10.

Pettengill, G. 1882. "Methods of Teaching Language." *American Annals of the Deaf,* 19, no. 1: 1–10.

Phillips, W. 1963. "Influence of Preschool Training on Language Arts, Arithmetic Concepts, and Socialization of Young Deaf Children." Ph.D. diss., Columbia University.

Piaget, J. 1926. *The Language and Thought of the Child.* New York: Harcourt Brace Jovanovich.

_____. 1952. *The Origins of Intelligence in Children.* New York: International Universities Press.

_____. 1970. "Piaget's Theory." In *Carmichael's Manual of Child Psychology.* Edited by P. Mussen. New York: Wiley.

Piaget, J., and B. Inhelder. 1969. *The Psychology of the Child.* New York: Basic Books.

Pickett, J. 1980. *The Sounds of Speech.* Baltimore: University Park Press.

Piers, E. 1984. *Piers-Harris Children's Self-Concept Scale: Revised Manual.* Los Angeles: Western Psychological Services.

Piers, E., and D. Harris. 1969. *Piers-Harris Self-Concept Scale.* Los Angeles: Western Psychological Services.

Pinker, S. 1997. *How the Mind Works.* New York: W. W. Norton.

Pintner, R. 1933. "Emotional Stability of the Hard of Hearing." *Journal of Genetic Psychology,* 43, no. 3: 293–309.

Pintner, R., J. Eisenson, and M. Stanton. 1941. *The Psychology of the Physically Handicapped.* New York: Crofts & Company.

Pintner, R., I. Fusfeld, and L. Brunswig. 1937. "Personality Tests of Deaf Adults." *Journal of Genetic Psychology,* 51, no. 4: 305–327.

Pintner, R., and D. Patterson. 1917. "A Comparison of Deaf and Hearing Children in Visual Memory Span for Digits." *Journal of Experimental Psychology,* 2, no. 2: 76–88.

Plann, S. 1993. "Pedro Ponce de Leon: Myth and Reality." In *Deaf History Unveiled: Interpretations from the New Scholarship.* Edited by J. Van Cleve. Washington, D.C.: Gallaudet University Press, 1–12.

Pollack, D. 1964. "Acoupedics: A Unisensory Approach to Auditory Training." *Volta Review,* 66, no. 7: 400–409.

_____. 1970. *Educational Audiology for the Limited Hearing Child.* Springfield, Ill.: Charles C Thomas.

_____. 1976. "The Crucial Year: A Time to Listen." *International Audiology,* 3, 243–247.

Pope, A. 1938. "A History of the Five Slate System." *Proceedings of the Twenty-Eighth Convention of American Instructors of the Deaf.* Washington, D.C.: U.S. Government Printing Office, 18–23.

Porter, S. 1868. "Professor Porter's Paper on Grammar." *Proceedings of the Sixth Convention of American Instructors of the Deaf.* Washington, D.C.: U.S. Government Printing Office, 144–145.

_____. 1869. "The Instruction of the Deaf and Dumb in Grammar." *Proceedings of the National Conference of Principals of Institutions for the Deaf and Dumb.* Alton, Ill.: Currier Steam Book and Job Printing House.

Powell, T. H., and P. A. Galladino. 1993. *Brothers and Sisters: A Special Part of Exceptional Families.* Baltimore: Brookes.

Powers, D., R. Elliot, D. Fairbank, and C. Monaghan. 1988. "The Dilemma of Identifying Learning Disabled Hearing-Impaired Students." *Volta Review,* 90: 209–218.

Powers, D., R. Elliot, and R. Funderburg. 1987. "Learning Disabled Hearing-Impaired Students." *Volta Review,* 89: 99–105.

Powers, S. 1999. "The Educational Attainments of Deaf Students in Mainstream Programs in England." *American Annals of the Deaf,* 144, no. 3: 261–269.

Premack, D. 1970. "A Functional Analysis of Language." *Journal of Experimental Analysis of Behavior,* 14: 107–125.

_____. 1971. "Language in Chimpanzees?" *Science,* 172: 808–822.

Pressley, M., and J. Levin. 1983. *Cognitive Strategy Research.* New York: Springer-Verlag.

Proceedings of the 1853 Convention of American Instructors of the Deaf and Dumb. 1853. Columbus, Ohio: Steam Press of Smith and Cox, 14.

Proceedings of the 1858 Convention of American Instructors of the Deaf and Dumb. 1859. Alton, Ill.: Courier Steam Book and Job Printing House, 15.

Public Law 94-142: The Education of All Handicapped Children Act of 1975. November 1975.

Pugh, G. 1946. "Summaries from the Appraisal of Silent Reading Abilities of Acoustically Handicapped Children." *American Annals of the Deaf,* 94, no. 4: 331–349.

Quigley, S. 1969. *The Influence of Fingerspelling on the Development of Language, Communication, and Educational Achievement of the Deaf.* Urbana: University of Illinois.

Quigley, S., W. Jenne, and S. Phillips. 1968. *Deaf Students in Colleges and Universities.* Washington, D.C.: A. G. Bell Association.

Quigley, S., and C. King. 1980. *Reading Milestones.* Beaverton, Ore.: Dormac.

_____. 1981. *Reading Milestones.* Beaverton, Ore.: Dormac.

_____. 1982. *Reading Milestones.* Beaverton, Ore.: Dormac.

_____. 1983. *Reading Milestones.* Beaverton, Ore.: Dormac.

_____. 1984. *Reading Milestones.* Beaverton, Ore.: Dormac.

Raifman, I. J., and Vernon, M. 1997. "Recognizing and Handling Legal Problems of Deaf Defendants Charged with Serious Crimes." *International Journal of Law and Psychiatry,* 20, no. 3: 373–387.

Rainer, J., and K. Altshuler, eds. 1966. *Comprehensive Mental Health Services for the Deaf.* New York: New York State Psychiatric Institute, Columbia University Press.

_____. 1967. *Psychiatry and the Deaf.* Washington, D.C.: U.S. Department of Health, Education, and Welfare, Social and Rehabilitation Services.

_____. 1970. *Expanded Mental Health for the Deaf.* Washington, D.C.: U.S. Department of Health, Education, and Welfare, Social and Rehabilitation Services.

Rainer, J., K. Altshuler, and F. Kallman, eds. 1963. *Family and Mental Health Problems in a Deaf Population.* New York: New York State Psychiatric Institute, Columbia University Press.

Randall, L. 1969. "A Comparison of the Self-Concept and Personality Characteristics of Deaf High School Students with Norms for the Hearing and with Norms for Delinquents." Ph.D. diss., University of Tennessee.

Rau, F. 1960. *Teaching Pronunciation to the Deaf.* Moscow: Moscow Institute of Defectology.

Ravitch, D. 1983. *The Troubled Crusade: American Education, 1945–1980.* New York: Basic Books.

Rawlings, B., and A. Gentile. 1970. *Additional Handicapping Conditions, Age of Onset of Hearing Loss, and Other Characteristics of Hearing Impaired Students, United States: 1968–69.* Washington, D.C.: Gallaudet College Office of Demographic Studies, Ser. D, No. 3.

Rawlings, B., M. Karchmer, and J. DeCaro. 1983. *A Guide to College/Career Programs for Deaf Students.* Washington, D.C.: Gallaudet College Press; Rochester, N.Y.: National Technical Institute for the Deaf.

Rawlings, B., S. King, J. Skilton, and D. Rose. 1993. *Gallaudet University Alumni Survey, 1993.* Washington, D.C.: Gallaudet Research Institute and Office of Institutional Research, Gallaudet University.

Rawlings, B., and R. Trybus. 1978. "Personnel, Facilities, and Services Available in Classes for the Hearing Impaired in the United States." *American Annals of the Deaf,* 123, no. 2: 99–114.

Rawlings, B., R. Trybus, and J. Biser. 1978. *A Guide to College/Career Programs for Deaf Students: 1978 Edition.* Washington, D.C.: Gallaudet College Press; Rochester, N.Y.: National Technical Institute for the Deaf.

_____. 1981. *A Guide to College/Career Programs for Deaf Students: 1981 Edition.* Washington, D.C.: Gallaudet College Press; Rochester, N.Y.: National Technical Institute for the Deaf.

Rawlings, B., R. Trybus, G. Delgado, and E. Stuckless. 1975. *A Guide to College/Career Programs for Deaf Students: 1975 Edition.* Washington, D.C.: Gallaudet College Press; Rochester, N.Y.: National Technical Institute for the Deaf.

Rawlings, B. W., M. Karchmer, J. De Caro, and T. Allen. 1999. *College and Career Programs for Deaf Students: 10ᵇ Edition.* Washington, D.C.: Gallaudet University; Rochester, N.Y.: National Technical Institute for the Deaf.

Ray, L. 1848. "Thoughts of the Deaf and Dumb Before Instruction." *American Annals of the Deaf,* 1, no. 3: 149–157.

_____. 1851. "On the Proper Use of Signs." American Annals of the Deaf, 5, no. 21, 182–193.

Read, E. D. 1921. "Americanization in Our Schools for the Deaf." *American Annals of the Deaf,* 66, no. 2: 137–146. Reprinted 1997, 142, no. 3: 49–52.

_____. 1852. "Family Education for Young Deaf Mute Children." *American Annals of the Deaf,* 5, no. 1: 32–35.

The Reading Report Card: Progress Toward Excellence in Our Schools. 1985.

Reagan, T. 1985. "The Deaf as a Linguistic Minority: Educational Considerations." *Harvard Educational Review,* 55, no. 3: 265–277.

_____. 1990. "Cultural Considerations in the Education of Deaf Children." In *Developmental and Educational Aspects of Deafness.* Edited by D. Moores and K. Meadow-Orlans. Washington, D.C.: Gallaudet University Press, 73–84.

Reese, C. M., K. E. Miller, J. Mazzeo, and J. A. Dossey. 1997. *NAEP Mathematics Report Card for the Nation and the States.* Princeton, N.J.: National Assessment of Educational Progress.

Reilly, J., and M. McIntyre. 1980. "American Sign Language and Pidgin Sign English: What's the Difference?" *Sign Language Studies,* 27: 151–192.

Report of the Joint Special Committee of the Massachusetts Legislature on the Education of the Deaf and Dumb. 1867. Boston.

Rice, J. 1973. *A Comprehensive Facility for Multiply Handicapped Deaf Adults: Final Report.* Fayetteville: Arkansas Rehabilitation Research and Training Center.

Ries, P. 1973a. *Reported Causes of Hearing Loss for Hearing Impaired Students, 1970–71.* Washington, D.C.: Gallaudet College Office of Demographic Studies, Ser. D., No. 11.

_____. 1973b. *Further Studies in Achievement Testing, Hearing Impaired Students, Spring 1971.* Washington, D.C.: Gallaudet College Office of Demographic Studies, Ser. D., No. 13.

_____. 1973c. *Additional Handicapping Conditions Among Hearing Impaired Students, United States, 1971.* Washington, D.C.: Gallaudet College Office of Demographic Studies, Ser. D., No. 14.

Rifkin, J. 1998. *The Biotech Century: Harnessing the Gene and Remaking the World.* New York: Tarchner/Putnam.

Rittenhouse, R., K. Morreau, and A. Iran-Nejad. 1981. "Metaphor and Conservation in Deaf and Hard-of-Hearing Children." *American Annals of the Deaf,* 126: 450–453.

Rittenhouse, R., and R. Spiro. 1979. "Conservation Performance in Day and Residential School Deaf Children." *Volta Review,* 81: 501–509.

Robinson, W., A. Park, and P. Axling. 1906. "The Industrial Status of the Deaf." *American Annals of the Deaf,* 49, no. 5: 460–464.

Rogers, D. 1888. "A Plea for Polytechnic Institute for Deaf Mutes." *American Annals of the Deaf,* 33, no. 2: 184–185.

Rose, D. E., M. Vernon, and A. F. Pool. 1996. "Cochlear Implants in Prelingually Deaf Children." *American Annals of the Deaf,* 141, no. 3: 258–261.

Rose, S., P. Conneally, and W. Nance. 1976. "Genetic Analysis of Childhood Deafness." In *Childhood Deafness.* Edited by H. Bess. New York: Grune and Stratton, 19–33.

Rosen, E. 1959. "A Cross Cultural Study of Semantic Profiles and Attitude Differences." *Journal of School Psychology,* 49, no. 2: 137–144.

Rosenstein, J. 1961. "Perception, Cognition and Language in Deaf Children." *Exceptional Children,* 27, no. 3: 276–284.

Rosenstein, J., and A. Lerman. 1963. *Vocational Status and Adjustment of Deaf Women.* New York: Lexington School for the Deaf.

Ross, A. 1964. *The Exceptional Child in the Family.* New York: Grune and Stratton.

Roush, J., M. Harrison, and S. Palsha. 1991. "Family-Centered Early Intervention." *American Annals of the Deaf,* 136, no. 4: 360–366.

Roush, J., and R. McWilliam. 1994. "Family-Centered Early Intervention." In *Infants and Toddlers with Hearing Loss.* Edited by J. Roush and N. Matkin. Baltimore: York Press, 3–21.

Rowell, E. G. 1987. "Learning Disability Assessment." In *Mental Health Assessment of Deaf Clients.* Edited by H. Elliot, L. Glass, and J. W. Evans. Boston: College Hill Press, 107–119.

Royster, M. 1981. "The Roysters: Deaf Parents: A Personal Perspective." *Deaf American,* 34, no. 3: 19–22.

Sanders, D. 1971. *Aural Rehabilitation.* Englewood Cliffs, N.J.: Prentice-Hall.

Sank, D., and F. Kallman. 1963. "The Role of Heredity in Early Total Deafness." *Volta Review,* 65, no. 1: 461–476.

Schiefelbusch, R., K. Ruder, and W. Bricker. 1976. "Training Strategies for Language Deficient Children: An Overview." In *Teaching Special Children.* Edited by N. Haring and R. Schiefelbusch. New York: McGraw-Hill, 49–73.

Schildroth, A. 1989. "Educational Placement of Deaf Students." Paper presented at Gallaudet Research Institute Symposium, May, Washington, D.C.

———. 1994. "Congenital Cytomegalovirus and Deafness." American Journal of Audiology, 27–38.

———. 1995. Personal Communication (Washington, D.C.: Gallaudet University, April 1995). Data from *Annual Survey of Deaf and Hard of Hearing Children and Youth,* 1993–1994.

Schildroth, A., and S. Hotto. 1993. "Annual Survey of Hearing Impaired Children and Youth: 1991–1992 School Year." *American Annals of the Deaf,* 138, no. 2: 163–171.

———. 1994. "Inclusion or Exclusion?" *American Annals of the Deaf,* 139, no. 2: 239–243.

———. 1995. "Race and Ethnic Background in the Annual Survey of Deaf and Hard of Hearing Children and Youth." *American Annals of the Deaf,* 140, no. 2: 96–99.

Schimmel, C., S. Edwards, and H. Prickett. 1999. "Reading?. . . . Pah! I Got It." *American Annals of the Deaf,* 144, no. 4: 298–308.

Schlesinger, H. 1977. "Treatment of the Deaf Child in the School Setting." *Mental Health in Deafness,* no. 1: 96–105.

———. 1978. "The Effects of Deafness on Child Development." In *Deaf Children: Developmental Perspectives*. Edited by L. Liben. New York: Academic Press, 157–172.

———. 1992. "The Elusive X Factor." In *A Free Hand: Enfranchising the Education of Deaf Children*. Edited by M. Walworth, D. Moores, and T. J. O'Rourke. Silver Spring, Md.: T. J. Publishers, 67–88.

Schlesinger, H., and K. Meadow. 1971. *Deafness and Mental Health: A Developmental Approach*. San Francisco: Langley-Porter Neuropsychiatric Institute.

———. 1972a. *Sound and Sign: Childhood Deafness and Mental Health*. Berkeley: University of California Press.

———. 1972b. "Development of Maturity in Deaf Children." *Exceptional Children,* 39, no. 5: 463–467.

Schmitt, P. 1966. "Language Instruction for the Deaf." *Volta Review,* 68, no. 2: 85–105.

———. 1968. "Deaf Children's Comprehension and Production of Sentence Transformations and Verb Tenses." Ph.D. diss., University of Illinois.

Schrag, P. 1967. *Village School Downtown: Boston Schools, Boston Politics*. Boston: Boston Press.

Scouten, E. 1942. *A Re-valuation of the Rochester Method*. Rochester, N.Y.: Rochester School for the Deaf.

Seguin, E. 1860. *Idiocy and Its Treatment by the Physiological Method*. New York: William Wood and Company.

———. 1932. *Jacobo Rodriguez Pereira: Primer Maestro de Sordomudos en Francia* (translated from French to Spanish by Jacobo Orellano Garrido). Madrid: Francisco Beltran.

Shulman, J., and N. Decker. 1980. *Readable English for Hearing Impaired Students*. Boston: Line Services, Inc.

Silverman, R., and H. Davis. 1970. *Hearing and Deafness*. New York: Rinehart.

Simmons, A. 1959. "A Comparison of the Written and Spoken Language from Deaf and Hearing Children from Five Age Levels." Ph.D. diss., Washington University.

———. 1962. "A Comparison of the Type Token Ratio of Spoken and Written Language of Deaf and Hearing Children." *Volta Review,* 64, no. 6: 417–421.

Sinnott, J., and M. Cancio. 1987. "Cytomegalovirus." *Infection Control,* 8: 79–82.

Siple, P., and S. Fischer, eds. 1991. *Theoretical Issues in Sign Language Research, Vol. 2, Psychology*. Chicago: University of Chicago Press.

Skinner, B. 1957. *Verbal Behavior*. New York: Appleton-Century-Crofts.

Slate, J. R. 1996. "Gender Differences in Wechsler Performance Scores of School Ages Children Who Are Deaf or Hard of Hearing." *American Annals of the Deaf,* 141, no. 1: 19–23.

Slate, J. R., and J. Fawcett. 1995. "Validity of the WISC III for Deaf and Hard of Hearing Persons." *American Annals of the Deaf,* 140, no. 3: 250–254.

Slobin, D. 1973. "Cognitive Prerequisites for the Development of Grammar." In *Studies of Child Language Development*. Edited by C. Ferguson and D. Slobin. New York: Holt, 175–208.

Soloman, J. 1943. "Psychiatric Implications of Deafness." *Mental Hygiene,* 17, no. 1: 37–52.

Somers, M. 1984. "The Parent–Infant Program at Kendall Demonstration Elementary School." In *Early Intervention for Hearing-Impaired Children, Total Communication Options*. Edited by D. Ling. San Diego: College Hill Press, 183–220.

Spence, C. 1973. "Relational Concepts in the Language and Thought of Deaf and Hearing Preschool Children." Ph.D. diss., University of Washington, Seattle.

Springer, N., and R. Roslow. 1938. "A Further Study of the Psychoneurotic Responses of the Deaf and Hearing Child." *Journal of Educational Psychology,* 29, no. 7: 590–615.

Stafford, C. 1967. "Fingerspelling in the Deaf Classroom." *American Annals of the Deaf,* 112, no. 5: 483–485.

Stagno, S. 1983. "Congenital and Perinatal Cytomegalovirus Infections." *Seminars in Perinatology,* 7, no. 1: 31–42.

Stanovich, K. 1980. "Toward an Interactive-Compensatory Model of Individual Differences in the Development of Reading Fluency." *Reading Research Quarterly,* 16, no. 1: 32–71.

Stedt, J., and D. Moores. 1983. "American Sign Language and Signed English Systems." *Focus on Infusion: Volume II.* Edited by F. Solano, J. Egelston-Dodd, and E. Costello. Silver Spring, Md.: Convention of American Instructors of the Deaf, 315–319.

———. 1990. "Manual Codes on English and American Sign Language: Historical Perspectives and Current Realities." In *Manual Communication: Implications for Education.* Edited by H. Bornstein. Washington, D.C.: Gallaudet University Press, 1–20.

Stedt, J., and D. Palermo. 1983. "The Morale of Teachers of Multihandicapped and Nonhandicapped Children in a Residential School for the Deaf." *American Annals of the Deaf,* 128, no. 3: 383–387.

Steele, K. P. 1998. "Progress in Progressive Hearing Loss." *Science,* 1870–1871.

Stein, L., N. Merrill, and P. Dahlberg. 1974. "Counseling Parents of Hearing Impaired Children." Paper presented at the American Speech and Hearing Association National Conference, Las Vegas.

Stewart, J., D. Pollack, and M. Downs. 1964. "A Unisensory Approach for the Limited Hearing Child." *ASMA,* 6, no. 2: 151–154.

Stewart, L. 1971. *Toward More Effective Rehabilitation Services for the Severely Handicapped Client.* Fayetteville: Arkansas Rehabilitation Research and Training Center.

———. 1974. *Multiply Handicapped Deaf People.* Keynote Address, Conference on Multiply Handicapped Deaf People, Brainerd, Minn.

———. 1979. *Hearing Impaired Developmentally Disabled Persons.* Tucson: University of Arizona.

———. 1990. "Sign Language: Some Thoughts of a Deaf American." In *Communication Issues Among Deaf People.* Edited by M. Garretson. Silver Spring, Md.: National Association of the Deaf, 117–124.

Stinson, M. 1972. "A Comparison of the Achievement Motive in Hearing and Hearing Impaired Children." Ph.D. diss., University of Michigan.

Stinson, M., and G. Walter. 1992. "Persistence in College." In *Deaf Students in Postsecondary Education.* Edited by S. Foster and G. Walter. New York and London: Routledge, 43–64.

Stockwell, E. 1952. "Visual Defects in Children." *Archives of Ophthalmology,* 48: 428.

Stone, C. 1851. "On the Use of Methodical Signs." *American Annals of the Deaf,* 4: 187–192.

Storrs, R. 1880. "Methods of Deaf Mute Teaching." *American Annals of the Deaf,* 24, no. 4: 233–250.

Strauss, M. 1999. "Hearing Loss and Cytomegalovirus." *Volta Review,* 99, no. 5: 71–74.

Streng, A. 1972. *Syntax, Speech and Hearing.* New York: Grune and Stratton.

Streng, A., W. Fitch, L. Hedgecock, J. Phillips, and J. Carroll. 1955. *Hearing Therapy for Children.* New York: Grune and Stratton.

Strike, K. 1985. "Is There a Conflict Between Equity and Excellence?" *Educational Evaluation and Policy Analysis,* 7, no. 4: 409–416.

Stuckless, E., and J. Birch. 1966. "The Influence of Early Manual Communication on the Linguistic Development of Deaf Children." *American Annals of the Deaf,* 111, no. 4: 425–460, 499–504.

Stuckless, E., and H. Corson. 1993. "Directory of Services." *American Annals of the Deaf,* 138: 2.

Stuckless, E., and G. Delgado. 1973. *A Guide to College/Career Programs for Deaf Students.* Washington, D.C.: Gallaudet College Press; Rochester, N.Y.: National Technical Institute for the Deaf.

Stuckless, E. R. 1995. "Directory of Programs and Services for the Deaf." *American Annals of the Deaf,* 140: 2.

Suchman, R. 1968. "Visual Impairment Among Deaf Children." *Volta Review,* 70, no. 1: 31–37.

Sullivan, P., and M. Vernon. 1979. "Psychological Assessment of Hearing Impaired Children." *School Psychology Digest,* 8, no. 4: 271–279.

Suppes, P. 1972. *A Survey of Cognition in Handicapped Children.* Stanford, Calif.: Stanford University, Institute for Mathematical Studies in the Social Sciences.

Supulla, S. 1992. "Equal Educational Opportunity: The Deaf Version." In *A Free Hand: Enfranchising the Education of Deaf Children.* Edited by M. Walworth, D. Moores, and T. J. O'Rourke. Silver Spring, Md.: T. J. Publishers, 170–181.

Sussman, A. E. 1988. "Approaches in Counseling and Psychotherapy Revisited." In *Two Decades of Excellence 1967–1987: A Foundation for the Future.* Edited by D. Watson, G. Long, and M. Harvey. Little Rock: American Deafness and Rehabilitation Association.

Sussman, A. E. and B. Brauer. 1999. "On Being a Psychotherapist with Deaf Clients." In *Psychotherapy with Deaf Clients from Diverse Groups.* Edited by I. Leigh. Washington, D.C.: Gallaudet University Press.

Taylor, N. 1983. *Family Literacy: Young Children Learning to Read and Write.* Exeter, N.H.: Heinemann.

Terman, L. 1916. *The Measurement of Intelligence.* Boston: Houghton Mifflin.

_____. 1944. *The Measurement of Intelligence: An Explanation and Complete Guide for the Use of the Stanford and Extensions of the Binet-Simon Intelligence Scale.* Boston: Houghton Mifflin.

Tervoort, B. 1961. "Esoteric Symbolism in the Communicative Structure Behavior of Young Deaf Children." *American Annals of the Deaf,* 106: 436–480.

_____. 1970. "The Understanding of Passive Sentences by Deaf Children." In *Advances in Psycholinguistics.* Edited by G. D'Arcais and W. Levelt. New York: American Elsevier, 163–173.

_____. 1975. *Developmental Features of Visual Communication.* Amsterdam: North Holland Publishing Company.

Tervoort, B., and A. Verbeck. 1967. *Analysis of Communicative Structure Patterns in Deaf Children.* Groningen, The Netherlands: A. W. O. Onderzoek, N.R.: 583–15.

Thoits, P. 1983. "Dimensions of Life Events That Influence Psychological Distress." In *Psychosocial Stress: Trends in Theory and Research.* Edited by H. B. Kaplan. New York: Academic Press, 33–103.

Thompson, R., A. Thompson, and A. Murphy. 1979. "Sounds of Silence, Sounds of Joy: Hearing Impaired Parents of Hearing Impaired Children." *Volta Review,* 81, no. 5: 331–351.

Thompson, W. 1936. "Analysis of Errors in Written Composition by Deaf Children." *American Annals of the Deaf,* 81, no. 2: 95–99.

Titova, M. 1960. "Peculiarities in Mastering Pronunciation Amongst Deaf Children Who Are Beginning to Learn Speech Through Dactilic Language." *Spetsial Skola,* 97: 26–28.

Tomas, T. 1920. *Juan Pablo Bonet.* Barcelona: Imprent de la Casa de Euritat.

Trybus, R. 1973. "Personality Assessment of Entering Hearing Impaired College Students Using the 16PF, Form E." *Journal of Rehabilitation of the Deaf,* 6, no. 1: 34–40.

Turnbull, H. 1975. "Accountability: An Overview of the Impact of Litigation on Professionals." *Exceptional Children,* 42, no. 6: 427–433.

Turner, M. D., and M. Traxler. 1997. "Children's Literature for the Primary Inclusive Classroom." *American Annals of the Deaf,* 142, no. 5: 350–355.

Turner, W. 1848. "Causes of Deafness." *American Annals of the Deaf,* 1, no. 1: 25–32.

_____. 1868. "Hereditary Deafness." *Proceedings of the National Conference of Principals of Institutions for the Deaf and Dumb.* Washington, D.C.: Gallaudet College, 91–96.

Valentine, P. 1994. "Thomas Hopkins Gallaudet: Benevolent Paternalism and the Origins of the American Asylum." In *Deaf History Unveiled.* Edited by J. Van Cleve. Washington, D.C.: Gallaudet University Press, 53–73.

Valentine, R. 1872. "Shall We Abandon the English Word Order?" *American Annals of the Deaf,* 17: 21–33.

Valli, C., C. Thumann-Preszioso, C. Lucas, S. Liddell, and R. Johnson. 1989. *An Open Letter to the Gallaudet Community.* Washington, D.C.: Gallaudet University Press.

Van Cleve, J. 1993. "Preface." In *Deaf History Unveiled.* Edited by J. Van Cleve. Washington, D.C.: Gallaudet University Press, pp. 1X–X.

Van Cleve, J., ed. 1993. *Deaf History Unveiled: Interpretations from the New Scholarship.* Washington, D.C.: Gallaudet University Press.

Van Cleve, J., and B. Crouch. 1989. *A Place of Their Own: Creating the Deaf Community in America.* Washington, D.C.: Gallaudet University Press.

Vernon, M. 1967a. "Rh Factor and Deafness." *Exceptional Children,* 34, no. 1: 5–12.

_____. 1967b. "Meningitis and Deafness." *Laryngoscope,* 10, no. 9: 1856–1874.

_____. 1967c. "Prematurity and Deafness." *Exceptional Children,* 34, no. 4: 289–298.

_____. 1967d. "Relationship of Language to the Thinking Process." *Archives of Genetic Psychiatry,* 16, no. 3: 325–333.

_____. 1968. "Current Etiological Factors in Deafness." *American Annals of the Deaf,* 113, no. 2: 106–115.

_____. 1976. "Psychological Evaluation of Hearing Impaired Children." In *Communication Assessment and Intervention Strategies.* Baltimore: University Park Press, 195–224.

_____. 1977. Editorial. *American Annals of the Deaf.* 122, 4, no. 3.

Vernon, M., and C. Alles. 1994. "Issues in the Use of Cochlear Implants with Prelingually Deaf Children." *American Annals of the Deaf,* 139, no. 5: 485–492.

Vernon, M., and J. Andrews. 1990. *The Psychology of Deafness.* New York: Longmans.

Vernon, M., and B. Daigle-King. 1999. "Historical Overview of Inpatient Care of Mental Patients Who Are Deaf." *American Annals of the Deaf,* 144, no. 1: 51–61.

Vernon, M., and D. Hicks. 1980. "Relationship of Rubella, Herpes Simplex, Cytomegalovirus, and Certain Other Viral Disabilities." *American Annals of the Deaf,* 125, no. 5: 529–534.

Vernon, M., and S. Koh. 1970. "Effects of Manual Communication on Deaf Children's Educational Achievement, Linguistic Competence, Oral Skills, and Psychological Development." *American Annals of the Deaf,* 115, no. 5: 527–536.

Vestberg, P. 1996. "My Opinion: A Skeptical Essay." *Nordisk Tidschrift for Döveundervisning,* no. 2: 14.

Voelker, C. 1938. "An Experimental Study of the Comparative Rate of Utterance of Deaf and Normal Speakers." *American Annals of the Deaf,* 83, no. 3: 274–284.

Vorce, E. 1971. "Speech Curriculum." In *Speech for the Deaf Child: Knowledge and Use.* Edited by L. Connor. Washington, D.C.: A. G. Bell Association, 221–224.

_____. 1974. *Teaching Speech to Deaf Children.* Washington, D.C.: A. G. Bell Association.

Vygotsky, L. 1962. *Thought and Language.* Cambridge, Mass.: M.I.T. Press.

———. 1989. *Thought and Language.* Translated and Edited by A. Kozulin. Cambridge: M.I.T. Press.

Walberg, H. 1984. "Improving the Productivity of America's Schools." *Educational Leadership,* 41, no. 8: 19–30.

Walberg, H., and T. Shanahan. 1983. "High School Effects on Individual Students." *Educational Researcher,* 12, no. 7: 4–9.

Waldo, M. 1859. "Early Home Instruction." *American Annals of the Deaf,* 11, no. 2: 170–192.

Walter, J. 1955. "A Study of the Written Sentence Construction of a Group of Profoundly Deaf Children." *American Annals of the Deaf,* 100, no. 3: 235–252.

———. 1959. "Some Further Observations on the Written Sentence Construction of Profoundly Deaf Children." *American Annals of the Deaf,* 104, no. 3: 282–285.

Walworth, M., D. Moores, and T. J. O'Rourke, eds. 1992. *A Free Hand.* Silver Spring, Md.: T. J. Publishers.

Waterman, J. 1970. *Perspectives in Linguistics.* Chicago: University of Chicago Press.

Watson, J. 1809. *Instruction of the Deaf and Dumb.* London: Darton & Harvey.

Watson, J. 1924. *Behaviorism.* Chicago: University of Chicago Press.

Watts, W. 1979. "The Influence of Language on the Development of Quantitative, Spatial and Social Thinking in Deaf Children." *American Annals of the Deaf,* 124, no. 1: 46–56.

Wechsler, D. 1974. *Wechsler Intelligence Scale for Children–Revised.* San Antonio: The Psychological Corporation.

———. 1991. *Wechsler Intelligence Scale for Children–III.* San Antonio: The Psychological Corporation.

Wedenberg, E. 1951. "Auditory Training of Deaf and Severely Hard of Hearing Children." *Acta Oto-Laryngologica,* Supplementum, 94: 1–130.

———. 1954. "Auditory Training for Severely Hard of Hearing Preschool Children." *Acta Oto-Laryngologica,* Supplementum, 110: 1–82.

Weed, J. L. 1859. "The Missionary Element in Deaf and Dumb Instruction. *Proceedings of the 1858 Convention of American Instructors of the Deaf and Dumb.* Acton, Ill.: Currier Steam Book and Job Printing House, 17–29.

Weiner, R. 1985. *PL 94-142: Impact on the Schools.* Arlington, Va.: Capital Publications.

Weinrich, J. 1972. "Direct Economic Costs of Deafness in the United States." *American Annals of the Deaf,* 117: 44–54.

Weir, R. 1963. "Impact of the Multiple Handicapped Deaf on Special Education." *Volta Review,* 65, no. 5: 287–289, 325.

Weld, L. 1844. *Twenty-Eighth Annual Report of the American Asylum at Hartford for the Education of the Deaf and Dumb.* Hartford, Conn.

———. 1855. *Thirty-Ninth Annual Report of the American Asylum at Hartford for the Education of the Deaf and Dumb.* Hartford, Conn.

Wells, C. 1942. *The Development of Abstract Language Concepts in Normal and Deaf Children.* Chicago: University of Chicago Press.

Welsh, W., and J. MacLeod-Gallinger. 1991. "Effects of College on Employment and Earnings." In *Deaf Students in Postsecondary Education.* Edited by S. Foster and G. Walter. New York and London: Routledge, 185–209.

Welsh, W., G. Walter, and D. Riley. 1989. *Earnings of Deaf College Alumni in the United States.* Rochester, N.Y.: National Technical Institute for the Deaf at Rochester Institute of Technology.

Werner, H. 1932. *History of the Problem of Deaf Mutism Until the 17th Century* (translated from German by C. K. Bonning). Jena, Germany: Verlag Von Gustav Fisher.

Westervelt, Z., and H. Peet. 1880. "The Natural Method Applied to the Instruction of Young Deaf Children." *American Annals of the Deaf,* 25, no. 3: 212–216.

Whorf, B. 1956. *Language, Thought and Reality.* Cambridge, Mass.: M.I.T. Press.

Wilbur, R. 1979. *American Sign Language and Sign Systems.* Baltimore: University Park Press.

Wilkinson, W. 1885. "Mechanical Arts Schools." *American Annals of the Deaf,* 30, no. 3: 177–187.

Williams, J. 1886. *Seventieth Annual Report of the American School for the Deaf.* Hartford, Conn.

Wines, F. 1888. *Report on the Defective, Dependent and Delinquent Classes of the Population of the United States as Returned in the Tenth Census (1880).* Washington, D.C.: U.S. Government Printing Office.

Wing, G. 1887. "The Theory and Practice of Grammatical Methods." *American Annals of the Deaf,* 32, no. 2: 84–89.

Winzer, M. 1981. "Talking Deaf Mutes: The Special Role of Women in the Methodological Conflict Regarding the Deaf." *Atlantis,* 6, no. 2: 122–133.

_____. 1993a. *The History of Special Education: From Isolation to Integration.* Washington, D.C.: Gallaudet University Press.

_____. 1993b. "Education, Urbanization, and the Deaf Community: A Case Study of Toronto, 1870–1900." In *Deaf History Unveiled.* Edited by J. Van Cleve. Washington, D.C.: Gallaudet University Press, 127–145.

Wolff, A. 1985. "Analysis." In *Cognition, Education, and Deafness: Directions for Research and Instruction.* Edited by D. Martin. Washington, D.C.: Gallaudet College Press, 79–81.

Wolff, A., and S. Brown. 1987. "Demographics of Meningitis-Induced Hearing Impairments." *American Annals of the Deaf,* 132, no. 1: 26–30.

Wolff, S. 1973. *Games Without Words.* Springfield, Ill.: Charles C Thomas.

Woodruff, L. 1848. "Primary Instruction of the Deaf." *American Annals of the Deaf,* 1, no. 2: 46–55.

Woodward, J. 1973. "Some Characteristics of Pidgin Sign English." *Sign Language Studies,* 3: 39–46.

Woodward, J., T. Allen, and A. Schildroth. 1985. "Teachers and Deaf Students: An Ethnography of Classroom Communication." *Proceedings of the First Annual Meeting of the Pacific Linguistics Conference.* Edited by S. DeLancey and R. Tomling. Eugene: University of Oregon, 479–493.

Wright, M. H. 1999. *Sounds like Home: Growing Up Black and Deaf in the South.* Washington, D.C.: Gallaudet University Press.

Wrightstone, J., M. Aranow, and S. Moskowitz. 1963. "Developing Reading Test Norms for Deaf Children." *American Annals of the Deaf,* 108, no. 3: 311–316.

Yale, C. 1939. *Formation and Development of Elementary English Sounds.* Northampton, Mass.: Clarke School for the Deaf.

Yarger, C. C., and J. Luckner. 1999. "Itinerant Teaching: The Inside Story." *American Annals of the Deaf,* 144, no. 4: 309–314.

Yoshinaga-Itano, C., and M. L. Apuzzo. 1998. "Identification of Hearing Loss after 18 Months Is Not Enough." *American Annals of the Deaf,* 143. no. 5: 380–388.

——. 1998. "The Development of Deaf and Hard of Hearing Children Identified Through a High Risk Registry." *American Annals of the Deaf,* 143, no. 5: 416–424.

Yoshinaga-Itano, C., and L. Snyder. 1985. "Form and Meaning in the Written Language of Hearing Impaired Children." *Volta Review,* 87: 75–90.

Yurkowski, P., and C. Ewoldt. 1986. "Semantic Processing of the Deaf Reader." *American Annals of the Deaf,* 131, no. 3: 243–247.

Zeckel, A. 1953. "Psyche and Deafness." *American Journal of Psychotherapy,* 321: 7–15.

Zemlin, W. 1968. *Speech and Hearing Science: Anatomy and Physiology.* Englewood Cliffs, N.J.: Prentice-Hall.

———. 1988. *Speech and Hearing Science: Anatomy and Physiology.* 3d ed. Englewood Cliffs, N.J.: Prentice-Hall.

Zwiebel, A., and D. Mertens. 1985. "A Factor-Analytic Study of Intellectual Development in Deaf and Hearing Children." In *Cognition, Education and Deafness: Directions for Research and Instruction.* Edited by D. Martin. Washington, D.C.: Gallaudet College Press, 151–155.

Name Index

Abernathy, E., 213
Abeson, A., 19
Abidin, R., 231
Adams, M., 236
Agricola, R., 36
Akamatsu, T., 184
Aldous, J., 145
Allen, T., 123, 124, 283, 284, 285, 322, 323, 349, 355
Allen, T. E., 114, 115
Alles, C., 113, 114, 115
Altshuler, K., 192, 194, 198, 199
Amman, J. K., 47, 51, 54
Anderson, R., 125, 126, 127, 130, 137
Anderson, R. T., 67
Andrews, J., 151, 165, 172, 185, 188, 190
Angelocci, A., 263
Anthony, S., 182
Aplin, Y., 113
Apuzzo, M. L., 158, 229
Aranow, M., 242, 282
Aristotle, 32, 33
Arnold, T., 33
Arnos, K., 109, 110, 111, 112
Augustus, C., 35
Austin, G., 194
Avicenna (Ibn Sina), 37

Avondino, J., 266
Axling, P., 342, 344
Ayres, J., 237, 238

Bailey, D., 230
Baker, C., 48
Baker, H., 44, 45
Balkany, T., 113
Ballard, M., 65, 170
Bargones, J., 158, 160
Barker, J., 34
Barnard, F., 255
Barnes, H., 342
Baroff, G., 192
Barry, K., 257
Bartlett, D., 235, 236
Beaver, D., 328
Behrens, T., 335
Belican, R. A. A., 49
Bell, A. G., 44, 72, 76, 78, 79, 80, 81, 82, 83, 86, 98, 99, 213, 260, 263, 265, 266
Bell, A. M., 78, 265
Belmont, J., 166
Bemiss, S., 94
Bender, R., 36, 47, 48, 50, 58, 59, 78, 79, 81, 82
Bernstein, M., 230, 231, 248

N-1

Subject Index

A

Appendix: World Wide Web Resources

This section provides a variety of Internet resources relating to education, advocacy, literacy, and the Deaf community in general.

Alexander Graham Bell Association for the Deaf, Inc.
http://www.agbell.org
The nonprofit membership organization works to promote awareness of deaf issues, strives to get more children tested for hearing loss, and gives scholarships and financial aid to qualifying children. Up-to-date news on political decisions that affect deaf and hard-of-hearing people can be found here.

American Annals of the Deaf
http://www.gallaudet.edu/~pcnmpaad/index.html
The *American Annals of the Deaf* is a professional journal devoted to quality in education and related services for deaf and hard-of-hearing children and adults. First published in 1847, the *Annals* has the distinction of being the oldest educational journal in the United States—as well as the oldest and most widely read English language journal in the world—dealing with deafness and the education of deaf persons. The *Annals* is the official organ of the Convention of American Instructors of the Deaf (CAID) and the Conference of Educational Administrators of Schools and Programs for the Deaf (CEASD).

American Speech-Language Hearing Association
http://www.asha.org
The ASHA is an organization/community of speech-language pathologists, audiologists, and scientists whose work relates to hearing loss. This site contains an abundance of useful medical and scientific information and news.

Association of Late-Deafened Adults
http://www.alda.org
The Association of Late-Deafened Adults works to create a community between people who have lost their hearing as adults by sponsoring a yearly conference and several regional meetings. Information on upcoming and past events, as well as membership, can be found here.

A-1

Emphasis on the impact of technology is integrated throughout the fifth edition, with coverage of

- current advances in medical technology, such as the increase in cochlear implants, digital hearing aids, and genetic engineering
- ways technology can assist deaf students, including the use of captioning, the Internet, distance education
- web resources in a new appendix